We Gain More Than We Give:
Teaming in Middle Schools

We Gain More Than We Give:
Teaming in Middle Schools

Thomas S. Dickinson
Thomas O. Erb
Editors

National Middle School Association
Columbus, Ohio

National Middle School Association
2600 Corporate Exchange Drive, Suite 370
Columbus, Ohio 43231
Telephone (800) 528-NMSA

ISBN: 1-56090-103-9   NMSA Stock Number: 1239

Library of Congress Cataloging-in-Publication Data
We gain more than we give: teaming in middle schools/Thomas S. Dickinson,
    Thomas O. Erb. editors.
        p.   cm
    Includes bibliographical references.
    ISBN: 1-56090-103-9 (pbk.)
    1. Teaching teams--United States.   2. Interdisciplinary approach in
education--United States.   3. Middle schools--United States.
    I. Dickinson, Thomas S.   II. Erb, Thomas Owen.
    LB1029.T4W4   1997
    371.14'8'0973--dc21   96--47731
                                                    CIP

Dedication

to Dr. Daniel Lips, M.D., F.A.C.C., and his team for keeping this project alive
— Thomas S. Dickinson

to the most important team in my life, one with a quarter century of history and a long future ahead: Karen, Chris, Greg, Brian, Emily, and Reggie
— Thomas O. Erb

Contents

Foreword

There are at least three kinds of people, one might say: those ahead of their time, those of their time, and the belated. The very same can be said of written works. Considering now several decades of works on teaming in the middle school, it is not difficult to determine in which of the first two categories to place this text. *We Gain More Than We Give: Teaming in Middle Schools* is indeed ahead of its time – yet ever so timely. Amidst the outpouring of articles and texts on teaming at the middle level, this text stands apart as the first to bring together all of the many voices who have played and are playing critical roles in the teaming drama. Parents, students, teachers, administrators, analysts, researchers, mature teams, rural teams, special educators, and more have been able to tell their stories here.

For the many educators who have labored long and hard in efforts to create and sustain successful teams, who have at times felt that they were giving more than they gained, reciprocity awaits you. From this text we gain more than the hard-won wisdom of those many years of committed and disciplined devotion to teaming. Here we find answers to questions we have asked for years, answers to questions we are just beginning to formulate, and answers to questions we have not yet realized should be asked. We are invited to enter worlds outside of our own teaming efforts, to confront struggles that echo our own, and to examine issues that pressures of the moment have compelled us to reserve for another time.

This rich compilation of readings arrives at a tenuous time in the middle school movement and in American education at large. Today's middle schools face a fragile future. In spite of enormous growth in the numbers of middle schools that have embraced teaming, many are struggling now more than ever before to articulate a clear defense for their teaming work in light of confounding and conflicting demands. The disenchanted public yearns for tangible results. The world cries out for complex, humane, and democratic results. Young people plead, often covertly, for personally and socially significant results. Advocates of teaming at the middle level have long clamored for most of these dividends and the reform eye has remained fixed on interdisciplinary teaming as a promising reform initiative. Yet the ensuing battles challenge us to uncover what we know about how and why this very hopeful construct rallies to all calls. Gratefully, this text does just that.

From its origins until the present, the concept of interdisciplinary teaming has been acknowledged as a piece in the larger educational portfolio of efforts to humanize America's middle schools. Long before the Carnegie Corporation's Council on Adolescent Development (1989) affirmed the middle school movement's fundamental precepts, advocates for teaming at the middle level celebrated the teaching team as a primary staffing plan needed to ensure the creation of small, personal communities for learning in which the lives of teachers and young adolescents could be transformed. Such communities have also been deemed the most viable means for teaching civility and democracy (Duke, 1990) and for designing a responsive and integrated curriculum (Beane, 1993).

While thousands of teaching teams are enhancing school and classroom life, too many teams have remained paralyzed by a limited vision of what teaming can and should be, naïve notions about the perils of collaboration, authoritative postures of leadership, and sketchy understandings about the rewards of thriving teams. Some of those teams were born in name only and never ventured to be more than an entitled unit. Some have fallen prey to school boards who have remained skeptical about the instructional merits of teaming. Other teams have disappeared as declining budgets have made team planning time a thing of the past. Still others are dying a slow, steady death as they battle conflicting visions, inadequate support, fading momentum, and little sense about just how to grow over time.

No doubt, two decades of teaming trials and triumphs have shown collaborative teaching is not simple. That teachers are organized in teams has been no guarantee of distinguishable changes in what students experience behind closed doors. In too many cases, teams of teachers who share common students, common planning time, and common schedules have only been able to dabble on the periphery of collaborative teaching. For a variety of reasons, visions of student-centered, humanistic communities fade behind a backdrop of control-dominated practices leaving students with little sense of being members of an empowered group. Hopes of planning an integrated curriculum get buried beneath fear-inducing state regulations or district mandates. Most importantly, the ultimate charge of creating synergism through collaboration is often met with exasperation and an occasional retreat to the safe confines of autonomy.

With the wisdom contained in this text, there is considerable reason to believe that the current generation of teaching teams, and those in the decades ahead will be able to become the transforming teams many once envisioned. In this era of teaming, we no longer can proclaim ignorance. Tom Dickinson, Tom Erb, and their colleagues have generated a work that will carry us forward, and beyond. Indeed, in reading this work, we will gain much more than we are called to give.

— Nancy Doda

References

Beane, J.A. (1993). *A middle school curriculum: From rhetoric to reality* (2nd ed.). Columbus, OH: National Middle School Association.

Carnegie Council on Adolescent Development (1989). *Turning points: Preparing American youth for the 21st century.* New York: Carnegie Corporation.

Duke, D.L. (1990). School organization, leadership, and student behavior. In O. Moles (Ed.), *Student discipline strategies* (pp. 11-25). Albany, NY: SUNY Press.

Acknowledgements

Books have lives and this volume is no different from any other text. We would like to recognize and thank the following who played an important part in bringing this volume to life:

- the individual chapter authors whose patience throughout the book's long development and publication process has been exemplary. Individually and collectively these authors are some of the finest minds in middle school education today and the editors have been sustained by both their kindness and their contributions.

- the teachers, administrators, students, and parents that allowed so many of us inside their lives so that we could understand firsthand the trials and triumphs of teaming. Without their kindness and indulgence this book would not have been possible.

- the administrators and colleagues at Indiana State University and the University of Kansas who provided both an intellectual environment and the support structure so necessary for such a book as this.

- Dr. Jerry Summers, Chair of the Department of Curriculum, Instruction, and Media Technology, School of Education at ISU, was especially helpful through his support, encouragement, and constant interest throughout the book's development.

- Karen Symms Gallagher, Dean of the School of Education, and Nita Wyatt Sundbye, Chair of the Department of Curriculum & Instruction at the University of Kansas, for facilitating this project through their support of a sabbatical application.

- Mary-Dean Barringer, Vice President of the National Board for Professional Teaching Standards for allowing her grandmother's story to be told.

- Deborah A. Butler and Karen Simmons Erb who listened, read, reacted, challenged, cajoled, and finally, who edited the editors' chapters. Love, hugs, and kisses.

- modern communication – overnight mail, e-mail, voice mail, fax, and the indispensable computer – played a significant role in this book's becoming. We knew we had arrived in the "Information Age" when we began to word process in the car while on vacation. And overnight mail from such locales as West Point, Virginia, to Lawrence, Kansas, was a reality that we came to depend on.

- Nancy Doda for taking the time to write the "Foreword" to the volume.

- National Middle School Association, John Lounsbury, and Mary Mitchell for their assistance in producing this volume.

Part I

The "Thingamabob" Called Teaming

The first two chapters in this book attempt to define the "thingamabob" that has come to be called "interdisciplinary teaming." Few practices in education are more often confused for something else than is interdisciplinary teaming. "Interdisciplinary teaming" consists of two words, one of which it shares with the concept "team teaching," the other it shares with "interdisciplinary curriculum." Therein lies the source of the confusion. Many educators, including scholars in the field of education, are not clear about the meaning of these three very distinct, though complementary, practices.

In Chapter 1 Tom Dickinson applies his almost poetic prose to looking inside successful interdisciplinary teams. He relates interdisciplinary teaming to five significant concepts that help to define the potential of this practice: mission, reciprocity, coming together, "cutting against the grain," and the impostor syndrome. Successful teaming is defined by far more than the mechanics of organizational features and procedures. Successful teaming is defined by the culture of schooling that it creates and sustains. Understanding culture is a more complex task than mastering mechanics.

In Chapter 2 Tom Erb tackles the confusion concerning interdisciplinary teaming, team teaching, and interdisciplinary curriculum head on. He places the development of interdisciplinary teaming in historical context by dealing with the evolution of school organization from 19th century one-room schools, through early 20th century one-room-schools-repeated-many-times in large junior and senior high schools and graded elementary schools, to the late 20th century move to teamed school organizations. Erb does this by telling some stories on himself as he reflects on his own experiences learning to become a team member.

The rest of the book

Subsequent sections of this book deal with interdisciplinary teaming from different perspectives. Part II, "Team Portraits," helps us see teams in action. We are offered five stories of real teams as they ebbed and flowed, learning from both successes and mistakes.

1

Part III, "Aspects of Practice," focuses on six important facets of teaming experience. Since teaming is a relatively new practice for many educators, it is helpful to read the reflections of a teacher who has spent a whole career as a team member. The contrasting experiences of getting started with teaming and continuing to develop as a mature team are discussed in the next two chapters. Learning how to provide a supportive administrative environment gets attention as well. The power of teaming to influence a single student is illustrated followed by a discussion of several parental perspectives on interdisciplinary teaming's impact on young adolescents.

Part IV, "The Knowledge Base," takes a very different approach to our understanding of teaming. Four different research bases are explored to give us the "big picture" on interdisciplinary teaming in a broad context. The first of these chapters documents the growth of interdisciplinary teaming in the middle grades. The second chapter in this part reviews the literature on team teaching and provides a perspective on team organization that challenges the premises in Chapter 2. The third chapter examines our knowledge about teaming elsewhere in society. Finally, the research base that documents the impact of interdisciplinary teaming on students and teachers in the middle grades is reviewed.

Part V, "Current Concerns," takes up six issues that often perplex educators attempting to make teaming work successfully. Getting beyond the "core four" to explore the meaning of teaming for elective and exploratory teachers is examined. The associated concerns of leadership and decision making are explained. The all important question of the relationship between interdisciplinary teams and curriculum gets further focus in this section. The relationship of two other current concerns of teachers about teaming are given thorough attention: language learning across the curriculum and inclusion.

In the final Part VI, "Coda," the book's two editors attempt to sum up where we currently are with interdisciplinary teaming and what the future may hold. For one thing is sure, the environment for education is not static. Teaming, to be successful, will have to adapt to this dynamic environment.

Pushing Humpty Off the Wall: Stories for a New Age of Teaming

1

Thomas S. Dickinson

> *Persons attempting to find a motive in this narrative will be prosecuted; persons attempting to find a moral in it will be banished; persons attempting to find a plot in it will be shot. By Order of the Author.*
>
> — Mark Twain, *Adventures of Huckleberry Finn*

■

Forming

Storming

Norming

Performing

— Bruce W. Tuckman,
Development sequence in small groups
Psychological Bulletin

■

I would like to tell you how to get there so that you may see all this for yourself. But first a warning: you may already have come across a set of detailed instructions, a map with every bush and stone clearly marked, the meandering courses of dry rivers and other geographical features noted, with dotted lines put down to represent the very faintest of trails. Perhaps there were also warnings printed in tiny red letters along the margins, about the lack of water, the strength of the wind and the swiftness of the rattlesnakes. Your confidence in these finely etched maps is understandable for at first glance they seem excellent, the best a man is capable of; but your confidence is misplaced. Throw them out. They are the wrong sort of map. They are too thin. They are not the sort of map that can be followed by a man who knows what he is doing. The coyote, even the crow, would regard them with suspicion.

There is, I should warn you, doubt too about the directions I will give you here, but they are the very best that can be had. They will not be easy to follow. Where it says left you must go right sometimes. Read south for north sometimes. It depends a little on where you are coming from, but not entirely. I am saying you will have doubts. If you do the best you can you will have no trouble.

(When you get there you may wish to make up a map for yourself for future reference. It is the only map you will ever trust. It may consist of only a few lines hastily drawn. You will not have to hide it in your desk, taped to the back of a drawer. That is pointless. But don't leave it out to be seen, thinking no one will know what it is. It will be taken for scribble and thrown in the wastebasket or be carefully folded and idly shredded by a friend one night during a conversation. You might want to write only a set of numbers down in one corner of a piece of paper and underline them. When you try to find a place for it – a place not too obvious, not too well hidden so as to arouse suspicion – you will begin to understand the futility of drawing maps. It is best in this case to get along without one, although you will find your map, once drawn, as difficult to discard as an unfinished poem.)

— Barry Lopez,
Desert Notes: Reflections in the Eye of a Raven

■

What we need today is not a number of Leonardos, but rather groups of interdisciplinarians. . . . Now it becomes clear that the focus of scientific knowledge is shifting from individuals to groups. Scientific knowledge has become a collective product that is only imperfectly represented in isolated individuals.

— Joseph Kockelmans, Why interdisciplinarity?
in *Interdisciplinarity and Higher Education*

■

Pseudo-team: This is a group [that] . . . **has not focused on collective performance and is not really trying to achieve it.** *It has no interest in shaping a common purpose or set of performance goals, even though it may call itself a team. . . . In pseudo-teams, the sum of the whole is less than the potential of the individual parts.*

— Jon R. Katzenbach and Douglas K. Smith,
The Wisdom of Teams

■

Wanted: Mission driven middle school teams

What I know about teams comes from my time in the military. And the most important lesson I learned in the military about teams was that they were mission driven. Mission – that was the focus, the goal, the reason for being. Everything revolved around mission. And for the team to be effective the mission also had to be clear, not vague, not ambiguous, not fuzzy, but clear and clear to all members of the team. In the military teams did not formulate mission, they implemented it. And they attempted to implement it in the most resource-effective manner possible in the quickest possible time frame. It was also important that all members of the team understood the mission, understood their part in implementing it, understood the parameters of their efforts.

In all my time in the military in small teams I never heard the mission challenged. While there were obviously individuals with concerns over almost any mission the prevailing attitude was articulated as "Ok people, we've got a job to do so let's do it." I also never heard any challenge to team composition. I never heard anyone state overtly "I don't want to work with this individual." That was not a choice. Personality conflicts did not exist in teams performing missions.

Middle school teams could learn from the military's orientation to teams, especially from their emphasis on mission-driven teams. I believe that there is too much emphasis in many middle school teams on the adults and not enough emphasis on students and their learning which is the real mission of the team at the middle school. Bottom line, teams exist for students and their best development, not for adults. And while I know full well the benefit that adults derive from teams – the ability to work together with a colleague rather than in isolation – I also know that that is not the mission of teams.

One of the most significant problems of teams, it seems to me, is their misplaced focus on themselves, especially when it comes to team composition and the continuing debates over who works with whom. Often I find the "personality conflict issue" to be a handy excuse to not invest in the development of the team, as a cop-out for any number of adult concerns that have nothing to do with student learning.

Being mission driven, and that should apply to all members of the team regardless of their background, means having a singular focus on young adolescents. It means working with colleagues with an eye on the needs of youth and not on petty conflicts, personal disagreements, potential slights, or imagined hurts. It means compromise, real listening, openly resolving problems, and confronting those problems readily so that the team can best devote its energies to accomplishing its stated mission.

■

More troublesome than apathy is social loafing. Research has shown that individuals, in general, tend not to work as hard in groups as they do as individuals. Known as "The Ringleman Effect" from the researcher by that name who conducted crude tug-of-war experiments in the 1880s, it has been established that two people don't pull twice as hard as one and three don't pull three times as hard as one, and so forth, as group size increases. More recent studies by social psychologists have established clearly a similar idea called 'social loafing.' Most social loafing occurs when it is not possible to distinguish the individual's contribution to the group output. On interdisciplinary teams, some individuals will naturally contribute more than others; a problem arises, however, when certain members are perceived as not contributing their share, forgetting assignments, failing to meet deadlines, never volunteering, letting others carry the load. When this happens, resentment eventually develops. Oddly enough, two people usually get blamed, the loafer and the leader who doesn't do anything about it. Soon, group cohesion begins to diminish. Like so many other problems that groups face, the answer is simple but painful: deal with it, either directly as a group, or through the team leader.

— James R. Davis,
*Interdisciplinary Courses and Team Teaching:
New Arrangements for Learning*

■

A team is a small number of people with complementary skills who are committed to a common purpose, performance goals, and approach for which they hold themselves mutually accountable.
— Jon R. Katzenbach and Douglas K. Smith,
The Wisdom of Teams

■

Barnston was struck by the way snow geese did things together. No other waterfowl are as gregarious; certainly no other large bird flies as skillfully in such tight aggregations. This quality – the individual act beautifully integrated within the larger movement of the flock – is provocative. One afternoon I studied individual birds for hours as they landed and took off. I never once saw a bird on the water move over to accommodate a bird that was landing; nor a bird ever disturbed by one taking off, no matter how tightly they were bunched. In no flight overhead did I see two birds so much as brush wing tips. Certainly they must; but for the most part they are flawlessly adroit. A flock settles gently

on the water like wiffling leaves; birds explode vertically
with compact and furious wingbeats and then stretch out
full length, airborne, rank on rank, as if the whole flock
had been cleanly wedged from the surface of the water. Sev-
eral thousand bank smoothly against a head wind, as pre-
cisely as though they were feathers in the wing of a single
bird.

— Barry Lopez,
A reflection on white geese, in *Crossing Open Ground*

■

Reciprocity

I am sitting in a middle school classroom after school one afternoon in the late fall. The last of the leaves are off the trees and cold is becoming a constant in the air. Roger, an eighth grade science teacher and team leader of a three-person team, and I are talking about moving from a traditional supervision model of working with student teachers to a performance based internship where the emphasis is on demonstrating competence. Questions of time, resources, and support dominate our conversations, set amidst black-topped tables with sinks, tall stools, and shelves of apparatus and equipment, most of which I cannot identify. I am trying, for the third time it seems, to emphasize that this change will be as much a challenge for me as for Roger and certainly for the student teacher, when Roger's eye is caught by some movement in the hall—

"Arnold," Roger yells across the room and into the hall. A shuffling of feet and into the doorway comes a young adolescent with backpack in hand. A smile and then "I forgot my math book."

"Come in for a moment Arnold, I want to ask you something." Now Arnold is not so sure – about the wisdom of forgetting his math book in the first place, or passing by Roger's door on his way to his locker to retrieve it. His face says it all: I-don't-think-I'm-going-to-like-this.

"Arnold, remember when you were having so much trouble with math at the start of school?"

"I'm doing good in math now Mr. Darhart. I'm making B's."

"Yes, I know you are Arnold, and all of us on the team are proud of you. I remember the fall when things weren't going so well and the conference with your father. I remember how I assured him that you would be able to catch up and bring your grade up. And I remember how Ms. Cates gave me the worksheets, and how hard you worked on them in advisory." Laughing, "And I remember how much math both of us ended up learning."

"Yeah." Arnold knows for sure that I-don't-think-I'm-going-to-like-this was right.

"How's English, Arnold?" Roger asks. Silence. Arnold's eyes are on the floor, watching the toe of his left shoe trace imaginary circles on the linoleum.

"I understand that you've been giving Mr. Hasty a hard time in English (the third member of the team, Erik Hasty is a first year English teacher)."

"Well, maybe some times. I don't like writing." Arnold is still watching imaginary circles.

"In the fall you told me you didn't like math."

Arnold puzzles over this connection for a moment. Then offers "Like I should lay off? Causing trouble?"

"That might help. And let me know if you need help on your writing during advisory. Besides," says Roger, laughing "you owe me."

Arnold turns to go "And don't forget to get your math book" Roger reminds him. And then Arnold is out the door, never again to cause Erik Hasty a problem. And Roger and I are back to questions of supervision and performances.

■

The strength of the pack is in the wolf
and the strength of the wolf is in the pack.

— Rudyard Kipling
The Jungle Book

Not power over but power with.

— Two signs over a teacher's desk at Chancey
Rose Middle School in Terre Haute, Indiana

■

I had three chairs in my house; one for solitude, two for
friendship, three for society.
—Henry David Thoreau, *Walden*

■

The best way to understand teams is to look at teams themselves. Their own stories reveal their accomplishments, skills, emotions, and commitment better than any abstract commentary or logical presentation. Real teams are deeply committed to their purpose, goals, and approach. High-performance team members are also very committed to one another. Both understand that the wisdom of teams comes with a focus on collective work-products, personal growth, and performance results. However meaningful, 'team' is always a result of pursuing a demanding performance challenge.

— Jon R. Katzenbach and Douglas K. Smith,
The Wisdom of Teams

■

Times of transition seem as difficult for nature as for people.

— Ann Zwinger, The Gates of Lodore
to Echo Park, in *Run, River, Run*

■

We operate that way often enough that a Yale economist, Charles Lindblom, even gave it a formal name, 'muddling through,' in a famous article published in the 1950s. At its best, Muddling Through recognizes that we are not really all that good at divining long-term, comprehensive solutions to problems – there are too many variables and imponderables involved. Instead we make admittedly incomplete, imperfect decisions, followed up by almost constant, incremental midcourse corrections.

— Tom Horton, Saving the Bay,
in *Bay Country: Reflections on the Chesapeake*

■

The team that came together

They were a team like many others. No real distinguishing characteristic. No claim to fame. Nothing that noted them as special. Just four teachers, two male and two female, representing math, science, language arts, and social studies. That is how they thought of themselves too, as subject matter teachers who taught eighth graders. Four individuals who had a common planning time, although they really did not do anything in common with it. Or at least they did not do anything with it before "The Day." Afterwards . . . well, that is what this story is about.

You may have read about it in the papers, but I will tell you the details anyway. It was a nice day in late August, about a week before school started. Constance had spent the day at WMS – Walker Middle School – putting the room in order, hanging her vocabulary mobiles, putting up her "Welcome Back" bulletin boards. She left to go by the grocery store for a few things and then home to fix supper for Ron who was to pick up the twins at day care. Everything was normal until she attempted to put her key in the back door lock, but it did not fit. She walked around to the front door, trying to figure why the lock was different when she ran right into their lawyer who handed her a piece of paper, mumbled something incomprehensible, and then fled back to his car in the main drive.

To say she was devastated is an understatement. Divorce is like that. Especially when your former partner takes the kids, changes all the locks on the house, and closes all of your joint accounts. And then sicks the lawyers on you while he was the one being unfaithful.

Why she showed up at Jean's, her science team mate, rather than anyone else's, she did not know, but in retrospect she (and the team) was glad she did. And Jean called Bill and Jamal.

When it hit the papers (Ron was heir to a major family fortune, a large construction company – you get the picture) Jean, Bill, and Jamal were already in "Flip" Stocker's office nailing down his commitment to Constance and the team. And they got it. As Bill said later, the job was all Constance had left.

So the team began the year holding a large group meeting for their eighth graders, both to welcome them and to lay a strong foundation—for the kids, for the team, and for Constance. And two weeks later they did it again, this time for parents at "Back to School" night. And Mr. Stocker was there as well – to answer parents' questions, to deal with their perceived fears, and to offer visible support to the team.

Team planning time became the focal point of their day. Because
Constance was a major concern, as well as the kids, they began the year with
more dialogue and discussion on what they were doing, how they could
support each other, which kids were doing what – all with an eye on keeping
track of their friend. And so they began to come together. And their teaching
got better as well.

They planned their first interdisciplinary unit together – which the kids
selected – on living in groups, which was wildly successful, including the
two weddings, the funeral, and the divorce hearing that they attended as field
trips. By then Constance had the twins (she had hired her own lawyer, a
barracuda who thought she could make a name for herself with this case, and
she did) and was able to see the humor in it all. And this was just the first of
four units that they did that year.

Their advisories took on a sensitivity they had never had before. And they
began to look at their overall instructional approaches, their failure rates and
the causes, and how their kids were working together. While the original
focus for much of their concern was Constance and the divorce, the team and
the kids quickly became the focus.

By the end of the year they were truly a team, on their way toward being a
high performance team. Constance, Jean, Bill, and Jamal were now a team of
four teachers who had much in common – their devotion to each other, their
pride in helping educate their students, their professionalism as middle
school educators, and their daily common planning time that was now a
celebration of life itself.

■

*If the essence of teams is 'teamwork,' then teams need to
function within a climate that fosters teamwork. The word
most often used to characterize this climate was 'trust,' and
trust was characterized as having four elements: honesty,
openness, consistency, and respect. When trust exists, team
members will stay focused on the goal, will communicate
more effectively, will compensate for each other's shortcomings, and will be more open to criticism and risk, thus improving the overall quality of outcomes. When a collaborative climate exists, team members are more likely to share*

information, admit problems, help overcome obstacles, and find new ways of succeeding. Such a climate is not easy to build, but appears to be related to the involvement that team members have and the autonomy the team has to do its job.

— James R. Davis,
*Interdisciplinary Courses and Team Teaching:
New Arrangements for Learning*

■

A group needs to contain a number of people sufficiently small for each to be aware of and have some relation to the other.
— John K. Brilhart, *Effective Group Discussion*

■

Finally, teams have more fun. This is not a trivial point because the kind of fun that they have is integral to their performance. The people on the teams we met consistently and without prompting emphasized the fun aspects of their work together. Of course this fun included parties, hoopla, and celebrations. But any group of people can throw a good party. What distinguishes the fun of teams is how it both sustains and is sustained by team performance. For example, we often see a more highly developed sense of humor on the job within the top-performing teams because it helps them deal with the pressures and intensity of high performance. And we inevitably hear that the deepest, most satisfying source of enjoyment comes from 'having been part of something larger than myself.'

— Jon R. Katzenbach and Douglas K. Smith,
The Wisdom of Teams

■

It is our belief that good quality is just plain cheap. Something made right holds up and does not have to be bought again soon. Common sense, of course, but a sense not so common in the commercial world. Occasionally a reporter will write an article about our 'upscale tools' and we wonder how the Swiss orchardist, the Japanese farmer, or the English landscaper would feel to hear that his or her everyday tools are now upscale. The term is a misnomer at Smith & Hawken. Consider the forks and spades on this page. They are made by an 800-year-old company that leads the professional market in England. This leadership has been earned over decades of meticulous attention to quality and detail. In England, unlike America, gardener-landscapers have to buy and maintain their own tools. This is true even for laborers. Because of that they simply can't afford forks that will splay, sockets that will bend or handles that will split. It's their money, and they spend it on tools that will give them the greatest value.

— From a Smith and Hawken
gardening catalogue entitled *Tools of the Trade*

■

Cutting against the grain

Mary-Dean Barringer, Vice President for the National Board for Professional Teaching Standards often tells an interesting story from her own childhood. One day she was at her grandmother's when she was working on her quilting. On this particular day her grandmother was cutting quilting squares. So Mary-Dean was plopped down next to her grandmother's rocker and supplied with a pattern piece, fabric, and scissors and after some basic instruction began to cut quilt pieces. It did not take Mary-Dean long to realize that cutting the pieces with the grain of the fabric was a lot easier than cutting them against the grain. And so she was merrily moving along, cutting with the grain, until her grandmother noticed her method and promptly said "Mary-Dean, cut the fabric against the grain, so that when tension is put on the quilt, it won't ravel and fray."

■

The formal study of groups and teams began in employment settings. A classic set of research studies conducted by Elton Mayo and his colleagues at Western Electric in the 1930s revealed the importance of 'human factors' in the productivity of workers. Although the variables being studied had to do with better working conditions, such as lighting, the personal attention being given to the workers as a group by the researchers proved to be the most important consideration. Now known for the classic 'Hawthorne effect' in social science research methods, the study set in motion further explorations of human factors in work environments where people work in groups.

— James R. Davis,
Interdisciplinary Courses and Team Teaching: New Arrangements for Learning

■

As for the best leaders, the people do not notice their existence. The next best, the people honor and praise. The next, the people fear; and the next, the people hate. When the best leader's work is done, the people say, 'We did it ourselves.'

— Lao-Tzu

■

In the seventh, the Dodgers loaded the bases with one out. Casey Stengel, out of first-liners, called on a tall, toothy left-hander named Bob Kuzava, who lost as often as he won. He struck out Snider. Now Kuzava was left to confront Jackie Robinson. It was always coming down to the best men. The count went to three and two. Robinson fouled off four pitches. The flags of Ebbets Field flapped in the wind. Robinson lifted an ordinary pop fly to the right side. The base runners ran. No Yankee moved. It seemed that the pop would bounce and that two runs or more would score and the Dodgers would win their first World Series. Who hits after Robby? Maybe we'll get six. What will I use for a lead? Billy Martin, the Yankee second baseman, sprinted, reached, lunged and gloved the pop fly when it was no more than two feet from the ground. It had been the first baseman's ball. No matter. Martin, an Oakland roughneck, had rescued the forces of U.S. Steel. The Dodgers never again threatened. The Yankees had won their fourth consecutive World Series. Next Year, the Messianic Time when the Brooklyn Dodgers become the best baseball team on earth, had not yet arrived. 'Every year,' I angrily began the page-one story, 'is the next year for the New York Yankees.'

— Roger Kahn, *The Boys of Summer*

■

Often, when individuals on pseudo-teams lament their failure to act like a team, they describe yet another irony. Each person faults the other people on the pseudo-team, especially the leader. The remedy prescribed inevitably sounds like 'we would do much better as a team if only the **rest of them** *would work as a team in the way* **I think** *makes the most sense.'*

— Jon R. Katzenbach and Douglas K. Smith,
The Wisdom of Teams

■

The impostor syndrome

I have always wondered why some individuals on middle school teams do not invest in the team, do not work within the structure, do not cooperate, do not become someone described as a "team player." I am not talking about those individuals who do not participate in their team because they do not want to be there, do not like kids, do not like their jobs, do not even like themselves. There is another solution for these individuals, but that is another story.

I am talking about good teachers, people who like young adolescents and working with them, creative people who enjoy coming to work every day and who transmit this joy to their charges. I wonder why they do not make the move, do not learn the lessons of becoming a team member, do not take the plunge.

Maybe they cannot.

Over the last ten years educational psychologists and researchers looking at teachers and teacher behaviors (Brems, Baldwin, Davis, & Namyniuk, 1994; Elbaz, 1987; Lieberman & Miller, 1991; Simon, 1992) have identified a condition that may identify why some middle school team members do not want to invest themselves in a team. Called "the impostor syndrome" it is characterized by a feeling of "I-don't-really-deserve-to-be-here-and-if-I'm-not-careful-people-will-find-me-out." Writing in *Leaders, Fools, and Impostors: Essays on the Psychology of Leadership* (1993), DeVries comments:

> *These people have an abiding feeling that they have fooled everyone and are not as competent and intelligent as others think they are. They attribute their success to good luck, compensatory hard work, or superficial factors such as physical attractiveness and likability. Some are incredibly hardworking, always overprepared. However, they are unable to accept that they have intellectual gifts and ability. They live in constant fear that their imposturous existence will be exposed – that they will not be able to measure up to others' expectations and that catastrophe will follow.* (p. 129)

The impostor syndrome can survive in teaching with our prevailing ethic of privacy. Behind closed doors, hidden away, a teacher with a feeling of impostorship can survive a crippling existence. But a middle school team, with its openness, its critical reflection, its debate and discussion, its cooperative, collaborative planning and execution is a massive threat to an impostor. And it may be the reason why some very talented teachers – highly creative and hardworking individuals – are repelled by teams.

The solution to the problem can only be openness and honesty about our own self-doubts about our work. For a teacher with a feeling of impostorship being on a team means that the impostor's overly critical and often incorrect view of their own work can be balanced by colleagues who offer honest and accurate appraisals as well as suggestions for improvement.

It may be a small point, but for some of our colleagues, being part of a team is a very scary situation.

■

Team crafted in Indiana.
— Sign on Subaru Outback stationwagon

References

Brems, C., Baldwin, M.R., Davis, L. & Namyniuk, L. (1994). The impostor syndrome as related to teaching evaluations and advising relationships of university teachers. *Journal of Higher Education, 65* (2), 183-193.

Brihart, J.K. (1982). *Effective group discussion.* Dubuque, IA: W.C. Brown.

Davis, J.R. (1995). *Interdisciplinary courses and team teaching: New arrangements for learning.* Phoenix, AZ: American Council on Education and Oryx Press.

DeVries, M.F.R.K. (1993). *Leaders, fools, and impostors: Essays on the psychology of leadership.* San Francisco: Jossey-Bass.

Elbaz, F. (1987). Teachers' knowledge of teaching: Strategies for reflection. In J. Smyth (Ed.), *Educating teachers: Changing the nature of pedagogical knowledge* (pp. 45-53). Bristol, PA: Falmer Press.

Horton, T. (1991). *Bay country: Reflections on the Chesapeake.* Washington, DC: Island Press.

Kahn, R. (1972). *The boys of summer.* New York: Harper and Row.

Katzenbach, J.R., & Smith, D.K. (1993). *The wisdom of teams.* New York: HarperCollins.

Kipling, R. (1894). *The jungle book.* New York: Century.

Kockelmans, J. (1979). *Interdisciplinarity and higher education.* University Park, PA: Penn State University Press.

Lieberman, A., & Miller, L. (1991). Revisiting the social realities of teaching. In A. Lieberman and L. Miller (Eds.), *Staff development for education in the 1990's: New demands, new realities, new perspectives* (pp. 92-109). New York: Teachers College Press.

Lopez, B. (1976). *Desert notes: Reflections in the eye of a raven.* New York: Avon.

Lopez, B. (1989). *Crossing open ground.* New York: Vintage.

Simon, R.I. (1992). *Teaching against the grain: Texts for a pedagogy of possibility.* Westport, Conn.: Greenwood Press.

Thoreau, H.D. (1950). *Walden.* New York: Random House.

Tuckman, B.W. (1965). Development sequence in small groups. *Psychological Bulletin, 63,* 384-99.

Twain, M. (1996). *Adventures of Huckleberry Finn.* New York: Random House.

Zwinger, A. (1975). *Run, river, run.* Tucson, AZ: The University of Arizona Press.

Thirty Years of Attempting to Fathom Teaming: Battling Potholes and Hairpin Curves Along the Way 2

Thomas O. Erb

Thirty years ago during the 1965-66 school year I decided to forsake a chance to enter the honors program in history at DePauw University in order to participate in a junior semester abroad program at Albert Ludwigs Universität in Freiberg, Germany. Among other life decisions that year, I was trying to figure out how to productively use my love of history while keeping a wary eye on the changing Selective Service laws. The thoughts in the back of my mind about high school teaching came increasingly to the fore.

After returning to Greencastle, Indiana, in the fall of 1966, I solidified my plans to go into teaching. What great news to tuition-paying parents: a senior decided to go into teaching without a single "education" course on his transcript! Not to fear, MAT programs abounded that were designed to address the teacher shortage by recruiting liberal arts majors into graduate teacher education programs.

So to pursue my dream of becoming a high school history teacher, I accepted Northwestern University's offer to fit me with the requisite credentials in five academic quarters. For this history buff, the Northwestern MAT program offered half of the graduate coursework in history with the bare minimum of coursework required for Illinois certification. I would be engrossing Chicago area high school students in the study of history with a minimum of bureaucratic hassle. Better yet, I would have a full-year, paid internship in a public secondary school while I completed my master's degree.

It should be coming clear by now that my interest in going into teaching centered around a love of subject matter. I had scant knowledge of adolescents. You should also know something about me that would not be revealed even to me until I entered my doctoral program ten years later: My Myers-Briggs Type, INTJ, has its most extreme score on the "I-E" dimension. For the uninitiated, I really get off by running ideas through my head; people just confuse me!

Now how did a subject-oriented introvert who did not understand much about adolescents, much less *young* adolescents, wind up devoting a career to interdisciplinary collaborative teaching arrangements in middle schools? As Yogi Berra says, "It's not over 'til it's over."

To be accepted into the Northwestern MAT program, one also had to be accepted as an intern by a public school district. After all they were paying the intern salaries. I flew to Chicago for an interview at Maine Township High School South. This venture allowed me to experience my first failed interview. No high school had hired me for an internship, and the end of my last semester at DePauw was fast approaching.

In late April, I received a call that a junior high in Wilmette was interested in hiring an intern for a core classroom. This intern would teach history – so far so good – language arts and group guidance in a three-hour time block to eighth graders. Being young, foolish, and desperate, I said "Yes!" And why not? They were going to pay me the sum of $3360 – my first professional contract!

So began my teaching career with 28 eighth graders. My immediate concern was to fill three hours with stuff engaging enough to keep the lid on! We started U.S. History that year relying on an old textbook to excite us about "the explorers." This approach produced a modicum of success. The low point came later in the semester when the father of one of my best behaved students called to question why I had kept the whole class after school for something that really involved only a few of the students. I was making all of the mistakes that someone who had a subject-matter focus and no specific training for teaching young adolescents could make.

Fortunately, I had the good luck to be assigned a room in Howard Junior High (don't let the name fool you, it was more of a middle school in the late 1960s than many "middle schools" are today) next to Yvonne Kuhlman. Mrs. Kuhlman had been both a high school and junior high English teacher for twenty-five years when I, a 22-year-old neophyte social studies intern, first encountered her. Yvonne Kuhlman and I had a common planning period, adjacent classrooms, and a common teaching schedule, though we did not officially share students as we were both separate core teachers.

Nonetheless, the common planning time – which is now well established as the key to effective teaming – provided time for Yvonne and me to discuss a number of common concerns. Dealing with student behavior, motivating 13 year olds, designing interesting lessons, dealing with administrators and parents, coordinating language skills and social studies topics were just a few of the ways that Yvonne oriented me to the profession of teaching young adolescents. What she was so skilled at doing was helping me come to understand how to see students as unique developing human beings – a much broader perspective than as mere students of U.S. History. The first task of our then informal teaming arrangement was to induct a new member into the profession. Later would come much more.

With all the other ingredients in place, by the second year we were exchanging students and had created our own two-person interdisciplinary team. I, the inexperienced, young, male, social studies oriented person, was being mentored by an experienced, female, English oriented teacher. She was full of ideas for active lessons. Students in her classrooms were always busily engaged in activities and creating projects to show what they were learning.

Yvonne was the most beloved teacher in the school. She perfectly fit the ideal of the caring teacher with high expectations for all students – including me. She so successfully inducted me into the world of middle school teaming that by the third year of teaching eighth grade, I was thoroughly committed to continuing in the middle grades, lost forever to the high schools of America. In the third year we were joined by a science teacher thus broadening our team's curricular responsibilities. With Yvonne leading the way, we developed a number of interdisciplinary units during the three and one half years we taught together. Some of the grandest units were under the themes "Cities," "Futures," "Civil Rights," and "Exploration." Making heavy use of cooperative groups, simulations, field trips around the resource-rich Chicago area, and student performances and presentations, we had students making decisions, solving problems, and using basic skills to express what they learned in unit-ending projects.

Teaching this way for weeks at a time kept students engaged in, some even excited about, what they were learning. The example that Yvonne set showed me how to become an effective middle grades teacher. When I made the shift to middle grades teacher education in 1978 at the University of Kansas, the first article I published, "Structure for Openness: An Eighth Grade Unit on Exploration," described an interdisciplinary unit that Yvonne and I developed and taught almost a decade earlier.

In the late 1960s and early 1970s I had walked, stumbling at times, into a juxtaposition of two educational practices, one with its routes early in the twentieth century (interdisciplinary curriculum) and one newly introduced into education (interdisciplinary teaming). The coming together of the two seemed so natural for meeting the professional growth needs of teachers and the learning needs of youngsters. Though I learned little of either in my preservice training, under Yvonne's leadership and with the support of the building administration, we grew teaming at Howard Junior High from the bottom up. Experiencing the effective functioning of interdisciplinary teaming, and only later studying the research, has propelled my personal and professional interest in promoting its use in middle schools.

What I did not understand then, but what has become clear in the past twenty-five years is that Howard Junior High School was on the cutting edge of a new era in school organization. Schools organized around teacher teams as opposed to teachers working in separate classrooms represented a shift in the work life of teachers more profound than the shift from one-room to multi-classroom schools that had occurred earlier in the twentieth century. The continuing debate about how best to plan curriculum and to instruct youngsters was to evermore take place against the backdrop of a new way of doing business in schools. Schools at the middle level were destined to take the lead in reforming school organization in this country.

Teamed Organizations vs. Cellular Ones

Successful schools mimic the success routes in society

How are teamed organizations, of which modern middle schools are a prototype, different from the cellular structures that most Americans have experienced in this century? To understand the profundity of the organizational change that is going on in American public education, it is useful to explore Broudy and Palmer's (1965) insight: "The success routes of an era dictate the dominant patterns of schooling" (p. 159). Comparing changing "success routes" from era to era can shed light on shifts in the way schools are organized to educate the young to take advantage of those success routes.

From colonial times through the nineteenth century the chief means of production (i.e., "success route" for adults) was the family farm and the small craftshop. On those farms and in those craft shops individual entrepreneurs would take orders from customers, secure raw materials and production tools, design products, manufacture the product or cultivate the crops, and market the products or commodities to customers.

Schooling, where a single teacher was in charge of delivering the entire curriculum to all students for the entire time they were in school, was a variation on this theme. The typical American receiving formal education attended an elementary school until about age 14 or 15 and then, having acquired the basic skills of literacy and numerary, left school to take his or her place in adult society. These schools tended to be small so that they were organized around a single teacher who delivered the total curriculum to the entire student body (see Kliebard, 1987). The classes in these dispersed one-room schools were heterogeneous. Students represented a wide range of ages, abilities, and levels of achievement.

According to Lortie (1975) during this period the "cellular" pattern for organizing schools was established. Teachers taught in small schools dispersed among widely scattered settlements. Teachers went for long periods of time without association with other teachers. In addition, these teachers spent each working day isolated from other adults. This pattern of schooling represented a series of self-sufficient "cells."

This small, dispersed single-teacher school pattern was so dominant that even at the beginning of the twentieth century only about twenty percent of elementary school pupils even began high school and only three percent graduated (Kliebard, 1987). However, late nineteenth century criticism of American public schools grew to a crescendo in the early twentieth (see Kliebard, 1987, for documentation of this criticism). By the turn of the century the Industrial Revolution had rendered a good agrarian education incapable of producing students who had the skills and habits necessary to take the jobs available in the factories of the Industrial Age. In addition, this Industrial Revolution triggered demographic changes that brought a new wave of immigration to America and fostered internal migration from the rural South to the growing industrial cities of the North.

By the 1920s a new type of school with two divisions, patterned after the factories that dominated the Industrial Era, came into prominence: the restructured high school, junior and senior division. At the same time, elementary schools in urban areas were becoming larger so that they came to consist of a number of self-contained classrooms. The era of the one-room, eight-year elementary school taught by one person who delivered essentially the same curriculum to the entire student body was coming to an end.

The newly created junior high school took the last two years of the old elementary school and the first year of high school to create a new type of school for grades seven through nine. The undifferentiated curriculum of grades seven and eight in the old elementary school was supplanted by a new curriculum that included new vocational subjects, student guidance, and the bringing of high school subjects such as foreign language and algebra into these middle grades. By placing a natural break after ninth grade, instead of after eighth grade as had been the case, and by placing new subject matter in grades seven and eight, it was expected that students who left school after ninth grade would have the skills necessary to be successful in the jobs opening up in industrial America (Van Til, Vars, & Lounsbury, 1961/1967).

At the same time that the junior division of the high school was created, the senior high school's role was expanded beyond college preparation for a small percentage of students to become a comprehensive school that would serve the masses whether the students were planning to enter the assembly line work force after high school or were planning to go on to college to acquire the training to become the managers in the new enterprises. Just as factories were larger and more complex than craftshops, junior and senior high school were larger and more complex than the elementary schools they supplanted. The new era demanded specialization. Schools responded by creating a departmentalized structure. Now instead of one teacher teaching the whole curriculum to all levels of the organization, teachers became specialists, each teaching only a portion of the curriculum to students. In addition to subject specialization, grade level specialization was adopted. With increased size and the complexity associated with dividing the curriculum among various subject and grade-level specialists, issues of management and control emerged. Consequently, new roles were created for those who could administer these complex organizations, and the profession of school administration was born. Now the large junior and senior high schools took on the hierarchical structure of the factories for which they were preparing students (McNeil, 1986; Skrtic, 1991b).

The means of production had been revolutionized. Instead of a craftsperson who managed the entire production process, what was needed was an assembly line worker who could perform assigned tasks without questioning authority or thinking too much about what he was doing. Indeed a premium was put on following orders and working in isolation (Skrtic, 1989). Factories, as opposed to craftshops, were hierarchical structures that required a small percentage of employees to design, organize, and manage the work for the majority laboring on the assembly lines.

The classrooms of the factory era schools were organized like assembly line work stations. Students were to learn basic facts and information that would render them literate enough to master the jobs being created in business and industry and to function as loyal Americans. However, they were not to become so skilled or knowledgeable that they could question what they were taught (Wrigley, 1982). The production quotas in business and industry had their educational counterpart in the form of curriculum to cover. The covering of the curriculum was measured by counting Carnegie Units. A "product" was complete when it had completed 18 units or whatever the locally prescribed standard (graduation requirement) was. The schools were organized, as were industries, to deliver efficient production (McNeil, 1986).

Though the size and organization of schools was greatly altered to reflect the new "success routes" of the Industrial Era, the work of teachers was not significantly affected by this shift. Lortie (1975) described teaching this way:

As cities grew in size and number, school patterns changed. The previously separated cells were combined under one roof and students were assigned to separate classrooms according to age....The creation of schools composed of multiple distinct classrooms, however, did not result in a sharp increase in task interdependence among teachers, since individual teachers either taught all subjects to a particular group for a year or, as later developed in the higher grades, taught a single subject to the same group for a stipulated period of time. ...Some teachers have begun their careers in one-room schools and moved on to urban multiple-room schools without, so far as one hears, experiencing serious difficulties. Teachers' work, in short, was not radically altered by the development of the multi-unit school. The principalship emerged, of course, and the beginnings of a hierarchy of officials took place. As before, the teacher continued to work largely alone with particular students but under the general surveillance of a full-time administrator appointed by the board of education. (p. 14)

In the transition from one-room schools to multi-unit schools what changed for teachers was not their isolated work with students, but the amount of the total curriculum they were responsible for. Teachers were reduced to being responsible for only part of the total curriculum of the school: either a grade level or subject specialization. Teachers were now to be supervised by a new breed of professional administrators. The hierarchical organization of the factory was carried one step further. Administrators managed the work of the teachers laboring on the curriculum assembly line.

From the 1940s through the 1960s, this economic and educational arrangement helped the United States win the Second World War and build one of the most prosperous nations in the history of the world. However, by the late 1960s all was not well in the land. Schooling came under attack for several perceived failures.

One area of concern among a few scholars and educators focused on meeting the developmental needs of the ten- to fourteen-year-old children who were starting the transition from childhood to adulthood. Although we had learned much about the rapid changes taking place in the pubescent bodies of young adolescents, about the changing ways in which they could think, and about the changes taking place in the social/emotional side of their personalities, critics blamed factory-model junior high schools for not doing a very good job of addressing these needs (Alexander, 1965/1995; Eichhorn, 1966/1987).

In short, junior high schools, organized to turn out academic products fashioned to fit a predetermined mold, were failing to address the developmental needs of many students. The school structure was too rigid to accommodate the diversity that kept walking in the front door. Typically the factory-model school, built on the hierarchical management of specializations, would create a new course or program to alleviate a problem when diversity got too complex to handle in the existing classrooms. After the initial division of work into subject and grade level specializations, it was found that many students were not learning well in the types of classrooms being provided. The result was the creation of classes for the learning disabled and various Title and Chapter classrooms. In addition, classes within subject areas were tracked to allow even further specialization within the prevailing school structures. Industrial era schools tended to respond to the increased diversity of their learners by creating additional specializations that further fragmented their programs (Skrtic, 1991a, 1991b).

Beginning about the same time that junior high schools were being criticized for their failure to successfully address the needs of young adolescents, senior high schools came under attack from the outside for failing to produce graduates with the skills needed to be successful in the work force (Boyer, 1983; Goodlad, 1984, Sizer 1984). While some people interpreted this attack to mean that the schools were deteriorating and that they needed to do a better job of the tasks that they had been doing for most of the twentieth century (National Commission on Excellence in Education, 1983), an alternative interpretation is more convincing. The "success routes" were once again changing.

The workplace know-how that is now needed includes basic skills, to be sure, such as the ability to read, write, perform mathematical operation, and listen and speak effectively. In addition, cognitive skills such as thinking creatively, making decisions, solving problems, visualizing, and knowing how to learn are needed. In order to succeed, workers also need to have personal qualities such as responsibility, self-esteem, sociability, self-management, and integrity. Five broad areas of competency have been identified by the U. S. Secretary of Labor:

1. *Ability to allocate resources such as time, money, materials, facilities, and personnel;*

2. *Ability to use interpersonal skills to work effectively on a team, to teach others new skills, to serve clients or customers, exercise leadership, negotiate, and work with diverse people;*

3. *Ability to acquire, evaluate, interpret, and communicate information as well as use computers to process it;*

4. *Ability to understand complex relationships and systems, correct performance, and design new systems; and*

5. *Ability to select appropriate technologies or tools for a task, apply technology to that task, and maintain and troubleshoot equipment.*

— U.S. Dept. of Labor, 1991

These are not the skills that led to living the American dream on the assembly lines of the early twentieth century. Just doing a more efficient job of what we had been doing for the last fifty years was not a useful response to the internal critics who were complaining about the inadequacies of the junior high school or to the external critics who were complaining about the poor skills demonstrated by school graduates. Just as America had undergone an Industrial Revolution in the late 1800s and early 1900s, America was undergoing another revolution in the way production was organized. Various labels have been attached to this new economic revolution: Post-industrial, Information, Service. Just as the craftshop-model elementary schools designed for an agrarian society were no longer viable for the Industrial Era, the factory-model junior and senior high schools, as well as the retrofitted multi-grade elementary schools, designed to meet the needs of the Industrial Era were becoming out of step with the needs of the Information Age.

A number of other societal changes began to occur in the decades following the Second World War. Economic and social factors resulted in young people receiving much less adult attention than they had received a generation earlier. The families that young adolescents were growing up in were much less likely to consist of two parents, one of whom was a bread winner and the other a homemaker. Two-worker families, one-parent families, blended families, and other nontraditional arrangements came to predominate. The intergenerational extended family was also less likely to be immediately available to assist the nuclear family in raising its young.

At the same time that young adolescents were getting less adult attention, a technological revolution was taking place that greatly altered the ways we communicate. Disappearing were the days when radios and black and white TV novelties were turned on a couple of hours a night. Cable television and VCR's have exponentially expanded the influence of media in our homes. The typical eighth grader now spends four times as much time watching television as doing homework (Office of Educational Research and Improvement, 1990). Computers have shrunk from room-sized calculators to desktop network terminals. There is so much more information bombarding people today.

In addition, the demographics of our society are undergoing major changes. A couple of changes are particularly sobering for those of us whose business it is to educate the next generation. In 1950 there where 17 workers supporting each retiree. By early in the decade of the 1990s there will be three workers for each retiree (Corrigan, 1990). Enlightened self-interest suggests that educators need to make sure this generation of young people can be gainfully employed in the new economy of the 21st Century. This challenge is made even more dramatic by the fact that various minorities who in the past have not always been well served by traditional public schools will make up more than half of the school age population by the year 2020 (Hodgkinson, 1989).

This last demographic statistic leads us to one other force of considerable magnitude that reshaped the playing field upon which schools operate: the social revolution taking place in the nation to advance civil rights and gender equity. Symbolized by the Supreme Court's 1954 decision in Brown vs. the Board of Education of Topeka and pushed by the civil rights movement of the 1950s and 1960s, society began to pay more attention to the rights, including the educational rights, of minorities. In the 1940s it was the practice to spend considerable resources on the education of white students in the North and virtually no resources on the education of blacks in the South. In 1946 the ratio of expenditures per pupil was at least 60 to 1 in favor of whites in New York compared to blacks in Mississippi (Fine, 1947)! In addition, Title IX symbolized society's attempts to provide females with the same access to educational opportunities that had been assumed for males. Since the 1960s, public schools have been expected to deal with human diversity that accompanies ethnic, racial, and gender differences in addition to the individual variations, including disabilities, that exist within ethnic and gender groups.

At the middle level, add to all of this diversity the differences associated with the developmental changes propelling youngsters from childhood to adulthood. Clearly, schools built on the factory model characterized by adding on new specializations to address every conceivable form of human learning diversity were simply not adequate to do the job of educating students for the post-industrial, post-modern America. Departmentalized school structures were simply not flexible enough to deal with the diversity of students growing up in an information-rich, attention-poor environment. A new approach for organizing schools that could accommodate increased complexity was called for.

During a seminar at Cornell University in the summer of 1963, William M. Alexander (1965/1995) first articulated a new type of school to address the needs of young adolescents. Refined over the years (George & Alexander, 1993; Lounsbury & Vars, 1978; Stevenson, 1992), the middle school concept has come to be characterized by several organizational and curricular characteristics. The idea of the middle school represented a fundamental break with the factory-model structures that had come to be accepted in the Twentieth Century as the way to do school. The complexity of life in post-modern America and the recognition of the immense diversity of the learners coming into schools demanded an organizational structure that was far more flexible, less hierarchical, and less dependent on isolated professionals teaching specialized subjects, levels, and tracks. What was needed was an organizational structure that thrived on diversity, rather than found diversity to be problematic as the bureaucratic school structures of the Industrial Age did.

Middle schools were to be organized around interdisciplinary teams. Each student was to be assigned to a group of teachers who shared common planning time and a common group of students. In establishing teams, several bureaucratic constraints characteristic of factory-model schools were removed from the path of teachers. To replace the bell schedule, teachers were given block schedules that allowed instructional time to be divided according to the learning needs of students and the logical time required to carry out different learning activities. Labs, speakers, writing assignments, simulations, videos, independent study time, project time, and field trips, were all easier to schedule by a team of teachers as opposed to the old isolated teacher-dependent-on-the-bell-schedule model that had come to dominate in bureaucratic schools. In addition to better control of time, teachers also had more control over the organization of learning groups in a team arrangement. Students could be grouped and regrouped within the team on a unit-by-unit or even lesson-by-lesson basis. All types of diversity could be accommodated in this way. Whether the critical factor was motivation, ability, learning style, self-management, or some combination of these, students could be grouped flexibly for learning. Further support for teachers teamed together was provided by assigning them to rooms that were close to each other to expedite student movement and encourage informal communication among teachers. In new construction, pods and "houses," that encourage teacher interaction, have come to replace individual classrooms as the basic building block of a middle school (Sullivan, 1996).

In summary, in the latter third of the twentieth century the success routes of the era have come to involve working collaboratively in teams to identify and solve problems. Very often the teaming process involves gathering relevant data to inform the decision-making process. More often than not some audience's, customer's, or client's needs are the subject of the team problem-solving process. To better understand the working of teams in Information Age organizations readers are referred to Larson and LaFasto (1989) and Hackman (1990) reviewed by Kain (1993).

The coming "adhocracy": School organization is changing

We didn't know what to call it; but we experienced a new way of working together. The longer we worked together, my teammate Yvonne and I grew professionally by adapting to each other as our planning for instruction become more and more interdependent. Before Slavin and Johnson and Johnson described and documented the results of various types of cooperative learning groups, we had discovered that young adolescents can accomplish a wide variety of learning outcomes when they work together in groups. But there certainly is no formula for setting up the perfect learning group. Whether we were planning learning groups to carry out some aspect of an interdisciplinary unit or whether I was seeking professional counsel in setting up groups within the context of social studies, Yvonne and I would discuss a number of factors. We were unburdened by any preconceived notion that learning groups should always be "heterogeneous" or should always be set up by "ability" to provide "appropriate" challenge levels. Classroom dynamics are too complex for such simplistic notions.

On one occasion she and I were discussing our concern that some of our students were quite passive regarding their involvement in class. These were students that appeared to us to be capable academically, but who had a rather "I'll sit back and watch the world go by" attitude. Perhaps part of their behavior was prompted by that of another set of students in class. These students were highly vocal and competitive. They tended to dominate class activities, including small group work, in a rather individualistic manner. They displayed a "Hey, teacher, look at me, aren't I great" attitude. They sought the limelight for themselves often at the expense of others. We grappled with how to deal with this dynamic as we planned activities to advance our curricular objectives.

On this particular occasion we decided to create six student work groups. On four of the teams we placed, by mutual agreement, students who we thought would work well together. However, in one of the other groups, we deliberatively placed the sit-back-and-watch students. We did this to force these students to take responsibility for their own learning. We hoped to create a situation where students who had not heretofore demonstrated leadership would have no choice but to do so. By isolating them in one group, Yvonne and I could supervise their interactions to promote their taking control of their own learning. In the sixth group, we placed the vocal, competitive individuals. For this group to succeed, these students would have to learn to cooperate and compromise. They could not dominate each other, for they were all too competitive to allow that to occur. Once again, however, Yvonne and I could devote considerable time counseling them on making the decisions that would advance their desire to get the learning task done right.

Though no single learning opportunity solved our problems, our strategy met with some success. All of the learning groups accomplished the task. Yet diverse needs of different learners were also addressed. Students who needed a nudge to get more involved in their own learning got one. On the contrary, those who needed help in toning down excessive competitiveness in order to carry out a cooperative learning task got what they needed. We were responding to the needs of different types of learners in the context of the regular classroom.

Had we discovered the secret for teaching this class? Of course not! On other occasions we let students group themselves. In teaching an interdisciplinary unit on space exploration we led whole-class discussions to help the students define what problems would have to be solved to carry out a space voyage to Alpha Centauri. The class settled on seven problem areas. Students then were allowed to select themselves onto the committee of their choice. In some cases negotiations with the teachers were necessary to finalize committee membership. However, in this case – ability, social maturity and other factors not withstanding – we were most concerned that all students were assigned to a problem area that they were interested in.

Pedagogical decisions were continually being discussed in team meetings. More and more, what each of us did in our own classrooms was filtered through dialogue. Even on those occasions when we were not specifically planning to carry out interdisciplinary units, the teaching that each of us did was influenced by the other teammate. These discussions of pedagogy caused Yvonne's teaching of language arts and my teaching of social studies to become influenced by insights from the other teammate. At the same time the two, later three, teachers on the team became more skilled at the craft of teaching through their mutual interactions.

When we were planning interdisciplinary units our teaching was explicitly interdependent. In the space unit three major projects were asked of students: multimedia group presentations, individual research projects, and a final essay. Each was designed by mutual give-and-take that allowed for there to be accountability for both language arts and social studies curricular objectives. The research projects were designed to be appropriate for a wide variety of student interests and abilities. Some students chose to do biographies of important figures in space exploration. At the other end of the continuum, some students evaluated the significance of quasars. Topics in the intermediate range included evaluating the planets in our solar system in terms of their suitability to sustain human life, classifying the myriad man-made satellites in terms of their purposes, and comparing space exploration to undersea exploration. In all three assignments a diversity of student products was encouraged. Each committee created a unique product, while each individual created two unique products: a report on a different analytical topic and a reflective essay.

School organization is changing. The teaching that we were doing was significantly different from that experienced by teachers who labor in separate enclaves. How different, I could not articulate at that time. However, unlike the earlier shift from one-room schools to factory-model schools that had a relatively minor impact on how teachers conducted their affairs, the transition to teamed schools significantly alters the day-to-day functioning of teachers. To understand how fundamental this change is requires understanding the differences between teamed and cellular organizations. Just as Yvonne Kuhlman was there when I needed her earlier in my career, in the 1990s I found a neighbor and colleague at the University of Kansas, Tom Skrtic, professor of special education, who was studying school organization. He provided analyses of organizations that helped to explain what makes successful teamed middle schools work, and unsuccessful ones flounder. In that process, he has helped me understand my own experience with interdisciplinary teaming.

Skrtic's work (1991a, 1991b) on organizations was foreshadowed by Toffler (1970): "We are, in fact, witnessing the arrival of a new organizational system that will increasingly challenge, and ultimately supplant bureaucracy. This is the organization of the future. I call it 'Ad-hocracy'" (p. 125). Skrtic's work has helped to explain the differences between the "professional bureaucracies" that characterize the work of teachers in twentieth century American schools and the "adhocracies" which characterize a more adaptive work environment. In addition, Skrtic (1991a, 1991b) has contrasted the way schools are managed from the way real work (teaching students) actually gets done. The earlier Lortie reference in this chapter alludes to this condition where large schools are run by a hierarchy of officials but the work of teachers takes place in separate cells much as it did when teachers worked alone in one-room schools. The term "factory-model" school is derived from how schools are administered as formalistic organizations which Skrtic calls "machine bureaucracies." However, our analysis here will focus on the functioning of teachers doing the real work of schools – teaching youngsters. Therefore leaving aside the differences between "machine" and "professional" bureaucracies, we shall concentrate here only on the differences between "professional bureaucracies" and "adhocracies." In this way the differences between teachers working in teams and working in separate cells can best be understood.

The differences between these two organizational structures can be grasped in terms of how work is organized in each type of organization (Figure 1). The work of different individuals in a school must be coordinated and the interrelationships understood. In addition, the nature of work outcomes and the organization's relationship to the outside world must be comprehended. Both professional bureaucracies and adhocracies are designed to carry out complex work whose processes cannot always be clearly prescribed in advance. Teaching, which involves the interaction of a teacher and multiple learners who are engaging in idiosyncratic ways with a curriculum, is complex work that requires on-the-spot decision making to successfully accomplish.

Beyond these similarities, professional bureaucracies and adhocracies begin to diverge. Work in a professional bureaucracy is coordinated through what Skrtic calls the "standardization of skills." That is, through professional training and socialization, different types of professionals acquire expert knowledge peculiar to their separate specializations. From an organizational perspective all social studies teachers are interchangeable as are all math teachers, physical education teachers, counselors, and so forth. Therefore, all professionals do what their specialized training has prepared them to do. Professionals each working in their own areas of specialization contribute to the total work of the organization – the complete education of the child. In an adhocracy, on the other hand, work (instruction of students in this case) is coordinated by the mutual adaptation of workers (teachers) operating as members of teams. Since the work of the organization (the education of youth) is too complex and uncertain to be left to professionals operating in isolation from each other, teams of teachers are required to work together to carry out the main function of the school.

Figure 1
Professional Bureaucracy Compared to Adhocracy[1]

Characteristics of or Assumptions About:	Professional Bureaucracy	Adhocracy
Work	Complex Uncertain	Complex Uncertain
Coordination of Work	Standardization of skills via training and socialization to a profession	Mutual adaptation (via teams of workers)
Coupling of Workers or Interdependency	Loose	Reciprocal/ Collaborative Discursive
Organization Type	Performance Delivers standard programs	Problem solving
Output	Standard product/service/ program	Novel product/ service Innovative programs
Environment	Stable	Dynamic

[1]Based on Skrtic, 1991a & 1991b

These two types of organization also differ in the way the work of one individual is related to the work of others. In a professional bureaucracy the work of teachers is loosely coupled, which means that there is a low level of interdependency. What a sixth grade teacher does has little bearing on what an eighth grade teacher does. The work of an English teacher is not related to what a science teacher does. A social studies teacher functions quite separately from a math teacher. Professionals in the work place can each carry out their fundamental duties independently of other specialists. However, in an adhocracy the work of teachers is reciprocally coupled through collaboration. The complex, uncertain work of the organization demands that professionals work together to exchange information and develop original responses to the learning needs that they encounter.

The professional bureaucracy can function (though not very well) on the backs of isolated professionals because the organization is performance oriented. The professionals are called upon to deliver the standardized performances that they are trained for and assigned to do. This explains the plethora of specialized "programs" in a bureaucratic school: honors science, remedial reading, sixth grade regular social studies, Chapter I math, learning disabled, gifted humanities, behavior disordered, and "at-risk" study skills just to name a few. There is a predetermined program available to meet whatever needs the school can determine that a student has. Skrtic has argued that a bureaucratic school's response to discovering a new need is to create another specialized, decoupled program to deal with it. That way the rest of the bureaucracy can continue to function as usual. Skrtic claims that bureaucracies are threatened by heterogeneity. Students either fit into the school's repertoire of standardized programs or get pushed out of the system. Separate "programs" for "at risk" youth would be seen from this perspective to be just the latest in a string of bureaucracy's attempts to create a new specialization so that the rest of the organization could continue as usual to deliver its other standard programs. On the contrary, "Student diversity is not a liability in a problem-solving organization; it is an asset, an enduring uncertainty, and thus the driving force behind innovation, growth of knowledge, and progress" (Skrtic, 1991b, p. 177). Adhocracies are organizations designed to solve problems. Teaching would be seen not as delivering programs but as solving learning problems. If a child is having problems learning, teachers collaborate to create a solution (see Bohrer, 1995).

These two different organizational types lead to different kinds of institutional outcomes. Professional bureaucracies deliver standard products, services, or programs. Adhocracies, however, create innovative solutions or novel products and services. A professional bureaucracy is designed to operate in a stable environment where standardized outcomes can be relied upon. Adhocracies are designed to function in dynamic environments that are constantly changing. Given the earlier discussion of the changing nature of society and of young adolescents themselves, it should be clear that an adhocracy is far better arranged to educate diverse learners than is a professional bureaucracy. Skrtic (1991a) summarizes his description of an adhocracy:

> *The adhocracy is premised on the principle of* **innovation** *rather than standardization; as such, it is a* **problem-solving** *organization configured to* **invent new programs***. It is the organizational form that configures itself around work that is so ambiguous and uncertain that neither the programs nor the knowledge and skills for doing it are known....[T]he adhocracy 'engages in creative effort to find a novel solution; the professional bureaucracy pigeonholes it into a known contingency to which it can apply a standard program. One engages in divergent thinking aimed at innovation; the other in convergent thinking aimed at perfection'* (Mintzberg, 1979, p. 436). *...Finally, under the organizational contingencies of collaboration, mutual adjustment, and discursive coupling, accountability in the adhocracy is achieved through a presumed community of interests – a sense among workers of a shared interest in a common goal, in the well being of the organization with respect to progress toward its mission.* (pp. 182-184) (emphasis in the original)

How can this perspective on organizations be useful in understanding the functioning of teams in middle schools?

To the extent that the characteristics of professional bureaucracies persist, teams become dysfunctional or, at the very least, plateau short of reaching their full potential. These characteristics can take the form of either perceptions or practices. As long as teachers see themselves as individually responsible for teaching a pre-specified area of the curriculum, they will self-limit their ability to function on a team. As long as administrators persist in the belief that they are ultimately responsible for what goes on in their schools so that they must make schoolwide decisions and hand them down for teachers to follow, teacher autonomy will be stymied. As long as a bell schedule dictates a pre-specified sameness for the duration of learning experiences, instructional planning will be constrained. The same can be said for the practice of assigning students to "classes" that they must remain in for the full semester or year. This last practice becomes even more debilitating for teaming when students are assigned during team time to special pull-out programs taught by people who are not on the team. When teachers assigned to whatever subject area or program see themselves primarily as guardians of their area of the curriculum, combining expertise to meet students needs is unlikely except as a hit-and-miss occurrence.

On the other hand, so far as teams are functioning as adhocracies, they will grow and continue to evolve into fully developed teams. When the complexity of teaching is acknowledged so that teachers come to believe that their effective functioning is dependent on reciprocal relationships with teammates, then teachers will work together to create unique pedagogical solutions for the learning problems that their students present them. Teachers will view teaching as a "problem solving" enterprise where learning activities are designed to meet the needs of specific learners – teachers, not bells, determine the duration of learning activities. Curricular and pedagogical adaptations, grouping and regrouping of students, and using a wide variety of learning strategies will become a natural part of teaching. When the permanent members of a team consult with those outside the team, their decisions regarding students, curriculum, and instruction will be better informed. When these practices are supported by interaction with teammates, block schedules, and flexible teaching spaces, they become a part of the reward system of teaching as opposed to being additional weights placed on already overburdened teachers. When teachers come to see that what they can contribute to the education of young adolescents can be multiplied by combining their talent and expertise with that of others, teams will flourish.

The answers to a few questions can help one see if the teachers and administrators in nominally teamed organizations are really functioning as adhocracies or have superimposed teams on an organization that is still functioning as a professional bureaucracy.

1. Do pull-out programs persist?
2. Are students still assigned to standardized programs rather than having their learning needs met in the context of a team?
3. Is disciplinary curriculum imposed from above so that teachers cannot plan interdisciplinary curriculum with their students?
4. Are standardized assessments more important in making curricular decisions than the needs of a particular group of students on the team?

5. Do bells ring to enforce a standardized schedule of set periods?

6. Are students assigned to tracked classes within the team setting?

Each of these practices was created in the twentieth century to serve the needs of bureaucratized schools. Skrtic goes so far as to describe tracking (all types including most special education programs) as "organizational pathologies." Each of these practices is unnecessary in an adhocracy where "work is distributed on the basis of a collaborative division of labor and coordinated through mutual adjustment, an arrangement that is premised on a team approach to problem solving and yields a form of interdependency premised on reflective discourse (Skrtic, 1991b, p. 173) (see Kain, 1995, for a discussion of team dialogue).

Finally, is "the classroom" still thought of as the place that teaching takes place? The classroom symbolizes the non-interdependent, specialized professional delivering a standardized program. In Lortie's (1975) words, it is the separate "cell," a collection of which makes up the "egg crate school" (p. 14). However, in a teamed middle school operating as an adhocracy, the "house" has replaced the classroom as the basic building block (Sullivan, 1996). A house, staffed by a team, is a collection of flexible spaces designed to support a wide variety of instructional activities.

Before leaving this somewhat theoretical discussion of bureaucratic (cellular) and adhocratic (teamed) organizations, let me share just a couple of observations from researchers who have recently been conducting on-site studies of interdisciplinary teams in action. Their findings give a glimpse of the manifestation of adhocracy in real middle schools.

- *[T]eachers who were less isolated and who shared the ordeal of teaching moved away from singular views of teaching. They also moved away from singular approaches to solving classroom problems as they shared ideas and suggestions.*   — Powell & Mills, 1994, p. 30

- *As students continued to recognize themselves as partners in the learning process, interesting negotiations occurred, and teachers continued to see students as resources for problem solving.*   — Mills & Ohlhausen, 1992, p. 110

- *Their planning emphasized decision making about flexible scheduling and grouping. They also emphasized planning about novel curriculum and instruction.*
    — Hart, Pate, Mizelle, & Reeves, 1992, p. 93

- *'Negotiation,' 'coaxing,' 'accommodating,' and 'simply requesting' were terms used to describe the decision-mak-*

ing processes used on the teams. Teachers reported that at first they worked on things that were 'tried and true,' but as trust and rapport developed among team members and they gained familiarity with their students, they addressed issues which required shared decision making.

— Polite, 1994, p. 71

Teams where teachers engage in dialogue about matters of mutual concern do reflect new levels of teacher interaction leading to the creation of novel solutions to educational problems.

It is crucial to understand how organizing a school around interdisciplinary teams can profoundly change the nature of that school. Interdisciplinary teams form the basis of a whole new way of engaging in teaching and learning, if those who implement them, administrators and teachers alike, really understand the organizational concept of adhocracy. Otherwise, if the practices that were created to make bureaucratic schools work (e.g., tracking, bell schedules, separate classrooms, specialized programs) are still being implemented by educators who view interdisciplinary teams as just another programmatic add-on, then teaming will fail and the educators will fail to create an adaptive, problem-solving, innovative organizational structure.

A caveat is in order. Changes in thinking and practice take time. Teachers in most schools will find themselves at some point in a transition period where a mix of organizational paradigms is working at cross-purposes. However, if educators understand the adhocratic nature of teamed organizations, they can plan to take the incremental steps that will move them ever closer to effective teaming. Effective teams do not spring full blown like Phoenix from the ashes. They are each created by educators who, armed with knowledge and foresight, dare to be better. Understanding that effective teams themselves change at the same time they are modifying how schools function is also important in interpreting the current discussion about the relationship between interdisciplinary curriculum and interdisciplinary teams in middle schools.

For "Teaming" and "Curriculum," What Does It Mean to Be "Interdisciplinary"?

"Interdisciplinary teaming" and "interdisciplinary curriculum" are two terms that even experienced educators can easily confuse. The former term refers to the way teachers are organized to do their work with each other and with students. The latter refers to the ways of organizing the learning experiences for students. It is easy to confuse these two terms because, although they refer to separate concepts, their most sophisticated levels of implementation are interdependent. An interdisciplinary team that has achieved its highest levels of functioning engages in delivering interdisciplinary curriculum. With the possible exception of a few core classrooms scattered around the country, interdisciplinary curriculum depends on interdisciplinary teams for its broadest and most enduring implementation.

The most successful middle schools in the past two decades are schools that have discovered how to make interdisciplinary teaming and interdisciplinary curriculum into mutually supportive processes. Though the two processes are separate and develop in different ways, at their highest levels interdisciplinary teams and interdisciplinary curriculum become intertwined practices. However, neither interdisciplinary teams nor interdisciplinary curriculum are unitary concepts. Both are best understood as occurring along separate four or five point continua from least complex to most complex forms of implementation.

As in most human enterprises, interdisciplinary teaming is practiced in ever increasing levels of competence and complexity. Tuckman (1965) and George (1982; Plodzik & George, 1989) have described four levels of team development. Tuckman contributed the following mnemonic to help remember his four stages: forming, storming, norming, and performing. During the forming stage team members seek a shared understanding of the team's purpose, its possibilities and limits, and their individual roles on the team. It is a time for testing and building relationships. This initial period of team building eventually leads to a stage of conflict where values, norms, procedures, and even purposes are questioned anew. The open expression of differences, sometimes aided by additional training or outside consulting, can lead to a clearer definition of common ground and increased levels of interpersonal trust among team members. With a renewed sense of purpose, refined procedures, and clarified expectations the team assumes greater risks as feedback is more freely exchanged in team meetings. With greater confidence in the teaming process and in each other, the team members advance to the performing stage. Garner (1995) has described this stage:

> *Teams in the performing stage experience high levels of cohesiveness and team identity. These teams are both efficient and effective. They can get the job done, and the team members enjoy the process of working together. Teams at this highest stage of development are characterized by their*

flexibility, being able to move easily from team tasks to in-
dividual issues to team concerns. Leadership is shared in
conducting the team meeting and in providing expertise on
specific issues. In the performing stage, team members are
more willing to take risks and to express their appreciation
and affection for one another. During this stage the team
provides a supportive environment in which team members
can further develop their individual personal and profes-
sional skills. (p. 13)

All teams go through these developmental stages. Teams cannot be initiated at the performing stage, only at the forming stage.

Focusing specifically on interdisciplinary teams in middle level schools, George (1982) identified four phases of development: organization, community, team teaching, governmental. The organization stage describes the essential building blocks upon which the later phases of teaming rest. These include two or more teachers of different subjects who share students, common planning time, and teaching schedules. These teachers are also located near each other in the school building. These conditions lead to opening up communication among teachers which leads to exchanges of perspective on student behavior and academic matters. When teachers internalize a sense of team identity so that they think of themselves as "we," they have advanced to the community phase of teaming. This phase also involves helping students identify with the team. With the sense of common purpose affirmed and a sense of trust developed, the team is ready for what George has called team teaching. This term refers to a wide variety of efforts to coordinate the planning and delivery of instruction to young adolescents: everything from coordinating exams and field trips to creating and teaching interdisciplinary units. George argued that the team teaching phase of inter- disciplinary team organization was not possible without the first two phases creating the foundation for this third phase. George then defined a fourth phase of teaming where teams are integrated into the governance structure of the school building. Teachers play an increased role in the decision-making processes of the school through their representation in schoolwide policy making bodies.

After interviewing hundreds of teachers on scores of teams in a half dozen states, Erb and Doda (1989) added their four-stage description of team development to the literature. Erb and Doda defined the stages in terms of the priorities for the use of team planning time. Subsequent observational studies of teacher talk in team meetings by Shaw (1993), McQuaide (1994), and

Powell and Mills (1995) have added credence to this description of team development. As teams develop they shift their emphasis (a) from dealing with procedural and management issues, (b) to addressing student needs, (c) to promoting their own professional growth and developing collective responsibility, (d) to coordinating instruction and integrating curriculum.

Teams that have not developed successful procedures for handling their business, including efficient ways to address student needs, and that have not grown professionally to view themselves as a team, have no hope of effectively integrating the curriculum.

Though the particular stages are defined differently, Erb and Doda, Tuckman, and George all agree that the highest levels of performance, which at the middle level involve instructional coordination and curriculum integration, are not possible without teams evolving through foundational stages. A team still in the foundational stages is properly called an interdisciplinary team if indeed its members are responsible for teaching more than one discipline or subject usually taught in the middle school. Some advocates of interdisciplinary curriculum have questioned the use of the term "interdisciplinary" when applied to teams not yet engaged in regular curriculum integration efforts. Some critics of teaming have argued that teams which were created to deliver an interdisciplinary curriculum are somehow deficient if they do not immediately engage in such practices. However, not taking account of the developmental nature of interdisciplinary teams has lead to disastrous attempts to force curricular integration before teams had the foundations laid for such an undertaking (see Chapter 6). Mary Gallagher-Polite (Chapter 10) makes the point eloquently:

> It is during these later phases of team development that teachers have the background knowledge, skill, and experience to begin to tackle the crux of the matter — changes in curriculum and instruction. Asking teams to do this too early can be a mistake, but not asking them to do it at all is an even greater one.

Teaching an interdisciplinary curriculum is a high level professional activity that relies on teachers of different subject areas collaborating with each other. It will not happen without the prerequisite knowledge, skills, and experience.

To defend the interdisciplinary character of teams that have not yet reached the higher levels of performance is not to excuse teams that have demonstrated arrested development. Teams that have become satisfied because the teachers feel they have a supportive environment and that discussing students' immediate needs is enough need a push to "tackle the crux of the matter." Yet the crux of the matter, which can only successfully take place at the third or fourth stage of team development, is not itself a one-stage matter. Anyone who has encountered more than one writer discussing interdisciplinary curriculum in the 1990s knows that each has defined four or five levels of interdisciplinary curriculum (see Figure 2). In discussing the history of interdisciplinary curriculum in the twentieth century Wraga (1996) has commented on the "lack of agreement on terminology in the field" (p. 126). As Figure 2 demonstrates the lexicon of curriculum integration is as varied as ever. Figure 2 is arranged in descending order from least amount of curriculum integration to most. I have attempted to arrange the terms of six different authors according to similar levels of meaning. Consequently, I can find different terms used for similar curricular practices [e.g., Beane's (1995) "multidisciplinary," Jacobs' (1989) "parallel disciplines," Schumacher's (1995) "reinforcement"] and the same terms applied to different practices. For example, "interdisciplinary" is used to apply to different things in the work of Vars (1993), Jacobs (1989), Brazee & Capelluti (1995), and Erb & Doda (1989).

For the purposes of this chapter, I have adopted Vars' (1993) usage of "interdisciplinary" curriculum: "any curriculum that deliberately links content and modes of inquiry normally associated with more than one of the scholarly disciplines" (p. 18). As does Vars, I am using the term "interdisciplinary" to refer to any level of cross-curricular linkages. Not all writers use the term as an umbrella for all levels of integration. For example, Brazee and Capelluti (1995) limit use of the term "interdisciplinary" to only the lowest level of curriculum integration which they describe as "exist[ing] OUTSIDE the 'regular' curriculum" (p. 31) (emphasis in the original). They use the term interdisciplinary to refer to a level of curriculum coordination that is considerably less than that associated with the "integrated" and "integrative" approaches that they advocate. However, this chapter uses the term in a broad way to distinguish any effort to coordinate the curriculum as opposed to teaching separate subjects.

Beyond the decision to use "interdisciplinary" curriculum in a broad sense, this chapter on interdisciplinary *teaming* cannot sort through all the nuances associated with interdisciplinary *curriculum* terminology. However, one of the writers featured in Figure 2 has based her discussion of interdisciplinary curriculum on observations of real interdisciplinary teams practicing various levels of curriculum integration. Therefore, I shall use Schumacher's (1995) description of curriculum integration to further my argument that the highest

Figure 2

Curriculum Organizing Principles – Several Views
From Least to Most Integrated

Beane (1995)	Vars (1993)	Jacobs (1989)	Schumacher (1995)	Brazee & Capelluti (1995)	Erb & Doda (1989)
Separate Subjects	Separate Subjects	Discipline Based	Departmentalized	Conventional	Preintegration/ Flexible Scheduling
Intradisciplinary Science Social Studies Whole Language					
Multidisciplinary	Multidisciplinary— Correlation	Parallel Disciplines	Reinforcement	Multidisciplinary/ Interdisciplinary	Coordinated or Overlap Teaching
Interdisciplinary	Multidisciplinary— Fused or Integrated	Multidisciplinary	Complementary		Cooperative Teaching
Integrated Curriculum Real Life Issues	Structured Core Problem Areas	Interdisciplinary Units Themes/Issues from Curriculum	Webbed		Interdisciplinary Thematic Units Curriculum Themes
Integrated Curriculum Student identification of Issues & Problem Areas	Unstructured Core Content & Themes Derived from Students	Integrated Day & Complete Program	Integrated Learning	Integrative & Beyond Integrative	Interdisciplinary Thematic Units Themes Derived w/students

levels of interdisciplinary teaming and interdisciplinary curriculum are interdependent. Schumacher's categories of integrated curriculum are in ascending order: departmentalized, reinforcement, complementary, webbed, and integrated learning (Figure 3).

FIGURE 3
Descriptors of Team Practices Associated with Different Levels of Interdisciplinary Curriculum[1]

Departmentalized
- independent planning and teaching
- separate distinct disciplines
- connections not made between discipline content
- strong single content backgrounds
- do not influence/interfere with other team member's content

Reinforcement
- resequence lessons with other teachers
- topics or units are rearranged to coincide with at least one other class
- "do" same things as when departmentalized, only the "when" changes

Complementary
- two or three teachers bring selected areas together in a unit that is less than a full interdisciplinary unit
- related classes are brought together to investigate a theme of issue
- shared planning and teaching of related areas, overlapping concepts, or ideas emerge as organizing themes
- teachers plan a unit of instruction
- teachers support each other's instruction

Webbed
- interdisciplinary units with connections
- connections are made between curriculum content and disciplines relative to a productive theme
- subjects use the themes to sift out appropriate concepts, topics, and ideas
- teachers work together to plan instruction and to make connections between the content areas
- may remain in class periods or use block of time
- may include all curriculum areas

Integrated Learning
- themes for study generated by students and teachers
- themes based on social and personal concerns
- blocks of time used
- investigation of themes is primary; learning of subject matter is woven into the investigation
- skills, competencies, concepts, and generalizations woven into the context of investigation
- based on student questions, investigations are authentic
- includes all appropriate subject areas

[1]Adapted from Schumacher, 1995. Used with permission.

What Schumacher has added to the dialogue about the relationship between interdisciplinary teams and interdisciplinary curriculum is that teams –
no matter what their level of development – do not always instruct students at
the same level of curriculum integration. The team that was categorized as
"departmentalized" did some reinforcement and complementary teaching
where teachers planned to support each other's units. The team that was
identified as engaging in the most "integrated learning" was also observed to
teach from time to time throughout the year at each of the four "lower" levels
of curriculum integration. Even teams that are capable of the highest level of
curriculum integration do not always teach at that level, though they may
spend 80% to 90% of their time teaching at some level of interdisciplinary
curriculum. What cannot be overlooked is that no team moves beyond what
Schumacher called "departmentalized" without first going through the
foundational stages of team development that Tuckman, George, and Erb and
Doda have described.

Even for teams that have developed to the team teaching (George) or
coordinating instruction and integrating curriculum (Erb & Doda) stage, the
levels of curriculum integration that they engage in vary from instructional
unit to instructional unit and even within those units. Schumacher (1995) has
helped us see that understanding the relationship between interdisciplinary
team development and interdisciplinary teaching is complex and textured.

Inexperienced teams have procedural issues to resolve; they need to learn
how to deal with immediate student needs without that activity devouring all
of their time; they need to acquire knowledge of both teammates and other
curricular areas before they can engage in the more complex interdisciplinary
curriculum levels. After the foundations of interdisciplinary teams are laid,
the further development of teams and the development of interdisciplinary
instruction become increasingly interrelated processes. Success with reinforcement or complementary levels of curriculum integration can be confidence builders to support subsequent attempts to move toward webbed or
integrated learning. Curriculum integration in a teamed school cannot be
understood, let alone successfully implemented, without taking into account
the developmental stage of the teams themselves. Figure 4 is an attempt to
visually show that the higher levels of interdisciplinary curriculum are
associated with the highest level of interdisciplinary team development.
However, once the foundational levels of procedures and student needs are
achieved, teams can begin to proceed up the interdisciplinary curriculum
ladder as they simultaneously continue to develop supportive teaming
processes.

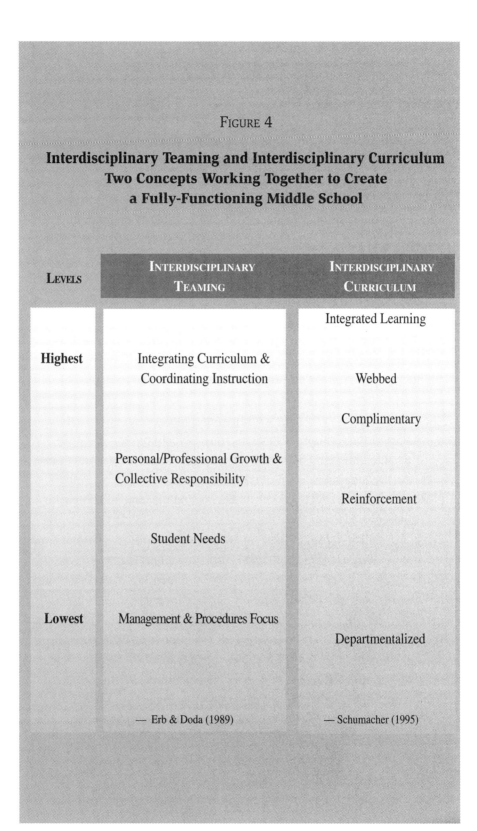

FIGURE 4

**Interdisciplinary Teaming and Interdisciplinary Curriculum
Two Concepts Working Together to Create
a Fully-Functioning Middle School**

LEVELS	INTERDISCIPLINARY TEAMING	INTERDISCIPLINARY CURRICULUM
		Integrated Learning
Highest	Integrating Curriculum & Coordinating Instruction	Webbed
		Complimentary
	Personal/Professional Growth & Collective Responsibility	
		Reinforcement
	Student Needs	
Lowest	Management & Procedures Focus	
		Departmentalized
	— Erb & Doda (1989)	— Schumacher (1995)

Schumacher (1995) has identified six aspects of teaming that are necessary for teams to successfully reach the upper levels of interdisciplinary curriculum. Though Schumacher's analysis is based on studying contemporary interdisciplinary teams, Van Zandt and Albright (1996) detail a parallel list of concerns derived from earlier efforts to integrate curriculum (Faunce and Bossing, 1958; Wright, 1950, 1952, 1958): (a) training that emphasizes the why as well as how of curriculum integration, (b) sufficient time for planning, (c) adequate instructional resources, and (d) the administrative leadership to allow all of the other concerns to be addressed adequately.

The first requisite that Schumacher found was that among the team members there is at least one "torch bearer" who takes a proactive stance for implementing integrated curriculum. This person is the catalyst for a curriculum partnership involving other members of the team. Second, the webbed and integrated learning levels are seldom achieved without preservice or inservice programs that address the philosophy of curriculum integration and provide practical experiences dealing with classroom management, student evaluation, teacher evaluation, resource procurement, and student achievement.

This observation is consistent with Erb and Doda's contention that the teaming stage of promoting personal and professional growth precedes the stage of coordinating instruction and integrating curriculum. Although in practice the two stages can overlap each other, it is clear that the highest levels of professional practice do not occur without accompanying professional development.

Third, team planning time where administrivia is kept to a minimum and "curriculum conversation" is one of the primary reasons for meeting is essential for getting to the webbed and integrated learning levels. The fourth element associated with higher levels of curriculum integration is team composition. Having teams made up of teachers with complementary personalities, working styles, and curriculum expertise is critical. These members need to stay together as a team for longer than a year to develop the foundational skills that support interdisciplinary curriculum. The fifth element is having a system by which teachers can access timely and appropriate resources for teaching an interdisciplinary unit. Using technology, the media center, and volunteer support to gather, catalog, and store materials is important.

A sixth element is having the administrative commitment to teaming and curriculum integration so that the other five elements get supported. Staff development, access to resources, encouragement of curriculum conversation, careful staffing of teams, and support for torch bearers all require administrative support so that these elements can in turn form the foundation for curriculum integration.

Where Does "Team Teaching" Fit?

Team teaching occurred in Wilmette; team planning took place more frequently. During the four years that I taught in Wilmette, I taught with five different teammates. In no two years was our team configured exactly the same. During most of that time we worked as a three-person team. One year science joined language arts and social studies to form the team. During the last two years I was there I teamed with two language arts teachers. Yvonne and I were constants for three and one half years. Each year we would initiate a new teammate. In the middle of the 1970-71 school year Yvonne resigned to follow her husband to a new job in San Francisco. In midyear she was replaced on the team by Karen Simmons, who coincidentally had just arrived from San Francisco. So after just three and a half years, this recent neophyte became the senior member of the team! Though our Wilmette years are long past, Karen and I have maintained a teaming relationship for more than a quarter century.

Whatever the combination of subjects and teammates, we met daily to discuss our students, our teaching, and future or current interdisciplinary units. As subject specialists we often taught subject matter and skills in our separate classrooms. Yet we often carried out what Vars (1993) calls "correlation" teaching. One year we planned to teach about ethnicity and race relations. Instead of a full-blown interdisciplinary unit we coordinated our teaching in language arts and social studies. Yvonne read *Raisin in the Sun* and *To Kill a Mockingbird* with our students while I studied "A Day in the Life of a Slave" with these same students, leading up to playing the simulation "Sunshine" where students assumed the roles of people with different ethnicities and socioeconomic circumstances. On numerous occasions, my teammates and I would plan our teaching together without benefit of integrative themes or being in each others' classrooms. Yet this joint planning allowed us to provide more coherence to our students' learning experiences than would have been possible with each of us operating in isolation.

The teaming also allowed us three or four times a year to teach more fully integrated units. Though we would provide for a great deal of student choice within the units we taught, we generally did not go beyond what Vars (1993) called "structured core." The previously mentioned unit on space exploration is such an example. We choose space exploration as a theme at a time when America's race to the moon was nearing its culmination in the late 1960s, though we let the students choose the destination, Alpha Centauri. It was during these interdisciplinary units that we not only team planned, but we also team taught. When students were working in their committees, they might be supervised by any adult member of the team. We adults teamed together not only to offer advice on process and on product, but also to help locate resources including people in the community such as a psychologist to assist the personnel committee and an aerospace engineer to assist the rocketry committee. Our teaching was influenced not only by our classroom interactions with each other, but by the emerging needs of our students as they pursued their learning tasks.

Team teaching is related to its big cousins, interdisciplinary teaming and interdisciplinary curriculum. As we have seen interdisciplinary teaming and interdisciplinary curriculum are not interchangeable terms. Nor is either interchangeable with team teaching. An interdisciplinary team can exist whether or not team teaching is occurring. Indeed in George's (1982) view, teams must proceed through two stages of development before they reach the "team teaching" stage. The opposite is also possible—if not long lived – where team teaching can occur in isolated pockets without interdisciplinary teams existing.

As was discussed earlier in this chapter, an interdisciplinary team can exist whether or not an interdisciplinary curriculum is being taught. The opposite, however, (an interdisciplinary curriculum without an interdisciplinary team) is impossible to imagine let alone accomplish – except in the unlikely event someone could figure out how to impose an interdisciplinary curriculum from above on a set of teachers operating primarily as department members! Palmer (1995); Pate, McGinnis, and Homestead (1995); Polite (1994), and Mills and Ohlhausen (1992) all describe teams in the act of negotiating the creation of interdisciplinary curriculum.

I must concede a historical point here to the guardians of core curriculum. Yes indeed, core curriculum can be taught without benefit of teaming by a single teacher with a block-of-time schedule (note my own humble beginnings mentioned above). However, the practice of self-contained or single-teacher block plans are a dwindling reality in middle level schools. Delivering curriculum to middle grades students via a self-contained approach has diminished by one half to two thirds form 1968 to 1993 (McEwin, Dickinson, & Jenkins, 1996). This is easily explained by pointing out that self-contained and single-teacher blocks are merely variations on the theme of isolated teachers in factory-model Industrial Era schools. So while the theoretical possibility exists to have interdisciplinary curriculum without interdisciplinary teaming, it is a historical curiosity rather than a possibility with a future.

While we have attempted to sort out both the differences and relationships between interdisciplinary teaming and interdisciplinary curriculum there is more to be said about team teaching, the simplest of the three practices to understand. When two or more teachers of the same or different disciplines jointly teach a course or instructional unit to the same group of students team teaching is taking place. The joint teaching implies some degree of joint planning as well. As has been often the case, a language arts teacher and a social studies teacher teaching social topics by integrating relevant literature and requiring that student ideas are written to meet appropriate standards of composition is a typical example of team teaching. Team teaching has been advocated for teaching at the middle and secondary levels since the dawn of the Progressive Era (Wraga, 1992/1993, 1996). However, team teaching never caught on as a predominate teaching strategy, primarily because for most of this century team teaching was the result of two teachers attempting to work together in an otherwise departmentalized school structure. Departmentalized junior and senior high schools provided little institutional support for these idiosyncratic teaching arrangements. While particularly imaginative and energetic teachers could be found dotted around the educational landscape engaged in team teaching, the practice was never widespread and remains a relatively insignificant curiosity in the history of departmentalized schooling in the twentieth century.

Though no hard data exist to verify the following statement, it is reasonable to assert that team teaching has seen a revival in the past two decades in schools where interdisciplinary teams have been established. In schools organized around teams of teachers, team teaching is supported by the larger organizational structure of the school. Once teams have progressed through the organizational and procedural stage of teaming past the community and student concerns stage, team teaching is compatible with further development of teams. In departmentalized schools, after two teachers have fought the structure of their school for a couple of years the departmentalized organization tended to swallow them up again. Today in those 50% of middle level schools organized around interdisciplinary teams, some form of team teaching can be expected to occur at least part of the time after foundational concerns are addressed.

On interdisciplinary teams the real power in team teaching lies in team planning for instruction. Whether teachers are planning to coordinate separate subjects or to create with students units integrated around problems to be solved or student questions to be answered, the instruction of students becomes more powerful. The joint planning of curriculum by teachers with different perspectives, backgrounds, and learning and teaching styles leads to more effective instructional experiences for students whether or not two teachers appear simultaneously in the same classroom with a group of students.

Teaming's Impact on Curricular Integration: Is the Glass Half Full or Half Empty?

The controversy continues in the field of middle level education regarding the extent to which the intended reforms have actually become institutionalized. There is some consensus among curriculum theorists that structural and organizational reforms have outraced curricular reforms in middle level education (Beane, 1993; Brazee & Capelluti, 1995; Lipsitz, 1984; Vars, 1993). They concede that interdisciplinary teaming is practiced in some form in far more places than is interdisciplinary curriculum and that it has been a faster growing practice: less than 10% of schools in 1968, between 20% and 30% in 1988 (Alexander & McEwin, 1989), 42% in 1990 (Epstein & Mac Iver, 1990), 57% in 1992 (Valentine, Clark, Irvin, Keefe, & Melton, 1993). The latest data suggest that interdisciplinary teaming is practiced in about 58% of sixth grades and in 40% to 50% of seventh and eighth grades (McEwin, Dickinson, & Jenkins, 1996).

Interdisciplinary teaming has virtually drawn even with departmentalization in the mid-1990s as the basic organizational feature of middle level schools. While this condition may dismay the impatient, as it does me sometimes since I witnessed the compelling nature of teaming in the late 1960s, this transformation is hardly short of spectacular. Consider that teaming does not represent just another way of doing business in the old way, but a completely different way of organizing the work life of teachers. Compare what you read in this book to Lortie's (1975) description of teaching as an isolating profession or Skrtic's (1991a, 1991b) description of professional bureaucracy. We have seen in less than thirty years a major restructuring of middle level schools in this country. When compared to the last such organizational change in America's schools – from the one room schools of the nineteenth century to the factory-like behemoths of the Industrial Era – which took place over the fifty-year period from the 1880s through the 1920s, we are well on track to institutionalizing team organization in America's middle level schools. When you further consider that the current change to adhocracy is requiring profound changes in the way teachers function compared to the less demanding move from one-room to factory-model schools, the current rate of change is spectacular.

But what of the impact of these organizational changes on the real work of schools – educating young adolescents? The advocates of increased curricular integration lament that interdisciplinary curriculum is not more prevalent. However, as Figure 2 demonstrates there are four or five generally accepted levels of interdisciplinary curriculum that can be practiced. These approaches can escalate from simply reinforcing skills or concepts in two different subject-centered classrooms by teaching related units simultaneously to creating curricular units that use themes generated from student concerns and societal issues to fully integrating skills and knowledge in the pursuit of student-created products and performances. Many curriculum integration advocates in the 1990s are motivated by a bias in favor of the latter. Some even profess a disdain for the former.

However, in the absence of interdisciplinary teaming (or the little used practice at the middle level of self-contained classrooms), *any* level of curriculum integration is hard to imagine. While some *ad hoc* team teaching arrangements have been found in departmentalized junior and senior high schools, the institutionalization of interdisciplinary curriculum without first establishing interdisciplinary teams as the way the school carries out its work is a naïve dream. Since team organization is a feature of only half of existing middle level schools, we need to look to those schools to assess the impact of teaming on curricular reform.

A second examination of Schumacher's (1995) data implies that interdisciplinary teams do indeed cultivate interdisciplinary curriculum, when *all* manifestations of it are considered in the way Vars (1993) uses the term. Even the team that she studied as the example of a departmentalized team practiced some instruction at the reinforcement, complementary, and webbed levels of interdisciplinary curriculum. The team that performed most of the time at the reinforcement level also spent some time teaching at the complementary level. Likewise, the team that did a great deal of teaching at the complementary level taught at both the reinforcement and webbed levels. The team that webbed its curriculum most of the time was detected teaching at each of the other three interdisciplinary curricular levels as well as at the departmentalized level occasionally. The team that engaged in the most integrated learning, spent almost as much time two levels below at the complementary level. This most advanced team could also be found teaching at each of the other three levels that Schumacher identified.

What Schumacher's data suggest is that when teams exists at all – even predominately at the departmentalized level – some degree of interdisciplinary curriculum is being taught. Granted most teaching is not done at the webbed or integrated learning levels for most teams. However, that more and more efforts are being made to teach interdisciplinary curriculum is a reasonable conclusion. This fact is often not appreciated because intermediate levels of curriculum integration have few advocates in the literature. Conservative critics of curriculum reform regard any attempts to dilute the disciplines as a step backward. On the other hand, advocates of interdisciplinary curriculum generally regard anything less that fully integrated approaches to be examples of incomplete, if not inferior, practice.

While some see the lag time between the implementation of teaming and the incorporation of interdisciplinary curriculum, especially at the highest levels of integration, and declare the glass half empty, I would argue that the impact of team organization on curriculum reform has been positive and will continue to exert pressure to move more frequently to higher levels of interdisciplinary curriculum. I look at thirty years of organizational and curricular reform and see a glass half full.

Indeed, thirty years ago the first tentative steps were being taken to transform a few middle level schools from professional bureaucracies into adhocracies, at about the time Toffler (1970) coined the term. Today 50% of middle level schools claim some attempts to implement interdisciplinary teaming. As encouraging as the changes at the middle level are, the current attempts to retrofit bureaucratic organizations at the elementary and secondary levels to include teams is downright validating (see *Breaking Ranks,* NASSP, 1996). Three years ago I attended a conference on educational innovations at Texas A&M University. One panel at that conference consisted of six Texas high school principals. To a person they described how they were implementing interdisciplinary teaming – some up through the senior year – to make their large schools more personable places. In the past several years the Association of Illinois Middle Level Schools has spawned a similar high school association to, among other things, assist the high schools of Illinois to implement teaming. Closer to home, I have worked this year with the University of Kansas's professional development high school to assist the work of the four freshman and one sophomore teams that are functioning there. I now hear high school teachers say "I don't know how you could teach freshmen without being on a team. Freshmen are so different from each other." Or to hear it asked: "Wouldn't it be better if we stayed with the students for two years and moved with them from the freshman year to the sophomore year?" Times, they are a changin'. With the organizational change will come what Gallagher-Polite (Chapter 10) calls changes in "the crux of the matter." We must refrain from making the mistake of expecting too much curricular change too soon. But neither can we afford to make the bigger mistake of not expecting it at all.

Teams throughout this country are at various stages of development. The teachers who populate them are in the process of creating adhocracies where only bureaucracies have stood before. Real change takes time. But where teachers are learning to share the responsibility for educating youth and in the process creating unique learning environments that emerge from their dialogues with colleagues, true personalized learning results.

What began to emerge three decades ago in places like Wilmette is changing the nature of schooling forever. It just made common sense to put two heads together in that year of 1967-68. What two (or three or four) people can do together for 60 (or 90 or 120) students is so much more than what those two can do working alone. Everything from helping students with learning or socialization problems, to coordinating the teaching of skills and knowledge, to providing a more coherent curriculum are made easier when knowledgeable adults work together. If single parenting is considered so difficult, why would we persist in thinking that single teaching would be better than doing it as part of a partnership?

References

Alexander, W.M. (1995). The junior high: A changing view. *Middle School Journal, 26,* (3), 20-24. (Reprinted from *Readings in curriculum,* pp. 418-435, by G. Hass & K. Wiles, Eds., 1965, Boston: Allyn & Bacon)

Alexander, W.M., & McEwin, C. K. (1989). *Schools in the middle: Status and progress.* Columbus, OH: National Middle School Association.

Beane, J.A. (1993). *A middle school curriculum* (2nd ed.). Columbus, OH: National Middle School Association.

Beane, J.A. (1995). Introduction: What is a coherent curriculum? In J. A. Beane (Ed.). *Toward a coherent curriculum* (pp. 1-14). Alexandria, VA: Association. for Supervision & Curriculum Development.

Bohrer, K. (1995). Diverse learning styles; A classroom's greatest asset. *Middle School Journal, 27* (1), 50-55.

Boyer, E.L. (1993). *High school: A report on secondary education in America.* New York: Harper & Row.

Brazee, E.N., & Capelluti.J. (1995). *Dissolving boundaries: Toward an integrative curriculum.* Columbus, OH: National Middle School Association.

Broudy, H.S., & Palmer, J.R. (1965). *Exemplars of teaching method.* Chicago: Rand McNally.

Corrigan, D. (1990). *Context for the discussion of the collaborative development of integrated services for children and families: The education side.* Paper presented at the National Symposium on Integrated Services for Children and Families, Alexandria, VA, March 5–6.

Eichhorn, D.H. (1966). *The middle school.* New York: The Center for Applied Research in Education, Inc. (Reprinted as Eichhorn, D.H. (1987). *The middle school.* Columbus, OH: National Middle School Association.).

Epstein, J.L., & Mac Iver, D.J. (1990). *Education in the middle grades: National practices and trends.* Columbus, OH: National Middle School Association.

Erb, T.O., & Doda, N.M. (1989). *Team organization: Promise—practices and possibilities.* Washington, DC: National Education Association.

Faunce, R.C., & Bossing, N.L. (1958). *Developing the core curriculum* (2nd ed.). New York: Prentice-Hall.

Fine, B. (1947). *Our children are cheated: The crisis in American education.* New York: Henry Holt & Co.

Garner, H.G. (1995). Teamwork in education and childcare. In H.G. Garner (Ed.), *Teamwork models and experience in education* (pp. 1-16). Boston: Allyn & Bacon.

George, P.S. (1982). Interdisciplinary team organization: Four operational phases. *Middle School Journal. 13* (3), 10–13.

George, P.S., & Alexander, W.M. (1993). *The exemplary middle school* (2nd ed.). Fort Worth, TX: Harcourt Brace Jovanovich.

Goodlad, J.I. (1984). *A place called school: Prospects for the future.* New York: McGraw-Hill.

Hackman, J.R. (1990). *Groups that work (and those that don't): Creating conditions for effective teamwork.* San Francisco: Jossey-Bass.

Hart, L.E., Pate, P.E., Mizelle, N.B., & Reeves, J.L. (1992). Interdisciplinary team development in the middle school: A study of the Delta Project. *Research in Middle Level Education, 16* (1), 79-98.

Hodgkinson, H.L. (1989). *The same client: The demographics of education and service delivery systems.* Washington, DC: Institute for Educational Leadership/Center for Demographic Policy.

Jacobs, H.H. (1989). Design options for an integrated curriculum. In H.H. Jacobs (Ed.), *Interdisciplinary curriculum: Design & implementation* (pp. 13-24). Alexandria, VA: Association. for Supervision & Curriculum Development.

Kain, D.L. (1993). Helping teams succeed: An essay review of *Groups that work (and those that don't): Creating conditions for effective teamwork. Middle School Journal, 24* (4), 25-31.

Kain, D.L. (1995). Adding dialogue to a team's agenda. *Middle School Journal, 26* (4), 3-6.

Kliebard, H.M. (1987). *The struggle for the American curriculum, 1893-1958.* New York: Routledge & Kegan Paul.

Larson, C.E., & LaFasto, F.M.J. (1989). *Teamwork: What must go right/what can go wrong.* Newbury Park, CA: Sage Publications.

Lipsitz, J. (1984). *Successful schools for young adolescents.* New Brunswick, NJ: Transaction Books.

Lortie, D.C. (1975). *Schoolteacher: A sociological study.* Chicago: University of Chicago Press.

Lounsbury, J.H., & Vars, G.F. (1978). *A curriculum for the middle school years.* New York: Harper & Row.

McEwin, C.K., Dickinson, T.S., & Jenkins, D.M. (1996). *America's middle schools: Practices and progress—A 25 year perspective.* Columbus, OH: National Middle School Association.

McNeil, L.M. (1986). *Contradictions of control: school structure and school knowledge.* New York: Routledge.

McQuaide, J. (1994). Implementation of team planning time. *Research in Middle Level Education, 17* (2), 27-45.

Mills, R.F., & Ohlhausen, M.M. (1992). Negotiating a workshop in middle school language arts: A case study of two team teachers. *Research in Middle Level Education, 16* (1), 99-114.

Mintzberg, H. (1979). *The structuring of organizations.* Englewood Cliffs, NJ: Prentice-Hall.

National Association of Secondary School Principals. (1996). *Breaking ranks: Changing an American institution.* Reston, VA: Author.

National Commission on Excellence in Education. (1983). *A nation at risk: The imperative for educational reform.* Washington, DC: U.S. Government Printing Office.

Office of Educational Research and Improvement. (1990). *National educational longitudinal study of 1988: A profile of the American eighth grader.* Washington, DC: U.S. Department of Education.

Palmer, J.M. (1995). Interdisciplinary curriculum—again. In J.A. Beane, (Ed.), *Toward a coherent curriculum* (1995 ASCD Yearbook) (pp. 55-61). Alexandria, VA: Association for Supervision and Curriculum Development.

Pate, P.E., McGinnis, K., & Homestead, E. (1995). Creating coherence through curriculum integration. In J.A. Beane (Ed.), *Toward coherent curriculum* (1995 ASCD Yearbook) (pp. 62-70). Alexandria, VA: Association for Supervision and Curriculum Development.

Plodzik, K.T., & George, P. (1989). Interdisciplinary team organization. *Middle School Journal, 20* (5), 15–17.

Polite, M.M. (1994). Team negotiating and decision-making: Linking leadership to curricular and instructional innovation. *Research in Middle Level Education, 8* (1), 65-81.

Powell, R.R., & Mills, R. (1994). Five types of mentoring build knowledge on interdisciplinary teams. *Middle School Journal, 26* (2), 24-30.

Powell, R.R., & Mills, R. (1995). Professional knowledge sharing among interdisciplinary team teachers: A study of intra-team mentoring. *Research in Middle Level Education, 18* (3), 27-40.

Schumacher, D.H. (1995). Five levels of curriculum integration defined, refined, and described. *Research in Middle Level Education, 18* (3), 73-93.

Shaw, C.C. (1993). A content analysis of teacher talk during middle school team meetings. *Research in Middle Level Education, 17* (1), 27-45.

Sizer, T. (1984). *Horace's compromise: The dilemma of the American high school.* Boston: Houghton Mifflin.

Skrtic, T.M. (1989). *School organization and adaptability: A structural perspective on equity and excellence.* Paper presented at the 3rd annual School Improvement Institute, University of Kansas, Lawrence, June 12-16.

Skrtic, T.M. (1991a). *Behind special education: A critical analysis of professional culture and school organization.* Denver: Love Publishing Company.

Skrtic, T.M. (1991b). The special education paradox: Equity as the way to excellence. *Harvard Educational Review, 61* (2), 148-206.

Stevenson, C. (1992). *Teaching ten to fourteen year olds.* New York: Longman.

Sullivan, K. (1996). Middle school program and participatory planning drive school design. *Middle School Journal, 27* (4), 3-7.

Toffler, A. (1970). *Future shock*. New York: Bantam Books.

Tuckman, B.W. (1965). Developmental sequences in small groups. *Psychological Bulletin, 63,* 384-399.

U. S. Dept. of Labor. (1991). *What work requires of schools: A SCANS report for America 2000*. Washington, DC: Author.

Valentine, J., Clark, D.C., Irvin, J.L., Keefe, J.W., & Melton, G. (1993). *Leadership in middle level education: A national survey of middle level leaders and schools* (2nd ed.). Reston, VA: National Association. of Secondary School Principals.

Van Til, W., Vars, G.F., & Lounsbury, J.H. (1961). *Modern education for the junior high years*. Indianapolis: Bobbs-Merrill Company. (Revised edition published 1967).

Van Zandt, L.M., & Albright, S.B. (1996). The implementation of interdisciplinary curriculum and instruction. In P.S. Hlebowitsh & W.G. Wraga (Eds.), *An annual review of research for school leaders* (pp. 165-201). New York: Scholastic, Inc.

Vars, G.F. (1993). *Interdisciplinary teaching: Why & how*. Columbus, OH. National Middle School Association.

Wraga, W. G. (1993). The core curriculum in the middle school: Retrospect and prospect. In T. Dickinson (Ed.), *Readings in middle school curriculum* (pp. 153-169). Columbus, OH: National Middle School Association. (Reprinted from *Middle School Journal,* 1992, *23* (3), 16-23.

Wraga, W.G. (1996). A century of interdisciplinary curricula in American schools. In P.S. Hlebowitsh & W.G. Wraga (Eds.), *An annual review of research for school leaders* (pp. 117-145). New York: Scholastic, Inc.

Wright, G.S. (1950). *Core curriculum in the public schools: An inquiry into practices*. Bulletin 1950, No. 5, Office of Education. Washington, DC: U. S. Government Printing Office.

Wright, G.S. (1952). *Core curriculum development: Problems and practices*. Bulletin 1952, No. 5, Office of Education. Washington, DC: U. S. Government Printing Office.

Wright, G.S. (1958). *Block-time classes and the core program in the junior high school*. Bulletin 1958, No. 6, Office of Education. Washington, DC: U. S. Government Printing Office.

Wrigley, J. (1982). *Class politics and public schools: Chicago 1900-1950*. New Brunswick, NJ: Rutgers University Press.

Part II

Team Portraits

Common planning time, shared students, block schedules, and team space do *not* make effective teams. These elements are to effective teaming as memorizing lines is to a successful play production. They are essential, but hardly sufficient. Indeed, the interpretation of a part in a play begins after the lines are memorized. So it is with effective teaming: the real work of conversing, negotiating, and decision making *begins* to take place *after* the aforementioned foundational elements are put into place.

"Team Portraits" presents the stories of five different groups of teachers attempting to become successful teams. The foundations for successful team development are present among these five groups to varying degrees. Readers of these five stories, contained in the next four chapters, can come to better appreciate the complexities and the nuances associated with becoming truly effective interdisciplinary teams.

The first story that George White tells in Chapter 3 challenges some of the shibboleths that we have come to accept about interdisciplinary teaming. In staffing teams we are cautioned to seek balance, including gender balance, and avoid putting the best of friends together on teams. Yet White describes a group of men that might too easily be dismissed as a group of "good old boys." As we follow their progress over several years, we see their development as an eighth grade interdisciplinary team. This team seems to have learned how to balance challenge and compassion in dealing with young adolescents. Because this development was neither instantaneous nor smooth, readers can see a vivid example of a team growing through ever higher levels of development.

Another rule of thumb is that younger teachers with middle level certification are better prepared to function on interdisciplinary teams. In his second story, White introduces us to a seventh grade team made up of five secondary-certified teachers, all of whom have taught for at least twenty years. Through staff development and long-range planning this team begins its path to development. However, only four of the five nominal members of the team appear to be committed to making teaming work. White describes how this team dealt with the question that often haunts teams: What do you do about the team member who will not pull his weight?

Deborah Thomas, however, lived with another group of experienced teachers who were together as an interdisciplinary team for the first time. In Chapter 4 she describes how this team struggled in that state of being between bureaucracy and "adhocracy." This eighth grade team tried to change old habits and patterns of thought while fighting the effects of such traditional practices as pullout programs. Yet triumphs did occur: the needs of individual students were addressed and several aspects of curriculum did get coordinated. There are lessons to be learned from the frustrations and false starts of this team.

As Sharon Lee points out in Chapter 5, most discussion of interdisciplinary teaming takes place in large urban and suburban schools. She focuses on the unique challenges of attempting to get teaming started in a small rural school. Even if all the pieces do not fall neatly into place, she shows the importance of getting off of dead center to try something. Without any formal team planning time, teachers used the time available in a graduate class to make their initial teaming plans. Out of this effort came unique adaptations of such essentials as team planning time: rotating team meeting attendance with study skills class.

In Chapter 6 Janet McDaniel provides a poignant portrait of the disintegration of a first year team. Her vivid description makes clear the need to understand team development and not push the process beyond its limits. We see in Chapter 6 the devastating effects of trying to integrate the curriculum before laying the foundations for teaming. While we would not expect the Golden Gate Bridge to stand majestically if its pylons had not been set on bedrock, we often proceed as if teams can produce miracles of curricular integration without first resolving organizational and procedural issues and creating learning communities. Chapter 6 should help readers clarify their thinking about the relationship between the development of teams and the integration of curriculum.

These team portraits are presented in Part II to provide concrete reference points for readers as they explore the chapters that follow. As you read about various aspects of practice, study the findings from formal research, and examine the current concerns about teaming, you should be able to evoke images from the stories of these five teams that will clarify the exquisite synergy that characterizes highly functioning interdisciplinary teams.

Team Maturity: Learning to Grow Together An Ethnography of Two Middle Level Teams   3

George P. White

> *I can't believe that it has been nine years. You know, I fought the change to a middle school, but I know now that I am a better teacher because of my teammates. Each year it gets a little easier. We help each other out, we support each other, we depend on each other, and we challenge each other to get better. We make a difference in the lives of the kids we teach and, just as important, we make a difference in each other's lives.* —Al, 8th grade team leader, Red Eight

> *Everyday I go to work is like a staff development day. I have learned so much about myself and about how to teach from my fellow teachers on the team. It took a while, about three years, before we would open up enough to one another and share what wasn't working, but once it happened it made teaching fun again. I hope they never decide to change our team make up because it is a lot of work to build trust and respect with four other people.*
> — Ed, 7th grade team leader, The Purple Team

You can't pick up a book or article or attend a conference on middle level education without being preached to about the benefits and intricacies of teaming. The same holds true in the fields of business and government. In both settings topics such as team membership, team organization, team development, team goal setting, and team conflict are thoroughly addressed. We learn how to select members for a new team, what type of staff development to provide them, and how to help them deal with the problems of the first year or two. Most of what we know about teams comes from observations and analysis of relatively young or immature teams, teams in their first through fifth year of development. What is lacking, however, is useful information on mature teams, teams where the entire membership has been together for five or more years. These are teams that have had the time to progress through the early stages of team development (establishing new rules, roles, and responsibilities) and who are now at the point of clarifying their norms and beliefs and refining their organizational culture.

What are the factors that keep a team together? What unique needs do mature teams have? How do rules, roles, and responsibilities change over time? Can a team be mature in years yet immature in its team development? What are the benefits of team maturity? What are the problems associated with team maturity?

This chapter will attempt to address these and other issues associated with the continued development of teams by sharing the experiences of two mature middle level school teams. These teams represent schools from different community types (urban and suburban) and different grade configurations (6-8 and 7-9). Through their eyes you will see the day-to-day experiences that help mold a team, and through their voices you will hear the joys, trials and tribulations of belonging to a mature team. These teams were selected for study not because they are excellent (although both are very successful, and get strong results from their students), not because they are models for all mature teams (different context makes such models impossible to find), nor because they posses some magical answer to the questions posed above. They were chosen because of their longevity, their willingness to be studied and to share their experiences, and their interest in growing professionally both as teams and as individuals. Like many teachers they feel that they have something to contribute to the profession and have a need to reflect upon what they do and why it works or does not work.

The Teams

Red Eight[1]
Formation and Membership:

> *To the outside observer we seem like a fairly macho group. Five guys, all of us either present or former coaches, somewhat gruff-looking. Our reputation as a team and as individuals is one of being tough, both academically and from a discipline standpoint. We work hard to foster this reputa-*

---

[1] **Note**: The team names and all persons' names throughout this chapter have been changed in order to provide anonymity to the participants.

tion, especially at the beginning of the year, because it gives our team character and defines expectations before we even get started. However, if you talk to the kids in a month or so I think you will hear that we can be a lot of fun and that we are very fair. The point is you don't always get what you see initially; you need to spend time with us so that we can grow on you.

This was the starting point, a discussion with Don early in the school year, as he described his team. Don is the language arts teacher on this all-white, all-male 8th grade team in a sixth through eighth grade urban middle school. The team has been together since the school changed from a junior high setting (departmentalization with grades 7-9) to a middle level program (teams, teacher-based guidance, flexible scheduling) nine years ago. Don has taught in this school for over twenty years, and he serves as the advisor to the student council and supervisor of the school store.

Two of Don's three colleagues on the team also taught at the school prior to the transition. Al is the math teacher and has served as the team leader since the team was formed. He is the former head football and wrestling coach at the school and now is assistant football coach. He organized and now serves as the director of the MathCounts program, an extracurricular program designed to provide academic challenge and competition to students. The school's MathCounts program won the state championship once and has been to the state finals three years. These are accomplishments that Al and his teammates are very proud of and speak of often to students, parents, and visitors.

Chris is the science teacher on the team. He has taught at the school for thirteen years, during which time he has run an environmental club when student interest is present. In addition, he has served as head soccer coach.

Bob, the team's social studies teacher, is the youngest member of the team. He began teaching seven years ago to replace a teacher who left the school because he disagreed with the middle school philosophy. Bob currently serves as the soccer and wrestling coach at the school.

The principal, Tim, indicated that he was aware of the conventional wisdom that when creating teams you work to have as much diversity among members as possible including gender, and in an urban environment, ethnicity. He indicated, however, that "…principals don't always have a choice when forming teams. Teacher contracts and certification requirements often dictate what the teams will look like. Therefore, you work with what you get and make the best of it."

He further indicated that when the teams were formed nine years ago, Al, Chris, Don, and the then social studies teacher Pete were strongly opposed to the transition and that even though they all had reputations as good teachers no one else in the building wanted to work with them. They became the "outlaw" team, a group that came together to fight the system. Don describes it a little differently.

> We liked each other, we socialized together before the team was formed, and we tended to think alike. It seemed natural that we should work together on a team. However, during the first few years, Pete, our first social studies teacher, struggled with the team. He was very independent and never would agree to do anything as a team. It finally came to a head with Tim when Pete refused to use the new textbook or to work on the development of an interdisciplinary unit. He was transferred the following year. When it came time to hire his replacement, we told Tim that we wanted a strong teacher that we could get along with. We thought that it would be important to hire a woman but agreed with Tim that we would hire the best teacher. Bob seemed to fit right in with who we were and what we believed in.

Chris goes on to state that the team had the opportunity to be part of the interviews and that they knew that they wanted someone who would be tough on discipline, had high academic standards, and was willing to get involved with kids outside of the classroom. According to Al, Bob met this profile and has provided the added dimension of sensitivity.

> We are very aware of our tough guy persona. Over the years we have had to work to provide opportunities for nurturing the more sensitive student. Bob has done this, in his own quiet way. I don't want to say that he is less manly than the rest of us, but he has tended to play the role of student supporter, being more sensitive than the rest of us to the needs of some kids, you know the role that a woman would typically play on a team. In addition we have worked with Tim each year to see that we have at least one female student teacher assigned to the team each semester. This provides the girls with a role model and someone they can talk with.

Students both past and present tell a different story about team member sensitivity. They indicate that each teacher, in his own way, has the ability to be nurturing. A former student, now in high school, describes how Al spent time just "hanging out" with him in the weight room when his mom and dad were getting a divorce. How, during that difficult period he offered extra time before and after school to help with his math when in reality what he was doing was providing the student the opportunity to talk about his troubles. The student indicated that he was not one of the "in-group" (a football player or wrestler) but just an average student that Al saw needed someone to talk with.

Sandy, a student teacher for Don, tells a story of the shy girl who was struggling with her writing but had a strong need to "tell her story." Don served as a mentor to this girl, meeting with her a few times each week before school and hooking her up with some of the more popular students on the team. He had her help with record keeping for the student council and encouraged her to send some of her stories to student publications. "By the end of the semester the student was sharing her writing in class and seemed to be much happier and more connected within the school."

The great majority of the students one talks with on the team state very clearly that their teachers care about them. They talk about the fact that the teachers are at *every* school activity, recognize when a student does something special in the community, are always at school to talk with, and seem to know when a student is having a problem.

Don was right. You do have to spend time with the team, at team meetings, in the hall, and after school to really get to know them. They each have a loud bark and a snarly disposition at times, but each cares about kids and they have found their own different ways of showing it. The students learn this very quickly as do their parents. But many of their colleagues are still unsure. They do not engage in the traditional activities of team award sessions, parties, or "special" days, but they do have a way of making their students feel that they belong to something special and that their teachers care about what they do in academics and in extracurricular activities.

Roles and Responsibilities:

> *It took us a while to learn exactly what a team was supposed to do. We had some staff development in the beginning but because we weren't committed to the idea we tended to blow these sessions off. We would act like we were interested but never got too involved. All of us were good teachers and very independent types and we knew what teaching junior high kids was suppose to look like. Our early team*

*meetings consisted of sitting around and talking about sports
or complaining about specific kids or about how the administration didn't know what they were doing. During the first
two years we never were able to get past this point. Pete
always seemed to want to deal with the negative aspects of
the 'new' program and we went right along. The turning
point came when Pete was transferred and Tim came to us
and asked for our involvement in hiring the new staff member. This forced us to share our ideas and to begin to talk
about what we could do and the benefits that the team could
have for each of us. Although we have been together for
nine years we really started to become a team seven years
ago. We now think we have it right. Our meetings now have
a purpose and a fairly regular format. We still mix business
with some pleasure and joking, but we get things done.*

— Al's reflections on the early years of the team

The team meeting began the same as the previous six had, with a discussion of how certain students were doing academically and behaviorally.
Three student teachers were present, two females and one male, along with
the male typing teacher who was attached to the team because the Red Team
students were taking typing/keyboarding for half the year. The team members
all sat in their "designated" seats, each bringing a drink to the meeting.
Friendly greetings were exchanged and some joking and personal chatting
occurred for the first five minutes. This was the normal beginning for a team
meeting.

Given that it was midterm, about half of the meeting focused on student
performance. Al asked each teacher to identify students who were in danger
of failing. Six students names came up three or more times. Bob suggested
that these students be brought in to meet with the team and that a specific
academic contract be developed for each one. He agreed to take responsibility for setting this up. Don suggested to Al that the team think about a way to
reward students who have had a good start. Chris agreed and suggested that
each person think about this idea and that a decision be made at the next
meeting. Al made note of the agenda item.

A student was brought in to the meeting for an "attitude adjustment"
session during which time the student heard from each teacher about what
she was doing that was not appropriate. The teachers made specific suggestions on how things could and should change, and the student was given time
to explain what she thought was happening. The session ended with Bob

agreeing to work with the student on the development of a performance contract and to serve as her "advisor" for the contract. Al indicated that these sessions occur about twice a week, and they are what the team sees as the greatest benefit of teaming, the ability to let students know that they are accountable for their actions to all of the teachers.

The meeting continued with a round robin review of upcoming events. Bob was planning to bring a speaker into his class to present information on the Civil War. Don made a joke about Bob not having a student teacher and needing a day off and therefore the kids would have to listen to some old reenactor. Everyone laughed (including Bob) and some friendly bantering occurred. Agreement was finally reached on a date that would be least disruptive to the other team members schedules. Chris asked Al to check during the next team leaders' meeting on the proposed schedule for district wide testing. He wanted Al to make sure that the team receives adequate notice and that the changes suggested after last year's session be implemented. The meeting ended with Don making a joke about the perceived difficulty one of the student teachers had with one of the team's more difficult students. He indicated to her that this type of situation was part of her "education" and that she would be a better person and teacher because of what she learned. Everyone laughed and the student teacher asked if anyone had any suggestions. A few ideas were offered.

After this meeting the three student teachers reflected on the functioning of the team and on the roles each teacher seems to play. Don's student teacher began.

> I have been here for over two months and as I see it each of the team members has a very specific role that he plays on the team. Don is the jokester, he makes people laugh. But through his humor he seems to guide the rest of the team to what is important. He also serves the role of social coordinator. He plans the friendly get togethers that the team has every so often. Al is the gatekeeper, he determines the agenda for the meeting, keeps the meeting moving, makes sure that everyone gets heard and that no one dominates. He also represents the team to the principal. Chris is the organizer. He makes sure that everyone knows exactly what they need to do and when it needs to be done. I find it interesting, however, that rarely does he end up doing any of the work.

Chris's student teacher agrees with this statement. "He is great at helping others see what needs to be done and how to do it and then assigning the work so he does very little of it."

Don's student teacher continues.

> *Bob is the peacemaker. He has the ability to bring the others to agreement when they have been fighting on an issue. He clarifies the different points of view and helps the others find common ground. He also seems to be the most creative member of the team. He is the one who comes up with new ideas or alternative approaches to dealing with a problem, especially when the problem deals with a student.*

In a series of individual interviews, each team member and the principal confirmed the observations of the student teachers. Tim (the principal) felt that this team dealt with responsibility better than any of his other teams because each member had a clearly defined role, and for the most part fulfilled that role. He did indicate that Chris's perceived "laziness" or disinterest in doing more than what he needed to do in his classroom had led to some conflicts in the past. He felt that this was, in large part, do to the fact that Chris runs a business after school hours and on weekends and that his other work has taken precedence over his work as a team member. Al confirmed this and indicated that it has been a real problem especially given the fact that in the past each of the other team members has worked for Chris.

> *...the problem comes to a head once or twice a year when Chris says that he will do something, such as make some calls to parents or set up a program, and than fails to come through. Team members then get angry and some just shut him out. But usually in a week or two things blow over and we are back together again. The nice thing about this team is that we don't carry grudges, and conflict never becomes a personal thing.*

As Don views it,

> *...a little conflict is good for the soul. We try hard never to get to a point where we are in a win-lose situation, either with each other or with our students. To help us with this Bob usually raises an issue or helps us vent our frustrations on a regular basis. He then helps us come back to what is important and to the decisions we need to make and not the people involved. In regard to Chris, we all have lives outside of this place, although sometimes some of us forget about them. He needs to do what he needs to do and some-*

*times we need to work as a team of three to get things done
instead of four, and we must remember that none of us are
perfect. Each of us has dropped the ball at times. It is not
like this happens all the time.*

Bob's perception of the roles members play on the team is somewhat
different from the other members of the team. He indicates,

*...that we all seem to play a certain role on the surface;
however, each of us at time does the job of somebody else on
the team. For example, Don is seen to be the disciplinarian
on the team. He is the one who can be tough on kids and
the one that we usually expect to play the role of the bad cop
when we have kids in for attitude adjustment sessions. However, Al will also play this role and at times Chris and I have
had to do the same thing. It depends on what we think will
work with kids. The same thing holds for the team itself. I
am seen as the peacemaker but I have been known to create
some conflict and Don or Chris will intervene and try to
resolve the conflict. Each of us is versatile in the skills we
bring to the team and we all have the ability to play the
different roles necessary to have success. I think this comes
from the fact that we have all coached and have learned
that it takes variety and skill to make a team successful.*

All members of the team indicated in one form or another that having
separate responsibility was important to getting work done but that it was
equally as important that each member maintain their individuality as they
worked as a team. Al's comments summarize the thinking of the team on
roles and responsibilities.

*We are individuals first, good teachers second, and then
team members. This is not to say that we don't believe in
the team , it is just that you can't lose yourself to the team.
You must behave in a way that is true to your beliefs.*

Activities: Team members spend the majority of their team time focused
on organizational and student issues with very little time spent on curricular
or instructional issues. According to Tim,

*I require each team to have students involved in at least
one interdisciplinary unit per year. That's all that the Red
Team chooses to do and they have done the same unit each
year. In addition, it is rare that team members will share*

*instructional tips or discuss what they are teaching. That's
just not what they are all about.*

Al concurs.

*As a team we believe that our primary responsibility is to
monitor students' performance. We have shown very little
interest in, as Tim says, 'connecting the curriculum.' We
have enough trouble in finding the time to teach what we
believe is important and what the district says we have to
teach. None of us wants to give up control of what we teach
or how we will teach. Occasionally, we will talk at a meeting about what we are teaching, but it is usually not planned.
We do, at times, talk about an activity we have tried with
the students, but again this just comes up at a meeting. It is
usually not planned.*

Don summed up the beliefs of the team best when he said,

*...we come together to help kids. We are willing to share
time and ideas to help the kids feel connected to the school.
But each of us also has a commitment to teaching them
something. In my case it is how to be better readers and
writers. Al teaches them math, and so on and so on. We all
have our individual style and are good at what we do. I
guess the adage that you can't teach an old dog new tricks
holds for us.*

Classroom observations, discussions with students and student teachers,
and the findings of two student shadow studies demonstrate that each teacher
is well prepared, provides numerous opportunities for interaction, and
presents a highly challenging course of study. These data also support the
team's commitment to individuality, in that little or no connections between
classes were observed or cited.

Students and parents indicate that they believe that the team has been a
very good experience. The students feel like they are part of something and
that all of the teachers care about what they do. One student stated: "Our
teachers are always at the school. They attend all of the events, they coach,
and work with the student council. I feel special because everyone knows that
our teachers make this a good school."

The Future:

*I would like to stay with these people until I retire. This is
a good team. We think alike, we value the same things, and*

we are good for kids. We trust one another, we have fun together and we share the same goals, and we get results. I think these are the major reasons that we are the most requested team by parents each year.

Each of the other team members in their own words shared the sentiment of Don on why the team works and why they are so strongly invested in staying together. There was a strong feeling that they are the best and that each one of the members views the other as a friend. Jokingly, Al felt that Tim would not change their team membership

...because no one else would have us and we would put him through so much grief that it wouldn't be worth it. He also knows that parents would be all over him because of our reputation in the community for getting the most out of kids.

Although they all want to stay together, Bob and Chris believe that the team would be even stronger if they could add a female member. According to Bob,

We still have to work hard to make sure we don't overwhelm the more sensitive students by our image and our style. If we could add a woman reading teacher I think that we would be the perfect team and have even greater success at meeting our goal of challenging and assisting all students to be successful. I don't think this will ever happen and I am not sure how we would all accept a new member, but I do think it would be the best thing for students.

The final session of the year occurred two days after school was out. It was a time for the team to reflect on their successes and failures during the year and make some plans for the next year. Tim had asked each team to identify what staff development they felt would be useful. The team talked about this for a while and finally decided that they really didn't need any staff development but could use some extra planning time to take care of paper work, to talk with students and parents, and to coordinate student IEP's with the special education teachers.

All of the members agreed that it had been a fairly good year. They had a few students that they did not reach and too many students failed too many subjects for the year (seven students failed two or more subjects). They agreed that this was an area that they would need to address next year. On the other hand, a large number of students showed great improvement throughout the year and a large majority participated in a variety of extracurricular activities. It was evident that they all took great pleasure in these successes.

Continuing a discussion that had began during a team meeting late in April, Don, and Chris decided that they would work to coordinate some of the English and reading selections to the topics being covered in social studies. They decided to do this with their first unit of the year and determine the results. This discussion was started because their student teachers had tried this type of coordination earlier in the semester and had had great success. According to Don, "The students liked the idea of studying the same topic in two classes. They felt they were getting away with something."

As he left the meeting Don said: "I guess it takes a young dog to teach an old dog new tricks."

The Purple Team
Formation and Membership:

> When we decided to make the change to a middle level program within our 7-9 structure six years ago, we knew that the most important area that we needed to address was the establishment of our teams. We decided to spend a year having the staff work together on the design of the program before we set up the teams. This way the teachers had an opportunity to get to know each other in relationship to the new program. We then gathered information on the work styles, grade and subject preferences, and general personality traits of each teacher. Finally, we asked the teachers to identify who they felt they could work with, and, who they knew they could not work with on a team. Along with our consultant, the assistant principal and I formed the teams. We wanted to ensure that there was gender balance along with a balance in teaching style and level of creativity. It was important to us that no one team got all the stars or all the turkeys. It was helpful that we had four vacancies that year. We were, therefore, able to accommodate all the teachers requests except for two.   — Ned, the principal

The seventh grade Purple Team is one of three seventh grade teams in this largely upper-middle class suburban middle level school. The team is made up of five teachers all of whom hold a secondary school teaching certificate in a specific subject area. The team has been together since the transition to a school-within-a-school model six years ago. All members of the team have at least twenty years of teaching experience, and all but one, Flo, had taught in the school prior to the transition. Flo came to the school as part of an involuntary transfer from the high school the year prior to the development of the teams.

> *I didn't want to teach middle school kids, I thought they were squirrely and were more interested in themselves than in learning. I was partially right. Their energy level is unbounded. However, I have found that this is a real plus for me. It has helped keep me alive and energetic. I also found that learning is important to many of these kids. You just have to find the right way to present the material so that it has meaning in their lives. The work we do on our team in developing strategies to connect the learning from our subjects to one another and to the needs of the kids has, in my mind, been the major strength of the teaming process. I had the opportunity to go back to the high school two years ago and decided that the middle school and especially our team is where solid education is happening. So here I am, a born-again middle schooler.*

Ed is the team leader of the Purple Team. He has taught English in the school at all three grade levels for twenty-three years and is considered by both the principal and assistant principal and many of his colleagues as the best teacher in the school. One of his colleagues stated, "He is tireless in his pursuit of innovative ideas which will help kids learn."

He is described by parents and students as tough, caring, and very creative. Ed was a member of the planning committee that designed and led the middle school program transition.

> *I knew I was a good teacher but I also knew that I could do so much more with and for kids if the structure would change. I was tired of hearing that 'the schedule won't let us do that' and I knew that there were other teachers who had great ideas and who were also having some of the same problems with kids that I was. After attending a conference by the Middle School Association and visiting some schools that had already made the change, I knew that teaming was the answer. The tough part was to convince my colleagues that this was right for them. Being part of the planning process and serving as a team leader has served to strengthen my resolve that this is the way all schools should be structured.*

According to his teammates it is Ed's passion for teaming that serves as the glue that bonds this team together.

Gail has taught seventh grade science in the school for twenty-two years. She grew up in the district and went to the school when it was a junior high. Parents and teachers describe her as the cheerleader for both the school and the team. According to Ed, she is always positive and has never met a problem that can't be solved. However, Gail remembers when she received her assignment to work with Ed on the team.

> *I was very upset. He had a reputation of not getting along well with women and always making sure that he got his way. I went to the principal and tried to have my assignment changed. I was told to 'just give it a year' and if things didn't work out that I might get changed. Learning to work with others so closely has been a real growing experience for me. I came to realize that we all had our way of doing things and yet our goal of getting the best out of every student was what has kept us together. The two best things we did during our first summer training were to spend quality time getting to really know one another and to establish some rules for how we would work together. After a two-day initial team building session with a consultan, the district provided us with six additional days to be used to 'get ready' for the first few weeks of the year. We met at each others' house and did some planning but what we really did was learn about each other. The rules we set during these sessions were very simple but they have served us well over the past six years. By the way, Ed is a joy to work with. He is demanding of himself and others, but it is obvious that he cares about the people he works with.*

Hal is the math teacher on the team and has taught for twenty-six years, the majority of which have been at the middle level. He has been in the district for ten years, coming from a middle school in a neighboring district where he had taught on a team for three years. In addition to his work on the team, Hal also serves as the department chairperson for the math department, a position he has held for the past seven years. He indicated that his previous experience as a team member was very rewarding and that even though he was being recruited to become the department chairperson at the high school he chose to stay and become part of a team.

I felt I had something to offer as the school moved to the middle level philosophy. I had learned what it takes to be a good team member and had lived through some of the problems associated with teaming, such as conflict between members, increased work load, and school structure inflexibility. I also knew who I wanted to work with and what I wanted to do once we got started. As I look back now I was probably pretty hard to live with that first year, a little Mr. Know-it-all. I probably slowed down our development more than I helped it.

The other members of the team agreed with Hal that it would have been better if everyone had started at the same point of development, or if someone had let Hal know that the others had to go through the experience of beginning a team. As Gail put it,

We were too polite in the early days. No one wanted to hurt anyone else's feelings, and we thought Hal knew what he was doing so we sort of let him make all of the decisions on what we would do and how we would act during that first year. It just about ripped the team apart.

As Ed recalls it, it was during the end of April that things came to a head.

At the direction of Ned (the principal) we were to evaluate how we were doing as a team. It was at that team meeting that Gail and I indicated that we didn't feel like we were a team but a loose connection of people under the direction of Hal. Flo and Jim agreed.

According to Flo they spent the next three meetings deciding what they wanted to change for the coming year. She felt that at that point the team started to become a team.

Jim is the reading teacher. He was a reading support teacher (Chapter I) prior to the establishment of the teaming concept. He has taught in the district for twenty-one years, his entire career. Jim started as a fifth grade teacher and taught at that level for twelve years before earning his reading specialist's degree and his assignment to the junior high. When the decision was made to require reading of all seventh grade students and assign a reading teacher to the team, Jim was not sure that he wanted to teach a regular classroom assignment at the middle level and requested a transfer to the elementary level as a reading specialist. There were no openings, so he was assigned to the team. In his role as reading teacher he teaches five classes and, as his duty period, has responsibility for partial supervision of the Chapter I program with his two colleagues from the other seventh grade teams.

Team Development: This is a team that knows they do not know everything there is to know about effective teaming. They are constantly assessing themselves and seeking new knowledge and experiences to assist them in their growth. As Ed stated, "We see the value in getting together each summer to take stock of the previous year, have some honest discussion about how well we did in meeting our goals, and check to see how well we are getting along with each other."

Flo adds,

> We set aside at least one team meeting a month to talk about how well we are functioning as a team. However we aren't always successful at using this time for self-assessment because something always seems to come up. A crises with a student, a parent meeting, a fire drill – you know how hectic schools can get. The point is we do value team assessment and make an attempt. That's why our summer work is so important. We appreciate the fact that the district pays us for two days of staff development during the summer to work as a team. This past summer I figure that we spent six days working on team business. The district gets its money's worth.

During the first full year, which included the summer prior to the establishment of the teams, most of the professional development time (a total of eight days) was used to assist team members in learning how to work with one another in a team setting. The topics included getting to know each other, team decision making processes, conflict resolution skills, and effective communication strategies. As team members continue to work together over the years, they indicate that they are spending more of their time on program development and on learning how to better use their team planning and instructional time. They also have noted that the way they use their team planning time (three periods every six day cycle) has changed over the years and they are now spending much more time on curricular and instructional issues and less on managerial items. Gail said it best following a team meeting with a student who was in danger of failing two subjects for not doing his homework.

> We have come a long way as a team in the past six years. We now understand that teaming involves more than meet-

ing a few times a week to talk about kids or to plan fun social activities. These things are important but effective teaming involves much more. It involves sharing my successes and failures. It requires learning to think beyond what works in my classroom to what will work best for students in a broader perspective. Being part of a team has helped me rethink what I teach and how I teach as well as how I solve problems with students. We work hard not only on addressing student problems but on identifying ways to assist students in understanding what they are learning and why it is important to learn, on making the connections between what each of us teach to the world in which they live. In order to do that we have had to learn to share with and trust one another.

For the most part the team seems to share with and trust one another. However, one of the major issues that they still have difficulty dealing with is the equable distribution of the team's work. Ed and Flo represent a type of individual who constantly identifies new ideas and develops new programs. Often they get frustrated when the other members of the team don't show the same enthusiasm or level of creativity. This has been the major source of conflict for the team, especially in recent years and is particularly true as it relates to Jim. Four of the team members separately identified Jim's lack of interest in team activities, his unwillingness to take on added responsibilities and his failure to participate actively in new program development as a major source of frustration. As Ed relates it,

Jim just doesn't want to be here and he makes that known through his passive behavior. I think it is because he doesn't have a good feeling about himself as a teacher of middle level kids. His unwillingness to try anything new or to take on added responsibility has caused some major problems on the team over the past three or four years.

You can feel the tension when you attend the team meetings. Jim sits at the far end of the table, usually with some of his class work in front of him. He will participate when asked a direct question, such as how a particular student is doing in his class or what items he may want on the monthly calendar. However, it was a rare occasion when he would offer a suggestion or volunteer to take on an added task. He was typically polite with his colleagues but rarely made eye contact with them and was usually the last to arrive at a meeting and the first to leave.

Hal stated that when the teams were formed,

> *I was very excited to have a reading specialists as part of the team. I thought that all of our students could use help with their reading skills, and that as we looked for ways to connect what each of us taught reading seemed to provide the natural bond. When Ed and Flo came to me with their concerns, I think it was near the end of our second year, I must admit that I was starting to have the same feelings. We agreed that I would try to work with him and see if I could be of help. He was struggling with the kids in class and was starting to let us down on things he was supposed to do. When I offered to help he told me that he appreciated anything that I could offer. But in most cases he failed to follow through. He is not the most organized person in the world or the most creative, but he is a nice guy and there-fore, hard to dislike.*

According to each of the team members they tried everything to function as a complete team of five members. They tried to talk about the problem frequently at their monthly team process meetings. They developed "work load" charts to ensure that everyone was contributing to the team. They even offered to cover classes for Jim so that he could shadow some of his students and see how they functioned in the other team members' classes. In each case some improvement resulted for a short time and then things reverted back to how they had been previously. Finally, they went to the principal and asked for help. None was forthcoming. Ned indicated that he had tried to move Jim to an elementary position but none of the elementary principals would take him. He refused to move him to another team stating that he was not willing to play with the chemistry of those teams and that the Purple Team was the strongest in the school and because of their strength this placement resulted in the least amount of harm to kids. Finally, he indicated that Jim is not 'incompetent' as defined by the law and therefore could not be removed.

As the year progressed it became obvious to this observer that the resolution to this problem had been decided. They now began operating as a team of four instead of five. By Thanksgiving they began to exclude Jim from the decision making process. As they set goals, made plans for speakers and field trips, developed thematic units, and met with parents, Jim was told where he was to go and what his students were to do and what schedule they should follow. Ed related what was happening.

The four of us met one Friday afternoon and just decided that we were spending too much energy on this problem and that we needed to get on with our work. The plan we developed was to work things out so that Jim could do what he wanted but we would plan things so that all students on the team would receive equal benefit from our activities. We decided not to battle with him or to make it personal, but to let him know that we were done holding back on what we wanted to do because of him. I agreed to meet with him and to tell him what we decided. I must say that he seemed relieved and recently he has pitched in at times to help with some of the team's plans. It was a tough decision, and at times I thought that the conflict was going to tear us apart. But I think we have grown stronger as a team because of the process we followed to get to where we are. I also think that we gained the respect of Ned, and strangely enough of Jim. I believe that something good will come of this problem for all five of us.

Goals and Activities:

At the first workshop we attended on teaming the presenter emphasized that effective teams have a clear goal that they strive to achieve. At the end of that first session he had us identify and write down two goals for our team for the first year. Every year since then we have developed at least two goals to guide us. — Ed

This team is definitely goal driven. They know what they want to achieve and develop a plan of action to achieve success. They dedicate much of their team time and resources to meeting their goals. Everyone involved with the team knows what the goals for the year are, and to some extent, what they can do to assist in achieving them. As one parent indicated

It was nice to read in the introduction letter that the team sent home in August that they were going to be working to have the students see the application of what they would be learning this year to the real world. I knew that my son would participate in a series of activities which would be designed to connect information from the various subjects to a community service project. I also liked knowing that the teachers wanted my help with these projects. It was ob-

vious from the start that they knew what they wanted to accomplish and that they valued my involvement in my child's education.

Throughout the years the nature of the goals have changed but every year the team has had goals. In the early years the goals tended to focus on student behavior and team spirit. More recently the goals centered on what students are learning, on helping students learn to learn, and on student success. This year the team had two new primary goals and one continuous goal from prior years. The continuation goal has become this team's signature. As Gail states,

About three years ago we became concerned with the high number of year-end failures we had. I think that year, out of a class of 132 students, we had over 40 who failed one or more subjects for the year and 14 students who had multiple failures. That summer we agreed that our goal for the coming year would be to eliminate year-end failures on the team while not lowering our academic standards.

As Hal recalls,

We spent a lot of time that summer working on a plan that would help us be successful. We set up a schedule so that each of us would be available at least one day a week before or after school for student assistance; we contacted the high school to arrange for students to tutor our students during the day; and, we agreed to keep parents more closely informed of student progress throughout the year.

According to Ed,

We worked hard that year, all five of us. We developed a monthly assignment calendar. We had parents involved as tutors. We held over 30 student/parent academic intervention conferences, and we began to work more closely with the special ed staff. We weren't completely successful, but we did reduce our end of the year failures from over 40 to 9, three of whom had multiple failures. Overall our standardized achievement test results remained stable and we all agreed that the quality of student work improved.

Flo recalls how excited they all were at having achieved what they set out to do.

We went out to dinner as a team and celebrated our success. It was at this dinner that we all agreed to make this a goal each year. This past year Hal and I were trained in

*Project Adapt and we now have a special ed teacher who is
assigned to the team as a support person. In addition, we
have an active parent tutor training program in place in the
school run by the counseling office. We believe we have made
a difference not only in our team but in the school.*

This year's goal focused on the development of an integrated service
learning program which the teachers hoped would bring some relevance to
the curriculum for the students.

*Over the past couple of years we have been feeling that
our students are more conscious about social problems then
we give them credit for and that they wanted to be more
actively involved in what goes on in their community. So
this year we decided to use a social problem as a theme to
connect the concepts we are supposed to teach to the students' world. In addition we all agreed that we wanted the
students to give something back to the community so we
added a service component to our units.*   — Ed

Flo described the process they used to develop this goal.

*We spent a lot of time last year talking with our stu-
dents, their parents, and some of the sixth graders to determine what issues were of greatest interest to them. From
these discussions we identified the topics of homelessness
and change as our major themes for the year. Each of us
agreed to incorporate these topics into our program throughout the year. We decided to develop a three-week unit for the
end of the year that would pull these topics together in a
unified manner. In addition, we determined that teams of
students would be responsible to complete an end of the
year project which addressed these themes. Finally, we felt
that it was important for the students to work directly with
these issues, so we connected the team with one of the home-
less shelters in the city and with the woman's shelter in our
community. We wanted to work as a team in providing support to these agencies and encourage our students to volunteer their time throughout the year to them.*

As Gail recalls,

*Each of us took responsibility for a part of the plan. Ed
made the cotacts with the shelters, I had responsibility with
Hal for developing the year-end project, Jim identified and*

*secured reading material that focused on the two topics,
and Flo worked with the administration to arrange schedules and get transportation. We all worked to find the natural links between the theme and what we teach. Even the
parents chipped in. One mother took responsibility for PR, a
father had his company give a grant to the team to provide
materials for the shelters and many parents volunteered their
time to assist the shelters. It turned into a true community
wide project.*

Classroom and team meeting observations throughout the year along with
interviews with students and representatives from the two agencies indicate
that the themes had been woven well into the curriculum and that students
were actively engaged in providing service to the two centers. As Hal indicated in a meeting at the end of the year,

*It was a lot of work but I feel that the students gained a
lot from it. I know I learned a lot. The added benefit was
that our kids got a lot of good PR from the local paper and I
know that many of them felt good about helping others. I
have heard that many of them will continue to work with
the shelters throughout the summer.*

Even Jim agreed that the project was very fulfilling.

*I don't remember when I have worked as hard and felt as
good. These kids really surprised me. They were interested
in what we were teaching and it was clear that even the
kids who normally were a pain got into this. I think for
many of them it was the first time that they felt that they
could make a difference in someone else's life. I think that
we should continue this next year.*

The Future: The team has developed three goals for next year. First, they
will continue with their signature goal of eliminating failure on the team
while increasing the overall level of achievement. Second, they plan to
expand their service learning theme by emphasizing the value of service in
other sectors of the community in addition to the shelters. Their new goal for
the year will be to teach students to be more goal directed and to improve
each student's organizational skills. The team has already begun to plan how
they will approach the achievement of this goal. They are organizing a series
of Saturday goal-setting workshops for both students and parents. They will
integrate organizational skill development into each of their programs, and

they intend to set up a reward and celebration program for students who make gains in achieving their goals. Their plan is to get together during the summer to make assignments and to secure the resources necessary to achieve all of their goals.

At the end of April, Ned (the principal) announced his intentions to return to teaching. He believes that he has achieved what he set out to do in the middle level reorganization and that he would like to finish out his three years prior to retirement in the classroom. This has caused some major concerns for the Purple team in that they viewed Ned as their key supporter. As Ed put it,

> He was our cheerleader. He ran interference with the central office for us, helped us get the extra resources we needed to do our job, and most importantly he set the direction for the school. We are as good as we are because Ned believed in what he wanted for the kids of this school and let each of us know that we could make it happen.

Each team member is concerned that the new principal (the former assistant principal) may break up the teams. He has already indicated to Ed that this may be their last year as a team because he "needed to spread the wealth". In a follow-up interview, Zack (the new principal) indicated that the Purple Team is by far the most effective team in the school.

> I am concerned that this is creating a problem for the two other seventh grade teams because parents want their children to have the same experiences as those students on the Purple Team and these teams don't have the skill or chemistry to make it happen. In addition, my eighth grade teams are not very creative and have not been functioning well since the beginning of the program. I am thinking about moving some of the Purple Team members to the eighth grade teams and assigning them the role of team leader.

He indicated however, that he had not made a final decision yet and was open for suggestion on how to improve the quality of the teams throughout the school.

As one can imagine, the members of the team are very concerned about the possible breakup of their team in order to save the other teams. In response they have begun to mobilize a subtle but organized "save the team effort" with both former and current parents. As Flo put it,

> Now not only do we have to spend time planning what we will do with our students next year but we must also

spend time figuring out how to keep us together as a team.
If there has been one benefit it has been that we, all of us,
have come together to brainstorm how we can make team-
ing work for everyone in the school.

Hal indicates that he hopes that Zack is serious about the fact that the decision has not been made yet.

I think we can all work together as a school-wide team to
make all of the teams work better. I don't think it will be
helpful to send the message to others that if you get too
good you will get broken up.

So the Purple Team continues with a new resolve.

To serve all of our students as best we can and create an
environment in the team where every student wants to learn
and learns how to learn. We are good as a team but we
know we can get even better if given the chance. — Ed

Comments

Background of the study

The selection of teams for this case study presented some interesting findings about mature middle level teams. First, team maturity is a relatively rare characteristic in most middle level schools. A survey conducted by the author in five mid-Atlantic states revealed that a very limited number of teams fit the definition of "all team members working on the same team for five or more years." Numerous reasons were provided by respondents for the lack of mature teams. The most common reasons were the newness of the teaming concept to the school, retirement of one or more team members, fluctuation in student population requiring personnel changes, and, school "policy" changing team membership on a three-to-five-year cycle (White, 1993).

Second, there seems to be reluctance on the part of more experienced teachers and some administrators to have someone observe and analyze what they do and how they do it. Even when offered the guarantee of anonymity, a number of prospective participants choose not to be involved:

We have a good thing going here and don't want to mess
it up by studying it;
We don't have the time, we are too busy doing what we
do to worry about what makes it work or not work;

We really aren't that good, we don't have anything to
offer other teachers.

One principal said, "I don't want to create professional jealousy among my staff so I try and make sure that no one team gets singled out as special." Many of these same teachers when questioned individually indicated that they keep professional journals and spend time with their friends and colleagues reflecting on what they do, why they do it, and how to get better. This issue of willingness to participate was not due to lack of interest in assessment, but rather to a concern about having an outsider observe and analyze their behavior. It seemed more a fear of "being found out" than a disinterest in the study. In fact, many of the individuals who chose not to participate requested that they receive the final results of the study.

If we are to learn from practice it is important that we work to address the concerns (expressed by many teachers) of the time involved, of the value received, and of the possible personal exposure associated with ethnographic research. Teachers must feel that they have control over the questions to be explored and they must be given the opportunity to have their voices heard by making meaning themselves out of the raw data. In order for teachers to risk involvement, they must have some control and believe that they are partners in the research.

This final section is therefore a collaborative work between the primary author and the members of each team. It is our effort to make collective meaning out of these team portraits, to identify some of the elements which seem to be important. Therefore, we ask that you join in and become an active participant in this analysis, to make meaning out of these stories and to add them to your collective knowledge on how teams work.

What have we learned?

Two mature teams. Two very different teams. Yet each with key similarities. What are the factors that seem to lead to successful team development and team maturity?

Time. Time is seen as a critical factor by both teams. It is not just the number of years, however, that a team has been together that leads to a team-maturing process, but how the time spent together is used. There seems to be two categories of time that are critical to team maturity: regular planning time and team longevity.

First is the regularly scheduled team planning time. Each of these teams had the same amount of team planning time (six periods in a six day cycle). They developed, however, distinctly different patterns of time usage during these meetings – one more businesslike, the other more friendly. Yet in both cases what was important was that a specific routine was established that permitted the team to accomplish the work they deemed important. Each team indicated that this routine took time to evolve (in one case it was well into year two). Until a pattern was established, members reported leaving many meetings with feelings of frustration and lack of control. As part of their routine now, the Purple Team uses at least one team planning meeting per marking period to talk about how they are working together as a team. They believe that this regular formative self-assessment time is critical to their overall functioning as a team. They indicate that spending time to "take stock of" the team process has led them to establish functional working norms and facilitated their growth to a higher level of performance. Self-assessment on the Red Team is very informal and non-scheduled. They believe that through their friendships with one another they are able to "work things out" as they go about the business of the team.

Both teams indicate that the second category of time important to a team's development is team longevity. In each case they indicate that it was not until some point in year three that they began to function as a team instead of as a group of individuals. It seems that team members must spend time together over an extended period to learn how to function as a team (Harvey & Drolet, 1994). This time allows them to go through the cycle of coming together (forming), learning how to deal with disagreement and conflict (storming), and beginning to establish routines for work and behavior (norming) (Scholetes, 1994). Both teams indicated that it is useful to understand this developmental nature of teaming – to understand that the act of becoming a team is a process, not an event. Their experiences would indicate that over an extended period, team members learn how to move from a position of talking *at* one another to talking *with* one another; or, as Senge (1990) states, that they move from participating in *discussion* where they get their point across and then listen to the points of others, to participating in a *dialogue* where the purpose is to create new points of view.

This act of moving from discussion to dialogue requires that team members trust one another. Trusting others takes time and involves risk. Each of the team members indicated that it was important to the trust building process to just spend time together working as a team. This permits them to learn what is important to each other and to establish a sense of togetherness.

Goal development and attainment. Time together as a team is one, but not the only, critical component of team maturity. The ability to set and work toward clear, challenging, yet attainable goals is another important element (Harvey & Drolet, 1994). It is through the goal-setting process that a team defines itself (Zoglio, 1993).

Over the course of time each of the teams developed a process for establishing its goals. Both teams have a clear philosophy that guides their actions. These philosophies seem to have emerged from a combination of the individual beliefs of team members in concert with the stated mission of the school.

The Purple Team, due in part to their original training, view goal setting as a formal process. They take time at the end of each year to evaluate what they have accomplished and to establish formal written goals for the upcoming year. Individual members then assume responsibility for various aspects of the work associated with the plan for achieving the goals. In addition, resources (time, money, and people) are allocated in accordance with goal-directed behavior. As the team has matured, the nature and complexity of its goals have changed. New goals are built on the foundation of previous goals and the activity and goal-directed behavior has been instrumental in changing the vision of the overall school.

The Red Team's process is much more informal. Their goals emerge from the needs of their students and have throughout the years been focused on behavioral issues and student accountability. The team does not write down its goals; however, all members seem to know what they are. There is no formal evaluation process of the goals nor is there discussion on how team resources will lead to goal attainment. This lack of formality should not be taken, however, as a sign that the team's behavior is not goal directed. Upon close inspection and analysis the behavior of each team member is directed at stretching students to achieve their maximum potential and to have them learn respect for the rights of others. This has become the unwritten yearly goal for this team. The level of specificity on how this goal will be accomplished, however, is lacking. In addition, there seems to have been no change in the activities associated with team function or individual teacher behavior over the course of years. In relationship to the goal development process the Red Team seems not to be maturing.

Start-up and membership. This sharp contrast in goal development between the two teams underlines the importance of a third component of healthy team maturity. What training a team receives, how it deals with conflict, and who its initial members are all help determine its future development.

Teachers are not natural team players. They are trained to assume an individual leadership role in a classroom, they learn on the job by observing other individuals at work, and they are rewarded individually as their careers progress (McLaughlin & Yee, 1988). Thus, when initial team formation takes place, it is essential that the members learn how to set group goals, how to deal with conflict, and to collaborate as a group to make decisions. Moreover, as the team grows together, it must continue to receive training and support in group dynamics in order to work through new issues as they arise (Corey & Corey, 1977).

As teams mature, they inevitably encounter roadblocks that affect their ability to continue in a progressive manner. Working through these conflicts actually promotes group development. Despite the difficulties and genuine pain associated with interpersonal conflict, the result of having worked through a challenging group issue often leads to a healthier group, a group capable of sustained and continued growth (Argyris, 1985). Both teams have had to work through difficult issues associated with a group member's unwillingness or inability to assume responsibility for team related activities. In each of the cases the remaining team members have employed a variety of problem solving approaches and developed a set of coping skills that have been useful in their overall development. These problem solving techniques required time, personal commitment, and a willingness to risk the anger of the other member. Because these strategies were employed, however, the team actually was strengthened and *all* of the members grew.

Most fundamental to the maturing process, perhaps, is the actual makeup of the original group. Background, learning styles, and sensitivity to interpersonal behavior are all key components (Merenbloom, 1991). Where appropriate, it is valuable to provide role models for students of this age level. Even more desirable, perhaps, is to have a team that has a mixture of concrete, abstract, sequential, and random learners represented for the benefit of both the students and the team itself. The more diverse the thinking approaches of the individual members the greater the opportunity that the team will become synergistic, a state where the products of the team is greater than the products of the sum of the individual team members. Finally, while many would assume that teams should be balanced in terms of gender in order that sensitivity to traditional "male" and "female" styles be present, the record of the Red Team shows that it is not the gender of the team members but their behavior that is key. In sum, the greater the diversity of the team members in terms of physical characteristics and philosophies, the greater the potential for early team difficulties, the resolution of which will lead to a higher level of team maturity. It must be noted that collectively the team members from both teams stated that the diversity of backgrounds, ideas, and philosophies served to add strength to the team. They also indicated that new teams must be made aware that in order for the team to fully develop, members must learn to accept and appreciate the unique perspectives brought to the team by each member. As Ed from the Purple Team stated,

> *I believe that I am a better teacher and that my team members are also because we have had to learn to look at our work through the eyes of people who hold different view points. These differences are what helps make us open to unique ways of serving our students. My advice to other teams is don't run away from your differences but embrace them and learn how to use them as strengths.*

Next steps

As is the case with all ethnographic research this study raises additional questions which need to be addressed through further study. The following questions are presented, not as a complete list but as a starting point to guide further inquiry. It is hoped that this study stimulates teachers and administrators to develop a field-based research agenda designed to answer these and other questions of importance related to team maturity.

1. At what point does a team reach its "half-life," the point in its development when it has stopped growing as a team and when future productive growth is minimal?
2. What is the difference between true team maturity and group think?
3. What are the reasons that a mature team should be disbanded? Who should make the decision and what criteria should be used?
4. At what point in a team's development should the leadership change?
5. What approaches are most effective in dealing with unwilling or non-productive team members?

The analysis of these two cases could and should continue. It is left to the individual reader to complete this process. It is suggested that the reader return to these and the other cases presented here after reading the chapters in the other parts of this text. It is only then that the richness and unique characteristics of these teams can be understood.

Summary

Based on the analysis of these rich case studies, a new definition of team maturity is proposed to guide future research and team development: a mature team is a team that has been together three or more years; has developed the ability to establish and work toward clear, challenging, yet attainable goals; can distribute work in line with individual member strengths, deal with conflict in a proactive manner, and frequently assesses both product and process.

> *Each year the team is together it seems like we give up something of each of us to create more of a we. It's hard work and at times very risky business. But you know the old saying, 'no pain no gain.' That's what team maturity means to me: giving up self to grow as a group to better serve our kids.* — Flo

References

Argyris, C. (1985). *Strategy, change, and defensive routines*. Boston: Pitman.

Corey, G., & Corey, M.S. (1977). *Groups: Process and practice.* Monterey, CA: Wadsworth.

Harvey, T.R., & Drolet, B. (1994). *Building teams, building people: Expanding the fifth resource*. Lancaster, PA: Technomic

Merenbloom, E.Y. (1991). *The team process in the middle school: A handbook for teachers* (3rd ed.). Columbus, OH: National Middle School Association.

McLaughlin, M.W., & Yee, S. M. (1988). Schools as a place to have a career. In A. Lieberman (Ed.), *Building a professional culture in schools* (pp. 23-44). New York: Teachers College Press.

Scholetes, P.R. (1994). *The team handbook for educators: How to use teams to improve quality*. Madison, WI: Joiner Associates.

Senge, P.M. (1990). *The fifth discipline: The art & practice of the learning organization*. New York: Doubleday Currency.

White, G.P. (1993). *A study of team maturity at the middle school level*. Unpublished manuscript, Lehigh University, Middle Level Partnership.

Zoglio, S.W. (1993). *Teams at work*. Doylestown, PA: Tower Hill Press.

"It's Not Like We Have Good Models to Follow. We're Learning As We're Doing It." A Case Study of the Dolphin Team

4

Deborah Thomas

Only by standing directly in front of the open, narrow window is it possible to feel the chill of this dreary February morning. At thirty-five degrees it is cold in Southeast Georgia. The overheated teacher's workroom at Mercer Middle School is stifling, making it difficult to breathe upon first entering the room. The aroma of brewing coffee and a Danish warming in the microwave merges with the odor of the chemicals just added to the duplicating machine. Its pulsating noise as it churns out study guides competes with the rhythmic drone of the copier spitting out science tests the eighth graders will take today. As the machines race to produce copies, the science teacher shares her concern about the test with two colleagues waiting their turns: "I hope they remembered to study. We reviewed yesterday and some acted like it was the first time they've heard of some of these terms."

By 8:15 most of the ten eighth grade teachers who will occupy this room during their ninety-minute planning period have arrived. Because of severe overcrowding at Mercer, they must leave their own classrooms during planning to allow "floating" teachers classroom space. The phone is already in use as a teacher makes the required calls to the homes of absent homeroom students. They stack the two planning tables, each formed by two cafeteria tables pushed together, with books and papers to be graded. The refrigerator door is opened and closed as teachers retrieve their morning snacks or breakfast. Laughter and social conversation dominate as the two teams of teachers greet each other and take their customary seats. Attempting to beat the bell signaling the beginning of first period, other teachers rush in and out of the crowded workroom to gather needed supplies from the closet, drop work into the copy box, or grab a quick cup of coffee. With a sigh of frustration, a seventh grade teacher escorts a disruptive student to the phone to call his mother.

I pass up the coffee for a cold Diet Coke from the soda machine and take my seat with the Dolphin Team. As I have done since joining this team in

October, I take out my notebook and turn on my cassette recorder to capture the complex and multifaceted team process.

Mercer Middle School

Mercer Middle School, built in 1963, is located in Garden City, Georgia, and serves approximately one-thousand students in grades six, seven, and eight. The student population is drawn from surrounding Chatham County communities of Garden City, Pooler, Port Wentworth, and Bloomingdale; and from Savannah's west side, including eight federally subsidized, inner-city housing projects. Fifty-one percent of the student population is Caucasian, and 49 percent African American. Approximately 60 percent of the students qualify for the federally funded free lunch program. Seventy-five percent are eligible for Chapter One services; however, the school is only able to serve the 250 students that score below the twenty-fifth percentile on the Iowa Test of Basic Skills. A program for students identified as gifted, called SEARCH, serves approximately sixty students.

The school schedule is segmented into seven, forty-five minute periods which includes a two-period team planning block. Each team has three to five academic teachers representing the basic skill areas of reading/language arts, math, science, and social studies. Sixth and seventh grades each have three teams with 100 to 112 students per team. Two teams of 150 students comprise the eighth grade. An exploratory or special area teacher is also assigned as a member of each team. However, since these teachers serve students during the teams' planning times, few formal opportunities are available during the school day for exploratory and special area teachers to meet with their assigned teams.

The school, an ominous brick structure with few windows, has three wings, one for each grade level. The wings connect to a wide hallway that leads to the media center, cafeteria, main office, counselor's office, and teachers' workroom on the side opposite the wings and ends at the gym, band room, music room, and special area classrooms. The school grounds can only hold two portable classrooms, thus the need to identify some teachers as "floating" teachers. Major renovations a year ago have transformed the school's former dark and dingy appearance. New lighting and bright colors create a lively interior. Benches and small tables create cozy seating areas throughout the hallways. A patio with concrete picnic tables offers an option of outdoor eating for small groups of students and teachers.

Mercer Middle School, as other public schools in Chatham County, is moving toward a school-based management system. A Building Leadership Team (BLT) that consists of ten appointed members was developed during the 1992-93 school year, with representatives from teachers, administrators, and parents. Mrs. DeLoach, the building principal for fifteen years, is a stanch supporter of the middle school concept and school-based management. She is a visible principal, serving hall duty with the teachers between class periods and visiting with teams during their planning times.

Instructional teams have been in existence at Mercer since 1984. Because of a variety of factors – teacher turnover, new programs, increasing student population, and changing needs – teams at Mercer have changed members each year. Previously a responsibility carried out by Mrs. DeLoach, organizing teams has been done by the Building Leadership Team since 1992. Each year teachers complete a survey indicating grade level and subject area preferences. BLT members discuss the needs of each grade level and, using the surveys, identify teachers they feel would best meet those needs.

The Dolphin Team

Doris Harn is the team leader and math teacher for the Dolphin Team. She is in her mid-thirties and has taught for twelve years. Her colleagues describe her as a good listener, extremely organized, and a reflective and analytic thinker. Considered an outstanding teacher, Doris relates well to others and is well liked by her students and colleagues. She has a calm demeanor, smiles frequently, and is an effective problem solver.

Tim Melvin, a former military officer, is in his third year of teaching. Tim is a large man in his early thirties who is as comfortable engaging in a stimulating intellectual conversation or debate as he is sharing one of his favorite jokes. He loves the study of history and is a gifted teacher who can make social studies relevant to the lives of the young adolescents he teaches. Although his size and distinctive voice create a certain amount of healthy fear that curtails most discipline problems, Tim maintains positive relationships with students.

Gina Layson is in her first year of teaching middle school after teaching high school English for six years. Bubbly, talkative, and creative, she is in her early thirties and teaches language arts. Though smaller than most of her students, Gina has a dominant presence that commands respect. She has a keen sense of humor and her laughter is contagious. As the only member of the team not certified in middle grades, Gina is taking staff development courses to obtain this certification.

Lattrell Myers is returning to teaching this year after taking last year off to stay home with her children. She is in her early forties and teaches science. Lattrell, who has been teaching longer than her team members, is sometimes distressed as she recalls memories when students gave teachers more respect and were more responsible and well behaved than today. She is very helpful and is always willing to change her schedule or make sacrifices for the team. Lattrell can envision the larger context when the team is planning a new endeavor, and alerts them to possible pitfalls or shortsighted plans.

Described as the idea person for the team, Mary McMurrain has taught for five years. She is in her mid-thirties and teaches reading. Whenever a team member needs a suggestion for a creative or clever activity, Mary has several to offer. New ideas and change are exciting for Mary and she is always ready to implement a new teaching technique. She enjoys taking students on trips, including excursions to Atlanta and Washington, D.C. Mary loves reading and talks about books and authors with great excitement.

During the 1992-93 school year these five eighth-grade teachers on the Dolphin Team allowed me to observe their team process in action. My role was mostly that of an observer as I sat in on team meetings two to three days per week. I also participated in selected team events and observed or participated in several classes. During my visits I wrote observation notes and audio-taped most planning sessions. The audio-taping was valuable because it allowed me to capture the variety and complexity of the planning process. This case study reflects how this group of teachers function as a team. Their successes, struggles, and questions are presented through descriptions of planning events and through their own voices.

Team planning

Merenbloom (1988) asserts that teams need to spend a minimum of two or three weekly periods planning together and addressing team issues in order to function effectively. He stresses that other tasks should not interfere with these sessions. The Dolphin Team met together daily, but separating teaching tasks from planning was nearly impossible. During this ninety-minute block, the teachers were involved in grading papers, making final preparations for the day's lessons, completing required paperwork, and making mandatory phone calls to the homes of absent students. In addition, the guidance office scheduled parent conferences during this time, with two to five conferences held each week. Though teachers expected notification at least a day in advance, it was not out of the ordinary to be summoned for a parent conference without notice. Additional interruptions occurred regularly such as questions from students, inquiries from other teachers, an administrator seeking information or issuing an additional task, or a request to cover an absent teacher's class.

Because of a lack of control over planning events, instructional planning and discussions of team issues took place while the team was simultaneously involved in completing required tasks. Students' strengths and weaknesses were discussed as papers were graded. Possible curricular connections, team assignments, field trips, and special team activities were generated as the teachers shared their teaching plans for the day, week, or month. Rather than identifying specific times to address instruction and curriculum issues, these discussions usually developed spontaneously, triggered by one teacher's comments about his or her own teaching goals or plans. Others would join in with suggestions for connecting additional content areas or ideas for involving the entire team. These discussions were not limited to the planning period but were just as likely to take place at other times during the day as Tim's comments reveal.

> Our team meetings can be described as ongoing. We usually don't have highly structured meetings. As we work during planning time, we discuss schedules, what's going on, etcetera. We also talk at lunch, during school breaks, after school, and even when we get together on Friday nights. I think both structured and informal meetings are effective. Whatever best fits the personalities of the team.

These five teachers genuinely liked each other, loved teaching, and enjoyed their students. The planning period was often chaotic, but usually productive. It was also a social time as teachers shared food, personal stories, and amusing anecdotes. The Dolphin Team socialized outside of school as well, often meeting for dinner at a local restaurant Friday evenings. This team's relationship exemplifies the climate of trust discussed by Stevenson (1992) that results in collaboration, open communication, and meeting the challenges of teaching young adolescents as a unified team.

Roles of team members

According to Erb and Doda (1989) teams that share responsibilities with defined roles for team members are usually more productive and experience less frustration than those that do not. Team leader and recorder are the only formal roles Mercer teams are required to identify. The faculty and administration have not clearly defined the roles and associated responsibilities. Each team selects its leader, although Mrs. DeLoach said she is sometimes asked by a team to appoint the leader, or occasionally a team cannot come to a consensus and she must intervene. Doris was the unanimous choice for team leader of the Dolphin Team. Her team members, other teachers in the school, and the administrators describe her as the ideal team leader. She possesses the qualities identified as characteristic of an effective team leader—strong organizational skills and the ability to analyze problems and provide helpful suggestions (George & Alexander, 1993). She is a good listener, respected, and well liked. Doris acknowledges her leadership abilities but was also comfortable discussing her weaknesses and how she relinquished responsibility for those areas to others.

> Doris: *I have come to the realization that we just spend too much time in parent conferences. And when you think about them individually, there's really no way you can dismiss any one of them and say it wasn't worth the time. But, in being team leader, I think I'm the one that is supposed to facilitate the meeting and make sure that, okay, we only need to meet for fifteen minutes and stay focused on the topic at hand. But they tend to get long and the parent has all this to say, and every teacher needs to talk. And they end up being very long. So, we decided to let Tim be the person who facilitates because I have not. For some reason I always think that every person should be able, if they have something important to say, so, we're going to listen. I don't really know where to cut people off, so it tends to go on long. So Tim is going to take that task on now. Tim is able to address the problem in this manner: What is the problem? What are we going to do about it? What are you going to do about it? If someone starts getting long-winded and off topic, he goes, 'No, we need to talk about what we're going to do.' So, as the parent would drift off, he would bring her back. He is really good at it.*
>
> Deborah: *How was it decided that he would take over?*
>
> Lattrell: *We just noticed his knack for it.*
>
> Doris: *Yeah, exactly. And we all appreciated that fact. I was the first one to admit that I was not doing that job very well.*

Mary assumed the role of team recorder. She keeps the team notebook, records minutes from formal team meetings once a week, and submits these to Mrs. DeLoach.

Since this is the first year these five teachers have worked together as a team, I was curious about how they learned to function productively and collegially. I asked Doris about their development as a team:

> Doris: *At the beginning I tried to have a meeting for everything. But, there's just no way. I don't think, or if you do it's just a waste of time. And we don't always have an allotted time to meet formally on a daily basis with parent conferences, calling parents, and all the paperwork.*
>
> Deborah: *What staff development did you have on teaming?*
>
> Doris: *None.*
>
> Deborah: *How did you learn to function as a team?*
>
> Doris: *Whoever you got on a team with and whoever pushes the others along to guide you and head you in the right direction or wrong direction.*

The organization of teachers in interdisciplinary teams does not necessarily result in teachers functioning effectively together (Erb & Doda, 1989). Staff development, essential for teams to understand the teaming process and learn how to work as a team (Smith, 1992), has not been provided for teams at Mercer Middle School. The success of individual teams seems dependent, as Tim stated in a discussion on teaming, on the personalities of team members and how well they work together. The Dolphin Team members felt positive about their team. During the eight months I interacted with them, I overheard many positive comments about the team and individual team members. Working on a team for the first time, Gina often expressed positive feelings about the teachers on her team.

> *I love my team! I am so fortunate to be on this team. If it wasn't for the people on this team, I don't know if I could have made it. They have helped me understand middle school kids, who are very different from my high school students. They've given me ideas, helped me with problems, and have just made teaching a lot of fun.*

The administration and other teachers recognized the Dolphin Team as the best team at Mercer. When asked to give reasons why it is such a good team, the responses focused on the personalities of the team members and their ability to work well with each other. Other teachers often remarked, "They were fortunate to be placed together." The faculty felt that finding the right personality mix is necessary for creating a productive, effective team; however, they view achieving the desired team composition a result of luck.

Planning a responsive curriculum

Merenbloom (1991) maintains that using some form of team planning or team teaching is one of the best ways a middle school can respond to the needs of young adolescents. It was apparent that the Dolphin Team teachers yearned to find ways to integrate their subject areas and develop learning experiences that were meaningful and relevant to their students. They struggled to balance the demands of their required teaching tasks with curriculum development. As do many other teachers organized in interdisciplinary teams (Mac Iver, 1990), the Dolphin Team complained that they did not have sufficient time to plan. During a team meeting (with Mrs. DeLoach attending) Tim and Mary addressed this dilemma.

> Tim: *Would it be possible to add an extra preplanning day to our schedule next year so we can get together as a team and plan? No meetings, no parent conferences, no interruptions. We need extended time to look at and plan our curriculum.*

> Mary: *There are so many things we want to do, but not having the time to plan is so frustrating. Planning things to do together takes so much time that we don't have.*

During the year the team developed several coordinated or cooperative units. These units were usually planned and implemented by two or three of the teachers. All five teachers usually participated in field trips, special projects, and culminating events. The unit themes usually evolved from a required topic of study, or as stated earlier, one teacher's idea. Initial plans were made and implemented and the unit expanded as it was being taught. In fact, the teachers described their unit planning as "planning while implementing." They said they never developed a written unit plan. Instead, each teacher wrote notes and ideas relating to individual responsibilities. Although the team expressed a desire to develop more teamwide, integrated units, most units concentrated on two content areas with the other teachers involved in field trips or a culminating activity.

In February, Mary and Gina implemented a theme unit using the genre of poetry as a vehicle for observing Black History Month and the celebration of Valentine's Day. The students read and created different types of poems from limericks to ballads. Poetry written by African Americans and poetry of the civil rights movement were highlights. Guests from the school and community read poetry to the classes almost daily and each student developed a scrapbook of favorite poems. Initially displaying a dispassionate response to being inundated with poetry, the students began to experience the wit and emotion inherent in it. They also recognized, through guided class discussions, that the questions, feelings, and experiences expressed in the poems often mirrored their own. Creating their own poetry was a natural progression. Students stopped by between classes and remained after school to share their poems with Mary or Gina. Besides writing poetry, students participated in a valentine contest with prizes for the most original, cutest, most romantic, silliest, funniest, and most artistic valentines.

The teachers required that each student write a research paper on a famous historical or literary couple. They emphasized the skills of organizing and summarizing information to diminish rote copying from an encyclopedia or book. Students explored the lives of Romeo and Juliet, Samson and Delilah, Anthony and Cleopatra, and others. Their findings became the focus for class discussions on topics such as relationships, love, gender roles, and gender expectations.

The culminating activity was a formal party held during the last two periods of the school day for students who completed all assignments for the unit. Parent volunteers decorated the cafeteria and supplied snacks. Mary and Gina had slipped in several etiquette lessons during the unit and students were expected to demonstrate their new skills during the party. Several students read their favorite or their own poems aloud. Mary awarded prizes to the winners of the valentine contest. The teachers also recognized other team achievements as the marking period had just ended.

Besides developing themed units, the team involved students in a variety of coordinated projects and assignments. For the schoolwide science/social studies fair, Tim and Lattrell worked together to help students develop their projects. Mary and Gina taught research and report writing skills, and the required paper that must accompany each project was a joint class assignment. Doris arranged three half-day trips to the main county library so students would have access to current resources and uninterrupted blocks of time to complete their research.

One team curriculum goal was to expose students to the world beyond their own communities. A teacher explained:

> *Many of our students have seen very little beyond their*
> *own neighborhoods. For many, that is a housing project. We*
> *have students who live forty-five minutes from the beach,*
> *but have never been. It's not enough to tell them to say no*
> *to drugs and not get involved in gangs and crime. We have*
> *to show them alternatives they do not see in their neighbor-*
> *hoods.*

The coastal area of Southeast Georgia offers an expanse of fertile marsh-lands, rivers, and the ocean with opportunities for firsthand learning to occur. Savannah is also a city rich with history. The team implemented numerous field trips to extend the students' learning beyond the classroom walls. Tim provides this view:

> *We can read about Georgia history in our textbook and*
> *for many it doesn't have any meaning. Or, we can go to*
> *places like Fort Pulaski and see history come alive. I believe*
> *the students are going to learn more about history if we*
> *start from where they are now, where they live, what affects*
> *their lives today. Then I try to help them see how history is*
> *a part of that, how history has had an effect on their lives.*

Besides exposing students to the Savannah area, the team worked with Mary to organize trips to Atlanta and Washington, D.C. The team involved students in reading about and researching the cities. Upon returning, they wrote about their experiences and discussed what they had learned.

Though not satisfied with their curriculum planning and development, the teachers recognized with pride that they were attempting to develop an interdisciplinary curriculum. They identified constraints hampering their work, but, as Doris' comments reveal, they did not allow the constraints to keep them from trying.

> *Though we're not where we should be, or where we want*
> *to be in developing curriculum for our students, I think,*
> *given the constraints we have – lack of time, QCC [Quality*
> *Core Curriculum] objectives, limited resources, limited con-*
> *trol over the time we do have to teach with so many kids*
> *being pulled for special areas – I think we're doing pretty*
> *good. Especially since we're fairly new at this. It's not like*
> *we have good models to follow. We're learning as we're do-*
> *ing it.*

Dealing with students

Research on students' perceptions of their teachers indicate that a sense of humor is an important characteristic of effective middle school teachers (George, Stevenson, Thomason, & Beane, 1992; Kramer, 1992). The Dolphin teachers believe that the exigencies of early adolescence and the accompanying challenges of teaching make humor a requirement. They also feel that humor should be genuine and never deprecating or wounding. Throughout the year they demonstrated the power of humor as it was effectively used to avert potential discipline problems or rescue a red-faced young adolescent from an embarrassing situation. Teachers and students exchanged jokes and lighthearted kidding was commonplace. During planning and at lunch, the teachers related humorous episodes from their classes, revealing the revitalizing nature of laughter.

Conversations with students were frequent and marked by an atmosphere of trust and mutual respect; teachers and students talked easily with each other during class, between periods, and at lunch. Students often visited the team during planning to get a late slip, turn in an assignment, or ask a question. Reprimands were rare; the teachers responded to the students courteously, sometimes accompanying the student to the office or another classroom as an advocate for the student. As they talked with students, the teachers often disclosed personal information that revealed their humanness and shared experiences as Gina's comments illustrate:

> Amy* showed me some of her poetry that she wrote. Did you read it? You should read her poems. They're all about love. I said, 'Amy, are these all about the same little fellow?' And she went, 'No (coyly).' And I said, 'You know, falling in love at thirteen is no different than falling in love at thirty-one, cause I feel the same way.' And she just smiled. She's so sweet.

Discussions of inappropriate behaviors and discipline problems were common topics during planning time. The teachers tried to find reasons for misbehavior such as students not getting enough rest, being over-stressed because of testing or a project due, or difficulties at home. They often asked that the school counselor join the team during these discussions to help develop a plan of action. During a discussion with the counselor in October, they realized that the large number of tests and projects scheduled close together contributed to a recent increase in behavior problems. To help ease this stress, they decided to develop a master schedule for their assignments,

*All student names are pseudonyms

tests, and projects so they would not overwhelm students in the future. When the team suspected that a student's actions were due to family problems, abuse, or the student's own high-risk behavior such as alcohol or drug use, they asked the counselor to intervene.

The Dolphin Team had more difficulty addressing problems involving academic performance. Rather than reaching a consensus, a compromise usually resulted. While planning a field trip, they discussed one student who had become lackadaisical with his work. One teacher mentioned that perhaps they should not allow him to go on the field trip. Mary questioned the fairness of this punishment:

> If we don't let this student go because he's not working as well as he should, we'll have to look at everyone else who is not performing as well as they should. Perhaps that's not a good reason for him to go, but we'll have to look at everyone, not just this one kid.

Many students on the Dolphin Team experienced life worlds apart from that of their teachers. Living in poverty in a housing project holds few similarities to the white, middle class backgrounds their teachers have experienced. Occasionally, a teacher expressed confusion and dismay at the lack of effort exhibited by students in the low-level group. Why, it was asked, does this group of predominately minority and low income students not work harder since getting a good education is the ticket out of poverty. The resulting discussions, such as the one presented below, offered opportunities for the teachers to wrestle with deep-seated beliefs and the conflicting evidence of their students' lives.

> Gina: *Yesterday I rode with the school's social service agent to visit Darnell's family. Let me tell you, it was a real eye opener. I now have a better understanding of this child's background. After doing that, I think every teacher should at least ride through the neighborhoods where these students live. I have lived in Savannah all my life, but I went to a part of Savannah yesterday I did not know existed. It was as though we turned into L.A., or Chicago, or Detroit.*

> Lattrell: *I don't know why these kids don't realize that school is a way out and make the most of it.*

> Doris: *They are unable to make that connection. I am amazed that they do as well as they do. When I look at my life, I really have it pretty easy. I don't have to worry about whether or not I'm going to have food to eat, or even if I*

have a place to sleep tonight. I think of Charnelle. She lives in horrible conditions in the project. Her mother kicked her out of the house and she stays with family members or friends as long as they will let her, taking care of their children and cleaning and cooking for them. She does good work at school and has the ability to go to college and have a promising future. She could just as easily end up in jail because of the way she has been raised.

Mary: *Are we going to have time to make a difference in the lives of some of these children?*

Tim: *We're going to have to take the time.*

Grouping students

Mrs. DeLoach groups students into teams striving for a heterogeneous mix based on race, gender, and ability level. It is not an easy task, she says, since 75 percent of the students are eligible for Chapter One services and the number of students identified as gifted is small. She expressed her dissatisfaction of having to put all SEARCH and algebra students on the same team because of scheduling difficulties. Once students are placed on a team, the teachers develop a plan for grouping students within the team.

Students on the Dolphin Team represented a wide range of ability levels with students pulled for SEARCH and Chapter One services for math and reading. Students were grouped according to low-level, average, and advanced, with each group of students remaining together for all their core classes. Grouping students for instruction created frustration for the team and conflict within individual teachers. They tried to juxtapose their knowledge of the negative effects of ability grouping with their experiences as teachers trying to meet the needs of a diverse group of learners. One eighth grade teacher expressed this frustration and conflict with these remarks:

I know the research does not support ability grouping. But the research does not tell me how to teach and meet the needs of a classroom of kids reading from second grade level to those who can handle college level material. In forty-five minutes each day how am I supposed to help my gifted students do advanced research and help my lower-level students just be able to read the majority of the words in the text. What about math? How can students ready for algebra

> *be grouped with students who still cannot multiply or di-*
> *vide? I'd be willing to try it if I knew what to do, but I don't.*

Student grouping arrangements were often topics of discussion during team planning. As the teachers shared information about a student's strengths, needs, and behavior, they often changed students' schedules in an effort to find the best class placements. One morning as the team attempted to make schedule changes for two students, the conversation centered on the number of discipline problems in the lower-level group. They discussed the possibility that grouping those students identified as lower ability together contributed to the development of discipline problems. Gina shared a journal entry from a female student placed in the low-level class:

> *If I were with different children I would act differently. I*
> *used to be with those smart kids and they were my friends.*
> *Now I'm in the lower group and they act like they don't*
> *know me.*

Mary expressed her belief that regrouping the students to eliminate the lower-level class would solve many of their discipline problems. The others agreed that it may be conceivable; however, they also felt that students who are discipline problems in the lower-level class would most likely continue their disruptive behavior in a heterogeneous setting. The team decided to move the author of the journal entry to a higher group and her behavior and academic work soon improved. Mary expressed her belief that this was evidence that they would better serve their students in a heterogeneous setting. She also shared her anxiety about being able to provide appropriate instruction for a wide range of ability levels in one class. Her colleagues agreed.

> Mary: *If I could just see it happening, see it working. I*
> *would feel better. I think I could do it if I knew, if I could see*
> *it taking place, and see what others do. But I don't know*
> *where it is working successfully. I need someone to tell me,*
> *to show me how to do it.*

> Lattrell: *The experts tell you what to do but not how to*
> *do it. You wonder how long it's been since those experts*
> *were in a classroom, or if they've ever taught.*

> Tim: *Our schedule prevents us from making major*
> *changes in the way we group students. We've spent forty-*
> *five minutes trying to change the schedule of two students.*
> *One is pulled for Chapter One math at a specific time and*

we can't alter that time. The other is pulled for Chapter One
math and reading and we can't change those times. It doesn't
leave us with a lot of options for making changes in our
schedule or in how we group students.

The teachers on the Dolphin Team recognized the diversity of their students and the needs represented. They struggled to determine the most appropriate and effective instructional means for meeting those needs. They did not reject research findings on ability grouping. However, they were frustrated with the perceived difficulty of implementing the research in the current classroom structure so that they may meet the learning needs of all students. They also struggled to feel comfortable with their teaching, to develop positive relationships with their students, and to maintain order and organization in a classroom of diverse young adolescent learners. They expressed a desire to learn more, to see good models of instruction with heterogeneous grouping, and to have more flexibility with the schedule.

Flexible scheduling

The team shared a block of instructional time, but, as their discussions about grouping students indicate, their inability to implement flexible scheduling was frustrating. Merenbloom (1991) identifies flexible scheduling as a key to teaming success. He offers suggestions for various flexible scheduling techniques such as rotating the schedule, using modular subdivisions of time, and alternate day rotations. Mrs. DeLoach supported the use of flexible scheduling and told teams to make schedule changes as needed. Discussions during planning often focused on reorganizing time to better address students' needs. Their attempts to implement flexible scheduling were unsuccessful, however.

Doris wanted to create a pre-algebra class during the second semester for students in the average and above average classes she felt were ready for more challenging and abstract work. Making the class changes for these students was a perplexing and daunting experience for her as the following transcript suggests.

I've got students that I need to get out of Mary's homeroom
and they need to come out of my fourth period. I need to
know who that's going to affect? (She reads the students'
names.) If I pull them and take them sixth period, that means
that they'll need to take science fourth so it's going to affect
Lattrell's fourth period science class.

Later, Doris talked with Lattrell about changing the students' schedule.

> *I need to find out about your sixth period class. These are the students I need sixth period. (She reads the names.) Would they work out in your fourth period class? Or, is that not a good combination?*
>
> Lattrell: *Those are my good ones from sixth period.*
>
> Doris: *Yeah, I know.*
>
> Gina: *It would only leave you the bad ones (laughing).*
>
> Lattrell: *Well, no. I mean academically more so than behavior. No, whatever you have to do. With science I can work around a lot easier than you can in math. Having taught math, I know that.*
>
> Doris: *But it also increases the number of kids you'll have to take to lunch. (The teachers take their fourth period classes to lunch.) I'm trying to work out a schedule with the algebra classes in third and fifth. I think I probably made myself think it was going to be easy.*
>
> Tim: *It would be easy if we didn't have all the constraints. The Chapter One constraints – Chapter One reading, Chapter One math, and SEARCH. Those are the three constraints that prevent schedule changes from being easy – or even occurring!*

George and Alexander (1993) describe the middle school schedule as "a unique and transitional type of schedule for any special type of program" (p. 367). They maintain that teams should be able to control the schedule. The Dolphin Team felt controlled by the schedule. The subject-centered, seven period day with large numbers of students pulled for special area instruction created constraints rather than options.

How problems are addressed

The literature on interdisciplinary teaming suggests that common instructional goals and a team discipline policy are two ways teams can respond to the developmental needs and characteristics of young adolescents. Doda (1992) asserts that having shared expectations and instructional goals is also beneficial for teachers as "this shared vision provides a supportive and useful frame of reference as they deal with common dilemmas in teaching" (p. 46). In January, the Dolphin Team teachers recognized their need to develop shared goals and policies as the following discussion illustrates:

Doris: *We need to discuss the issue of make-up work. We seem to have different expectations and rules for make-up work and it is confusing to the students and doesn't make us look unified. Either we don't do it, give a certain amount of time for it to be completed, or only allow it to be done at Saturday School.*

Lattrell: *In the past I would have never accepted late work like I'm doing now. However, now I feel like I am under so much pressure because of grades to let the students do make-up work.*

Mary: *I feel pushed in the corner because of grades. But I also feel it's our own fault. What have you, or I, the teacher, done?*

Gina: *I think we need to get together tomorrow and talk about what we want to accomplish as a team. That we get the kids together and have a team meeting. Tell them that we are not pleased with them and this is what we need to do. Let's have Mrs. DeLoach attend.*

Mary: *I'm having problems with kids having to go to the bathroom just as class begins. Other kids are coming in late to class with excuses of 'I didn't have time to go to the bathroom and get to class on time.'*

Doris: *Let's meet during planning tomorrow and decide what we need to do about these issues. We need to develop policy.*

Gina: *They're going to high school next year and I think a part of our job is to get them ready for that. I think we need to develop, as a team, a list of accomplishments we want to see at the end of this year.*

Erb and Doda (1989) state that teams will become frustrated and will not make progress if they do not have a sense of direction. There were times, like the example above, when the team recognized they did not have a sense of direction. They felt a need to meet with a structured agenda to develop team guidelines on challenging issues.

Erb and Doda (1989) discuss the benefits of teams working together to find solutions to problems:

...using collaborative planning, teamed teachers can in-crease the consistency and clarity of the discipline policies and behavior expectations that they apply to students on

their teams. Moreover, difficult management situations can be analyzed and resolved in a collaborative fashion, resulting in richer discussions and sounder solutions. Finally, teamed teachers can jointly generate strategies to improve student motivation, student responsibility, and student performance in each classroom represented on the team. (p.76)

The most difficult problems this team faced involved balancing the students' need for socialization and the team's need for order and organization. There were times when the team was unable to achieve effective solutions for these problems. In mid-October, they met to address the extreme noise and inappropriate behavior in the cafeteria during lunch. Everyone agreed that since all eighth graders ate at the same time, both teams should work together to develop a solution. In an effort to involve students in generating possible solutions, they decided that homeroom representatives would talk with the students in their homerooms about the problem and brainstorm ideas, including rules for conduct and consequences.

Homeroom representatives met with several eighth grade teachers the next day in the library conference room with Mr. Melvin leading the discussion. The students sat at the table and the six other teachers stood around them. Most of the students came with suggestions for consequences for inappropriate behavior, but they did not have rules for behavior developed. The consequences included silent lunch, offenders would eat lunch on the stage for all to see, and cleaning the cafeteria. Mr. Melvin asked the students to identify offenses that would result in each consequence. No student immediately responded, so a teacher mentioned the problems in the cafeteria such as chairs not pushed in, food left on the table, students wandering, and loud talking. A student spoke up and said that the students wanted to sit wherever they want, and not with their homerooms. Justifying the impossibility of that request, a teacher responded that she may have to speak to a student but may not know the person's name. The student suggested that the teacher could ask someone. Another teacher mentioned possible incentives such as setting up an area outside for students to go after eating and playing music during lunch. These suggestions excited the students, and the meeting ended with the following comments:

> Mr. Melvin: *When do you want to start?*
>
> Student: *Today. (Laughter)*
>
> Teacher A: *You're really going to have to get this over to your friends. It's up to you whether this works or not.*

> Teacher B: *I think we need to start this Monday so that you will have time to talk to your homerooms.*
>
> Teacher C: *Can we have a student discuss this on the T.V. during morning announcements Monday?*
>
> Teacher D: *I think before we do this we need to know what the routine is going to be.*
>
> Teacher C: *Why don't we have these people tell those they go to lunch with.*
>
> Student: *The LD class wants to do this, too, but they're still eating lunch with the seventh graders.*
>
> Teacher D: *I think this is too soon. We need a trial run. We need to get everything worked out. If we haven't thought it out there will be problems.*
>
> Teacher A: *This is going to be up to you if this works or not. You have to tell your friends they must make it work. You have a lot of muscle of your own. It's going to be on your shoulders. You're going to have to talk with these people hard.*

The team did not discuss the lunchroom situation during their planning times for several weeks. In early January the teachers were lamenting the fact that eighth graders would be eating lunch in their classrooms because of the noise in the cafeteria the previous day. I asked about the plan they had attempted to develop in October.

> Lattrell: *Well, we had good intentions, but it was time to start the science projects and the behavior problems were extensive in the cafeteria. And the students do not appear to be interested.*
>
> Doris: *We sometimes have a problem following through.*
>
> Lattrell: *We gave it the college try.*

Since they had been unsuccessful, the teachers hoped to involve students in developing solutions to the constant noise and inappropriate behaviors in the cafeteria. The meeting with students and teachers resulted in limited input from students and teachers' voices dominating. No decisions or plans for future discussions or actions were developed. As a result, the noise in the cafeteria continued to be a problem. The teachers' reasons for not following through with their initial plan reveal their own frustration with the process of finding a workable solution. With so many other demands on their time, they shifted their focus to areas where they felt more secure, the science and social studies fair. Lattrell's comment, "We gave it the college try," reflected a note of cynicism. She may be saying, "We did what the experts told us to do. Not only was it not as easy to do as the experts suggest, but it did not work." Her comment also suggests a need for good models of teams solving problems, and the type of staff development discussed by Spear (1992) that "centers on the needs of teachers as they perceive them" (p. 121).

Lessons learned from the Dolphin experience

The voices of the Dolphin Team teachers tell of the joys, frustrations, successes, and failures they experienced as a team of middle school teachers. Most of all, their voices present the struggles, concerns, questions, and desires of middle school teachers nationwide as they strive to provide appropriate and effective learning experiences for their middle level students. The following five points reflect the experiences of the Dolphin Team teachers as well as suggestions for all middle level educators as they work together to find answers to the difficult questions confronting all who work with or have an interest in young adolescents.

1. **Teaming is more than an organizational feature – it affects the school's culture.** Most schools, including Mercer Middle School, view teaming primarily as an organizational feature. Implementing teaming is seen as strictly a matter of forming teachers and students into groups called teams. Although subject matter expertise and grade level preference must be considered when forming teams, schools that organize teams using only information about content and grade level fail to recognize that teaming affects all facets of the school's culture. Without attention to the wider social, cultural, and power implications, the organization of teachers on teams is left to luck, as perceived by the Mercer teachers. Rarely is a systematic process used to analyze personality, learning styles, beliefs about teaching and learning, teaching experience, pedagogical knowledge, or cultural awareness and understanding especially in relation to the school's ethnic and socio-economic population. An atmosphere for effective teaming cannot develop without attention to these broader issues.

   When viewed as an organizational arrangement, teams are more likely to change membership regularly as they do at Mercer. The annual re-combination of team members prevents teams from evolving through identified phases (George, 1982) or stages (Pickler, 1987) of effective teaming. Thus, each year repeats the first year of teaming. A lack of team stability inhibits the development of good models of teaming and perpetuates the feeling expressed by the Dolphin Team that teaming is "learned by doing." There is an expectation that teams will learn through the process of teaming, but there must be continuity and a support system in place so that each new learning experience builds upon and extends prior learning.

2. **Teaming requires new ways of viewing schooling**. When teaming is viewed as an organizational feature, the former structure of the school remains intact. Grade levels are maintained with separate subject area teachers. At Mercer, an exploratory or special area teacher is assigned to each team but their teaching assignments and planning remain unchanged. Because exploratory and special area teachers teach students during a team's planning time, opportunities for team planning and discussion are limited. At other schools, teams of exploratory and/or special area teachers are formed. Both models are ineffective if teachers who teach a common group of students are unable to meet and plan together. Organizational arrangements that exclude certain teachers from the teaming model create a feeling of being disconnected to or less important than subject area teachers. The current trend to mainstream special area students presents new possibilities for teaching and school organization. Most middle schools still use the junior high model for developing and scheduling exploratory courses. These courses are often seen as separate from and inferior to subject area courses. Exploratory teachers frequently remark that students don't take their classes seriously because they don't "count." Taking to heart John Lounsbury's and Gordon Vars' description of the exploratory program as the "component of the curriculum that comes closest to mirroring the bewildering transience and diversity of the transescent student" (p. 83), may result in unique, appropriate exploratory experiences for young adolescents as well as enhanced teaming experiences for teachers and students.

3. **Staff development is necessary for effective teaming to develop.** Staff development was not provided for Mercer Middle School teachers and as a result teaming success was viewed as dependent on the personalities of team members and how well they worked together. The literature on teaming emphasizes the necessity of initial staff development to facilitate the formation of teams and to help teachers learn how to function as a team. Ongoing staff development is required to provide

assistance as teams make plans to utilize flexible scheduling, employ
alternative student grouping arrangements, develop integrated units, and
implement other curriculum innovations. To achieve these goals, staff
development must focus on bridging the gap between research and
school practice.

The Dolphin Team teachers developed positive relationships with
each other and with their students, but often struggled to understand the
lives of those students from disparate backgrounds. This struggle was
most evident as they grappled with grouping students for instruction.
Although they did not reject the research on ability grouping, they were
unable to visualize learning environments that would provide students
from diverse backgrounds and ability levels appropriate and adequate
instruction. The current structure of schooling, with an inflexible,
seven-period day combined with students identified with specific
learning needs being pulled from classes at specified times prevented
any formation of this vision. The teachers yearned for good teaming
models and effective staff development to help them interpret and use
research as they developed curriculum and teaching strategies that
would respond to the learning needs of all students.

4. **The realities of middle school teaching and students must be recog-
    nized and addressed by administrators and middle level experts**.
    Educational literature on teaming abounds but it often fails to address
    the realities of teaching in most schools. Mercer Middle School, like
    many other schools, is overcrowded and all available space is utilized
    for classes. Planning must take place in a cramped workroom which
    does not allow for uninterrupted blocks of time. The paperwork and
    required tasks that teachers must complete are enormous and take
    precedence over curriculum planning. Unexpected requests and fre-
    quent interruptions are the realities of planning time at Mercer and other
    schools.

    The unique developmental characteristics of young adolescents are
    addressed in nearly every middle level text and licensure or university
    course. Middle school teachers who have obtained middle level certifi-
    cation, like the Dolphin Team teachers, are usually well versed in these
    generalizable social, emotional, intellectual, and physical characteristics
    of the age. While this emphasis on developmental characteristics has
    broadened our knowledge of middle school students as a whole, it has
    also had the effect of marginalizing some students. What is missing in

the middle school literature is a knowledge base and understanding of how race, class, and gender as well as societal and cultural values intersect with these developmental characteristics. Only through a broader exploration of these factors can we gain insight into the variety of ways our middle level students experience early adolescence. Perhaps then we will be better equipped to plan learning environments and experiences that will ensure success for all students.

5. **Enhanced collaborative relationships between schools and universities are needed.** University faculty concerned with middle level education have, in recent years, become actively involved in research on middle school organization, curriculum, and instruction. This has resulted in a substantial body of literature that continues to inform the middle school movement. An increasing number of State Departments of Education are responding by creating middle school endorsements or licensure requirements. Teacher education programs are developing specialized middle level courses as well as undergraduate and graduate programs in middle level education. Unfortunately, many middle schools have not been profoundly impacted by these significant developments. Good models of teaming, interdisciplinary curriculum and instruction, flexible scheduling, exploratories, advisory programs, and other components of the middle school concept are not widespread. The Dolphin Team teachers, like many others, feel as though they must learn how to team through the process of teaming as adequate models are not available. It appears that although the literature provides a framework for transition to a middle school, this transformation requires a change in attitudes and beliefs, new views of teaching and learning, and enhanced interaction among students, teachers, parents, and administrators. Reading available teaming literature needs to be complemented with staff development, teacher action research, school evaluation studies, and school based plans for change.

Enhanced collaborative efforts between universities and middle schools are needed. Research in middle schools that actively involve teachers and students as researchers and participants will provide a greater awareness and understanding of students, the realities of teaching and learning in middle schools, and appropriate ways of responding to each. Rather than telling teachers they must "look internally to discover and develop the tools necessary to create effective classroom environments..." (Spear, 1994, p.129), university faculty must be willing to work side-by-side middle school teachers as co-learners and re-searchers in order to find more meaningful and effective responses to the problematic issues facing teachers and schools. These collaborative efforts must be valued and rewarded for middle school teachers and university faculty by their respective institutions.

References

Doda, N. (1992). Teaming: Its burdens and its blessings. In J.H. Lounsbury (Ed.), *Connecting the curriculum through interdisciplinary instruction* (pp. 45-55). Columbus, OH: National Middle School Association.

Erb, T.O., & Doda, N.M. (1989). *Team organization: Promise—practices and possibilities.* Washington, DC: National Education Association.

George, P.S. (1982). Interdisciplinary team organization: Four operational phases. *Middle School Journal, 13* (3), 10-13.

George, P.S., & Alexander, W.M. (1993). *The exemplary middle school* (2nd ed.). Ft. Worth, TX: Harcourt Brace Jovanovich.

George, P.S., Stevenson, C., Thomason, J., & Beane, J. (1992). *The middle school and beyond.* Alexandria, VA: Association for Supervision and Curriculum Development.

Kramer, L.R. (1992). Young adolescents' perceptions of school. In J.L. Irvin (Ed.), *Transforming middle level education: Perspectives and possibilities* (pp. 28-45). Boston: Allyn & Bacon.

Lounsbury, J.H., & Vars, G. (1978). *A curriculum for the middle school years.* New York: Harper and Row.

Mac Iver, D.J. (1990). Meeting the needs of young adolescents: Advisory groups, interdisciplinary teaching, and school transition programs. *Phi Delta Kappan, 71*(6), 458-464.

Merenbloom, E.Y. (1988). *Developing effective middle schools through faculty participation* (2nd ed.). Columbus, OH: National Middle School Association.

Merenbloom, E.Y. (1991). *The team process: A handbook for teachers* (3rd ed.). Columbus, OH: National Middle School Association.

Pickler, G. (1987). The evolutionary development of interdisciplinary teams. *Middle School Journal, 18* (2), 6-7.

Smith, H.W. (1992). A guide for assessing the development of teaming. In J.H. Lounsbury (Ed.), *Connecting the curriculum through interdisciplinary teaming* (pp. 145-148). Columbus, OH: National Middle School Association.

Spear, R.C. (1992). The process of change: Developing effective middle school programs. In J.L. Irvin (Ed.), *Restructuring middle level education: Perspectives and possibilities* (pp. 102-138). Boston: Allyn & Bacon.

Spear, R.C. (1994). Teacher perceptions of ability grouping practices in middle level schools. *Research in Middle Level Education, 18* (1), 117-130.

Stevenson, C. (1992). *Teaching ten to fourteen year olds.* White Plains, NY: Longman.

Teaming in a Rural Middle School   **5**

Sharon Lee

Interdisciplinary team planning is but one of the many organizational structures of middle level education that teachers and administrators are implementing in both just established and recently reorganized middle schools. There is a wealth of information available in the literature for those interested in implementing a team approach. George and Alexander (1993), leaders in the middle school movement, speak of the importance of teaming in middle level education:

> *In the presence of a stable interdisciplinary team organization, other components of the middle school program function more smoothly. In the absence of the interdisciplinary team organization, they operate with considerably more difficulty, if they exist at all.* (p. 247)

The virtues of team decision making, planning, and teaching can be found in the work of Erb (1995), Erb and Doda (1989), George and Stevenson (1989), Plodzik and George (1989), and Merenbloom (1991); however, the implementation of middle level teams has often been found to be more difficult in rural areas of the country. Most of the information available about the functioning of interdisciplinary teams is gathered in urban areas, suburban communities, or otherwise large school districts. Parke (1989) asserts that students from sparsely populated areas face different barriers to learning than their urban counterparts due to the conditions of size and remoteness. The same is true for teachers and administrators who wish to implement interdisciplinary team organization into their middle schools. Recent studies of rural middle schools in Georgia, Illinois, Kansas, and South Dakota revealed that these schools are indeed very different from urban and suburban ones (Allen, Sheppard & Bath, 1994; Benenson & Steinbeck, 1994; Sardo-Brown & Shtlar, 1994). Lee & Milburn (1994) found that the constraints to middle school transition are quite different in rural and remote settings than in most urban areas. While urban teachers are concerned with overcrowding and how to make students feel a part of a small team, rural teachers are concerned with small budgets, diminishing student populations, and large distances. Studies conducted in rural settings provide a rationale for the view that team planning is qualitatively different in rural areas of the country than in large urban centers. Middle schools in rural and remote areas make up a large percentage of middle schools in this country. According to Meyer (1994), "51% of all schools in the United States are located in small towns or rural areas; nearly 40% of students nationwide attend either small town or rural schools. Twenty-three states have 50% or more of their students in these categories" (p. 12). This chapter focuses on the plight of these rural middle schools by providing an in-depth description of one such school where teaming was effectively implemented despite the constraints, problems, and concerns present in rural America.

Middle school philosophy and rural educators

While many middle level teachers in rural America understand their special problems due to size and geography, they are continuing to participate in the middle school movement. The National Middle School Association has responded by creating a special task force on rural and small schools. Around the country teachers in rural areas are leaders in local, state, and regional affiliates of the National Middle School Association. Small budgets, small students populations, and small teaching staffs are common in these areas, but not small ideas. Lee and Milburn (1994) found that teachers in rural middle schools generally understand and support middle school concepts, despite the constraints of size, geography, and resources.

Information about middle level philosophy has reached the rural and remote areas of our country through a variety of avenues. Numerous publications of the National Middle School Association are available to support teachers and administrators in the transition from junior high to middle school. Tadlock and Barrett-Roberts (1995) focus specifically on the condition of small rural schools. Workshops, consultants, university coursework, research, and opportunities for networking are available at the state and national levels. Although regional conferences held by state middle school associations are an especially effective way of providing staff development for rural middle schools (Johnson, 1994), "staff development for middle level rural educators suffers from the realities of distance, isolation, and financial restrictions" (p. 15). Based on their study in another state, Tadlock and LoGuidice (1994) found that "professional development opportunities for staff [in rural areas] simply don't exist or are extremely limited" (p. 5).

New state and federal guidelines for accreditation and licensure are also reaching rural areas. New standards are being adopted that require knowledge of middle level concepts as well as experience with young adolescents to become newly licensed middle school teachers. Many of these new teachers are educated in colleges and universities, however, that are not located in rural communities. Many complete their early field experiences and student teaching in urban and suburban centers. Even states that are considered largely rural do not provide middle school licensure programs in all colleges, especially those with connections to rural communities. The Middle Level Alliance of Rural and Small Schools (MARS) Project from the Center of Education for the Young Adolescent (1991) found that the lack of middle level licensure among rural middle school teachers was a significant problem for rural educators.

Yet, when the desire to make the transition to middle school is evident in these rural communities, many colleges and universities are ready to meet the challenge and are willing to provide continuing staff development for those transition years. This is a story of just such a rural community in a rural state with a strong desire to improve – and the university that provided the assistance that was needed.

A rural middle school decides to change

The state of South Dakota became concerned about middle level licensure in the early 1990s largely in response to a push from the National Middle School Association/National Council for Accreditation of Teacher Education (NMSA/NCATE) requirements for accrediting middle level teacher education programs. The South Dakota Division of Education and Cultural Affairs (DECA) engaged in discussion with middle level teachers, administrators, teacher educators, and state association leaders about the easiest way to ensure appropriate teacher licensure. The conclusion drawn was that state mandates were the best way to ensure that all teachers of young adolescents were adequately prepared and licensed. In 1991, the discussion culminated in a proposal that required all new and practicing middle school teachers to have at least eight semester hours of coursework in middle school curriculum and/or methods to receive middle level licensure. This instantly posed a problem particularly for teachers in rural and remote areas of the state. The mandate created a situation that put many teachers at risk of not being licensed because of remoteness from state colleges and universities that offered the necessary coursework. Access to these classes was difficult if teachers had to drive two or more hours to attend them. However, in one district, George, a farsighted middle school principal, began discussions with a local university to solve this problem.

In consultation with one of the university professors dedicated to middle level concerns, George arranged for all eight semester hours of coursework to be brought to the school site through extension education over the span of three semesters. Courses on middle school curriculum, interdisciplinary teaching, and middle level literacy were planned and scheduled. All of the middle school staff were invited to participate in the courses. All did participate in the first two courses in order to gain middle level licensure. A change in regulations made the third course voluntary. Consequently, only about two-thirds of the staff took the middle level literacy course.

These courses began in the fall of 1991. Four university professors were involved in teaching the three courses. Some professors travelled 90 minutes to get to the school on a weekly basis for the duration of a sixteen-week course. The commitment to rural, extension education is a major part of the mission of this university. Many colleges and universities in rural states have a similar commitment to extension education. It is vital that teacher education programs in these states further the cause of middle school transition through continued commitment to rural and distance education (Lee & Milburn, 1994; Meyer, 1994).

Unfortunately, as is typical of state mandates, during the middle of the second course on team planning, DECA reversed its stand on middle level licensure and announced that all practicing middle school teachers would be licensed under a "grandfather clause." It was determined that the task of educating all current middle school teachers was too ambitious in a state with so many rural and remote areas. The challenge to the colleges and universities was overwhelming, and the state was not certain that it could hold the standard for all districts. Consequently, even though the intent of the mandate was to strengthen middle level education throughout the state, the constraints confronting rural districts seemed insurmountable. Middle schools and young adolescents lost out.

While this unfortunate turn of events could have become the excuse to stop the coursework and to continue with business as usual, the principal and the staff would not hear of it. They had made a commitment to change, and the majority chose to continue. Nineteen teachers and administrators, including the counselor, the activity director, and the principal enrolled in the final course on middle level literacy. This was the course that was instrumental in the transition to team planning and teaching.

The state and the district

South Dakota is a large state with a small population and a small budget. There are currently about 700,000 people living in the state; the total state budget for FY 1993 was $1.4 billion. Most readers will recognize that these figures are comparable to some suburbs of large cities in our nation. Of the state budget in 1993, only $180 million was set aside for aid to local governments and schools. In other words, only about 14.5 percent of the state budget is allocated for education. The majority of the money to fund education in South Dakota is the responsibility of local districts and comes from local property taxes. South Dakota has a very large portion of the state that is federal land which is not subject to local property taxes: there are seven Indian reservations in South Dakota which are under the control of tribal law as well as the Bureau of Indian Affairs. Furthermore, agricultural land is levied at about 60 percent of nonagricultural land in South Dakota. Farmers and ranchers hold a very powerful lobby in this state, and while property taxes are considered high by many rural citizens, South Dakotans have a relatively low tax burden with no personal income tax and a small sales tax. In 1993, schools received $329 million from property taxes which caused South Dakota to be ranked 42nd in per pupil spending: about $4,000 per student. In 1994 reductions in force occurred in 90 percent of South Dakota's school districts. In 1995, an initiative to reduce property taxes by two-thirds failed in the general election. However, in 1995, the newly elected governor – through legislative action – reduced the property tax burden by 20 percent, modified the school funding formula, and capped per pupil spending at $3,350 for all districts in the state. Many districts are faced with significant reductions in services and staff. Currently, South Dakota ranks 51st in teacher pay nationwide. The average teacher salary in 1993 was $24,125, a 1.2 percent increase from 1987.

On the other hand, South Dakota students consistently score in the top 10 percent in the nation on SAT tests. Also, 86.6 percent of public school students complete high school placing South Dakota in the top 10 nationally. Taxpayers in South Dakota have gotten a high return from the resources spent on education.

The rural school that is the focus of this chapter is part of this larger context. It is decidedly rural! The district buses about 70 percent of its students from outside the city limits. It incorporates seven small communities within a 40-mile radius. The district is considered poor even by South Dakota standards. They currently spend about $2000 per student and pay their teachers below the state average.

In 1991, this school was a junior high. The principal, George, explained the school in this way:

> We were totally departmentalized. We had no team plan-
> ning, no interdisciplinary units, and no discussion of ways
> to work together. We had no advisor/advisee program, mainly
> because we had never heard of it. We had assigned electives
> rather than exploratories. We were not a middle school.

The school and the staff were an extension of the high school. The junior high was housed in the old part of the high school building and shared many rooms and teachers with the high school. Middle level students went "up to the high school hallway" to attend band, choir, home economics, and special education (including gifted programs). There were 12 rooms in the middle level portion of the building, and all the teachers shared these rooms. Four of the teachers did not even have a room assigned to them. They called themselves "the teachers on a cart." They wheeled their supplies and books to different rooms each period. In 1991-92, only the 7th and 8th grade rooms were housed in the middle level, while the 6th grade teachers taught in self-contained classrooms in the elementary school.

It is important to note that the transition from a junior high to a middle school was "not the result of a ground swell of feeling that we need to change." As Gwen, the art teacher, stated, "We were lost and unaware of the middle school philosophy nationwide." George convinced the school board that they needed a new middle level building. The research concerning implementation of the middle school concept began as a result of this push. The three courses that were brought to the prospective middle school staff by the university were instrumental in effecting the slow and methodical changes in thinking that led to the implementation of the middle school philosophy.

The first attempt at curricular coordination

The courses that were conducted in the school during 1991-92 provided an overview of middle school curriculum, the elements of an effective middle school, and some organizational arrangements present in middle schools. In the fall of 1992, the staff who chose to continue in the middle level literacy class were given more information about the merits of interdisciplinary team planning. They had heard it before in the middle school curriculum class and the interdisciplinary teaching class. When the complaint came to the instructor that they needed more practical information and a chance to try out some of the ideas, the instructor was ready with some real-life examples and an authentic team planning task. Example units from other schools and other grade levels were shared with the teachers through lesson plans, slides, pictures, and testimonials of successful practitioners. The course assignment was to prepare a thematic unit that could be incorporated into the regular curriculum – while creating new literacy tasks for students. The teachers went to work. They negotiated the topic, the time frame, the assignments, and the outcomes. They asked questions of the instructor and asked advice from their colleagues and community people. They did it during class time in this graduate level seminar. In 1992-93 there was no team planning time incorporated into the middle school schedule, so there was no other time for them to share ideas or create the unit.

By the end of the course, the team had developed a week-long plan that involved not only themselves but all the middle school teachers in a thematic unit on Japan. The objectives of the unit were jointly written and agreed upon by the team, providing the opportunity for all middle school students to have the opportunity to learn about:

1.   the education system of Japan,
2.   family life in Japan, and
3.   the traditions and customs of Japan.

The objectives were broad in scope to allow all teachers great latitude to find the activities or methods that most appropriately fit with their regular curriculum. The team was excited about the unit, and was ready to share the idea with the rest of the staff that had no role in its planning. In December, the principal and a few of the teachers introduced the idea to the entire teaching staff during a weekly faculty meeting. George supported the idea and answered questions for the staff, but he found that "there was some initial resistance." The teachers who were enrolled in the class were a little concerned about this resistance. Donna, the seventh grade science teacher, noticed that "they didn't want to do something new." The art teacher, Gwen, realized that "this unit would require a break from their own curriculum, and that was just too uncomfortable." Randy, the seventh grade social studies teacher, believed that the resistance came from teachers who "still viewed the curriculum as a constraint to thematic planning."

Time was the biggest issue raised as a reason that the unit might not work. Many teachers were still locked into the mode of teaching the textbook chapters in order and planning to get all chapters taught before the end of the year. Some of the teachers who were hesitant at first said that they feared "this would require extra work to get ready." One teacher announced in the meeting that, "we already have enough to do in order to teach our regular classes. This unit would require research that is not always a part of other units of study."

One class participant was concerned that some teachers might need to "change their attitudes" in regards to a study of Japan. A few of the staff had negative attitudes about Pearl Harbor and other Japanese actions. Consequently, several staff members harbored negative stereotypes about the Japanese people.

Some teachers were worried about how they could get involved. Even though all students took his classes, Todd didn't know how he could participate as a typing teacher, "I eventually decided that students could type the pen pal letters that they were writing in communications class. It worked out OK, but I hadn't planned this in my curriculum. I just had to move something around to make room for this activity."

Not everyone "bought into the idea" of curricular coordination and interdisciplinary teaching when it was first introduced. Some were still reluctant even after the unit was completely planned. Comments like "Why are we doing this?" and "What are the benefits for kids?" were continuing in the teachers' lounge long after the decision was made to proceed with the unit. One teacher complained that "there are too many questions left unanswered."

Social studies teacher Randy was concerned about the initial response. "They didn't want to do something new. This would require a break from the old curriculum plus work and extra research to get ready." When asked why *he* took to the idea so quickly, he responded, "I guess, I'm more bent that way than other teachers. They haven't taken the classes in middle school teaching that I have. I am more receptive, I understand it, and I want to try this to see if it works."

In previous discussions involving the middle school staff, they had agreed that they wanted to move to interdisciplinary team planning. They had listed team planning time as their first priority for change. Although this top priority had not yet been incorporated into the middle school schedule, since the unit was virtually "classroom ready" when it was introduced to the staff, the teachers laid aside their initial complaints and decided to try the idea. The only thing teachers had to do was make time for a few activities in their classes that revolved around the topic of Japan. The concepts had been established, the outcomes had been written, and the culminating activity had been finalized using planning time during the graduate seminar. So, even though the initial resistance was troubling, all of the teachers agreed that it was time to try the concept of curricular coordination, and this unit seemed to be the best alternative for experimenting with the idea.

Dan, the 7th grade English teacher, planned to teach the students Haiku. Gwen, the art teacher would have the students make rice paper on which to write their Haiku. The students had already learned calligraphy in art, and this would be an opportunity to practice that skill. Gloria's communication students wrote pen pal letters that were typed in Todd's keyboarding class. Instructional technology students with Terry videotaped a typical school day to exchange with the Japanese pen pals. Donna helped her science students make homemade root beer as part of the culminating activity. When the teachers finally got involved, they found that they could be creative. The math teachers, Ed and Brad, had students make wind socks by incorporating a study of dimensions and percentages along with metric conversions. Roberta, the home economics teacher, provided time for students to sew the wind socks. Everyone could become involved with just a little bit of imagination.

The music and PE teachers were the only teachers who did not get actively involved in the unit. Since students only took their classes two days of the week, the teachers did not feel there was enough time for them to participate adequately in an activity tied to the Japan unit. With all of the 7th graders in one class, they especially did not feel they had the space nor ability to get all students doing an "extra" activity. One of the constraints to teaming and curricular coordination in rural schools is the lack of time for joint planning caused by special area teachers shuttling between the elementary, middle, and high school just to teach a full load of classes. When teachers are not housed in the middle school area, they do not have the opportunity for formal planning nor the advantage of informal collaboration that is necessary. Joint planning time for special area teachers with a team of grade level teachers was not available when those teachers had responsibility for all students in the district.

The special teachers who were exceptions during this experiment were the teachers who were enrolled in the class and thus afforded joint planning time – Gwen in art, Roberta in home economics, and Todd in typing. The involvement in the initial planning was a motivator for these teachers to carry out the unit, no matter how much extra planning time was needed to ensure its success.

Reflections about the unit

As an interested observer of this experiment in curricular coordination, I spent several hours with teachers and students during the week that the Japan unit was taught. I was able to observe many classes and became involved in the culminating activity. I interviewed all of the teachers and a few dozen students to ask them to reflect about the success of the unit. Their comments provide some interesting insight into the actual and perceived success of the first attempt at interdisciplinary planning, as well as the students' and teachers' attitudes toward future teaming efforts.

Teacher Reactions. After the unit was completed and teachers had a chance to reflect on the positive and negative aspects of the week, there were many comments on both sides of the issue. Many agreed with Gwen that this unit was very positive for kids. "There is a continuity in their learning in this kind of unit." One of the many positive dimensions of the unit was that "the kids knew what to expect. They knew what was going on each day." The role of expectations in the teaching/learning process can not be overemphasized in this case. The fact that students knew the goals and objectives throughout the unit only enhanced their ability to learn about Japan and apply it in new ways. Randy noted in his classes that "anticipation of the activities leads to increased excitement – both for me and for the kids." Brad said that "this is different for [the kids]," but he was pleased with what they learned. Roberta agreed and added, "they learned more than if it was taught the regular way." Gloria, the 8th grade communications teacher, was impressed that "they learned the culture, the system of honor, and the tradition as well as the content concepts we taught in our regular classes."

In order to fully understand the power of the unit, the teachers engaged in some reflective group discussions about both the unit and the planning process after the unit was completed. They noted that "we tended to work together more than we normally do" because of the extra planning that was involved to make sure everything fit together in the unit. "We had to know what everyone else was doing for this to work." At the end of the week, when they usually were tired and ready to start their weekends, teachers were walking in and out of other classrooms to see the many displays of student work that accompanied the unit. They became more interested in the other curricular areas to see how the concepts in another class tied in with the concepts they had been teaching.

The unit was a success, but success was not achieved without a few "bumps" along the way. Craig admitted, "we don't do team planning very well right now, but we know what we need to aim for in the future." The challenge of working with other teachers for the success of a unit was new to them. Valerie said, "I knew when I had to teach the concept and how long I had to do that. Before, I could go at my own pace without worrying about what the teacher next door was doing." Randy summed up the feelings of the teachers when he stated "we learned how much planning is necessary in a team situation."

Student Perceptions of Interdisciplinary Teaching. At the conclusion of this first coordinated unit, I spent some time with the students at the school to gather their perspectives on the unit, their feelings about the thematic teaching, and their understanding of team planning. Powell (1993) indicates that talking to students about teaming can provide insights into interactions between students and teachers as well as help them better understand the teaming process. Because the team planning process and interdisciplinary teaching were so new to students, I thought I would have to explain that they had been taught using a thematic approach. They understood the concepts and the objectives of the unit because teachers had spent more time explaining the unit than with the previous units. "I knew what we were going to do for the whole week," was a comment offered by a 7th grade girl who had never had much trouble with the regular curriculum. For her, the team planning approach gave her an opportunity to expand her knowledge and to strengthen her skills through an extra-credit project concerning Japanese art. Her friend added, "we would never have learned everything we learned this week in just one class."

Although teachers commented that there were some possible negative effects for students, the students did not comment on negative aspects of the unit in my interviews. One teacher thought that "one week may have been too long for a unit on Japan in some of the related classes. It was a big adjustment for kids." Several other teachers agreed that perhaps they should have planned for a two or three day unit rather than a whole week for the first attempt. Students did not agree. One 8th grade boy said, "one week was too short. This was much better than normal school." A 7th grade special education student added, "This is the way we should do it every day." Other comments from students indicated their reasons for enjoying the unit were, "we learned by ourselves;" "we like being independent;" and "I like activities rather than worksheets."

Students certainly saw and felt the benefits of this coordinated unit. When given this feedback, the teachers were surprised and pleased. By the end of the week, the teachers saw how easy it would be to plan for two or three weeks of thematic teaching. Some were concerned about the level of interest for the kids. However, when they found out that their concerns were unfounded, many teachers had renewed commitments to team planning, and agreed with George when he stated, "we will do this again."

Effective teaming principles

Observations of the thematic unit planning process coupled with analysis of the oral and written reflections of a first attempt at curricular coordination revealed that many of the principles of effective team planning were evident in this school. Although they were not well established before the fact, nor even recognized by some of the participants, they were nonetheless observed. The success of the first attempt at thematic teaching paved the way for the future of team planning.

Team Leader. There was no formally designated leader of this team during the planning process. However, Randy, the 7th grade social studies teacher, took over the role of informal leader by virtue of his interest and organizational skills. He had taken courses in middle school curriculum and philosophy in his undergraduate coursework, and was active in the state middle level association. He was the strongest advocate for middle level principles and according to his self-report, "most wanted team planning to succeed." He became the unofficial leader during team planning times and in ensuing discussions with the other staff members who were not involved in the original unit writing.

George & Alexander (1993) advocate for either formally identified leaders or some type of informal designation. According to their research, both methods seem to work equally well as long as someone serves as a liaison between the administration and the team and functions to coordinate the program within the team. Randy served this role well – so well that he became a team leader when the more formalized leader designation was established the following year.

Administrative Support. As principal, George had a key role in the success of the transition to interdisciplinary team planning. He was the one who made the initial contact with the university and supported the courses with a classroom in his building each week.

In addition, he enrolled in all of the courses along with the teachers. Most researchers dealing with school change and school effectiveness speak of the importance of the principal in any change process. Thomason and Thompson (1992) state that "the building principal . . . . must set the tone for the necessary changes and . . . . {must} articulate the goals and objectives not only to teachers but to other tiers of schooling as well" (p. 10). George did this with both words and actions. His commitment to the middle school philosophy was clearly demonstrated to the middle school staff and the administration of the entire district. The transition to team planning was a high priority for him.

Team Planning Time. The time that the teachers were given to plan the first unit in the middle level literacy course was invaluable for a number of reasons. Even though team planning time was identified as the first priority for the new middle school schedule, no team planning time was incorporated into that schedule! In addition, there were still some teachers who remained unconvinced of the need to use time for curricular coordination. They still viewed potential "team time" as time limited to talking about students and other school concerns such as workloads, extracurricular activities, and union issues. They did not see the value in curriculum planning on a regular basis. So when the first attempt at team planning involved a major break from the traditional curricular model, many teachers offered resistance, especially since they had not been involved in the initial planning of the unit. Jumping into the thematic unit planning without having the time to "learn how to work together" or even involve all affected teachers in the planning process proved to be quite problematic.

Schroth, Dunbar, Vaughn, and Seaborg (1994) make a strong statement about the need for team planning time to include important curricular concerns:

> Learning to share information about students that they have in common is one thing; cooperative team planning about common thematic units is altogether different regardless of how much they learn about the process of shared planning. Simply stated, even the best staff development will not work until teachers learn how to work together. (p. 34)

Clear Goals and Expectations. Since the teachers who had written the original unit in the Middle Level Literacy class had a common goal and common expectations of the unit, they could evaluate their success at the end of the unit. Many of these teachers stated their "feelings" of success with the unit, but the important criteria were not just that kids had fun or that the teacher had a break from the regular curriculum. Most teachers felt that they accomplished the goals of the unit as well as the broader goals associated with the team planning approach. "I feel that we accomplished the goals. Kids got the message that different is not bad, not odd, not derogatory – just different."

When teachers discovered that they could come together to work toward these common goals, they were able to collaborate and cooperate much more effectively. When one activity got a little out of hand in the cafeteria (did you know that homemade root beer has terrific "fizzing" properties?), teachers were not as quick to point a finger of blame to one teacher. They had all agreed that the project was worthwhile and were themselves interested in the results of the scientific experiment. It was a little easier to enlist the help of all the teachers and students when it was time to clean up the mess.

The next step

The middle school staff agreed that "this was an important beginning to our interdisciplinary teaming." Dan, the English teacher, admitted that "it wasn't perfect; there were some problems; but we will definitely do this again." Teachers learned from the unit and from the team planning process what to expect in the future. The teachers knew what they needed to do in order for this type of unit to become the rule rather than the exception in their school. As they thought about plans for the future, they generated the following list of expectations for the coming year.

1. **More planning time.** All teachers agreed that two 20-minute sessions in weekly staff meetings did not provide enough time to fully enlist the support of all teachers. Many just went along because of the people who introduced it. They did not have the time to do the research and planning that was necessary. One teacher admitted, "I should have started planning and researching sooner. I can't wait until I'm in the middle of teaching the unit to go to the library and find out the information I need."

   Increased planning time was needed so that all teachers could meet together to discuss ideas about curriculum culminating activities, and student projects. In the first unit, there were some tense moments when the teachers "argued about which teacher should introduce which activity." In a truly interdisciplinary unit, there are many activities that could naturally fit into a variety of content areas. Considerable discussion is necessary to ensure that there is adequate overlap of concepts without too much repetition of activities in the different classes.

2. **Team leader.** "We need a coordinator!" was the cry from many of the teachers during the initial planning session. All the teachers felt this lack of leadership and were frustrated by it. "We kept asking each other 'So who's in charge?' Someone had to make some final decisions and move us forward." Everyone agreed that Randy and George were the leaders in the class project, but were not sure if that was acceptable to the entire staff. When teachers needed to ask questions, they did not know whom to ask or when and how to ask them.

There was a problem with one of the teachers wanting to start some of the activities a week sooner than everyone else. Since there was no agreement regarding how to resolve this issue, the teacher went ahead, thus creating some tension among the staff.

3. **Stay small until there is time to allow everyone to be comfortable.** The excitement that surrounded the first unit was contagious. Once teachers got a taste of the freedom allowed in a unit like this, some of them went wild. "I think some of us bit off more than we could chew in this first attempt," says Donna. But the teachers learned how much can be planned for one week with limited time to plan. They adjusted their expectations during the next unit. Finally, teachers agreed that two weeks should be devoted to schoolwide interdisciplinary projects, since those units were indeed bigger than one week would afford. The small steps were critical to the bigger development in the future.

4. **Encourage teachers to be flexible.** In a schoolwide interdisciplinary unit, some teachers have to be willing to sacrifice their regular plans. The comfort that was present in the traditional curriculum was disturbed by doing something different. Some teachers were not as willing as others to rearrange their schedules. Specific curriculum guidelines were still seen as barriers to this type of unit. The administrative support here was invaluable to assure teachers that it was acceptable to put some activities "on hold" until after the thematic unit was completed.

Teaming becomes formalized

In response to the schoolwide commitment to teaming and the success of the first coordinated unit, the district provided additional financial support to the teachers. Five middle school teachers were employed by the district during the summer of 1993 to plan for interdisciplinary teaming. This group included a 6th, 7th, and 8th grade teacher, one special area teacher, and an administrator. They met, with pay, for one week during the summer to begin the official planning for interdisciplinary teaming. Randy served on this committee and shared what he considered the goal of the group when the committee met for the first time:

> As a staff, we need to make decisions. Since some people were left out of the planning in the first unit, we have to decide when we plan for interdisciplinary units, when we can meet for teaming, who should be involved, and how to effectively use our time and energies.

The committee was charged with writing a philosophy for interdisciplinary teaming that was to include interdisciplinary teaching and planning. One of the major goals of team planning appeared in the philosophy statement:

> The goal of interdisciplinary team planning is to foster a sense of middle school unity by focusing efforts of all teachers and students on a single thematic unit for approximately two weeks each semester.

The members of the committee were in agreement about the importance of team planning, and after reaching consensus, developed a philosophy that was presented to the whole staff.

> The purpose of teaming is to increase communication and cooperation among staff and administration through implementation of interdisciplinary units.

In addition, the committee decided to recommend to the faculty that it plan two schoolwide interdisciplinary units for the 1993-94 school year. Schoolwide units were seen as the natural transition to grade level teaming for the next year. The success of the first one led to continued experimentation the next year.

When the committee presented their philosophy statements on teaming and interdisciplinary teaching to the middle school staff at the pre-school inservice in the fall, there was unanimous agreement with the statements. The teachers repeated their desire for more team planning. The planning committees for the two-week units were appointed and work began. The first unit was organized around the theme *Elections* to coincide with the upcoming

South Dakota gubernatorial election. Every teacher was planning to discuss this anyway, so it was a natural choice for the fall unit. The spring unit centered around the theme *Environment* and involved a range of community service options. Students and teachers spent time at the river and provided a variety of services to local businesses while helping to raise their awareness of environmental issues.

With this background behind them, the entire staff began discussing how best to incorporate regular team meeting time in the daily schedules of all middle school teachers. The successes and the challenges posed by the first thematic unit were fresh in the minds of the teachers as they paved the way for more formalized teaming in the future. George, as a strong instructional leader, charged the staff with considering other changes in the middle school schedule and curriculum as they tried to adopt more and more of a true middle school philosophy.

A transition to teaming

The 93-94 middle school schedule provided time for teachers to meet in teams. Because of the small school staff and the number of special classes that were available to students, teachers rotated through team planning time. Although a team meeting was held each day, individual teachers did not attend all meetings. All teachers were assigned to monitor a directed study time for their grade level. Each week, teachers met the directed study at least once, thus giving the other team teachers a chance to meet. There was never a a chance for all grade level teachers to meet together during the school week, but each teacher met with their team at least three days most weeks. The teachers found new and inventive ways to make connections to each other and to the principles for effective teaming they knew from the research literature. Rules for participation were clearly delineated so that all teachers knew their responsibilities. If a teacher was not in attendance at the meeting on Monday, someone provided them with notes when they were able to attend on Tuesday. They always began their unit planning discussions with academic outcomes to insure the continued rigor involved in interdisciplinary units. They also accepted diverse points of view when teachers presented new and different ideas. There were some tense moments when there were disagreements, but no more so than in any team planning situation. The diversity and acceptance gave the grade level teams a sense of community that is important in effective teams (George & Stevenson, 1989).

Leadership positions rotated on a weekly basis so that each teacher had the opportunity to lead the group. This type of rotating leadership allowed all teachers to feel the responsibility that falls to a team leader, and encouraged more support for the leader of the week. As they planned for the opening of the new middle school building, the teachers had a renewed sense of the importance of team planning and team teaching. They insisted that it was the most important element in their middle school. Team planning time and team meeting rooms were built into the new middle school. There was no going back for these teachers.

Teaming today

The faculty had made tremendous strides towards effective team planning when the new middle school building, situated between corn fields and bean fields, opened in 1994. There is a team room in each of the grade level sections of the building. Creative scheduling and some flexibility by the staff have allowed for teaming to be successful. Currently, each grade level has between 28 and 40 minutes a day to meet together. One teacher from each grade level has to give up some individual planning time in order to meet with the team, but it is working well for them. Most teams have four teachers: English, social studies, math, and science. All teachers currently teach a section of reading, so all core areas are included. Teachers of exploratories and electives are not currently included in the team planning. One team has only three teachers as one teacher is responsible for both math and science. When asked how the school is different now, all the teachers have something to say.

The special education teacher says that "more kids are being served in the regular classroom now. I am getting fewer referrals than previous years. I definitely think it is because the teachers have a chance to discuss the needs of kids as a group." Dan, the 7th grade English teacher, reported that he thinks fewer kids are failing this year, because "we spend about half of our team time discussing student progress." Gloria, 8th grade communications teacher, says that parents are involved more with team time. "We often invite a parent to team planning time to discuss students. We can decide on parent contacts and help kids before little situations become big problems."

Randy sums up the feelings of the group when he says, "I feel like we're more important now. Our teaching is more challenging and more work, but it is also more useful. The whole climate of the school is different. The interdisciplinary teaching adds variety to our teaching, and the responsibility for the success of the school gives us a feeling of satisfaction."

Now that time is being provided, team planning is working for them, and they are pleased with the progress they have made. While they know that some larger schools may do it differently, they still feel they are "light years ahead of where we were even two short years ago." "We see people on our team a lot more than we ever did in the past," says Todd. "It did something to us as a staff when we started team planning," said Randy. George, who is now the superintendent of schools in this district, says that this is the most significant thing he has ever done as an educator. "We designed a school around what we knew a middle school should be. We are proud of our efforts, of our teachers, and our students."

In their small, rural school, they have had to reshape team planning time to fit the needs and constraints of the district. They are satisfied with the results so far.

Teaming: A review

In the two years since attempting that first unit on Japan, the faculty of this school has effectively planned about a dozen schoolwide thematic units and have successfully implemented team planning time into their daily schedules. The teams continue to involve teachers, community members, parents, and administrators in these units. They see the first unit as the initiating activity that fostered the schoolwide commitment to team planning. Many teachers are certain that if they had not had the time to experiment with interdisciplinary teaching with that first unit, they would have never made the "leap" to daily team planning time that they enjoy today.

This school went through a three-year process to come to the point where they are satisfied with their team planning approach. They started with a coordinated unit in which it was easy for all teachers to become involved. The teachers knew that that unit was the first step towards the fully developed team planning necessary to design true interdisciplinary units. Randy commented, "our goal with this unit was to eventually have a regularly scheduled team planning time in all grade levels. We needed more staff support for this to happen. The unit was the push to encourage others to join our efforts." He knows that some people became involved in the unit "just because everyone else did," but he still sees the Japan unit as pivotal. The middle school now has an exploratory on Japanese culture that was designed as a result of this one unit. George commented in a written note to an instructor after the unit was complete, "I feel this class continued bringing the staff together in a joint effort to develop a philosophy of trying some interdisciplinary projects and to organize their own ability to work as a team." It was the beginning of the process.

As schools begin the transition to interdisciplinary team planning, they can take courage from the story of this rural South Dakota community. While teaming was a priority, the constraints of the small school were problematic. Yet, they were never seen as insurmountable. George and his staff were restricted by their size and the rural nature of the community – but they understood the community and learned how to overcome the restrictions. Other schools can do the same thing.

Many middle schools are in the throes of change as they are attempting to implement teaming and other elements of effective middle schools. While not all are constrained by the rural issues affecting this school, they may be constrained in a variety of other ways. The research and theoretical literature available to middle school teachers and administrators may be daunting unless it is considered in light of how to modify and experiment within the constraints of an individual school.

This middle school was able to effectively make the transition to interdisciplinary team planning, and their story may be a challenge and a vision of hope to other schools attempting the same changes. These were ordinary teachers and administrators with an extraordinary desire to change. Over a three-year period they accomplished what they could within the limits of their district and community. The lesson for us all is powerful when we are tempted to say that something cannot be done because of our special circumstances that prohibit change. In the face of the constraints of a rural mentality in a state that is content to see obstacles rather than challenges, these teachers did what others only hope they can – they changed.

References

Allen, M.G., Sheppard, R.L., & Bath, D. (1994). Changing a rural school to better meet the needs of its young adolescents. *Middle School Journal, 26* (1), 18-20.

Benenson, W., & Steinbeck, E. (1994). An opportunity for ownership: Developing a sense of community in a rural middle school. *Middle School Journal, 26* (1), 21-22.

Center for the Education for the Young Adolescent. (1991). *MARS Project research report.* Platteville, WI: Author.

Erb, T.O. (1995). Teamwork in middle school education. In H.G. Garner (Ed.), *Teamwork models and experience in education.* Boston: Allyn and Bacon.

Erb, T.O., & Doda, N.M. (1989). *Team organization: Promise – practices and possibilities.* Washington, DC: National Education Association.

George, P.S., & Alexander, W.M. (1993). *The exemplary middle school* (2nd ed.). Fort Worth: Harcourt Brace Jovanovich.

George, P.S., & Stevenson, C. (1989). The "very best teams" in the "very best" middle schools as described by middle school principals. *TEAM: The Early Adolescence Magazine, 3* (5), 6-17.

Johnston, W.F. (1994). Staff development for rural middle schools through regional conferences. *Middle School Journal, 26* (1), 15-17.

Lee, S., & Milburn, C. (1994). Implementing middle school concepts in rural areas: Problems and solutions. *Middle School Journal, 26* (1), 7-11.

Merenbloom, E.Y. (1991). *The team process: A handbook for teachers* (3rd ed.). Columbus, OH: National Middle School Association.

Meyer, R. (1994). Rural middle level education: Challenge for the 90s. *Middle School Journal, 26* (1), 12-14.

Parke, B.N. (1989). Educating the gifted and talented: An agenda for the future. *Educational Leadership,46* (6), 5.

Plodzik, K.T., & George, P.S. (1989). Interdisciplinary team organization. *Middle School Journal, 20* (5), 15-17.

Powell, R.R. (1993). Seventh graders' perspectives of their interdisciplinary team. *Middle School Journal, 24* (3), 49-57.

Sardo-Brown, D., & Shetlar, J. (1994). Listening to students and teachers to revise a rural advisory program. *Middle School Journal, 26* (1), 23-25.

Schroth, G., Dunbar, B., Vaughan, J. L., & Seaborg, M. B. (1994). Do you really know what you're getting into with interdisciplinary instruction? *Middle School Journal 25* (4), 32-34.

Tadlock, M., & Barrett-Roberts, J. (1995). *Middle level education in small rural schools.* Columbus, OH: National Middle School Association.

Tadlock, M., & LoGuidice, T. (1994). The middle school concept in small rural schools: A two year inquiry. *Middle School Journal, 26* (1), 3-6.

Thomason, J., & Thompson, M. (1992). Even if it isn't broken: A proposal for wholesale change. *Middle School Journal, 23* (5), 10-14.

The Brief, Bright Light of the Village 6

Janet E. McDaniel

The village began with the principal and ended with the principal. No one could deny the persuasive power of her personality and her leadership style – least of all, her teachers. What Katie wanted, Katie got. Usually, this turned out for the best. In the case of the interdisciplinary team known as "The Village," what Katie got was a bright but brief illumination of the potential power of teaming.

This was Katie's first middle school principalship, and she had made a point of being out in front in terms of middle school reform. The state department of education was forming ten regional partnerships of middle schools, each of the ten comprised of ten middle schools with "an uncommon commitment" to middle school reform. The one hundred schools chosen for the regional partnerships would have some nominal support from the state department, but as everyone said with a laugh, "an uncommon commitment" was operationally defined as "the willingness to undertake restructuring all out of your own pocket." It was widely accepted that Katie was a gung-ho principal if ever there was one, and with or without state funds to support the effort, her school was going to be a leader in middle level reform. When her school was selected as a partnership school, Katie became one of the leaders of the principals' group. Within a year she was chair of the partnership principals, and with four years of experience as a middle school principal, she was leading her school to make strides in middle school reform.

Katie believed strongly in having the teachers buy into the new reforms before they were formally adopted. Her modus operandi was to tell the faculty about a wonderful program she had heard about, and then invite any of them who might be interested in learning about that program to travel to a school where she knew the program was doing well. Through the partnership of 100 schools, Katie heard about exemplary middle level practices on a regular basis. She invited her teachers to look at advisement, parent involvement, and portfolio assessment to see how these might be incorporated into the school program. Naturally, none of the programs should or would be imported wholesale. Local conditions would demand some modifications if any of these were deemed worthy of adoption.

The local conditions at Katie's school (herein called "Desert Middle School") had changed considerably in the last decade. What had once been a small, agricultural community had become a sprawling suburb for a major metropolitan area. The student population was burgeoning, with a new school opening almost every year to accommodate the growth. Different neighborhoods in the district were quite different in ethnic, socioeconomic, and linguistic diversity, although every school was diverse enough to require some second language acquisition instruction for a certain proportion of the students. The predominant second language at Desert was Spanish, although a smattering of other languages were also spoken by the students. The school population grew steadily over ten years, with more than 1,300 sixth, seventh and eighth graders attending the school in the mid-1990s. The students represented the working class neighborhood surrounding the school. More than half were from ethnic minorities, with the largest group being Hispanic. The school buildings – set on a full city block in an open campus setting that made up Desert Middle School – were filled to capacity, with barely enough classrooms to allow all the teachers to have their own rooms. The four permanent classroom wings and two dozen modular classrooms hosted departmentalized groups of teachers. The science wing was the least flexible set of classrooms, as these were the only eight rooms with built-in laboratories. Most of the other 40 classrooms were nondescript, although the teachers were definitely grouped by subject areas and many had not moved in many years. The physical setup of the school, then, suggested a departmentalized system as one might expect in a traditional junior high school.

In the first few years of her principalship at Desert, Katie won over the teachers in many ways. Her genuine caring for the kids and staff members, her casual demeanor, her frequent visits to classrooms, her willingness to perform the "down and dirty" duties, her oft-expressed belief in the teachers' wisdom ("I'll do whatever you guys want to do.") – all these contributed to a near-universal attitude of admiration and trust in Katie. So when Katie approached the teachers with some new scheme, she usually walked away with a new project underway.

The statewide network of regional partnership schools was an excellent vehicle for learning about exemplary practices in operation. Katie was a sponge at regional and state principals' meetings. Upon returning from the meetings, she reported to the staff on whichever practices seemed to be most promising for a too-large, too-old, too-unchanging school such as Desert.

With professional development funds from the state, Katie sponsored trips for the Desert teachers to visit schools to see the programs in place. Almost without exception, the visitors returned with rave reviews, and the teachers agreed to try out some version of the program.

Katie was convinced that interdisciplinary teaming was an appropriate way to address the problem of having 1,300 young adolescents on the school campus at the same time. The students needed a sense of belonging; they needed focused attention from their teachers; they needed a coherent curriculum and sense of orderliness in their day. All these were more likely with an interdisciplinary team, Katie figured. When she broached the topic of teaming at a staff meeting, the teachers agreed to investigate. During the next month, Katie arranged for every teacher to visit a middle school that had already adopted some version of interdisciplinary teaming. There were sufficient exemplars in the greater metropolitan area that the teachers did not need to venture far. One middle school in their own district had adopted teams schoolwide. They called their teams "villages" to connote the sense of interdependence and identity they hoped to promote.

Every teacher at Desert had engaged in a conference or a school visit or a workshop connected to new middle school practices by the spring of the year. In general, the teachers seemed impressed with some of the organizational aspects of the teams they observed, but no team seemed to have the integrated curriculum that they imagined must be possible with teaming. At a staff meeting, Katie called for consensus on which new programs should be written into the school's Five Year Plan document, and which ones should be piloted the next school year. There was general agreement on interdisciplinary teaming, and Katie asked the teachers to think about their interest in being on a team the coming year. Sara, a sixth grade language arts/social studies teacher, was immediately interested. In 20 years of teaching K-8, she had taught everything and was willing to try anything. She caught the eye of Ann, a first year science teacher, while Katie was making her pitch. During a break in the meeting, Sara and Ann started to talk about the possibilities of teaming. They would need a mathematics teacher and an additional language arts/social studies teacher to complete the core curriculum team. As if in answer to their thoughts, their favorite sixth grade mathematics teacher, Harry, approached them and was soon drawn into the planning. Finding a second LA/SS teacher proved more difficult, as none of the teachers seemed an immediate likely teammate. Harry finally suggested Brooke, with whom he had once shared ideas and resources when he taught LA/SS for a short time. The deal was struck when Brooke walked into Harry's classroom while

Harry and Ann were in the midst of mulling over their next step. Within a few days of Katie's "Let me know," the sixth grade village pilot teaching team was constituted. The experienced dynamo, Sara; the enthusiastic novice, Ann; the agreeable problem-solver, Harry; the good neighbor, Brooke – here were Katie's pioneers. Katie hired substitutes for the pioneers for one day in the late spring so that they could begin to put together a game plan for their team. Sara took a leadership role in suggesting projects, a grading system, classroom discipline, and celebratory days. The task of designing curriculum units was more daunting, and for this, Katie had a plan.

During the ensuing summer, Katie arranged two planning experiences for the "village people," as they began to call themselves. The first was a three-day teaming workshop sponsored by the state middle school association. This was held at a resort area a few hours away from home, and would include two nights away. Sara, Ann, and Harry made arrangements to go. Brooke was not so sure that the workshop was more important than some personal business she needed to do, and she promised the other three that she would be very supportive of whatever they decided during the workshop. So three-fourths of the village met with teams from across the state to learn the rudiments of designing interdisciplinary curriculum and coordinating other aspects of their classroom lives. The workshop facilitators – an educational consultant and two experienced middle school teammates – used Heidi Hayes Jacobs' (1989) *Interdisciplinary Curriculum: Design and Implementation* as their guide. The workshop participants were led through a step-by-step process for creating interdisciplinary units. Worksheets that neatly laid out "guiding questions," "interdisciplinary activities," "levels of thinking," and "procedures" became familiar tools for Sara, Ann, and Harry. In the Jacobs model, the school subjects represented by each teacher were left intact, so the villagers retained their own curricular content, assignments and assessments. They recognized the goal of having the different subject areas relate to overarching themes, and this was their most difficult task. Intense working periods were relieved by social time, which the three enjoyed a great deal. Sara considered the social hours as "bonding time," when the three excitedly talked and dreamed about how successful and fulfilling the coming year would be. By the time the three returned home, the village had an overall motto, "Reach for the stars!", and the first six-week unit, "You are a part of the world," was on paper. When the three met with Brooke, she was (as promised) delighted with their work.

The second phase of team planning came in mid-August with eight paid half-days of curriculum planning for the four villagers. They met every morning to continue to construct the village. The *Reach for the Stars!* motif was elaborated by Ann, who had organized her science classes the previous year around a "Super Stars" theme. Ann had found success with a system of classroom rewards based on "stellar dollars," squares of colored paper decorated with stars and denominations of 10, 20 and 50 dollars. These were liberally given to the students for any form of good behavior or achievement. The students redeemed the dollars for privileges such as sharpening a pencil. When the teacher's stellar dollars supply was low, a classroom auction would be held to exchange the paper money for inexpensive items from the store or the storeroom. Ann swore by the stellar dollars. "The kids will do *anything* for the stupid money!" she told her teammates. The villagers also adopted a discipline plan that Ann had created for science. This was the PRIDE approach:

> **P**repared when the bell rings
>
> **R**espect each others' rights
>
> **I**n your seat at all times
>
> **D**irections to be followed the first time
>
> **E**xpectations will be kept high

Rewards for compliance with PRIDE were posted in each room. They ranged from stellar dollars to "teacher's respect" to "five-minute passes." Consequences followed an assertive discipline (Canter & Canter, 1976) routine, from warnings to referral to the principal's office.

At the end of the eight days of summer planning, the teachers had agreed on six six-week themes for the year. Three of the four – Sara, Brooke and Harry – were familiar and comfortable with the sixth grade social studies curriculum of the ancient world. As LA/SS teachers, Sara and Brooke had already established connections between the social studies content and their language arts curriculum. Harry and Ann agreed to relate their mathematics and science content to the six social studies-based themes:

- You are a part of the world.
- Prehistoric world.
- We are a world of societies.
- Gifts from our world (Egypt).
- Gifts to the world (Greece).
- A world of roads (Rome).

For the first theme, "You are a part of the world," Harry would teach the students to calculate percentages using measurements of the human body and large population groups. This tied in with Ann's science content – atoms as the building blocks of human bodies. Sara and Brooke would address autobiographical writing for language arts and designing a family tree for social studies.

The villager teammates were optimistic when they met their 120 sixth graders on a warm day in early September. They spent the first hour of school on get-acquainted activities so that the students would begin to feel a sense of belonging with the team and their peers. The students had been randomly assigned to the teachers for their four periods of common time. The village students also had three periods outside the village, taking exploratory courses and physical education. Each day started with a 20-minute Advisory period. The village students were assigned to one of the four team members for this period. While the students went to a non-village course first period, the village teachers had a common planning period. Then the teachers saw their village students four of the remaining six periods of the day. Each teacher taught two additional sections of students to fill out their teaching load. To complicate matters, of the 120 students, about 15 took advanced mathematics, which was taught outside the village. In return, Harry taught 15 students who were otherwise not in the village during his four periods of village math. This "contamination" of the self-contained village repeatedly plagued the village teachers when they planned whole-village, multi-period events such as field trips and festivals. Another logistical problem to be accepted was that the village teachers' classrooms were not connected to one another, and the science room was in a different area of the school from the other three. Sara's room was slightly larger than the other three, and by removing all the furniture from it, the 120 students could be seated for a production or a meeting.

The village teachers agreed to meet during first period twice each week to launch the year. At their first village meeting of the year, Sara, Ann, Harry and Brooke congratulated each other on their star-oriented room decorations and their exciting first days with the village students. Each class was sticking to the program. The first unit, "You are a part of the world," was off to a good start. The villagers were "on the same page," they agreed. Ann reported some skepticism from her science department colleagues. The science teachers had always kept their curriculum in sequence and taught the same lessons in tandem, but now Ann was already out of sync. Brooke said that the language arts teachers had questioned her use of language arts money in the budget. They wanted to be sure that Brooke's allocation would be used entirely on language arts items. They did not want their departmental budget to be spent freely for village programs in general. The four teachers were quiet following this conversation; they recognized the beginning of school politics at work. Then they moved on to talk about discipline situations. The summer conference had emphasized the need for proactive parent contact, so Sara volunteered to write the first newsletter to parents. The letter described the village as "a unique guidance-oriented learning environment which focuses upon the specific needs of young adolescence." The PRIDE discipline plan was explained and grading systems for each of the four courses were described.

The village worked well from the beginning with regard to helping individual students who experienced academic and behavioral difficulties in school. Even in the first week, the village teachers had their eyes on a couple of students. They agreed to watch for further developments, and within three weeks the villager who was the advisory teacher for one student had made contact with the parents by telephone. A parent conference was held within the first six weeks. Throughout the year, this system of advisory teacher as parent liaison for the team proved efficient for the village. Another system that worked well was Ann's elaboration of the Super Stars rewards. Every week the village students received a calendar that kept track of the homework for the five weekdays and the four courses. As homework was collected, the teacher signed the appropriate box. If at the end of the week, all the homework boxes were signed for all courses, the students were given "Super Star" status and tickets to dine with a teacher one day the following week. The students brought their own food to Super Star lunches, and the village teacher provided a cookie or candy treat for dessert. The villager teachers marveled at how the students apparently valued such small material rewards.

The interdisciplinary unit designed during the summer, "You are a part of the world," pleased all the villagers. Usually Sara and Brooke, the LA/SS teachers, taught map and globe skills, but in this unit, Harry taught the concepts of latitude and longitude in math class, and he showed the students how to construct their own globes. In all four courses, the students were to bring to class relevant news articles to share. The LA/SS teachers provided instruction on reporting current events. The fall election polling results were translated into graphs in math class after being discussed in LA/SS. For a culminating project, all 120 students participated in an "Eyewitness News Broadcast" video presentation. Each student contributed to the videotaped broadcast by writing news stories, reporting or illustrating the news clip or commercials, building sets, or working on the technical production. The day of the videotaping, all the students met in Sara's room for the first time. It was hot; there was not enough room; the program ran longer than expected.

Nonetheless the village people congratulated themselves for pulling off the first unit plan. At their next village meeting, Sara exuded enthusiasm: "I'm just *so* proud of us and of all the kids! I think the village readily bonded. They got a lot out of the videotaping; their performances were *great!*" One of Sara's strongest interests within language arts was drama, and her interest in performance was a thread that ran throughout the year.

The village people met every Monday morning during first period unless some other obligation interfered. While their original plan had been to meet two to three times weekly to plan curriculum and talk about students, by late October it was all they could manage to make the meeting once each week. At first, leadership in the village was left fluid. But since Sara and Ann were self-described "stronger personalities," one or the other of them usually drew up an agenda for the meetings. Ann suggested that the village people take turns at the team leader role. Each teacher could take the responsibilities as "captain of the ship" for one grading quarter. Sara volunteered to be the leader for first quarter, and Ann agreed to take second quarter.

It was soon apparent to Sara and then to Ann that the captain would have to run a tight ship, for the days inexorably passed by and the curriculum plans for the remaining five units were in reality only sketches. The activity plans that constituted daily lesson plans for each unit demanded detailed objectives, vocabulary, procedures, and materials/resources. The planning for the second unit, "Prehistoric World," was underway when the school year began. Although it was not as polished as the first unit, the villagers were happy with their work. At meetings, there were some regular complaints about lack of time to complete the plans. At one meeting, Brooke suggested that perhaps the activity plans did not have to be quite so detailed. "All of us have taught our parts before; can't we just agree on what we're going to do without writing it all out?" Sara and Ann were opposed, as the summer institute training had been explicit on the value of writing out the unit plans. Harry remembered that the institute facilitators had emphasized the commercial value of unit plans. Even though he was not interested in publishing, Harry had been impressed by the notion that their work could be so valued. Brooke remained a skeptic. Her approach to instructional planning was to have the skeleton in place and then allow the details to come out of the daily work. Sara wanted the plans written out in detail.

With some last-minute scrambling, the second unit was written and ready to enact in October. The culminating activity was a field trip to two museums in the metropolitan area. The anthropology museum illustrated the curriculum on the prehistoric world, and the space museum focused the students on the future. The field trip was a logistical nightmare, with half the students going one day and half the other. Non-village teachers served as chaperones, and the carefully laid plans for learning activities fell apart. Ann was so disappointed with the students' rambunctious behavior that the following day in class, she put aside her usual cheerful disposition and resoundingly chewed out the village students in class. She suggested that no further field trips or big productions would be possible if they could not change their behavior. The village teachers were "terribly disappointed" in their students; they felt "almost betrayed" because the students did not represent them or the school well. For Ann, the unit had worked well overall, but the field trip debacle was a big disappointment.

In the last few weeks of the second unit, Sara and Ann had become concerned that Brooke and Harry exhibited less interest in planning the third unit, "We are a World of Societies." The unit was only a sketch when the school year began. Well into the Prehistoric World unit, planning the next unit was yet to be done. Week after week, Sara or Ann came to meetings with an idea for a village-wide production or a event. Their interest was not infectious; Harry and Brooke gave lukewarm or downright chilly responses. Sara tried to keep the villagers on task at meetings, and the response was increasingly, "Well, Sara…" with rolling eyes. Sara tried to convince the others of her vision: "Just look what we could do to wrap up the unit." Brooke began to share with Harry her reluctance to undertake another big production. She was not at all certain that the results justified the teachers' efforts. Harry increasingly felt uncomfortable as he tried to balance his admiration for Sara (who had been a mentor to him on cooperative learning strategies) with his good working relationship with Brooke (who had been so generous with her help when he had taught LA/SS). He genuinely liked all his village colleagues, but his own "laid back" style of curriculum planning was closer to Brooke's than to Sara's or Ann's.

Throughout November, village meetings became less pleasant for all the teachers. Brooke and Harry felt that Sara and Ann were running full-speed ahead without taking into account their wishes. Sara and Ann felt that their "stronger personalities" had to serve as the "driving force" to accomplish the curriculum plans. Sara repeatedly insisted that she did not want to be in control, but she had what she believed were good ideas for the "bonding experiences" that would make the village a success. "I had to plan these, but that's how I can get what I want," she reasoned. She created a teacher evaluation of the village program and gave it to all the village teachers to "bring to Thursday's meeting." Brooke complained that Sara was telling her what to do, even though Brooke had made it clear she did not like some of the ideas under consideration. Sara was definitely trying to take charge; she and Ann had an agenda to which Brooke and Harry were not party. Harry was concerned. He remained silent in village meetings, but beneath his calm appearance, he began to feel the stress. After a meeting in which little was accomplished, Brooke and Harry agreed they should talk to the principal, Katie.

Katie was not overly concerned by what she heard from Brooke and Harry. She knew all the teachers well, and she could well imagine the clash in styles between the two stronger and two quieter teachers. Katie asked how she could be of help – perhaps by attending a couple of village meetings? Brooke and Harry agreed that was an excellent idea. At the next two meetings, Katie sat in. She praised the teachers for doing "an outstanding job." She knew the statewide scene well, and the village was doing what few other teams had done – made the curriculum the driving force behind the team. The two meetings were productive. Sara and Ann were less insistent about what Brooke thought of as their "grandiose" ideas. Katie's praise for the village raised the notion of the teachers putting together videotape clips of their activities to date and showing the finished product to the rest of the faculty. As the video wizard of the village, Harry agreed to oversee that project.

For the moment, the crisis was averted. The third unit was implemented without a wholesale production or field trip. As the winter holidays approached, village meetings were increasingly consumed with attention to individual students, with parent conferences, and with planning celebrations to mark the season. In classes, the stellar dollars continued to be awarded; Super Star lunches were held; an auction of odds and ends helped to bring back to the teachers the stellar dollar papers. Still, the curriculum plans were not moving forward.

In late January, the unit connected with ancient Egypt began. The village teachers called this unit "Gifts from our world." Sara suggested a final project of creating an Egyptian newspaper. Brooke had done a similar project in the past; it sounded fine to her. Ann and Harry were agreeable, but understood that there was little planning that would include the science and math classes in the newspaper. The LA/SS teachers, Sara and Brooke, would do the newspapers. This plan worked for the "Gifts from our World" unit. Team meetings continued to focus on individual students and on ongoing activities to reinforce the PRIDE discipline plan. The village teachers compared notes on their use of the stellar dollars. Since the new year, the teachers had used the little paper squares less and less. The students seemed to be responding well without the carrot of the dollars. Thereafter, the stellar dollars were used only sporadically by the village teachers. By February, the village was still functioning as a unit, but much of the initial enthusiasm and drive behind the curriculum integration was missing in action. Serious problems with a few village students consumed most of the meeting time. For Brooke, the hiatus in curriculum planning was a relief. For Harry, it was no problem. For Sara, it was a sign – a sign that the other teachers were not as ready as she to take on interdisciplinary teaching. For Ann, it was a puzzlement that what had started so well was in such doldrums.

While the village teachers began to contemplate the last third of the year, including the units called "Gifts to the World (Greece)" and "A World of Roads (Rome)," an opportunity presented itself. Brooke and Harry were experienced master teachers for preservice teacher education, and they had agreed to take in student teachers for the spring semester. When the Greece unit began, the two student teachers would be in place. Their presence might serve as a safety valve in the village, Ann thought. With two enthusiastic, hard-working apprentices, there might be a greater likelihood of Brooke and Harry reentering the curriculum arena with Sara and Ann.

The student teachers became part of the village people when they arrived for part-time and then full-time student teaching. As their responsibilities in Harry and Brooke's classrooms increased, however, they found less time to devote to village meetings. The challenges of putting into effect on an ongoing basis the kinds of lessons they had envisioned during their coursework and earlier student teaching proved more daunting than imagined. Brooke's student teacher encountered difficulties brought on, Brooke thought, by an inability to deal well with discipline situations. Harry's student teacher was having ongoing problems making lessons clear for the students, and then responding appropriately when students expressed their confusion. Both student teachers demanded more time of Brooke and Harry. As the spring wore on, Brooke's student teacher became more capable in discipline and Brooke was able to relax her vigilance in the classroom. Harry's student teacher continued to have more rough spots than Harry would have liked, so he stayed close to home in the classroom for most of the spring.

At a village meeting in early April, Sara reminded her teammates that neither Brooke nor Harry had taken leadership in the curriculum planning earlier in the year. Now that they both were assisted by student teachers, surely they were in better shape to take that leadership. Sara preferred that the curriculum planning be done by the village people as a whole, but this had not been working out well since before the winter holidays. Thus, if four village members were unable to agree on a plan, at least there were two who had more time than the others. It made perfect sense to Sara that Brooke and Harry should take responsibility for the "bonding production" of the Greek unit – an Olympic festival. Ann agreed. Besides her unwillingness to be more confrontive with Brooke and Harry at this point, Ann was preoccupied by a personal matter. Her longtime boyfriend was about to become her husband on a long weekend in May. Ann's happiness and busyness on this account precluded her from wanting to deal with any unpleasantness in the village. When Sara suggested that Brooke and Harry plan the Olympic festival, they agreed. This was the same Olympic festival that all the sixth grade LA/SS teachers had organized the year before. Brooke knew that there was a great deal of work to accomplish so that the students could make up teams of players for mock Olympic events out on the athletic field. Equipment, signs, timetable, rewards – all must be carefully constructed so that 120 students were well occupied. Harry was willing to work with Brooke on the plans. His student teacher seemed to be progressing a little, and he wanted the end of the school year to pass smoothly for the village.

While Brooke and Harry began their festival planning, the specter of the following school year appeared on the horizon. An elementary school building was slated to be converted to a new middle school in the district. Rumor was that Katie was in line to be principal at the elementary school for a year and then oversee its conversion to middle school. If that were to happen, some teachers from Desert would likely request transfers to Katie's school. The members of the village, like the rest of Desert's teachers, did not talk about wanting to transfer. Katie would have the final say, and no one wanted to be embarrassed if left behind. Throughout the school, next year's plans were low key. Nonetheless, plans must be made. The village members discussed their class schedules for the next year as if they would all be present. The school faculty had decided that a teacher would keep the same group of students for three years of advisory. This meant that the villagers would have seventh graders for advisory while continuing to teach sixth grade. That they would be missing a connection with the village sixth graders did not seem an insurmountable problem. Harry felt excited and weary at the same time when thinking ahead to the next year: "At times I want the village to go on for another five years, and at times I just don't have the energy to deal with it. It's not good to put in that much energy for so long – not good for me or for the kids."

When Katie approached the village people to determine their interest in attending a second statewide institute on interdisciplinary teaming—this would be a follow-up to the one Sara, Ann and Harry had attended the year before – the teachers were ambivalent. Ann had travel plans with her new husband, and the other three villagers were inclined to say "No, thanks" to Katie. Ann had in mind that she might not be at Desert Middle School the following year. With the possible leave-taking of Katie to another school, Ann was actively seeking employment in school districts closer to her home, an hour's drive from Desert. Sara, too, had some reservations about making the commitment. Sara wanted to follow Katie to the new school. Katie and Sara possessed similar spirits – both balls of fire looking for somewhere and something exciting to ignite. As for Brooke and Harry, they were playing a waiting game at the end of the year. There were options for longtime teachers such as they were; it was too soon to commit to the village or to Desert Middle School for the coming year.

While their student teachers implemented the ancient Greece curriculum in LA/SS and the geometric shapes curriculum in math, Brooke and Harry brought together the Olympics festival plans. During village meetings at this juncture, Harry took the lead in presenting their plans. Brooke was occasionally testy as she presented a chart showing all the separate tasks that needed to be accomplished. When Brooke sarcastically asked, "Are we over-planning? Does it have to be perfect?," Harry tried to lessen the tension: "Oh, something will definitely go wrong. There's still lots of flexibility in the plan, so let's just see what happens." Harry suggested asking a seventh grade teacher for the use of his color printer to make signs. Brooke feigned horror: "What? Go outside the village?" Harry again tried to ease the tension: "God help us! We've got a pure village so far!" The laughter of the village people was nervous. The camaraderie they experienced at the beginning of the year had worn mighty thin.

A week later, a successful Olympics festival was held – "the last goddamned big village production I'm doing this year," Brooke promised herself. At the next village meeting, Brooke asked for assurance that "we aren't planning any other big 'do.'" Sara replied, "Well…," to which Brooke muttered, "Oh ____." Sara suggested that an end-of-the-year party was needed to give the students a feeling of accomplishment and closure. No one suggested that there be another curriculum-connected "big production." Clearly, Brooke and Harry had done their piece, and as the year came to a close, all the village people wanted was a sense of closure for themselves and their students. The major obstacle in their way was Katie, who had forbidden year-end parties. Sara figured a way around the ban. The village would hold an awards ceremony. She was certain that she could prevail upon Katie to allow it. No food would be served, so Katie could not possibly call it a party. And Katie had just announced that she was indeed leaving to take the elementary principalship so that she could plan the new middle school. So, Ann reasoned with a smile, "Who cares if Katie objects?"

Sara received permission from Katie to move ahead on the awards gathering. On the final day of school, the 120 sixth graders gathered in Sara's room for the last time. Sara started the ceremony by asking everyone to close their eyes and to visualize what the village had been like for themselves. Sara cried quietly for those few minutes. Then she composed herself and began the awards that the teachers had designed. These included Best Dressed, Most Academic, Best Comedian, Most Helpful, Tallest Boy and Girl, Best Couple, and many more. The students accepted their certificates for these awards amid much laughter and many catcalls. All the leftover stellar dollars were then disposed of by having the students write their names on the back of the dollars and drawing for prizes. Baseball cards, pencils, and a Polaroid camera were among the giveaways.

Sara brought the gathering back to a serious note when she asked for volunteers to come up to the small stage to say what they thought of the village. A dozen students shared their thoughts: "The village helped us because we have more friends;" "The teachers are real caring;" "It helped me get through sixth grade;" "I liked it because we got to have field trips and festivals and stuff." Two of the students were comforted by Ann and Sara when they started crying while they spoke. Barely holding back her own tears, Sara told the students that each of the teachers wanted to say something, too. The teachers, she said, "wanted to bring you together because we really do care about you. We are people who care. And now if I don't stop, I *will* cry." Ann complimented the students: "Through good times and bad, you've been fabulous. Thank you from the heart – thank you for being you." Harry told the students, "You have made this the best year since I've been at Desert. Thank you, and I wish you the best of luck." Brooke was upbeat as she addressed the students: "It's been fun, and I want you all to come back and see us when you are big seventh graders."

At the end of that final day, Brooke was visibly relieved to be done with the village for the year. She could appreciate the benefits of the village for herself and her students. She felt supported by her village colleagues; they had worked well together, especially in addressing student problems. But the clashes dating back to late autumn had taken their toll. Brooke felt that she simply was not comfortable working with powerful personalities. She was not enthusiastic about continuing to work with Sara and Ann. It wasn't that she did not respect them, for clearly they were terrific teachers with many good ideas; but their "take charge" personalities and their preference for big performances exhausted Brooke. There had been perhaps too much emphasis on doing everything well the first year, Brooke suspected. Maybe a more gradual approach to designing and implementing interdisciplinary curriculum was advisable.

Sara, too, reflected on the difficulties the village people had encountered during the year. She realized the effect she had on Harry and Brooke when a grand scheme would occur to her. She knew that they had approached Katie to "pull the cheerleaders off," as she thought of it. Katie pointed out to her that the teachers were in different comfort zones with interdisciplinary teaming. Sara looked back on those days: "I wanted to fly to the moon, and they weren't ready. So I had to back off and quit being the mama driving the truck." But looking ahead, Sara was already forming a vision of the next two to three years in the village. Katie would have supported the villagers to write more complete curriculum units in the succeeding years. Without Katie, how much support would there be? The incoming principal was being moved from an administrative position at the district office. He had no middle school experience. Although he was well liked in the district, he was certainly no Katie in terms of the infectiousness of his personality. Sara was inclined to wait and see what developed over the summer.

Katie's leaving was the icing on the cake for Ann. With few regrets, she accepted a teaching position closer to home. Within a couple of weeks, Sara found that her request for transfer to Katie's school was accepted. One of her charges at the new school would be to start a sixth grade village and assist the other teachers to form teams of their own. With Sara and Ann leaving Desert, the dynamo and the enthusiast had left the village. Brooke and Harry admitted to some relief. Their feelings of ambivalence were lessened. They would continue the village because they felt it was good for the students. But they would be careful about who to invite in to their team.

The village continued to exist the next year, with Brooke and Harry paired up with Sara's and Ann's replacement teachers. No new curriculum units were planned; no new "big production" activities were held. A couple of village-wide events that were already "in the can" – like the Olympics festival – were repeated, but without the fanfare associated with them the year before. The student discipline plan continued, but since the village people were not the advisory teachers for the village students, the teachers were pulled in different directions to make parent contacts for two sets of

students. The new principal supported the idea of the village, but he took a
"hands off" attitude toward the teachers school-wide, as he did not want to be
viewed as the outsider who came in to change a school and individual
programs that were already working well. So in its second year, the village
existed as a loosely connected team of four teachers, comfortable with one
another but not ambitious in pressing the interdisciplinary curriculum.

Why did the village fail to thrive? According to the four village people,
their own personality clashes, fueled by differences in instructional planning
styles, spelled disaster for the village. Clearly Sara and Ann were more
desirous of the productions that they saw as necessary to the "bonding" of the
village students to one another and to the teachers. Harry and Brooke supported a coordinated curriculum effort – Harry especially enjoyed teaching
some social studies concepts in math – but they were less impressed with the
necessity for labor-intensive detailed lesson planning and "boffo" culminating activities. Harry and Brooke began to feel they were being "told what to
do," and as competent professionals with long records of success, they
resisted. The delicate balance achieved by the end of the year – proceeding
with the units agreed upon at the beginning of the year, but with less detailed
plans – was the best the village people could do under the circumstances.
When Katie left Desert, the villagers no longer had an admired administrator
whom they liked to please. Sara and Ann found greener pastures; Harry and
Brooke scaled back their commitment to interdisciplinary curriculum work.

Although none of the village people identified other sources of trouble, the
efficacy of their interdisciplinary curriculum approach may be questioned.
Early on, the villagers decided to build the curriculum around the social
studies scope and sequence for the year. This required little change for Sara
and Brooke, as their curriculum would proceed more or less as before.
Simply add in some village-wide productions, and coordinate homework and
test days with Harry and Ann – and the curriculum would carry on as usual.
While the first interdisciplinary unit – You are a Part of the World – was
more topical, most of the units were clearly identified with the chronological
study of ancient history. The later units were only slightly renamed from
what they would have been in an LA/SS course. Thus the Egypt unit became
"Gifts from the World: Egypt," and the Greece unit was "Gifts to the World:
Greece." Harry and Ann made more pronounced adjustments, at least initially. They changed the sequence of their math and science topics, and they
had to coordinate with the LA/SS curriculum. Still, Harry was definitely
teaching math using the same materials he had always used; likewise Ann
was still a science teacher covering the same concepts as before. The curricu-

lum structure, perfectly in line with the method that was used at the summer workshop, was built around the disciplines. This made it easy for the teachers to fall back on just teaching their own subject areas, for that was their primary responsibility even within the village. Their assignments and assessments fell perfectly within their usual frames of reference. The "big productions" certainly involved all of them in the planning and execution, but the separate disciplines were easily distinguished in daily classroom activity. One might speculate as to the village's staying power had the curriculum been less discipline-centered and more integrated across the disciplines, perhaps even to the extent of erasing the boundaries among the courses. Other curriculum structures such as great ideas, life problems, and mind constructs (Harter & Gehrke, 1989) might have forced the villagers to become more interdependent as they enacted the curriculum. The disciplines were strong in the village people and strong in their activity plans. To dismantle the curriculum entirely – to put all the curriculum pieces on the table and re-configure them without the preconceived notion of "language arts," "social studies," "mathematics" and "science" – was never an expectation of these teachers. Thus when they fell back on their prior work experience and prior successes as disciplinary teachers, they were comfortable with themselves.

The fact that the team did not have a daily team meeting time in addition to individual planning time also took its toll. Taking two, maybe only one, common planning times a week made it difficult to carry out an ambitious team agenda. Trying to carry out any interdisciplinary units, let alone six, while learning how to plan together, dealing with individual student needs, planning and executing a reward system, and holding joint parent conferences would prove too much for four people who had never teamed before.

The village of Sara, Ann, Brooke, and Harry has not been emulated by the other teachers at Desert. While they were admired for their attempt, the other teachers thought that the results just did not seem worth the effort. The clashes of personality and style could have been repeated many times in the faculty of longtime independent teachers.

Without adequate meeting time to work out differences and reach consensus, teaming did not appear to be worth the effort. While informal mentoring and cooperation were encouraged, these were mostly done within subject area departments. Some departments were particularly hard-working in terms of the professional development of their teachers. None was inclined to cut across disciplines to reach out to colleagues. Without Katie there to push the buttons to start another team, the teachers were inclined to work on curriculum issues from other angles. The village had been a singular light at Desert Middle School, but only for that one year, and only with some difficulties along the way. Thereafter, interdisciplinary teaming seemed more a mirage than a likely reality in a school that professed the middle level concept but could not see its way to making teaming an integral part of the school program.

References

Canter, L., & Canter, M. (1976). *Assertive discipline: A take charge approach for today's educator.* Seal Beach, CA: Canter & Associates.

Harter, P.D., & Gehrke, N.J. (1989). Integrative curriculum: A kaleidoscope of alternatives. *Educational Horizons, 68* (1), 12-17.

Jacobs, H.H. (Ed.). (1989). *Interdisciplinary curriculum: Design and implementation.* Alexandria, VA: Association for Supervision and Curriculum Development.

Part III

Aspects of Practice

From one point of view, teaming is the pursuit of answers to a number of fundamental questions: How is teaming practiced? How do two or more teachers meld together into a new whole that creates opportunities for student learning beyond what individual teachers can do on their own? Beyond these fundamental questions there are other questions as well: How do middle school teachers go through their careers as team members, growing and learning their craft over several decades? How is "the wisdom of teams" developed by new teams and how is it passed on? How do mature teams continue to grow, how do they move beyond elemental transitional concerns? How do administrators work with teams, both new and experienced? How do teams maximize their strength in teaching their students? And what does having a child on a middle school team mean for a parent?

Part III: "Aspects of Practice," provides answers to these questions about practice that individual team members, teams of teachers, and those that work with teams face day in and day out. These six chapters, written by and about experienced team members, hold a wealth of insight gained from years of collaboration with students, teachers, administrators, and parents. The authors provide "close encounters" that lay bare fundamental issues of teaming in middle schools – sometimes disturbing and painful, often joyous, always true.

This section begins with the question "What would it be like to spend an entire career as a member of teams?" Ross Burkhardt's career offers an answer. Through an intimate and engaging portrait we meet Ross's teammates, his students and their parents, experience his classroom and his curriculum and instruction, and how working together can be as natural as breathing in and breathing out. We come to know, in Ross's own words, how "we gain more than we give" as members of teams.

The "wisdom of teams" has been hard-earned by numerous teams from a wide variety of middle schools throughout the nation. Stacey Burd Rogers, Marge Bowen, and Judy Hainline comprise one of those teams that has forged itself together through the heat of practice. In their chapter "Starting A New Team: Advice and Best Practice" these three classroom teachers offer to new teams windows on their own experience that reveal mistakes not to make, insights on how to deal with colleagues who become stumbling blocks to team advancement, and their mistakes in implementing theoretical practice without adaptation to site and situation. Their private experience, now made public, should allow new teams to move further down the road of teaming with less pain, ultimately arriving where these teachers now are – using teaming both creativity and flexibly and with insight. Ultimately the authors pass along a rich range of "wisdom of teams" such as: "As subject lines have blurred, so have our classrooms expanded."

Drawing on her long and rich experience as a team member as well as her current university position, Jeanneine P. Jones provides mature teams with a set of standards and cautions for their advancement to new levels. While much of the middle school movement, and this is true of teams as well, has been focused on making the transition, Jeanneine moves all of us further along the road of development with a wise and insightful exploration of what can and should be done as well as what dangers lurk to snag development.

Teams do not exist in isolation, they are part of a climate and a culture. How do administrators, charged with working with teams at the middle level, provide the support, guidance, and structure that they need? Using a theoretical paradigm drawn from Bolman and Deal's work with reframing organizations, Mary Gallagher-Polite provides both a theoretical framework and practical advice for administrators working with teams in middle schools. In the final analysis Mary cuts to the heart of teaming in middle schools: "But real teaming is not just something we do. It is something we believe."

Richard Powell is an example of a rare researcher who can get students and teachers to talk about their feelings, concerns, and motivations and embed that dialogue in a larger context for a reader. "The Case of Jimmie" is a powerful portrait of what teams can do for individual children. Slowly, over time, we watch the "rescue" of an individual student and the discovery and affirmation of his sense of self. This chapter provides an example of "the power of teams" when theory and practice are combined for student development and learning.

If teaming is good for students then one of the strongest sources of support for teams should be parents. Using a case study approach from the Blue Valley School District in eastern Kansas, Sue Carol Thompson, Maria Harper, Karen King, Stan Smith, and K.O. Strohbehn (the last four coauthors are parents of students who were on teams) explore teaming from a parent's perspective and conclude that to involve parents more fully in their children's education "team organization is the foundation for much of that involvement."

The "aspects of practice" provided in Part III continue the development of a richer, deeper, stronger knowledge base for teaming in middle schools. These six chapters expand the exploration of fundamental practices of this critical element, and, married to the case studies in Part II, give the reader abundant learning opportunities.

Teaming: Sharing the Experience   7

Ross M. Burkhardt

Eighth grader Bonnie Snyder gave me a handwritten letter on the last day of school. Our team had just returned from a three day trip to Boston where, among other events, we held a closure ceremony called "Memory Minutes." Bonnie's reflections about Boston and the entire year, penned on the penultimate day of her middle school career, raise several implications for teaming.

6/22/92

Dear Mr. Burkhardt,

Thank you for giving me the best year of my life, so far of course, but I doubt anything else could come this close. I am so glad that I got to be part of this wonderful team, and I'm glad I got to know everyone.

In the beginning of the year, we were all quiet and mostly self contained. Then, during PEEC [a three-day outdoor education whole team field trip in September], we all just connected, and we began to open up. You made the year so great, and not just for me. I believe I speak for everyone when I say that you're the best, and that you're right about life being unfair.

I realized so much at Boston. I realized by looking around at everyone during 'Memory Minutes' that we were all so high on ourselves. We were all confident. Not one person in that room could've felt low or depressed because they had a whole team cheering for them, supporting them, just listening — it was great! Everyone was so close to each other.

A little while ago I was talking to a friend on another team. She said how jealous she was of our team because we were all so close. At first I didn't understand, but before I

163

could say anything Dennis came in and said, 'Anyone have a dollar?' Someone gave him a dollar. Sue said that on her team you just didn't ask for a dollar or for anything. I knew what she meant. This team is like a family and I am very sad to see us all split up.

This year has been so great for me. I never thought I could be so happy going to a classroom. Every day I looked forward to English and Social Studies because I loved them so much. Everything I did in that class was to please only 2 people, me and you.

I don't know how to express all the thanks I have towards you in words. Just thanks. Thanks for a great year, thanks for being a friend, thanks for talking to me, and thanks for taking a bunch of scared kids and turning them into a strong, confident team.

Is this part of the reason you teach? So you can see all these kids grow and work together and so you can reflect on all the great things you've done and see how you've helped so many people?

Well, one more day, then I'm just a visitor in your class and visit I will. I may be going to high school, but I'm not moving. I'll be back!

Love always,
Bonnie Snyder

Bonnie's letter is clearly out of the ordinary. In my experience most 8th graders do not engage in metacognition about their schooling. What prompted Bonnie to write what she did? What were the team experiences that led her to those reflections and assertions? Some of them I know, and some I may never fully understand. For teaming is a group experience shared singularly; each individual has a slightly different perception, and the collective whole is difficult to see, assess, or explain. But ask kids who have been on dynamic teams and they delight in the memory. Ask teachers who have helped create and maintain successful teaming situations and they know the value of their efforts. Teaming works, for middle school kids and teachers.

What constitutes a team? And what benefits does a teacher derive from being part of a teaming arrangement? How are the lives of young adolescents affected by a team setting? How do teachers balance the academic purposes and social opportunities of teaming? What responsibilities do students have to their team? What should teachers do to help their team grow and flourish? Useful questions, all.

Many educators, and I am one, see the team as a home away from home, a place where middle school students gain a sense of belonging. A passage from Robert Frost's *The Death of the Hired Man* offers this definition:

> *Home is the place where, when you have to go there,*
> *They have to take you in.*
>
> *I should have called it*
> *Something you somehow haven't to deserve.*

Young adolescents, those children of the universe currently inhabiting our classrooms, have an absolute, undisputed right to be there. They don't "deserve" home – it is their due, automatically, by virtue of the fact that they exist. In middle schools, team structures provide that "home away from home" for students, an increasingly important accommodation in today's world of working parents and latchkey kids. A well organized team creates a sense of place and belonging. Teams often mean fewer teachers with whom students interact; consequently, a rich set of relationships frequently develops between students and teachers. Teams offer greater stability for kids, a home base (which is further reinforced when advisory groups are formed from within the team), a more consistent learning environment, enhanced possibilities for social development, more occasions for students to emerge as leaders, and increased opportunities for adjustments to schedules, class lists, and curricula during the year. In short, a team setting provides enormous benefits to young adolescents.

Similarly, teachers are served by participating on a team. Support from colleagues, shared responsibility, assistance in planning the learning activities, a lessening of the sense of isolation that some teachers experience – all these are immediate benefits of teaming. Those new to a building encounter veterans who can show them the ropes; in return, experienced teachers are energized by the buoyancy of youth. Team structures place colleagues in shared decision-making roles. Teams encourage and enable integrated curriculum activities, and they help teachers see possibilities beyond their normal frames of reference. Team settings expose teachers to different methods and teaching practices, and they give teachers a sense of identity.

I've participated in two kinds of teaming situations during my career: first, when a group of teachers worked cooperatively, and at times voluntarily, on behalf of a larger group of students, whether or not the students they served saw themselves as a team; second, when the school administration specifically designated a smaller number of students and a specific set of teachers as one of several teams in the building. My work with both kinds of teams goes back more than thirty years, and those experiences inform my teaching.

In 1965 I began teaching 9th grade social studies in my home town, located near West Point in the Hudson Valley. A returned Peace Corps volunteer, I had lots of energy and very little training, but my work on a team of two American and two Tunisian physical education instructors at an orphanage/trade school for boys aged 10 to 16 had taught me a great deal about compromise and cooperation. For seven years at Monroe-Woodbury High School I was a member of a voluntary academic team; the four of us decided to plan units and prepare lessons together. We team taught large groups of students, organized whole grade activities, took each other's teaching schedules and taught the same lesson fifteen or sixteen times to the entire 9th grade, and slowly developed both a common philosophy of teaching and a set of common experiences that engaged our students. We did not start out with any grandiose plans to "do" teaming; rather, we knew very little about the new 9th grade social studies curriculum, we were all relatively inexperienced teachers, and we saw the opportunity to cooperate as being more productive and less scary than going it alone. In retrospect it is clear that we were predisposed to working collaboratively. In fact, our teaming went further than that.

We ate lunch together, socialized after hours, and shared our developing ideas about what kids needed and what teaching could be. Marty was the veteran (he'd been teaching five years), and we counted on him for strength and guidance. Howie made up in dedication and compassion what he lacked in organizational skills. Diane, fresh from her Peace Corps experience in Guatemala, provided boundless enthusiasm and unconditional love for her students. And I read pertinent passages from *Education & Ecstasy* and *Teaching As a Subversive Activity* to the three of them, eager to expand our horizons with radical teaching strategies.

I recall a collective nervousness when Marty, Diane, and I first got three classes together for a joint lesson on the Soviet Union in the fall of 1967. Then there were the intricacies of scheduling a six week unit on Vietnam for the entire 9th and 10th grades that began shortly after the 1968 Tet offensive, ending in a series of debates between "hawks," "doves," and moderates just prior to the assassination of Dr. Martin Luther King, Jr. By the time Diane and I left Monroe-Woodbury, we were committed to teaming as a way of teaching. It had brought out the best in the four of us; each made unique contributions to the larger team. I did preliminary scheduling, Marty provided vision, Diane asked hard-nosed questions, and Howie offered unflagging support. Collectively we created an innovative social studies program and taught a "team" of over four hundred students – the entire 9th grade.

Diane and I eventually married; our professional relationship developed long before we shared a personal one. Today we both teach on different 8th grade teams at a middle school on Long Island. Our years at Monroe-Woodbury High School, however, were where we learned how to teach and how to team together.

Shoreham-Wading River Middle School opened its doors in 1972 with advisory groups and teaming in place from Day One. Dennis Littky, our principal, was a brilliant educator who encouraged experimentation, raised appropriate questions, and served as the leader of a team of sixth, seventh, and eighth grade teachers dedicated to the idea of excellence in middle level education. Dennis' vision created the school; a quarter of a century later his ideas continue to resonate among SWR staff and students.

My first year I was one of six teachers responsible for the entire 7th grade. I moved to eighth grade in 1973 as a member of a three person English/social studies team. This grew to four teachers a year later, then shifted to a two person academic team in 1976, our current organizational structure. My partner, Nancy Lukoski, teaches math and science and I teach English and social studies to the same forty-nine students. Each team in our middle school is composed of four advisory groups, and the advisors meet regularly to discuss both academic and social concerns related to students on the team.

At SWR I have engaged in teaming in many ways. For example, two years in a row the eighth grade social studies teachers and a student teacher team taught a three week unit on conflict. After we each gave similar introductory lessons to our own students, they selected either the Civil War, World War I, World War II, Korea, or Vietnam for further study. In my Civil War group (only three of the 18 students were mine) we read *Andersonville*; Diane's group viewed *Hearts and Minds* during their study of Vietnam. As teachers we enjoyed specializing in a particular area of interest and meeting other students. The eighth graders got to select a learning activity and work with a different teacher. It was a successful teaming experience for all of us.

One year George Dorsty (English), Ed Hopkins (science) and I (social studies) did a unit on evolution. We began with a large group presentation. I put together a ten-minute slide show of various flora and fauna. George read passages from *Genesis*. Then, as Ed was explaining *Origin of Species*, the principal (whom we had invited to observe) suddenly stood up and stopped the lesson. She informed us that what we were doing – teaching evolution – was against school policy, that we were not to continue teaching any more Darwin, and that we were to meet in her office the following period to discuss the situation. She then turned and abruptly walked out of the large group instruction room, leaving fifty 8th graders and three teachers stunned; no one knew what to say. Ed, George, and I began complaining loudly among ourselves. The kids, upset that the lesson had been stopped, listened to us argue for a while. Soon they were planning to march *en masse* to the principal's office and protest. Before the period was over, however, we let our team in on the secret: they had just experienced a "staged" simulation akin to what John Scopes underwent in 1925; the principal had acted her role well. During the rest of the four-week unit students read *Inherit the Wind*, held debates, studied the history of the twenties, and went further into Darwin's scientific ideas. Again, three teachers working together provided a team of students with a memorable learning experience.

At our middle school, students stay together as a team for three years; they move as a group from 6th to 7th to 8th grade. Each September my eighth graders and I work with our team's 7th grade social studies teacher and her students (they will be mine the following year) to create a United States timeline around the walls of the library. Her pupils select dates from the years 1600 to 1865. Nancy, my math/science partner, works with me on this project, and our 8th graders cover the period from 1866 to the present. They research important cultural, historical, technological, scientific, and mathematical developments. The final result is a chronological array of some 400 posters depicting major events in our nation's history over four centuries. The collective work of almost one hundred 7th and 8th graders provides the rest of the school with a valuable resource. The United States Timeline is now an annual cross-discipline, cross-grade, multi-year project that begins our academic year on Team 8-IV.

Each spring my students do The Inquiry Project, another example of integrated learning. In this culminating activity, every student selects a topic for investigation, then begins research in the library. Eventually students create individual magazines containing fifteen or more "items" from math, science, foreign language, English and social studies; "items" may include graphs, illustrations, poems, first and third person narratives, biographies, interviews, editorials, interior monologues, maps, glossaries, letters, charts, reports and analyses. Working in writing groups, students improve their written expression through a drafting and revising process. Using a family learning style, they also help one another by explaining complex computer applications, critiquing each other's magazine covers, participating in surveys, and suggesting ideas for new inquiry items. The entire team participates in an intense six-week, multi-discipline academic experience that ties together all the skills they learned during the year.

Eight Essential Truths About Teaming

Working with others over the decades has taken many forms, and through those experiences I have come to realize eight essential truths about teaming:

- **A team functions best when its members agree on a shared set of common expectations.**

   Before we began teaming together in 1988, my math/science partner Cliff Lennon and I scheduled several meetings to exchange views on kids, teaching, and middle level education. Out of those conversations came The Distinctions, a set of terms to guide our work with students. While the specific words we came up with (appreciation, acknowledgment, communication, risk, respect, etc.) are a matter of personal choice and other teams might agree on a different set, it was the fact of our creating the list together and committing ourselves to abide by those expectations that made the difference on our team.

   To enroll students in The Distinctions, Cliff and I set aside a double period on the second day of school and discussed them thoroughly with the kids. In January 1989 at "Lessons Learned" (a team meeting at which students reflect on the first four months of school) , the very first student to share, Jason Ragona, observed,

   > I learned that you guys are serious about The Distinctions. When you first mentioned them in September, I thought, 'Oh sure, here's something the teachers are bringing out to tell us how to behave, but we won't see these again after September.' But you kept bringing them back, and referring to them, and using them. You guys are serious about The Distinctions.

   How does discussing terms such as *compassion, individuality, trust,* and *cooperation* on the second day of school impact the way students see their education? How do The Distinctions affect student thinking about relationships and the way they can be with teachers and advisors and fellow students on the team?

Jen Hodess, commenting on The Distinctions at the end of 8th grade in 1994, said:

> *I think that The Distinctions were not only goals that we set for our team to accomplish, but we did accomplish them. They really helped my relationship with the teachers on the team because I knew that both you and Ms. Lukoski had Compassion for each and every team member. That helped all of us Trust you. And both of you had every single Distinction; there was some part of you or something you did that demonstrated each Distinction. The Distinctions also helped my relationships with everybody on the team. When we started 8th grade, I knew everybody but I wasn't really friends with them. The Distinctions helped me become friends with everybody on the team. Everybody was different, and each Distinction was different, so using each different Distinction with each person helped me become friends with them. With Kristin, for example, I became pretty good friends with her because I knew that whatever she was saying was what she was thinking. This was Kristin practicing the Distinction of Communication.*

If teachers and students can agree on a way of being with one another, and then live out the school year according to those expectations, their time together will be something special. Experience suggests that The Distinctions work for many, provide direction for all, and help a team stay focused on what is truly important. To keep The Distinctions visible, we display typed student definitions on the wall outside our adjoining classrooms. In October we publish a team anthology containing each student's perspective on two or three Distinctions. As the year unfolds we also conduct regular activities that recall and strengthen our collective understanding of and commitment to The Distinctions.

Our Day Two conversation about The Distinctions is crucial to the success of the team because through that discussion we create an agreement for what is important, a framework for what happens, and a structure of organization, purpose, and intent. The Distinctions are our social contract; they bind us together as a team and remind us of what we are about.

- **A significant whole team experience early in the school year pays great dividends later on.**
  This past September for the seventh year in a row, my partner and I

organized a team trip to the Pocono Environmental Education Center (PEEC). Fostering a sense of community is a declared goal for this trip. After a three hour bus ride from Long Island to Pennsylvania, we spent three days canoeing, orienteering, square dancing, and being together. At a team meeting late on the second night in 1991, I noted that through the Confidence Course, Talent Show, Pond Study, Sunrise Hike, and other activities, "We've built the foundation" for a successful school year. Nick Naccarato, another team advisor and the school's technology teacher, added, "We can now build the house." At that, Liz, a particularly astute 8th grader, predicted, "Come June when our house is finished, I know it will be beautiful." And it was, as Bonnie Snyder's opening letter attests. PEEC had us in the trenches together, sharing the rain and the cabins, the physical challenges, and the not-quite-home-cooked meals. Charlie Maciejewski, one of Liz and Bonnie's classmates, expressed it this way during January's Lessons Learned gathering:

> PEEC was an experience that helped me learn and understand some of the people I did not know too well. PEEC even brought me and my friends closer and more understanding of each other. It also taught me to respect the people on my team better. PEEC really was a good way to bring the whole team closer together. I can now understand and respect all the students I did not know well last year.

Teams need opportunities to grow together. The importance of a common team experience early in the school year through which to build community and collective memories cannot be overstated.

- **Successful teams need regular activities to keep the spirit alive during the year.**

Nurturing kids is part of what teams are about, and that takes work. Each month Nancy and I do a different activity to connect members of the team. We play Jeopardy using categories such as Team Trivia, PEEC, Math/Science, English/Social Studies, or SWR Middle School. We recognize student participation in a variety of ways so that each student is acknowledged several times ("All members of the soccer team, stand up!" "Everybody in chorus, stand up!" "Everyone who got 100 on a math quiz, stand up!" "Everyone who *did not* get 100 on a math quiz, stand up!" "Everyone who went to PEEC, stand up!"). We celebrate birthdays, share family traditions, reflect on Lessons Learned and acknowledge individual and group accomplishments. At the end of the year we do "Memory Minutes," a closure ceremony during which each person on the team has an opportunity to speak to the rest of the team, say farewell, and be complete with the experience.

All of these activities have a positive impact on our classrooms. They address the social and emotional needs of our students, who learn better when they know they are in a caring, supportive environment.

• **Academic projects link team members together**.

Students become part of something larger than themselves when they undertake a team project, and as a result they share common memories. In my English classes, we publish several team booklets during the year: collections of poems, interior monologues, and narratives; also, reflections on various learning activities (The Distinctions, PEEC, Lessons Learned). Every student contributes to each booklet, and when an anthology is published, students write to fellow team authors about their entries. In this way team members are continually reminded that they are part of a community of writers, and they interact regularly with one another about their learnings.

Last year in social studies my students created a new version of Billy Joel's 1989 hit song, "We Didn't Start The Fire." In just six weeks they produced a three-screen slide show based on the major figures and events of their lives from 1979-1993: "Jimmy Carter, Rockefeller, Three Mile Island, Margaret Thatcher . . . ." At the Parent Premiere in November each student explained some aspect of the project: taking notes from visiting guest speakers, researching the 120 terms we finally agreed upon, finding visual images for each term, arranging the slides, recording the lyrics, selecting the title ("The Fire Burns On . . ."), designing the logo, printing sixty t-shirts. Student ownership of the learning experience was clear to all. Danielle Lyle summarized her involvement two months later during our annual Lessons Learned meeting:

> We had to research and coordinate the entire project on our own. To have a successful project we all had to act responsibly and do our assignment as well as we could. We had to be committed to working together or we would never have been able to communicate our ideas through a smoothly run show. The project was meaningful to me because I felt good to have contributed my best to making a great slide show possible. I also learned how to use the slide show projectors and work them in a precise timed program.

Danielle's sense of team identity was strengthened by participating in this curricular activity with the rest of the students on Team 8-IV; she became part of something larger than herself.

- **Young adolescents need to belong, and teams address that need.**

The team can become a "home away from home." When kids feel that they belong, they do not engage in antisocial behavior. Students on well-run teams feel less alienated, less prone to misbehavior and vandalism, and less likely to act out. Most kids do not deliberately mess up their own homes, and while an occasional early adolescent bedroom or school locker might resemble a disaster area, kids respond with courtesy to environments where they feel welcome and respected. When problems on a team do occur, the students often help in cleaning them up because they have a stake in the success of the team; it's theirs, and they care about their reputation.

Question – should teachers work to create a family atmosphere on a team if the following year that atmosphere is not continued? Once again, a poem by Robert Frost, *Happiness Makes Up In Height What It Lacks In Length,* supplies the answer. I say it is better that kids have a great year than a mediocre one. Holding back because of what might or might not happen in the future does not make a lot of sense and does not serve kids.

Teams are communities. If we want kids to understand how a successful community operates, we have to provide a working model. In May 1992 following the Rodney King verdict, Los Angeles experienced a massive breakdown of community. If we expect young adolescents to function well in the larger society, we need to give them positive community experiences in school.

- **Two (or more) heads are better than one.**

When it comes time to plan team activities, I am grateful that Nancy is there with me developing class lists, designing our schedule, suggesting team activities, writing Jeopardy questions, making signs, listening to my concerns, sharing her issues with me, and at times reining me in. When the advisors on our team meet each week to discuss kids, I get to exchange information about specific students and see them more completely as their advisors relate useful information back to me. I also am able to enroll the other advisors in assisting me as I work with individual students; we all want the kids to be successful, and this mutual interest serves our students well. The team partnership also lets me know that I am not in it alone, that I have colleagues to whom I can go for support, for reactions to a new curriculum idea, for advice about a kid or a lesson, or simply for opportunities to share something interesting that happened in class.

- **Teachers are exemplars for students when they model cooperation, caring, and common sense.**

If we believe in cooperative learning and collaboration among students, we need to provide concrete examples in real life. Middle school students are keen observers of what occurs around them. Some of the most powerful lessons we offer come from the ways we handle adversity or unexpected situations. When students see several adults cooperating, speaking civilly, sharing responsibilities, and supporting each other during the year, they are viewing powerful illustrations of how to be successful adults. As teachers working together on a team Nancy and I are careful neither to contradict nor criticize one another in front of our students, and yet we are also comfortable discussing open-ended or unresolved questions publicly. We believe that when students see us struggling to reach a decision, they will accept the final result more readily because they know it was not arrived at arbitrarily.

Learning to work with others is part of what school is about for students and for teachers. Over the years I have had numerous partners, and I have learned that what is needed most on a team are agreement, cooperation, compromise, and a sense that your own ideas, while important, are not necessarily the best solutions. Every teacher on the team needs to feel included, wanted, a part of what is happening. Individuals need to experience ownership of the team goals, direction, and agenda.

- **Adult team members need to build for the long term result, not scramble for the short term gain.**

Successful teams, like Rome, are not built in a day, nor do they happen by accident. Rather, they are the result of cooperation, planning, and maintenance where teachers see and seize opportunities as they come along. More often than not, successful teams result from intentionality, compromise, and hard work. Good ideas and appropriate practices emerge slowly over time. Year after year I knew that my team partners and I would add and sift and discard, and I was always thinking, "Next year we can do it this way." We functioned as a team in it for the long run, sharing a collective responsibility for what happened and keeping an eye on the future. Through conversation and compromise we gradually built a successful context that made a difference in the lives of kids.

Teaming evolves from year to year, so these eight "essential truths" will undoubtedly change over time. Currently they constitute state of the art teaming as I understand it. But I am also sure that next year Nancy and I will initiate activities we have not even dreamed of yet as well as recycle some current activities that, experience tells us, work well for kids. Above all, we will continue to nurture our students and help them grow emotionally, physically, socially, morally, and academically.

The most difficult experience I have ever been through on a team was the death of my teaching partner to cancer. Cliff Lennon, a Notre Dame lacrosse player and Grumman computer systems analyst, went into teaching at age forty because he wanted to work with kids. He was a natural, and his students loved him beyond measure. He taught exciting hands-on math and science classes; chaperoned countless dances and field trips; accompanied eighth grade Spanish students to Madrid; coached soccer, basketball, and baseball; and gave unstintingly of his time to students and staff. Cliff organized our first team trip to PEEC, which became the cornerstone of our academic year, and he constantly sought new ways to integrate learning. His impact on my teaching was considerable.

Having spent the previous spring developing The Distinctions to guide our work with kids, Cliff and I began working together in the fall of 1988. In 1990 Cliff suggested that my end of the year English magazine project could easily become a math/science and English/social studies activity called The Inquiry Project, which we could do together to culminate the school year. It is now some of the best work I do with kids. As we taught year after year, Cliff and I developed a close friendship; we shared meals, movies, and moments of relaxation along with the highs and lows that are a natural part of working with eighth graders.

When Cliff's cancer was diagnosed in March 1991, we held a team meeting to announce it to our students. That fall, Cliff missed opening day; he was just too sick to come in. Again, we began the year with a team meeting and informed our new students about Cliff's condition. He went with us to PEEC one last time in late September, and just before Thanksgiving he completed his last lesson, a hot air balloon unit that culminated on the soccer field with the launching of nine colorful tissue paper balloons, each constructed by a small group of students.

Cliff died on January 27, 1992. The following morning I met our students at the door, told them the sad news, hugged them silently, and led a brief team meeting to announce the schedule for the day. Later, we spent 4th and 5th periods together as a team, talking about Cliff and giving kids an opportunity to share their emotions. All along we had kept them informed of Cliff's deteriorating condition, but his death still came as a shock.

Two things kept me going through this difficult time – the support of my teammates, plus the kids and their need to grieve and be comforted. Neither

my students nor I recall what was taught during February and March –
classes met, periods began and ended, and the weeks slowly passed. Cliff's
death was a daily topic of conversation as we attempted to come to grips with
our loss. In May, many students on the team participated in a memorial
service held by the school district to honor Cliff. Over seventy of his past and
present students, eighth graders to college freshmen, performed in music
groups, delivered speeches, recited poetry, presented a slide show, passed out
programs, made presentations, and escorted members of the Lennon family.

The experience of Cliff's untimely death still links those of us on the team.
Two years later Kristi, who loved Cliff like a father, tearfully dedicated the
last of the candles at her Sweet Sixteen birthday party to his memory. As a
team we went through what no one should have to go through, and yet what
all of us must go through eventually. In her letter Bonnie Snyder noted that I
was right about the unfairness of life. A sign in my classroom quotes JFK
during a Cold War military buildup: "Life is unfair." Bonnie and her classmates suffered brutal unfairness. But the team got through a devastating
experience because we shared our grief openly with one another, and because
we all supported each other. The team structure helped each of us move on
from the tragic loss of Cliff Lennon.

At the end of the 1992-93 school year Andy McIlwraith, one of my
advisees, handed me a three-page, typed letter containing his recollections of
the school year. Andy's words touched me deeply, and I felt fully acknowledged by his many compliments. As I re-read his letter now, I see from a
student's perspective the many threads of teaming that came together to form
the powerful experience that Andy had that year.

6/19/93

Dear Burk,

*Not only is this a letter of memories but it is a letter of
appreciation and acknowledgment from yours truly, Andy
McIlwraith. I wanted to thank you for all you have done for
me this year. Every experience has been wonderful.*

*Let's start with Advisory. Without your constant enthusi-
asm and wit, the advisory probably would have been bor-
ing. The stories of neat things that have happened in your
life have always added a little fun to everything. The stories*

of 'Secret Santa's' at your own home when you were younger were enjoyable to listen to and made us all very anxious to find out who was our 'Secret Santa' and if it was you. Boy, was I glad when I found out it was you! The gift you gave me was very thoughtful, and it was nice of you to spend your time making a funny tape for me, including sound effects.

The advisory traditions such as the milk bag, secret Jolly Rancher hoard, flame thrower guy drills, etc., were very exciting and a great way to start or end the day. Also the way that you always inform us of current events is always interesting. I usually don't read the news but some of the articles concerning Long Island or one of the WDSTF terms that you find are always good to hear about.

Speaking of 'We Didn't Start The Fire . . .', the WDSTF slide show project was definitely an awesome learning by doing experience. I have never learned so much from one project. It was really fun and a great way to teach us kids about the Cold War. I don't know how many times you have heard this but the projects you do with us teach us more than any textbook. Believe me, keep this project.

Another project I would like to address would be the Inquiry. This was the best project of the year, and here's why. I liked the idea of choosing my own topic to research. I didn't have to waste all my time researching some stupid thing like spinach to get a good grade. I could waste my time researching something that has an impact on my life, something I enjoyed, and something that was fun. I think the best example of why this is such a good project would be Seth. When something motivates Seth, it has to be a great project!!

I think that's one of your best qualities, motivation and making things fun to do. Everything is a challenge in your classes, and that is what makes you such a good teacher.

One of the things that I know each of us on Team 8-IV will remember are The Distinctions. You express The Distinctions every day in different ways which helps your classes to work and to be efficient. The Distinctions are like the characteristics of you.

- *Your **Acknowledgment** and **Appreciation** of everything good on the Team is always a mood booster. The Acknowledgment and Appreciation Activities are prime examples.*
- *The **Cooperation** you use with students every day, during projects and disagreements, is also a great quality you express while working.*
- *The **Commitment** you show to students and getting things done is immense.*
- *The **Trust** you show for students by making us feel so at home and having such things as the couches, microwave, and stereo in your room. You trust us to treat these things right and not to take advantage of the advantage.*
- *Your **Compassion** for your advisees and the rest of the Team members.*
- *The **Responsibility** and **Risk** you show when taking us on such trips as PEEC, Boston, Williamsburg or West Virginia.*
- *The **Respect** for us and other Team teachers and advisors.*
- *Your **Contributions** to advisory and the Team.*
- *The **Individuality** you possess that no other teacher can.*

One of the things that I told about in my recent 'Lessons Learned' was the phrases you used every day in class. These are something that are very true and that most everyone should know. Ones such as 'Life is Unfair,' and 'Do what works,' are two that will help each and every one of us in future life. **(You should hear John's impressions of these!)**

Now let's talk about PEEC. I had never been on an overnight trip before and I was a little nervous. I knew that all my friends would be there, but I still wasn't sure about how it would be there. The way everything worked and was planned made it the best trip ever! I had the best room ever! I was put in a room with all my friends and some that I wanted to get to know better. The activities were great, and I definitely had one of the best experiences of my life, so far. I loved this trip and learned about teamwork, risk, and many other Distinctions and just some other stuff. The best memory of mine from PEEC was the advisory competition activity and the dance. Thanks!

Now, how about the various out of school trips. This is part of the motivation. You make learning fun and recre-

ational. The trips such as Williamsburg, West Virginia, Albany and Coxsackie were fun for everyone on them, and they learned and taught from them. Other trips like movie trips and advisory trips were very cool. I usually never went to the movies often, but you gave my parents an excuse to let me go. Also I would like to compliment you on the way that the advisory trip went. It was really fun, and it was great spending time with you and the advisory. It ruled all other advisory trips!!!

Poetry memorization is a good memory of mine. It was fun doing them, most of the time, and I know that this will help me in high-school. Even Bryan did it. He usually does not participate in these kinds of activities, but I think the way you make all of us feel so comfortable, and the way the kids on the Team act, he felt comfortable doing it.

There are many other projects and activities that I would like to address, but I do not want to write too much so here is a brief summary.

'Things That Concern Us' Slide Show

newyorKids slide show

Letter to Chelsea Clinton

The Nine Dots

School Newspaper

Poems

This list represents some of the various informative projects that Mr. B. presented to Team 8-IV this past year. They have readied kids for the high-school and have made learning fun.

I think that I have covered everything that I want to say so I am now going to 'shut down' my computer but before I do . . .

. . . You have helped to make this year the best year of my life, all the things that you have taught, all the things you do for me, and the way you run your classes. I think that you are a prime example of a great teacher.

Sincerely,

Andy McIlwraith

P.S. Keep up the good work. < Follow those instructions.

Andy was a quiet student for much of the year, one who observed from the sidelines, certainly not a major player or participant in advisory, class, team, or school affairs. I was just doing what I normally do as I taught, unaware of how important it was to Andy. But his letter revealed to me the significance of his team experience. Nancy and I created and maintained an intentional context on the team; Andy found a home and delighted in it. Sometimes we never know the impact we are having on our students; letters like Andy's remind me that we need to keep on doing what is right and good for kids, whether they let us know so or not.

Nancy and I are interested in nurturing kids. Each year we set out to create an environment where they feel accepted, at home, part of the team. Eric Hoffer said maintenance is the key to Western civilization. Teaming is no different; we need team traditions that occur on a regular basis no matter what, for through them we strengthen the attitudes of the kids and the behaviors we seek to inculcate. To maintain traditions, Nancy and I continue to do affective activities such as Lessons Learned and Memory Minutes. Most kids respond positively to such a setting. Nothing is guaranteed, however.

In late June after school ended, Simon's parents asked for a meeting. Simon [not his real name] had an unsuccessful team experience. At the end of the year, after PEEC and Lessons Learned and Boston and the Inquiry Project and Jeopardy games and everything else, he still did not feel part of the team. His parents, assistant principal Bonne Sue Adams (also an advisor on our team), and I spent almost two hours discussing Simon's year, what happened, and what went wrong. We talked about how to help future team members be more successful. While the vast majority of the kids on our team had a great year, Simon clearly did not bond with his classmates, nor did he develop a sense of belonging as did so many others. Even the best of intentions and an array of team bonding activities did not work for Simon.

As teachers on a team, we need to be sensitive to the loners and isolates, recognizing that it is our obligation to make every student feel part of the larger community and integral to the team's success. Even then, we may not always get the job done.

But over the years, most of the time, we do make a difference with kids. Danielle Susskraut, one of Simon's classmates, spoke for many students at Lessons Learned in January 1994. She said,

> *Self-worth – I feel that being on this team gives not only
> me but others the chance to see that whatever advances
> they make towards a goal help. Like with the Billy Joel slide*

show, we had something to do, and we knew that if we
wouldn't have done it we might not be proud of our project.
I know I mean something when Mr. Burk or Ms. Luke say,
'Good job!' I love being on this team; it's a good feeling.

Just as kids are nurtured by a team setting, so too are teachers. The team provides support, friends with whom to hang out, and a place to share successes and failures. Stability helps. In general, the fewer changes of personnel over time, the more likely a team will flourish. Yes, new team members can shift the social dynamics and provide opportunities for growth. But frequent changes in staff retard the emergence of a shared team philosophy and a functioning partnership. Problems in teaming also occur when individual members cannot agree on a common philosophy. In these instances, if team partners cannot resolve their differences, building administrators need to step in. Teachers who work together year after year get to know one another's styles and adjust accordingly. Yet sometimes we get trapped in forced relationships, a group of teachers who have worked together for a while and have developed negative habits.

Sometimes it is difficult to support the actions of a fellow team member. I recall a strong student coming to me in tears a few years ago, crying because one of my team partners had treated her harshly over an academic matter. As I consoled her, I struggled with the dilemma of walking that thin line between being understanding of her complaint and supportive of my colleague.

Another pitfall occurs when one team member does not pull his or her weight. You meet, you discuss an issue, you agree on responsibilities, and then the day arrives and something vital has not been handled. Every adult on the team looks bad because one teacher did not keep a promise. Instances such as these are more likely to occur in the early development of a team. Whenever they happen, though, they provide team members wonderful opportunities for healthy discussion about the ground rules of teaming and the meaning of commitment. No one ever said teaming was easy.

As I look back on my teaching career, I can see many changes in my understanding of and appreciation for the possibilities of teaming. Where school was once a disjointed schedule – fragmented into separate students, classes, periods, and units – I now see the whole academic year as a flowing entity of time from September to June, and all the students under the umbrella called Team 8-IV as my responsibility.

Regarding teaming, I'm clear that the three best decisions I made during my career are (a) agreeing on The Distinctions, a set of expectations to guide our team's work with kids; (b) developing a series of affective activities such as Memory Minutes to keep the team connected during the year; and (c) teaming with others rather than going it alone.

One morning in late May 1994 Colin MacKenzie handed me a letter from his parents, prompted by my distributing to each student on Team 8-IV an article I had written for the Spring '94 issue of *In Transition*, the journal of the New York State Middle School Association. Many students, including Colin, were quoted in the article, which described Lessons Learned, our team reflection activity in January '94.

May 19, 1994

Dear Mr. Burkhardt and the entire 8-IV team advisors,

This morning I read the article you wrote for the New York State Middle School Journal and for me, it tied all of Colin's school year together. The purpose of PEEC, Distinctions, Reflections, etc., all made sense. When these class booklets come home, I generally do not get an explanation of what their purpose is, I am only asked to sign them. Not getting an explanation is as much my fault as it is my son's. Too often I am given things to sign on the fly, and there is no time for discussion. Other times, there is time, and I, for whatever reason, choose not to ask. Too often I am unaware of the 'why's' of what he is doing, but when I take the time to ask, I am happy to say that Colin has always been able to fill me in. This says a lot about his instruction. Reading the article also showed me what else the kids learned, besides 'book stuff.' To have a son that has learned some 'Distinctions' and 'Lessons Learned' about himself and others is, in many ways, far more important than knowing an equation or academic fact. Facts can be looked up in a book. Being a sensitive human being cannot. My husband and I think Team 8-IV has done an incredible job in giving its team members gifts and skills for the future. Team work, cooperation, caring and sharing will take these kids much farther than any one piece of information ever will. This entire year was well executed, carefully planned and integrated so skillfully that I don't think the students realize how much they have learned.

*We just wanted to take a moment to thank you for all the
outstanding work you have done this year with Colin. We
see his growth and development, and have heard from each
of you how much you appreciate and like our son. How
many parents are as fortunate to have teachers take the
time to recognize the good in their child, and then have the
teacher take the time to tell the parent? Thank you for taking the time. Thank you for continually keeping us informed
about student progress, expectations, due dates and activities. You've done a great job! Keep up the good work! We
hope our other children are as fortunate as Colin when they
are at the Middle School.*

Sincerely yours,
Mr. and Mrs. James Mackenzie

It is gratifying to receive such a letter from parents, to have our team
acknowledged in such a comprehensive and complimentary manner. Not
every parent would write an identical letter, and not every student would see
the school year the same way. But most of the kids and most of their parents,
most of the time, would agree that the shared experiences and intentional
activities on Team 8-IV were a significant factor in their ownership and
enjoyment of middle school.

Teaming as I experience it, a panoply of successful policies and practices
assembled over three decades, wasn't always like this, nor will it be in the
future. Specific activities will evolve and change, new ideas will occur, and
old practices will be discarded. What will remain constant are the beliefs that
every kid belongs, every kid has the right to a great year, and every kid
deserves, no, *earns* just by virtue of showing up, a place he or she can call
home, a safe and supportive environment where respect, acceptance, and
engagement are the watchwords.

What kinds of students do we want to emerge from middle school classrooms after three years of nurturing? How do we create those students? And
how do teaming arrangements affect student performance and outlook? The
three letters cited, each one from a different academic year, give some
indication of what most students experience on our team. Bonnie speaks
about community and a "family atmosphere." Andy cites the Distinctions as
a reason why his classes worked and were "efficient." The MacKenzies
appreciate the fact that Colin became a more sensitive human being. These

letters stand on the shoulders of more than thirty years of trial and error, success and failure, learning and living. In that sense, Nancy, Nick, Bonnie Sue, and I represent only the most recent members of a much larger team of people whose collective actions shaped the present operational structure of the team. While much of what occurs is the direct result of intentional decisions made by Nancy and me, we are also aware that we have been assisted in creating a positive teaming experience through the active participation of our students, their parents, and our middle school colleagues. To them we owe an enormous debt of gratitude.

In particular, I cannot conceive of what my teaching would be like without the constant influence, inspiration, and support of my wife Diane, who challenges me to grow as an educator as she demonstrates exemplary teaching skills with the young adolescents on her 8th grade team. I come home each evening to my ultimate teaming partner, as I have since Diane and I were married in 1969, and we reflect on the day together. Our conversations provide both valuable insights and brilliant coaching. I am a better teacher because of Diane's unflagging support. In a nutshell, she taught me how to team.

Finally, I cannot imagine the past three decades working with young adolescents without it being a team experience. Life is a joint venture, teaching is essentially an exercise in cooperation, and celebrating kids is part of our mission. The many teaming partners with whom I have worked over the years – Diane, Howie, Marty, Jerry, Don, Cliff, Nancy, Jim, and others – all contributed greatly to my development as a teacher. I learned from them, and I suspect they learned from me as we shared kids, ideas, space, time, activities, philosophy, and vision. For when we share the experience, we gain more than we give. And that is really what teaming is all about.

Starting a New Team: Advice and Best Practices   **8**

Marge Bowen, Stacey Burd Rogers, and Judy Hainline

There were five of us when Oxford Middle School opened in 1988. It was a beautiful new school in an upscale suburban neighborhood near Kansas City in the Blue Valley School District. Fortunately, the district had strong financial backing, and parents were interested and involved in their children's educations. We looked forward to a formidable, yet challenging task.

Our job was to design a middle school team that would make everyone, especially our sixth graders, happy and successful students. Initially, it did not seem too difficult. After all, three members of our team came to their new positions seasoned with many combined years of upper elementary teaching experience. Another was new to teaching, enthusiastic, and arrived highly recommended by her university. She brought us fresh theoretical knowledge and we valued her input, even though we tempered it from time to time with our "real life" perspectives. A fifth member joined us with a year of teaching experience which can only be described as "trial-by-fire" from an inner-city junior high school. So here we were – five women ranging in age from 22 to 50 something. We were single, divorced, married, with and without our own children at home, ready to begin our new journey as a team with someone else's children whom we had been trained to refer to as the "transescents."

Transescent was a middle school term later replaced by *young adolescents* which we came to understand as describing the sixth, seventh, and eighth graders soon to be in our charge. It was a word we heard often during our two-week training period prior to the opening day of school. Our district administration and our newly-hired Middle School Director, Sue Thompson, had planned extensive inservice activities for over a hundred of us who would become colleagues in the middle school movement. The majority of those in attendance were inexperienced in teaming, and the middle school teaming concept was totally new to the Blue Valley District. We needed training, and we appreciated the opportunities we had during this inservice time.

We gathered much general information about young adolescents and their needs. We were able to participate in small group experiences, some of which served as models of what might be expected to occur during an advisory time. We were introduced and reintroduced to ourselves and to each other. We understood that as we were able to become more comfortable with who we were both in and out of the classroom, it would be easier for us to facilitate our mentor relationships with youngsters.

We were fortunate enough to hear several nationally known experts in middle school education. Among them were Nancy Doda and Tom Erb.

Nancy Doda made us aware of our multifaceted roles as middle school instructors and described us as people who would be "wearing many hats." She provided us with numerous memorable examples of young adolescent behaviors and characteristics. We realized through her comments how important it was going to be for our students to have an identity with their team and a strong feeling of belonging to the group. She brought us suggestions for organizing our students so that a constructive identity could be built through the team, without setting forth a competitive atmosphere among coexisting teams. Additionally, she was able to suggest appropriate classroom management techniques that would help us set limits for students, yet allow students to maintain self-respect and personal differences.

Tom Erb acted as an advisor to us through the initial days of training. Later in the growth of our middle school life, he would return to hear our suggestions and experiences along the way and to provide us firsthand assistance through the process. Initially, he emphasized for us the importance of establishing clear lines of communication with parents and school support personnel. He provided techniques for us to use in establishing a positive middle school classroom climate. He acknowledged and encouraged our personal teaching styles while simultaneously helping us think in a "teaming work mode." From Erb we received some of our first information about how to develop thematic, interdisciplinary teaching units.

As our two weeks of preparation continued, we became familiar with *Middle School Journal* and other useful publications. It was the hope of our trainers, no doubt, that we might show some initiative and interest in educating ourselves. Some of us did. Along the way we were informed of the procedure for joining the National Middle School Association. Some of us did. We heard from various speakers that social adjustment was more important than academic achievements. Many of us did not believe it. Some of us did.

Many of us participating in this training came from fourth and fifth grade teaching backgrounds. We had more than a small investment in the academic performances of those students we sent to middle schools. Often we had watched with concern and dismay as bright students had seemed to become underachievers when they left elementary school. Occasionally, the reverse was true. Names appeared on the middle school honor roll, which we never expected to see there when we worked with them at a younger age. We felt a degree of professional vindication and relief when we learned that these kinds of fluctuations in performances were normal and expected among young adolescents. Such academic behaviors in most instances were neither damaging nor permanent. It would be our job as middle school educators to make sure they were not.

After a few weeks of working with sixth graders, we had firsthand appreciation of the social, emotional, and physical changes that occur at middle school age. We watched six foot eighth graders walk down the hall with their five foot friends of the same age and saw nearly as much variance among our sixth graders.

Even when differences in physical maturity were not obvious, differences in emotional maturity were manifest. Still, we had not forgotten that our school district valued achievement and intellectual challenge. We puzzled over this new direction and wondered aloud how we would marry traditionally high standards with the social priorities of this age level. We began to sense some of the difficulties that lay ahead.

If the middle school concept was challenging and confusing for teachers, it is fair to say that it was, perhaps, doubly so for parents and patrons. Middle school no longer resembled the junior high they had experienced in their early adolescent years. This new concept had removed from them a familiar base of old experiences. Because it was unfamiliar, in some minds it was untrustworthy. A smattering of phrases like "self-image" and "social interests" had trickled into the community. Although the district had made deliberate and prolonged efforts to educate patrons about ensuing changes, every person did not interpret the same message in the same way. Reluctance is always a part of change and the new middle school concept was no exception. Its progress was watched closely by the community. Some parents expressed their concerns that our focus on the child would mean a sacrifice in academic emphasis. Too much nurturing, they feared, would mean too little preparation for the rigorous competition of the "real world."

Admittedly, our team of teachers shared a part of this concern. While we embraced what we had learned and were learning about middle schools, at the same time we spoke with reluctance among ourselves about the possibility of compromising high expectations in student performance. We searched for resources to help us weld academic proficiency and social development. Eventually, we discovered that there were ways to unite these learning goals with the social explorations so significant to middle school age. Our research and the knowledge gained from our two week training session resulted in responsive strategies that we felt were supportive of student interests and also met district curriculum expectations. We were now working in daily team meetings, trying to solve daily kinds of instructional problems. We were beginning to really feel what it was like to be together for nearly an hour every day, five days a week.

Trust and risk taking

As we spent an increased amount of time with one another, we found among our five members philosophical and attitudinal divisions which greatly affected our ability to function wholly as a team. For some of us, this daily 47 minute team meeting was a very stressful time. We were highly diverse, strong personalities, five strangers trying to come together on both a professional and, to some degree, a personal level. As a result of our exposure during training to middle school structure, we believed that we needed team roles. We never discussed or questioned this need, we simply proceeded with it as a "given." Consequently, we agreed upon a team leader, a parent contact person, and a recorder. In addition, one team member would communicate with the counseling department and the special services resource people. Another member became responsible for keeping exploratory class teachers informed. We further agreed, verbally, that these roles would rotate from time to time. We settled upon a nine-week rotation, since this was the span of a grading period in those first years.

It did not take long for us to realize, silently, that we were uncomfortable with these structured assignments. However, because we truly believed that what we thought the literature said would work effectively for us if we persevered, we plodded on with our efforts to stay role oriented during team time. It took nearly two years before we were confident enough to openly defy our team structure. Roles did not work for our teaching team. They inhibited our flexibility. Each person's duties were not evenly balanced. Sometimes a member forgot her job, but no one else felt free to pick up the slack, since we all had our own responsibilities. No one wanted to risk infringing on another's territory, for fear that in so doing one of us might imply that the other was lax. Initially, we expected our team leader to come prepared with a printed agenda. This was abandoned in favor of handwritten notes when time constraints infringed upon the leader, or when the current leader was not computer-literate. Over time and with familiarity, any formal sort of agenda was abandoned altogether. The recorder took voracious notes, not really knowing at this juncture why they might be needed. The parent contact person found it awkward to call parents about problems that were occurring with a student in the classroom of another team member. Parents who had questions were uncertain who they were supposed to call. Similarly, counselors and special services staff often needed direct conversation with a specific teacher. These people found it unnecessary, as we now believe it was, to relay messages through only one member of our team. Exploratory teachers who wanted to communicate with us were never sure who our representative was at any given moment, despite our best efforts to notify them of our rotations. In short, we found that specific roles created disharmony among the team and confusion outside of it. Bluntly stated, sometimes roles were used as a license to boss each other around. "You need to do this or that," we found ourselves saying to each other. "It's your job." We had misused roles to create an inflexible, restrictive situation for ourselves. Teaming should never put professionals in the demeaning position of having to ask permission from other team members to make instructional decisions. Neither should teaming create a situation in which its members feel "used" by other group members. We blame, retrospectively, our loyalty to roles for a large part of these behaviors.

By the third year we had abandoned our adopted roles. We created a position which we designated as "team representative." We continue, in our sixth year, to use this model. Under the umbrella of team representative falls the responsibilities for contacting administrators, exploratory people, and special services personnel. We are fortunate to have had the same person in the representative position for three years. Her position has greatly simplified our ability to function and communicate, since everyone in our building knows who to contact. We jokingly "boss" her around daily, and she takes our chiding good naturedly, rarely pushing us around in return. Our administration has arranged for team leaders, or in our specific case, the team "representative" to receive a small stipend. We continue to maintain a written record of our meetings, but we have learned to take more sparing, relevant notes, which document for us when we contacted staff or parents about concerns or what steps we took to proceed with an instructional objective. Each of us now contacts parents whenever we have a need, although we usually check with the rest of the team to see if anyone else has a reason to speak with that parent before we call. Occasionally, because we checked, we discover that several of us have concerns, and so the call becomes a request to the parent for a team conference.

Three of our original five members now remain. Administrative policies in our building dictate the number of people allotted to a team. For four years we functioned with five people. We worked as a four member team for two years and now we are three, teaching three subjects each and handling an advisory period. Along the way we have relaxed and laughed much and learned to be each other's best support. We would like to clarify who we are.

Marge is the oldest member of the team. Her early teaching career was in a small, rural Kansas community where she taught first and second graders. She left teaching for marriage and children. Marge and her husband have three grown children and three grandchildren. She returned to teaching when her youngest graduated from high school. She taught fifth grade for ten years in the Blue Valley School District. As our district moved to a true middle school model Marge transferred to sixth grade at Oxford Middle School. She has a master's degree with an emphasis in reading.

Judy is a 40-plus elementary education major with teaching experience in first through sixth grades. She has a M.S. in educational psychology and taught educable mentally handicapped students before returning to school where she entered a specialist's program in elementary counseling. Following a stint as an elementary counselor, she completed Ph.D. coursework in counseling and personnel services. Her study led to a position as a therapist in a public mental health facility and some part-time teaching in a junior college. After marriage and the birth of her son, she came to the Blue Valley School District as a fifth grade instructor. In this same district she began teaching at Oxford Middle School the year it opened.

Stacey joined the team during the final week of middle school orientation. Many of the team-building activities had already occurred, but the other four team members were adamant from the beginning that she be included in all decision making. She had an eighteen-month-old son and her daughter was due to be born that December. Stacey came with a bachelor's degree in elementary education with concentrations in math and science. She had a year's experience in an inner-city junior high. The structure of this new middle school was wonderfully child-centered compared to the restrictive departmentalization she had experienced in the junior high. Stacey has received technology training at the Biological Science Curriculum Studies ENLIST Micros Leadership Institute in Colorado Springs, Colorado. Following this training, she conducted technology classes in the evenings for teachers in the Blue Valley School District.

Our diversity, we feel, is perhaps a little unusual. Our hope is that by relating it, we can emphasize that homogeneity of age and backgrounds is not a necessary prerequisite for effective teaming. The attitudes we share today often coincide, but they were rooted very differently in our past, and have been cultivated similarly as a result of diligent team work and shared experiences over the past six years. In this vein, we have arrived at certain precepts to which we as a team ascribe.

We believe in risk-taking behaviors. Sharing on a professional level is one kind of risk. It is the easiest kind. Sharing on a personal level is quite another responsibility. While we do not feel that personal sharing is necessarily a prerequisite for effective teaming, it has been a mainstay of our working relationship. We have evolved the ability to share openly without fear of put downs or frowning judgments. We have a trust level among us of immense intensity.

Perhaps we owe this closeness to the daily stresses we experienced through dealing with difficult team members. Our team was definitely not "born" feeling wonderful toward each other. We are in our sixth year. The first three were spent tiptoeing our way through a jungle of personal relationships. We strove for harmony. We were five personalities trying to get along with each other, yet not knowing enough about each other to question when we had doubts, express our own beliefs freely, or confront when we disagreed. We appeared to lack personal confidence. For reasons yet uncovered, we found it tough to brainstorm and found the greatest part of our security at this early time in our assigned recipe-like roles. Even in the discomfort of the roles we were taking our time, assessing one another's personalities, trying to become middle school teachers and friends all at the same time.

We later recognized that we had allowed one particularly strong personality to dominate the group. We spent too much time placating and appeasing this person. We nearly destroyed the balance of our team in the process. We later confided that none of us could handle conflict well and each of us would go to great lengths to avoid confrontation.

The first attempt at making a team quilt is a telling example of our passivity. In our early years we enthusiastically developed over several days a terrific plan for producing a team quilt. The quilt would have a block in it from every child and would be a grand culminating activity for our African unit. We used crayons to create a sample block. We spent considerable effort explaining the procedure to our students, gathering ideas and examples through team research in the library, developing individual practice blocks with our sixth graders, and finally creating the perfect individual projects.

Students were excited and involved. Our goal was to have the quilt done in time to display it for parents at Fine Arts Open House night. The date was drawing near. We teachers spent additional time ironing the blocks to set the crayon color in place. The moment arrived in team planning time for teachers to sew the blocks together into strips as we had discussed and then to make final decisions about sewing the strips together, adding a backing and tying the final piece. On that fateful day in team meeting, the quilt died. "Ladies, you surely aren't going to make a quilt! I'm not spending my weekend sewing blocks and strips together! We never talked about this!"

Silence overtook us. We thought for a mutual moment perhaps we had dreamed the whole experience. Our mouths hung open, we looked fleetingly around the circle at each other, but no words came. Meanwhile she droned on about the impossibility of such a thing ever becoming a reality, and reiterated that she had been uninvolved in any such planning. Passivity ran rampant. Someone in the silent majority caught her breath and suggested we staple the completed muslin blocks to the hall bulletin board, so that they might leave the impression of a quilt when viewed from a distance. Meekly we gathered our staplers and toddled like the baby egos we were toward the hall. Dumb-founded, we stapled with grace and shame.

So great was our mutual desire to appear harmonious, we remained ethically closed-mouthed about our unhappiness to other staff members and to the administration. We barely hinted at it among ourselves. Generally, we left an exterior impression of functioning cooperatively, not reflecting our discontent. Communication happened extremely slowly. No one was willing to take the risk which could unleash so many dangerous feelings. First we talked privately in twos. We were so good at hiding our feelings we were not sure who was unhappy or where the lines of loyalty were drawn. As much as anything, the quilt incident served to unify us. We could not deny the obvious problem in our midst, and through joking over the quilt, three of us began a long overdue dialogue. We know now that we owe to this experience a great leap in our personal growth levels. As we recount today our behaviors at the time, we invariably question our paralyzed attitudes and marvel that we have come so far.

We eventually realized we were lacking laughter, spontaneity, and openness. Until now, laughter and joking-had served primarily to relieve tension, which in turn enabled us to move on with our pseudo-group-togetherness behaviors. As openness among the three of us grew, our confidence levels grew also, and we were able to abandon our teaming roles and increase our risk-taking behaviors.

We resolved to be more assertive in decision making, even at the expense of incurring our fourth person's wrath. For example, we were involved at one point in an integrated unit on space. Our fourth member brainstormed with us, appeared to plan enthusiastically and agreed to the necessary flexing of schedules. Midway through the experience with half of our exciting plans still ahead of us, she quit! She announced that she "was finished" with the integrated project and would have nothing more to do with it. "It was time," she thought to "get back to real school." The remaining three of us decided to continue in spite of our cohort's stubborn refusal to carry through. It meant we had to confront her with our decision. She would have to take the students in the order we had previously agreed upon, which she found annoying. It was not possible to teach her established classes. Our sixth graders were in their "space groups." Furthermore, it was not possible to have equally distributed time slots. Students would have to remain arranged for our convenience, not hers. Lastly, it was not possible during this period to maintain team harmony. The division was openly contentious. When it finally became apparent to her that we were determined to function as-a threesome, if not a full four, she reluctantly, albeit grudgingly, rejoined us with minimal participation. She had lost control, and we had learned something.

We learned to relax and genuinely laugh. We know now that our confidence would permit any one of us, with or without the others, to avoid a similar pitfall, should it occur again. We still dislike confrontations, but we have learned the value of taking risks.

Creating community

We believe in relinquishing psychological ownerships which interfere with the good of the group and its charges. There is no place in teaming for exclusivity. None of us owns her classroom, her materials, her ideas, her time, or her subject specialty. Possessiveness of materials, ideas, and time on a team does not result in effective team instruction for children. Along the way we have worked hard coordinating our instructional efforts for students. When one team member is uncooperative or unwilling to share in this effort, our job becomes immensely more complicated. Occasionally we have had to structure activities around a team member who has committed to remaining uninvolved. This is not to say that a teacher who makes such a choice is ineffective in the classroom. People who may be excellent instructors in their own right are not always comfortable sharing their skills and resources on a team. When excessive ownership from one individual remains unaddressed in a teaming situation, the results are wasted time for everyone, a general loss of enthusiasm and energy, and, perhaps the most potentially destructive, a greatly increased level of personal stress. Compromise, flexibility, and complete willingness to share skills and resources are important factors in making teaming work. Without these behaviors a teaching group cannot function at its maximum level of effectiveness. Initially, we endangered our group's ability to operate at its fullest because we failed to be appropriately assertive with members who were reluctant to become team players. As team members have come and gone, we have learned from experience what works, and we have committed ourselves wholly to the middle school concept. Consequently, we have made the decision to be up-front in the future about our philosophies of teaming with new members who join our group.

We believe in encouraging among team teachers the sharing of subject areas. By our standards, good teaming cannot occur when resistance or possessiveness toward this end exists in one or more members. Ownership in subject matter can create a kind of self-enhancement for an individual member, resulting in an esoteric atmosphere on a team that only serves to inhibit group cooperation and flexibility. Conversely, there are instances in which a team associate may not be willing to commit the time and effort necessary to become familiar with his cohorts' subject areas. The existence of either of these situations restricts team functioning.

Our team members feel it is important to acknowledge the pride and expertise each of us has in our particular subject areas, but we nonetheless consider ourselves to be coachable by the member most experienced in a subject. When we plan units, we use our "expert in the field" as a lead teacher for activities. We rely on that person as our resource to provide appropriate objectives, suggest teaching strategies, and to assemble materials. Because we work together so closely, it became necessary to increase our familiarity with district curriculum goals and objectives in all subjects. Each of us keeps copies of the others' curriculum guides and manuals on our professional shelves. This sometimes means we must not be too proud to admit to students our inability to fully answer a question stemming from another discipline. We are a team, and students see us operate in that way, when we openly refer to each other for solutions and suggestions.

As subject lines have blurred, so have our classrooms expanded. We all easily share our rooms for team activities. We understand and accept that sharing often means we must rearrange furniture, take down posters, and open bulletin board space. We have really strong feelings that being connected to each other academically and logistically is very important. Sometimes we have requested changes in our classroom assignments to accommodate physical proximity among ourselves. One of the major factors contributing to our eventual cohesiveness as a team was the willingness of our principal to make these logistical changes in our behalf. We were allowed to move our science person from a fully equipped science room on the other end of the building to a regular classroom near our other rooms.

Mr. Wilson was willing to equip the room with a portable sink to make this move possible. We all felt that the benefits of being next door to each other were well worth disturbing the status quo to make the change. It enabled us to move our students among our classrooms more efficiently and to make last minute adjustments in instructional plans.

We have found that students are sensitive to the physical placement of classroom locations. When we are in different parts of the building, they tend to see us as less "team-oriented." We recall early in our teaming experience, when our classrooms were still spread out, the student who saw our science and reading teachers laughing together one day and said with surprise, "You mean you two are *friends*?" This comment strongly emphasized to us the need to work in overt ways as a team, so that as we planned for students, they would at least sense our close attitudinal, if not physical, proximity. When we were finally able to arrange our rooms near each other, students much more readily recognized us as their "team." In turn, we felt our nearness served as an obvious model, helping them visualize their own peers as a more identifiable team. We now, as a matter of course, take regular steps in this direction by periodically changing students' class schedules. In this way we are able to facilitate for them increased opportunities to interact with teammates they might not otherwise learn to know very well. We typically hand schedule our students before school begins, or very shortly thereafter. We take the time to do this because we feel we get a better mix of children among our three feeder elementary schools. We have found the office computer program unreliable in this respect, and we agree that the short amount of time it takes for us to do the work is worth the payoff in new friends for our sixth graders.

Having given ourselves permission to flex room arrangements and student schedules, we found it somewhat natural to flow into a more interrelated teaching style. Once we became a team able to function more freely, we welcomed honing our skills with new instructional strategies. Among them was a stirring interest in integrative teaching. We had previously worked thematically through the development of interdisciplinary units. Moving into a more thoroughly integrative style would require even greater flexibility from each of us. We shared an eagerness to begin.

We recognized quickly that rigid, bell-driven schedules would have to go. We devised block schedules and flexed subjects. As we had hoped, instructional objectives overlapped and blended; students and parents could see new purposes in learning. Often, we found we could plan entire days around one or two objectives we had in common. We rallied around curricular demands and children's interests, often revising our students' days so that they could experience a particular event such as an election, an eclipse, or an academic field trip.

For instance, to begin our Martin Luther King, Jr. unit, we elicited questions from our sixth graders. We were surprised and pleased at the depth of their concern and interest in that period of recent history. In small groups youngsters planned activities which would serve to answer the questions they had proposed. From these sessions a wide variety of lessons were generated by students. We saw "The Road to Memphis," a documentary about King. We read several of Mildred Taylor's novels about the South. Some students created a mural of "The Road to Memphis."

Others wrote poetry about discrimination. Interviews with adults who lived through the era contributed much to our learning. We played music from the time period. As a culmination experience, we invited a parent to speak. She grew up Mississippi during the 1960s and became the first African American to be admitted at one of the southern universities. Her life experiences were a powerful message for our sixth graders!

Many such units followed. Sometimes we came together as a large group, used a sturdy table as a makeshift stage, borrowed a microphone from the media center, and took notes as we watched and listened to presentations of student projects from integrated units. Follow-up activities for events on these days were shared jointly.

Every rearranged day on our team does not necessarily stem from a significant outside event. A shared teaching plan might be devised if we discover that we have an objective which can most easily be taught with the help of all team members. It is not unusual for us to rearrange our time frames to teach to that need. When we had an opportunity to use graphing, all four of us taught four-quadrant graphing. As a logical follow-up to this instruction, we all shared the instructional responsibilities for teaching integers.

Similarly, if we assess a general weakness of skills in a particular area, it may become appropriate to "stop the world" again until we have remedied the problem. Often sixth graders need specific instruction in notetaking strategies or developing graphic organizers. Sometimes they have difficulty writing good paragraphs or using strong topic sentences. What ever skill may be needed, we feel strongly that it is our responsibility as teachers to help that child conquer his or her particular deficit.

None of us, as professionals, feel thwarted in meeting these types of instructional objectives. We agree as a team of professionals that we wish to communicate to our middle school students high expectations for behavior and skills, while still maintaining our awareness and acceptance of their developmental characteristics. District curriculum is always kept at the forefront of whatever we plan. We never rearrange our teaching day to accommodate what we feel is "fluff." We flex time to allow valid learning to occur.

Flexing time can imply a wide variety of specific schedules. Needs dictate schedule changes, not bells. We are responsible for teaching five subjects. How these subjects become incorporated into our day often changes. If we have a speaker for only our team or a sixth-grade, cross-team event, we might simply block off that section of time and divide the remaining minutes among all of our subjects. If it is an event that properly requires followup, then we might schedule the rest of our day as a block time to reinforce related concepts. Block time, for us, means that each teacher keeps the same group of students for two or three class periods to fulfill instructional obligations. Occasionally, we have found that an alternating block schedule works well for us. On an alternating schedule each class meets for a two-hour time slot. For example, on Monday and Wednesday we would see hours one and two. On Tuesday and Thursday we would meet hours three and four. Fifth hour is seen daily. We have found that when we are following this alternating block, Friday is a good day to culminate the week's activities by meeting with all classes. Generally, we make a point of thinking about time as a commodity we control, and we use it to enhance our teaching.

We have trained our students to take responsibility for informing themselves about each day's schedule. A dry erase board hangs in the hall near our rooms where students congregate. Each morning we write on the board, listing materials needed for the day and noting any schedule changes. Students and parents have consistently reported that the breaks in routine are refreshing and sometimes fun.

Our experience has cautioned us that specialist teachers who work with our students do not always find it easy to adjust their established case loads to our flexible routine. Sometimes in our enthusiasm, we forget to inform these people. Our students are involved with teachers of Learning Disabilities, English as a Second Language, Behavior Disorders, Gifted, Speech and the Semi-independent Learner Program. At this juncture, these are all pullout programs, although the state has mandated inclusion of specialists. When inclusion fully occurs, we anticipate our changing routine will become less problematic in specialized areas. Meanwhile, we are working to help them understand why we seemingly behave so unpredictably.

Involving parents

It is also of great importance to us that parents understand clearly how our routines change, how teaming works, and why we know these approaches serve their children well. Our district has an established Meet the Teacher night for parents, but it typically is scheduled two or three weeks after the school year has begun. Our team decided that we needed to meet with parents on the evening before the first day of school. Many parents attend orientation meetings the previous spring, but by the time school starts in the fall, they indicate to us that much of what they heard earlier has been forgotten. They appreciate the timely update. We find it advantageous to discuss with parents our expectations, policies, and procedures before meeting their children. They know we do not have impressions of their students yet and feel less need to conference with us at this informational session. They hear from us about the important role they play in our teaming effort. We emphasize to them that teaming is a triad of shared responsibilities among parents, students, and teachers. We try to impart to parents our strong feeling that school is most successful for a child when that child's parents and family are deeply invested in it.

In preparation for this early meeting, we prepare a handbook that is specific to our team. The handbook contains explanations of team operations. We describe the curriculum that we teach, who is primarily responsible for each curricular area, our grading systems, our discipline procedures, how we will communicate with parents, and important dates for team events and conferences. We tell parents during this first meeting that we are always available for conferencing and that they do not have to wait until the assigned district conference days arrive to visit with us about their child.

We encourage parents to conference with us not only out of concerns or fears, but just to keep the lines of communication open. Our team conferences are round table discussions, where parents and teachers sit in a random circle. We always conference in the same classroom so that parents will know where to come, if they have made an appointment. We do not follow a printed agenda. Each teacher speaks freely about what is occurring in her classroom.

If there are problems, we report them honestly, but we always keep in mind that we are talking about someone's child. We try to speak with hopefulness and diplomacy. If a change in behavior is deemed necessary, we strive throughout the conference to involve everyone present in a plan of action toward that end. An overriding objective for us during the conference is to establish a comfortable rapport with the parent(s). Occasionally, parents and teachers feel that the child should attend the conference, too. We may, in this instance, pull the child from one of his exploratory classes, so that we may involve him in the discussion.

While one or two parents meeting with as many as five teachers might seem potentially intimidating, our parents have expressed themselves to the contrary. After experiencing the format, they tell us they found it very beneficial to understanding their child. A more complete picture is seen by a parent when they are able to hear how their student functions during all five core hours of the day. Sometimes it becomes apparent that students have proclivities or deficits in particular curriculum areas that parents might not have realized had they visited with only one teacher. Parents of Attention Deficit Disorder students particularly appreciate being able to hear from all of us at once about how a youngster is performing during particular times of the day. They may seek from their physicians adjustments in medication based on our observations.

Team conferences work well for us, we feel, because we spend so much team planning time discussing individual student performance. This regular dialogue enables each of us to keep abreast of the progress of specific students. We know who is working well in which areas and what needs must be meant to strengthen other areas. The result of our team discussions allows us to present an informed, united, supportive front to parents. It further leaves a genuine and accurate impression among parents that we are concerned about their particular student, working appropriately with him to encourage his achievement potential.

Creating team identity

We believe in the importance of establishing a team identity. Before we taught even one day of middle school, we had named our team the "Wizards." We did not seek student input for this designation, since we were eager to put up bulletin boards and establish a structure for them to enter from the first day.

Because our school identifies itself as the "Knights," our name seemed appropriate. We promote our Wizard identity in various ways. One of our favorite activities to do with students is to design team t-shirts. The colors in the shirt are the colors we adopt for ourselves during that school year. One of our first year students designed a crest for the team. We each have a copy of the crest in our classrooms. We have periodically published a monthly Wizard Newsletter. We teachers made full length, purple Wizard costumes during that first year. We have since worn them for many different Wizard occasions. Students love the outfits and ask, even after becoming seventh and eighth graders, when we will be wearing our costumes. The academic activities we plan are frequently structured to encourage team identity and spirit. Large group presentations by small groups of students promote the feeling; so does an instructional technique we are fond of, "Teams, Games and Tournaments."

Learning and growing through teaming

The summer following our fourth year of teaming, we were presented with an opportunity to attend as a team the Colorado Middle School Conference in Dillon, Colorado. Our team had expressed a strong interest in learning more about integrated instruction. Coincidentally, movement toward a more integrated curriculum was becoming a primary area of focus and study in our district at that time. Integration of curriculum was to be the primary emphasis of the conference.

During this informative week we were afforded opportunities to meet with national leaders of the middle school movement. Among them was Ed Brazee from the University of Maine, who was assigned as our district's resource person for the duration of the conference. We asked many questions of him, as we took advantage of this intensive time together to plan integrated activities for the upcoming school year.

Even though we have nearly an hour of team planning time every day at school, we find as we do more joint instruction, we need even more hours together. We accomplish the most, it seems, when we remove ourselves from the school setting. Sometimes this means we meet on Sunday afternoons and in the summer to accomplish our goals. We function more effectively at such times, with fresher mental outlooks, away from the distractions and demands of school business.

Through the years since the implementation of the middle school concept in our district, our director and administration have continued to support us by inviting to inservice sessions experts in middle level education to speak and work with us. We have been offered multiple opportunities to attend relevant workshops outside our district. On occasion our team has been invited to conduct inservice programs in nearby districts on the teaming concept. Additionally, we have presented at middle school conferences.

The opportunities we have had since we became a team are obviously numerous. The discoveries we have made, in spite of the bumps along the way, have served us well. We believe that one of our primary discoveries revolves around the importance of power in the structuring of a team's life. Handled with wisdom, we found that the distribution of power became the most positive, motivating, and driving force behind our successful teaming experience. Had we continued to allow the misuse of power, we would no doubt have risked destroying our team. When groups are newly forming, it is a natural phenomenon for members to seek a power base. We believe that on healthy teams power rotates continuously. It is our experience that when there is shared respect and acknowledged separation of expertise, there is less need for one or two individuals to always be the driving force. Too much power centered in too few people can strip everyone of dignity and enthusiasm for the group experience. We discovered effective teaching to be very difficult under such circumstances. Team members need to be willing to work hard toward acceptance of every person in the group. This was not an easy task for us. To accomplish it required a consistent, friendly dose of assertiveness. We have made concerted and deliberate efforts toward sharing our teaching strategies and methodologies. We have not been reluctant to share pieces of our personal selves. These efforts have contributed much to our unification as a team. We have recognized each other's intelligences, personalities, creativities, strengths, and weaknesses. We make authentic efforts to support each other and to make each member feel safe. We are our own support.

Sometimes our close working relationship is misperceived by other staff members, who are left with the impression that we have separated ourselves too much from the rest of the faculty. It seemed to us that as we spent increased amounts of time working toward common goals, we chose to put greater demands on ourselves. Consequently, we found our need for mutual time increased. Not only did we have an allotted planning period during the day, we often used our personal planning time. Very frequently, we chose to eat lunch together in one of our classrooms. These extra minutes spent meeting enabled us to discuss student issues, while still planning integrated instructional units. Separatism, as a perception among others, became a side effect of our efforts.

As we were learning to take more personal risks, we also became more professionally adventurous. When we manipulated our instructional time to fit a more integrated teaching style, we inadvertently invited a barrage of questions and judgments from our building colleagues. It became commonplace to hear:

> *What schedule are you on?*
>
> *No one told me you were doing something different today.*
>
> *Where are your kids? You have to notify the office every time you do these changes.*
>
> *How can you teach science in a regular room?*
>
> *You want to buy a $1000 sink? But you have room at the other end of the building. Why do you want to move?*
>
> *You're showing a video in the hall?*
>
> *What? You want your whole team to do research in the library at the same time?*
>
> *It's ten-thirty at night in July! What do you mean you want to know next year's master schedule?*
>
> *Why are your kids in the hall when it's not a real passing period?*
>
> *I thought you taught math. Why do you need a globe?*

We chose to treat these comments with lightness and humor. We knew we were on the right track, and we refused to be derailed by the implied doubts of others.

In spite of our diversity at the onset, the three of us who remain share some common beliefs. We are all child-centered. We all believe in the middle school concept. We all want to maintain effective communication with parents. We are enthusiastic about teaming, always open to new possibilities. From the start we judged each other as competent. All of us were coachable. Above all we were invested in the potential success of our team, and our determination carried us forward.

We have categorized for ourselves, but not finalized, some specific tenets which we feel have allowed us to operate as an effective unit. We believe in sharing our personal and professional resources. We believe in making every effort to accommodate the needs of our students. We believe in being flexible in all arenas. We believe in distributing power among team members. Most of all we believe in measured and reasonable risk taking.

We are still learning about the chasms which separate us, and we are still working daily to bridge the differences through compromise and constant communication. We expect this effort to be a never-ending one, for to halt its movement would leave us in danger of stagnation. We are proud that we can share, laugh, work, socialize, celebrate, and still maintain our privacies and our families.

We believe there is no such thing as a best model or a good recipe for making a team gel. Just as no two individuals are the same, nor should they be, neither will two teams operate identically. Each group must take the most general, prudent path and find a formula that makes them work, produce, feel satisfied often, be happy, and laugh frequently. Our advice? Enjoy your students. Look forward to your day. Be proud. Relax, relate, rejoice with one another, and find excitement in the journey.

Epilogue:

The day we completed the writing of this piece, Stacey Burd Rogers tearfully told us she had resigned to accept an eighth grade position in a district nearer to her home. We wish her well, but we will miss our good friend dearly. And now we are two.

Mature Teams at Work: Benchmarks and Obstacles 9

Jeanneine P. Jones

The two sat side-by-side on the green couch near the folding wall that separated their classrooms. Legal pads and grade books, ink pens and coffee cups, imaginations and curriculum guides lay around them in stacks of organized clutter. The walls beside and in front of them were piled high with enormous garbage bags that were packed with many, many thousands of aluminum can tabs. They laughed as they talked. Their eighth graders had really gotten the joke on them, although these kids had no clue that they had so totally surprised their teachers.

That fall semester had started out with a traditional review of estimation by the math and science half of this two-person team. Heavy into the lesson, she'd stopped and admitted that it was pretty hard to discuss a million when she had no clue what a million of anything actually looked like. The kids were quick to chime in their agreement, and why not collect a million of something? 'Yeah, why not?' had been the general attitude and so the idea of collecting the can tabs eventually settled the discussion, and the race was on. Mid-December was established as the deadline because that was the most distant date guessed by individuals as to when the goal of gathering a million tabs would be reached.

The fifty-eight students on this team worked in competitive groups of four, with each Monday designated as Can Tab Day. They hauled aluminum tabs into class in gallon bags and grocery bags and lunch bags, in purses and gym bags and pockets. Their parents collected them and their friends from other classes collected them, and some of the students even coerced downtown businesses and local mills to collect them. The two teachers were overwhelmed at the

volume of tabs that each Monday produced, at this sugges-
tion-gone-deliciously-out-of-control; they'd expected the ex-
citement to hang on for several weeks or perhaps even a
couple of months, but never this long. Oh, the teaching pos-
sibilities that jumped out of that one classroom confession!
The enthusiasm that resulted from these students setting
the agenda for their educations was absolutely contagious,
absolutely middle school, and absolutely teaming from both
students' and teachers' perspectives.

Janet Thompson and I were not new to the middle school concept that
year, rather far from that. Although we had been together for only three
years, we had each team taught for about fifteen. Both our students and their
parents knew and respected that knowledge base. Working with a team
partner, with young adolescents, and with the middle school concept in
general all made a smooth road for us, as experience had taught us well. We
understood this age group and were mesmerized by them and by the dynamics that brought us, and kept us, all together as a team of fifty-eight youngsters and two teachers.

Like other middle school educators in our system, we were proud of our
team and our school. We were risk takers, not only because it was an effective attitude, but because our principal expected us to be. Put simply, teaming
worked and worked well, and we were happy to be a part of it.

Designing an interdisciplinary unit around our students' can tab collection
idea was therefore both fun and natural for us, just as this type of curriculum
continues to be for most other middle school teachers in Alamance County
Schools (North Carolina) where middle level education has been both firmly
and fully established for some twenty-five years. The idea of integrating the
curriculum is as instinctive for teams of teachers here as talking and teaching
and learning are. That stance stems from educators who are highly trained
experts in not only curriculum design, but also young adolescent development, exploratory classes, adviser-advisee sessions, block scheduling, and a
panoply of other components that, together, make schooling for the young
adolescent something that this system is very proud of.

The task of capturing these positive attitudes and team dynamics on paper
is incredibly difficult. Teaming, and teaching, are based on human relationships, and those are so very hard to describe, particularly when they work
with the seeming ease of good symphonies in concert, Shakespearian players
on stage – those groups that are well beyond the rudimentary and are now at
a place that is smooth, seasoned, and difficult to dissect. Mature teams

operate at times from an almost "mind melt" approach that defies language.

This chapter attempts a description of these mature teams. What makes them function so smoothly? What problems must they address in order to ensure growth toward a higher level of mastery? What advice can they share? These difficult and nebulous issues are explored through a compilation of observations and spontaneous interviews in over fifty schools across the state of North Carolina and particularly Alamance County. Woven throughout are results from more extensive interviews with and observations of teams at one of Alamance County's oldest middle schools, Woodlawn Middle. This chapter therefore examines several issues, including benchmarks of success for the mature team, obstacles they must address in order to maintain mastery, and finally, general advice from experienced team members for those ready to move beyond the initial stages of teaming.

Benchmarks of success for the mature team

> *Instinctively knowing when to run forward, when to ease back and when to let someone else take over... these are the marks of a great team and a great team player... knowing when to lead and when to follow.*
>
> — Georgia-Pacific Corporation, 1993

The eight teams of 43 teachers at Woodlawn Middle slide from leader to follower and back again with the confidence of those who have long practiced their craft. They maintain the hallmarks of basic teaming: team identity, common work space, connection to the school's mission statement, respect for the position of team leader, and flexible policies for discipline, homework, parental involvement, community service, remediation, and enrichment. These attitudes speak for themselves:

> *We really love the concept of teaming here. It's the basis of middle school; it's where everything begins. The teaching is very important to us, and that includes dealing with the kids individually. We have the freedom to treat them like adults; for example, when we feel like we need a conference, our team has one with the student first and encourages him or her to take responsibility before we contact the parent or anything. You get to know these kids very well. They really feel like they have a family at school. That family, is, of course, the team.*
>
> — Team member, Woodlawn Middle

Woodlawn's teams are interdisciplinary in structure and their members range from two to four core teachers and extend to embrace all other "special (exploratory) teachers" who regularly teach the children on the core's team. Students are heterogeneously grouped and for the most part, always have been.

These teams are unique because they have had time to gain expertise beyond the basics of classroom curriculum, student interactions, parental involvement, administrative concerns, and organizational skills. However, it should be noted that time in and of itself does not guarantee a mature team. Perhaps a minimum of five years of middle school experience is a good baseline to establish, for that allows teachers an opportunity to master the basics and begin to stretch beyond them. The average teacher at this school has, in fact, taught for a number of years in a true middle school setting, and so has moved into a depth of experience that is uncommon among many middle school faculties in this country.

While teams at Woodlawn Middle include individuals who have practiced teaming for a significant number of years, they have not necessarily been together. Rather, members have flowed in and out of newly configured teams on occasion, with little if any break in success. This is possible because both teachers and administrators here know and understand the middle school concept, including a deep commitment to the young adolescent, responsive curriculum, scheduling, and program development. Their knowledge base, experience levels, professional dedication, willingness to take risks, and their administrator's expectations provide them with a like focus. This common direction then allows them the freedom to reorganize their teams when necessary, while maintaining their high levels of success.

This consistency in understanding extends across members of this faculty, the three additional middle school faculties in Alamance County, and the school systems in neighboring counties. This also contributes heavily to teachers moving in and out of different teams with continued effectiveness. Each member understands the task at hand and can immediately begin to tackle it together because a firm foundation has been laid through knowledge, commitment, experience, and a willingness to work together for the good of the children involved.

When attempting a description of the mature teams at Woodlawn or any number of other schools, it becomes evident that there are several bench-marks that they have mastered. Identifying these is important for two primary reasons. First, they enable mature teams to recognize their accomplishments and thus the next stages necessary for continued growth, and second, they identify common standards that provide direction to others less experienced in the concept of teaming.

The five benchmarks discussed here are by no means an inclusive list; rather, they represent broad and common standards that mature teams effectively master and beyond which they grow, some in short periods of time and others in longer. Their level of expertise has not come easily, although observations of these teams lead others to believe that everything they do is synchronized, slick, and effortless; rather, they have worked hard and tenaciously to achieve this level of efficiency and success. Many hold degrees beyond the required bachelor's level, maintain relationships with university faculties, regularly attend and participate in professional conferences, and interact with staffs from neighboring schools in order to compare and share classroom strategies and concerns. You will often find these team members carrying dinner to a sick colleague's home, spending Saturday telephone time discussing problems or curriculum development not covered during the week, and maintaining their professional attitudes in the grocery store or at their child's dance recital when community members initiate discussions of school. These are teachers for whom the philosophy of middle grades education parallels their own personal philosophies about caring, nurturing, giving, and being.

> *What makes us good? It's not always the number of years that a team has actually been together, but rather a meshing of personal commitments and philosophies. It also includes the freedom to be both creative and spontaneous. It's having the autonomy to teach, really teach, in every sense of the word.* — Team member, Woodlawn Middle School

BENCHMARK 1: Mature teams are experts who recognize that the acquisition of professional knowledge is a lifelong process.

Although many of these teachers hold advanced degrees, their pursuit of *knowing* has gone well beyond a graduate school classroom. It has moved, instead, into an area of quiet and deep reflection that has awakened in each teacher individually, and the team collectively, the understanding that teaching and learning are lifelong pursuits – very sophisticated, often enigmatic, and generally beyond the trappings of college course work. Experience has provided them with individual depth and they now use that as a solid and proven base for continued growth across the team. Former training has supplied the methodology, past successes the motivation, their students the fuel.

Rachel, for example, began her career twelve years ago as a science teacher who had a passing interest in the local health curriculum. After the Carnegie Council's report *Turning Points* (1989), her school's faculty wrote a Professional Development Plan that included an intense reworking of the current health curriculum, a revision that focused on students' poor social decision-making skills.

A faculty vote resulted in the agreement to add one period of health to each licensed teacher's instructional day, regardless of content training. This gave health issues, and particularly social decision making, the emphasis that it needed, unlike the current nine weeks of health taught as part of an exploratory rotation.

Rachel volunteered to take over the lead responsibility for her team. As a result, one team meeting per week was devoted to discussions of this particular curriculum and how it applied to the team's current students. Rachel based her team's discussions on *Turning Points*, expanded readings that she was doing, formal and impromptu student interviews across the team, guidance from the school's health instructor, and conversations with other health teachers from neighboring schools.

What caused the faculty, and Rachel, to take on this task? It was certainly not mandated by the district administration, nor was it the result of community demands. If anything, it added community education as well. Rather, it was simply something that needed to be done for the well-being of the students, and that was reason enough. Mature teams are aware of student needs at different levels and in different ways. By sharing candid and regular discussions about those needs, teams are both motivated and competent to address students' concerns successfully, no matter the extra effort or cost.

Mature teams must, of course, prioritize their recognition of these needs. The best of these tell us that they usually acquire the necessary information in three primary ways:

- They ask their students about specific topics or for general concerns through team-designed questionnaires and group discussions, including those found in advisory. The feeling of family found within these classes lends itself to honesty, although anonymity is accepted in written remarks. These responses are discussed across the team of teachers, with general and specific conclusions drawn. These outcomes are then confirmed with the students, with misperceptions corrected and directions refocused when necessary. Finally, teachers ground these perceptions and directions with professional conference attendance and professional journal readings. Information supplied by both is shared across the team, with each member adding to the collective knowledge base.

- Several teams report ongoing professional reading groups that are fashioned verbally after the written reaction papers that many had to complete in graduate course work. This format serves a threefold purpose: It keeps the entire group abreast of current paradigms and methodology, and it provides a sounding board for testing new ideas and the applications of them. Finally, it supplies positive reinforcement to the fact that teaching is a difficult, but highly rewarding, opportunity.

- One result of the team's conference attendance and reading is that they come to recognize exemplary schools within a reasonable distance from their own. Aided by their administration, these teams travel to other classrooms to observe teachers who have mastered the technique or issue with which they are concerned, or who are implementing new concepts that they, too, would like to try. This information is then discussed not only among themselves and their students, but with the entire faculty as well. In this way, all benefit from the travel time of a few.

Once the necessary information is acquired, it is discussed thoroughly within the team, prioritized and addressed, and, when utilized and understood, is shared out in a variety of ways. Common among these are the following:

- As has been stressed already, information gained and perspectives realized are always shared among other teachers in the school. This lends to the atmosphere of continuity across the grade level and with the transition from one grade to the next.

- This sharing among teachers leads easily to the mentoring of less experienced faculty members and student teachers. In this way both the process and the resulting information are maximized.

- Several of these teachers are quick to share at regional and state conferences, for they realize that the most powerful model is that of teachers training teachers. This same thought sometimes leads to team publications in both state and national journals.

BENCHMARK 2: Mature teams are confident, express job satisfaction, and are proud of their schools.

The two sat side-by-side on the green couch near the folding wall that separated their classrooms....They laughed as

they talked; their eighth graders had really gotten the joke
on them....The two teachers were overwhelmed at the vol-
ume of tabs that each Monday had produced, at this sug-
gestion-gone-deliciously-out-of-control....The enthusiasm
that resulted from these students...was absolutely conta-
gious, absolutely middle school....

Confident? Sure. Enjoy their job? Certainly. Proud of their school and
their kids and the opportunity to teach? Oh, absolutely. These are people
who cannot *not* teach; it is as much a part of them as living and breathing and
getting up in the mornings. They represent teams that are both effective and
successful, and which consist of individuals comfortable with and knowledgeable about their roles as positive models, instructional facilitators,
leaders and followers, empathetic human beings, and respectful citizens. This
is, in part, the direct result of specific training, experience in human relationships, and the security of knowing that a strong support system surrounds
them. George and Alexander (1993) add other critical characteristics:

For teamwork at its best, individual members must like
teaching at this level and enjoy their role as team member.
They must be optimistic as persons, about themselves, their
students, and the process of teamwork. Maturity, in terms
of patience and tolerance, are high on the list. (p. 293)

Positive adult attitudes are reflected in students' attitudes as well. These
attitudes set the tone for the classroom. Teachers report high levels of student
enthusiasm and few repeat disruptions that require disciplinary action.
Purkey and Schmidt's philosophy of invitational education (1987) applies
here. It reports that in order for schools to be successful, they must be the
most inviting places in town. These students *are* invited, for they feel special,
that they have a choice, and that there is something happening at their school
every day that they do not want to miss, and so they come to school to
participate in whatever that is. For some it may be the fact that a teacher is
reading an exciting piece of adolescent fiction aloud in the classroom, for
others that spark lies in band or drama or a shop class. Still others may be
excited about intramurals or an interdisciplinary unit or the fact that the math
teacher is bringing in a grocery store's worth of food and soap containers
with prices attached for basic budgeting.

These are the teams of teachers and students who end up sitting together
at a ball game even though they have just spent an eight-hour day in the same
space. These are the same teams who sponsor School Spirit Day on campus
or who visit a rest home twice monthly for an "Adopt a Grandparent" pro-

gram. The message is clear: You belong here, for you are special and important and very, very needed.

BENCHMARK 3: Mature teams constantly nurture the relationship among team members.

These team members usually become good friends who have fun with what they do. Teaching together is to them a festival, a celebration, a group challenge, an opportunity to share and learn from one another. When coming together for the first time, teams may choose to solidify their relationship through activities after school and off campus. These sometimes include a cookout, shopping, or perhaps a movie in order to expedite the process of getting to know one another better. Others opt for on-campus activities such as eating lunch together, sitting with one another at faculty meetings, or bringing snacks for after-school paper grading sessions. They may wear team t-shirts on occasion or recognize birthdays and holidays among themselves, just as they do with their students. Regardless of their approach, team members move to a closer personal connection, with a positive correlation witnessed in their professional relationships.

Once an initial comfort zone and understanding are established, these relationships are nurtured and therefore grow on a steady basis. For example, a team social life may be maintained through time spent together aside from class or from afternoon conversations that involve personal interests, families, fun, sorrows, and traditions. Intellectual stimulation is pivotal, as well, and is found in a team's professional reading circle, conference attendance, or staff development. Educational publications like regional newsletters and state or national journals provide an outlet for a particularly strong curriculum unit or common observations and concerns. Grant writing is often seen as not only a source of funding for special projects but also as a challenging and stimulating group effort. The spiritual side is equally as important, for every educator knows that teaching young adolescents requires a serious emotional investment; therefore, team members bolster spirits or offer sympathetic ears when a colleague feels especially concerned, stressed, or simply needs a shoulder to lean on. As is obvious, honesty is at the heart of these relationships, and truthful feedback can be shared in the mature team without hesitation, for these alliances form a foundation that is both solid and professional. In short, these teachers motivate each other as well as they do their students.

Finally, it must be added that teams occasionally do not mesh on a personal level. This is not the determent that it seems, for mature teams have found that they can still be quite effective professionally. They have grown well beyond the initial stage of novice individuals who grapple for personal recognition and reputation. Rather, they view themselves as a single unit that moves in tandem with students' needs and interests, their own met within the adult team when possible, and if not, then through some other source. Regardless, they are clearly focused on the task at hand and the population whom they serve, and as professionals, have found that they can put personal interests and conflicts aside and look to one another's strengths as expert educators. They purposefully address each other's skills and use them to advantage, moving beyond the temptation to focus on a difference of opinion or a conflict in individual interests.

For example, one team at Woodlawn Middle found that they worked together quite well, despite the fact that they did not always agree on personal issues. They strongly noted:

> Interpersonal skills are critically important, with both the teachers on your team and the students within it. There's a lot of give and take involved; you have to be open-minded enough to see another's point of view. You don't have to love each other to work together, although it does make things click faster. If not, you learn to use each other's strengths to advantage.

Another team added that "One drawback [to team success] is that team members make or break it on their willingness to get along with others." They emphasized that personal relationships are sometimes difficult to separate from professional ones when you are in close daily proximity with the same group of people. They stressed, however, that the separation must be made because we are role models to impressionable and vulnerable young adolescents. All agreed that directly focusing on the relationship among team members, either personally, professionally, or both, is integral to the team's successful accomplishment of its mission.

BENCHMARK 4: Mature teams are curriculum risk-takers who are given the autonomy to accomplish their goals.

These teams are allowed to be both creative and spontaneous, and they feel free to do so. They are not overly concerned with standardized testing; scores seem to take care of themselves. Their administrators encourage them to rework curriculum mandates that are inappropriate for their developmentally and culturally diverse students. They view textbooks as supplementary tools rather than documents to be poured over page by page and question by question. They are thoughtful in their planning, interactive in their discussions, rigorous in their academic expectations, and clear in their communications. They monitor their instruction to be certain that it is integrated with literacy skills and relevant life experiences. They reference what other team members are teaching and often join them for lessons. In short, they endorse each other's content area in class as naturally as they teach their own. Students recognize that their team is led by a bank of educators who operate as a smooth, cohesive, and aware unit.

Like our opening scenario surrounding the can tab collection, these teachers see themselves as facilitators of student-directed instruction rather than as teachers who control textbook wisdom. Dismayed, they nod in full agreement when Arnold (1991) cautions:

> *Unfortunately, developmental responsiveness has become a cliche...seldom understood or applied to curriculum...a school will have a flowery mission statement about developmental responsiveness, but its practice amounts to little more than a few hands-on activities, an occasional field trip, a dash of Piagetian jargon, and business as usual.* (p. 10)

Not them and not their school...not any longer. Although these teams have certainly spent time at this level in their initial stages of growth and development, they have moved past it now, in part because their students demanded it and they listened. Therefore, they no longer talk about young adolescents as if they are some theoretical age group detached from today's history lesson or basketball drills. Instead, they plan based on the immediate needs and developmental levels of their individual students.

A part of this planning involves the identification of basic criteria to be used with selecting a topic or listing skills and strategies to be covered. The Middle Level Curriculum Project (1991), for example, identified a set of eight questions that successful teams must answer before designing new curriculum:

— *Who are young adolescents?*
— *What questions do they have about themselves and their world?*
— *What questions does the world pose for them?*
— *In what kind of future world might they live?*
— *How can adults help all students learn?*
— *What activities should young adolescents engage in at school?*

> — *How do we design a curriculum that is good both for young adolescents as well as for the adults who share their world?*
> — *In the school experience, how do we utilize all ways of knowing and all areas of human experience?* (p. 30)

When considering these questions, and perhaps others, one example of appropriate curriculum comes to mind. It is important here not only because it met these requirements, but because it also involved a significant risk, both emotionally and in the spontaneous planning required.

This topic was taken directly from a world event that particularly affected a team of students. Desert Storm, the Middle Eastern conflict of 1991, hit North Carolina and this group hard, as there is no question that this is a key military state. Emotions were edgy at best and confusions frequently voiced.

The topic of Desert Storm dominated one team's classrooms and filled students with fears, questions, and bewilderment; therefore, it was not only appropriate to plan a study of the conflict, but necessary. The result was an interdisciplinary unit that teachers intended for one day's inquiry; however, the reality was that students' demands led to more than a week of passionate interaction.

That entire team, teachers and students alike, learned much more than oil and statistics and the history of war. They learned that we are a society sharing the same concerns and fears, that we are all a part of the continued success of America, that we are an unconditional support system for one another, and finally, that it is OK to not understand how you feel about a complex issue that is close to home. Instead, we can all sort through our feelings together until they make sense to us individually.

You will note, of course, that this study was not pulled directly from a single textbook or designed with the exclusive objective of producing high scores on the end-of-course standardized test. Rather, it was pulled from life, designed with both students and curriculum mandates in mind, connected to past and future, and rich in interpretation for every person involved, from students to teachers to parents and beyond.

When designing this type of curriculum, or any lesson, successful teams use approaches that are not traditional and safe, for they realize that they serve a different clientele from that which they taught at the beginning of their careers. This understanding leads them to use cooperative learning groups and other social approaches on a constant basis. They devise learning centers, games, simulations, role playing, and other activities often, and they use the computer lab regularly. They consider ethnic identities, learning styles, and individual developmental needs. Their classrooms are noisy and their desks are always all pushed together or around the perimeter or outside on the sidewalk or wherever is necessary to accomplish the lesson's task. In short, their students make and talk and do and research and teach daily, interactively, and with integrity. These teachers understand the needs of their students and they act on them with tenacity, confident that they are doing their jobs well. They support each other through the long-range planning required to accomplish such student-oriented tasks, and they are never afraid to risk trying a new concept or instructional approach. These are teams of professionals who are respected as experts in their field.

BENCHMARK 5: Mature teams are in harmony with the administrative leadership.

Mature teams generally agree that they teach for administrators who not only allow autonomy and flexibility, but who expect it. The result is a central faculty that teaches together for many years, which in turn creates conditions ideal for the development of mature and effective teams. These administrators have contributed to this team cohesiveness by deliberately assembling instructional leaders who are totally committed to young adolescents. Less dedicated faculty have been encouraged to move to other grades that more readily suited their interests, or to select other professions that were more aligned with their needs. These administrators have the same standards for their faculty that they expect faculty to have for their students – spontaneity with intent, creativity with abandon, achievement with integrity. Mature teams flourish within this atmosphere of harmony, trust, and respect. These teams address a variety of campus concerns, decisions, and policies that are critical to the school's success and which have traditionally been the domain of the administration.

One initial example of decision making is the structure of the teams themselves. Teachers are surveyed at the close of the school term as to which grade level they prefer for the coming year and with which team members they would enjoy working. For some, the request is for the same team that they've worked with for many years; for others, the choice is a new shake-up. Principals who nurture harmony respect these requests and honor them when possible, in this way allowing teams to participate in their own organization. Lynn Briggs, principal of Woodlawn Middle School, adds, however, that an administrator must consider "what's best for both the students and teachers, but the students must always come first; teachers may not like that, but those teams that function well together will accept it and go on." Certainly mature teams do "accept it and go on," for they recognize that students' needs take precedent over personal wishes.

Once their organization has been confirmed, mature teams are entrusted with a variety of decisions and issues. For example, they often design their school schedules by grade level, chart curricular directions, determine how students will be divided for the school year, and submit budgetary requests that are honored. They meet weekly with an administrator to express concerns, consider problems, and discuss questions. There is an open door policy in the main office that extends beyond these scheduled sessions and which invites teams in at any time and for any reason. Their administrators occasionally teach content classes and often host a daily student advisory group. In summary, it is clear that these teams not only respect their leaders but are fiercely loyal to them, an attribute that is clearly reciprocated.

Lynn Briggs illustrates this, for it is clear that Woodlawn's teams do work in close accord with her office. She actively participates in each team on her faculty, for she considers herself a member of each. Although young in this role, she has been a middle school teacher for a number of years; therefore, she fully understands the realities of the classroom, the mission of middle schools, the contributions of mature teams, and the vision of the successful principal. She champions her faculty with a vengeance and supports her students with a loyalty that they never question. She is rarely in her office, as she considers team events her purpose. Every person in her school is happy, necessary, and successful, and every team is focused, challenged, and responsive. The result is a school population that works smoothly and effectively as a larger single team bound by a common vision.

As has become obvious to all who teach, administrators are in key positions to either hinder the work of mature teams or to encourage them forward. As central figures, those who are successful perceive themselves as team players with resources to be spread out before teachers, tapped into, and used wisely. When this happens and harmony between faculty and administration is achieved, many obstacles that block the growth of mature teams can be successfully addressed and eliminated.

Obstacles to address

> *Great teams aren't built overnight. They evolve...slowly*
> *and through shared experiences. And, always at the heart,*
> *are the steadfast elements of trust and commitment.*
>
> — Georgia-Pacific Corporation, 1993

Any task that results in greatness requires much of the giver. This is especially true in middle grades education, where teaching is emotional, demanding, and intense. The concept of teaming at this level is therefore even more important today than it was thirty years ago, for the task of preparing young adolescents for the world is simply too overwhelming to face alone.

Indeed, our understanding of teaming has evolved slowly, but the result has been a knowledge base that is deep, experiential, and rich. The majority of this knowledge base lies in an exploration of those teams that have operated at successful levels for an extended period of time and who share common benchmarks and beliefs.

Included among these beliefs is a complete commitment to both young adolescents and the profession which serves them. It is this deep sense of responsibility that must carry these same teams forward as they strive for an even greater understanding of this age group and the pedagogy appropriate to their needs. With this in mind, there are three immediate obstacles to continued growth that need to be addressed by the majority of mature teams. Included among these are the complacency that many teams exhibit after reaching this level of success, the fact that most mature teams restrict meaningful team functions to the core teachers, and the lack of self-designed research studies which address specific team concerns.

OBSTACLE 1: Mature teams often become complacent after reaching a high level of success.

Just as any difficult accomplishment deserves a period of quiet and evenness, so reaching a level of mastery in team teaching does too, for everyone needs an opportunity to recharge. When the time comes, it is natural to sit back and enjoy the smooth workings of a team that has reached success after years of driving hard to achieve its goals. Indeed, entire faculties occasionally come to know the easy stride that results from the pursuit of this common vision. These plateaus are not only justified, but should be shared and celebrated, for they represent a well-earned measure of high-level achievement.

Too often, though, these plateaus stretch on and quickly become prolonged periods of complacency that spawn a decrease in energy and focus for everyone involved. It is during these times that teams rely heavily on past curriculum that has proved effective. Field trips and interdisciplinary units are still used on a regular basis, but they are the same ones that have always been called upon with little to no revision for the current class of students.

Team meetings tend to become mechanical and result in simple approval of the same homework, discipline, or grading policies employed in the past. Parent conferences begin to center around teachers who tell more than they inquire. The thoughtful reflection that was important in the past now has the unspoken designation of belonging to those teams who are still striving to achieve this level of mastery.

Constant evaluation is perhaps the best way to avoid this attitude of prolonged complacency. This type of review should be conducted by both the team itself and an outside evaluator.

In exploring the suggestion of objective self-evaluation, Merenbloom (1991) designed a flexible instrument that is appropriate for team use, and particularly for those new to the process of teaming. A great many of Merenbloom's suggestions also apply to mature teams, however, and can easily be reworked according to their specific needs. For example, among the 42 questions that he suggested are the following six:

1. Do members of the team explore their role and function as a team?
2. Does the team work effectively with resource personnel?
3. Are leadership responsibilities shared?
4. Does the team evaluate goals and objectives periodically?
5. Does the team utilize sub-groupings of the team when appropriate?
6. Do team members participate in staff development activities? (pp. 122-23)

There are several possibilities that surface. For instance, the first and fourth questions are excellent tools for general reflection. The second could be reworked to focus on the inclusion model of bringing both exceptional children and their teachers into the classroom to team with the regular teacher. The third might target the problem of team leaders who are selected by the administration and not rotated on a regular basis, creating a power play among older team members. The fifth could easily be used to disseminate responsibilities for planning interdisciplinary units, festivals and celebrations, field studies, and the like. Finally, the sixth could be reworded to spotlight team members who conduct staff development and present sessions at conferences. Again, the possibilities abound and should be explored within each team according to individual needs. Instruments could then be designed and shared across faculties and either the best of each collapsed into one or each team given multiple copies for the sake of variation and reference.

When considering outside evaluation, mature teams must be certain that the evaluator spends an ample amount of time in data collection and that she is well versed in middle grades philosophy, has personal classroom experience with it, has served on a team for a number of years, and is knowledgeable about appropriate program evaluation practices. As stakeholders, team members should ensure that they are kept abreast of all findings and that the process is ongoing, whether continued through an outside researcher or through team self-evaluation.

Teams should request that school districts supply these outside evaluators for their use in order to streamline strengths and identify areas that lack positive growth. Merenbloom (1991) suggested that systems might add these evaluations of teams to those of individual teachers, and he noted that these could be conducted by a variety of individuals ranging from state accrediting groups to peers. Although Merenbloom stressed the use of self-evaluation as being perhaps most beneficial, mature teams are ready to add to the ongoing process, and indeed must if they are to continue growth beyond present levels of mastery.

OBSTACLE 2: Mature teams often isolate themselves and the result is a membership that rarely extends beyond core teachers.

A team must relate to every single person who touches the lives of the students on the team, from core teachers to exploratory, from the school nurse to the principal, from learning disabled to academically gifted, from parents to business personnel, and well beyond. This community of instructional leaders is not only important to a child's full education, they often provide the incentive for a student to come to school regularly. For example, a child may not be fully convinced that mathematics is a critical life skill as evidenced through math classes, but when those same concepts are presented by the art teacher as a part of an exciting project, that student may well find it hard to wait to get off the bus in the mornings.

We are all educators first, and we are all responsible to these young adults. It is our professional commitment. Teams tend to get comfortable and overlook this, however, including those at highly experienced levels. Core and exploratory teachers rarely share common planning times; therefore, it is easier to simply prepare and do within the core team of math, language arts, social studies, and science, rather than find before or after school time to extend the boundaries to other instructional leaders. This takes an obvious commitment to cooperation, communication, and additional time. When we recall our art student, however, it becomes clear that those beyond the core enrich the existing program in such a powerful way that the extra effort is worthwhile. An example will underscore this reality.

Those teachers not on the core teams are called "special teachers" at Woodlawn Middle, a label that is both positive and earned. These teachers have worked hard to address this problem of revolving on the periphery with no integration into core curriculum or methodologies. One result of this ongoing undertaking has been that the special teachers not only participate in core team operations when possible, but that they also design curriculum using many instructional strategies that are often left exclusively for the use of the core teachers.

An illustration is found in the interdisciplinary unit on Mexico that they initially taught in 1993 and have since repeated each school term due to demand from both students and faculty. It has proven so successful, in fact, that it is not only celebrated at school but is also shared publicly through both the media and state conference presentations.

The first of these annual events was wrapped around a study of Mexico and included an examination of everything from Spanish music to a taste of Spanish culture. The students were so enthusiastic about what they were reading and experiencing that they decided to share it with faculty, and so a gala dinner was set into motion.

With a Southern Bell grant providing funding, art students went to work making bright tissue flowers for decorations, maracas for table favors, and Mexican bread boxes. After a taste-testing party and a study of native culture, Spanish students pitched in with woven placemats and pinatas, while the shop teacher focused on candle holders and painted carts. With that, the cafeteria became a festival of color and lights.

Reading students enjoyed literary selections and discussions that, too, provided a look at native culture, and they then used their enriched perspectives to design invitations for the faculty and to add huge chalk drawings to the cafeteria's decorations. With donated fabric, the career exploration teacher guided students through sewing bow ties and cummerbunds for the waiters and waitresses and then discussed how to cater a large party.

All of the students enjoyed the cooking, and the majority of it was done in classrooms, with the home economics lab supplying appliances at scheduled times. The menu provided a Mexican feast featuring chicken with rice and other dishes that won rave reviews from the faculty. The chorus and band both shared Spanish music as dinner entertainment and the student waiters and waitresses not only served but also danced. This one single event has been referenced time and again by teachers from across Woodlawn's faculty, leaving no doubt as to the evening's success.

This was, in fact, so exciting that it returned for a repeat performance the following year, with a school dance supplying funding and the country of Costa Rica providing focus. Can't you just picture the decorations that came from that country? In addition to similar activities from the previous year, a prompt sheet was added so that teachers could chat with the students in Spanish. Team leader Debbie Schoderbek and members Debbie Hipp, Julie Canovai, and Kathy Boynton were chief organizers of the event which involved about 150 students for each of the two years mentioned.

Fun stuff! There is no doubt that this faculty and these students are headed in a positive direction. Fortunately, through public sharing of this event and others similar, teams from other schools have found this an exciting model and have, like Woodlawn, begun to evaluate the role that exploratory teachers currently play in both team dynamics and curriculum design.

Other teams, however, will find it much easier to stick by their original complaints about a lack of common planning time or a core curriculum that is more important than an exploratory class. That attitude is so inappropriate when we again consider that drama, physical education, or art often provides the very spark that brings many youngsters to school when math, language arts, social studies, or science simply do not. Those mature teams who strive for continued growth and thus greater levels of achievement will certainly focus on this issue, for it is critical to the totality of a child's school day.

OBSTACLE 3: Most mature teams are not researchers.

No one is closer to the core of influential educational data than the class-room teacher. Mature teams must recognize and respect this rich abundance of information and, as a result, should deliberately gather, analyze, incorporate, and report it on a constant basis. It is already found in team meetings as teachers agree to observe a student whose behavior has changed dramatically or as they evaluate a curriculum unit that they have just taught. This process must be formally acknowledged, brought to the forefront of team discussions, and practiced for its inestimable value. Results that are of interest to all teachers should then be shared through other team meetings, faculty gatherings, conference presentations, and journal publications.

Action research, whether done individually or in collaboration, allows teachers to "experience problem solving and to model it for their students" (Calhoun, 1993, p. 62). It involves traditional methodology in that the problem is identified, data are collected and analyzed, a solution is decided and acted on, and the results are evaluated. Its implications for growth seem almost endless to the mature team, who might consider tackling even larger problems on a school-wide scale or collaborating with other teams across the district. Consequently, professional research should be purposefully added to a team's immediate agenda.

Consider this illustration. Gene, like others on his team, had long been concerned with the entire advisory program at his school. He recognized that several things provided a solid foundation for these frustrations: a lack of detailed staff development both at the onset of the program and as an ongoing process, an administration that placed little emphasis on program evaluation, a guidance counselor who did not recognize that her office must provide specific direction, an advisory period that was too long, and classes that ranged in number from twenty to thirty. Determined to make a change at least in his own classroom, Gene approached the team and asked for some time to be set aside at a meeting the next week so that this could be discussed and they could help him find some direction.

Faithful to their team procedure, he kept an anecdotal journal until that time, recording such things as student behaviors during AA, attention to the topic or task assigned, the class attitude in general, comments the students either made to him or that he overheard concerning the day's agenda, and his own personal feelings. He presented this to his team a week later, prefacing it with the fact that his students simply showed no interest in AA and that he felt like it was time to either give up or rework the program. Opening that door was like opening Pandora's Box, and others began to spill over with similar frustrations and problems that they had been reluctant to admit. Most of the meeting became a productive venting session, and they closed determined to find a way to research the problem.

Team meeting two days later began with several members explaining that others across the school felt the same as they, and with one person producing an article on action research that she'd received at a graduate class the semester before. Sharing copies, she suggested a few steps that they might want to take.

The first involved the design of a survey that they could pilot test with their own team and possibly use later with the entire school. This was agreed upon and initial background reading on advisory programs and survey design was initiated next. With that done and discussed, work on the actual instrument became the third step. The math teacher suggested that her classes tabulate the quantitative section and that they as a team analyze the qualitative portion. This data analysis became the fourth step.

The survey produced some interesting results and gave Gene's team some insight into how they could work within time and class size constraints to improve both curriculum and class atmosphere. The students' suggestions and dislikes were carefully considered, and the next step produced a new curriculum and topical plan based on them. With that done, the team put the new plan into action for a period of six weeks, carefully monitoring the revised program through spontaneous interviews with students, class discussions, and anecdotal journals. After that the same instrument, with slight revision, was re-administered and follow-up interviews were conducted as evaluation. The results were very encouraging!

Gene's team discussed their findings with their administrator, who suggested that it be brought up in the team leaders' meeting the following Monday morning. It was thoughtfully discussed and then carried back to the remainder of the faculty, who asked that it be shared in the next teachers' meeting. A decision was made to use the efforts of Gene's team as a pilot for school-wide research. Through expanded data collection and persistent efforts, one team's original concern made quite a difference in the entire school's refinement of an important program. Like Gene's, other mature teams must recognize the reformation and thus contribution that is found through professional classroom research. There is perhaps no other source of involvement that can reap such credible results as a carefully planned investigation. Too often even mature teams assume that change comes through a top-down model, leaving them tied to current agendas until an administrator designates the steps necessary to address the situation. As Gene's team has proved, this attitude is both untrue and unnecessary. Teams who research open a window that reveals change, empowerment, control, and an unprecedented source of both professional and personal growth.

A few words of advice

Because mature teams are in the position to provide leadership for those who are younger in the concept, it is appropriate to constantly solicit advice from them. With that in mind, the teams and principal from Woodlawn Middle offered these do's and dont's:

DO's:
- Try everything! This includes cooperative learning groups and an inclusion model. Be patient. The good things take time.
- Make certain that teams share common space, planning periods, students, and visions.
- Exercise team choice and expect your students to do the same.
- Expect two planning periods.

- Develop appropriate relationships with both team members and students.
- Be flexible and open-minded about everything.
- Both lead and follow.
- Understand fully the entire concept of middle grades education in general, and teaming in particular, before you begin. Request staff development and a professional reading list if you feel like you need additional information.
- Keep up with the National Middle School Association, your state league and association, journals, and conferences. Young adolescents change constantly, and so does our knowledge base. Share your information. A great deal of this is available on both audio and video cassettes.
- Give teams the freedom to do what they know how to do best: teach adolescents, in every sense of the word. This includes curriculum, coping skills, decision making, and life in general.
- Be a willing faculty. It's worth it.
- Make certain that every adult in the school puts students first.
- Blend teachers' strengths and personalities carefully when organizing teams.
- Maintain a positive attitude at all times. Education won't work without one.

DON'T's:
- Take on too much at first. This includes later years when you've accomplished one goal and you're setting the next. Quality makes the difference.
- Implement teaming, or anything, without rigorous, quality staff development.
- Look back to the past with an "that way was good enough for me; it should be good enough now" attitude.
- Stay in middle school if you'd rather work somewhere else. Our kids deserve teachers who want to teach them.
- Be governed by test scores and curriculum mandates at the expense of real learning.

In closing

What makes some teams work? What makes them function with an ease that seems as effortless as children jumping rope on a playground? Spending time with seasoned teams dramatically deepens our understanding of their synchronized ease of thought and movement, and it therefore brings us a bit closer to an answer.

For example, we know that mature teams who are successful share certain benchmarks of achievement. We know that they are treated as professionals whose expertise is both respected and valued, and that they are supported by the administration, the student body, and the surrounding community. We know that they take care of one another just as they do their students, for that sense of caring and giving are simply a part of who and what they are. We know that they are confident enough to take important risks in the name of their children, their school, and their profession.

We realize, too, that their continued growth is critical to us, for they are in the very unique position of having practiced teaming for many years. This is a badge that the majority of middle school teachers cannot yet wear, and so these seasoned teams stand available to teach many things about their experiences. This is their obligation to the profession, and so they must carefully evaluate themselves if they are to chart directions that will ensure their continued growth and mastery. Their moving beyond common obstacles in order to teach others who follow their path is their torch, their special contribution.

In closing, it is certainly obvious that these mature teams do not realize that they are good, really good. They simply see themselves as cohorts of professional friends who enjoy kids and love what they are doing. For them, there is no other job on earth that is more important than the one they do in their school with their children. That, too, is their special contribution.

References

Arnold, J. (1991). Towards a middle level curriculum rich in meaning. *Middle School Journal, 23,* 8-12.

Calhoun, E.F. (1993). Action research: Three approaches. *Educational Leadership, 51* (2), 62-65.

Carnegie Council on Adolescent Development. (1989). *Turning points: Preparing American youth for the 21st century.* New York: Carnegie Corporation.

George, P., & Alexander, W.M. (1993). *The exemplary middle school* (2nd ed.). Fort Worth, TX: Harcourt Brace Jovanovich.

Georgia-Pacific Corporation. (1993). *What makes a great team?* Atlanta, GA: Author.

Merenbloom, E.Y. (1991). *The team process: A handbook for teachers,* (3rd ed.). Columbus, OH: National Middle School Association.

Middle Level Curriculum Project. (1991). Middle level curriculum: The search for self and social meaning. *Middle School Journal, 23* (2), 29-35.

Purkey, W.W., & Schmidt, J.J. (1987). *The inviting relationship: An expanded perspective for professional counseling.* Old Tappan, NJ: Prentice Hall.

The Art of Creative Composition: An Administrative Perspective on Interdisciplinary Teaming 10

Mary Gallagher-Polite

The emerging melody

A melody runs through your head like a constant voice; echoing from an abstract part of you. You know it is there but you cannot capture it completely. The constancy of its presence creates a feeling of friendship; yet it is a friend without a face or a name. It is almost close enough to touch, yet it remains elusive.

As you sit down to try to capture the essence of this new friend on paper, your melody takes on a life of its own. Like writing with words, as you release your control over the melody and let it emerge, you find that it will take shape and form unencumbered by your own restrictions, expectations, or predictions. Like the written word, your melody will begin to flow onto the page, note by note, phrase by phrase, until the completed melody is before you for inspection and review.

You then have the opportunity to fine tune your melody. With artistry, you can begin to build and massage it with your knowledge and skill about theory, harmony, balance, timbre, and tone. From a once haunting voice that ran through your head abstractly calling you to give it life, you now hold the beauty of creation; the birth of a melody becomes a song at your hand.

Traditional views of schooling have yet to capture the essence of creation. Instead of writing new melodies, schools tend to constantly remake hits from the past, changing the artist instead of the melody and form. We redo instead of create. We revise instead of produce. And while it is important to learn from the successes and failures of the past, becoming restricted by preexisting parameters prevents us from writing the new melodies which could inspire and motivate.

Being a middle school principal is akin to composing music. Administrative preparation programs should and do provide a background of knowledge and skill designed to enhance the effectiveness of prospective school principals. Combined with an individual's professional and personal experience, this preparation can equip the new principal with the foundation for effective leadership. But the choice remains with the individual. Principals can choose to lead or choose to manage; they can choose to remake hits from the past or they can choose to compose a new creation. Young adolescents need composers willing to create new ways to meet their needs in this ever-changing world. What has worked in the past can inform the present, yet past achievements should not limit emerging paths that have yet to be blazed. Middle school principals who choose to compose accept a challenge that is often frustrating, frightening, and wrought with ambiguity. There are no clear answers for the middle level composer, but if you begin with a strong foundation, at least you'll know you're starting on the right note.

The foundation

As schools implement the practices associated with the national middle school movement, they typically implement interdisciplinary teaming as a core component of the transition process (Carnegie Council on Adolescent Development, 1989). If putting teams of teachers together with a common group of students in a designated area of the school is approached as only an organizational strategy, the school will become nothing more than a teamed junior high school. "Unfortunately, the experiences of the last two decades have shown that changes in the content of schooling do not automatically follow from organizing teams" (Lounsbury, 1992a, p. 2). The way schools look might change, but a change in how people behave in them does not necessarily follow. To realize the full potential of interdisciplinary teaming, individuals in the school need a supportive teaming mentality. If teaming is to be more than an organizational change, people on teams have to change. And change occurs one person at a time.

Developing a teaming mentality is a process which for many of us requires substantive work. We hear a lot today about teaming. We are assailed with buzzwords like teacher empowerment, collaboration, shared decision-making, and participatory management. But real teaming is not just something we do. It is something we believe. It is a way of looking at an organization which is different from the old top-down hierarchy. If those who have historically been at the bottom of that hierarchy are to move up, then those at the top have to get out of their way. And getting out of the way is not always easy. An administrator who wants to build teams on the *outside*, needs to develop a teaming mentality on the *inside* first.

Developing a teaming mentality: Five steps in the process

(1) Know yourself. Knowing who you are, how you tick, what your values are, and how they will guide your behavior empowers you with the self-knowledge imperative for a leadership role. Managers, perhaps, can operate in isolation of self-awareness simply by making sure they *do things right* (Bennis, 1989). Tasks become the priority, and the principalship becomes defined by a list of expected duties. The formal job description outlines expectations for the administrator who then simply conforms to what has been tradition. To lead, however, takes more.

Middle school principals who choose to lead, to *do the right things* (Bennis, 1989) know that leading is not easy and that the *right things* are not always predictable. Knowing what is right comes from a deep understanding of self; an identification of a moral and ethical code rooted deeply in personal values and beliefs. Knowing what is *right* in a given situation means that you know what is not. It means knowing that the gray area in between what is right and what is not is often expansive and that intuition is a needed companion to reason when attempting to navigate your way through the quagmire. Schools are seldom logical and rational. Neither is leadership.

Coming to know yourself is an ongoing process of discovery, confrontation, acceptance, and courage. Covey (1989) encourages individuals to develop a personal mission statement to define a set of guiding principles which can serve as the center for effective living. The development of a mission statement allows an individual to uncover important underlying principles which become the focus for short and long-range planning and goal setting. Similarly, I have found that in working with prospective administrators, that taking time to define what we call "Principal's Principles" is a worthwhile endeavor. Administration students come to better know and understand themselves in a way that informs their leadership potential. Defining a personal mission statement (Covey, 1989), or outlining your guiding principles, lets *you* determine how the role of principal in a teamed middle school can be performed instead of giving that responsibility away to someone else. Who you are is who you will be as a principal. So you had better know well who you are taking with you to the job.

(2) Know your stuff. Self-knowledge is a beginning, but that is not all you need to know to work effectively with interdisciplinary teams. The literature is replete with calls for the principal to act as the instructional leader of the school (See for example, Smith & Andrews, 1989). This redefinition of the role of principal from manager to leader outlines the need for knowledge of

curriculum and instruction. As a middle level administrator, that means you will need a thorough grounding in the developmental characteristics of young adolescents, an understanding and belief in the middle school philosophy, and an awareness of the research on effective middle school practices. In addition, however, knowing your stuff means also that you understand the change process and how adults work in and through change in schools.

Cuban (1988) defined first and second order change as alternative outcomes of reform. First order change leaves the basic organizational features of the school undisturbed by focusing on the school's efficiency and effectiveness without transforming the people in them. Second order change alters the basic design of the school and challenges those in and around them to redefine their roles and responsibilities. First order change has focused on correcting problems in existing structure and practice rather than to alter basic beliefs, values, and visions of schooling. And some would argue that the time has come to push beyond the surface-level tinkering of first order reform in order to redefine the basic character of schools through second order transformation (Deal, 1990; Lounsbury, 1996). If middle level schools are to be the hope of tomorrow's young adolescents, then principals in them need to know their stuff about middle schools, to understand the differences between first and second order change, and how to bring about the latter.

(3) Know your limits. Know how to find out what you do not know, but do not expect to know everything. If you intend to create and bring about second order change, expect the unexpected. Accept that you will not know everything but that often others will expect that you do. As new research is conducted and more is learned about teaching and learning, you will need to find ways to maintain your own professional development. You will teach others by your example and promote the value of lifelong learning in the process.

When others ask you a question, try staying focused on whether or not it was the right question to ask before you rush off to find the right answer. If the question is right, then taking time together to find the answer is worthwhile. If not, you will simply be spinning your wheels in yesterday's ruts.

If you intend to simply manage and revise, you can take existing checklists of middle school practice and simply implement them. You can recreate someone else's innovation and do nothing more than replicate what has been done somewhere else. But working in a middle school with the complexities associated with interdisciplinary teaming calls for a diverse set of responses. Leave the door to innovation ajar. If you stop learning, the door closes and locks.

(4) Listen to the voices. Effective team leadership is a relationship with others (Bolman & Deal, 1991). And if leadership is distributed throughout the school (see for example, Johnson, 1993; Polite, 1993), then your voice should blend with the chorus and not always stand out as the solo part.

Listening to other voices in the school — the voices of students, teachers, staff, parents, and community – could be undertaken as only a perfunctory chore. Typical communication strategies – such as surveys, questionnaires, phone conversations, interviews, and public meetings – meet the technical requirements for interaction between and among various constituency groups in the school. Hearing voices, however, means that you set aside your own agenda for a time and listen to both the content and the feelings expressed. If you can get underneath the obvious message, you will hear the underlying meaning in their words. Listen hard and long enough to know what is meant, not just what is said. Make quiet time for yourself as a priority so that you can reflect on the thoughts and ideas of others. If you expect that you do not know everything and live with the ambiguity of change, then you will more likely be able to respond to the expressed and unexpressed needs of others.

Stevenson (1992) told a personal and heartwarming story in his book *Teaching Ten to Fourteen Year Olds*. He described his experience as a beginning teacher intent on helping students enjoy classical literature. With good intentions and prerequisite planning, he set out to entice his young readers into an exciting experience with the classics. When his plan failed and students didn't master the content, he admittedly looked to them as the source of blame. Over the years he came to know and accept that the ideation (Pearce, 1971) of teaching and learning that drove his early behavior needed to be reshaped into one which was responsive to his students' needs. If they did not learn the way he taught, he had to teach in ways that they did.

Likewise, as a well-intended beginning principal, I set out to reshape the school into what I had envisioned it could be. With vigor and excitement, well-defined goals, and a notebook full of lessons on effective leadership, I pushed and prodded people into action. And when they did not want to do what I wanted them to do, I admittedly looked to them as the source of blame. Like Stevenson, over the years I have come to know and accept that the ideation (Pearce, 1971) of leadership that drove my early behavior had to be reshaped into one which was responsive to individual needs. If they did not follow, I had to lead in ways that made them leaders too.

Listening to the voices in the school will allow you to come to better know the individual needs of those who live there. Listening is a requisite for team leadership. Giving voice to those in the school will model for others what is important for them to do too.

(5) Define your role broadly. Typically, the role of a building principal has been defined around the broad categories of leader and manager, but anyone who has done the job knows there is more to it than that. The middle school principal has myriad roles and duties which fluctuate, often daily, depending on the situation at hand. As principal, you act as:

Facilitator	Mediator	Negotiator
Decision Maker	Participant	Delegator
Motivator	Evaluator	Doer
Coordinator	Director	Observer
Follower	Listener	Consensus Builder
Crisis Strategist	Arbitrator	Problem Solver
Risk taker	Entrepreneur	Promoter
Politician	Parent	Organizer
Poet	Engineer	Architect

If you limit your roles, you also limit your ability to respond. If you define your repertoire of roles broadly, you can more flexibly respond to the varying needs of individuals and teams in the school. Reflecting on those roles which you readily assume and those you could assume will open up a new way of looking at your position and allow you to step outside normal limits. Defining your roles broadly will help you get out of the way so others can assume leadership positions too.

Providing the needed leadership to work effectively with interdisciplinary teams on the outside begins with a critical and reflective look on the inside. In looking inside, you create a composition that begins on the right note. My impression is that most people either skip this step entirely, or realize too late that developing self-awareness is important. Given the pressures to get the job done, many dive in head first before making sure they are in the deep end of the pool. Knowing yourself and your stuff, recognizing that you need to learn but that there will always be more to know, responding flexibly with a broad array of roles because you have listened to the voices in the school, will help you approach your role with a firm foundation. With a teaming mentality, you can then begin to develop a framework for action as interdisciplinary teams in the school begin to develop and grow.

The framework

George has identified four stages, or life phases, through which interdisciplinary teams tend to progress in their developmental process: organizational, community, teamed instruction, and governmental (George, 1982/1992;

Plodzik & George, 1989). There are, however, other authors (see for example Erb & Doda, 1989) who have identified different developmental stages. Knowing what typically happens at each phase can help the middle school administrator better know how to relate to each team and to determine the responses which will most effectively promote growth. "The principal can facilitate or frustrate the growth of the team, depending on whether he or she understands the phases through which teams grow..." (George, 1982/1992, p. 141).

Working with interdisciplinary teams in the middle school, however, can be a lot like herding cats. Not everyone will want to go where you think they should, when you think they ought to go, and in the manner that you might think best. Teams, in this regard, are a lot like cats. Each team develops its own unique personality and requires specialized treatment. While it would be much tidier if teams would all progress at the same rate, like young adolescent learners, they tend to move through these developmental phases in their own time and at their own pace. If you expect rocky terrain, yet can refrain from bulldozing, teams will more likely be able to fully realize their full potential and move through all four phases rather than becoming fixated at a beginning stage.

In addition to understanding the developmental stages in the life of an interdisciplinary team, it is important for the principal to have a framework for responding to the needs of the team at each phase. As a leader it can sometimes be truly hard to imagine why people do the things they do. And when they get into groups, it can become even more perplexing. Others' behavior, attitudes, and style can seem almost foreign at times and making sense out of it all can often be problematic. "Whenever others' actions seem to make no sense, it is worth asking whether you and they are using different frames" (Bolman & Deal, 1991, p. 325).

Understanding organizations, how they function, and how and why people in them act as they do is a complex study, and certainly one which is too extensive for full review here. Schools are organizations, however, so having a framework for better understanding what goes on there is worthy of some discussion.

Major schools of organizational thought have been consolidated into four perspectives, or frames (Bolman & Deal, 1991).

> *Frames are both windows on the world and lenses that*
> *bring the world into focus....The truly effective manager and*
> *leader will need multiple [frames], the skill to use each of*
> *them, and the wisdom to match frames to situations.* (p. 11-12)

When leaders fail to view the context in which they work from multiple vantage points, they are less able to deal with the wide variety of issues they encounter, and less able to understand the wide range of behaviors, attitudes, and styles of others in the organization.

The *structural, human resource, political,* and *symbolic* frames defined by Bolman and Deal (1991) are based on the four major schools of organizational theory and research. Each has a distinct set of assumptions and propositions, strengths and weaknesses, interpretations and applications. The following summaries, adapted from *Reframing Organizations* (Bolman & Deal, 1991), provide an introduction for the middle school administrator on the various vantage points available for looking at the school and its teams (Figure 1).

The *structural* frame emphasizes the division of labor, specialization of tasks, formal roles and responsibilities, policies, structures, and procedures in the organization. Line-staff relationships are detailed on charts which outline the chain of command, communication channels, and decision makers. From this vantage point, people exist to serve organizations, where goals are clearly articulated as the driving force. When things do not work, restructuring or reorganization is the prescribed remedy.

The *human resource* frame emphasizes individual and group needs, interaction, and involvement. Individuals bring their feelings, strengths, limitations, and needs to the workplace, along with a capacity to both learn new things and fervently hold on to the old. From this vantage point, organizations exist to serve people, and effectiveness is enhanced when organizations are designed to fit the needs of its people rather than the other way around. When things do not work, finding an organizational form that enables people to get the job done while feeling good about what they do is the prescribed remedy.

The *political* frame views organizations as places where coalitions form over special interests to compete for limited resources and power. Conflict is inevitable from this vantage point, and negotiation, bargaining, coercion, and compromise are all seen as part of the reality of working in an organization. When things do not work, power is concentrated in the wrong places or distributed so widely that nothing gets done. The remedy calls for political skill in bringing people together on fair playing fields where differences can be aired and new agreements reached.

The *symbolic* frame departs from the rational, logical perspective of the preceding frames. It describes the rituals, ceremonies, stories, myths, symbols, and players as pieces which build the culture of the organization.

FIGURE 1

Multiple Perspectives on the Administrator's Role in the Life Phases of Interdisciplinary Teams

	Preliminary Phase	Organizational & Community Phases	Teamed Instruction & Governmental Phases
√ **Structural Frame**	Organize the planning team Determine mission & goals Establish needed policies Develop supportive structures Outline roles & responsibilities	Carefully organize team membership Encourage team mission & goals Clarify team roles & responsibilities Establish expected procedures Use curriculum as organizing principle	Remove bureaucratic barriers Provide technical data Use multiple indicators of success Define shared governance Design leadership structures
√ **Human Resource Frame**	Communicate effectively & often Determine individual & group needs Facilitate active involvement Provide needs-responsive inservice Attend to the affective needs of staff	Build a teaming mentality Administer personal inventories Encourage open dialogue Develop group maintenance processes Provide needs-responsive inservice	Acknowledge feelings Nurture risk-takers Reshuffle with caution Provide needs-responsive inservice Empower others for leadership
√ **Political Frame**	Expect conflict Identify important stakeholders Build networks & coalitions Secure needed resources Build power base	Allocate needed resources Distribute power brokers Mediate erupting conflicts Create fair arenas Nurture external support	Broaden base of support Increase resources to teams Expect controversy Beware the floating flotsam Horse-trade to keep momentum
√ **Symbolic Frame**	Identify core values Provide passionate inspiration Tell illustrative stories Embrace the rites of mourning Create new school symbols	Identify the actors Facilitate team identification Develop team rituals Promote team storytelling Celebrate successes	Be visible & available Promote humor & play Practice what you preach Energize through ritual & ceremony Help the school find its soul

From this vantage point, the organization is a stage where actors play their parts, tell their stories, and use their symbols, rituals, and ceremonies to provide meaning and cohesiveness. When problems occur, improvements are made by rebuilding the culture through inspiration and symbolism.

"Each of these frames has its own vision or image of reality. Only when [leaders] can look through all four are they likely to appreciate the depth and complexity of organizational life" (Bolman & Deal, 1991, p. 16).

Given the complexities associated with working with interdisciplinary teams in the middle school, it seems reasonable then to use this multi-framed approach to identify strategies which could facilitate the development of interdisciplinary teams as they progress through the stages in their life process.

Getting ready for teaming: The preliminaries

If you are getting ready to work with interdisciplinary teams, your school has made a commitment to fundamentally change the way it is organized, how it operates, and what happens in it. "Of the many suggestions offered for reforming American public education in the 1990s, team organization is one of the most powerful" (Erb & Doda, 1989, p. 13). In order to capitalize on the potential inherent in the teaming process, some preliminary steps are needed.

From the structural frame
    √ Organize the planning team
    √ Determine mission and goals
    √ Established needed policies
    √ Develop supportive structures
    √ Outline roles and responsibilities

People will need a sense of structure as you begin to plan for and implement interdisciplinary teaming in the school. Structures increase predictability and provide assurances that the change has been well thought out and developed. Change is risky and as people travel new ground they will need to know how decisions will be made, who will make them, and what impact decisions will have on their daily life.

The need for careful and thorough planning for the implementation of middle school concepts, including interdisciplinary teaming, has been well documented (see for example, Williamson & Johnston, 1991). Collaboration early enhances the commitment from key constituency groups and provides

the school with the benefit of a wide variety of perspectives and talents.
At this stage, data that support the need for the change should be gathered
and shared. National as well as local information and facts provide the basis
for data-based decision making.

In addition to an overall plan which details how and when interdisciplinary
teaming will be implemented in the school, a clear and driving mission
statement based on the developmental needs of young adolescents needs to
be developed to guide the process. "Developing a mission statement is one of
the essential early planning activities" (Williamson & Johnston, 1991, p. 22).
The mission, when developed as a joint venture with staff and community,
reflects the shared values of the school. From the mission statement, specific
goals, objectives, activities, and timelines can emerge. Expectations, clearly
defined, will set the stage for a more productive transition.

Equally important are the decisions related to district and school policies,
rules, regulations, and standards that can either support or hinder the school's
efforts to organize teams. The type of involvement needed at the district level
will be dependent on the situation; however, expectations from the district
will need to be clarified so the school will better understand the parameters in
which it must work (Williamson & Johnston, 1991). Of particular importance
will be the degree of freedom allowed the school in the development of
curriculum and instruction appropriate for young adolescents. District and
school policies need to be linked, and if negotiated contracts are in place,
these too will need to be reviewed so that violations do not occur. School
policies, rules, and procedures need to be aligned with district expectations,
rooted in mission and goals, and communicated clearly through appropriate
handbooks, policy documents, and standard operating procedure manuals.

Supportive organizational structures then need to be designed that support
the mission and goals, and are in line with established policies and procedures. For example, a flexible block-of-time master schedule and common
planning time for interdisciplinary teams have become trademarks of effective middle schools (George, Stevenson, Thomason, & Beane, 1992). Typically, this results in a bell-free school so that teams can take full advantage of
the flexibility inherent in the schedule. Decisions need to be made about how
the facility will be utilized to maximize teaming, where team meetings will
occur, and how common areas in the school, such as the media center, library,
cafeteria, and auditorium, will be used. How teams will be organized and
who will be on each team will be important decisions, and much will need to
be considered in making this determination (Erb & Doda, 1989). It will also
be important to establish a building budgetary process that will support

school and team activities if current procedures are not aligned with the goals of the school.

An outline of specific roles for individuals in the school, along with a description of responsibilities associated with each role, will further clarify expectations. What exactly is expected of the principal? assistant principal? counselor? team leader? team members? support staff? What are the lines of communication between and among individuals and teams in the school? What is the expected chain of command? How will decisions be made? by whom? when? And if decision making is to be shared, how will human and material resources be allocated to facilitate this process?

From the human resource frame
   √ Communicate effectively and often
   √ Determine individual and group needs
   √ Facilitate active involvement
   √ Provide needs-responsive inservice programs
   √ Attend to the affective needs of staff

"Organizations and people depend on one another" (Bolman & Deal, 1991, p. 130). From the human resource perspective, the middle school administrator would focus on finding ways to match the school's needs with individual's needs so that both will benefit. Understanding and accepting the human condition and the resultant economic, personal, and social needs of staff members will communicate a sincere desire to establish a nurturing and caring work environment. People need acceptance and fulfillment and can become subversive and destructive when they feel disenchanted by their treatment in the school.

How and when you communicate as an administrator will informally send the message that you see staff members as whole human beings, capable of meeting and even rising above what is expected of them. Taking time at the onset to meet with individuals and groups to build and establish personal and professional relationships will reap benefits later when issues arise that may be uncomfortable or unpleasant. Accepting that everyone has different needs and placing a priority on finding out what they are will send the message that you accept their uniqueness. Actively involving staff in meaningful ways based on their needs will not only promote esprit de corps but will also demonstrate your recognition that people need to have opportunities to develop to their maximum potential.

As you come to know the needs of individuals and groups in the school, you can then more effectively work together to develop appropriate professional development activities. It is quite common for schools to design staff development for the transition process (Clark & Clark, 1987) and typically as part of this plan teachers visit other middle schools, share and discuss middle level literature and research, and attend sessions on young adolescent characteristics, teaming, advisory, curriculum, instructional strategies, and the change process. A "boiler plate" approach used in other schools, however, might not necessarily meet the specific needs identified in your school. Making your staff development program needs responsive, allowing for differentiated options which accommodate varying needs and learning styles, not only increases the likelihood that the activities will be meaningful, but also models for teachers what you hope they do for their students.

Likewise, when you provide for the affective as well as the cognitive needs of staff members as they prepare to team, you model the importance of integrating both in the learning process. Schools which have taken time to not only learn new content, but have also provided opportunities for individuals to express their feelings about the content, have been better able to heighten understanding and acceptance of what it means on a personal level to change (Polite, 1993). And since change can often be hard, painful, and slow, the efforts you make to ease the way for staff members will pay dividends when they begin teaming and can transfer their new insights to their students.

From the political frame
    √ Expect conflict
    √ Identify important stakeholders
    √ Build networks & coalitions
    √ Secure needed resources
    √ Build a power base

Organizations are "…alive and screaming political arenas that have a complex variety of individual and group interests" (Bolman & Deal, 1991, p. 186). The administrator who does not recognize this can unfortunately be easily consumed. Looking at the school through the political frame helps the administrator remember that conflict in the school will be inevitable given that everyone wants what they want but there are rarely enough resources to go around. So groups get together around special interests to round up enough clout to get their agenda met. The administrator needs to create arenas where fair negotiations can result in acceptable compromises. School politics do not have to be dirty, but they have to be.

In the political frame, you will need supportive networks and coalitions to move ahead with plans to implement interdisciplinary teams. "The first task in building networks and coalitions is to figure out whose help you need" (Bolman & Deal, 1991, p. 211). The identification of major stakeholders early in the transition process will allow you to develop relationships with them so they can support teaming rather than oppose it. Your first major stakeholders will be the superintendent and appropriate central office personnel. How and when members of the Board of Education become involved in the process will depend largely on the district context. However, you will need to know these key players are in your corner as you proceed with changes in the school. Working with the district curriculum coordinator will be of particular value. You will need a knowledgeable and supportive curriculum coordinator in your corner, one who is able to negotiate curriculum policies which promote integrated curriculum and active, hands-on instructional practices. Parents too should be included so that they too can become part of the supportive network for change. Knowing who the other power players are both in the school and community will give you access to a network that will eventually mobilize its resources one way or another anyway, so getting them on your side early will reduce the chance for what could later become a battle between groups with competing interests. Put simply, to get done what you need to get done, you need allies. Building the necessary relationships to make others your allies will take time, effort, and energy. You can either put the time in up front to build supportive coalitions, or spend it later dealing with the fallout.

Shoring up the needed human and financial resources for the transition process becomes part and parcel of the coalition building process. Different people have access to different resources; some have money, others have time. Some have power, others have influence. And still others have the authority to make decisions that you need to go in your favor. If you are in a unit district, often overlooked allies in the transition process are the high school and elementary administrators. If your district is facing the common dilemma of declining financial resources, their support will be particularly important. Shared staff, for example, can become problematic when you begin to build a flexible block master schedule. You need to have the cooperation of other administrators in order to have access to these staff members when you need them, and bitter fights can ensue if your administrative colleagues in the district do not understand the complexities of building a flexible block schedule. Likewise, it is often necessary to add staff members when reorganizing into teams to provide the diversity in program and team planning time so critical for success. If money is tight, you can bet that other administrators will be in there fighting for their agendas, so you will need to muster all of your political savvy to negotiate effectively to achieve your goals.

Building a base of power can be risky business, yet without it little can be done. As the administrator you already have some power in the authority vested in your position, but it is rarely enough to get the job done. Anyone who has spent anytime in a school knows that power is often widely distributed and can come in various forms. Some teachers, for example, have power due to their reputations, knowledge, or expertise. Others have charisma, or access to resources, or are skilled in ways that are valued by others giving them power and prestige (French & Raven, 1959). Likewise, parents and community members may have power through their networks or positions. You will need to not only assess how power is distributed inside and outside of the school, but you will also need to clarify what the preferences are of those in power related to the proposed changes and how they intend to mobilize that power to get what they want.

"The question is not whether organizations will have politics, but what kind of politics they will have" (Bolman & Deal, 1991, p. 223). As you begin to implement interdisciplinary teams in the school, you will stir the political waters. And if you are not careful, those waters could get muddy. They don't have to. "Constructive politics is a possibility" (Bolman & Deal, 1991, p. 204), and a necessary possibility if teaming is to be successfully implemented in your school.

From the symbolic frame
- √ Identify core values
- √ Provide passionate inspiration
- √ Tell illustrative stories
- √ Embrace the rites of mourning
- √ Create new school symbols

Up to this point, the preliminary steps in the transition process have been, for the most part, fairly rational, logical, and linear. Often our common sense tells us that structure, people, and power have to be considered when moving in a new direction. But from the vantage point of the symbolic frame, things do not always look so neat and orderly.

> *The symbolic frame centers on the concepts of meaning, belief, and faith. Human beings have always found life bewildering. Events often cannot be explained....Circumstances cannot always be controlled.... Contradictions often cannot be reconciled.*   — Bolman & Deal, 1991, p. 253

So people find meaning in their lives through symbols which help them understand what otherwise does not make sense.

In schools, this is quite evident. American education has traditions, practices, and a rich history that even Rip Van Winkle would recognize were he to wake up today. Moving from a traditional junior high school to a middle school with interdisciplinary teams means that you are breaking away from traditional practice to something quite different. And to do this, you need some glue to hold everything together.

While the development of a mission statement, goals, and objectives in the planning process can be viewed logically through the structural frame, it can also be viewed through the lens of symbolism to see that it can be even more powerful than that. A mission statement represents the core values that are shared by those involved with the school and gives people faith that they are going somewhere together rather than alone. The importance of a common mission can be elevated to a higher status if instead of letting it becoming a dusty document on the shelf, you use it to give meaning to people as they risk the rough terrain of change. One way to translate the mission of the school into a symbolic representation of shared values is to create a school-wide theme to use at the preliminary stages of implementation. Themes schools have used, such as "We're on the move", "Kids come first, second, and third", "Change isn't easy but our students are worth it", or "Hang on to your hats...We're going places" can give people a sense of unity to reduce the feelings of uncertainty that may emerge as people confront new experiences.

With a rallying point of mission and theme, you can then provide the passionate inspiration that will generate faith in the school's ability to implement something new. Like actions in the other three frames, this too can be risky business. You can fall flat on your face if you misread the underlying values people revere and you could end up looking rather the fool if you are passionate about things to which they have no connection. By starting with the best of the school's rich traditions and values, you provide a symbolic link between what has been and what is to be. Your stories can interweave examples of successful middle schools and dynamic teams outside the school with tales of your own school's rich heritage so that you can begin to alter beliefs about what is possible. With passion, communicate a vision of the school's "unique capabilities and mission" (Bolman & Deal, 1991, p. 364), so you can inspire others to begin to see themselves that way as well.

"From a symbolic perspective, transition rituals must accompany significant organizational change" (Bolman and Deal, 1991, p. 391). As people in the school begin to embrace changes inherent in the adoption of a middle school philosophy, they naturally go through stages of grief and will need to mourn the loss of what has been. As with any mourning process, there are stages that the school will move through in order to let go of the past and embrace a new future (Bolman & Deal, 1991). One school which understood this need held a summer retreat prior to implementing interdisciplinary teams and included activities which promoted a healthy opportunity for staff members to mourn. Each teacher had a poster with his or her name at the top. For 30 minutes, each took a marker and wrote compliments to each other on the posters about who they were and what they had accomplished in the past. When they were finished, each stood by their own poster, and amidst tears, they said good-bye to their "old" school and reminded one another that they would be taking who they had been with them into their "new" school. Some reported that they have kept their posters during their first year of teaming as a reminder that they are competent professionals, admired by their colleagues, and capable of meeting the many challenges of change.

As people move through the mourning process and begin to let go of the past, they will need new symbols, rituals, and ceremonies to reduce the ambiguity and uncertainty of an untried future. Learning to work together in teams rather than in isolated classrooms can be a frightening experience. The closing of the classroom door has been symbolic of the autonomy of the teacher, and when those doors are opened and teachers are challenged to learn and work together, they can often feel the overwhelming need to slam the door shut again. The transition planning process and documents themselves can be used as powerful symbols that there is a certain path that has been forged and that all will be well if those plans are followed. Likewise, stopping to celebrate along the way will not only help provide assurances that you know where you are going, but that you are getting there. Schools have used planning meetings, retreats, inservice and committee meetings, open house, orientation sessions, and presentations of progress to the Board of Education as rituals which renew faith in the school's new venture. Ceremonies which provide recognition for both accomplishment as well as effort can infuse newfound energy into the process. "Schools with records of success report spending time and money on whole faculty fellowship" (Doda, George & McEwin, 1987, p. 4), and they end up with symbols, rituals, and ceremonies that become part of their new tradition.

Using the structural, human resource, political, and symbolic frames at the preliminary stages can remind the middle school administrator of the numerous issues which need attention prior to the implementation of interdisciplinary teams. Just as students are asked to do their homework, you too must do yours. Using a multi-framed approach to assess what needs to be done before teaming begins will provide greater assurance that you are starting off on solid ground. And once teaming begins, you will need to continue to look through various lenses to promote team growth and development.

Let the teaming begin: Early phases in the life of a team

The *organizational* and *community* stages in the life of a team represent the early phases in their development. The organizational phase represents a time when teachers begin to see the potential of teaming and generally, a high level of enthusiasm is characteristic. The same teachers and students begin to learn the fundamentals of collaborative work. As they feel more comfortable working together, teams enter the community stage and begin to identify with their group. A spirit of unity develops and they take pride in their uniqueness and successes. Parents too will begin to acknowledge the changes taking place at the school, especially if teams have made efforts to make them a part of the life of the team (George, 1982/1992). Using a multi-framed approach at these early stages, the administrator can see a variety of strategies to support and encourage team success.

From the structural frame
 √ Carefully organize team membership
 √ Encourage team mission & goals
 √ Clarify team roles & responsibilities
 √ Establish expected procedures
 √ Use curriculum as organizing principle

"Long before the first team meetings take place, careful planning must occur to lay the foundation for successful teaming" (Erb & Doda, 1989, p. 14). Consideration should be given so that both the core teams (teachers of language arts, math, science, social studies) and encore teams (teachers of the unified arts, typically including such areas as home economics, industrial arts, technology, physical education, fine arts, foreign language) are organized to meet the goals of the school. Needed considerations in determining team membership have been well defined (see for example, Erb & Doda, 1989, p.14-15). Thought needs to be given not only to legal issues (licensure and qualifications of staff members), but also to personal issues (individual preferences, balance, diversity). Often, the administrator is faced with the dilemma of placing on teams one or two staff members with whom nobody seems to be compatible. From the structural perspective, preestablished policies and procedures could help make the appropriate determination. For example, if you have already determined that teams need diverse characteristics, to include both inexperienced and veteran teachers, elementary and secondary licensed members, and a balance of gender and race, then your decision can be made based on these criteria. The wise administrator knows, however, that the structural frame alone is not enough to use in making this important decision. Issues related to the human resource frame (personal style, strengths and weaknesses of individuals), political frame (power players, proponents vs. opponents of teaming), and the symbolic frame (history and reputation) need to also be considered.

Just as the development of a mission statement, goals, objectives, and timelines are important for the school as a whole, teams need to do the same thing. Team mission statements and goals should link directly to the district and school documents, and once developed, can then be shared with students and parents through appropriate team handbooks and materials. Given that most teams lack experience in this type of activity, your involvement in this process may not only be instructive, but necessary. While some freedom and flexibility should be given to teams to set their own course, you need to be sure that they are headed in the right direction. Trying to redirect the course of a misguided team later in their development could hinder growth and lead to disintegration. Carefully set parameters early that provide linkages to district and school mission and goals so teams will come to understand the need for a careful balance between autonomy and cohesiveness.

Specific titles and roles for members of the interdisciplinary teams define expectations and responsibilities. While team job descriptions vary, a typical team has a designated team leader that is either assigned, elected by the team, or a volunteer. Leaving this designation to chance at the early stages is risky, and having an established list of qualifications for determining the team leader may be helpful. This position can rotate on a yearly, semester, or even monthly or weekly basis, but regardless of the length of term, this person is responsible for the formal leadership of the team. Often team leaders set agendas for team planning time and conduct the meetings, serve as a liaison to a school-wide team leader committee, and lead the team towards accomplishments of its goals. Likewise, team members generally have specified job descriptions which outline expectations for their role on the team. Like cooperative learning groups, each member is given a specific role to assume in the group, and each has specific responsibilities for tasks which need to be accomplished (Erb & Doda, 1989). At the organizational phase of the life of the team, members need to be clear about what is expected and what each is to do. As teams mature, they can more easily determine for themselves what roles are needed because they will have learned through experience the value of this process.

Linking the core and encore teams in the school to support personnel and programs requires that coordinating structures be in place to outline communication and decision-making channels. At the early stages, teams are generally more concerned with intrateam communication, decision making, and dynamics than they are with linking to others in the school. But as they grow and mature, they will need to be able to identify the procedures which will link them directly with other teams to solve broader student and school problems.

At the early stages, however, the more important procedures to clarify are those that will promote effective and efficient use of team planning time. Teams will need to know expectations for the use of team planning time and be held accountable for making productive use of it (see for example, Merenbloom, 1991). Many schools develop team meeting agendas; notebooks for team members; strategies for maintaining team minutes; forms for student and parent conferences held during team planning time; and forms to organize team homework, test schedules, projects, and activities (see for example, Erb & Doda, 1989). In addition, many teams develop student behavior management, homework, absence and tardy policies which have been coordinated with district and school policies. These tools help teams get organized and focused, communicate expectations, and provide a sense of security for the novice team. As the team matures, they can adapt forms and procedures as needed; however, if you ask them to do that too early, teams can quickly fall apart, find the teaming process too cumbersome, and retreat to the isolation of their individual classrooms.

As part of the process for establishing expected procedures, policies, roles, and responsibilities, set the expectation that the organization of teams in the school in the first place was prompted by the need for reform in the process of teaching and learning, not in the process of schooling. "The central organizing determinant of the school should be the curriculum" (Hawkins & Graham, 1994, p. 39). While it will be important to analyze the use of curriculum as the central organizing principle in the school from all four frames, from the structural perspective, it should be firmly embedded in the structures, expectations, policies, and procedures of the school from the onset (Lounsbury, 1992a). The roots of the interdisciplinary team should be planted in the knowledge of the developmental characteristics of young adolescents. And while it may already be "old hat" to talk about the social, emotional,

physical, and intellectual needs of students, their needs are still the driving
force for middle grades reform. The hat may be old, but it still fits. And in
veteran middle schools when teachers say things like, "We've already
covered the characteristics of young adolescents. We don't need to do that
again, do we?", it becomes clear that they need to find their roots again. To
communicate this message clearly, one school used the characteristics of
students in all team documents. Their mission, goals, forms, and policies all
included the development needs of kids and their implications for practice. A
monthly team evaluation form was used to be sure they stayed on target and
when they got off course, they quickly knew how to get back on it. They
knew at the beginning they were teaming to change the teaching and learning
process, and not simply to make cosmetic changes in how the school looked.
Policies at the district, school, and team levels should establish curriculum as
the central organizing principle for the transition process, and this vision
should be clearly communicated in all that you say and do.

From the human resource frame
√ Build a teaming mentality
√ Administer personal inventories
√ Encourage open dialogue
√ Develop group maintenance processes
√ Provide needs-responsive inservice

Just as many administrators often dive into the transition process without
first developing a teaming mentality, so too do members of the staff if they
are not encouraged to first take a look at who they are, what they need and
believe, and how they will fit into the school and the team. Using the "five
step process" previously outlined, plan reflection and analysis time for staff
members to engage in this process. Encourage each person to develop his or
her own personal mission statement. If each person first identifies their own
guiding principles, they can lay them on the table when it comes time to
develop a mission with their teammates. If each person can identify their own
knowledge base, strengths and weaknesses, and can share these with one
another, they will be better prepared to work as a team.

The traditional role of the teacher as "sage on the stage" needs to be more
broadly defined as "guide on the side" in a teamed middle school
(Cummings, 1991). Just as your role as an administrator varies, so too does
the role of the middle level teacher. Staff members need to identify the
numerous roles they need and have opportunities to acquire the knowledge
and skill to use them. For example, as an advisor, the middle level teacher

builds relationships with students, serves as their advocate, and strengthens home-school partnerships. Assuming this new role can be quite challenging for many teachers and having time to develop new skills and understandings will be needed (Bergmann & Baxter, 1983). Teachers will also need time to reflect on which voices they will need to hear and how to listen and respond effectively to do their job. The time you spend working with staff members to develop a teaming mentality may seem unnecessary at first. The pressures to get underway will mount and you and your staff may feel pushed to act. However, if you consider building a teaming mentality as an important action in the process, you will lay the foundation for more productive work relationships, and you will find, as many schools have, that the time is well spent.

The use of inventories and instruments to identify individual style and preference has become more common as schools prepare to team (see for example, Erb & Doda, 1989; Hawkins & Graham, 1994). The use of the personality inventories, such as the *Myers Briggs Type Indicator* (Myers & Briggs, 1976), or the *Keirsey Temperament Sorter* (Keirsey & Bates, 1984), can help staff members know themselves better and understand and accept one another. Teacher learning and teaching styles inventories, such as the *Dunn & Dunn Profile* (Dunn & Dunn, 1985) or Kolb's *Learning Style Inventory* (1976), are also helpful tools in the self-exploration process and can support teams as they grow through the organizational to community phase. Promoting the acceptance of diversity on the team helps teachers come to see that they need not be clones of one another to be successful and that the team is actually better served when members are different and diverse. This translates into a deeper acceptance that students are diverse and should also be prized for their uniqueness. Sharing information from personal mission statements and personality or learning styles inventories can open up dialogue on the team. If you model a willingness to be open yourself by participating in activities alongside the staff and attend team meetings on a regular basis, you can facilitate team solidification. If you work directly with each team at the early stages, you will nurture the cohesiveness on the team and in the school. In your role as coach, mentor, and model, you can influence the process without disabling the team by taking over leadership. You can help them put issues of concern on the table early so they will not come up later to eat away at the fabric of the team.

Regardless of the structure we place on groups by outlining goals, formal roles, and procedures, what is known about group dynamics tells us that an informal process will also emerge (see for example, Gorton, 1983). At their early stages, teams may need some help determining appropriate process or maintenance skills and strategies to determine "how" the group will work. Issues related to how the team will make decisions, resolve conflict, and deal with resistance and incompatibility need to be articulated before problems arise. Waiting for a crisis when emotions can run high is the wrong time to try to figure out the best way to deal with problems. If you anticipate that problems will eventually surface and proactively help the team derive possible solutions, they will be better able to move through their problems and continue to grow.

Ongoing, needs-responsive inservice programs should emerge from the issues related to initial implementation. At the organizational and community stages, teams need to be empowered not only with continuous content information related to middle grades education, but also with the knowledge and skills they need to work together. Topics, such as writing a personal and team mission statement, group dynamics, conflict resolution, decision making, and consensus building could also be included in the plan. By assessing faculty needs and gathering impressions through your involvement with teams, you will be able to develop with staff appropriate and diverse activities for professional development.

From the political frame
  √ Allocate needed resources
  √ Distribute power brokers
  √ Mediate erupting conflict
  √ Create fair arenas
  √ Nurture external support

Regardless of the structural or human emphasis you place on enhancing team development in the early stages, political realities will surface. "[The political frame] acknowledges the existence and importance of human and group needs but focuses on situations of scarce resources and incompatible preferences where different needs collide" (Bolman & Deal, 1991, p. 193). And when people get together on a team, you can count on some collisions.

Because of the focus on scarce resources in the political frame, you will need to attend to the dispersement of resources and often will have to arbitrate between equally important competing demands. While teams will not necessarily all need the same resources at the same time, they will all need some, and they will mobilize their power if they feel they have been overlooked in the allocation process. A structural response might direct you to develop policies which specify how resources will be distributed assuming that one way is better than another for the school as a whole. A human resource response might focus on finding forums for people to come together to discuss their needs and find a solution that would allow everyone to win. From the political perspective, you might want to assess how power is distributed and how those power brokers are likely to take action to get what they want.

Conflict can also erupt as individuals on teams confront change on a personal level. Teams will not always agree on how discipline should be handled, what the expectations for students should be, or on how they should define their new roles. In dealing with these conflicts, one solution is not necessarily better than another from the political perspective as long as a fair playing field is provided for the negotiation process that is likely to ensue.

Establishing a fair playing field with rules and referees prevents the bargaining process from deteriorating into a bloody battle where long lasting damage can be done by people wielding their power to get what they want. In the bargaining process, it is often not what is gained that is the issue, but what is lost. And if what is lost is more important to a team or individual than what they won, you can be sure they will be heard from again. The changes that teams are experiencing will not benefit everyone equally at the same time. They will need opportunities to air differences without fear of reprisal so that new agreements can be reached that are palatable to all involved. Your role will often be that of referee, though in some schools the informal leadership in the school gives this role to someone else. Like a sports referee, however, that role is a critical one in making sure the rules of the game are well established and that they are followed. If you underestimate the power of the political frame, you can easily get burned, because for certain there will be those in the school who do not.

Cultivating external support will not only be necessary at the preliminary stage, but should continue as an important priority as teams move through the early stages of development. Regional, state, and local networks can link the school with others who are facing similar challenges. Involvement in professional associations interested in middle level education can give you and your staff access to valuable information and provide opportunities for shared problem solving. Collaboration with area colleges and universities can also enhance your base of support. In one area, for example, the local university sponsored a "Middle Level Educators' Network" so that teachers and administrators could come together monthly to discuss their common problems and share their experiences with one another. Schools at various stages of the transition process were thereby linked to one another giving them an external network to support the internal changes being made back home.

From the symbolic frame
- √ Identify the actors
- √ Facilitate team identification
- √ Develop team rituals
- √ Promote team storytelling
- √ Celebrate successes

In the symbolic frame, actors have a part to play in the school as theater. As powerful as formal roles and identification can be, attending also to the informal or symbolic roles individuals play will provide important insights. The *priest or priestess*, *historian*, *gossip*, *hero or heroine*, *mother or father superior* in the school hear confessions and minister, remind others of their past, spread information, establish standards, and keep order (Bolman & Deal, 1991). Knowing who plays these parts can help you better understand the culture of the school, how and if it is changing, and where problems might arise during the process. For example, in one school the priestess "gave blessings" to struggling team members, listened when they needed to complain, understood when they made mistakes, and helped to promote new ceremonies which celebrated their successes. She had a part and she played it well. And in doing so, she was instrumental in facilitating team development. Her efforts were encouraged and supported by the administrator, who was wise enough to know that she played an important part in keeping things together. Individuals who hold informal roles in the school can help keep the transition running smoothly or they can derail it. Working with and through these people early on can help promote a culture which will be needed to support more substantive changes later in the process.

"How someone becomes a group member is important" (Bolman & Deal, 1991, p. 293), so developing rituals for staff and student orientation into the school and team should be developed. Rituals for joining a group could be as simple as organizing a "signing up" activity to give individuals a chance to declare their commitment to the school or to the team. Schools have typically engaged in such activities when they send home the school discipline plan for parents and students to sign as a symbol of their willingness to adhere to policy, yet stop short of using the same strategy to build school and team cohesiveness. Giving people a chance to pledge their support can be a powerful way of engaging them to give their best efforts so that the school and team can prosper and grow.

Building team identification is yet another aspect of team development at the early stages (see for example, Doda, 1992). Both teachers and students on the team need to feel a sense of belonging, and teams can promote this by developing symbols, rituals, and ceremonies of their own. Promoting the development of symbols, such as a team name, logo, and motto can develop unity. Many schools have team shirts, hats, buttons, and banners to further identify membership on the team. Whole team meetings, field trips, and projects can be the rituals which teams use to create meaning. Ceremonies, such as team birthday parties or student and parent recognition programs, provide places for the team to come together to play and celebrate. These activities are valuable not only because they promote a sense of camaraderie and fellowship, but also because they symbolize the emerging culture of teaming. Teams in the early stages may need your support and assistance in finding ways to build identity and to understand why efforts to do so are valuable.

As teams begin to move into the community stage, they will have accumulated stories of "the way we do things around here" which can become part of the oral tradition of teaming in the school (Bolman & Deal, 1991). When you model storytelling as a way to build culture, you can help teams learn to use storytelling as a tool of their own. Through storytelling, teams will begin to develop their own language that further highlights their uniqueness. One team, for example, used nicknames for one another that had emerged from their team meetings. These were special names they had created for each other based on their early experiences, yet years later they still used their nicknames for one another. Their nicknames had become part of their team vocabulary as symbols of their shared history.

Schools that do not wait until the end of the first year of teaming to stop and celebrate their achievements have a head start on building a positive school culture. Some schools experience a period of letdown after the first semester of teaming. The honeymoon is over and the real work of teaming is underway. At this point, teachers may need recognition for their efforts and accomplishments. One school had an end of semester party in the school. They toured the building together to visit each team's area, where teachers shared something they had done of which they were especially proud. The superintendent was invited and gave each team a flower to symbolize pride in their hard work. Needless to say, those teams were energized and ready to continue. Each school will have its own unique needs and timetable, so you will need to read the vibrations in your school to know when its time to stop and celebrate success.

Let the teaming continue: Later phases in the life of a team

The *teamed instruction* and *governmental* stages in the life of a team represent the later phases in their development. Time and skill are needed to empower teachers to move into the teamed instruction phase, which is characterized by a move from doing things separately to doing things collaboratively in the areas of curriculum and instruction. Teams plan joint assignments, common projects, and interdisciplinary thematic units across two or more content areas.

> *Research and experience in the area of team organiza-*
> *tion indicate that teachers who successfully negotiate the*
> *first three phases of team life frequently find themselves*
> *motivated to assume more responsibility, professionally, for*
> *the decisions that affect their lives and the school experi-*
> *ences of their students.*   — George, 1982/1992, p. 139

At the governmental phase, fully functioning teams become more actively involved in school decision-making processes so that they can authentically participate in the important decisions in the school (George, 1982/1992).

At these later stages, a multi-framed view of the school can help the administrator see a variety of strategies to support and encourage team development. While it is typical to assume a "hands off" approach as teams mature, they still need support in order to maximize their full potential. "Increasingly it is being recognized that there will be no significant 'restructuring' of schools until reform efforts attack and make fundamental changes in the curriculum of content and the instructional approaches utilized—what and how kids learn" (Lounsbury, 1992a, p.1). It is during these later phases of team development that teachers have the background knowledge, skill, and experience to begin to tackle the crux of the matter, changes in curriculum and instruction. Asking teams to do this too early can be a mistake; but not asking them to do it at all is an even greater one.

From the structural frame
   √ Remove bureaucratic barriers
   √ Provide technical data
   √ Use multiple indicators of success
   √ Define shared governance
   √ Design leadership structures

Learning to work together to change curriculum and instruction requires more than a supportive schedule and common planning time. Bureaucratic barriers standing in the way of change will need to be removed so that more supportive structures can be designed to take their place. As teams begin to take a serious look at the curricula in the school, district policies which allow flexibility will be needed. Your earlier efforts to coordinate district expectations and work with appropriate central office personnel will pay off now. Integrating the middle school curricula is more than just developing one or two interdisciplinary units during the year (Lounsbury, 1992b), so clear goals for curricular and instructional innovation should define expectations.

Likewise, if teams have been burdened with "administrivia" that diverts their time and attention from curricular and instructional issues, then new structures will be needed to take these burdens off their backs. When this became a problem, one school went to their parent organization and asked them to hire a full-time clerical assistant for teachers. Given the thousands of dollars some parent groups can generate, it may be more advantageous for them to allocate their money that way, than to divide it up among individual classrooms who often end up with so little they reap no real benefit. Another school went to the superintendent with a plan to reallocate staffing resources. They replaced a part-time reading teacher with additional clerical assistants for teams; integrated reading across the content areas, developed a community volunteer program to promote reading for pleasure, and made reading achievement a school goal to assure that students previously helped by the part-time reading teacher would not fall through the cracks. While neither of these solutions might work in your school, if you review the structures, policies, and procedures in place you can increase their alignment with school goals and remove unnecessary bureaucratic barriers in the process.

Structures also need to be developed which enhance inter-team communication. As teachers begin to integrate content, core and encore teams will need new ways to connect with each other as it is often difficult for these teachers to find time to work together (Lounsbury, 1992b). Flexible scheduling, team leader meetings, inservice and summer workshops can all help to increase the opportunity for cross-team integration. However, other competing demands will also need to be reduced so that teams are able to give the needed time and attention for instructional planning.

"At critical strategic crossroads, a rational process that focuses on gathering information and carrying out analyses may be exactly what an organization needs" (Bolman & Deal, 1991, p. 325). As teachers begin to let go of traditional content, they will not only need moral support, but will also need technical assurance that the new way is the right way. Evidence which supports curricular innovation should be gathered and shared. Ask, "what information do we have to analyze this situation?" Then provide it. Help teachers understand how to change by providing models for curriculum development (see for example, Beane, 1993a,1993b; Fogarty, 1991; Hawkins & Graham, 1994; Jacobs, 1989) and then expand your data bank to include multiple indicators of success. In addition to norm-referenced testing, authentic assessment tools will be needed which provide additional information on student progress. Performances, exhibitions, and portfolios, for example, can enrich teachers' understanding of what works for students and what does not. Before teachers can realize the potential of their team to impact the teaching and learning process, they will need support and guidance on how this can best be accomplished and technical data to let them know when they're successful.

Designing structures which give teachers the opportunity to become meaningfully involved in building governance has been recommended by the Carnegie Council on Adolescent Development (1989). Shared decision-making models, including school councils, leadership teams, and advisory boards have all been used to include teachers in "school level problem solving and policy development" (Plodzik & George, 1989, p. 15). As structures are designed, initial emphasis placed on clarifying a common definition of what shared governance and decision making mean will establish parameters for the group's work. Although the terms are common, individuals attribute different meanings to them and have different expectations of what it will mean to become involved and what responsibility they will have as a result of their participation.

Hawkins and Graham (1994) recommend the development of three leadership structures in the school to promote shared governance; problem solving groups, long range planning groups, and communication groups. Each group needs a "clearly understood purpose and a designed method of operation including how it will be led, how it will make decisions, and how its meetings will be conducted" (p. 79). You will also need to decide how membership on each group will be determined, length of term, and how groups will interface with each other and the teams. Clearly establishing structures for shared governance which are well articulated and communicated will let everyone in the school know how decisions will be made, who will make them, and how they can be involved.

From the human resource frame
   √ Acknowledge feelings
   √ Nurture risk-takers
   √ Reshuffle with caution

√ Provide needs-responsive inservice experiences

√ Empower others for leadership

"It is well known that teachers can be very successful in resisting a teaching innovation that they do not like" (Bolman & Deal, 1991, p. 236); so motivation and commitment are critical to help teams move into and through the later stages in their development. How teachers feel about curricular change needs to be uncovered. Both on teams and through established inter-team structures, teachers need to spend time talking about their problems and concerns. You may need to facilitate these discussions so they do not deteriorate into group gripe sessions yet allow needed catharsis to occur. Change is risky, awkward, and threatening. If teachers are to be committed to change, they need individual support and encouragement. Some principals have found that having lunch with individual teachers gives them time together to talk through the issues. Others have found it valuable to meet with teams to enhance their motivation. In one school, teams went out to dinner together once a month with the administrator and support staff to talk through their concerns. "School administrators must attend more closely to the interpersonal dimensions of school life as a staff ages" (Evans, 1989, p.12), and those that have find that it pays off for everyone.

Risk takers can be particularly vulnerable, especially at the later stages of team development. In one school, a team that moved quickly into integrated curriculum, was ostracized and ridiculed, although they had not previously related this way with one another. In subtle, but powerful ways, they were being sent the message to "slow down." One teacher in fact made the comment that the team made "everyone else look bad." People do not like to lose face, and if they feel they are, they can wreak interpersonal havoc in the school. One principal gave weekly awards to teachers who had taken a risk on their team. In not every case were these awards given for curricular innovation, yet the activity clearly communicated that going out on the limb a bit to try something new was valued in the school.

At the teamed instruction phase, teachers will be immersed in the work of planning, implementing, and evaluating new curriculum. The work of integration can be labor intensive and team effort and energy can quickly be depleted. If they had doubt about the value of teaming before, that doubt can intensify now. Many schools report that it is at this point that some teams become dysfunctional and often changes are made in team membership as a way of solving the problem. Just as students who are passed from group to group in a cooperative learning classroom soon learn that their lack of cooperation and resistance will result in getting moved around, team members too can learn that being passed around from team to team may keep them from ever having to change. When team membership changes, they start over in their developmental process, even though they may be able to move through the earlier stages more quickly given their prior experience. Administrators should be cautioned about reshuffling teachers on teams too quickly as a way to either help struggling teams or to separate individuals finding it hard to learn to work with their colleagues. It may be better to intervene and help them establish a stronger sense of community rather than to move people around.

While it is important to provide needs-responsive staff development at the early stages of implementation (Clark & Clark, 1987), that practice should be continued as teams enter the later stages. At the teamed instruction and governmental stages, several issues emerge which may be appropriate topics to explore. How to develop integrated curriculum, as well as sessions which help teachers learn how to use active, hands-on instructional practices may be worthy of consideration. Alternative assessment may need to be explored, along with opportunities to learn to read and utilize standardized test scores. Leadership training programs, which include information about the legal parameters of building-level decision making, could help teachers ease into shared governance roles. Process and content issues both need to be addressed in planning for appropriate teacher inservice activities, and administrators might explore the value of a "training for transfer" model which includes opportunities for feedback and follow-up (Joyce & Showers, 1988). Additionally, if one is not already in place, a clinical supervision program could help you work directly with staff to improve instruction (Oliva, 1993).

Needs-responsive staff development should empower teachers with the knowledge and skills they will need for leadership roles on the team and in the school. Until teacher preparation programs provide courses and experiences on shared governance, schools are left with the task of retraining staff members for these new roles. As teachers become active in the decision-making at the school level, you will be able to gather input about what they need to function effectively. Yet in order to move beyond *empowered conformity*, letting teachers make decisions that have already been sanctioned, to *distributed leadership*, recognizing that teacher leaders emerge naturally in the school (see for example Diedrich-Reilly & Zenz, 1993; Grant, 1993; Johnson, 1993: Polite, 1993), you have to give up the traditional view of the top-down hierarchy. Participation increases both morale and productivity (Bolman & Deal, 1991), but if it is to be more than a fad, you have to believe that teachers have the human need and potential for leadership and be willing to help them acquire the knowledge and skill to exercise that potential.

From the political frame
√ Broaden base of support
√ Increase resources to teams
√ Expect controversy
√ Beware the floating flotsam
√ Horse-trade to keep momentum

From the political perspective, teacher empowerment as we know it just does not make sense. When people talk about "sharing power" they obviously do not understand that some people already have it; that it is not something that can be given away; and that all we can really share in "shared-governance" is a common playing field where people with power can negotiate reasonable agreements. You can bargain and swap resources, but power is not a tradable commodity. You can broaden your base of support to get those with power on your side, but they cannot give their power away.

Coalitions and special interest groups can become quite active as teams move into later life stages and confront what it really means to develop a student needs-responsive school. You can build internal alliances, but you will also need external support, especially at the district level where you may need to renegotiate for curricular flexibility and shared governance. Through your involvement in regional, state, and national professional associations and activities, you can tap into broader networks for support. One principal, for example, sought national and state recognition for the school as a way to not only validate the school's agenda, but also to insulate the school from internal district pressure. Skillful public relations strategies were used to get the word out, and once the recognition had been received the district was then hard pressed to force the school to abort an agenda that had brought notoriety to the district and school.

It can sometimes be easier to say something cannot be done, rather than to admit you do not want to do it. Not having enough resources can be a real roadblock to innovation or it can be an excuse for some teams who may want to avoid real change. If resources are particularly tight, you may need to assume an entrepreneurial role to secure the human and material resources teams need at these later stages. If you are not a skilled grant writer, you will need to find someone who is. If you do not already have a school-business partnership, you may need to get one started. When one school faced the problem of meeting the high technology needs of students without available district resources, they organized a committee of staff and community members to find ways to get the materials they wanted. Another school went to the community to solicit business sponsors so teachers could attend a summer institute. Still another held fund raisers throughout the year to buy additional materials teachers needed to integrate the curriculum. Administrators in these schools would not take *no* for an answer. When the door seemed to slam in their faces, they found ways to go under it, around it, or through it, and their students were the beneficiaries.

When resources are tight, conflict is inevitable, so expect controversy. People have differing views and opinions about what the curriculum in a middle school should be, and they will mobilize their resources to have their agenda heard. Controversy at the school and team levels can pit individuals and groups against one another not only over how to integrate curriculum, but over why. Breaking with tradition can escalate tension and often those in power strengthen their existing arsenal by expanding their coalition and resource base. Thus, power brokers have more to take to the table to swap and trade to get what they want. And in this sea of controversy, sometimes the ship can get wrecked.

Shipwrecks can and do occur in schools and flotsam can interfere with team progress. When controversy escalates, and it often does as teams move into substantive changes in teaching and learning, teams can become the ships that are wrecked in the absence of an ethical code to guide negotiations. "Organizations can take a moral stance. They can make it clear that they expect ethical behavior, and they can validate the importance of dialogue about the moral issues facing [the school]. Positive politics absent moral dialogue and a moral framework is as likely as successful farming without sunlight or water" (Bolman & Deal, 1991, p. 223). Not only will you face moral dilemmas as an administrator, but team members too will face the challenge of negotiating how power could and should be used on the team and in the broader school context to get what they want. While it would be unwise to impose a narrow ethical code on the school, it would be equally unwise to avoid open discourse about ethical issues and expected moral behavior. As a "benevolent politician" (Bolman & Deal, 1991, p. 224), administrators need to recognize the political realities in the school and help others see them too. Adversarial strategies for resolving conflict, as well as more collaborative ones, can be appropriate if they are embedded in an ethical context. Getting what you want at all costs will have its price and everyone in the school needs to know that the price could be higher than anyone is really willing to pay.

"Horse trading" which occurs on a playing field with rules, referees, and open dialogue about expected ethical behavior, allows individuals to swap and trade resources in exchange for rewards (Bolman & Deal, 1991, p. 211). Rewards at district, school, team, or individual levels could be traded for risk taking and growth. Horse trading with the superintendent so that the school can move ahead with integrated curriculum could mean that you swap public recognition for the superintendent and Board of Education for resources you need in the school. Sharing success can further build the alliance between the district and school. Individual horse trading on teams could mean that teachers share ideas, plans, and units with one another in exchange for additional resources to the team. As you and others horse trade inside and outside of the school, you will continue to build the base of support needed to make second order change a reality in the school.

From the symbolic frame
    √ Be visible and available
    √ Promote humor & play
    √ Practice what you preach
    √ Energize through ritual & ceremony
    √ Help the school find its soul

The notion of "MBWA," managing by wandering around, was popularized by Peters and Waterman (1982) as a way to keep a pulse on the organization. But wandering around is not aimless. In the symbolic frame, wandering is a way to promote and build school culture, communicate shared values, and gather important information on the health and well-being of the school. Peters and Waterman (1982) identified the impact on the organization when managers got out of the office and interacted with employees and customers. Middle level administrators also know that being visible in the school and in the classrooms can be a powerful symbolic activity. And when teams struggle, they need to know that you are available to support and affirm them. Telling stories as you wander around which communicate what the school believes to be important for young adolescents and reading the needs of teams as they begin to change curriculum and instruction cannot be done if you spend your day behind your desk. Being available during the day is not easy though and you could get sucked into a system which gives only lip service to the importance of being visible. Yet wise administrators know that in even in the midst of mixed messages about what is expected, scheduling time to interact with students and staff during the day should remain a top priority.

"Groups often focus single-mindedly on the task at hand and discourage any activity not related to work. Seriousness replaces godliness as a desired virtue. But effective groups encourage both play and humor" (Bolman & Deal, 1991, p. 298). Work should be fun and creativity can be hard to muster if putting your nose to the grindstone means that you get ground up in the process too. Playful banter can help teachers release the tension that can build up on the team. "Inside" jokes can help teams learn to laugh together and better cope with the serious student issues that challenge them daily. Humor and play do not have to be occasional diversions from work; they can become part of the work itself and can provide teams with sources for "relaxation, stimulation, and renewal" (Bolman & Deal, 1991, p. 299). Given the serious nature of your work, you too need to remember to play. If you make having fun part of the culture of the school, you send a powerful message that work does not have to be grueling to be important and teams can enjoy one other and their students as they face the challenges of moving into and through the later stages in their development.

The basis for change in the school and on the teams needs to constantly be refocused on meeting the developmental needs of young adolescents and if you practice what you preach, that means what you do should send the clear message that you are committed to building a needs-responsive school. One principal did this by asking "Why are we here?" when there was uncertainty about what an appropriate course of action might be. One team went so far as to create a three-dimensional model of a young adolescent which was present at their team meetings as a reminder of their commitment to meeting students' needs. Part of practicing what you preach means that you also acknowledge the personal and professional needs of the adults in the school. Teachers are hard pressed to remain responsive to students if they are ignored. By focusing on their needs rather than their wants, you can help them learn the difference. Giving teachers what they want may not always be possible, but meeting their needs should be if that is what we expect them to do for students.

"Ritual and ceremony provide opportunities for reinforcing values and bonding individuals to the organization and to one another" (Bolman & Deal, 1991, p. 299). As teams move through the later stages of their development, they may need to be re-energized and this can be accomplished by inventing new rituals and ceremonies to sustain momentum. For example, in one school during the teamed instruction phase, samples of interdisciplinary units written and used in other schools were routinely shared with teams. Sharing units not only communicated to teachers that what they were being asked to do was possible, it allowed them to critique the work without fear of losing face since it was not yet their own. They not only could talk about what was effective, but they could also discuss problems more openly because they did not yet own the material. Ceremonies which celebrate effort and progress in addition to those which acknowledge success, need to become part of the norm in the school. Celebrate approximations to team goal attainment. School and team ceremonies which include not only all certified and non-certified staff members, but students and their parents as well, can keep the vision of change in the forefront. For example, one school recognized the important role of the parent in moving to an integrated curriculum by giving awards which expanded the traditional definition of parental involvement. In addition to awards which recognized contributions parents made by being active in the school during the day, other awards acknowledged that involvement takes many forms. Because it is often hard for parents to imagine how their child can possibly learn in ways that are different from how they were taught, some were given "Flexible Parent" awards for supporting the changes in the school. Others were given "Home Helper" awards to acknowledge the importance of supporting learning at home, while others received "Role Model" awards to acknowledge the example they provided by being dedicated to their own work.

Other ways to build rituals and ceremonies to celebrate staff and student achievement should be developed. Hunt (1993) suggests that teams use the "Cracker Jack" theory to develop student recognition programs. Each box of "Cracker Jacks" has a surprise inside and so does every student. Instead of first defining criteria for student awards and then matching students to those criteria, she suggests that teams look at students, one at a time, and develop an award which recognizes what is special about that individual. The same approach could be used to recognize other members of the school community, and if distributed routinely, this approach could become an important energizing ceremony in the school.

According to Bolman and Deal (1991), "soul is the secret of success" (p. 302). There is more to an effective organization than designing structure, meeting needs, and allocating resources. Looking through the symbolic frame reminds us that people need to find meaning in what they do to help them accept a world which does not always make sense. Bad things do happen to good people and sometimes all you ever thought you wanted is not really enough (Kushner, 1965). You can help the school find a part of itself that many do not even know is there. You can help the school find its soul.

> *Our souls are not hungry for fame, comfort, wealth, or*
> *power. Those rewards create almost as many problems as*
> *they solve. Our souls are hungry for meaning, for the sense*
> *that we have figured out how to live so that our lives matter,*
> *so that the world will be at least a little bit different for our*
> *having passed through it.* (Kushner, 1965, p.18)

Individuals struggle to find meaning in their lives and need to feel that who they are and what they do really does matter. This struggle does not just occur away from work, but is also profoundly affected by it (Moore, 1992). Work can either provide a spiritually rich environment which gives people hope or it can leave soul elements to chance (Moore, 1992) and run the risk of being a desolate island devoid of meaning.

Helping the school find its soul means that you attend to the school culture and realize that people need to see themselves in the products they produce, whether those products are machines or minds. While it is common to think that we find our work, it is probably more accurate to say that our work finds us (Moore, 1992). Work as a vocation can be more exciting and fulfilling for individuals; schools which have a vocation can be too.

Your school's vocation to meet the developmental needs of young adolescents is a challenging one. You and your staff need to know that all of you do make a difference in the lives of your students, yet that impact is often not visible during the short time span of a typical middle school. The influence of your efforts may be intangible and invisible and are not always appreciated at the time by those you serve. Yet you need to remain rooted in your vision of hope and the promise of tomorrow. The school and the people in it have a relationship which needs to be mutually fulfilling. Teachers should not be seen only in terms of what they can do for the school; the school needs to do for them too. When the spiritual side of the person is ignored, a feeling of emptiness can permeate the school. If souls are nurtured, the school can create a rich spiritual dimension which enriches the lives of all those who live there. But helping the school find its soul means you have to find yours. And doing that brings us back where we started.

Summary: The art of creative composition

Letting the melody emerge is often easier said than done. As you sit down to compose, you may think that the next phrase in the melody should rise into the upper octaves. But if you allow the melody to flow, you may find that bass notes are really more pleasing to the ear. As a composer, you may need to look inside yourself so that you can do more than just remake hits from the past. You will need to know and understand yourself and your stuff; play many roles which respond to the variety of voices in the chorus; confront your need to control outcomes, predict the future, and have all the answers; and accept that omnipotence is neither desirable nor possible. If you want to create a teaming mentality on the outside, you have to make time to be sure you have one yourself. And then you will have to encourage others to do the same.

The development of a teaming mentality in the school is a journey not a destination (Johnson, 1993). As you work with interdisciplinary teams to develop a collaborative foundation, you may find it helpful to look through a variety of lenses in order to see a fuller picture of the school and its teams. A four-framed view (Bolman & Deal, 1991) was offered as a way to analyze the structural, human resource, political, and symbolic dimensions of teams as they progress through their organizational, community, teamed instruction, and governmental life phases (George, 1991/1992). You are encouraged to read the full works of these authors, but more important, you are challenged to use your artistry to create your own composition for working with interdisciplinary teams in the middle school.

Being a creative composer is most certainly not easy and no one knows that better than you. Your challenges are great but they are not insurmountable. Your belief that the adults and young adolescent learners in your school are worth the time, effort, and energy it will take to build a school with not only sound structures, healthy relationships, and positive politics, but also one which has a soul, will sustain you when times are hard and the melody remains elusive. And when the melody begins to flow again, it can emerge at the hand of one who knows well the art of creative composition.

References

Beane, J.A. (1993a). *A middle school curriculum: From rhetoric to reality* (2nd ed). Columbus, OH: National Middle School Association.

Beane, J.A. (1993b). The search for a middle school curriculum. *School Administrator, 50* (3), 8-16.

Bennis, W. (1989). *Why leaders can't lead: The unconscious conspiracy continues.* San Francisco: Jossey-Bass.

Bergmann, S., & Baxter, J. (1983). Building a guidance program and advisory concept for early adolescents. *NASSP Bulletin, 67* (4), 49-55.

Bolman, L.G., & Deal, T.E. (1991). *Reframing organizations: Artistry, choice, and leadership.* San Francisco: Jossey-Bass.

Carnegie Council on Adolescent Development. (1989). *Turning points: Preparing American youth for the 21st century.* New York: Carnegie Corporation.

Clark, S., & Clark, D. (1987). Interdisciplinary teaming programs: Organization, rationale, and implementation. *Schools in the Middle.* Reston, VA: National Association of Secondary School Principals.

Covey, S. R. (1989). *The seven habits of highly effective people: Restoring the character ethic.* New York: Simon & Schuster.

Cuban, L. (1988). Constancy and change in schools: 1990s to the present. In P. W. Jackson (Ed.), *Contributing to educational change: Perspectives on research and practice* (pp. 85-106). Berkeley, CA: McCutchan.

Cummings, C. (1991). *Managing a cooperative classroom.* Edmonds, WA: Teaching Inc.

Deal, T.E. (1990). Reframing reform. *Educational Leadership, 47,* (8) 6-12.

Diedrich-Reilly, I., & Zenz, K. (1993). *Dr. Charles E. Gavin School: A case study.* Technical Report. Urbana-Champaign, IL: University of Illinois, National Center for School Leadership.

Doda, N. (1992). Teaming: Its burdens and its blessings. In J. H. Lounsbury (Ed.), *Connecting the curriculum through interdisciplinary instruction* (pp. 45-55). Columbus, OH: National Middle School Association.

Doda, N., George, P., & McEwin, K. (1987). Ten current truths about effective schools. *Middle School Journal, 18,* (3) 3-5.

Dunn, R., & Dunn, K. (1985). *Learning styles model* (reprint). Lawrence, KS: Price Systems.

Erb, T.O., & Doda, N.M. (1989). *Team organization: Promise—practices and possibilities.* Washington, DC: National Education Association.

Evans, R. (1989). The faculty in midcareer: Implications for school improvement. *Educational Leadership, 46,* (8) 10-15.

Fogarty, R. (1991). *How to integrate the curricula.* Palatine, IL: Skylight Publishing.

French, J.R., & Raven, B.H. (1959). The bases of social power. In D. Cartwright (Ed.), *Studies in social power* (pp. 150-162). Ann Arbor, MI: Institute for Social Research.

George, P.S. (1992). Four phases in the life of a team. In J. H. Lounsbury (Ed.), *Connecting the curriculum through interdisciplinary instruction* (pp. 135-142). Columbus, OH: National Middle School Association. (Reprinted from George, P.S. (1982). Interdisciplinary team organization: Four operational phases. *Middle School Journal, 13* (3), 10-13.)

George, P., Stevenson, C., Thomason, J., & Beane, J. (1992). *The middle school — and beyond.* Reston, VA: Association for Supervision and Curriculum Development.

Gorton, R.A. (1983). *School administration and supervision: Leadership challenges and opportunities.* Dubuque, IA: Wm. C. Brown.

Grant, L. (1993). *Roger L. Sullivan High School: Success by exhibition.* Technical Report. Urbana-Champaign, IL: University of Illinois, National Center for School Leadership.

Hawkins, M.L., & Graham, M.D. (1994). *Curriculum architecture: Creating a place of our own.* Columbus OH: National Middle School Association.

Hunt, K. (1993). *Fifty things that great teams do.* Presentation at the Association of Illinois Middle-Level Schools Summer Institute, Fairview Heights, IL.

Jacobs, H.H. (Ed.). (1989). *Interdisciplinary curriculum: Design and implementation.* Alexandria, VA: Association for Supervision and Curriculum Development.

Johnson, M. (1993). *Redefining leadership: A case study of Hollibrook Elementary School.* Technical Report. Urbana-Champaign, IL: University of Illinois, National Center for School Leadership.

Joyce, B., & Showers, B. (1988). *Student achievement through staff development.* New York: Longman.

Keirsey, D., & Bates, M. (1984). *Please understand me: Character and temperament types.* Del Mar, CA: Prometheus Nemesis.

Kolb, D. (1976). *Learning style inventory.* Boston: McBer.

Kushner, H. (1965). *When all you've ever wanted isn't enough.* New York: Simon & Schuster.

Lounsbury, J.H. (1992a). Interdisciplinary instruction: A mandate for the nineties. In J. H. Lounsbury (Ed.), *Connecting the curriculum through interdisciplinary instruction* (pp. 1-2). Columbus, OH: National Middle School Association.

Lounsbury, J.H. (1992b). Interdisciplinary instruction: A voyage not a harbor. In J. H. Lounsbury (Ed.), *Connecting the curriculum through interdisciplinary instruction* (pp. 155-158). Columbus, OH: National Middle School Association.

Lounsbury, J.H. (1996). Please, not another program. *Clearing House, 69* (4), 211-213.

Merenbloom, E.Y. (1991). *The team process: A handbook for teachers* (3rd ed.). Columbus, OH: National Middle School Association.

Moore, T. (1992). *Care of the soul* (reprint). New York: Harper-Collins.

Myers, I.B., & Briggs, K.C. (1976). *Myers-Briggs type indicator* (reprint). Palo Alto, CA: Consulting Psychologists Press.

Oliva, P. (1993). *Supervision for today's schools* (4th ed.). New York: Longman.

Pearce, J.C. (1971). *The crack in the cosmic egg.* New York: Julian Press.

Peters T.J., & Waterman, R.H. (1982). *In search of excellence: Lessons from America's best-run companies.* New York: Warner.

Plodzik, K.T., & George, P. (1989). Interdisciplinary team organization. *Middle School Journal, 20,* (5) 15-17.

Polite, M.M. (1993). *The story of Cross Keys Middle School: Learning to ask the right questions.* Technical Report. Urbana-Champaign, IL: University of Illinois, National Center for School Leadership.

Smith, W. F., & Andrews, R. L. (1989). *Instructional leadership: How principals make a difference.* Alexandria, VA: Association for Supervision and Curriculum Development.

Stevenson, C. (1992). *Teaching ten to fourteen year olds.* New York: Longman.

Williamson, R., & Johnston, J. H. (1991). *Planning for success: Successful implementation of middle level reorganization.* Reston, VA: National Association of Secondary School Principals.

Teams and the Affirmation of Middle Level Students' Voices: The Case of Jimmie

11

Richard R. Powell

Teachers would invite students into modes of dialogue as participants rather than pawns, as collaborative interlocu-tors instead of slates to be filled. — Gergen, 1991, p. 250

It is not a matter of determining the frames into which learners must fit, not a matter of having predefined stages in mind. Rather, it would be a question of releasing poten-tial learners to give them voice. — Greene, 1993, p. 219

Innovations such as interdisciplinary unit planning will fail to fulfill their promise without the nurturing of student voices. — Oldfather & McLaughlin, 1993, p. 21

W e sat in desks facing each other in an empty classroom at Thurman White Middle School, one of the middle schools in Clark County School District (CCSD), Nevada. At the time of this study CCSD, which has grown the past decade at an unprecedented rate, was the eleventh largest school district in the USA. Sitting across from me was Jimmie, a quiet seventh grader, rather tall and filled out for his age. My immediate impression of Jimmie was that of a keenly bright student, al-though his school grades in earlier years had been marginal. Jimmie had an earring in his right ear, a fashionable sign of the times, and he was wearing a black t-shirt that hung loosely on his broad frame.

I asked Jimmie to describe himself to me, to tell me what his life was like both in and out of school, and to tell me why he thought I was talking to him. I asked Jimmie many questions, I listened to him talk; I listened silently, openly, affirmingly. As he continued talking our conversation deepened and turned to Jimmie's home and family life; the story behind Jimmie's voice unfolded before me. As Jimmie talked to me he took me places I had not been before. He took me into the deeper, even darker, corners of his life. Jimmie showed me how deeply emotional, profoundly personal, and totally cultural is this elusive concept, student voice, that educators have now idealized.

As I heard Jimmie describe himself I realized that at that moment he was the teacher: Jimmie was teaching me about his voice, about student voice. I also realized that we were collaborative researchers: I was helping Jimmie explore the origin and meaning of his own voice; he was helping me explore student voice on deeper, highly personal levels.

This chapter describes how an interdisciplinary team of teachers successfully affirmed the voice of one of their students. Reports are available on how student voices have been silenced, marginalized, and neglected (Fine, 1991; Trueba, Jacobs, & Kirton, 1990). In response to these reports I elected to focus on how four middle school teachers, working together as an interdisciplinary team, succeeded (rather than failed) to lift a student's voice from passive silence to active expression.

During the past few years middle level practitioners and researchers alike have begun to better understand the many dimensions of interdisciplinary teaming, including the influence of teaming on the academic and social growth of students. Interdisciplinary teaming typically involves a cadre of teachers from diverse subject areas working together in many ways including collaborating on instructional units (Beane, 1993b; Erb & Doda, 1989). Over time team teachers develop instructional units that link subject areas in academically useful ways. Team teachers also share aspects of their teaching, in addition to developing instructional units, as they meet together in team meetings to solve student problems, talk to parents, and plan team activities (George, 1992; Powell & Mills, 1995).

One of the initial purposes of interdisciplinary teaming was to create school environments that were more developmentally appropriate for young adolescents than traditional junior high school environments (George & Oldaker, 1985; George & Shewey, 1994). Studies completed over the past few years have provided insight into benefits that both teachers and students derive from a middle school environment that includes teaming. For example, several recent studies (e.g., Oldfather & McLaughlin, 1993; Powell, 1993) indicate that students feel more confident in school after being with the same team of teachers for more than one year; this is because they know their teachers personally and they know what teachers expect academically. Additionally, students have more meaningful relationships in and out of school with peers who are in their team (Powell, 1993). Related studies

(Mills, Powell & Pollak, 1992; Powell & Mills, 1995) suggest that team teachers who meet together in team meetings on a regular basis feel less isolated in their classrooms. Teachers like collegial team support when solving student problems, and they appreciate collaborative team comments in parent conferences. Teachers engage in various kinds of discourse during their team interactions (Shaw, 1993), which fosters intra-team mentoring and professional knowledge sharing among team teachers (Powell & Mills, 1995).

While studies like those above are helping middle level educators understand the benefits and challenges of teaming, what happens on very personal levels to the lives of team students and their teachers as they interact over time is less clear. To more clearly understand what happens in the personal lives of team teachers and students, we must look closely at their lives; that is we must capture the personal stories of middle school teachers and their students as they live out their school lives together.

Some educators believe that the true test for the success of a middle school is an increase in standardized test scores, a measuring stick that aligns more closely with junior high school factory models of schooling. Other educators, especially those who understand the initial intent and true spirit of the middle school movement, including the dimension of interdisciplinary teaming, realize that creating a developmentally appropriate learning environment that enriches individual lives of students personally, socially, and academically is the true test of school success. This is not primarily measured with standardized testing. Exploring the personal experiences of team teachers and their students as they unfold over time, and as they are shared together, is a useful and feasible way to understand the influence of the middle school model interdisciplinary team on shaping the social, academic, and personal lives of young adolescents.

An important concept that is providing a means to explore personal lives of students and teachers is *student voice* (Oldfather & Mclaughlin, 1993; Powell, 1993; SooHoo, 1993). In a manner that is consistent with the student-centered ideology of middle schools (Carnegie Council on Adolescent Development, 1989), the notion of student voice draws our attention to students' experiences, and makes their lives central to understanding the efficacy of interdisciplinary teaming. Consistent with this view, and using the construct of student voice, I studied the school experiences of Jimmie, a seventh grader who had been in the same team for two years.

The case of Jimmie

When I asked him to choose a name for himself other than his own that I could use in this report, he chose "Jimmie." Jimmie was recommended to me by Darleen Birdman, an educator in an interdisciplinary team at Thurman White Middle School. Darleen and I had worked together on various middle school projects, and over several years I have grown to trust her intuitive sensitivity for how to meet the many needs of middle school students (see Mills, Powell, & Pollak, 1992; Powell, 1993; Powell, Birdman, Huff, Havas, & Bednar, 1992). I talked to her about my interest in learning about the voices that middle level students have in school. As we talked about the idea of student voice, Jimmie's name surfaced in our conversation. Darleen's description of Jimmie's personal and academic development during his two years in her interdisciplinary team made me deeply curious about his voice, a voice that was once silent at school, that felt unwanted, but at the time of this study felt needed and heard. I was equally curious about the strategies Darleen and her team teachers used to affirm Jimmie's voice. With Darleen's assistance I arranged a time to talk to Jimmie individually, and a separate time to talk to the team teachers as a group.

At first I was unsure how to talk to Jimmie about factors that gave shape to his student voice. Should I ask him directly about what voice means to him? Just how do you ask another person to talk about their "voice?" As I began talking to Jimmie I realized that mentioning voice, as an abstract concept, would be academic and meaningless to both of us. So I put that aside, and I simply asked him to tell me about himself. Jimmie's "voice" then came forward.

Affirming Jimmie's voice: His perspective

The earlier years. My conversation with Jimmie took place toward the end of the school year. By then he had been a member of the same interdisciplinary team for two years. I knew from conversations with Darleen Birdman, one of Jimmie's team teachers, that he skipped school a lot in previous years. After listening to Jimmie I attributed his skipping school in part to his life at home and in part to the structure of his former schooling. Jimmie's parents were divorced several years earlier, and after the divorce he flew to Los Angeles almost every weekend to be with his mother, then flew back to his father's home the same weekend to be in school by Monday morning. He told me: "My parents have been divorced for a while. And I got really frustrated one time when my mom moved out to California and for one year I went there every weekend on the plane."

Dealing with his parents' separation was not the only problem Jimmie had at home. He and his brother had some tough times. He related that his brother continuously abused him verbally and called him names. Erupting from this tension were many fights between Jimmie and his brother; some fights according to Jimmie were "real brawls." When I asked him if he had any protection from his older brother he said, "Not really. I'm pretty much on my own at home."

I asked Jimmie to tell me about his earlier years as an elementary school student and about his participation in school. He said: "Since third or fourth grade I've been cutting class and stuff. When I came to this school I started cutting a little less. But I still did it too much even though I shouldn't do it at all."

Darleen told me that in sixth grade, the first year Jimmie was on her team, he missed over ninety days of school. "Not only was Jimmie absent from school a lot, but when he was in school he was very quiet, choosing to remain silent and unheard. I asked him why he felt like being quiet in school."

He said: "The year before last [in fifth grade] I felt like nobody wanted me to be in school. I was afraid that if I answered out and got something wrong they would think differently of me, dislike me in some way."

Jimmie's transformation. With obvious pride Jimmie told me about his improved grades and his almost perfect attendance in seventh grade. He said, "I'm coming to school now and doing my work." Coming to school regularly, and getting better grades was not something that happened in only a few weeks. It was an arduous two-year, uphill journey for Jimmie through some fairly rocky terrain that took the ongoing efforts of both him and his team teachers.

For most of our conversation I avoided talking to Jimmie about idealized notions of student voice. I knew, however, that talking to Jimmie about student voice as an idealized construct was necessary if I was to adequately explore the part his voice played in his personal and academic progress in middle school. I then decided to ask him directly about student voice. I have included my own comments, which I indicate with "R," in the conversation below to provide a context for his responses.

> R: *The year before last [in fifth grade] you said you felt like no one wanted you to be in school and you said you were very quiet in school. Then last year [in sixth grade]*

was your first year with the team. You said you started sixth grade as a very quiet person and that you cut school a lot. Now I want to ask you sort of a weird question about all this. What do you think your teachers were hearing you say when you were being quiet in class and when you were cutting school all the time? What voice were they hearing with your silence and with your absence?

J: *(long pause) They must have been hearing that I was (pause) shy (pause) and that I didn't really care about school or school work. (long pause) And probably that I was very (pause) I was also very morbid last year and maybe a little morbid this year. I would say those are the things they heard.*

R: *What do your teachers hear when they listen to you as a morbid person?*

J: *They hear (pause) that I am very dark. Shy. Maybe mean. (pause) Certainly very dark.*

Jimmie's responses like those above prompted me to continue our discussion about voice as an abstract concept. So I talked to him about the idea of "being heard." I asked him,

R: *Do you feel like you are being heard by your teachers this year?*

J: *Yes!*

R: *In fifth grade did you feel heard by your teacher?*

J: *No, not nearly as much.*

R: *What about last year in sixth grade?*

J: *I did. I felt more heard.*

R: *What were your teachers hearing?*

J: *They were hearing me. They were hearing that I wanted to do my school work, that I could do my school work and come to school. (pause) And also that they knew I could do it. (pause) They believed in me.*

As Jimmie began feeling heard by his team teachers, he began connecting with school. Being heard changed his view of self as morbid person to view of self as valued person. Throughout this process Jimmie experienced a personal transformation as his team teachers, through persistent and patient effort, helped him find his voice.

To better understand the roots of Jimmie's personal transformation, I knew that I needed to more fully explore factors that facilitated this. In searching for this understanding I discovered how his team teachers, working together, helped Jimmie find his voice and in turn find himself. I asked Jimmie to talk openly about why he was more engaged in school during seventh grade. Jimmie immediately said:

> *The teachers really influenced that. I remember last year*
> *when I missed so many days Mrs. Birdman called my home*
> *almost every time. The teachers were convincing me that I*
> *could do it, that I could get good grades and come to school.*
> *And this last grading period I almost got an honor card.*
> *Only one little grade in English kept me from it.*

I asked him what it meant for him personally when teachers showed an interest in him. He told me: "It means they care. That they really care about me and their students. That means a lot to me."

The caring that Jimmie felt from his teachers began to influence him during sixth grade. Toward the end of sixth grade Jimmie acknowledged a change in his attitude toward school:

> *About half way to the end of [sixth grade] something just*
> *snapped. And I was doing my work and coming to school.*
> *And that's carried over to this year. I'm doing other activi-*
> *ties too, like Knight Flight. And I took some Judo classes for*
> *a while outside school. And this year I really got into it.*

One activity in particular that Jimmie's team teachers got him involved in was Knight Flight, a tumbling team comprised of approximately ninety students at Thurman White Middle School. Knight Flight, which was sponsored by Craig Whitley, one of Jimmie's team teachers, puts on anti-drug and self-esteem performances for thousands of students in other district schools each year. As Jimmie talked about Knight Flight I noticed an excitement come over him.

> *I've been in Knight Flight for most of this year. We prac-*
> *tice three hours on Mondays and Wednesdays, and we put*
> *on shows at other schools. It's really fun doing the shows.*
> *And doing shows is important to other kids who watch. A*
> *lot of my friends are in Knight Flight, and they are new*
> *friends.*

By the end of our conversation I had succeeded in talking to Jimmie in both abstract and concrete terms about the notion of student voice. Returning to this as a means to finish our time together, I asked Jimmie:

> R: *You told me that you feel your voice is heard now at*
> *school. What does it mean when you hear me say your voice,*
> *[Jimmie's] voice?*

J: *That means I've been known. I've been discovered.*
That some people realize that I can actually do it. Being
heard means showing other people that I can do good in
school.

R: *I wonder if any of this carries over to outside of school?*

J: *(Immediate response) Oh yeah! Now if my brother*
makes me really mad I don't really beat him up. Last year
we fought all the time. But this year I think being in school,
being on this team, has really calmed my temper down.

R: *Why is that?*

J: *I'm less frustrated. I'm glad I'm not fighting as much*
with my brother. I feel a lot better.

R: *In what way?*

J: *I have confidence in myself now that I didn't have*
before. I can feel it.

After listening closely to Jimmie during our conversation at school, then
after listening again to the taped conversation several days later, I was
reminded of Penny Oldfather's description of student voice: "Voice comes
from a deeper place than our throats. Voice comes from our heart, from our
minds, and from the deepest places of knowing and feeling" (Oldfather &
McLaughlin, 1993, p. 9).

Jimmie's silent school voice, hushed for much of his elementary school
years, was embedded in the deepest places of his knowing and feeling. His
silent voice was rooted in feeling angry and feeling unwanted. Jimmie's four
team teachers collectively heard and affirmed this voice.

Affirming Jimmie's voice: The teachers' perspectives

Prior to talking to Jimmie I had a lengthy conversation with his team
teachers during one of their team planning periods. For the conversations I
had with the teachers and with Jimmie I followed the suggestions offered by
Oakley (1981) on conducting interviews. By doing this I assumed the role in
these conversational interviews as participant and co-discussant rather than
detached interviewer. I also held many informal conversations with the
teachers, and made impromptu observations of them when I visited the
school at unscheduled times throughout the school year.

Darleen Birdman, the reading teacher on the team, was the team leader.
Other team teachers were Craig Whitley, the mathematics teacher and
sponsor of Knight Flight; Lisa Rollins, the special education teacher for the

team; and Vivian Wiley, the language arts teacher. The conversations I had with teachers were informal, yet highly focused. As I talked to these teachers, I realized that I was in the midst of serious middle level educators who were deeply committed to middle school ideology. They, too, were interested in student voice, and they were very willing to join me in this project.

By almost every standard, this team of teachers was a fully functioning unit, working closely together in all school functions and spending much of their school time outside of class together. They also gave each other freedom to move in and out of their classrooms as needed throughout the school days. Thurman White Middle School (TWMS), a new suburban school where the team was housed, was fully committed to the middle school concept. Teachers at the school had individual preparation periods in addition to separate team meetings. High expectations were placed on TWMS teachers to exemplify the middle school ideology; Darleen Birdman and her team colleagues exceeded these expectations. The year prior to this report, for example, the team was the recipient of the 1994 Sandra Babich Memorial Award for Quality Teaching, which was presented to them at the Western Regional Middle Level Consortium (Middle Level Educator, 1994).

The team had been together for two years, since TWMS opened. As a group they collectively had many years of teaching experience, and all were highly dedicated to working with young adolescents both in and out of the classroom. They were also dedicated to continuous learning about middle schools, which was evidenced by their active participation in regional and national middle school conferences.

From my interactions with the teachers for this study, and at numerous other times that I visited the school, I always found the teachers to be focused on students. Whether they were alone in their classrooms, together in team meetings, monitoring hallways together between classes, or chatting at lunch, their focus, both explicitly and implicitly, was on helping students be successful at school. If they felt that one of their students was "falling between the cracks," they would discuss ways to bring the student more into the team and school cultures. Consequently, much of their effort was spent on appraising student growth, monitoring student progress, and meeting the daily challenges that students created for them.

Interacting with the team for this study and at other times of the school year, I further observed that the teachers had an obvious team focus on their instruction, not the kind of focus demonstrated by teachers who work alone in departmentalized schools (Johnson, 1990). Darleen and her team teachers had a team consciousness; that is, they thought together as a team, worked collectively to solve daily problems, depended on each other for assistance in their teaching, and produced relevant and useful interdisciplinary units. They attended middle school workshops together and demonstrated team learning for their students.

This was the team environment that Jimmie associated with during sixth and seventh grades. To provide the context for how Jimmie's voice was affirmed by this environment, I first highlight the teachers' perspectives about student voice in general. I then consider their perspectives of Jimmie.

Perspectives on student voice. The teachers talked to me about student voice, as an abstract concept and as a lived experience in daily classroom and school life. Darleen's perspective of student voice was embedded in her belief that teachers, especially at the middle level, should be facilitators of student learning. She noted:

> To be a facilitator is what teaching is all about. And facilitating also applies to the voices of students. By this I mean for teachers to facilitate what they see and hear. And you can't do that without recognizing the student's voice. And that voice is basically everything that happens with students; the way they walk, the way they carry themselves, the things they are doing, the actions they are taking. Everything they do is their voice.

Vivian believed that letting students express their opinions and ideas was central to facilitating students' voices. Vivian was concerned that this was not happening for many students. She said:

> I think the whole idea of student voice is so complex. It's made complex because kids feel now that their opinions and ideas are not being heard by adults, by teachers. As a team we work very hard at overcoming this, at helping students express opinions and views. And we listen to our students, we hear them, and we let them know that.

This comment by Vivian about listening to students corroborated a comment made by Lisa. Lisa described the difference between teachers as listeners and teachers as talkers:

> There's an important difference between being a listener and a talker as a teacher. I think some teachers are listeners and maybe that's where the connection to voice comes in. The voice is there if you're willing to listen to it and pay attention to it. Some teachers are task masters and they do

*all the talking but they're really not hearing. They're more
curriculum and task oriented. When the classroom is this
way I'm not sure which is the most important to teachers,
the voices of students or the curriculum. On our team we try
to help students feel that their voices are the most important.*

To bring student voices into the team curriculum, and then into the school
curriculum, Craig believed in helping students develop two kinds of voices,
what he called the *autonomous voice* and the *performance voice*. One way
Craig helps students develop these voices is through Knight Flight, the
student organization he sponsors. Craig explained:

> *One thing I do for students in school is to build an au-
> tonomous voice in my tumbling team called Knight Flight.
> It's a self-esteem building group for boys and girls that re-
> ally helps develop two kinds of voices, the autonomous voice
> and the performance voice. If kids want to be in Knight
> Flight and they can't tumble for some reason, then I have
> them set up mats for performances and other kids set up the
> PA [public address] system. All this helps make them au-
> tonomous. And whatever kids in Knight Flight are doing,
> whether its only tumbling or only setting up mats, they are
> performing. I think every kid should be given the opportu-
> nity to be on some kind of stage at some time during the
> school year. Helping them succeed in their performance,
> whatever the performance is, helps them build their self-
> esteem and confidence and self-respect.*

Perspectives on Jimmie's voice. The comments above give a general idea
of the teachers' perspectives that framed Jimmie's team environment for sixth
and seventh grades. This environment, which was influenced by these
perspectives, helped Jimmie find his voice. Lisa described Jimmie this way:

> *I think Jimmie is the kind of kid that would just love to
> fade into the woodwork if he could. He isn't interested in
> getting a lot of attention for anything. And I think maybe
> he fought that with us as a team at first. You know, he
> probably asked himself, "Why do they want to be such a
> part of my life? Why do they keep getting involved with
> me?" And now I think he realizes we really do care.*

Darleen explained what Jimmie was like at the beginning of sixth grade:

> I think he came to school feeling absolutely no commitment to himself, to the school, to academics, to even possibly staying in school. I think he came occasionally sort of checking in once in a while. Then he found himself in an atmosphere where he couldn't become anonymous. Even though he tried very hard to become part of the wall, I mean to be invisible, he wasn't able to do it. He realized that there were people here that were not only going to notice him but going to insist that he make some kind of stand and that he find his voice among the other students.

Vivian told me how she heard Jimmie's silent voice:

> I think Jimmie really felt disconnected from school in sixth grade. He didn't have anyone to identify with. I think his voice inside was saying, 'Nobody cares about me. They don't care whether I'm in school or not. They won't notice me. I can be gone ninety days and nobody will care.' And I think that was what his silent voice was saying.

Early during the sixth grade year the teachers first brought Jimmie's voice into their team learning environment, and then into the school environment. Darleen explained how they did this:

> Last year in sixth grade we just kept bringing [Jimmie] in for talks, and kept calling home every time he was absent. When he didn't come to school I'd run down to the phone and call his home and ask, 'Where's Jimmie, what's going on?' We first started helping Jimmie in small ways. We didn't start with, 'We want all A's and we want you involved in this and that.' We started with attendance, with the request, 'Just come to school.' From attendance we went to academics. From academics we've gone to involvement in Knight Flight and performing. We're working on helping Jimmie have a more influential voice in our [interdisciplinary] team. We kept trying different avenues with Jimmie until we found some that would help him.

Another comment for how the teachers brought Jimmie into the team was made by Craig. This comment, which can be viewed metaphorically, suggests the strength the team gave Jimmie to express himself and to build his self esteem. In the seventh grade Jimmie, quite literally, began carrying his peers on his shoulders. Craig noted:

We did our Knight Flight Christmas show for the school.
Jimmie's part of the show was that he was the base and two
other people stood on his shoulders. One person stood on
Jimmie's shoulders, and then another person stood on top
of that person's shoulders. So we had a three person stack
with Jimmie holding the whole stack up.

After talking to the teachers about Jimmie I realized facilitating the development of his voice, bringing him into the collective conversation of school and of the team, was not the effort of any single teacher. When I listened to the teachers I heard the collective voice of four teachers that was filled with harmony and sincerity. The teachers talked about student voice, and about Jimmie's voice, with serious intention. After learning about Jimmie I knew that no one teacher, by her or himself, could have done for Jimmie what the four teachers, working concertedly and harmoniously as a team, did over two years. I also realized, after hearing the following comment by Darleen, that one school year would not have been sufficient time for Jimmie's teachers to reach him. Darleen said:

I don't think we could have helped Jimmie like we did if
we, as a team, hadn't been with him for both sixth and
seventh grades. It takes that long to get students like Jimmie
to trust you and for them to let you come into their space.
Being with students two years lets them know that you're
not going away, that you're a source of security.

Most middle level educators would surely agree that many young adolescents, especially those with backgrounds like Jimmie, need stability in their lives. Long-term teaming, where a group of teachers and students are together for several years, is one means to provide this stability, as so clearly reflected in Darleen's comment above. In the case of Jimmie, who was quiet, shy, and self-marginalized at school, Darleen and her team colleagues took most of sixth grade to develop a deeper understanding of him, and to realize his keen potential to do well in school. Toward the end of sixth grade, and throughout seventh grade, trust between Jimmie and the team teachers grew. Jimmie realized that these four teachers, who continuously called his home when he was not at school, who constantly encouraged him to do well in school, who invited him to be part of meaningful extracurricular activities, were going to be there for him whenever he needed them. Darleen believed that this would not have happened in only one year, that Jimmie needed the stability they provided him over two years.

One factor that contributes to the power of teaming, which was demonstrated by Darleen's team, is building trust with students over time in a stable team culture. Teams that are restructured every school year, or who only partially attempt to implement teaming, may not be able to establish the kind of trust that Jimmie built with his team teachers. Working together, however, in a consistent and concerted manner, as demonstrated by Jimmie's teachers at TWMS, increases the likelihood that students will feel that they are part of school, that they will feel they can build trusting relationships with teachers.

As I reflected more on Jimmie's relationship with his team teachers, a line in one of Peter Shelly's poems, *Love's Philosophy*, became relevant. In this short poem Shelly (cited in Noyes, 1956) wrote, "All things by a law divine in one spirit meet and mingle" (p. 1059). In exploring the school life of Jimmie, I had taken part in such a meeting and mingling; I had become part of the teachers' collective spirit, if only momentarily. I felt energized, I felt a sense of hope for young persons in our middle schools that I had not felt for many years. My wish at that moment, and as I wrote this paper, was that Jimmie, in his own way, experienced a similar hope. If he did not experience hope, I know that he experienced the same meeting and mingling of spirit that I felt. But unlike the limited time I had with the teachers, Jimmie had two academic years. I knew then what brought new life to Jimmie's voice; a spirit that these four teachers created out of their beliefs about building trusting relationships with students. When I realized this I was strangely disquieted. For a moment I was not sure that I could even capture all of this in a story.

Rethinking student voice: From ideology to reality

The case of Jimmie made me aware of how shallow and academic recent attempts have been at making 'student voice' a topic for politicizing, idealizing, and objectifying (Nolen, 1994; Thorkildsen & Jordan, 1994). The teachers were working with voice in ways I had not imagined, had not envisioned, and certainly had not read about in academic literature. I also realized at that moment how student voice, as understood in the practical lives of teachers and as understood by the lived experience of students, must be further explored and described, not just by educational researchers but by all educators, especially those who spend each day shaping the lives of young persons. Jimmie's story helped me realize, too, that the recent calls for viewing teaching and learning in new ways, using new metaphors, has immediate practical implications for classroom teaching (Apple, 1993;

Banks, 1993; Bullough, 1994; Doll, 1993; Gay, 1988; Gergen, 1991;
Kincheloe, 1993; McLaughlin, 1994; Perkinson, 1993).

Prior to talking with Jimmie and his team teachers I had become, like so
many other educators, enamored with the idea of student voice. In some
ways I had romanticized the concept, which only further distanced my
idealized notion of student voice from the reality of the classroom. The
concept I held of student voice when I talked to Jimmie and the teachers was
embedded within an emancipatory ideology. From this ideology I view
students as being mostly "pawns" in school decision making rather than
"collaborative interlocutors" (Gergen, 1991). And I view students as young
persons who are often silenced by a bureaucratized power hierarchy. Align-
ing with Freire (1972), I also believe that curriculum, if it is to be useful in
preparing students for a democratic society, should empower them with
knowledge and skills, and consequently help them become independent
thinkers. Such curricula help students think, act, and make decisions according to their own personally constructed principles rather than conforming out
of habit, and in an unquestioning manner, to someone else's values and
beliefs (Boomer, Lester, Onore, & Cook, 1992).

The interactions I had with Jimmie and his team teachers did not necessarily cause me to do away with my ideology for students; I still believe this to
be evermore appropriate for students in the twenty-first century. What talking
to Jimmie and the teachers did, however, along with talking to other colleagues and with reviewing the literature on student voice, was to help me
realize that by abstracting, romanticizing, idealizing, and objectifying student
voice I have failed to think critically about two very key issues in classroom
teaching. These issues are the approaches we employ to interact with students
in the classroom, including the metaphors we use to depict these interactions,
and the loose and fashionable manner by which we, as an educational
community, are now approaching student voice.

Toward a curriculum of voice: New metaphors

Interacting with students as part of a team is very different than interacting
with students as an individual teacher, not part of a functioning interdisciplinary team. As young adolescent education moves from traditional, content-
centered departments of instruction to interdisciplinary teams, there is a
corresponding need to rethink the nature of teacher and student interactions.
For example, building long-term trusting relationships with students, as
Darleen's team did with Jimmie, involves radically new kinds of ethical and

moral considerations for teaching. One way to rethink your interactions with students, to reconsider your moral and ethical obligations to them, is to reconceptualize teaching – that is to place teaching in new metaphorical frameworks as Bullough (1994) and McLaughlin (1994) suggest.

Using new metaphorical frameworks to view teaching helps us rethink the perspectives we have of ourselves as middle school educators. Without this rethinking, teachers can easily go through the motions of being a middle school teacher but still hold fast to junior high school ideology. For example, teacher as classroom manager and subject matter authority are metaphors that align with traditional junior high settings. For middle school settings, where teams of teachers collaborate to deliver instruction to cadres of students and where students have a shared voice in their teams, the metaphors of teacher as collaborator, teacher as facilitator, and teacher as content guide are more suitable. Thinking in terms of *teacher as content guide* evokes a very different mental image than *teacher as content authority*. The notion of guide suggests a teacher who helps students explore various pathways to learning, with no one pathway being necessarily definitive. The notion of teacher as content authority suggests one pathway which leads to the teacher as central to all learning (Apple, 1993: Doll, 1993). Middle school teachers who fundamentally believe they are subject authorities for their students, rather than guides or facilitators, will likely transport junior high school philosophy into middle school environments. This makes collaboration among middle school teachers, especially for developing interdisciplinary units of instruction, more complicated and arduous.

Thinking in terms of middle school and interdisciplinary teams, rather than in terms of junior high school, requires not just restructuring the school schedule, but more importantly restructuring our whole conceptual and metaphorical thinking about the very nature of middle level schools. Such restructuring may very well challenge long held beliefs about classroom relationships between teachers and students (Bullough, 1994; McLaughlin, 1994). Much of our previous thinking about these relationships has been in terms of political, emotional, and psychological factors. Few of us would argue with the importance of these things. However, making these factors central to teaching young adolescents has resulted in an over reliance on controlling student behavior, managing and directing student learning, and enforcing school rules that maintain traditional, long-standing power relations in school. The combined effect of these factors has been to disengage students like Jimmie from meaningful learning and to thwart the kind of instruction that helps students become thoughtful, critical, and informed

decision makers about important social and environmental phenomena
(Apple, 1993; Kincheloe, 1993; Perkinson, 1993).

To reengage students in meaningful learning there has emerged a focus on
making students' voices central to curriculum decision making (Erickson &
Schultz, 1992; Oldfather and McLaughlin, 1993). Ascribing to this focus
requires an acceptance of three factors, in addition to those mentioned above,
that give shape to the learning process. More specifically, if the relationship
between Jimmie and his teachers reflects the kind of relationships that are
inherent in middle school ideology and that are required for teaching in
today's classrooms, then future discussions of student voice must consider
anthropological factors (Erickson, 1982), cultural factors (Banks, 1993; Gay,
1988; Powell, Zehm & Garcia, 1996), and standpoint factors (Harding,
1991). I discovered these factors in the relationships that existed between
Jimmie and his team teachers. The teachers were anthropologists in that they
tried to understand how Jimmie related to the school and to their team. The
teachers were cultural workers in that they continuously tried to bring
together Jimmie's tendency to be part of a self-appointed school outcast
culture with their team culture. And rather than discounting Jimmie because
he initially demonstrated an overt aversion to school, his team teachers
affirmed his voice by beginning from his standpoint, not the teachers' stand-
points. Beginning from his standpoint meant trying to understand, from
Jimmie's point of view, how and why he was not fitting into the school and
team cultures. This in turn required the teachers to hear what he was saying,
even in his silence and in his absence. From what they heard the teachers
were able to bring Jimmie into the team culture. By doing this they affirmed
his voice without negating his standpoint. Such negation would have turned
Jimmie even further away from school than he was at the beginning of sixth
grade.

When Jimmie's teachers did these things, they were teaching from a
different set of assumptions, and alternative metaphors, than what has
previously framed teacher and student relationships in traditional classrooms.
The teachers' assumptions aligned with what Doll (1993) calls a transformative curriculum, where students are viewed as key stakeholders in creating
classroom curricula (Boomer et al., 1992). To construct this kind of curricula,
according to Doll (1993), "passages [between students and teachers] are
negotiated...where each party listens actively to what the other is saying. The
point is to find ways to connect varying viewpoints through engagement with
another" (p. 250). Darleen and her colleagues listened actively to Jimmie,
and they heard what he was saying. They eventually found ways, after

hearing and listening, to first connect with him personally, then connect with him academically.

Figure 1 compares the assumptions and related metaphors of a transformative, voice-centered curriculum to the assumptions of a traditional, content-centered curriculum. I interpreted the team learning environment and classroom curricula created by Jimmie's team teachers to be framed by the assumptions, metaphors, and precepts of a transformative curriculum.

FIGURE 1

Assumptions for Curricula That Awaken and Curricula That Manage Student Voices

Curriculum for awakening voice and sharing subject matter	Curriculum for managing voice and prescribing subject matter
CLASSROOM DYNAMICS	
negotiating shared curriculum	implementing prescribed curriculum
sharing power with students	maintaining centralized power
resolving classroom conflict	managing classroom problems
fostering responsible behavior	disciplining behavior
constructing shared meaning	imposing fixed meaning
promoting student-student relations	promoting teacher-student relations
CURRICULUM AND INSTRUCTION	
creating transformative curriculum	implementing prescribed curriculum
using interdisciplinary instruction	using single subject instruction
using nongraded types of evaluation	using graded types of evaluation
STUDENT METAPHORS	
student as empowered learner	student as controlled learner
student as active learner	student as passive learner
TEACHER METAPHORS	
teacher as anthropologist*	teacher as psychologist
teacher as facilitator	teacher as authoritarian
teacher as listener	teacher as talker

* focus on cultural dimensions of learners

Understanding the multiple dimensions of student voice

Moving toward a transformative curriculum as shown in Figure 1, where student voices are genuinely part of the classroom curriculum, means hearing multiple dimensions of student voices. When you listen to voices of students, and when you approach the classroom as an anthropologist and cultural worker, you gain valuable insights into the multiple dimensions of student voices (see Barone, 1989). You also learn how your school and classroom curricula and how your classroom instruction, while engaging some dimensions of student voices but overlooking others, connects some students to the classroom curriculum in meaningful ways while alienating other students (Eckert, 1989; Fine, 1991; Gay, 1988).

How do you know which dimensions you acknowledge with your classroom curriculum and instruction, and which dimensions you unawaringly, perhaps even innocently, overlook? In the conversation I had with Jimmie's teachers, Darleen Birdman, the team leader, made a statement relevant to this question. She said, "Everything a student does is voice." This comment is central to understanding one kind of voice, namely the behavioral voice. You must consider yet another kind of voice, however, if you are to really hear the fullness and richness of student voices. You must consider not only what a student *does* (i.e., behavioral voice) but also what a student *is* (i.e., cultural voice).

In this final section of the paper I propose, within an anthropological orientation, that everything a student is, as well as does, represents voice. Returning momentarily to Jimmie's case exemplifies what I mean here. To agree with Darleen's definition of student voice above means also to agree that Jimmie expressed a voice when he skipped school and when he was mostly silent in class. That was what he *did* at the beginning of sixth grade. What he *was*, however, was feeling lonely, angry, unwanted, unneeded, and upset over having to live in two different households. He was also consistently angry over the tension between him and his brother. Without responding to what Jimmie *was* as well as to what he *did*, his teachers might have further disengaged him from school.

What a student does in the classroom suggests a behavioral expression of some kind. These are the things that we actually see students do, and the things that we actually hear them say. Teachers mostly interact with students overtly on a behavioral level. Lesson objectives, classroom rules, and evaluation instruments are, for example, usually written in behavioral terms. What a student does tends to predominate traditional classroom instruction; for most of their professional lives educators, in very general terms, try to control, manage, and correct student behavior. The same occurs for politicians, policy makers, and school board members who also believe that managing and controlling the behavior of students should be part of school curriculum. When the entire focus is on what a student does, however, we hear only a portion of students' voices.

What a student is in the classroom suggests a cultural expression, or cultural voice, of some kind. This kind of voice is not always explicit, and may be expressed as habits, customs, beliefs, predispositions, and tendencies. Educators who are insensitive to certain cultural voices may demonstrate unintentional cultural bias that alienates some students from classroom learning (see Contreras and Lee, 1990, for a fuller discussion of unintentional cultural bias).

Student voices emerge from a number of cultural sources, such as home, family, race, ethnicity, language, deafness, religion, economic status, and gender. Also giving shape to the cultural dimension of student voices are biographical experiences, including problematic experiences at home where parents and/or siblings are engaged in addictive behaviors, such as alcoholism or drug addiction (see for example Powell, Gabe, & Zehm, 1994; Powell, Zehm & Kottler, 1995). In a society that is profoundly multicultural and global and in middle school settings where students are just beginning to search for and express the many voices they have, we must acknowledge the cultural dimensions of students' voices, we must bring light to what students are as much as we have brought light to what students do. Bissinger (1990) does a good job of this for student athletes and school athletic programs. This account questions an over-reliance on what students do, and openly challenges the deification of students' performance voices by both schools and their surrounding communities.

Viewing voice from the dual perspectives of the behavioral and the cultural requires educators to look more closely at the multiple dimensions of voice. As a means for doing this I suggest a typology of student voices in Figures 2 and 3. Figure 2 contains behavioral voices, and Figure 3 contains cultural voices. Although the voices are shown as separate and distinct, in reality they meld together.

Two classroom challenges are inherent in Figures 2 and 3 which all middle level educators must ultimately face. The first challenge is to determine which of the voices you acknowledge and how you acknowledge them. The second challenge, perhaps the most crucial one, is to determine which of the voices you unawaringly overlook, and to determine the consequences of this oversight.

FIGURE 2
Student Behaviorial Voices

autonomous voice	what tasks or duties that students carry out by themselves in a responsible manner
classroom social voice	what students incidentally say during social interactions
content knowing voice	what students academically learn and express
democratic voice	what classroom and school activities students are allowed to, or choose to, participate in
developmental voice	what students say that reflects their independence or separation from parents and other authority figures
fun-loving voice	what students demonstrate relative to the innocence of their early adolescence
rebellious voice	what retaliatory actions or expressions that students demonstrate, often (but not always) a function of early adolescence
shared voice	what ideas students share with each other; also collaboration
spontaneous voice	what students express honestly and sincerely without provocation

Figure 3

Student Cultural Voices

biographical voice	when students bring to the classroom their prior personal experiences
social class voice	when students demonstrate behaviors, actions, or expressions that reflect their socioeconomic background
ethnic voice	when students demonstrate unique behaviors, actions, or expressions that reflect their ethnicity
gender-specific voice	when students demonstrate behavior that typifies being socialized into male or female societal roles; when students express gender-specific needs
internal voice	when students have internal dialogues with themselves that may be unheard by others
racial voice	when students demonstrate behaviors, actions, or expressions that reflect their race
religious beliefs voice	when students explicitly or implicitly express their religious beliefs or values in the classroom toward peers, teachers, and the curriculum
silent voice	when students choose to remain silent in school, to become "invisible"
silenced voice	when students are alienated from school because of intentional or unintentional cultural bias by educators, peers, or curriculum
survival voice	when students living in dysfunctional home environments demonstrate inappropriate survival behaviors at school

Conclusion

Beane (1993a) writes, "If we truly mean to have a school that is responsive to young adolescents, then we must ask, 'Where are their voices in this effort?'" (p. 195). One way to make student voices part of this effort, to honor them as Oldfather and McLaughlin (1993) suggest, is for interdisciplinary teams of teachers to proactively focus on affirming the various voices that students express. As the case of Jimmie demonstrated, student voices do have various forms. Which forms, if appropriately affirmed, would make interdisciplinary teams more responsive to young persons? How can interdisciplinary teams, by their very design, incorporate the voices of students in their curricular decision making? Perhaps most pressing is the question, do middle schools really want to bring the voices of students into their learning environments? Jimmie's team teachers and his middle school clearly wanted this. What might have happened to Jimmie had he been in a school environment where student voices were less affirmed, where instruction was more content-centered, and where interdisciplinary teams were not part of the school (see Oldfather and McLaughlin, 1993, for important insights into this question)?

When a team of middle school teachers works concertedly to give their team students a voice in school, then students are brought into the harmony of the team culture, just as Jimmie was brought into the harmony of the team culture created by Darleen and her colleagues. When team teachers help students find their voice then students are heard, just as Jimmie was reportedly heard. Hearing voices, as Jimmie's teachers demonstrated, depends ultimately on the instructional choices you make and the beliefs you hold about student learning. Bell Hooks (1989) writes, "What is true is that we make choices, that we choose voices to hear and voices to silence" (p. 78). Which voices do you choose to hear, to affirm, to encourage, or to silence?

Acknowledgements

I am deeply grateful to Jimmie, who confidently and openly shared his personal experiences with me. I am also grateful to Darleen Birdman who helped organize this study, and to Frank Lamping, who was the principal of Thurman White Middle School at the time of the interviews. Mr. Lamping always held open the school doors for me as an educational researcher. Thanks also go to the remaining three team teachers (Lisa, Vivian, and Craig) who shared their valuable time and insights; to Heather Sabadin who provided essential feedback to me on earlier drafts of this chapter; and to the insightful middle school teachers and administrators in my class, Trends in Middle School Research, who reviewed this paper, and provided me with important suggestions for improving it.

Dedication

This chapter is dedicated to the memory of Cindy Lowery, whose excellent teaching at the middle level, while lasting only a few years, will always be remembered by the students who learned from her, by team and non-team teachers who worked closely by her side each day, and by others, including the author of this chapter, who learned about middle school teaching by exploring her classroom instruction. Nothing is more important than truly dedicated teachers working in small corners of the world with students whom they genuinely care about, as Cindy Lowery so fully demonstrated.

References

Apple, M. (1993). *Official knowledge: Democratic education in a conservative age.* New York: Routledge.

Banks, J. (1993). Approaches to multicultural curriculum reform. In J. Banks and C. Banks (Eds.), *Multicultural education: Issues and perspectives* (2nd ed) (pp. 195-214). Boston: Allyn and Bacon.

Barone, T. (1989). Ways of being at risk: The case of Billy Charles Barnett. *Phi Delta Kappan, 71,* 147-151.

Beane, J. (1993a). *A middle school curriculum: From rhetoric to reality* (2nd ed). Columbus, OH: National Middle School Association.

Beane, J. (1993b). Turning the floor over: Reflections on *A Middle Level Curriculum.* In T. Dickinson (Ed.), *Readings in middle school curriculum: A continuing conversation* (pp. 193-204). Columbus, OH: National Middle School Association.

Bissinger, H.G. (1990). *Friday night lights: A town, a team, and a dream.* New York: Addison-Wesley Publishing Company.

Boomer, G., Lester, N., Onore, C., & Cook, J. (1992). *Negotiating the curriculum:Educating for the 21st century.* Bristol, PA: The Falmer Press.

Bullough, R.V. (1994). Digging at the roots: Discipline, management, and metaphor. *Action in Teacher Education, 16*(1), 1-10.

Carnegie Council on Adolescent Development (1989). *Turning points: Preparing American youth for the 21st century.* New York: Carnegie Corporation.

Contreras, A., & Lee, O. (1990). Differential treatment of students by middle school science teachers: Unintended cultural bias. *Science Education, 74*(4), 433-444.

Doll, W. (1993).*A post-modern perspective on curriculum.* New York: Teachers College Press.

Eckert, P. (1989). *Jocks and burnouts: Social categories and identity in the high school.* New York: Teachers College Press.

Erb, T.O., & Doda, N.M. (1989). *Team organization: Promise — practices and possibilities.* Washington, DC: National Educational Association.

Erickson, F. (1982). Taught cognitive learning in its immediate environments: A neglected topic in the anthropology of education. *Anthropology and Education Quarterly, 13* (2), 149-180.

Erickson, F., & Schultz, J. (1992). Students' experience of the curriculum. In P. Jackson (Ed.), *Handbook of research on curriculum* (pp. 465-485). New York: MacMillan Publishing Company.

Fine, M. (1991). *Framing dropouts: Notes on the politics of an urban public school.* Albany, NY: State University of New York Press.

Freire, P. (1972). *Pedagogy of the oppressed.* London: Penguin Books.

Gay, G. (1988). Designing relevant curricula for diverse learners. *Education and urban society, 20* (4), 327-340.

George, P.S. (1992). Four phases in the life of a team. In J.H. Lounsbury (Ed.), *Connecting the curriculum through interdisciplinary instruction,* (pp. 135-142). (Reprinted from George, P.S. (1982). Interdisciplinary team organization: Four operational phases. *Middle School Journal, 13* (3), 10-13.) Columbus, OH: National Middle School Association.

George, P.S., & Oldaker, L.L. (1985). *Evidence for the middle school.* Columbus, OH: National Middle School Association.

George, P.S., & Shewey, K. (1994). *New evidence for the middle school.* Columbus, OH: National Middle School Association.

Gergen, K. (1991). *The saturated self: Dilemmas of identity in contemporary life.* New York: Basic Books.

Greene, M. (1993). Diversity and inclusion: Toward a curriculum for human beings. *Teachers College Record, 95* (2), 211-221.

Harding, S. (1991). *Whose science? Whose knowledge? Thinking from women's lives.* Ithaca, NY: Cornell University Press.

Hooks, B.(1989). *Talking back:Thinking feminist, thinking black.* Boston: South End Press.

Johnson, S.M. (1990). *Teachers at work: Achieving success in our schools.* New York: Basic Books.

Kincheloe, J. (1993). *Toward a critical politics of teacher thinking: Mapping the postmodern.* Westport, CT: Bergin & Garvey.

McLaughlin, H.J. (1994). From negation to negotiation: Moving away from the management metaphor. *Action in Teacher Education, 16* (1), 75-84.

Middle Level Educator.(1994). Sandra Babich Memorial Award for quality teaching. *Middle Level Educator, 2* (2), 3-5.

Mills, R., Powell, R., & Pollak, J. (1992). The influence of middle level interdisciplinary teaming on teacher isolation: A case study. *Research in Middle Level Education, 15* (2), 9-25.

Nolen, S. (1994, April). *Learning from students.* Paper presented at the annual meeting of the American Educational Research Association, New Orleans.

Noyes, R.(Ed.). (1956). *English romantic poetry and prose.* New York: Oxford University Press.

Oakley, A. (1981). Interviewing women: A contradiction in terms. In H. Roberts (Ed.), *Doing feminist research* (pp. 30-61). London: Routledge.

Oldfather, P., & McLaughlin, J. (1993). Gaining and losing voice: A longitudinal study of students' continuing impulse to learn across elementary and middle level contexts. *Research in Middle Level Education, 17* (1), 1-25.

Perkinson, H. (1993). *Teachers without goals: Students without purposes.* New York: McGraw Hill.

Powell, R.(1993). Seventh graders perspectives of their interdisciplinary team. *Middle School Journal, 24* (3), 49-57.

Powell, R., Birdman, D., Huff, B., Havas, K., & Bednar, J. (1992, January). *Toward a deeper understanding of interdisciplinary teaming: Collaborative research.* Paper presented at the annual meeting of the Western Regional Middle Level Consortium, Phoenix, AZ.

Powell, R., Gabe, J., & Zehm, S. (1994). *Classrooms under the influence: Reaching early adolescent children of alcoholics.* Reston, VA: National Association of Secondary School Principals.

Powell, R., & Mills, R. (1995). Professional knowledge sharing among interdisciplinary team teachers: A study of intra-team mentoring. *Research in Middle Level Education Quarterly, 18* (3), 27-40.

Powell, R., Zehm, S., & Garcia, J. (1996). *Field experience:Strategies for exploring diversity in classrooms.* Columbus, OH: Merrill.

Powell, R., Zehm, S., & Kottler, J. (1995). *Classrooms under the influence: Addicted parents, addicted students.* Newbury Park, CA: Corwin Press.

Shaw, C. (1993). A content analysis of teacher talk during middle school team meetings. *Research in Middle Level Education, 17* (1), 27-45.

SooHoo, S. (1993). Students as partners in research and restructuring schools. *Educational Forum, 57* (4), 386-393.

Thorkildsen, T., & Jordan, C. (1994, April). *Negotiating a moral community of scholars.* Paper presented at the annual meeting of the American Educational Research Association, New Orleans.

Trueba, H., Jacobs, L., & Kirton, E. (1990). *Cultural conflict and adaptation: The case of Hmong children in American society.* New York: The Falmer Press.

Parental Perspectives

12

Sue Carol Thompson, with Marla Harper,
Karen King, Stan Smith, and K.O. Strohbehn

The combined impact of societal changes and early adolescence make the need for home and school to work together more critical than it has ever been. Myers and Monson (1992) have outlined the following benefits of parent involvement in schooling:

1. Academic performance improved.
2. Parents become closer to their children as school becomes a shared experience, a family experience.
3. Relations between home and school, as well as between the school and community, improve.
4. Parents have the skills needed to help students in the classroom, both academically and socially.
5. Students need all the extra support and understanding their parents can give them, both at home and at school.
6. Services performed by parents and other volunteers stretch limited school funds.

If Myers and Monson are right, what are middle schools doing to capitalize on the power of parental involvement in the education of their young adolescents?

In the mid-1980s, the Blue Valley School District in eastern Kansas, like many across the United States, decided to evaluate its middle level programs and determine a future direction based on current research and practice regarding the most effective ways to educate young adolescents. During the 1987-88 school year, a committee composed of teachers, parents, administrators, and board members met to study and share information about the characteristics and needs of young adolescents and the organizational structure needed to best meet those needs.

As a result of their efforts, the Middle Level Study Committee recommended to the Board of Education five organizational changes to be implemented over a three-year period. The first of these changes was the implementation of interdisciplinary teaming, followed by a full range of exploratory classes, an expanded activity program, and an advisement program. The fifth component of the plan, staff development, has been ongoing over these past several years. The decision was also made to hire a middle level director who would oversee the new program.

When the Middle Level Study Committee was meeting to determine the philosophy, organizational structure, and program components necessary to plan schools that would truly be responsive to the needs of young adolescents, committee members were told time after time that the current level of communication between home and school needed to be improved.

No wonder! The organizational structure was based on a departmentalized model where students in grades six through eighth traveled throughout the school changing classes every forty-five or fifty minutes and interacting with as many as seven adults a day who could not, because of scheduling restraints, share the same students.

Consequently, if students were experiencing difficulties in their classes or with their peers, teachers did not know which of their colleagues had these same students, and teachers certainly did not have common planning periods to discuss such concerns with each other, much less parents. While teachers were certainly caring and compassionate individuals, the organizational structure of the school was a roadblock to the development of a satisfactory communication system with parents.

While the organizational culture of a middle school must be looked at holistically and the components of a middle school are just parts of a much larger picture, the decision to implement interdisciplinary teaming, where every student is assigned to a two- to five-person team with a common group of students, significantly improved the home-school connection in the five middle schools of the Blue Valley School District.

It is not surprising that the superintendent and school administrators were able to "sell" the community on the transition from the old junior high model to a middle school model by emphasizing an increased amount of interaction and communication between home and school. When some parents became unhappy about the changes in the activities/athletics program, they made it very clear that they were quite pleased with the interdisciplinary teaming occurring in their child's middle school.

At the end of the third year of the implementation of the middle school concept in the Blue Valley School District, an in-depth evaluation was conducted by two independent consultants, Thomas Erb of the University of Kansas and John Lounsbury of Georgia College. The findings of the evaluation were based on examinations of data from several sources including: staff and student interviews; data collected from middle school Site-Based Leadership Councils; parent, teacher, and student surveys and comment sheets; activities participation data; district standardized testing results; and several measures of subsequent high school performance.

The teaming concept was recognized in the report as a very successful element. The concept was found to encourage teachers of various disciplines to coordinate and integrate their planned curriculum and to provide a much better communication system for parents. In fact, 73 percent of the parents strongly agreed or agreed with the statement "Communication from the school concerning my child is adequate," and 76 percent of the parents surveyed believed that the school kept them adequately informed of their child's academic progress. Eighty-five percent of the parents surveyed believed that the middle school had provided a smooth educational transition for their child from the elementary school they attended, and 81 percent of the parents believed that their child's middle school provided a warm, supportive learning environment for their child.

For the 1990-91 school year, the rate of parental contacts, both face-to-face conferences and phone calls, reported by teachers ranged from over 1600 to over 2600 per school. This averaged to between three to five school-to-home contacts concerning an individual student. These totals did not include written communications such as notes or assignment sheets. These figures were corroborated by the fact that both parents and teachers ranked the statement "It is easy to contact teachers if I have questions about my child" first among all items on their survey forms.

The experience in Blue Valley demonstrates the capacity of interdisciplinary teaming to improve home-school communication and encourage continued parental involvement in their children's education. Teams acted as an antidote to the problem of inadequate communication and declining involvement. This result is especially significant since young adolescents often resist parental "interference" in their lives at school.

Parental involvement in school plays a key role in the success of young adolescents as students. According to Eccles and Harold (1993), there is increasing evidence that the quality of the links between parents and schools does influence children's and adolescents' school success. Not only does active parental involvement in school play a critical role in a child's educational success at all grade levels, parents and teachers are positively affected by good parent-school links. When their parents demonstrate caring by being involved in their schooling, students' attitudes, behaviors, and achievement are positively influenced. Parent involvement does make a difference (Henderson & Marburger, 1990).

Many researchers have looked at groups of high and low achieving students and studied the differences in how their families and schools have behaved. Benson, Buckley, and Medrich (1980) questioned families of 764 sixth graders about how they spend their time and found that children with parents who engage them in educational activities tend to do better in school, even if they are from very disadvantaged backgrounds. Rankin (1967) found that high achievers are much more likely to have active, interested, and involved parents than low achievers.

The Carnegie Council on Adolescent Development's (1989) landmark document *Turning Points: Preparing American Youth for the 21st Century* states that if middle schools are going to meet the needs of their students, families must be reengaged in the education of young adolescents. The Council recommended giving families meaningful roles in school governance. Although the evidence is clear that parental involvement in all of its forms improves student achievement and attitudes toward school, such involvement declines progressively during the elementary school years. By the time a student reaches middle school, there is a diminished relationship between school and home.

A survey by the National Center for Educational Statistics (1990) that sampled 25,000 eighth graders revealed that the level of parent involvement both with their schoolchildren and with their children's school is frighteningly low. Nearly two thirds (62%) of students say they never or rarely discuss their classes or school programs with their parents, one quarter (26%) say their parents rarely or never check their homework, while 57 percent of parents say they rarely (once or twice a month) or never help their children with homework. Only half (50%) of the parents have attended a school meeting since the beginning of the school year, and fewer than three in ten (29%) have visited their children's classes.

Scales (1991) compared a young person moving through the period of early adolescence to a caterpillar metamorphosing into a butterfly, but, points out that a young person's metamorphosis is not predictable. He states that:

> Young people both cling to and struggle against the co-
> coon. Changeability and ambivalence are normal, a fact
> that can drive parents to distraction.
>
> It is an unanswered question as to who is having the
> harder time in early adolescence, young persons trying to

develop their own identity without losing connection to oth-
ers or parents trying to accept that change while still hang-
ing on to their children. (p. 11)

Parents bring many fears into a middle level school as their youngster moves from a small close knit elementary school where everyone knows everyone else into a larger, often less personalized, middle school setting. Further exacerbating the concerns of parents are the increasingly high risk activities that young adolescents might choose to engage in as they search for independence and autonomy.

Although it is true that young adolescents desperately want to belong and are striving to form positive peer relationships, they are also seeking positive social interaction with adults. As Scales (1991) points out, "Popular culture follows in depicting the period as one of rejection of parents, whereas rejection is really temporary and on a superficial level for most" (p. 15). The great majority of young adolescents give their parents grades of *B* or better, and say they agree with many of their parents' values on sex, politics, and religion. The message that parents need to hear is that while peers are a powerful force in the socialization process, they do not replace parents. Parents need to remain in close contact with their young adolescents and show interest in school and extracurricular activities.

Unfortunately, some teachers see parental involvement as an intrusion into their work. They are fearful that parents will be critical of their work or not understand the instructional methods they are using. Various school and teacher practices, according to Eccles and Harold (1993), have disenfranchised parents from schools. These practices involve poor reporting practices, hostility toward parents, lack of understanding of how to effectively involve parents, and lack of interest in involving parents.

In addition, the behavior of young adolescents sometimes conveys the message that they do not want their parents to be involved in school. Eccles and Harold (1993) state that while parents may feel that their youngsters do not want them to come to school, as evidenced by a common adolescent plea not to have their parents chaperone school activities, this belief is too extreme. Young adolescents want to know that their parents support their educational endeavors. They also want positive structure and support from both home and school and this can best be achieved when they see parents and teachers communicating and working together.

Parents Express Their Views on Teaming

Four parents of eight middle school students in the Blue Valley School District were asked to share their perceptions of the effects of interdisciplinary teaming, not only for their children but also for themselves. Although interdisciplinary teaming is a core organizational element of middle schools, if teaming does not improve the learning environment for young adolescents, the full potential of teaming has not been reached. Vars (1993) has expressed the view that since life is "interdisciplinary," if the curriculum is to help young people relate to life, at least some portion of it should also be interdisciplinary.

Interdisciplinary teaching

The parents were asked if they had seen evidence of this kind of interdisciplinary teaching on their child's team. All four parents talked about their student's team teachers working hard to find ways to "connect" the separate subjects. They were knowledgeable about their children's learning experiences because they came home excited about what was happening in their classrooms, and parents received communication about these activities from the teams. Stan Smith, father of two middle school students at Leawood Middle School and a Junior High Principal in a neighboring district, commented on the benefit of several of the culminating activities that had been planned in the evening so students could showcase to their families their work on thematic units.

Marla Harper, former PTA president at Harmony Middle School and mother of a daughter who started high school this past year, stated:

> *I am a big fan of the middle school concept and the way students learn now. The teaming of teachers is a wonderful concept. There is a greater chance of success for all students in this system. No longer are students getting a fragmented education like I experienced in the old junior high program.*
>
> *During her seventh grade year my daughter experienced the best example of a multidisciplinary unit. The team studied the rainforest. Every subject area dealt with this topic which even included a field trip to Omaha, Nebraska, to visit a rainforest. Projects were done in every discipline— that helped students to see the connectiveness between the disciplines in relationship to the topic they were studying. This is a wonderful way to learn.*

Mrs. Harper continued by saying:

> *In addition to the thematic learning experiences that each team provides for their students, as a parent and member of PTA I have also had an opportunity to work with the media specialist in planning a one day event centered around the theme of "Building Harmony at Harmony Middle School." Parents and the media specialist and her staff have worked closely with all of the interdisciplinary teams in relating this theme to the work that is occurring on their team. During the 1994-95 school year this project was ongoing throughout the entire year. I believe that this kind of event can only take place in an environment where teachers are encouraged to connect their disciplines through multidisciplinary and interdisciplinary units. Teaming allows this to happen.*

Board of Education member and middle school parent K.O. Strohbehn also talked about student learning in relation to interdisciplinary teaming. She said, "Project G.R.O.W. is an eighth grade program at Leawood Middle School that provides students with a 'real-life' experience of starting a business, developing a product, marketing, and selling the product. While students may not recognize the value of this style of learning, I support the hands-on approach to academics whenever possible."

She also shared information about a language arts project that her son experienced where each student had to identify a societal problem, research the problem, visit and interview a community organization that dealt with the problem, write a summary report, and perform an interpretive activity before the class.

She concluded by saying:

> *I believe students learn in many ways. Teachers must be able to identify how their students learn so that they can construct their lesson plans to accommodate all learners. Ideally, this identification is made in elementary school. Teaming helps in this regard. By meeting regularly as a group the team is able to share insights on students and this should help the teachers provide better individual instruction for each child.*

Karen King, an elementary teacher in the Blue Valley School District and mother of a sixth grader, a seventh grader, and an eighth grader, said that she believed that all three of her children benefited both academically and socially from the teaming approach. She stated,

Teaming made it possible for the teachers to provide a more flexible and varied service delivery model for their students. My children were involved in a variety of different learning experiences where teachers worked diligently to show students the connections between language arts, social studies, math, and science.

Stan Smith was so impressed with the benefits of interdisciplinary teaming for his children that he decided to study the teaming concept for his school. He consequently promoted and piloted interdisciplinary teaming in his school, and it has now been adopted in the junior high schools in his school district. Stan Smith found teaming to be really powerful in restructuring a middle level school to be more responsive to the needs of young adolescents. "Often times," he stated, "in non-teaming situations, kids are thrown to the wolves. They are having to adjust to seven different teachers who don't communicate, sometimes as many as seven different philosophies, and seven different set of rules and expectations." He concluded, "Even the worse team is still better than what you had in the old junior high departmentalized system."

Creating a supportive environment

There are several key transition points in a student's educational career and the transition into middle school is one of those points. During this transition youngsters are experiencing many changes simultaneously. According to Epstein and Mac Iver (1990), they enter puberty, change schools, revise peer and friendship groups, begin new interactions with their parents, and begin to expand their social boundaries and participation in their communities. Transitions are both difficult and exciting as they mark points of risk and opportunity for student development. All four parents talked about the importance of a smooth transition from elementary school to middle school. One of the primary goals of an interdisciplinary team is to create a small community of learners that reduces the isolation, anonymity, and alienation that young adolescents often feel in large, impersonal schools and that reduces the possibility of serious problems resulting from dealing with so many changes simultaneously. The parents talked about how the teaming organization provided a sense of security for their children and how the special activities the team planned for students helped them build a sense of identity with their team.

Marla Harper talked about activities that her daughter's sixth grade team had used to help students get acquainted with the school and with each other. Her daughter's team designed a team t-shirt and a team logo and students felt less intimidated in the larger middle school because they were a member of a smaller group of students with which they could identify. In addition to being a member of an interdisciplinary team, her daughter was also a member of a small advisory group.

Marla Harper stated:

> At Meet-the-Teacher night, I was pleased to have the team teachers give their goals and expectations for the students. The school theme was reiterated, and the team goals supported the schoolwide theme. Life Skills were posted in every classroom. This was obviously something that the team teachers felt very strongly about and was woven into everything they did. Many times I heard them refer to having students do their personal best, which was one of the Life Skills.

Articulation activities are equally comforting to parents. These activities assure that parents are better informed about the school programs, requirements, procedures, opportunities, and responsibilities at the new level of schooling. Many of the teams in Blue Valley have Meet-the-Teacher night before or during the first week of school. This significantly reduced the anxiety both parents and students felt about the new school, new school year, and new teachers.

Stan Smith shared the concern that he and his wife had about their son's lack of organization skills when he entered middle school. They had decided to wean him off the dependency he had on them as parents. He said the team was extremely helpful in picking up where the parents left off as they coordinated efforts, provided an assignment notebook and calendar of important deadlines, and established a telephone hotline. "Teaming," according to Stan Smith, "allowed my son to be more successful with managing his own time."

When the Smiths attended parent conferences with the team, they not only wanted to hear about grades, they also wanted to hear about how their son and daughter were doing in other areas, such as making friends and getting along with their peers. Interdisciplinary teams could give a much more complete picture of the students since they shared information across the school day in a variety of settings. Karen King, mother of three middle school students, felt that meeting with the whole team provided a broader and more accurate picture of a student than meeting with individual teachers in isolation from each other.

Ms. King also talked about her children's smooth and somewhat uneventful transition from elementary to middle school:

> *In the spring of their fifth grade year, each child spent a day visiting the middle school in anticipation of the coming school year. This helped build excitement and quell some fears. As parents we also attended an open house before school began for both parents and students. Tours of the building were conducted and newsletters were received throughout the summer. Students had an opportunity to buy school supplies, receive their team assignment, practice locker combinations. and visit with their friends on enrollment day.*

Some of our middle schools are now sending students their team assignments at the beginning of the summer so that they do not have to worry and wait until fall to find out which team they have been assigned to.

Most parents in the Blue Valley School District have been very supportive of the interdisciplinary teaming concept at the middle school level. Over the past eight years, teams have worked diligently to build positive relationships with parents in order to more effectively meet the needs of young adolescents. Teams continually strive to find more and more ways to communicate with parents and include parents in the educational process.

Teaming's roles in improving learning environments

Over these last several years, Blue Valley middle school administrators and teachers have looked at the organizational, philosophical, and psychological assumptions that we believe should drive decisions at our level. We identified six components to address as we continue to improve the learning environments in our middle schools. These six components are:

1. School climate and culture
2. Structure and organization
3. Management and school administration
4. Family and community
5. Instructional techniques
6. Assessment and accountability.

The component of structure and organization emphasizes the belief that the middle school should create a community of staff, students, and parents that work together to achieve academic and personal goals for each student. We believe that the public school system was founded on the principle that the participation of families and communities in school decision making is essential to its success. We recognize the increasing diversity of public school children and the changing composition of families and the need to change certain practices that create hardships for some families.

And lastly, in the area of assessment and accountability, we have committed ourselves to the implementation of a cross-curricular portfolio process for every middle school student in our district. Each middle school interdisciplinary team is in the process of developing its portfolio system. Each middle school team is also determining how to share portfolios with parents during the course of the school year.

We know that parents want to know more about what their child knows and can do, and more importantly, how their child learns. Parents will be able to see evidence of growth over time in the four areas of academic development:

1. *Knowledge and skills* across all content areas and the ability to use those skills and knowledge across disciplines to complete projects and assignments

2. *Communication* that demonstrates effective written and oral student expression

3. *Problem solving and critical thinking*

4. *Personal and social awareness* through application of life skills such as effort, goal setting, responsibility and cooperation.

The cross-curricular portfolio is a meaningful way to involve both students and parents in the learning process that focuses on the importance of student responsibility. Real student work, gathered in the portfolio, can show the student, teacher, and parent, what the student knows and can do.

There are a multitude of reasons and ways to involve parents in the education of their children. In the Blue Valley School District, interdisciplinary team organization is the foundation for much of that involvement.

References

Benson, C., Buckley, S., & Medrich, E. (1980). Families as educators: Time use contributions to school achievement. In A. Henderson (Ed.), Parent Participation-student achievement: The evidence grows (NCCE occasional papers, pp. 19-21). Columbia, MD: National Committee for Citizens in Education.

Carnegie Council on Adolescent Development. (1989). *Turning points: Preparing American youth for the 21st century.* New York: Carnegie Corporation.

Eccles, J., & Harold, R. (1993). Parent-school involvement during the early adolescent years. In R. Takanishi (Ed.). *Adolescence in the 1990s* (pp. 110-129). New York: Teachers College Press.

Epstein, J., & Mac Iver, D. (1990). *Education in the middle grades: National practices and trends.* Columbus, OH: National Middle School Association.

Henderson, A., & Marburger, C. (1990). *A workbook on parent involvement.* Washington, DC: National Committee for Citizens in Education.

Myers, J., & Monson, L. (1992). *Involving families in middle level education.* Columbus, OH: National Middle School Association.

National Center for Educational Statistics. (1990). *A profile of the American eighth grader.* Washington, DC: U. S. Department of Education, Office of Educational Research and Improvement.

Rankin, P. (1967, February). The relationship between parent behavior and achievement of inner-city elementary school children. Paper presented at the annual conference of the American Educational Research Association, New York.

Scales, P. (1991). *A portrait of young adolescents in the 1990s: Implications for promoting healthy growth and development.* Chapel Hill, NC: The Center for Early Adolescence.

Vars, G. (1993). *Interdisciplinary teaching: Why & how.* Columbus, OH: National Middle School Association.

Part IV

The Knowledge Base

After exploring interdisciplinary teaming in middle schools from a number of different practical perspectives, we turn our attention to more formal ways of understanding teaming. Four different knowledge bases are presented in this section. Each one of them looks at a different aspect of teaming.

In Chapter 13 C. Kenneth McEwin provides a type of epidemiology to describe the spread of teaming across the country. He traces the growth of interdisciplinary teaming from the first studies conducted in the 1960s to recent 1990s studies that show that teaming has "infected" approximately half of all middle level schools in the country. Each successive study over the past thirty years has reconfirmed the trend toward teaming in America's middle level schools. McEwin also documents trends in various teaming practices such as use of flexible scheduling and the selection of team leadership.

William Wraga takes on the challenging task of explaining the research on a practice often confused with interdisciplinary teaming – team teaching. These two concepts, both containing the root word "team," have been confused by educators ever since interdisciplinary teaming entered educational practice about thirty years ago. Based on his reading of the literature on team teaching, William Wraga presents an analysis that suggests that interdisciplinary team organization is a latter-day middle school adaptation of the "team teaching" concept. By contrasting Wraga's perspective to that in Chapter 2, readers will be in a position to better assess the roots and meaning of teaming as an organizational feature of middle schools.

The growth of interdisciplinary teaming in middle schools is not occurring in a vacuum. Jane and Fred Page introduce us to the research that has been conducted on teaming in settings other than schools. Part of the justification for teaming in schools is based on the fact that teams are becoming more prevalent in other areas of human endeavor. Educators can gain useful insights into the practice of teaming by knowing how it is functioning in non-school settings.

What do we know about the effects of teaming? After thirty years what does research show about the impact of teaming on teachers and students?

David Strahan with his associates Nan Bowles, Vanessa Richardson, and Sarah Hanawald provides readers with a review of research findings showing the differences that teaming makes. After examining the perceptions of students and teachers about teaming, Strahan examines the effects of teaming on the work life of teachers. Chapter 16 also discusses the emerging findings related to teaming's effects on student behavior and achievement. This chapter is indeed a work in progress. Research on teaming in middle level schools has exploded in the 1990s. Every volume of *Research in Middle Level Education Quarterly* and *Middle School Journal* contains current updates of research on the effects of interdisciplinary teaming on teachers and students.

This section of *We Gain More Than We Give* is designed to provide readers with answers to questions about the "big picture." Whether readers are concerned about how extensive is teaming and various teaming practices, how teaming relates to similar educational practices, how middle school teaming relates to teaming outside of schools, or how teaming affects the teacher and students who experience it, this section will provide valuable answers.

Trends in Establishing Interdisciplinary Team Organization in Middle Schools   **13**

C. Kenneth McEwin

Interdisciplinary team organization is now widely considered an essential component of developmentally responsive schools for young adolescents. It is an essential feature of middle school reform since it is an organizational plan that provides increased opportunities for teacher planning and instruction (Oakes, Quartz, Gong, Guiton, & Lipton, 1993). It is a crucial component because it allows and encourages teachers to teach a diverse student body in developmentally responsive ways to accomplish important goals such as the integration of curriculum.

As documented throughout this book, interdisciplinary team organization, when carefully planned, implemented, and maintained, is a key component of highly successful middle school programs. It is gaining popularity not only in the United States, but also in the middle grades of schools in Canada as well as in international schools in Europe, South America, and Asia (George & Shewey, 1994; Waggoner & McEwin, 1992). Additionally, significant numbers of American senior high schools have established teacher teams (Cawelti, 1994a; 1994b).

This chapter describes the growth and current status of interdisciplinary teaming in America's middle level schools. Comparisons with past practice are made so a historical perspective may be gained. The data base drawn upon includes several major studies, most notably a comprehensive study of middle schools conducted by Alexander in 1968, a 20-year follow up study by Alexander and McEwin (1989a; 1989b), and a 25-year partial replication study by McEwin, Dickinson, and Jenkins in 1993 (1996). Results from other studies are used to supplement these data.

Putting teams in historical perspective

Interdisciplinary team organization is a reform recommendation of the past 30 years that has often been ignored or poorly carried out in thousands of middle grades schools. Though it is not a brand new experimental idea or practice, in historical time it is a fairly recent concept. It has, however, too frequently been implemented in isolation without being part of a comprehensive reform plan.

The rationale for team organization has its roots in the junior high school movement where it surfaced as a call for core curriculum (Van Til, Vars, & Lounsbury, 1967; Wright, 1958). Proponents of core curriculum had many of the same goals in mind as do present day advocates of interdisciplinary team organization. For example, Gruhn and Douglas (1956) noted that core curriculum proponents were concerned by the extreme departmentalization which was common in junior high schools and indicated that it needed to be modified so that "pupils may have the security of knowing a few teachers well, that teachers may become intimately acquainted with their pupils, and that better integration may be achieved" (p. 84). The junior high school modification that supported the core curriculum was for one teacher to integrate two or more disciplines for a common group of students. Today, the advocates of teaming in middle schools use much of the rationale for core to further their cause – a case of different means (core and team organization) aimed at a similar end (e.g., integrated curriculum and developmentally responsive instruction).

Since core classrooms developed in fewer than one in five middle grades schools (Wright, 1958), early proponents of the middle school included interdisciplinary team organization as the new means to address the needs of young adolescents. William M. Alexander, in his historic 1963 speech at Cornell University in which he proposed the new middle school stated: "It would facilitate the introduction in grades five and six of some specialization and team teaching in staffing patterns" (Alexander, 1963/1995, p. 24). He recommended: "A team of three to five teachers could be assigned to each group of 75 to 150 pupils, organized either on a single grade or multi grade basis" (p. 24). The importance of interdisciplinary team organization was also emphasized in early books that helped shape the middle school movement, for example *The Emergent Middle School* (Alexander, Williams, Compton, Hines, Prescott, & Kealy, 1968) and *Perspectives on the Middle School* (Grooms, 1967).

Despite the advocacy for interdisciplinary team organization in the middle school, many questions remain. What is the extent of its implementation in middle level schools? Which grade organization patterns are most likely to be closely associated with interdisciplinary team organization? What is the extent of its use at various grade levels in middle level schools? These and related questions are explored below.

The extent of interdisciplinary team organization in middle level schools

The use of interdisciplinary team organization has increased significantly in the past 25 years. For example, the percentage of 6-8 middle schools in which sixth grade language arts is taught on an interdisciplinary team has increased from 8 percent in 1968 (Alexander, 1968) to 33 percent in 1988 (Alexander & McEwin, 1989b) to 59 percent in 1993 (McEwin, Dickinson & Jenkins, 1996) (Figure 1). Although the increase may not seem dramatic for the first 20 years, the use of interdisciplinary team organization for teaching sixth grade language arts increased 26 percentage points in the five years between 1988 and 1993. While this change was taking place, the use of the self-contained organizational plan declined from 30 percent in 1968 to only 11 percent by 1993.

The use of departmentalization first increased between 1968 and 1988, then declined in popularity to only 29% between 1988 and 1993. This decrease in the use of departmentalization is especially noteworthy since its use has traditionally worked against teaming. Departmentalization separates teachers into departments and has students taking separate courses from specialists in each subject. It is a traditional practice that has posed a difficult roadblock for schools that seek to become developmentally responsive to the needs of young adolescents.

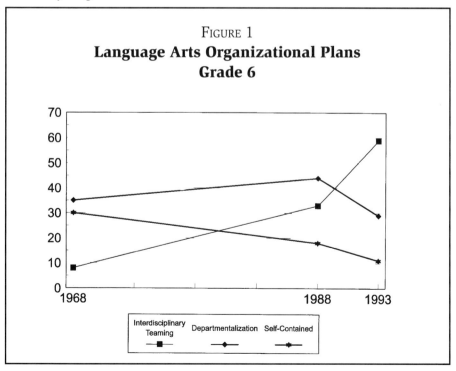

FIGURE 1
**Language Arts Organizational Plans
Grade 6**

The use of interdisciplinary team organization has expanded to include other grade levels and other basic subject areas (Table 1). For example, in mathematics at the eighth grade level where teaming has been perhaps the most difficult to implement and sustain successfully, its use has grown from 6 percent in 1968 to 23 percent in 1988, to 42 percent in 1993. Similar increases have occurred in science and social studies during these same periods. McEwin, Dickinson, and Jenkins (1996) report that 12 of every 20 (60%) middle schools practice interdisciplinary teaming at the sixth grade level. This ratio is 9 of 20 (45%) schools at the eighth grade level.

TABLE 1
Percents of Middle Schools Utilizing Certain Plans for Organizing Instruction in Basic Subjects, 1968, 1988 & 1993

Subject Area	Grade	Interdisciplinary Team			Departmentalization			Self-Contained		
		'68	'88	'93	'68	'88	'93	'68	'88	'93
Language Arts	5	3	41	46	20	26	20	60	38	34
	6	8	33	59	35	44	29	30	18	11
	7	6	40	53	74	66	43	1	6	5
	8	6	31	45	74	71	50	1	6	5
	Av.	6	36	51	51	52	36	23	17	14
Math	5	3	31	44	33	31	23	50	36	33
	6	8	37	58	50	48	32	24	16	11
	7	6	27	49	88	71	46	0	5	5
	8	6	23	42	89	75	53	0	4	5
	Av.	6	30	48	65	56	39	19	15	14
Science	5	3	30	48	30	26	22	55	39	30
	6	7	36	58	50	47	32	26	16	10
	7	5	26	49	87	71	46	0	4	4
	8	6	22	44	87	76	52	0	5	4
	Av.	5	29	50	64	55	38	20	16	12
Social Studies	5	3	29	47	28	27	20	60	27	33
	6	7	37	59	39	46	31	32	17	11
	7	5	28	58	80	68	38	1	4	4
	8	6	23	45	76	72	51	2	5	4
	Av.	5	29	52	56	53	35	24	13	13

1968: Alexander definition of middle schools
1988: Grades 5-8 schools data are used for fifth grade and grades 6-8 schools data for other grade levels
1993: Grades 5-8 schools data are used for fifth grade and grades 6-8 schools data for other grade levels
Av: Average for all four grade levels

Closely associated with successful interdisciplinary team organization is the use of flexible scheduling. It is difficult, if not impossible, to have highly successful interdisciplinary team organization plans without also having flexible scheduling to support them. However, only about 5 percent of respondents to the 1968 Alexander study reported the use of flexible scheduling at the sixth grade level. This percentage had increased to 30 percent by 1988 (Alexander & McEwin, 1989b), and to 40 percent in 1993 (McEwin, Dickinson & Jenkins, 1996). Increases were also found at the seventh and eighth grade levels (Figure 2). However, the unfortunate conclusion to be drawn from these data is that only approximately two-thirds of middle schools using team organization employ flexible block schedules. On the positive side, the number of middle schools implementing flexible schedules has risen by one-third or more in the five-year span from 1988 to 1993.

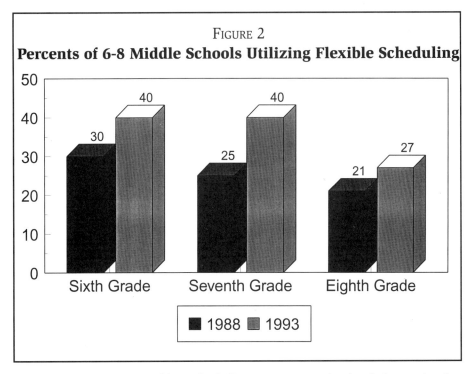

FIGURE 2
Percents of 6-8 Middle Schools Utilizing Flexible Scheduling

In summary, the use of interdisciplinary team organization is increasing in middle schools in all four basic subject areas. This practice seems to be a more common occurrence in middle schools with especially good reputations. George and Shewey (1994) reported a study of 108 middle schools that had made serious attempts to implement developmentally responsive programs; 87 percent had established interdisciplinary teams. Seventy-five percent of these schools had also established flexible schedules.

There is a trend toward flexible scheduling, but 84 percent of middle schools continue to utilize a schedule of daily periods, equal in length (McEwin, Dickinson & Jenkins, 1996). It should be noted, however, that many of these schools block some of these equal periods so that basic subjects can be blocked and core teachers can have common planning periods. Additionally, six percent of 6-8 middle schools report having daily periods of varying length, with the seven period day being the most common plan.

Interdisciplinary team organization and grade organization

There is a clear correlation between different grade organization patterns and interdisciplinary team organization. For example, Epstein and Mac Iver (1990a), in a comprehensive national study of 1,753 schools with grade organizations that included grade seven, found that more 6-8 middle schools (just more than 40%) used interdisciplinary teaming and provided that experience to more students (53%) than did other grade organizations. Further, they found that principals of all grade organizations, except K-8 schools, expected to increase their use of interdisciplinary teams in the three years following the survey (Epstein & Mac Iver, 1990b). This study also reported that middle schools and 7-8 schools used more developmentally responsive practices, including interdisciplinary team organization, than other grade organizations. Grades 7-9 junior high schools and 7-12 schools, by contrast, used fewer responsive practices.

McEwin, Dickinson, and Jenkins (1996), in their 1993 study of 1,798 middle level schools, found that grades 5-8, 6-8, and 7-8 middle schools were much more likely than 7-9 junior high schools to have developmentally responsive practices such as interdisciplinary team organization. For example, 58 percent of 6-8 middle schools, as compared to 28 percent of 7-9 junior high schools, reported using interdisciplinary team organization in social studies at the seventh grade level. Similar findings were reported in other national studies (Alexander & McEwin, 1989a; Cawelti, 1988; McEwin & Clay, 1983; Valentine, Clark, Irvin, Keefe, & Melton, 1993), as well as in several state studies including Arizona (Clark & Clark, 1990) and North Carolina (McEwin & Farmer, 1992). It is beyond question that interdisciplinary team organization is most likely to be found in middle schools that begin with grade 5, 6 or 7 and end in grade 8. Further, it can be concluded that this plan is least likely to be found in elementary/middle schools (K-8), middle/senior high schools (7-12), and junior high schools (7-9). Arriving at these conclusions does not mean, of course, that interdisciplinary team organization is found only in middle schools, only that it is less likely to be found in other types of schools at this time.

Grade levels and interdisciplinary team organization

According to 1995 figures assembled by Market Data Retrieval of Shelton, Connecticut, the most common middle grades found in the 12,623 public middle level schools across the nation are grades six, seven, and eight. There were 6,898 6-8 middle schools during the 1994-95 school year as compared to 1,266 5-8 schools, 2,360 7-8 schools, and 1,062 7-9 junior high schools. Examination of research results from these three grades reveals that the degree of implementation of interdisciplinary team organization has been highest at the sixth grade level and has declined with each higher middle grade (Table 1).

Epstein and Mac Iver (1990a) reported that teaming was used in sixth grade more than in grades seven and eight and hypothesized that this was in part because new middle schools may begin implementation in grade six and proceed to the higher grades over a period of time. An additional possibility is that the use of interdisciplinary team organization is purposely decreased in the higher middle grades to "help prepare young adolescents for the transition to the senior high school." Greater resistance to change from eighth grade teachers, who are more frequently prepared in a single-subject-matter secondary degree program than are sixth grade teachers, is also a likely factor. Whatever the reason, the good news is that the use of interdisciplinary team organization is increasing at all three of these grade levels as well as at the fifth grade level in 5-8 middle schools and ninth grade level in 7-9 junior high schools (Cawelti, 1988; McEwin, Dickinson, & Jenkins, 1996).

Team membership and team leader selection

The assignment to teams is most often made by school administrators. In about 40 percent of all middle level schools teachers have the autonomy to decide which team to join. The subjects most likely to be taught on core teams are social studies, English, mathematics, science, and reading. Fewer than 20 percent of schools with interdisciplinary team organization teach subjects such as foreign language, home economics, or industrial arts in a team setting. Only about 8 percent of middle level schools have more than five teachers on a core team. When this does occur, foreign language, home economics, or industrial arts teachers are most likely to be added to these teams (Epstein & Mac Iver, 1990a; Mac Iver & Epstein, 1993).

When the results of the 1988 and 1993 (McEwin, Dickinson & Jenkins, 1996) studies are compared, it is evident that a shift has occurred in the ways team leaders are selected (Figure 3). Within this relatively short period of five years, the number of teams without team leaders has decreased from 40 percent to 20 percent. Also, fewer team leaders were appointed by administrators while more were elected by team members or the position was being rotated among teammates. These trends seem to support a growing recognition of the importance of having team leaders and to recognize that teachers should play a larger role in the decisions that select those who serve in team leadership positions. A 1992 study reported that about 10 percent of team leaders received released time for leadership responsibilities, and 27 percent received monetary compensation. Middle schools that contained grade six were the most likely to offer monetary compensation (Valentine, et al., 1993).

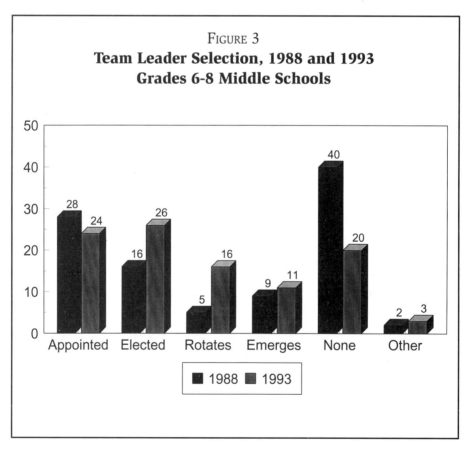

FIGURE 3
Team Leader Selection, 1988 and 1993
Grades 6-8 Middle Schools

Teacher planning times

Epstein and Mac Iver (1990a) found that 70 percent of all schools that contained grade seven and claimed to have implemented interdisciplinary team organization provided at least some common planning time for team members. About 36 percent of these schools which used interdisciplinary team organization scheduled two or more hours of common planning time per week. In a 1992 study 56 percent of 6-8 middle schools and 54 percent of all middle level schools reported having two daily planning periods for team members (Valentine, et at., 1993).

Although there was no specific item on the 1993 survey which asked about common planning time, data were collected on the number of teacher planning periods provided for faculty members (Figure 4). It was found that the majority of all schools of all grade organizations included in the study (5-8, 6-8, 7-8, 7-9) provided at least one planning period for teachers. More specifically, 36 percent of 6-8 middle schools provided two planning periods for most or all teachers. Grades 6-8 and 7-8 schools most frequently provided most or all teachers with two planning periods with teachers in 7-9 junior high schools being least likely (18%) to have two planning periods (McEwin, Dickinson, & Jenkins, 1996).

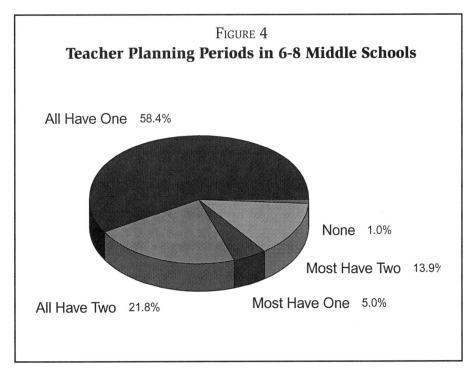

FIGURE 4
Teacher Planning Periods in 6-8 Middle Schools

All Have One   58.4%

None   1.0%

Most Have Two   13.9%

All Have Two   21.8%

Most Have One   5.0%

Concluding remarks

Examining the levels of implementation of interdisciplinary team organization in America's middle schools is both encouraging and disheartening. On the one hand the use of interdisciplinary teams is increasing at all grade levels, in all basic subjects, and in all middle grade organizational plans. There are now several thousand middle schools where interdisciplinary team organization is being practiced, in many cases with documented success (George & Oldaker, 1985; George & Shewey, 1994; George & Stevenson, 1989). The dedicated, insightful, and courageous faculties, administrators, parents and others that have invested the efforts necessary to achieve this success are to be congratulated for what they have accomplished for young adolescents.

On the other hand, there are still thousands of middle schools that have not successfully implemented this organizational plan which provides rich opportunities to improve the education of young adolescents. Unfortunately, in the majority of all middle level schools, departmentalization continues to dominate – isolating teachers, fragmenting curriculum, and letting thousands of young adolescents "fall through the cracks." Recent research has indicated that departmentalization is associated with poor student-teacher relationships, heavy student loads, and the development of negative beliefs on the part of both students and teachers (Lee & Smith, 1993; Mac Iver, 1989).

Furthermore, in some middle level schools, interdisciplinary team organization is predominately a "paper plan." In these schools, it is usual for some teams that recognize the powerful potential of teaming to be experiencing considerable success while colleagues on other teams are permitted to continue to operate as if teaming were no different from departmentalization. Circumstances such as these must be reversed so that teaming becomes established in all schools that house young adolescents.

References

Alexander, W.M. (1968). *A survey of organizational patterns of reorganized middle schools.* Washington, DC: United States Department of Health, Education, and Welfare.

Alexander, W.M. (1995). The junior high school: A changing view. *Middle School Journal, 26*(3), 20-24. Reprinted from G. Hass, & K. Wiles (Eds.). (1965). *Readings in curriculum.* Boston: Allyn & Bacon.

Alexander, W.M., & McEwin, C.K. (1989a). Earmarks of schools in the middle: A research report. Boone, NC: Appalachian State University. (ERIC Reproduction Service No. ED 312312)

Alexander, W.M., & McEwin, C.K. (1989b). *Schools in the middle: Status and progress.* Columbus, OH: National Middle School Association.

Alexander, W.M., Williams, E., Compton, M., Hines, V., Prescott, D., & Kealy, R. (1968). *The emergent middle school.* New York: Holt, Rinehart and Winston, Inc.

Cawelti. G. (1994a). *High school restructuring: A national study.* Arlington, VA: Educational Research Service.

Cawelti. G. (1994b). Let's reinvent high school. *The American School Board Journal, 181*(7), 19-22.

Cawelti, G. (1988). Middle schools a better match with early adolescent needs, ASCD survey finds. *Association for Supervision and Curriculum Development Curriculum Update.*

Clark, S.N., & Clark, D.C. (1990). *Arizona middle schools: A survey report.* Phoenix, AR: Arizona Department of Education.

Epstein, J.L., & Mac Iver, D.J. (1990a). *Education in the middle grades: National practices and trends.* Columbus, OH: National Middle School Association.

Epstein, J.L., & Mac Iver, D.J. (1990b). The middle grades: Is grade span the most important rule? *Educational Horizons, 68*(2), 88-94.

George, P.S., & Oldaker, L. (1985). *Evidence for the middle school.* Columbus, OH: National Middle School Association.

George, P.S., & Shewey, K. (1994). *New evidence for the middle school.* Columbus, OH: National Middle School Association.

George, P.S., & Stevenson, C. (1989). The very best teams in the very best schools as described by middle school principals. *TEAM: The Early Adolescent Magazine, 3* (5), 6-14.

Grooms, M.A. (1967). *Perspectives on the middle school.* Columbus, OH: Charles E. Merrill.

Gruhn, W.T., & Douglass, H. R. (1956). *The modern junior high school* (2nd ed.). New York: Ronald Press Company.

Lee, V.E., & Smith, J. (1993). Effects of school restructuring on the achievement and engagement of middle-grades students. *Sociology of Education, 66*(3), 164-187.

Mac Iver, D.J. (1989). Effective practices and structures for middle grades education. *Policy Issues.* Charleston, WV: Appalachia Educational Laboratory.

Mac Iver, D.J., & Epstein, J.L. (1993). Middle grades research: Not yet mature, but no longer a child. *The Elementary School Journal, 93* (5), 461-480.

McEwin, C.K., & Clay, R.M. (1983). *Middle level education in the United States: A national comparative study of practices and programs of middle and junior high schools.* Boone, NC: Appalachian State University.

McEwin, C.K., Dickinson, T.S., & Jenkins, D.M. (1996). *America's middle schools: Practices and progress — a 25 year perspective.* Columbus, OH: National Middle School Association.

McEwin, C.K., & Farmer, N.J. (1992). *Middle level education in North Carolina: A status report on programs and practices.* Raleigh, NC: North Carolina League of Middle Level Schools.

Oakes, J., Quartz, K.H., Gong, J., Guiton, G., & Lipton, M. (1993). Creating middle schools: Technical, normative, and political considerations. *The Elementary School Journal, 93* (5), 461-480.

Waggoner, V.C., & McEwin, C.K. (1993). Middle level practices in European international schools and Department of Defense schools. *Middle School Journal, 24* (5), 29-36.

Wright, G. (1958). *Block-time classes and the core program in the junior high school.* Washington, DC: United States Department of Health, Education, and Welfare.

Valentine, J.W., Clark, D.C., Irvin, J.L., Keefe, J.W., & Melton, G. (1993). *Leadership in middle level education: A survey of middle level leaders and schools.* Vol. I. Reston, VA: National Association of Secondary School Principals.

Van Til, W., Vars, G.F., & Lounsbury, J.H. (1967). *Modern education for the junior high school years* (2nd ed.). Indianapolis: The Bobbs-Merrill Company.

Interdisciplinary Team Teaching: Sampling the Literature

14

William G. Wraga

Interdisciplinary team teaching has long been a recommended practice in the literature dealing with both middle level and secondary education. In fact, team teaching predates the middle school movement and has been encouraged as a viable instructional option at every level of schooling and involving any number of subject area configurations. The range of problems this approach purportedly addresses would seem almost to endow team teaching with the mantle of educational panacea.

The perennial popularity of interdisciplinary team teaching has inspired a vast literature about the practice. Two separate on-line literature searches yielded nearly 1,500 citations on the topic – and these searches extended back only to 1966 and included just journal articles. This chapter attempts to orient the reader to the literature on interdisciplinary team teaching, to glean useful information and insights from a sampling of available writing on the practice, and to recommend sources that seem pertinent especially to middle level educators. The reader should be aware that the following discussion is neither a comprehensive nor even a representative review of the literature about interdisciplinary team teaching. Rather, it is a sampling of the literature that, it is hoped, will whet the appetites of those who are contemplating the approach and serve as a preliminary resource for those embarking on the practice.

Clarification of Terms

Some clarification of terms related to the two "interdisciplinary" concepts of "team teaching" and "team organization" is necessary to provide focus for the present discussion. It is not uncommon for the terms "interdisciplinary team organization" and "interdisciplinary team teaching" to be used inter-changeably in the literature. Additionally, any given term can have a variety of definitions, as is the case with "team teaching" (e.g., Beggs, 1964; George,

1984; Merenbloom, 1986, 1991; Shaplin & Olds, 1964; Vars, 1966, 1993). To confuse matters further, the same term can have different meanings at different grade levels, as is the case with "interdisciplinary team teaching," discussed shortly. In an attempt to clarify this matter a distinction will be drawn between the terms *team teaching* and *interdisciplinary team teaching*, both of which will be subsumed beneath the generic term, *teaming*.

The term *team teaching* is often used to describe a situation in which two or more teachers on the same grade level share students and common planning time. In middle school education such teaching teams are referred to as grade-level teams, academic teams, multidisciplinary teams, and even interdisciplinary teams (George, 1984). In the literature of middle school education, team teaching is commonly viewed largely as a way to organize teachers and students in order to monitor and improve student work habits and discipline, confer with parents, consult support staff, coordinate assignments and instruction, plan large events, and effectively complete other tasks that benefit from communication and coordination not afforded when teachers are isolated in their respective classrooms. In the present discussion a group of teachers collaborating on such tasks is considered a teaching team. The critical attribute of teaching teams is that though teachers share students and meeting time, during their actual teaching duties they work individually and make no connections between or among their respective subject specialities. In this arrangement, the term "interdisciplinary team" is a misnomer since teachers' work is discipline-centered. The possibility of a teaching team engaging in interdisciplinary teaching is not ruled out, but neither is it guaranteed (Vars, 1966).

Interdisciplinary team teaching, on the other hand, involves a team of two or more subject teachers who share students and planning time and who work to draw connections between their subjects; often these teachers actually teach together. When a team of teachers attempts to articulate the subject curriculum horizontally they are expanding the function of their team to include matters of curriculum integration. As they do this, they will invariably become involved in one or more of the common forms of interdisciplinary curricula: correlation; fusion; or core (Vars, 1987, pp. 10-12; Vars, 1993, pp. 17-25; Wraga, 1993). The real distinction between team teaching and interdisciplinary team teaching, then, is a curricular one; that is, a team of teachers becomes an interdisciplinary team when its members engage in purposeful efforts to integrate learnings from normally disparate disciplines.

This distinction between team teaching and interdisciplinary team teaching in practice is important because it points to a discrepancy in the conception of teaming in the literature. On the secondary and college and university levels the practice of "interdisciplinary team teaching" (or simply "team teaching") almost invariably involves making purposeful connections between and among specialized disciplines. Although noted middle level advocates such as Vars (1966), Beane (1976), and Lounsbury (1992) have called for greater attention to the curricular possibilities of team teaching, and although the term "interdisciplinary team teaching" is ubiquitous in middle level literature, middle school educators often neglect the curriculum possibilities inherent in bringing together teachers from separate subjects into a team setting. The implications of clarifying these terms are revisited in the conclusion.

Origins and purposes of teaming

The history of teaming in the schools dates at least to the Platoon School, the Winnetka Plan, and the Pueblo Plan of the early 20th century (Polos, 1965; Shaplin, 1964, pp. 45-50). Teaming was also a feature of Hosic's short-lived Cooperative Group Plan (Shaplin, 1964) and of the Eight-Year Study (Aikin, 1942) during the 1930s. During the 1950s teaming was promoted as a solution to a number of perceived educational problems, most notably to the chronic teacher shortages the nation faced following World War II (Bair & Woodward, 1964; Shaplin, 1964). By the mid-1960s, teaming had assumed the proportions of an educational fad. The *Second Handbook of Research on Teaching* gauged the popularity of "team teaching" by observing that while between 1955 and 1957 *Education Index* carried no entries for the topic, over the next decade more than 200 entries were listed (Travers, 1973, p. 21). Indeed, in 1965 the editor of *The Clearing House* proclaimed, "Team teaching is today's educational bandwagon" (Polos, 1965, p. 456). Four years later, Funaro (1969) observed, "Like many educational innovations, team teaching has become a panacea for known and suspected problems and, in some instances, a preventative for potential problems" (p. 401). Funaro warned that the bandwagon effect "has been responsible for the distortion and even the failure of any number of meaningful curriculum and instructional innovations" (p. 401) and attempted to analyze objectively the educational potential of "team teaching."

Teaming has been touted as a solution to a variety of educational problems, including the following: utilizing staff in a cost-effective way; making instruction relevant to students; mainstreaming classified students; providing effective special education services; delivering basic skills instruction at the college level; rejuvenating "burnt out" staff; and integrating a variety of subjects including literature and science, law and social work, health and physical education, English and photography, separate psychology specializations at the college level, and academic and vocational learnings. Interestingly, the purposes teaming is purported to serve at a given time often parallel the prevailing educational reform sentiment.

During the 1950s, for example, when the United States faced a shortage of qualified teachers due to the war and to a post-war enrollment surge, teaming was offered as a way to teach larger groups of students using fewer teachers and as a means of recruiting, training, and expanding career prospects of teachers (Shaplin, 1964). When the Soviet launching of Sputnik precipitated myriad discipline-centered curriculum projects conducted under the auspices of the National Science Foundation (NSF) (Hlebowitsh & Wraga, 1989), teaching teams would allegedly contribute to the development and implementation of these projects (Shaplin, 1964). When regionalization as promoted by Conant was embraced as a way to provide comprehensive programs to high school youth, team teaching was touted as a means of supporting smaller, personalized groups of teachers and students within the context of the larger high school (Shaplin, 1964) – an idea not unlike the "houses" concept prevalent among middle school educators and touted by small school advocates during the late 1980s and early 1990s. When the application of new educational technologies (e.g., television, teaching machines) seemed to promise great results, team teaching was depicted as a critical component of such efforts (Shaplin, 1964).

During the late 1960s and early 1970s, when the school curriculum was attacked for lacking relevance to the lives of learners and to the life of society (Tanner & Tanner, 1990), interdisciplinary team teaching appeared in the educational literature as a way to foster individual efficacy and social amelioration. Interdisciplinary, team-taught courses, usually integrating science and social studies and co-taught by a teacher from each subject, focused on helping students make sense of and even act upon a range of societal problems (Meyer, 1969; Geller, 1973; Dillingham, Kelly, & Strauss, 1975). Ironically, the interdisciplinary team-taught course described by Geller (1973), entitled "Crisis in America," grew out of the teacher's dissatisfaction with the NSF-sponsored BSCS program's lack of direct application to pressing social issues.

It should come as little surprise that an approved practice such as teaming would reflect popular educational reform trends. Instructional practices certainly should be harnessed to solve important educational problems and success at such an endeavor could garner needed support for approaches that are more difficult to implement than the conventional single-teacher-standing-in-front-of-the-class format. The danger of associating an instructional approach like teaming with a current fashion in educational reform, however, is that it could be viewed as a superficial, passing fancy and fall victim to the next fad that dominates the educational scene – as Funaro (1969) prudently warned.

Teaming at Different Grade Levels

While initially emphasis was placed on implementing this approach on the secondary level, both team teaching and interdisciplinary team teaching have been recognized as an approved practice on all grade levels. Let us look briefly at the roles team teaching and interdisciplinary team teaching have played on the elementary, secondary, and college and university levels before turning to the middle level.

Elementary level

During the late 1950s and early 1960s team teaching on the elementary level received some attention in the educational literature. Elementary team teaching tended to emphasize individual teachers teaching to their strengths and interests in a particular subject area over the integration of subject matter (Lambert, 1960; Critical Look, 1961). The curriculum function was viewed as one of providing enhanced specialized subject-related experiences for students, rather than as one of providing interdisciplinary experiences (Dean, 1962). Since that time, however, the elementary level is the least likely place one will find either kind of teaming discussed in the literature. This is probably due to the general lack of departmentalization on the elementary level, the generalist nature of preservice education for elementary teachers, and the survival of the self-contained classroom despite the imposition of ability grouping down through the kindergarten.

Secondary level

Teachers working in teams on the secondary level usually aim to serve the curriculum function of integrating subject matter in order to provide students with a sense of the inter-relatedness of knowledge and with opportunities for applying academic competencies in new contexts. The early work of Trump (e.g., Trump & Baynham, 1961), which emphasized the role of team teaching in capitalizing on teachers' specializations, is the notable exception to this rule. Later, however, Trump placed greater emphasis on the interdisciplinary possibilities of team teaching (Trump & Miller, 1973). The projects described by Geller (1973) and Dillingham and associates (1975), cited above, integrated subject matter from science and social studies to help students grapple with pervasive societal problems such as pollution, health care, and housing as well as with issues such as racism, elitism in the environmental movement, and ethical questions about the use of scientific knowledge. Tyler and Holden (1972) described a program that correlated vocational training and instruction in mathematics and English and sometimes science to encourage the application of basic academic skills.

Blew and McLean (1976) described in detail the inception, development, and implementation of a team-taught, block-time class that attempted successfully to integrate American history and literature, as well as art, philosophy, and music to provide students with a comprehensive impression of the American experience. Ingram, Henson, and Crew (1984) described a team-taught, four-hour block-time course that integrated American history, literature, writing, and environmental science to focus on historical preservation. Clapsaddle and Thomas (1991) described an interdisciplinary course called Applied Biology/Chemistry that was team taught by a biology teacher and a health occupations teacher to make science content more applicable and accessible to students enrolled in a health occupations program. Gentzler (1991) developed a compelling case and provided useful suggestions for integrating social studies and home economics through staff collaboration from the two departments to encourage in the students the ability to deal with societal issues that face them on a daily basis. Krovetz, Casterson, McKowen, and Willis (1993) described performance assessment techniques employed to evaluate tenth grade students enrolled in a three-period, block-time course integrating biology, United States history, and American literature.

Occasionally, education journals will devote an issue to an interdisciplinary theme that will include suggestions for integrating subject matter from the separate disciplines. Often, articles describing interdisciplinary team teaching approaches may be found in such issues; if not, articulation suggestions contained therein could certainly serve as a resource for organizing interdisciplinary team teaching. Two such theme issues have been published by *The English Journal*. The October 1976 issue offered a section on "Humanities and Interdisciplinary Studies" and another on "Interdisciplinary Teaching—Methods and Materials" and included a description of two interdisciplinary team-taught courses: American Studies (Trump & Hunter, 1976) and World History/English (Clark & Van Nostrand, 1976). The February 1980 issue carried a section on "Interdisciplinary English" and included a description of a course taught by an interdisciplinary team comprised of an English teacher, a social studies teacher, a biology teacher, and a geometry teacher (Seeberg, 1980). In what was probably a singular event in educational publishing, the editors of seven education journals (*The Science Teacher, American Biology Teacher, Man/Society/Technology, Social Education, Art Education, Chemistry,* and *The Physics Teacher*) devoted a portion of the February 1975 issue of their respective journals to addressing their particular discipline to the problem of water purification. In a joint "Declaration on Interdisciplinary Environmental Education," appearing in all seven journals, these editors claimed, "if teachers from several study areas attack the same topic at the same time, the students are almost forced to draw the conclusion that there are relationships between these areas or that they are all part of a whole." While only one article in these journals described an interdisciplinary team teaching project per se (Dillingham, et al., 1975), the many suggestions for applying subject matter from a variety of disciplines to the topic of water purification could serve as a practical resource to those planning to pursue interdisciplinary team teaching.

College and university level

Perusing the literature about interdisciplinary team teaching at the college and university level, one is struck by its frequency considering the high value attached to research specialization and the resulting "territorial imperatives," as one interdisciplinary team (Davis & Richter, 1981) put it, that tend to dominate the world of academe and discourage cross-department interaction and collaboration. While occasionally references are made to interdisciplinary team teaching as a strategy for responding to institutional problems such as faculty renewal, shrinking budgets, and declining enrollments (Rinn & Weir, 1984), most often it is embraced as a means for overcoming the fragmentation of knowledge wrought by hyper-specialization of research fields. Sophisticated epistemological rationales and references to C.P. Snow's critique of the "two-cultures" gap are common in the interdisciplinary team teaching literature at the post-secondary level.

Interdisciplinary team teaching is used most frequently but not exclusively to fulfill the general education function of the undergraduate curriculum. Projects described in the literature range from introductory units for freshman (Ehntholt, 1978) to introductory courses (Malachowski, 1990), to sophomore general requirement courses (Davis & Richter, 1981), to upper level college electives (Lerner & Gosselin, 1975), to required courses for first-year medical students (Begun & Rieker, 1980). A variety of curriculum organizations are used (Rinn & Weir, 1984), including separate courses taught back-to-back with their content correlated (Frankel & Hiley, 1980) and single courses that integrate knowledge and perspectives from two or more fields (Goodwin and LeBold, 1975; Lawless & Pici, 1977; Lerner & Gosselin, 1975; Zander, 1975). While such efforts usually involve subject matter and faculty from traditional science and humanities departments, a wide range of specialized disciplines have participated in interdisciplinary team-taught courses including biology, creative arts, economics, history, political science, philosophy, sociology, aeronautics and astronautics, industrial management, administrative science, and chemical, civil, mechanical, and nuclear specializations in engineering.

Aside from the obvious need for collaborative planning among team members, the most commonly cited key to the success of an interdisciplinary course at the college and university level is that all instructors on the team (ranging in number from two to five) attend each class session and interact with each other as appropriate. Although this literature depicts many successful interdisciplinary team-taught courses, the longevity of these "experiments," as they are frequently labeled (especially when supported by grant monies, as they often are), is difficult to ascertain through journal articles. Whatever the case may be, this literature offers many ideas for integrating academic subject matter that may be translatable to the secondary or even middle levels and used in an interdisciplinary team teaching format. Indeed, Lerner and Gosselin (1975) extended their interdisciplinary project by collaborating with teachers from a local high school.

Middle level

In the literature of K-12 schooling, teaming is most often associated with middle level education. That teaming on the middle level outlived the fad period of the 1960s and since then has consistently been identified as an approved practice in middle schools perhaps attests to its relevance there (e.g., Beane, 1990; Carnegie Council on Adolescent Development, 1989; George, Stevenson, Thomason, & Beane, 1992; Superintendent's Middle Grade Task Force, 1987). Teaming is a hallmark of genuine middle school education.

Erb (1987) identified four necessary features of effective team organizations at the middle level: common planning or meeting time; shared students; common block-time teaching schedule; and spatial proximity of team members' classrooms. Team organization and interdisciplinary team teaching have been intended to serve a variety of functions in middle level education. Prominent among these functions are coordinating instructional programs, delivering guidance services to students, attending to the individual needs of pupils, teaching skills across the curriculum, and planning interdisciplinary units and activities (Merenbloom, 1986). Team organizations are valued also for the positive impact they can have on the quality of teachers' professional lives, as discussed below. It seems, however, that the function that makes a team truly *interdisciplinary* – the correlation of curriculum – is the function most difficult to realize at the middle level.

As noted earlier, the existence of a team of teachers does not guarantee the emergence of efforts aimed at curriculum articulation. Vars (1966) offered a trenchant critique of team teaching arrangements with respect to implementing interdisciplinary curricula, especially the core curriculum. DiVirgilio (1972) outlined three reasons for the establishment of interdisciplinary teams in terms of teams' three principal functions (to provide effective guidance, selection of instructional strategies, and organization of curriculum) and emphasized both the complementary nature and the necessary coexistence of these functions. "It is one thing to say interdisciplinary teams meet to discuss children," he cautioned, "but if that is all that is done the learning process would collapse, resulting in purposeless activity resembling chaos" (p. 210). DiVirgilio (1972) drew attention to the curriculum function when he suggested that "teams get bogged down in problems of discussion about maladjustment of children, when in actuality the children are reacting normally to a poorly organized, undefined, purposeless learning environment" (p. 211).

DiVirgilio (1972), Beane (1976), Merenbloom (1986), Vars (1987, 1993), and Funaro (1969) offered practical suggestions for implementing truly interdisciplinary teams that purposefully seek to develop and implement correlated, fused, and integrative curriculum experiences for students. Funaro (1969) also discussed the roles of principals and supervisors in promoting team teaching. Phillips (1969), Meyer (1969), George (1984), and Merenbloom (1991) offered general guidelines for establishing successful teaching teams. Garner (1976) emphasized the importance of tailoring team teaching arrangements to the local educational situation, and Fox (1975) identified "common reasons" for the failure of teaching teams and proposed a practical planning cycle developed by teachers.

George (1982) identified four "operational phases" in the life of teaching teams. The "organizational" phase is characterized by the emergence of common procedures; the "community" phase is marked by the conscious promotion of team identity among teachers and students; the "team teaching" phase, which George considered nonessential to the existence of team organization, involves team members planning and teaching together; the "governmental" phase is characterized by the involvement of team members in participatory decision making. George (1982) deemphasized the curricular function of teams and pointed to the importance of administrative leadership to successful implementation of team organization. Plodzik and George's (1989) study of the implementation of seventh grade teams in 159 New England middle schools corroborated George's (1982) four operational phases, pointed to the importance of inservice activities to implementation efforts, and reaffirmed the critical role of constructive leadership emanating from the principal. Hart, Pate, Mizelle, and Reeves' (1992) study of the implementation of team organization in a middle school in the South identified the kinds of planning strategies teachers use to make decisions in team contexts.

Descriptions of middle level team-taught, interdisciplinary units and activities are available, as well. For example, Brodsky (1987) described an interdisciplinary unit on the 1920s for eighth graders that involved teachers from all subject areas in the school (including exploratory subjects). Stromberg and Smith (1987) explained how a simulation model was used to structure interdisciplinary, team taught units on the sixth grade level involving social studies, mathematics, English, science, and reading teachers. Kerekes (1987) described a schoolwide unit on the 1920s, discussed other correlated units, and offered guidelines for implementing such units based on the local experience at her school. Gillespie (1990) described in detail a two-month seventh grade interdisciplinary unit on the Great Depression team-taught by a language arts and a social studies teacher. Waltz (1976) discussed the important role played by an "exploratory team," comprised of teachers from home economics, art, industrial arts, speech/drama, and music, in highlighting concepts common to these areas and briefly described a unit on colonial American that correlated the exploratory and academic subjects of the whole school curriculum.

Middle level educators looking to implement team teaching or interdisciplinary team teaching would do well to consult many other resources about the practices too numerous to summarize here. The following sources will likely prove useful in such an endeavor: Baker (1976); Golner & Powell

(1992); Kain (1993); Merenbloom (1991). Lounsbury (1992) provides an indispensable anthology of articles about interdisciplinary teaming.

Communicating across the grade levels

The lack of vertical communication within our educational system is manifested in the literature about interdisciplinary team teaching. While communication is probably best among the levels within K-12 schooling, even there it occurs less often than one might expect. Communication between K-12 schooling and post-secondary education regarding team teaching, even in the form of bibliographical acknowledgement, is too rare. Yet with proper adaptation to the particular developmental stage of students, selected ideas and strategies can probably be transferred among levels. It is obviously advisable to pursue articulation of both curriculum and instruction across the various grade levels, since such provisions can go a long way toward fostering sequence, continuity, and transfer of student learning from year to year, making students' school experience more coherent over time.

Impact of Teaming

The widespread advocacy of team teaching and interdisciplinary team teaching is not yet matched by research that gauges the effectiveness of these strategies. While anecdotal accounts of the success of local team projects usually accompany descriptions of such projects, empirical evidence about the impact of teaming on students and on staff is scarce relative to, say, the research about the effectiveness of cooperative learning. Let us briefly review what the research suggests about the effectiveness of team teaching and interdisciplinary team teaching at the elementary and secondary levels, the college and university level, and the middle level.

The first edition of the *Handbook of Research on Teaching* (Gage, 1963) included neither a chapter nor an index citation on teaming. The *Second Handbook* (Travers, 1973) mentioned "team teaching" in a chapter on "Research on Teaching in Higher Education," documenting the increased interest in the strategy and indicating the lack of conclusive evidence of any positive effect of it on student achievement (p.21). Like its predecessors, the third *Handbook* (Wittrock, 1986) had little to say about teaming, again mentioning "team teaching" only briefly in a chapter about college and university teaching (p. 756) while summarizing Schustereit's (1980) study, discussed below. The latest edition of the *Encyclopedia of Educational*

Research, however, includes a partial summary of research on teaming in a section of the chapter devoted to "Staffing Patterns." Here, McPartland and Fissler (1992) observed that little research on the impact of team teaching on student achievement had been conducted through the 1970s, citing a notable study by Armstrong (1977). They also described various configurations of teaching teams and concluded that "research has not yet become available on the effects of teacher teams on student outcomes" (p. 1258) again citing Armstrong. McPartland and Fissler, however, overlooked research conducted subsequent to Armstrong's 1977 study.

Schustereit (1980), for example, reviewed 10 studies conducted during the 1960s and 1970s on the impact of teaming on the achievement of college students. His summary of this research is worth quoting at length:

> Of the ten studies reviewed, five reported results favoring team-teaching. One study found evidence favoring methods other than team teaching. Two studies presented no significant differences between the methods compared, and two other studies had mixed findings. . . . While the reviewed studies gave a plurality of support to team-teaching, a generalization that team-teaching is a superior instructional technique would not be justified based on the various studies. (p. 88)

Schustereit noted that Armstrong (1977) had reached these same conclusions after reviewing research on the effect of teaming on the achievement of students in precollege education with the difference that Armstrong had found a greater number of studies revealing no significant difference between team teaching and other teaching strategies. Similarly, a review conducted by Cotton (1982) yielded no significant difference between the effects of interdisciplinary team teaching and conventional single teacher instruction on student achievement. Interpreting this small body of research, then, is probably a matter of choosing to view the team teaching glass as half empty or half full. It is important to note, however, that all but one of these studies assessed only student achievement and left other important functions of teaming unexamined. Further, these studies typically drew no distinction between team teaching and interdisciplinary team teaching, making interpretation of the findings additionally problematic.

The relatively persistent interest in teaming at the middle level has yielded a wider range of research into the practice's effects there. In terms of practice, Mac Iver and Epstein (1991) found that roughly 42 percent of students in the United States were taught by teachers who were members of teaching teams between grades 5 and 9, that teams of teachers from several subjects (usually social studies, English, mathematics, and science) were most common in middle schools versus other schools within the K-12 system of education, and that such teaching teams were most prevalent in the Northeast region of the country. Epstein and Mac Iver (1990) also found that "schools committed to departmental organization, . . . are not less likely to be committed to interdisciplinary teaming, indicating that a departmental emphasis and interdisciplinary teaming can co-exist" (p. 37). This finding is significant if true interdisciplinary team teaching means focusing team attention and energy on curriculum articulation, to which a departmental, subject-centered mindset can easily serve as an obstacle.

Middle level researchers have examined the effect of team teaching on areas other than student achievement. Cotton's (1982) review, for instance, found that "interdisciplinary teaming is at least slightly favored by the majority of studies . . . And significantly favored by some" in promoting "affective outcomes such as self-concept and school attitudes" (p. 5). George, Spreul, and Moorefield (1987) surveyed students to find that they viewed the team organization as having a positive impact on their relationships with peers and with teachers. Students also felt that academic expectations were clearer and more challenging in a team setting. Powell (1993), using structured student interviews, followed-up this study with an exploration of the impact of team teaching on personalizing students' middle school experience. Powell's findings corroborated those of George, Spreul, and Moorefield (1987) and found also that students involved with a team felt less isolated in school. Powell discussed several implications of his study for implementing effective teaching teams as well. Stefanich, Mueller, and Wills (1992), however, found no significant difference in self-concept between students in schools employing teaming and those not.

Team teaching has long been regarded as an effective tool for improving the professional lives of teachers (Shaplin, 1964) and recent research has found positive effects in this area. Erb (1987) reported that team teaching tends to transform teachers' peer relationships and to increase the quantity and quality of teachers' input to decisions that affect them. Summarizing several studies, Erb (1987) noted that teachers almost invariably report greater satisfaction with their work environment when they work as members of a team. Similarly, Walsh and Shay (1993) found that "the participative climate of the team structure was associated with increased teacher and student sense of responsibility for meeting the goals of the school" (p. 59). Kasten, Short, and Jarmin (1989) found that teaching teams could manifest the characteristics of self-managing work groups often discussed in management literature accompanied by positive effects such as reduced teacher isolation. They also noted the importance of the principal's leadership to successful implementation efforts and found that "interdisciplinary teaming" (i.e., teaching teams) is no guarantee of interdisciplinary curriculum and instruction. Mills, Powell, and Pollack (1992) found that teaming reduces teachers' sense of personal isolation but can have the effect of isolating team members from subject departments and from other teams. Gatewood, Cline, Green, and Harris (1992) found that teaming can yield lower stress and a heightened sense of professional identity among team members.

This small sample of the research on the effects of teaming will hopefully prompt the reader to examine this literature more closely. Accessible summaries of research on the effects of team teaching include the reviews prepared by Arhar, Johnston, and Markle (1988/1992a, 1989/1992b), and Chapter 16 in this volume. Clearly, research on team teaching at the middle level has focused on effects beyond student achievement, reflecting the wider range of purposes middle level educators hold for teaming. The research has, however, yet to address the question of whether true interdisciplinary team teaching fosters the ability of students to perceive and make connections among the conventional subjects.

Finally, it may be of interest to note that team teaching has enjoyed some notoriety overseas as well. Geen (1985) examined the longevity of team teaching in secondary schools in England and Wales and found that "very few of the [team teaching] schemes which had been devised during [the 1960s] have survived to the present" (p. 33). While these schemes generally did not involve interdisciplinary team teaching as defined here, the reasons for abandoning these schemes summarized by Geen can be useful to educators embarking on such an endeavor today. Geen (1985, p. 37) concluded that teacher commitment and administrative leadership were the most important factors in the longevity of team teaching arrangements in Britain and Wales.

Conclusion

Hopefully this sampling of the literature about interdisciplinary team teaching has served the purposes of orienting the reader to the literature on interdisciplinary team teaching, gleaning useful information and insights from a sampling of the available literature on the practice, and pointing to sources that seem pertinent especially to middle level educators. If middle level educators are to benefit from the successes and failures of their colleagues teaching on other grade levels and vice versa, it is imperative to clarify the terminology we currently employ when discussing team teaching arrangements. On the secondary and college/university levels the term and practice of "interdisciplinary team teaching" (or simply "team teaching") almost invariably involve making purposeful connections between and among specialized disciplines. It is predominantly on the middle level that the term interdisciplinary team teaching does not necessarily carry curriculum connotations. Meanwhile, the literature on middle level teaming embraces a wider range of purposes and a correspondingly wider research agenda than writing about teaming in any other phase of schooling. It seems that the strength of this concept at the middle level is also its weakness: while middle level educators ambitiously embrace a wider range of goals for interdisciplinary team teaching, in the process the curriculum function of the strategy is diminished, despite warnings by noted advocates of middle level education. Indeed, this paradox is one of the dilemmas upon which Beane (1990) bases his provacative call-to-arms for genuine efforts to transform the middle school curriculum. Middle level educators can begin to heed Beane's call by making interdisciplinary team teaching just that.

References

Aikin, W.M. (1942). *The story of the eight-year study*. NY: Harper.

Arhar, J.M., Johnston, J.H., and Markle, G.C. (1992a). The effects of teaming and collaborative arrangements. In J.H. Lounsbury (Ed.), *Connecting the curriculum through interdisciplinary instruction* (pp. 15-22). Columbus, OH: National Middle School Association. (Originally published in *Middle School Journal,* 1988, *19* (4), 22-25)

Arhar, J.M., Johnston, J.H., and Markle, G.C. (1992b). The effects of teaming on students. In J.H. Lounsbury (Ed.), *Connecting the curriculum through interdisciplinary instruction* (pp. 23-35). Columbus, OH: National Middle School Association. (Originally published in *Middle School Journal,* 1989, *20* (3), 24-27)

Armstrong, D.G. (1977). Team teaching and academic achievement. *Review of Educational Research, 47,* 65-86.

Bair, M., & Woodward, R.G. (1964). *Team teaching in action*. Boston: Houghton Mifflin.

Baker, J.A. (1976). Interdisciplinary, grade-level teams: From jargon to reality. *Middle School Journal, 7* (1), 10-11.

Beane, J.A. (1976). Options for interdisciplinary teams. *Dissemination Services on the Middle Grades, 7* (5), 1-4.

Beane, J.A. (1990). *A middle school curriculum: From rhetoric to reality*. Columbus, OH: National Middle School Association.

Beggs, D.W., III. (Ed.). (1964). *Team teaching: Bold new venture*. Indianapolis: Unified College Press.

Begun, J.W., & Rieker, P.R. (1980). Social science in medicine: The question of "relevance." *Journal of Medical Education, 55* (3), 181-185.

Blew, R.W., & McLean, J. (1976). American history and literature: Team teaching high school history. *The History Teacher, 9* (4), 556-565.

Brodsky, M.A. (1987). The Roaring Twenties—an interdisciplinary unit. *Middle School Journal, 18* (4), 7-9.

Carnegie Council on Adolescent Development. (1989). *Turning points: Preparing American youth for the 21st century*. New York: Carnegie Corporation.

Clapsaddle, J., & Thomas, J. (1991). A healthy start for team teaching. *Vocational Education Journal, 66* (6), 28-29.

Clark, J.A., & Van Nostrand, L. (1976). World history/English: An interdisciplinary approach. *The English Journal, 65* (7), 51-52.

Cotton, K. (1982). *Effects of interdisciplinary team teaching*. Portland, OR: Northwest Regional Educational Lab. (ERIC Document Reproduction Service No. ED 230 533).

Critical look at team teaching. (1961, October). *The Instructor, 71*, 39-42.

Davis, W.E., & Richter, P.E. (1981). Integrating science and humanities—A modular approach. *Journal of College Science Teaching, 10* (3), 176-177.

Dean, R.B. (1962). Team teaching in the elementary schools. *The American School Board Journal, 145* (6), 5-6.

Dillingham, C.K., Kelly, C.A., & Strauss, J. (1975). Environmental studies: A noncosmetic approach. *The American Biology Teacher, 37* (2), 116-117.

DiVirgilio, J. (1972). Guidelines for effective interdisciplinary teams. *The Clearing House, 47* (4), 209-211.

Ehntholt, D.J. (1978). "How do you know that?" An interdisciplinary introductory unit. *Journal of College Science Teaching, 8* (1), 45-46.

Epstein, J.L., & Mac Iver, D.J. (1990). National practices and trends in the middle grades. *Middle School Journal, 22* (2), 36-40.

Erb, T.O. (1987). What team organization can do for teachers. *Middle School Journal, 18* (4), 3-6.

Fox, J.H. (1975). Planning interdisciplinary units within a team structure. *Middle School Journal, 5* (4), 49-51.

Frankel, R.J., & Hiley, D.R. (1980). Course-pairs: Team-teaching without tears. *Liberal Education, 66*, 340-346.

Funaro, G.J. (1969). Team teaching: The danger and the promise. *The Clearing House, 43* (7), 401-403.

Gage, N.L. (Ed.). (1963). *Handbook of research on teaching.* Chicago: Rand McNally.

Garner, A.E. (1976). Interdisciplinary team teaching: Is your middle school ready? *NASSP Bulletin, 60* (403), 98-102.

Gatewood, T.E., Cline, G, Green, G., & Harris, S.E. (1992). Middle school interdisciplinary team organization and its relationship to teacher stress. *Research in Middle Level Education, 15* (2), 27-40.

Geen, A.G. (1985). Team teaching in the secondary schools of England and Wales. *Educational Review, 37* (1), 29-38.

Geller, L.R. (1973). Team-taught course "crisis in America" has broad appeal. *The American Biology Teacher, 35* (2), 88-90.

Gentzler, Y.S. (1991). Developing social responsibility by having social studies and home economics departments collaborate. *The Social Studies, 82* (5), 198-201.

George, P.S. (1982). Interdisciplinary team organization: Four operational phases. *Middle School Journal, 14,* 10-13.

George, P.S. (1984). Middle school instructional organization: An emerging consensus. In J.H. Lounsbury (Ed.), *Perspectives: Middle school education, 1964-1984* (pp. 52-67). Columbus, OH: National Middle School Association.

George, P.S., Spreul, M., & Moorefield, J. (1987). *Long-term teacher-student relationships: A middle school case study.* Columbus, OH: National Middle School Association.

George, P.S., Stevenson, C., Thomason, J., & Beane, J. (1992). *The middle school—and beyond.* Alexandria, VA: Association for Supervision and Curriculum Development.

Gillespie, J.S. (1990). Reliving the Depression: Integrating English and social studies. *English Journal, 79* (6), 64-69.

Golner, S.J., & Powell, J.H. (1992). Ready for teaming? Ten questions to ask before you jump in. *Middle School Journal, 24* (1), 28-32.

Goodwin, W.M., & LeBold, W.K. (1975). Interdisciplinary and team teaching. *Engineering Education, 66* (2), 247-254.

Hart, L.E., Pate, P.E., Mizelle, N.B., & Reeves, J.L. (1992). Interdisciplinary team development in the middle school: A study of the Delta Project. *Research in Middle Level Education, 16* (1), 79-98.

Hlebowitsh, P.S., & Wraga, W.G. (1989). The reemergence of the National Science Foundation in American education: Perspectives and problems. *Science Education, 73* (4), 405-418.

Ingram, J., Henson, K.T., & Crew, A.B. (1984). American studies at central high. *Phi Delta Kappan, 66* (4), 296-297.

Kain, D.K. (1993). Helping teams succeed: An essay review of *Groups that Work (and Those that Don't): Creating Conditions for Effective Teamwork. Middle School Journal, 24* (4), 25-31.

Kasten, K.L., Short, P.M., and Jarmin, H. (1989). Self-managing groups and the professional lives of teachers: A case study. *The Urban Review, 21* (2), 63-80.

Kerekes, J. (1987). The interdisciplinary unit: It's here to stay. *Middle School Journal, 18* (4), 12-14.

Krovetz, M., Casterson, D., McKowen, C., & Willis, T. (1993). Beyond show and tell. *Educational Leadership, 50* (7), 73-76.

Lambert, P. (1960). Team teaching for the elementary school. *Educational Leadership, 18* (2), 85-88.

Lawless, G.W., & Pici, J.R. (1977). The elementary effectiveness of team teaching. *Engineering Education, 67* (5), 403.

Lerner, L.S., & Gosselin, E.A. (1975). Physics and history as a bridge across the 'two-cultures' gap. *American Journal of Physics, 43* (1), 13-19.

Lounsbury, J.H. (Ed.). (1992). *Connecting the curriculum through interdisciplinary instruction.* Columbus, OH: National Middle School Association.

Mac Iver, D.J., & Epstein, J.L. (1991). Responsive practices in the middle grades: Teacher teams, advisory groups, remedial instruction, and school transition programs. *American Journal of Education 99* (4), 587-622.

Malachowski, M.R. (1990). A cluster approach to teaching nonmajors science. *Journal of College Science Teaching, 20* (1), 22-26.

McPartland, J.M., & Fissler, R. (1992). Staffing patterns. In M.C. Alkin, (Ed.). *Encyclopedia of Educational Research* (pp. 1252-1258). 6th Ed. NY: Macmillan.

Merenbloom, E.Y. (1986). The interdisciplinary team approach. *Transescence, 14* (1), 6-11.

Merenbloom, E.Y. (1991). *The team process: A handbook for teachers* (3rd ed.). Columbus, OH: National Middle School Association.

Meyer, J.A. (1969). Teaming a first step for interdisciplinary teaching. *The Clearing House, 43* (7), 406-410.

Mills, R.A., Powell, R.R., & Pollak, J.P. (1992). The influence of middle level interdisciplinary teaming on teacher isolation: A case study. *Research in Middle Level Education, 15* (2), 9-26.

Phillips, E.L. (1969). Team teaching: Where do we begin? *The Clearing House, 43* (7), 404-405.

Plodzik, K.T., & George, P. (1989). Interdisciplinary team organization. *Middle School Journal, 20* (5), 15-17.

Polos, N.C. (1965). Team teaching: Past, present, and future. *The Clearing House, 39* (8), 456-458.

Powell, R.R. (1993). Seventh graders' perspectives of their interdisciplinary team. *Middle School Journal, 24* (3), 49-57.

Rinn, F.J., & Weir, S.B. (1984). Yea, team. *Improving College & University Teaching, 32* (1), 5-10.

Schustereit, R.C. (1980). Team-teaching and academic achievement. *Improving College & University Teaching, 28* (2), 85-89.

Seeberg, M.S. (1980). All the king's men. *The English Journal, 69* (2), 33-36.

Shaplin, J.T. (1964). Antecedents of team teaching. In J.T.Shaplin, & H.F.Olds, Jr. (Eds.), *Team teaching* (pp. 24-56). NY: Harper & Row.

Shaplin, J.T., & Olds, H.F., Jr. (Eds.). (1964). *Team teaching.* NY: Harper & Row.

Stefanich, G.P., Mueller, J.C., & Wills, F.W. (1992). A longitudinal study of interdisciplinary teaming and its influence on student self-concept. *Research in Middle Level Education, 15* (2), 41-56.

Stromberg, R.B., & Smith, J.M. (1987). The simulation technique is applied to an I.D.U. *Middle School Journal, 18* (4), 9-11.

Superintendent's Middle Grade Task Force. (1987). *Caught in the middle: Educational reform for younger adolescents in California public schools.* Sacramento,CA: California State Department of Education.

Tanner, D., & Tanner, L. (1990). *History of the school curriculum.* NY: Macmillan.

Travers, R.M.W. (Ed.). (1973). *Second handbook of research on teaching.* Chicago: Rand McNally.

Trump, J.L., & Baynham, D. (1961). *Guide to better schools.* Chicago: Rand McNally.

Trump, J.H., & Hunter, J.F. (1976). American studies. *The English Journal, 65* (7), 50-51.

Trump, J.L., & Miller, D.F. (1973). *Secondary school curriculum improvement.* (2nd ed.). Boston: Allyn & Bacon.

Tyler, H.B., & Holden, H.D. (1972). VIP integrates academic and vocational subjects. *American Vocational Journal, 47* (3), 46-48.

Vars, G.F. (1966). Can team teaching save the core curriculum? *Phi Delta Kappan, 47* (5), 258-262.

Vars, G.F. (1987). *Interdisciplinary teaching in the middle grades.* Columbus, OH: National Middle School Association.

Vars, G.F. (1993). *Interdisciplinary teaching: Why and how.* Columbus, OH: National Middle School Association.

Walsh, K.J., & Shay, M.J. (1993). In support of interdisciplinary teaming: The climate factor. *Middle School Journal, 24* (4), 56-60.

Waltz, T.F. (1976). Exploratory teaming: An interdisciplinary approach to the fine and practical arts. *Middle School Journal, 7* (2), 18-19.

Wittrock, M.C. (Ed.). (1986). *Handbook of research on teaching.* (3rd ed.). NY: Macmillan.

Wraga, W.G. (1993). The interdisciplinary imperative for citizenship education. *Theory and Research in Social Education, 21* (3), 201-231.

Zander, A.R. (1975). Science and fiction: An interdisciplinary approach. *American Journal of Physics, 43* (1), 9-12.

TEAM me: A Philosophy Bigger Than Sports   **15**

Jane A. Page and Fred M. Page, Jr.

Erk Russell was the Assistant Head Football Coach at the University of Georgia in 1980, the year the Georgia Bulldogs won the national championship. Coach Russell provided several reasons for the success of the 1980 Bulldogs:

> We had Herschel Walker. We had a lot of good players. The kicking game was good. The offense and defense made timely plays. We did so many good things. Yet, deep down, I really and truly believe our guys became a TEAM because five good seniors...caused 'The Hog Incident' to take place in the spring that year. — Russell, 1991, p. 91

In his autobiography, Coach Russell shared the story in which five seniors were caught as ringleaders in a mischievous activity (conducted for the "benefit" of the team) and made to pay dearly for it with their work during the summer. It seems that the entire team sought ways to support these seniors and a new sense of unity was inspired. Head Coach Vince Dooley attempted to extend this unity to the playing field.

> During spring practice of 1980, Coach Dooley made it a point every day during squad meetings to emphasize the importance of TEAM play as opposed to individual play. If the TEAM was successful, each individual player would be successful. If the TEAM won, everyone was a winner. There is enough for everybody when the TEAM does well. The theme was TEAM and he did an outstanding job of getting their attention focused on that point. (p. 91)

Coach Russell sought to emphasize the theme in a more concrete manner.

> . . . during the summer I designed the first 'TEAM-me' t-shirts. (The word 'TEAM' was very large, with the word 'me' in very small letters underneath.) Every player became a walking picture of the theme. (p.91)

In 1981, Erk Russell brought that theme to Georgia Southern University where he would build a football team "from scratch." Georgia Southern players wore the TEAM-me t-shirts and practiced that philosophy. By the time Coach Russell retired in 1989, his teams had won *three* I-AA National Championships!

The sports arena has been the typical setting for the team concept, perhaps because athletics can be so cleanly divided into "individual sports" and "team sports." Additionally, the "goals" do not have to be "envisioned" since they usually involve concrete outcomes like scoring more points in the allotted time. The individuals on the team share the common purpose to achieve that goal. This unification is so complete that the members even wear the same clothing. The boundaries and rules are clear in sports, and neutral officials are designated (and have the authority) to reinforce the boundaries and rules. The timeframes are also clear. You know when you have begun and you know when you are done. The "plays" are completely synchronized and everyone must do his or her part for the play to be successful. And so, it is on the playing field (and on the scoreboard) that we can quickly observe the results of good teamwork or poor teamwork.

However, businesses, industries, government associations, and other organizations have also learned that the results of using the team concept surpass those of rewarding individual efforts. In fact, in a recent survey of Fortune 1,000 companies, half the managers questioned said they are converting to self-directed teams (*Implementing*, 1995).

Real world teams are changing American institutions

What are teams? Dyer (1995) succinctly defined teams as "collections of people who must rely on group collaboration if each member is to experience the optimum of success and goal achievement" (p. 4). Teamwork, of course, is not a new concept. However, Americans have tended to keep teamwork in its place. Where is that place? According to Wellins, Byham, and Wilson (1991), it is "on playing fields, in films, and through the use of stale clichés" (p. 5). In their book entitled *Empowered Teams*, these authors deliberate on the reasons for the suppression of real teamwork.

> *We may talk about the value of teamwork with our chil-*
> *dren, but much of the real world they see is oriented toward*
> *the individual. We are proud of our children when they hit*
> *home runs; we urge students to compete for individual rec-*
> *ognition through high grades. And when work begins, per-*

*formance systems continue to reward individual accomplish-
ments. All through life we celebrate the individual.* (p. 5)

Although the celebration of the individual will be continued, many organizations have moved to also celebrate the team. In 1992, the Rochester
Institute of Technology's College of Business teamed with *USA Today* to
recognize outstanding teams through the presentation of Quality Cups. These
awards have been presented annually to teams that made stunning improvements in products or services. The teams are recognized in five categories: (a)
service, (b) small organizations (fewer than 500 employees), (c) manufacturing, (d) nonprofit, and (e) government. The 1994 awardees (recognized in the
April 8, 1994 issue of *USA Today*) are representative of the kinds of progress
that can be made with teamwork (Wiseman, Ramon, Jones, Memmot, & Cox,
pp. B2-B3).

Military Electronics and Avionics Division of TRW, the winner of the
manufacturing team award, provides an excellent model for organizations
willing to risk change in order to realize big improvements. Before they
moved to the team approach, people across the various departments were not
communicating.

> *Designers were toiling in isolation. They would figure
> out which computer chips to use and how to package them,
> then throw the plans "over the wall" to manufacturing. En-
> gineers and parts buyers would see the design and reject it
> or argue about whether it could be built at a reasonable
> cost. Delays would pile up.* (p. B3)

That working arrangement (which had been undertaken for decades) was
abandoned after Bob Mason, TRW's director for production of F-22 fighter
jets, read a book that proclaimed the positive outcomes of Japanese
automaking methods. In August 1992, he asked contract and material manager Mike Carosella to initiate a team approach which crossed division and
even company lines. In addition to seven TRW managers, Carosella brought
in contractors and suppliers from other companies including Lockheed,
Motorola, Rockwell, Texas Instruments, ITT, and GEC. The initial working
relationship was somewhat difficult. Committed team members, however,
persevered and were successful.

> *. . . they kept at it and began to grasp the benefits. Parts
> experts realized they could head off trouble by examining a
> design early in the process before the designer called for
> parts that couldn't be made at a reasonable cost. Working
> face to face helped the team concentrate on common goals,
> not pet interests.* (p. B3)

The team eventually slashed the cost of its F-22 systems from $2.1 million to $1.6 million a jet.

> *Mason indicated that a key to TRW's success was the commitment of management. He felt comfortable turning the team loose because his supervisor, TRW Vice President Richard Kohler, did not attempt to micro-manage the F-22 project.*
>
> *According to Kohler, 'To get the best results, you've got to empower your people. It's the only thing I can see to do if you're a manager these days.'* (p. B3)

The teaming concept has been borrowed from abroad

American organizations have traditionally been arranged with top-down leadership, direct control management, and individualized rewards. Many experts indicate that this work philosophy can be attributed to Frederick Taylor, the father of modern industrial engineering. At the turn of the century, he recommended that the best way to run manufacturing organizations was to provide standardized activities that workers could do in simple, repetitive tasks and then closely supervise them (Taylor, 1947). The assembly line idea seemed ready-made for an American work force that included many poorly educated immigrants. And, indeed, work production was deemed efficient. However, all effects were not positive.

> *In a culture based on independence, an ironic thing happened. Many workers were forced to surrender their independence and the freedom they had enjoyed as members of small, craft-based teams. The captains of industry operated on a model that was large scale, high volume, and machine paced. Central control became more important than individual autonomy. Power reverted back into the hands of a few leaders, and workers gave up control and ownership of their work in the move toward a new way of getting things done. Although centralizing power may have made sense at the time, the regrettable result was a loss of worker empowerment.* — Wellins, Byham, & Wilson, 1991, p. 7

American organizations using high-control management began to lose some of their competitive edge as experiments began in other countries that facilitated more self-direction and teamwork. In fact, the semiautonomous team idea originated in the late 1940s in experiments at British coal mines.

Behavioral scientists at London's Tavistock Institute of
Human Relations, led by Eric Trist...concluded that indus-
try needed a new paradigm of work organization. By stress-
ing autonomous work groups, jobs of wider scope, and
worker involvement in decision-making, Trist and his col-
leagues said, companies could adjust much more easily to
fast changing market and political conditions.

— Hoerr & Pollock, 1986, p. 7

Trist and his co-experimenters developed the "socio-technical systems" concept of work design which calls for the involvement of workers whenever possible in planning a new or redesigned plant. The STS concept moved from Britain to Norway and Sweden. Volvo used the concept in designing its plant at Kalmar, Sweden, which began operating in 1974. The work force at this plant is divided into about 20 production teams with each team assembling a major unit of a car in an average of 20 minutes to 40 minutes. The company reports that production costs at Kalmar are 25% lower than at Volvo's conventional plants (Hoerr & Pollock, 1986).

While the STS concept in Europe had as its major emphasis plant design (therefore affecting work relationships after the design), the Quality Circle movement in Japan became a stimulus for investigating alternative strategies focused on the quality of the product. According to Nonaka (1993), this movement in Japan actually began long before the words "Quality Circle" became associated with it. In her article, "The History of the Quality Circle," Nonaka organized the movement into three phases. Phase 1 began before World War II when quality control (QC) pioneers existed in some Japanese companies. However, there was no organization to promote QC until 1949 when the Union of Japanese Scientists and Engineers (JUSE) was established to educate people about QC. Seminars on statistical quality control were provided to engineers in 1950 by W. Edwards Deming. The book published from these lectures was widely read and Deming donated royalties to JUSE. JUSE used these funds to establish the Deming Prize, which became the hallmark of good quality in Japan. With this foundation, Japanese companies established QC departments. The Japanese workers were surprised at the success of the techniques and tried to increasingly use them. However, they found that some alterations needed to be made to actually fit the Japanese workplace. The Quality Circle was conceived as a part of these alterations.

The second phase of the Quality Circle history began in the early 1960s with the publication by JUSE of a magazine that advocated the use of gatherings where workers studied and discussed QC. The publishers referred to these groups as Quality Circles. They also served as a network for registering the circles. The magazine (now called *QC Circle*) has kept the same mission which includes the following statement:

> The magazine should encourage readers to organize, at the workshop level, a small group called the 'QC Circle,'"headed by the foreman and participated in by subordinate workers and should encourage them to study QC techniques using this magazine as a textbook among the groups.
>
> — Nonaka, p. 83

Phase 3 was the actual formation and registration of Quality Circles. The increase in quality of products made in Japan and services rendered was remarkable.

The circle or team concept really did not move forward in the United States until the early to mid 1960s with pioneering groups like the Procter & Gamble Company and the Gaines dog food plant in Topeka, Kansas (Ketchum, 1984). Wellins and associates (1991) reported that the movement began to spread "like wildfire" in the late 1980s. Since the mid '80s, scores of pattern-setting organizations have adopted the concept including industrial manufacturers such as General Electric, Ford, most General Motors divisions, and Westinghouse. High tech companies including Xerox, Honeywell, and Digital Equipment have also made the move. Service industries (e.g., Shenandoah Life) and governmental organizations have followed, some more cautiously than others. Although many of the original borrowed concepts (e.g., Quality Circles) have been modified and renamed, the basic movement toward the team approach appears to be alive and well.

Making teams good, avoiding the bad

In their book, *Teamwork: What Must Go Right, What Can Go Wrong*, Larson and LaFasto (1989) described factors determined through their interviews and investigations that were important for a team's success. They reported that the interviewees in their sample consistently said that it was imperative to select the right people.

> All too often, people are chosen as team members for the wrong reasons. 'Harry should be on the team because he's interested in the topic.' Or 'Bill's feelings would be hurt if he were left off.' Or 'Mary should be included because she reports to Bill.' These may be important considerations, but

> *they don't necessarily lead to successful teams. Instead, what*
> *should be paramount is selecting people who are best*
> *equipped to achieve the team's objective.* (p. 59)

Two types of competencies are identified by Larson and LaFasto: "(1) the necessary technical skills and abilities to achieve the desired objective and (2) the personal characteristics required to achieve excellence while working well with others" (p. 62). The first type is more easily defined by team builders and more easily evaluated. However, these *technical skills* differ from team to team depending on the purpose and objectives. Larson and LaFasto (1989) indicate that it is important to know what the critical technical skills are and to know what the necessary balance of those skills should be. After these are defined, team builders can select individuals who show competence and expertise in these areas. The second type of competency, *personal characteristics*, refers to the qualities, skills, and abilities necessary for the individual team members to function as a team. These characteristics are often overlooked by those who are responsible for the selection of team members. The result may be a group of people with high technical skills working individually in different directions. Ruth Rothstein, CEO of Mount Sinai Hospital in Chicago, summarized the problem:

> *One person who doesn't work well with others can set*
> *the team off into oblivion. One person like this can ruin a*
> *team. When that happens, you give feedback to that indi-*
> *vidual and help them make the necessary changes. But if*
> *they can't adapt, then you have an obligation to remove*
> *them from the team. Otherwise, the rest of the team can*
> *become pretty resentful.*   — Larson & LaFasto, 1989, p. 71

Red Auerbach, the former coach, and now general manager and President of one of America's most successful sports franchises, the Boston Celtics, provided this explanation.

> *I've turned down a lot of trades where I might have got-*
> *ten a better player, but I wasn't totally sure of the chemistry*
> *of that new player coming in. Even though he might possess*
> *golden ability, his personality and the way he gets along*
> *with teammates might be things you just don't want to cope*
> *with.*   — Webber, 1992, pp. 58-59

The personal characteristic that is often hardest to define but most important in the success of the team is commitment. This is the quality sometimes referred to as "team spirit." Coach Erk Russell would describe this factor as dedication to the TEAM-me philosophy. It is a very intense identification

with a group of people. Jim Lynch, captain of the 1966 championship Notre
Dame football team, described the commitment on the Notre Dame team:

> *When I was captain of the team I took it so damn seri-
> ously it's unbelievable. To this day I still believe that's the
> greatest honor I ever had in playing. I made All-American,
> All-Pro, and won the Maxwell trophy, but those things never
> meant as much to me as being captain of that football team.
> I believed in it so much; I believed in the people who were
> there; and I believed in Notre Dame. . . . It was kind of a
> magical time. It was a time when everybody worked their
> hind end off. I can hardly explain it, but it really was a
> group of guys that believed in what they were doing. The
> coach instilled that. He took a team that was two and seven
> my freshman year, and the next year [1964] we went nine
> and one and almost won the national championship. . . .
> We had the players, we were coached so well, and we be-
> lieved so much in what we were doing. You would have kids
> that would get hurt in the middle of a game and would
> literally crawl off the field so they wouldn't have to call time
> out. It wasn't like that was a big deal, that's just what you
> naturally did. I never felt that again with any other team.
> Amazing stuff.   — Larson & LaFasto, 1989, pp. 73-74

When team members are not committed, the results are efforts in futility.
John Brodic, president of United Paperworkers Local 448, expressed his lack
of commitment to the team concept in this quote attributed to him in *Business
Week*:

> *What the company wants is for us to work like the Japa-
> nese. Everybody go out and do jumping jacks in the morn-
> ing and kiss each other when they go home at night. You
> work as a team, rat on each other, and lose control of your
> destiny. That's not going to work in this country.*
>
>   — Hoerr, 1989. p. 56

Brodic and other critics of employee team involvement in the auto industry, however, are outnumbered by their fellow union members who favor the
changes. Through their input, the team concept in the United States has
become one that increases workers' autonomy and assists management in
making decisions at higher levels.

The focus on *commitment* to the team is reinforced by Wellins and associates (1991) in their identification of key factors in team development. (Figure

1). These factors (commitment, trust, purpose, communication, involvement, and process orientation) are not developed by teams overnight. Teams go through stages of trial and error, bumps and bruises, and roller coaster excursions as they work to attain the level of an empowered, self-directed team. A breakdown in any of these areas can result in an unsuccessful team. As teams develop, evaluation of these six areas will provide the feedback needed for team maturation and success.

FIGURE 1

Key Factors in Team Development

Commitment

Team members see themselves as belonging to a team rather than as individuals who operate autonomously. They are committed to group goals above and beyond their personal goals.

Trust

Team members have faith in each other to honor their commitments, maintain confidences, support each other, and generally behave in a consistent and predictably acceptable fashion.

Purpose

The team understands how it fits into the overall business of the organization. Team members know their roles, feel a sense of ownership, and can see how they make a difference.

Communication

Communication refers to the style and extent of interactions both among members and between members and those outside the team. It also refers to the way that members handle conflict, decision making, and day-to-day interactions.

Involvement

Everyone has a role in the team. Despite differences, team members must feel a sense of partnership with each other. Contributions are respected and solicited, and a real consensus is established before committing the team to action.

Process Orientation

Once a team has a clear purpose (why it's together and where it's going), it must have a process or means to get there. The process should include problem-solving tools, planning techniques, regular meeting, meeting agendas and minutes, and accepted ways of dealing with problems.

From *Empowering Teams* (1991) by Richard Wellins, William C. Byham and Jeanne Wilson. Reprinted with permission from Jossey - Bass Publishers.

Put me in, Coach

Teams may eventually take over many of the jobs traditionally reserved for managers and supervisors. As these teams assume more responsibility, the roles of managers change. This may be a difficult transition for many managers to make.

> *After all, we have been taught that leadership is reserved for the 'elite' few and that the leaders of our organizations make the difference, not the people on the floor or in the back office. Just look at the dozens of books written in the past decade that have exalted leadership. We spend our entire careers trying to climb up the organizational ladder – not down.* — Wellins et al., 1991, p. 128

According to most experts, the role of the leader is not eliminated, but it does, indeed, change. But change to what? This question was addressed by Emery (1980) in his article about socio-technical systems:

> *The role of the foreman is so central to the traditional authoritarian system, that the first question to ask of any proposed scheme for the democratization of work is, 'What does it do to the foreman's role?' If it leaves that role intact, then the scheme is fraudulent.* (p. 21)

Fifteen years later, many organizations are still dealing with this concern. Most are realizing that the new leader works to encourage and coach fellow workers to internalize and self-manage much of the control imposed previously by managers and other supervisors. Wellins and associates (1991) recommended that organizations involve managers and supervisors in the change process:

> *Moving supervisors and managers into new roles is best done with them rather than to them...Adolph Coors Company's brewery warehouse operation firmly believed that the team concept did not mean doing away with leadership. As a result, it relied heavily on supervisors to create empowered work teams. In essence, these supervisors led the change.* (p. 139)

The TEAM-me philosophy is especially important for leadership personnel to develop. Studies by Larson & LaFasto (1989) indicated that the most effective leaders were those who subdued their ego cravings in favor of the team's goal.

> *Whether it was in the context of college or professional football, mountain climbing, cardiac surgery, project teams,*

*or executive management teams, the following observation
held true: Effective leaders bring out the leadership in others. Effective leaders give team members the self-confidence
to act, to take charge of their responsibilities, and make
changes occur rather than merely perform assigned tasks.
In short, leaders create leaders.* (p. 128)

Bosses, (Wall, 1986) provides stories told by leaders in a variety of fields.
One of the stories is told by a Quality Circle leader. This leader shared his
transformation from a traditional supervisor to a facilitator and coach:

*Once we're in the QC meeting, my job is to keep the meet-
ing moving. I'm not supervising that group. I am a member
just like they are, but I'm the chairman, who makes sure
that things keep moving rather than getting bogged down....
The circle, as it improves quality, really develops the personnel. The members of the circle learn problem-solving techniques.... They're becoming better decision makers and problem solvers on the job, not just in the circle. So it's beneficial
to the company from that standpoint. The QC is also good
for me. It's good exposure, and along with the younger members, I've developed.... I'm finding that it's broadening me,
exposing me to technical areas that I previously knew little
about.... Because I get so participative with the circle (I see
benefits from participation – my QC people are so free to let
their ideas flow) I say, 'Why can't it work over here in my
group?' I've changed and developed a different vocabulary,
a different way to express myself, and now I conduct myself
interpersonally in a way that better taps the resources of my
subordinates.* (p. 257)

This Quality Circle leader has discovered the joy of using "power-with"
rather than "power-over" his subordinates. Graham (1991) described the
advantages of the "power-with" philosophy as compared to "power-over" and
"power-sharing:"

*It stems from the pooling of powers. By pooling, no one is
giving any of his own away. When a car breaks down, its
driver is not able alone to move it to the curb. A helpful
person comes along, adds his weight to the driver's and the
car is on the curb in a couple of minutes. There has been no
sharing of powers. The separate powers of the two persons
have been pooled together to create the joint power which*

> *moves the car. Pooling increases total power. By pooling*
> *powers, we get not only the addition of the separate powers*
> *but also something extra, the extra value created through*
> *their joint interaction.* (p. 114)

Effective leadership facilitates the fundamental change to the team concept. Leaders help members feel connected by assisting them in understanding the mission or vision of the entire team. They provide feedback which leads to team members becoming more confident in their abilities. They encourage individuals to take risks for the sake of the team. If they lead well, team members will not realize the leader's contribution. Instead they will say, "we did it ourselves." An example of this type of leadership is provided in a story told by Red Auerbach of an exchange he had with Bill Walton that made a difference:

> *One day he told me he was down in the dumps. I asked*
> *him what was wrong, and he said he didn't feel like he was*
> *contributing to the team. 'Of course you're contributing.'*
> *'But I'm not scoring,' he said. 'That's the trouble with you,'*
> *I said. 'You're worried about statistics.'*
>
> *I told him that we didn't care about what he scored. All*
> *we were interested in was what he contributed. Did he roll*
> *down? Did he play defense? Did he run the court? Did he*
> *pass?*
>
> *He asked, 'You mean you really don't care about scoring?' I told him, 'Not at all. It won't affect you one iota.'*
>
> *You could see his face light up. And from that point on,*
> *he was a different guy. He was always great to begin with,*
> *but this made him even better. He became loose. And he*
> *never looked to see what he scored. All he looked at was,*
> *did we win. And it was 'we,' not 'I.'* — Webber, 1992, p. 64

A winning concept: Lesson for educators

What lessons can middle school educators learn from teaming experiences in non-educational settings? Certainly many of the factors that have proven to be effective in business, industry, and athletics are also factors that are important in school situations. Three of the most important lessons are these:

1. Select teachers and staff members who have not only the technical skills needed for working with the team, but also the personal characteristics for positive interpersonal relations. Staff development opportunities

may be necessary in the area of interpersonal relations if personnel do not exhibit these characteristics.

2. Everyone on the school team should have a role that is important for the success of the team. And, each team member needs to be accountable for his or her role. This is a lesson not only learned from outside teaming, but also learned from cooperative learning research conducted in schools. Slavin (1995) has stressed the importance of cooperative learning which uses positive interdependence and individual accountability.

3. The principal and other school administrators must develop a commitment to gaining "power with" rather than "power over" teachers and staff members. The initial step is for the school administrators to recognize the power that teachers already have. By pooling their power, educators will be able to realize their goals more efficiently and effectively.

Although, there are many implications from these non-school settings, it is important for educators to realize that much of the discourse may not be applicable. Middle school children are not "products" that are designed, manufactured, marketed, and sold. In a report released in 1989 by the Bookings Institution, Levine and D'Andrea Tyson of the University of California reviewed all major research studies of employee involvement. The conclusions indicated that meaningful team participation has a very positive effect on productivity (Hoerr, 1989). And if the bottom line is the product, teams are a winning concept. But most organizations have found that the by-product of human development has become as important and profound as the increase in productivity. And of course, human development is more than a by-product in our schools.

Several years ago, Coach Erk Russell was asked how he motivated his teams. He responded by talking about caring: "I believe that if you really *care* about the players, and they *know* that you care about them, they will do their best to be the best they can be." The team concept is a winning concept because it is based on relationships. And when it comes down to the *real* bottom line, people matter.

References

Dryer, W.G. (1977). *Team building: Current issues and new alternatives* (3d ed.). Reading, Massachusetts: Addison-Wesley.

Emery, F.E. (1980). Designing socio-technical systems for green field sites. *Journal of Occupational Behavior, 3,* 19-27.

Graham, P. (1991). *Integrative management: Creating unity from diversity.* Oxford: Basil Blackwell.

Hoerr, J. (1989, July 10). The payoff from teamwork. *Business Week,* pp. 56-62.

Hoerr, J., & Pollock, M.A. (1986, September 29). Management discovers the human side of automation. *Business Week,* pp. 70-77.

Implementing self-directed work teams (1995). Boulder, CO: CareerTrack.

Ketchum, L.D. (1984). How redesigned plants really work. *National Productivity Review, 3,* 246-254.

Larson, C.E., & LaFasto, F.M. (1989). *Teamwork: What must go right, what can go wrong.* London: Sage.

Nonaka, I. (1993, September). The history of the quality circle. *Quality Progress,* pp. 81-83.

Russell, E., with Mandes, R. (1991). *Erk: Football, fans, and friends.* Statesboro, GA: Southeastern Sports Marketing.

Slavin, R.E. (1995). Synthesis of Research on cooperative learning. In H. Pool & J. Page (Eds.). *Beyond tracking: Finding success in inclusive schools* (pp. 165-179). Bloomington, IN: Phi Delta Kappa.

Taylor, F.W. (1947). *Scientific management.* New York: Harper.

Wall, J. (1986). *Bosses.* Lexington, MA: Heath.

Webber, A.M. (1992). Red Auerbach on management. In Harvard Business Review's, *Leaders on leadership* (pp. 55-64). Cambridge, MA: Harvard University Press.

Wellins, R.S., Byham, W.C., & Wilson, J.M. (1991). *Empowered teams: Creating self-directed work groups that improve quality, productivity, and participation.* San Francisco: Jossey-Bass.

Wiseman, P., Ramon, S., Jones, D, Memmot, M, & Cox, J. (1994, April 8). Meet this year's quality cup winners. *USA Today,* pp. B2-B3.

Research on Teaming: Insights from Selected Studies

16

David Strahan, Nan Bowles, Vanessa Richardson,
and Sarah Hanawald

W hen the editors of this text asked us to review the research on teaming, we gladly agreed, believing that systematic studies of teaming might offer us answers to some of our questions about middle school improvement. We soon found that "research on teaming" encompassed a wide variety of perspectives and methodologies. We found several strong quantitative analyses and a number of rich case studies. We are still searching for the sophisticated, large-scale, long-term studies we originally envisioned.

As we might have predicted, we learned that relationships among team organizations, team processes, student outcomes, and teacher perceptions are complex and contextual. We decided to focus our review on studies of the "effects" of teaming on students, teachers, and schools. We defined effects broadly to encompass measurable outcomes such as achievement test scores and attitude scales as well as naturalistic descriptions derived from observations and interviews.

One of the first things we learned was that systematic "research" on teaming was not as plentiful as we had hoped. Many of the articles we reviewed were not really studies. They offered helpful ideas but presented little data. We soon established three essential criteria for our review:

1. All of the studies included in this synthesis are data-based. Directly or indirectly, they report information gathered in classrooms and schools. Some studies report quantitative measures, some qualitative observations and interviews, others combine the two.

2. All of the studies have been published in a reviewed fashion, either in refereed journals or as doctoral dissertations.

3. All of the studies are recent, published within the past nine years.

Our review reports 30 studies and is organized by the type of study reported (research syntheses, comprehensive investigations, studies of student perceptions, studies of teacher perceptions, studies of team processes, and case studies). To provide a more comprehensive bibliography for the reader, we also cite some of the major works referenced in the studies we report. Following our summaries of these 30 studies, we offer tentative conclusions and suggest directions for future research.

Research syntheses

A number of books and articles have presented syntheses of research on teaming. As background for our report, we reviewed three of these syntheses as well as a major meta-analysis of factors related to student achievement.

We found the three-part series by Arhar, Johnston, and Markle (1988-89) in the *Middle School Journal* to be most helpful. The first of these articles, "Cooperation, Collaboration, and the Professional Development of Teachers" (Johnston, Markle & Arhar, 1988) is a compilation of the literature on collaboration and cooperative learning. This first article focuses on the "theoretical and empirical justification for interdisciplinary teaming" (p. 28). The authors reiterate that interdisciplinary teaming should lead to a decrease in teachers' feelings of isolation and an increase in their sense of effectiveness. In addition, teaming may help teachers form more positive interpersonal skills. Johnston, Markle, and Arhar (1988) cite studies by Meyer, Cohen, Brunetti, Molnar, and Lueder-Salmon (1971) and Cohen, Deal, Meyer, and Schoot (1979). These investigations found that increases in teaming do not, in and of themselves, result in higher levels of teacher job satisfaction. The degree to which teachers feel involved and effective in the school and classroom plays a crucial role in job satisfaction.

Arhar, Johnston, and Markle's second article in the series (1988), "The Effects of Teaming and Other Collaborative Arrangements," is a review of studies which led the authors to conclude that, "team arrangements reduce teacher isolation, increase satisfaction and improve individual teachers' sense of efficacy" (p. 25). They also found that in most teaming situations teachers discussed students' needs and operational details, rather than curriculum integration or curriculum planning. In coming to these conclusions the authors cited several studies:

- George (1984) found the lack of conversation about curriculum evident in the early developmental stages of teams;
- George and Oldaker (1985) found that teaming contributed to an improved staff morale;
- Bloomquist, Bornstein, Fink, Michaud, Oja, and Smulyan (1986) also found improved morale, but noted that non-team teachers (support personnel like music, art, P.E. teachers, etc.) felt isolated and wished to

be a part of a team; Lipsitz (1984) found that teaming was a part of the four exemplary schools in her study, but only one school identified it as the "most representative feature of the school."

The final Arhar, Johnston, and Markle article, "The Effects of Teaming on Students," is the third of the series (1989). This article compared the literature and research available concerning the question "does teaming really have an effect on students?" The authors pointed out mixed results in this area. The first two articles indicated that "teaming has an important effect on the organizational climate of the school, the satisfaction and professional development of teachers, and collaboration within the workplace," therefore, one would expect teaming to have a positive effect on students. However, not all the results of studies supported this conclusion, even though the *belief* was strong that teaming did benefit students.

The authors cite several studies which showed that teaming had little effect on student achievement. Armstrong (1977), in "Team Teaching and Achievement" examined 11 studies done between 1959 and 1970 for his findings that teaming does not affect student achievement. In "Effects of Interdisciplinary Team Teaching, Research Synthesis," Cotton (1982) examined 13 studies and three large scale reviews to conclude that there was little data to indicate much difference between the effectiveness of teaming and the effectiveness of the traditional (non-teamed) approach. Georgiades and Bjelke (1966), Zimmerman (1962), Gamsky (1970), and Cooper and Sterns (1973) all found the same lack of improved student performance. These older studies are difficult to interpret given the possibility that researchers may have considered "team teaching" as well as interdisciplinary team organization at that time.

Arhar, Johnston, and Markle (1989) then cited a series of studies which indicated that teaming did lead to higher academic achievement for students. Sinclair (1980) demonstrated that teamed students had higher CAT scores than non-teamed students. George and Oldaker (1985) found that in their study 62% of those who participated found academic achievement tied to teaming. They also found improved school discipline and better peer relationships as a result of teaming. George, Spreul, and Moorefield (1987) found that teams staying together for longer than one year reported improved discipline. Doda (1984) also found that these longer arrangements were an improvement, because they kept teachers from "writing off" low achieving, difficult to manage students (p. 26). Finally, other researchers found that the benefits of teaming depended on the specific course areas (Noto, 1972; Sterns, 1968). After surveying these articles, Arhar, Johnston, and Markle

(1989) came to the conclusion that teaming probably did make a difference in student outcomes, "but not in direct, easily discernible ways" (p. 27).

These analyses demonstrate the complexity of relationships among organizational arrangements such as teaming and subsequent "outcomes" such as achievement and attitude. One of the most comprehensive syntheses of studies of these relationships is that conducted by Wang, Haertel, and Walberg (1993). Labeled "the mother of all educational research syntheses" by Levin (1993, p. 245), Wang, Haertel, and Walberg integrated three different analyses of research related to student achievement. First, they conducted a content analysis of 179 reviews of research, identifying 228 variables and averaging their effects by categories. They then asked the authors of research reviews to rank variables and aggregated mean ratings by category. Finally, they updated a meta-analysis originally conducted by Fraser, Walberg, Welch, and Hattie, (1987). The synthesis of these three efforts resulted in an analysis of over 11,000 relationships.

Wang, Haertel, and Walberg (1993) found that the clusters of variables most associated with student learning were student characteristics and classroom practices. Two other clusters, home and community educational contexts and design and delivery of curriculum and instruction, were less associated. The clusters least associated with student learning were school-level demographics and practices and state and district governance and organization (p. 270). The five most influential categories of variables (in descending order) were classroom management, metacognitive characteristics, cognitive characteristics, home environment/parental support, and student and teacher social interactions (p. 272). The researchers concluded that "proximal" variables, those closest to classrooms, have more impact on learning than "distal" variables at the school, district, or state-level (p. 276).

While teaming was not one of the variables they addressed directly, the conclusions drawn by Wang, Haertel, and Walberg (1993) suggest that "effects" and "outcomes" from teaming are likely to be indirect rather than direct. Teaming probably enhances learning when team processes create a climate in which teachers can improve their classroom management, create more engaging instruction, and establish more supportive relationships with students and parents.

These inferences echo Arhar, Johnston, and Markle's (1989) conclusion that teaming probably makes a difference in student outcomes "but not in direct, easily discernible ways" (p. 27).

Comprehensive investigations

We identified six studies that examined the complicated relationships among teaming and outcomes in a "comprehensive" manner, that is, they gathered empirical data regarding several variables related to teaming in a systematic fashion.

Mac Iver (1990) used data from a national survey on the practices and trends in middle grade education conducted by Johns Hopkins University to study "Meeting the Needs of Young Adolescents: Advisory Groups, Interdisciplinary Teaching Teams, and School Transition Programs." The survey indicated that about 42% of students between the grades 5 and 9 receive some type of interdisciplinary instruction. About 40% of the grade 6-8 middle schools surveyed use interdisciplinary teaming.

The degree to which middle schools commit to the teaming model varies significantly. In order to be successful, teams need a common planning time, yet only 36% of the schools that are using the interdisciplinary team approach have this planning time available. Furthermore, when team planning time was available, the time was not always used to coordinate the teaming situation. Yet it was agreed upon that the teaming situation had a positive effect on the teachers from the standpoint of social support and understanding.

Mac Iver found that while 32% of all public schools that use teaming in the seventh and/or eighth grade, only 10% of the schools show real commitment to interdisciplinary teaming by providing significant planning time (p. 461). However in that small group of schools, teaming does seem to make a difference. "Our data support the claim that a well-organized interdisciplinary team approach can strengthen a school's overall program for students in the middle grades" (p. 461).

The data also showed that "self-chosen" teacher teams seemed to spend more of their common planning time on team planning than did administratively appointed teams. These self-chosen teams were also more likely to engage in integration of subject areas than were principal-appointed teams. Mac Iver found that teams with a leader functioned more efficiently than did teams without a leader, regardless of whether the leader was appointed, elected, or whether the leadership rotated.

These findings led Mac Iver to state, "...interdisciplinary teams of teachers – if they have an appropriate leader, sufficient common planning time and the willingness to use this planning time for team activities – were reported to produce a wide variety of benefits" (p. 464). Some of the benefits produced include: effectiveness of instruction, improved teacher support, attentiveness to student problems and needs, and an improvement in students' work and attitudes.

In his dissertation study, *A Program Evaluation of Interdisciplinary Team Teaching in a suburban Northern California Middle School,* Ferrara (1993) attempted to find out how effective teaming was in meeting the needs of the student population and if there was a correlation between the use of thematic units and student learning. His research methods included the use of cross-sectional survey, observation, and interviews.

Ferrara chose one middle school in suburban Northern California and administered a researcher created survey to 276 students, 276 parents, and the 48 staff members of the school. Ferrara used a Team Effectiveness Observation Form to gather data on the teachers and their interaction involving both units and teaching. He then interviewed a sample from each group to elicit additional information in regard to the areas addressed in the questionnaire.

Each group reported finding a strong correlation between teaming and students' attitudes toward learning. An overall improvement in schoolwide achievement was noted based on testing. There was not an indication that an overall improvement in student behavior had occurred as a result of teaming. The program was deemed effective and the observations indicated that thematic teaching and interdisciplinary practices were in existence.

Hall's (1993) dissertation study, *Effectiveness of Interdisciplinary Team Organizational Pattern of One-half of a Seventh-grade Class Compared with Traditional Departmentalized Pattern of the Other Half of the Seventh-grade of a Selected American Middle School in Europe,* addressed three areas of student development which might be affected by exposure to interdisciplinary teaming. Those areas were academic achievement, behavior, and attendance.

During the 1991-92 school year, a seventh grade class at an American Middle School in Europe was divided so that one group continued to operate in the traditional departmentalized way and the other group used interdisciplinary teaming. The departmentalized students were the comparison group and the interdisciplinary students became the experimental group.

Hall examined grades and the results of the Comprehensive Test of Basic Skills to determine achievement levels. To determine behavior results, Hall assessed both discipline referrals and conduct grades. Attendance was measured through quarterly attendance reports. The results indicated that there was statistically significant improvement in academic achievement for the experimental group based on the achievement test, but the attendance data was statistically significant for the traditional group. There were no significant differences found for either group in discipline referrals, conduct grades, or academic grades.

Ernest (1991) discussed both student achievement and attitude in her article "Effectiveness of an interdisciplinary team teaching organization on student achievement and student attitudes toward school in selected middle schools." She analyzed student achievement and positive attitude toward school in an interdisciplinary team and compared her findings to a non-team organization. Ernest selected an experimental team-taught group and a traditionally-taught control group through a random cluster sampling procedure. Students were assessed by both The Iowa Test of Basic Skills and The Student Attitude Measure. No significant differences were found between the interdisciplinary team organization and the traditional organization in promoting positive attitudes toward school. Students in the control group scored significantly higher than team-taught students in social studies achievement; other achievement tests showed no significant differences. Ernest concluded that the two types of organization are equally effective except in regards to social studies teaching.

Spillman's (1993) dissertation study, *The Effects of Interdisciplinary Teaming and Parent Contacts on the Academic Achievement, Motivation, Attendance, and Suspension Rate of Students Identified to be At-risk of Repeating the Ninth Grade*, followed 100 "at-risk" students. These students were identified through poor attendance and weak academic performance in eighth grade, and were deemed to be at-risk for leaving school. The students were selected through an application process and were put into two groups. One group followed the traditional high school approach in curriculum and served as the control group. The other group became part of an interdisciplinary team which focused on the four core subjects – math, science, English, and social studies. Teachers in the experimental group made more frequent parent contacts than did the control group. At the end of the year both groups' grades, attendance, and suspension rates were analyzed. The results showed that the increased parent contact had a statistically significant effect on achievement and attendance. No statistically significant correlations were noted between interdisciplinary teaming and gender or motivation.

Bradley's (1988) dissertation, *The Effectiveness of an Interdisciplinary Team Organization Pattern Compared with Departmentalized Organizational Pattern in a Selected Middle Level School Setting*, focused on the influence of teaming on student achievement, attendance, discipline problems, and parental attitude. Bradley asked, "how effective is the interdisciplinary team staff organizational pattern (ITSOP) when compared to the traditional departmental staff organizational pattern (DSOP)?" Bradley administered evaluative instruments to matching pairs of 78 randomly selected students. There were no statistically significant differences found between the ITSOP and DSOP students in the areas of reading achievement, student attendance, or discipline referrals. However, high ability math students in the DSOP program did significantly better than the high ability ITSOP students in math achievement. Parents of students who participated in ITSOP held more positive perceptions of their students' performance.

Studies of student perceptions

We found five studies that examined affective factors related to young adolescents and teaming. Three of these studies focused on self-concept; one on bonding; and one on perceptions of team practices.

In *A Survey of Interdisciplinary Teaming in Iowa Middle Level Public Schools*, Wills (1988) studied various teams to learn if there were generally agreed upon components of interdisciplinary teaming. He also studied the attitudes of students, teachers, and administrators towards teaming in Iowa middle level public schools.

Wills examined 18 schools in Iowa with any configuration of grades six, seven, and eight. Researchers administered a series of instruments to identify demographics, configuration of interdisciplinary teaming, concerns, level of use, and student's self-concept. A comparison was made between schools using teaming and those with a non-teamed approach.

Interdisciplinary teaming was not very widespread. Both teamed and non-teamed schools perceived the five components of interdisciplinary teaming as highly desirable but the perceived implementation level was considerably lower. Students in teamed schools did have a higher self-concept score.

Wills recommended that researchers replicate the study in five to seven years since interdisciplinary teaming was in the early stages of utilization in Iowa public middle schools. Wills also recommended assessing teacher preparation to implement the interdisciplinary teaming concept and the teacher morale of those using interdisciplinary teaming. In addition, Wills advocated long range studies to determine the effects of interdisciplinary teaming on students in terms of student achievement and self-concept.

Five years later, Wills joined with other researchers in a follow-up to his 1987 study. Stefanich, Mueller, and Wills' (1992) study, "A Longitudinal Study of Interdisciplinary Teaming and Its Influence on Student Self-Concept" was the result. While the 1987 study used 18 schools in Iowa with any configuration of grade six, seven and eight, the 1992 studies used six schools selected from the original 18. Three of the schools were teamed and three were non-teamed. Teachers from these six schools completed the Interdisciplinary Teaming Innovation Configuration Checklist and the Interdisciplinary Teaming Stages of Concern. Each school also administered the Piers-Harris children's Self-Concept Scale to a heterogeneous class of English or social studies students at grade levels six, seven, and eight.

The results indicated that there is limited use of teaming in Iowa schools. Even schools which have been practicing teaming for five years have not reached a high level of comfort with the process. The researchers found that using interdisciplinary teams over a period of time does not necessarily mean that the teams will move to higher levels of implementation. These schools were still in the early stages of teaming. In the 1987 study, students at schools where teaming was in place reported a higher self-concept than did those students from schools without teams. In 1992 there was no reported difference in self-concept between the two types of schools.

Nolke (1991) studied the issue of student self-esteem. *Interdisciplinary teaming and student self-esteem*, discusses his research concerning the influence of organizational structure on the self-esteem of middle school eighth grade students. Nolke used the Coopersmith Self-Esteem Inventory at the beginning and the end of the school year to evaluate both a teamed group of students and a non-teamed group of students. Nolke found significant relationships between total overall self-esteem scores, the home parent self-esteem sub-scale scores, and male and female students' scores on school academic self-esteem. Females showed significantly higher post-test scores in the school academic self-esteem area. These results led Nolke to conclude that interdisciplinary teaming does have a significant effect on students' self-esteem.

Arhar (1990), in "Interdisciplinary Teaming as a School Intervention to Increase the Social Bonding of Middle Level Students," addressed the degree to which students exposed to teaming develop stronger social bonds than students in non-teamed schools. Arhar studied 5000 seventh graders, half of whom attended middle schools with teams, the other half attended non-teamed schools. The study involved 22 schools that were matched according to size, socioeconomic status (determined by the percentage of students receiving free or reduced price lunches), and the percentage of minority students.

Arhar administered a twenty-five item Likert-type Social Bonding Scale from the Wisconsin Youth Survey to each student. The scale was used to measure student bonding to peers, teachers, and school. The survey revealed that, with some exceptions, students attending teamed schools were more strongly bonded to both the school and their teachers. Students in teamed schools were also somewhat more likely to feel bonded to their peers; however, low socioeconomic status proved to have a depressing effect on student social bonding to peers, thereby countering the effect of teaming (p. 8).

Arhar found some explanations for situations in which teaming did not help students form stronger bonds to their schools. One school had a staff that the principal described as "considerably resistant" to teaming. Another teamed school drew from two communities of students who would go on to attend different high schools, while a non-teamed school had implemented many of the characteristics of middle schools that did not involve teaming (integrated study, collaboration among teachers, student advisory). Arhar recommended further research be done to shed more light on the effect of school organization on the social bonding of middle level students.

In "Are Interdisciplinary Units Worthwhile? Ask Students!," Strubbe (1990) based her study on the fact that very often researchers fail to ask those persons most involved in a situation how they perceive it. She collected students' feedback on interdisciplinary units over a five year period. She used a Likert-type questionnaire with five statements to which the students were to indicate their level of agreement and give evaluative comments. There were a total of about 700 sixth, seventh, and eighth graders involved. The responses were overwhelmingly positive in all five areas addressed. These areas included: (a) were topics interesting, (b) did students feel they learned something, (c) was the class sharing of information learned beneficial, (d) was working with others beneficial, and (e) a self-ranking of the student's involvement in the project. Strubbe examined students' responses and developed several criteria for identifying successful interdisciplinary units: (a) relevant topics; (b) clear goals and objectives; (c) variety in topics, structures, activities, and grouping; (d) choice in topics and project groupings; (e) adequate time, processes, and products; (f) field trips; (g) group cooperation, sharing, and community involvement. Strubbe concluded with a statement to the effect that teachers sometimes sense that an approach appears to be working, but feedback (such as she received from the students in this study) can verify these hunches with concrete data.

Studies of teacher perceptions

We identified five studies that investigated the effects of teaming on teachers' perceptions. The focus of these analyses were teachers' perceptions of their roles, of isolation, of stress, of climate, and of job satisfaction.

In her dissertation study entitled *Teacher Perspectives and Practices in Two Organizationally Different Middle Schools*, Doda (1984) explored teachers' perspectives and the ways those perspectives influenced practices. Doda conducted an ethnographic study of teachers from two schools, one a middle school using teams, the other a non-teamed school. The two schools were different in organization, curriculum, and administration. Teachers from the non-teamed school defined themselves as curriculum disseminators and suggested that their instruction was information-centered and teacher-directed. They seemed to view teaching as an individual enterprise with little autonomy. Teachers from the teamed school revealed a greater sense of personal responsibility for student socialization and academic learning. They seemed to view themselves as part of a collective effort and expressed a stronger sense of autonomy.

In "The Influence of Middle Level Interdisciplinary Teaming on Teacher Isolation," Mills, Powell, and Pollak (1992) reported a year long study conducted at Burkholder Junior High School in Nevada that involved the sixth, seventh, and eighth grade teachers at the school. Researchers randomly selected one team from each grade level and used interviews (structured and unstructured) and observations to collect their data, logging over two hundred hours of observation. The researchers asked teachers about different types of isolation in reference to school structure. They found that teamed teachers did not feel personally isolated, even early in the school year. However, teachers did report other types of isolation. Some reported feeling like "islands in the stream" as the school flowed around their particular team, teachers felt isolated within their grade level. Teamed teachers felt isolated from other teachers in their subject area, and some team teachers perceived an isolation from support personnel and other non-teamed staff and students. The researchers found a need for further research investigating ways to keep the team intact and yet overcome the "islands in the stream" phenomena.

In "Middle School Interdisciplinary Team Organization and Its Relationship to Teacher Stress," Gatewood, Cline, Green, and Harris (1992) compared the amount of stress felt by teachers in schools where interdisciplinary teams were used to that in schools where a non-teamed structure existed. Six research inventories (Teacher Stress Inventory) were sent to each of the 50 schools with instructions for teams to select one member to complete the survey and return it directly to the researchers (rather than through building administrators). Of 300 potential responses, 111 of 150 came back from the 25 schools using team structures (74% return rate), and 113 of 150 were returned from the 25 non-team schools (75%).

The results indicated a slight reduction in reported stress when a teacher was a member of a team; however, there was no reduction in the number of physical complaints which usually accompany stress, nor was there decreased concern over work-related concerns such as time for planning or completing paper work. Those respondents who were a part of a team reported an increased feeling of professionalism.

Walsh and Shay's (1993) "In Support of Interdisciplinary Teaming: The Climate Factor" compared levels of teacher and student involvement in both interdisciplinary teaming and the traditional departmental model. The researchers asked, "Do middle level teachers working within the two different organizational structures – team versus departmental – differ significantly in their perceptions of school climate? And if so, how do the variables of certification type, experience, sex and age interact on their perceptions" (p. 58)?

The researchers used a Likert Questionnaire, (Profile of a School – Teacher Questionnaire, 1978) sending it to 400 seventh and eighth grade teachers employed in New Jersey middle schools. They received 310 completed surveys from 173 teachers on interdisciplinary teams and 137 from teachers working within a departmentalized structure. Walsh and Shay found statistical differences between the two groups in all areas of involvement. Teachers involved in interdisciplinary teams viewed their school climate more favorably concerning decision making and their roles as supporters to students. These team teachers also saw their students as being more involved and more open with their teachers than did teachers from more traditional models. The researchers stated "the results of this study provide further evidence as to the effectiveness of the interdisciplinary team structure in creating an environment which is conducive to students and staff working together at the middle school level" (p. 59).

Laven's (1992) dissertation, *A Study of Teacher Perceptions of Job Satisfaction Related to the Use of Interdisciplinary Teams at the Middle School Level in the State of California*, examined how participation with an interdisciplinary team affected teachers' feelings about their jobs. Two hundred teachers from 115 middle schools in California, who were currently a part of an interdisciplinary team, were surveyed using parts of a previously developed instrument (Education in the Middle Grades: A National Survey of

Trends and Practices, developed by Epstein and Mac Iver) as well as new questions designed to be more specific to job satisfaction. One hundred seven teachers answered the survey. The significant relationships which emerged from the results were in the area of teacher collegiality. The study found that strong ties of collegiality exist when team members have a common planning time. Teachers reported that their team members provided social support as well as understanding. There was no significant relationship between teacher job satisfaction and the use of interdisciplinary teaming. Laven suggested that the study indicated a need for further research in the areas of teacher personality types, interdisciplinary teams, and job satisfaction as well as the effect of interdisciplinary teams on discipline and academic achievement.

Team processes

We identified five studies that carefully examined basic processes of teamwork, that is, they explored how teams function and the nature of their work together.

One of the most straightforward of these studies was George and Stevenson's (1989) "The very best teams in the very best schools as described by middle school principals." The authors conducted a survey of 154 middle schools that had been recognized for excellence by professional organizations. They asked principals to identify and describe the "very best" teams in those schools. They found that administrators emphasized both academic and affective practices. Principals often noted that students on the "very best" teams made dramatic progress on achievement tests and were recognized accordingly (p. 9). They noted that teams developed strategies for monitoring progress and stressed students' progress in their conferences with parents and with each other. Principals also described the ways successful teams developed relationships. One respondent, for example, noted that team members were often "close professional friends but not necessarily close personal friends" (p. 13). Other principals highlighted the animated nature of team meetings and the need to balance personal issues with team priorities. Many principals emphasized the student-centered nature of team interactions and shared illustrations of teams that held frequent case discussions, met beyond team time, and worked to promote teamwork. One of the major themes to emerge from these data was the importance of team identity. Among the emblems of team membership cited were names, logos, mascots, shirts, buttons, pins, and colors. Ceremonies and recognition were also important: award celebrations, field trips, picnics, intramurals, parent meetings, and team dinners. In highlighting these results, George and Stevenson (1989) emphasized the essential nature of commitment:

> *Distinctive threads in the fabric of this data* [sic] *further indicated that teachers recognized the importance and urgency of helping every child succeed in specific ways, then publicly recognizing those achievements within the teams.*
> (p. 9)

Schumacher's (1992) dissertation study, entitled *A Multiple Case Study of Curriculum Integration by Middle School Interdisciplinary Teams of Teachers*, analyzed curriculum integration at five specific levels. Using the work of Vars (1987) and others, Schumacher developed a continuum of curriculum integration that involved five levels: departmentalized, reinforcement, complementary, webbed, and integrated learning. Schumacher used naturalistic inquiry and questioned interdisciplinary teams of middle school teachers from five middle schools, each at one of the five levels. Using interviews, documents, observations, and artifacts Schumacher was able to more clearly define each level and to find some common themes. For example, curriculum integration is more likely to occur in teams that are together for longer than one year. In addition, teams that spend more time discussing curriculum during team planning are more likely to achieve integration.

The Educational Specialist Practicum Report, *A Program To Increase Effective Teaming in the Middle School* by Sevick (1989) analyzed the effect of a "curriculum-connection" packet in helping interdisciplinary teams see more clearly how to integrate their curricula. Sevick focused on two seventh and two eighth grade teams consisting of 18 teachers and 588 students. These teams were among those judged "ineffective" during a districtwide survey. Teachers received packets that included each grade level's curriculum, a skills checklist for each subject, a list of possible objectives in curriculum integration, and seven activities which could fit into a thematic unit. The purposes were to show teachers the viability of integration and to give them tools to make connections. The packet was used in staff development. Survey results indicated that teachers considered the packets a positive way to move towards integration.

For her dissertation study, *Factors Present During the Development of Exemplary Interdisciplinary Teams in Middle Level Schools*, Gibson (1992) surveyed and observed team members at twelve Virginia middle schools in order to identify "common elements in the experience of exemplary interdisciplinary teams in middle schools." The teams were selected as exemplary based on criteria set up by Erb and Doda (1989) which delineated four stages of team development: (a) organization, (b) attention to students, (c) shared responsibility and growth, and (d) instructional coordination. Gibson's results were mixed. She found the following absent in her exemplary teams: (a) coordination with non-team faculty, (b) uniform discipline policies, (c) observation of peer teaching, (d) uniform scheduling guidelines, and (e) ideas relating to staff development. The exemplary teams focused either on administration, curriculum, or changing to new activities.

Kain (1993) observed one middle school team over the course of a year. He examined the ways in which the three teachers on the eighth grade team worked together to exploit opportunities for integrated units that arose during the year. Kain was particularly interested in learning what determined a teacher's level of interest in and commitment to an integrated unit that developed from a propitious event. Kain found that teachers focused on two factors in deciding whether to participate with their colleagues in an integrated unit. Kain calls these factors curricular content and subject intent. High curricular content occurs when a potential unit relates directly to the curriculum assigned to a particular course. Conversely, subject intent occurs when the propitious event relates to the processes a teacher wishes students to engage in or understand. For example, Kain found the eighth grade team showing a film that involved several scientific experiments. The experiments were not aligned with the curriculum for the eighth grade; however, one of the science teacher's goals was to encourage students to engage in the scientific method.

Kain found that in order for a teacher to become fully committed to an integrated unit, the teacher needed to believe that the unit should have either a high curricular content or a high subject intent. When neither of these elements was present, the teacher (if they participated at all) gave minimal class time to the effort and did not evaluate students with relation to the activity.

Kain developed a matrix to predict the level of teacher involvement based on the content of the propitious unit. His Interdisciplinary Judgment Matrix offers a view of teachers' decision making processes that shows how teachers weigh the influence of an official curriculum and that of their own professional expertise. The matrix also challenges notions that teachers should engage in any integrated opportunity that arises, asking instead that teachers critically evaluate integrated units and reject those that place integration above meaningful, related connections for learners.

Case studies

In our final section, we summarize five very specific profiles of teams in action. Each of these case studies offered detailed descriptions of teams based on at least one full year of observations and interviews.

Kotler (1991) conducted a three year study of students' responses to interdisciplinary curricula and instruction in one particular middle school. Through observation, interviews, and instruments, Kotler found that the interdisciplinary unit encouraged students to cooperate, relate history to their own experiences, and to understand historical analysis in more sophisticated ways. Teachers emphasized the importance of working together, trying new ideas, and developing connections across the curriculum. These findings suggested that interdisciplinary curriculum and instruction was highly compatible with the cognitive development of these young adolescents. Based on her study, Kotler advocated a thoughtful balance between discipline based and interdisciplinary approaches.

"The Delta Project: A Three-year Longitudinal Study of Middle School Change" by Pate, Mizelle, Hart, Jordan, Matthews, Matthews, Scott, and Brantly (1993) described the efforts of one school in a small community in rural Georgia to become a "pocket of excellence" – a school that has changed its curriculum, methods of instruction, and organization to be more in keeping with what we know about adolescents and how they learn. The impetus for the project was a conference, "Project 2061: Science for All Americans," attended by two of the teachers at the school. The teachers learned of a school in Cologne, Germany, where teachers and students remained together for six years. The school had found that this format resulted in positive experiences for both the teachers and the students. As the Georgia teachers considered this model, they brainstormed ways they could adapt it to their school. They attempted to create a family environment by keeping a group of students and teachers together for all three years of middle school.

The school invited professors from the University of Georgia to participate as collaborators. The professors acted as sounding boards, information disseminators, and evaluators for the project. They analyzed the projects' impact on both students and teachers, gathering their data from student questionnaires, teacher and student interviews, and transcriptions of team planning sessions. The students were randomly assigned to a team of four teachers by gender, race, and achievement. The teachers used alternate schedules allowing for larger blocks of time when needed; they also used cooperative learning and higher order thinking skills in their activities. Teachers coordinated the curriculum through a variety of materials, including current issues, specific content, and themes.

According to both teachers and students, the Delta project has been a success. With few exceptions the group remained intact for three years. Students reported feeling like one big family and enjoying the support this framework provided. They also indicated that not only their teammates but also their teachers "stood by them." The teachers see the Delta Project as one that will continue to develop.

Powell's (1993) study, "Seventh Grader's Perspectives of Their Interdisciplinary Team" is based on the year he spent with the Tort Team at Burkholder Junior High, Henderson, Nevada. This was the second year the team had been together; most of the students had been together in sixth grade, and all but one teacher was the same. Powell's data were gathered from observations and interviews. He was originally interested in three questions: (a) What is the influence of teaming on students' attitudes and feelings toward their school work? (b) How has teaming influenced students' intra-team and inter-team relationships with peers? (c) How does teaming influence students' personal existence at school? What are the benefits for students from being on a team?" (p. 50).

Powell cited a study by George, Spreul and Moorefield (1987) that addressed the first two questions through a survey of about 900 middle school students. These students felt that long-term teaming helped them with relationships with teammates, other peers, and teachers. Students also felt that long-term teaming encouraged them to do better academically because the teachers knew them better. Powell explored his third question through interviews with 14 students selected by him and the Tort teachers. All students selected had been on the Tort team for all of the sixth grade and for these first few months of seventh grade. In order to have a wide perspective, Powell and the teachers selected four students who were high achievers, six who were average, and four who were below average. None of the students created serious behavior problems and none were identified as learning disabled. The interview questions were compiled by the Tort teachers and the researcher.

Once the interviews were completed and the transcripts examined three themes emerged from the students' comments: "(1) feeling like a school family, (2) students' social connections, and (3) expectations of teaching and learning" (p. 52). The students found that being on a team for two years gave them a sense of family and a closeness to those team members and teachers; however, they indicated a lack of time to get to know other peers. Students felt that they did better academically because they knew their teachers well and knew what was expected of them. They also thought that their teachers, in turn, expected more from them both academically and personally for much the same reasons.

Powell found four implications from his study. First, schools should attempt to structure themselves so that students and teachers have at least two years together in order to develop their relationships. Secondly, those teams which develop a close, trusting, collaborative relationship stand the best chance of enhancing both academic achievement and personal skills, as well as a reduction in the feelings of isolation for both students and teachers. Thirdly, principals who have these established teams should be very cautious in moving students from one team to another. Students need to feel secure in their team. Fourth, because long-term teaming can create a feeling of isolation from the rest of the school, officials should be sure to include activities in which teams can interact.

In "Beginning Curriculum Integration," Burnaford (1993) described three teams she worked with as they moved toward interdisciplinary study. Each of the teams had achieved a different level of teamwork when they began working with Burnaford. By examining the growth of the three teams, Burnaford was able to generate some principles about teaming.

The first team Burnaford described was a new sixth grade team preparing to move from an elementary school to a new middle school. The teachers had been self-contained in the elementary school and were apprehensive about the move. Burnaford was able to determine that the major point of contention was the teachers' perception that they were acting under a mandate from the administration to become a team. However, some of the teachers were eager to begin planning integrated units with other team members. Eventually, the teachers' successful transition in becoming a team led Burnaford to the realization that "not all team members need to be equally invested initially for coordination and cooperation to occur" (p. 50).

The second "team" Burnaford discussed was a group of eighth grade teachers that had worked together for several years. However, this group of teachers did not have many of the characteristics associated with teaming, such as a common planning time. The teachers wanted help in designing an integrated unit. When they first met Burnaford, the teachers seemed to have gotten stuck on "how to do" an integrated unit. Burnaford discovered that the teachers had never examined "why" they wanted to attempt an integrated unit; instead, they had just assumed that they should, and moved from there. The group articulated their reasons for engaging in an integrated unit, and addressed many of the logistical difficulties integration would entail. After this process, they were able to plan the "how" part of a unit without great difficulty.

The third team (actually four teams at one school) Burnaford described had been working together at the team level for several years. The decision to work with Burnaford in deepening their level of integration was theirs, the teams had selected "personalized learning and integration of curriculum" as one of their school goals for the year (p. 55). Burnaford observed these teams successfully coordinate their efforts in large scale integration. These units brought new dilemmas to light: teachers were concerned about methods of evaluation and the degree to which themes were "inclusive, yet welcoming of diversity" (p. 59).

From her observations, Burnaford generated three principles that may serve as the bases for future professional development efforts. The first principle was that teachers expect a certain degree of autonomy and individuality in their work. Secondly, change in methods and curriculum can happen only after teachers have personally clarified and investigated the reasons for such change. Finally, professional development is most productive when teachers are willing to view themselves as learners and view students as participants in the educational process.

Like Burnaford, McDaniel and Romerdahl (1993) investigated integrative efforts at three separate schools in writing their "A Multiple-case Study of Middle Grade Teachers' Interdisciplinary Curriculum Work." Their central question was "how do middle grade teachers develop and maintain interdisciplinary curriculum?" (p. 66). The first team examined was a four-teacher ninth grade team in a high school setting. This team focused on a skills approach to integrated learning. Each teacher made specific efforts to support other teacher's curricula in their classrooms. For example, vocabulary from language arts texts were used in math, science, and social studies classes. The teachers refer to the process of exposing students to knowledge in the most appropriate course as "bridging" from one subject area to another (p. 69).

The second school studied was a middle school with a sixth grade team that served as a development program model for the district. The team consisted of two full-time teachers, along with a part-time teacher. The teachers make an effort to keep the curriculum process oriented rather than fact oriented; however, over time they have made many changes to their original concept. These changes include a return to math texts and workbooks, along with a reinstatement of the districtwide spelling curriculum.

The final integrative effort studied involved the work of one teacher at a middle school. This English teacher was given a block of time in which to teach social studies and language arts and was initially overwhelmed and intimidated. Over time, the teacher has developed a nearly fully integrated curriculum for these two subjects. This curriculum has come about almost entirely through her own efforts during the past fifteen years.

From their examination of these three situations, McDaniel and Romerdahl developed three hypotheses that provide implications for other teachers attempting to create interdisciplinary experiences for their students. These hypotheses suggest some preliminary directions for further research:

1. While small groups of teachers find planning logistics easier, the interplay of a team provides a much richer interdisciplinary curriculum;
2. When interdisciplinary programs coexist with disciplinary programs, curricular compromises will be made by the interdisciplinary program;
3. For an interdisciplinary program to succeed, it must be supported by those outside its confines (pages 76-78).

Conclusions

These 30 studies demonstrate that research on teaming has become more systematic and they suggest some tentative conclusions. Interdisciplinary team organization seems to be clearly associated with the overall success of middle school programs (Arhar, Johnston, & Markle, 1989; Doda, 1984; Ferrara, 1993; Mac Iver, 1990). Associations among team organization, team practices, and student achievement are inconsistent however. Some studies document strong associations between team arrangements and achievement (Ferrara, 1993; Hall, 1993) Others demonstrate little difference (Bradley, 1988; Ernest, 1991). Teaming is more consistently associated with positive student attitudes. Students in teamed settings report a stronger sense of bonding (Arhar, 1990), appreciate interdisciplinary units (Kotler, 1992; Strubbe, 1990), and feel a strong sense of community (Pate et al. 1993; Powell, 1993). Associations with self-concept are less predictable (Nolke, 1991; Stefanich, Mueller, & Wills, 1992).

Teaming seems to be most clearly associated with teacher perceptions of collegiality and professionalism. Teaming can reduce personal isolation (Mills, Powell, & Pollak, 1992), foster collegiality (Laven, 1992), increase feelings of professionalism (Gatewood, Cline, Green, & Harris, 1992), and enhance perceptions of school climate (Walsh & Shay, 1993). Essential team processes seem to include clear organization (Gibson, 1992), responsiveness to students as individuals (Pate et al, 1993; Powell, 1993), extensive discussions of curriculum (Burnaford, 1993; McDaniel & Romerdahl, 1993;

Schumaker, 1992) and ongoing negotiation of connections among content areas (Kain, 1993). Team processes may become more sophisticated when teams remain together for more than one year (Pate et al., 1993; Powell, 1993; Schumaker, 1992).

These tentative conclusions suggest several implications for improving middle level schooling. First, we need to remind ourselves that forming interdisciplinary teams is not likely to automatically improve the quality of education. Relationships among team organization, team processes, student outcomes, teacher perceptions, and school improvement are complex and contextual. Rearranging schedules and assigning teammates does not guarantee teamwork. The things that seem to matter most about teaming are personal and interactive. When teams create a sense of community, students and teachers may perceive themselves as members of a "family" (Pate et al., 1993; Powell, 1993). At the same time, teaming may create an "islands in the stream" mentality that results when teachers feel isolated from the rest of the school (Mills, Powell, & Pollak, 1992). As more schools create interdisciplinary team organizations and as teachers grow more experienced with team processes, learning to balance team bonding with school membership will become increasingly important.

Another major implication is that team arrangements are not as prevalent as we might wish (Mac Iver, 1990). Moreover, the type of collaborative, "exemplary" teaming we envision seems to be a rare phenomenon (Gibson, 1992). Encouraging teams to work together for more than one year may enhance the development of exemplary teams (Pate et al., 1993; Powell, 1993; Schumaker, 1992). At a minimum, teamwork requires time, nurture, support, and ongoing leadership. The other chapters in this text can provide guidance for enhancing teamwork.

We continue our search with as many questions as tentative conclusions:

1. **How do teachers learn to team?**
    What types of teacher education experiences encourage teamwork?
    What types of staff development experiences encourage teamwork?
    How do experienced team members invite new members to be successful teammates?
    How can administrators foster teamwork?

2. **How do students form more caring relationships?**
    What types of school bonding can teachers nurture?
    How can teams create a sense of community?

What are the effects of practices such as teaming across grade levels or keeping teams together for three years?

What types of team projects can extend a sense of community responsibility?

What types of team processes can enhance positive discipline and personal responsibility?

3. **How do teams get beyond organizational considerations to meaningful integration of classroom experiences?**

How can team leaders encourage more meaningful discourse?

How can administrators guide teams to think beyond immediate questions to consider new possibilities?

How might teams integrate measures of subject-area accountability with assessments of integrated reasoning development?

4. **How do schools form "communities" among teams that have strong identity?**

How can teams interact with each other to foster stronger school bonding and shared identity?

What types of school activities might foster collaboration among teams toward common purposes?

How might teams work with parents and members of the community to create ongoing partnerships?

How might teams collaborate with elementary or high school teachers to articulate purposes across levels and create more supportive transitions?

These questions and others merit more systematic studies. The complexity of the interactions affecting teaming warrant more sophisticated investigations.

We particularly need longitudinal studies of students and teachers working together in teamed settings. The case studies we reviewed have helped illuminate some of the dynamics of teamwork. However, we need to know more about long-term "effects" of teaming. We especially need to know how teaming enriches learning in the content areas. Comprehensive longitudinal studies could gather data regarding academic and affective outcomes over time.

We need to encourage studies from student and teacher perspectives. Very few of the studies we found were written from teachers' perspectives. None were written from students' points of view. We need more studies written with the voices of teachers and students.

We especially need to promote action research. Teachers can address many of the issues they face on their teams with their own action studies. Faculties can monitor the success of innovations. Individual teachers can chart the effects of integrated instruction and other team efforts in their own classrooms. Sharing these action studies would help all of us find more sophisticated ways to connect theory, research, and practice.

Our search has convinced us that systematic study of teaming is only beginning; so the search continues. We hope that readers will join us.

References

Arhar, J. (1990). Interdisciplinary teaming as a school intervention to increase the social bonding of middle level students. *Research in Middle Level Education: Selected Studies 1990*. Columbus, OH: National Middle School Association.

Arhar, J., Johnston, J.H., & Markle, G. (1988). The effects of teaming and other collaborative arrangements. *Middle School Journal, 19*(4), 22-25.*

Arhar, J., Johnston, J.H., & Markle, G. (1989). The effects of teaming on students. *Middle School Journal, 20*(3), 24-27. *

Armstrong, D. (1977). Team teaching and achievement. *Review of Educational Research, 47*(1), 65-86.

Blomquist, R., Bornstein, S., Fink, G., Michaud, R., Oja, S. & Smulyan, L. (1986). *Action research on change in schools: The relationship between teacher moral/job satisfaction and organizational changes in a junior high school* (Report No. 81-0040). Washington, DC: National Institute of Education.

Bradley, E.M. (1988). *The effectiveness of an interdisciplinary team organizational pattern compared with a departmentalized organizational pattern in a selected middle level school setting*. Unpublished doctoral dissertation, State University of New York at Buffalo.

Burnaford, G. (1993). Beginning curriculum integration: Three middle level case studies in professional development. *Research in Middle Level Education, 16*(2), 43-65.

Cohen, E.G., Deal, T., Meyer, J., & Schoot, W. (1979). Technology and teaming in the elementary school. *Sociology of Education, 56*, 20-33.

Cooper, D., & Sterns, H. (1973). Team teaching, student adjustment and achievement. *Journal of Educational Research, 66*, 323-327.

Cotton, K. (1982). *Effects of interdisciplinary team teaching, research synthesis*. Portland, OR: Northwest Regional Laboratory. (ED 230 533)

Doda, N.M. (1984). *Teacher perspectives and practices in two organizationally different middle schools*. Unpublished doctoral dissertation, The University of Florida, Gainesville.

Erb, T.O., & Doda, N.M. (1989). *Team organization: Promise—practices and possibilities.* Washington, DC: National Education Association.

Ernest, K.F. (1991). *Effectiveness of an interdisciplinary team teaching organization on student achievement and student attitudes toward school in selected middle schools.* Unpublished doctoral dissertation, University of Idaho, Moscow.

Ferrara, R.L. (1993). *A program evaluation of interdisciplinary team teaching in a suburban Northern California middle school.* Unpublished doctoral dissertation, University of San Francisco.

Fraser, B.J., Walberg, H.J., Welch, W.W., & Hattie, J.A. (1987). Syntheses of educational productivity research. *International Journal of Educational Research, 11*, 145-252.

Gamsky, N. (1970). Team teaching, student achievement and attitudes. *Journal of Experimental Education, 39*, 42-45.

Gatewood, T., Cline, G., Green, G., & Harris, S. (1992). Middle school interdisciplinary team organization and its relationship to teacher-stress. *Research in Middle Level Education, 15* (2), 27-40.

George, P. (1984). Middle school instructional organization: An emerging consensus. In J.H. Lounsbury (Ed.), *Perspectives on middle school education* (pp. 52-67). Columbus, OH: National Middle School Association.

George, P., & Oldaker, L. (1985). *Evidence for the middle school.* Columbus, OH: National Middle School Association.

George, P., Spreul, M., & Moorefield, J. (1987). *Long-term teacher-student relationships: A middle school case study.* Columbus, OH: National Middle School Association.

George, P., & Stevenson, C. (1989). The very best teams in the very best schools as described by middle school principals. *T.E.A.M.: The Early Adolescent Magazine, 3* (5), 6-14.

Georgiades, W., & Bjelke, J. (1966). Evaluation of English achievement in a ninth grade three period team teaching class. *California Journal of Educational Research, 17*, 100-112.

Gibson, P.K. (1992). *Factors present during the development of exemplary interdisciplinary teams in middle level schools.* Unpublished doctoral dissertation, Virginia Polytechnic Institute and State University, Blacksburg.

Hall, L.K. (1993). *Effectiveness of interdisciplinary team organizational pattern of one-half of a seventh-grade class compared with traditional departmentalized pattern of the other half of the seventh-grade of a selected American middle school in Europe.* Unpublished doctoral dissertation, The University of Arizona, Tempe.

Johnston, J., Markle, G., & Arhar, J. (1988). Cooperation, collaboration, and the professional development of teachers. *Middle School Journal, 19* (3), 28-32.*

Kain, D.L. (1993). Deciding to integrate curricula: Judgments about holding and stretching. *Research in Middle Level Education, 16* (2), 25-43.

Kotler, W.I. (1991). *Interdisciplinary study in a middle-level school. Student and teacher perspectives: A case study.* Unpublished doctoral dissertation, University of Virginia, Charlottesville.

Laven, D.L. (1992). *A study of teacher perceptions of job satisfaction related to the use of interdisciplinary teams at the middle school level in the state of California.* Unpublished doctoral dissertation, University of the Pacific, Stockton, California.

Levin, H.M. (1993). Editor's introduction. *Review of Educational Research, 63* (3).

Lipsitz, J.S. (1984). *Successful schools for young adolescents.* New Brunswick, NJ: Transaction Books.

Mac Iver, D. (1990). Meeting the needs of young adolescents: Advisory groups, interdisciplinary teaching teams, and school transition programs. *Phi Delta Kappan, 71*, 458-464.

Meyer, J., Cohen, E., Brunetti, F., Molnar, S., & Lueder-Salmon, E. (1971). *The impact of the open space school upon teacher influence and autonomy: The effects of an organizational innovation* (Technical Report No. 21). Palo Alto, CA: Stanford University, Center for Research and Development in Teaching. (ED 062 291)

McDaniel, J.E., & Romerdahl, N.S. (1993). A multiple-case study of middle grade teachers' interdisciplinary curriculum work. *Research in Middle Level Education, 16*(2), 65-87.

Mills, R., Powell, R., & Pollak, J. (1992). The influence of middle level interdisciplinary teaming on teacher isolation. *Research in Middle Level Education, 15* (2), 9-26.

Nolke, R.F. (1991). *Interdisciplinary teaming and student self-esteem.* Unpublished doctoral dissertation, University of Missouri-Columbia.

Noto, R. (1972). *A comparison between traditional teaching and interdisciplinary team teaching at the seventh grade level.* Unpublished doctoral dissertation, St. Louis University.

Pate, P.E., Mizelle, L., Hart, L., Jordan, J., Matthews, R., Matthews, S., Scott, V., & Brantley, V. (1993). The delta project: A three-year longitudinal study of middle school change. *Middle School Journal, 24* (1), 24-27.

Powell, R.R. (1993). Seventh graders' perspectives of their interdisciplinary team. *Middle School Journal, 24* (3), 49-57.

Schumacher, D.H. (1992). *A multiple case study of curriculum integration by middle school interdisciplinary teams of teachers.* Unpublished doctoral dissertation, The Florida State University, Tallahassee.

Sevick, M.J. (1989). *A program to increase effective teaming in the middle school.* Educational specialist practicum report: NOVA University, Ft. Lauderdale, Florida.

Sinclair, R. (1980). *The effect of middle school staff organizational patterns on student perceptions of teacher performances, student perceptions of school environment and student academic achievement.* Unpublished doctoral dissertation, Miami University, Oxford, Ohio.

Spillman, K.E.C. (1993). *The effects of interdisciplinary teaming and parent contacts on the academic achievement, motivation, attendance, and suspension rate of students identified to be at-risk of repeating the ninth grade.* Unpublished doctoral dissertation. Virginia Polytechnic Institute and State University.

Stefanich, G., Mueller, J., & Wills, F. (1992). A longitudinal study of interdisciplinary teaming and its influence on student self-concept. *Research in Middle Level Education, 15* (2), 41-56.

Sterns, H. (1968). *Student adjustment and achievement in a team teaching organization.* Unpublished doctoral dissertation, University of Michigan, Ann Arbor.

Strubbe, M. (1990). Are interdisciplinary units worthwhile? Ask students. *Middle School Journal, 21* (3), 36-39.

Vars, G.F. (1987). *Interdisciplinary teaching in the middle grades: Why and how.* Columbus, OH: National Middle School Association.

Walsh, K.J., & Shay, M.J. (1993). In support of interdisciplinary teaming: The climate factor. *Middle School Journal, 24* (4), 56-60.

Wang, M., Haertel, G., & Walberg, H. (1993). Toward a knowledge base for school learning. *Review of Educational Research, 63*, 249-294.

Wills, F.A., Jr. (1988). *A survey of interdisciplinary teaming in Iowa middle level public schools.* Unpublished doctoral dissertation, University of Northern Iowa, Cedar Falls.

Zimmerman, W. (1962). *Departmental and unified seventh grade programs in English and social studies, a study of changes in subject matter achievement and personal adjustment.* Unpublished doctoral dissertation, Syracuse University.

* Editor's Note:

Arhar, Johnston, and Markle (1988, 1989) and Johnston, Markle, and Arhar (1988) have all been reprinted in J.H. Lounsbury (Ed.).(1992). *Connecting the curriculum through interdisciplinary instruction.* Columbus, OH: National Middle School Association.

Part V

Current Concerns

The practice of teaming, like much in middle school education, is constantly undergoing changes as new practices and programs develop. Part V includes six chapters exploring current concerns in middle school education that influence the practice of teaming – issues such as team leadership, integrative curriculum, and inclusion of students.

Jacqueline Anglin explores team configurations beyond the standard core four team of mathematics, science, language arts, and social studies. Various configurations, both permanent and temporary, for both exploratory and core teams are examined as well as schoolwide efforts. The focus here is on meeting student needs "without the constraints of traditional models – either departmentalized ones or stereotyped teaming ones."

As teams come to be the signature of middle schools, questions of team leadership have emerged. Daniel L. Kain examines the role of the team leader and team leadership. Moving from a foundation of effective teaming based in the current literature on teams, Kain outlines six leadership roles that arise from effective teaming which are organized around purpose, norms, and boundary-spanning issues. Kain offers us direction for the future – direction toward effective team leadership and away from current practices of "leaders as clerks."

Participatory decision making is a practice that many middle school teams use to make decisions. Elizabeth Pate offers four vignettes of middle school teams using this collaborative practice and in doing so provides new insights into both how teams of teachers make decisions and why decisions about time, curriculum, and facilities should be shared responsibilities at the team level.

"Surprisingly, relative little has been written about the role that interdisciplinary teams can play in developing and facilitating curriculum," begins John Arnold's chapter on "Teams and Curriculum." No longer, however, will this be the situation. Arnold, well known for his curriculum leadership in the middle school, offers insights into three major topics that facilitate curriculum: team structure and procedures, fundamental principles of responsive curriculum, and appropriate instructional approaches. "Teams," Arnold concludes, "must be in the forefront" of the middle school's curriculum efforts.

Whole language has arrived at the middle school. Deborah Butler and Tom Liner connect the assumptions behind this language movement with the assumptions behind interdisciplinary teaming. Using rich portraits of a variety of teams integrating whole language across the disciplines, Butler and Liner sketch out key guidelines for collaborative thinking about reading and writing across the team.

The last chapter is this section deals with another broader educational movement that affects middle schools and middle school teams. Inclusion, like whole language, is a practice that fundamentally fits with the middle school concept. Chriss Walther-Thomas demonstrates how, through thoughtful planning and collaboration, teams can provide for all their students. Supported by significant research Walther-Thomas weaves theoretical concerns with actual practice drawn from a middle school and its teams.

Part V, with its emphasis on current concerns, provides the reader with an opportunity to look at contemporary issues that will, over the next decade, loom large for middle school teams and those middle level educators who are working hard to meet students' needs in a dynamic environment.

Teaming Beyond the Core Four $\qquad$ **17**

Jacqueline Anglin

It never dawned on me in my first years of teaching that I was not part of a team. As the middle grades art teacher, I was busy enough teaching my forty-minute art classes, working with students during explorations, and meeting with the art club at lunch. I served as the consultant for anything "visual" around the school (props, costumes, and scenery for plays, decorations for dances, pep signs, banners, and bulletin boards). I was busy enough! I never felt left out, and everyone in the school valued art.

But after several years of teaching art, I wanted to share what I was feeling about integrating my art activities with other disciplines. I was seeing connections between art concepts and knowledge, students' interests, and activities in other subject areas. I became increasingly dissatisfied with the narrow view of the visual arts at my school. I felt alone and isolated. I began to share and show my frustration with other teachers and found that the music and physical education teachers related to this sense of separation. After all, the students were in art, music, and physical education while the "academic" teams were meeting. Team planning time for the "core four" took place while students were in the "specials." Being catalogued as a "special" by many experts in the 1970s did not feel *special* any more.

The organization of the school did not support teams or collaboration. The art, music, and physical education teachers did not function as an interdisciplinary team at my school. We did not plan among ourselves for an integrated view of the arts. The music teacher and I tried several times to work together, focusing on a common concept (such as pattern in art and rhythm in music) but because our classes were not block scheduled, we could not team teach the concepts. Rather, we merely referred to each other's examples during instruction. We had no team structure. Any planning that we did occurred before or after school on our own time, and quite often other school commitments took precedent. Rarely did we evaluate the results of these attempts at interdisciplinary instruction so we continued blindly celebrating our small joys and successes but sharing them with no one else. Certainly, these occasional attempts at teaming did not reflect the students' needs, nor did they change our curriculum, which remained discipline-based and totally unassociated. Nevertheless, the music teacher and I continued our feeble attempts to coordinate our subjects until he was transferred to the high school.

The next music teacher and I rarely worked together except on the spring program (making costumes to *fit* the music). The conversation with the music teacher usually went like this, "I don't have time to team teach. I've got the local, state, and national curriculum to follow and I feel really pressured to get the kids interested in band and choral programs so they will elect them in high school." I felt the pressure, too, to motivate the students to elect art in high school if they showed an interest in art as a vocation or avocation. Eighth grade art was the terminal point in my students' formal art instruction unless they chose to enroll in high school art courses.

My school district art curriculum guide was a K-12 model and was mainly written by secondary art teachers and a curriculum specialist. Nowhere in the curriculum guide did it mention teaming, integrating, or interdisciplinary themes. That art curriculum document received state recognition so I am sure that it is still solidly in place in the school district. I had no ownership in that curriculum document, so any visions of team teaching with other content area teachers came directly from my imagination.

The female physical education teacher and I had much better luck with our teaming attempts without benefit of organized meeting times. We worked as an *ad hoc* team, coming together for a specific need, and then going back to our traditional, self-contained teaching structure. We found common goals. She was interested in creative movement, so she saw many "art forms" correlating with her activities. We were driven by the desire to team teach, something neither of us had done before. We actually pulled off units like "masks and movement." We looked at the origin and types of masks, had the students construct and use them as a motivation to create dance forms, and performed with them several times during the year. Too bad we did not know enough to ask a social studies teacher to team with us and integrate history and culture into our thematic unit. I wonder what she would have said.

Even the exploratory program at the school limited my attempts to team teach. Our exploratory program consisted of minicourses, which offered threat-free settings for students to discover their strengths, weaknesses, likes, and dislikes. But the inherent instructional nature of the minicourse, one teacher/one subject, isolated me even further. Teaching photography, sculpture, and ceramics left me solitary in the art room (because of the equipment and materials needed for instruction). No one asked me, but I would have loved to teach computer graphics as an exploratory class with the eighth grade math teacher.

The principal was very supportive of the academic teams. A former high school history teacher, he team taught a unit on the civil war with one of the core-four teams. They attended team-building and planning workshops. The "special teachers" did not even have to go to building-level planning sessions because we were not on a team. I always wondered what went on at those meetings.

I stretched the curriculum boundaries to the breaking point in the next few years, gained valuable experience, and learned important lessons on how to integrate art with other subjects and work with other teachers. I learned there is no one way to team or no one name to describe the process. The terms *multidisciplinary* and *interdisciplinary* describe who is on the team, not what curriculum integration is truly taking place.

An element that further led to my isolation was my enrollment in graduate school. Here I met a mentor who lived and breathed interdisciplinary teaching. Gordon Vars, my major advisor, had literally written the books! I was intrigued by his discussions of interdisciplinary teams, thematic units, core curriculum, and webbing. I had not heard of these concepts in my undergraduate art education program. Now, my need to team teach art finally had philosophical grounding. I developed wonderful thematic units for the graduate class. I asked thousands of questions and spent hours reading about teams. When I went back to my building and tried to implement my new ideas, I found the same teaming boundaries and constraints in my way:

1. no common planning
2. little communication with the core academic teams
3. departmentalized instructional organization
4. curriculum guides developed at the state level
5. discipline-based curriculum in the "special subjects"
6. an exploratory curriculum structured around purely elective minicourses
7. other teachers who had little or no formal training in or practice with curriculum integration
8. other teachers who had little or no formal training in or practice with collaboration.

This is where my story stopped and my search for answers began. What I found was that teaming can take many forms for elective and exploratory teachers in middle schools. They can be organized into permanent exploratory teams where teachers of such subjects as art, industrial technology, foreign languages, and music meet regularly to discuss mutual concerns, students, instruction, and curriculum. In other schools the elective teachers retain their departmentalized organizational structure, even in some schools that have organized the core teachers into teams. However, these elective teachers come together in *ad hoc* or temporary arrangements to plan and carry out special events or specific interdisciplinary units of study.

In other schools there is a more permanent arrangement tying elective teachers to core teams. For example, in some schools all sixth graders may take art and industrial technology. Therefore, the teachers of these exploratory subjects are attached permanently to the sixth grade core teams. At other schools, all students are required to take physical education all three years that they are in middle school. In this case a physical education teacher may be assigned to the core teams on a permanent basis. A variation on this theme occurs when an exploratory wheel is employed to expose all students to a series of learning experiences. For example, if all seventh graders are exposed to nine-week experiences in family and consumer education, foreign language, art, and keyboarding, the teachers of each of these four subjects are assigned on a rotating basis to a core team for the nine-week period that the students are studying in that area.

Even in those schools where exploratory teachers are not assigned to meet regularly with core team members, temporary teaming arrangements do occur to plan grade-level themes or special student performances. In one school where exploratory teachers were not assigned to teams, at one grade level each year the students produced a Renaissance Festival that involved not only English, social studies, and math, but also music, art, industrial technology, physical education, and family and consumer education. The unit culminated in an evening festival that attracted the entire school community.

In almost all schools, opportunities exist for elective teachers to serve on standing or *ad hoc* schoolwide committees. Teamwork is required to represent the interests of the exploratory teachers in curriculum committee meetings or on site-based management teams. These groups continue on an ongoing basis. On other occasions schoolwide special events (Earth Day, Martin Luther King Day) or projects require input from exploratory teachers in order to plan successfully.

Exploring the teaming options

Recent literature on middle school teaming offers hope to the struggling exploratory or elective teachers who are trying to find a rightful place on teams. Erb (1994), Arhar (1992), Bergmann (1992), and Alexander & McEwin (1989) offer insights on scheduling teams in nontraditional configurations. According to Arhar, "Typical school organization often promotes isolation and the individuality of teachers" (p. 150). Conventional daily school schedules are restrictive as individual teachers can do little to change the length of periods or times they teach. However, teams of teachers – both permanent and temporary – are more powerful. Teachers can form *ad hoc* or temporary teams so that they can adjust their schedules and work within the existing daily time frame, meet before or after school, to work together on special projects or units. Other more ongoing or permanent team organizations can be created to permit elective or exploratory teachers to meet regularly with each other, with a core team, or to serve as a representative on a schoolwide committee. These team configurations are represented in Figure 1 and will be discussed in the following sections.

FIGURE 1

Three Types of Team Configurations for Teachers Beyond the Core Four

Type of Teaming	Ongoing/Permanent	Ad Hoc/Temporary
With an exploratory team	Regular meeting time with other exploratory/elective teachers	Temporary collaborations with one or more other exploratory teachers to plan interdisciplinary activities or team teach a unit.
With a core-four team	Regular meeting with a core team	Short-term collaboration with one or more core teams to coordinate a special event or interdisciplinary unit
With a schoolwide effort	Service as exploratory team representative on schoolwide leadership team or curriculum committee	Service on an *ad hoc* committee to plan a special theme event or theme week or study trends and issues

Configurations involving an exploratory team

Ongoing or permanent exploratory teams. An ongoing or permanent team could be formed to consist of the art, music, physical education, foreign language, industrial technology, family living, and computer technology teachers. This kind of teaming could give these teachers common planning time, an opportunity to block schedule their classes and integrate the curriculum. This team carries out the exploratory and elective part of the curriculum and meets regularly to discuss "learning experiences that it is thought all young adolescents should experience regardless of talent or aspirations" (Erb, 1994, p. 395). It is an opportunity for the "special" teachers to start talking.

> *Like any other type of team, exploratory/elective teams must have regular, common planning time. Team members cannot discuss mutual concerns, student needs, or curricular issues without a regular meeting time. However, since teachers of exploratory and elective classes may not share students on a daily basis as do core team teachers, they may not need to hold team meetings as often as do core teams. However, if one takes the long view extending over the course of the whole school year, if not the full two or three years that students spend in a middle school, the teachers on exploratory/elective teams also share the same students. Therefore, they are able to provide assistance to each other in understanding the learning needs of the students they share.*   — Erb, 1995, p. 180

There are many more similarities than differences among these elective and exploratory teachers and their curricula for the middle grades. Each curriculum includes production and performance of relevant skills. There should be many joint opportunities for plays, performances, shows, festivals, and exhibitions. These exploratory teams of teachers and their students could showcase their skills and talents in very visual, public ways. By working together, exploratory teachers can enliven the school day with demonstrations, displays, and simulations. It is not unusual for the specialist teachers to expend piles of energy when putting on a play, musical, art show, or physical education event. These productions are much easier to pull off when several teachers, lots of students, and abundant enthusiasm are available.

Bergmann (1992) warns however, "When teachers are labeled academic, special, or exploratory, they may not be seen as equal in the eyes of the students, faculty, or administrators" (pp. 188-189). However, all teachers in the middle grades play important curricular roles. Students' developmental needs are diverse; they require a wide range of learning experiences. Erb (1994) made the point: "Some critics have mistakenly asserted that this exploratory/elective part of the curriculum is less important than the core curriculum. From the perspective of meeting the developmental needs of a diverse set of learners, such view is very inaccurate" (p. 395).

Ad hoc and temporary exploratory teams. In an *ad hoc* or temporary situation, an exploratory team of art, music, and home economics teachers could meet and team teach a common concept, such as aesthetic appreciation (of musical and design forms), or a time period such as the 1960s, or a culture such as Indonesia, all pulling from their content to make planned thematic connections. When the common concept or historical period has been team taught by teachers and assimilated by students, the teachers return to their traditional teaching structures and curriculum.

Exploratory teachers may, at times, want to slide into a minicourse or an activities configuration where they teach concepts based on students' special interests. This frees teachers to explore topics which do not have rigid content boundaries. Computer graphics, stock market games, and genealogy are examples of topics which cross disciplines.

At other times teachers return to teaching in their own classroom. Teachers draw from their own rich background and teach specific content, often from a required or standardized curriculum such as the district or state curriculum document. There are times when this type of instruction is the best way to deliver content and build the students' knowledge base. Teachers should not apologize for teaching by themselves some of the time. Consequently, working from the base of separate elective subjects, teachers can emerge from time to time to team for special events or units.

Configurations involving a core-four team

Ongoing and permanent teams within the core four. When the planning and scheduling stereotypes begin to fall away, the concept of interdisciplinary teaming can be intriguing to middle school specialists. Interdisciplinary teaming has been identified as a key organizing element of the middle school (Plodzik and George, 1989) and is defined as "a group of teachers who together represent more than one subject area who share the same students, the same space and the same schedule" (p. 15). These authors concluded that the interdisciplinary team ... "is the most frequent mode for organizing teachers and students for instruction in middle school" (p. 17).

There is no theoretical reason why exploratory teachers cannot be mutual partners with core-four teachers in planning and carrying out interdisciplinary curricular approaches. In fact, it may be possible for an art or music or foreign language teacher to be a permanent part of a core team. The issue becomes one of scheduling, both teaching schedules and planning time.

Whenever an exploratory teacher presents a part of the curriculum that is required of students at some point in their middle school careers, that teacher could be scheduled to meet regularly with the core teachers. If, for example, all sixth graders were required to experience foreign language instruction, then foreign language teachers could be permanent members of the sixth grade core teams. This would be true for any exploratory subject that was required for a period of time in the middle school curriculum (e.g., industrial technology for all seventh graders, or consumer education for all eighth graders). Under these conditions, foreign language teachers would be permanent members of sixth grade teams, as would industrial technology teachers of seventh grade teams and consumer education teachers of eighth grade ones.

Another way that exploratory teachers can become members of core teams is on a rotating basis. This arrangement is akin to "serial monogamy." Exploratory teachers meet regularly as members of a core team; however, they change their partners as their students rotate through an exploratory wheel. When the students on one core team are taking keyboarding, the keyboarding teacher participates as part of that team. After six or nine weeks the keyboarding teacher may move to the next team that is taking keyboarding only to be replaced on the first team by an art teacher who will work to integrate art into the core curriculum for the next cycle.

Ad hoc and temporary teams with the core four. Interdisciplinary teaching requires a structure or model so that each teacher, even if not permanently a member of a team, is familiar with how planning for interdisciplinary teaching can take place. If everyone understands interdisciplinary curriculum planning, then teachers will be more likely to "team up" and will enter the planning cycle whenever their content or curriculum allows them to participate. Also, once teachers have been through the planning cycle, they will be more likely to join in when they feel comfortable. Jacobs (1989) points out, "As in any 'marriage,' attachment to an interdisciplinary team promises to bring into one's life, along with stimulation or even inspiration, a sizable set of not fully predictable vexations. The payoff and risk of interdisciplinary education can both be high" (pp. 32-33).

Jacobs (1989) recommends a step-by-step approach for developing integrated units of study based on target themes. These steps can be used by either *ad hoc* or permanent teams of teachers as a model for developing interdisciplinary themes. The steps in her planning model include:

> 1. *Selecting an organizing center which can be a theme, subject area, event, issue, or problem. Concepts such as observations, patterns, light, revolution, humor, flight, pioneers, the future, and world hunger have proven highly effective as organizing centers.* (p. 54)

> 2. *Brainstorming associations encourage deliberate exploration of a theme from all discipline fields (which include but are not restricted to mathematics, the arts, social sciences, language arts, humanities/philosophy, and science).* (p. 56)

> 3. *Establishing guiding questions to serve as a scope and sequence and serve as a framework for investigating the organizing center. Examples of guiding questions in a unit on flight may be: What flies? How and why do things in nature fly? What has been the impact of flight on human beings? What is the future of flight?* (p. 59-60)

> 4. *Writing activities for implementation come from the guiding questions and tell us what students will be 'doing' to examine the interdisciplinary organizing center.* (p. 60)

Two other especially good sources for interdisciplinary planning are Beane (1993) and Stevenson and Carr (1993).

Specialist teachers may see natural connections between their curricular areas and the organizing center or they may wish to sit out that unit of study and become involved in subsequent units. No teacher should ever feel forced to get involved in a unit. They must philosophically agree with the direction the unit is taking and be willing to assume ownership from initial planning through final assessments. However, when exploratory and elective teachers see connections between what they teach and other subject areas, they may go out of their way to plan special units, events, or projects that combine elements for core subjects with their own.

Another temporary arrangement for teaming would be to open the lines of communication with the core team by inviting one exploratory teacher to meet with each core team as they develop long-range plans. This teacher would serve as a "broker of learning experiences" (Vars, 1993, p. 23), watching for points in the curriculum where the expertise of the arts or physical education or foreign language teacher might be creatively applied. This "curriculum broker," also described by Gardner (1991), works ahead, during the planning stage, and makes sure all teachers are aware of how their unique contributions and content specialties could benefit other teams and themes. Other school personnel and members of the community can be called upon to collaborate with students and teachers as they explore topics of common interest.

If the elective teachers know the core teams are planning to cover time periods or topics, they may want to correlate or fuse their curricular areas (see Vars, 1993). Most specialists have the freedom to change the order or pattern of their teaching within a given semester or school year in an attempt to correlate their curriculum but may not have the time to do the additional research or have the funds to augment their existing materials. On the other hand, the specialist can often bring a rich background of musicianship, artisanship, or craftsmanship to the study of the liberal arts or humanities.

Within a schoolwide effort

Ongoing and permanent teaming within a schoolwide effort. The notion of exploratory teachers, as well as guidance teachers and other school personnel serving on schoolwide teams is a common practice in middle schools. Placek (1992) in her article "Rethinking Middle School Physical Education Curriculum: An Integrated, Thematic Approach," urged physical educators to volunteer to serve on curriculum committees as one way to communicate with all teachers in the school. The schoolwide team can be called a leadership team, a collegial team, or a site-based management team. No matter what the name, the schoolwide team (or committee) is ongoing and permanent having these same components as an interdisciplinary team, permanent members and meeting time. The schoolwide team members should consist of teachers who represent the core-four teams, the exploratory and elective areas of the curriculum, the activities program, and the advisory program. Administrators and students should have representation as well. Schoolwide teams can study issues such as scheduling, curriculum, and instructional resources, and assess and recommend changes in team configurations and build team policy. For example, a site-based leadership team at Armuchee Middle School in Rome, Georgia, studied and recommended a math/science/computer cross-grade team be formed because the new science curriculum could not be taught developmentally and sequentially without the combined efforts of the math, science, and computer faculty. The site-based management team continues to meet regularly and give their input on all team-related matters.

Ad hoc and temporary teams within a schoolwide effort. There are times when an entire school will participate in an activity or theme event such as Earth Day or Black History month. Teachers and students from all grade levels will participate, but a team of teachers representing all other team configurations is designated to work on an *ad hoc* or temporary basis to plan the event. The team will function together long enough to plan, implement, and evaluate the event and may not work together again until another event is planned. At that point, a different team may be organized to plan the event.

Schoolwide events such as this occur in middle schools all over the United States. A good source of schoolwide programming ideas come from books of the National Middle School Association, such as *Exploration: The Total Curriculum*, Compton and Hawn (1993), and videos such as *A Learner-Centered School* (Phi Delta Kappa, 1994).

Another type of team, which is considered *ad hoc* or temporary, occurs when educational trends, innovations, or problems affect a middle school, and they choose to have a team of teachers focus on what this means for their school. For example, a team of teachers may study cooperative learning (Slavin, 1983) or multiple intelligence theory (Gardner, 1991) to determine if these strategies should be implemented. On the other hand, an *ad hoc* task force may form in order to look at common concerns such as the risks of students during non-school hours. Schoolwide teams that look at what adolescents do with their time after school could be composed of teachers, counselors, students, community members, and social service agencies. *Ad hoc* teams or task forces may become permanent teams if the situation or innovation is deemed important enough to warrant adoption or ongoing study.

Curriculum and team configurations

The most encouraging insights on middle school curriculum integration come from authors such as Beane (1993) and Stevenson and Carr (1993). These authors embrace middle school curriculum reform that reflects thematic approaches to teaching and learning based on content, skills, and concepts grounded in students' needs. Beane (1993) expressed his challenge this way:

> *Middle school advocates have claimed from the begin-*
> *ning that their primary concern is with the characteristics of*
> *early adolescence. If those characteristics are extended into*
> *a discussion of the curriculum, it becomes apparent that the*
> *persistent organization around a collection of academic and*
> *'special' courses, with emphasis on the former, is not a de-*
> *velopmentally appropriate nor genuinely responsive ap-*
> *proach to the curriculum. Surely there must be a different*
> *and better answer to the curriculum question, an answer*
> *that more closely matches the curriculum with ongoing rheto-*
> *ric about middle schools.* (p. 2)

In his book *The Middle School Curriculum: From Rhetoric to Reality*, Beane (1993) envisioned a curriculum designed around three dimensions, "themes that emerge from the intersection of personal and social concerns, the skills necessary to fully explore those themes, and the enduring concepts of human dignity and cultural diversity" (p. 68). These are components all educators can identify in their discipline-based curriculum and should be able to envision how they transfer to curricular themes Beane advocates. These integrated themes are the centerpiece of the "new curriculum." There is encouraging news here for specialists and exploratory teachers. This thematic configuration could bring:

> *so-called 'special' or 'exploratory' teachers out of the far*
> *reaches of the curriculum and into the mainstream of gen-*
> *eral education. Indeed, it is very likely that many of these*
> *teachers will have much to offer in light of the kind of cur-*
> *riculum they have been engaged in for years.* (p. 91)

Stevenson and Carr (1993) describe reformed curriculum as one which invites teachers to go "dancing through walls; breaking through and remov- ing the walls of "…mental barriers that derive from a textbook-workbook- recitation-test orientation to instruction; the submission to vague pressures to 'cover' one curriculum or another, the isolation of colleagues in different disciplines; incongruities between child development theory and prevalent instructional practices" (p. 2). Their accounts are encouraging and invite every teacher in the school to "go beyond the everyday routines and obstacles to meet the needs of all their students" (p. 200). "Weather Watch," "Go With the Flow," and "Climb Every Mountain" are integrated units with the study of nature as a basis. Studies, such as "On the Road Again," "Richmond Four Corners," and "A View from The Park," invite community involvement. These authors describe an intriguing study which began with a walk along the road and ended in an integrated study called "Garbology." As the art teacher, I would have joined with the students to make a sculpture out of all the car bumpers and hub caps they found.

Lessons learned from practice

In retrospect, there are several lessons I learned from practice. One, if teachers have not been trained in or experienced team-building activities, they will find it difficult to open lines of communication, facilitate continual communication, and be receptive to the different configurations teams can take. Inservice and preservice course work for middle school teachers should include opportunities to explore team member relationships. Prospective middle grades teachers who major in art, music, foreign language, or physical education and find themselves teaching young adolescents must know about teaming. Ideally, all teachers should take a methods course in the school or college of education that models team teaching and places them on teams with other students to develop units and actually team teach during field experiences or practica. Team teaching scenarios must be part of *all* student teaching experiences for every student, specialist, and education major alike who will be certified to teach young adolescents.

Secondly, a middle school does not need to commit to only one team configuration. A healthy team atmosphere would allow and encourage teachers to move back and forth using a combination of permanent and temporary structures to serve students. A teacher could teach in a self-contained classroom in the morning, be a member of an interdisciplinary team in the afternoon, and still participate in exploratory experiences for students. In many cases, a teacher may be a member of more than one team during a given school year when their expertise can contribute to a variety of themes, units, or activities. Perhaps the idea of a "floating" exploratory teacher could be investigated. For example, a foreign language teacher could be available during the exploratory schedule to teach minicourses, electives, or team teach exploratories with the art teacher (Renaissance Art) or the music teacher (Renaissance Music) or the physical educators (folk and traditional dances from other cultures).

Finally, if students are truly the center of the curriculum, teachers will do what they can to meet their needs. Most of the models and curriculum reform movements today put students at the center of planning, teaching, and assessment. If we start and remain focused on students' needs, then territorialism and teacher isolation will naturally disappear. Teachers will become "free agents," able to move from one teaming configuration to another without the constraints of traditional models – either departmentalized ones or stereotyped teaming ones.

Final reflections

I returned to my former middle school often – this time as a college student teaching supervisor. I helped three art students through a semester of middle level student teaching. The cooperating art teacher, who had taken my place, was six years into her career. I asked her if she ever felt frustrated or isolated from the academic teaching teams. She said, "Not at first, but I see lots of places where art would fit in." I could see a cycle was beginning to repeat itself.

Right at that moment, I stopped and asked her if she and her student teacher would like to go and talk to the social studies teacher about team teaching a thematic unit on artists from Ohio. (I knew the core four teamed up for an Ohio history unit every year.) She and the student teacher were very excited about planning a unit, especially since I agreed to help. As we walked down that very familiar hall together, I said to myself, "Maybe this time I can make a difference in lives of both of these young teachers by introducing them to team planning and teaching. These are the first steps; this is how teams begin."

References

Alexander, W., & McEwin, K. (1989). *Schools in the middle: Status and progress*. Columbus, OH: National Middle School Association.

Arhar, J. (1992). Interdisciplinary teaming and social bonding of middle level students. In J. Irvin (Ed.), *Transforming middle level education: Perspectives and possibilities* (p. 139-161). Needham Heights, MA: Allyn and Bacon.

Beane, J. (1993). *The middle school curriculum: From rhetoric to reality* (2nd ed.). Columbus, OH: National Middle School Association.

Bergmann, S. (1992). Exploratory programs in the middle level school: A responsive idea. In J. Irvin (Ed.), *Transforming middle level educational: Perspectives and possibilities* (p. 179-192). Needham Heights, MA: Allyn and Bacon.

Compton, M., & Hawn, H. (1993). *Exploration: The total curriculum*. Columbus, OH: National Middle School Association.

Erb, T.O. (1995). Teamwork in middle school education. In H. Garner (Ed.), *Teamwork models and experience in education* (pp. 175-198). Boston: Allyn and Bacon.

Erb, T.O. (1994). The middle school: Mimicking the success routes of the information age. *Journal for the Education of the Gifted, 17* (4), 385-406.

Gardner, H. (1991). *The unschooled mind: How children think and how schools should teach*. New York: Basic Books.

Phi Delta Kappa (producer). (1994). *A learner-centered school* [video]. (Available from Phi Delta Kappa, P.O. Box 789, Bloomington, IN).

Jacobs, H.H. (1989). Design options for an integrated curriculum. In H. H. Jacobs (Ed.), *Interdisciplinary curriculum: Design and implementation* (p. 13-24). Alexandria, VA: Association for Supervision and Curriculum Development.

Placek, J. (1992). Rethinking middle school physical education curriculum: An integrated, thematic approach. *QUEST, 44*, 330-341.

Plodzik, K.T., & George, P. (1989). Interdisciplinary team organization. *Middle School Journal 20* (5), 15-17.

Slavin, R. (1983). *Cooperative learning*. New York: Longman.

Steffans, P. (1991). Exploration-the final frontier. *Middle School Journal, 22* (3). 30-33.

Stevenson, C. & Carr, J. (1993). *Integrated studies in the middle grades: Dancing through walls*. New York, NY: Teachers College Press.

Vars, G. (1993). *Interdisciplinary teaching: How and why*. Columbus, OH: National Middle School Association.

Misplaced Camels, Crowded Captains, and Achieving Greatness: Leadership of Interdisciplinary Teams 18

Daniel L. Kain

It's 10:00 a.m. on a Friday morning in September. The halls of Waterfront Middle School are dark and quiet, having stayed empty this day due to high winds and crashing trees that cut the power to the school and neighborhood, closing down the day's activities. The eighth grade interdisciplinary team is meeting, taking advantage of the break from instruction to select the team leader for the school year.

Trent: *So who's going to go for it?*

Catherine: *There's some documentation required, isn't there? We have to produce an agenda.*

Trent: *It's asinine! There's three of us. We'll work it up afterwards.*

Catherine: *I'm really reluctant to take on another position.*

Trent: *We know from last year that time is essential.*

Jeremy: *Isn't it Catherine's turn? I mean, you did it last year, Trent, and I'm new.*

Trent: *Yeah. You could do it next year. It'd be your turn.*

Catherine: *How seriously do we take this job description?*

Trent: *We don't take it seriously at all.*

Catherine: *I'm feeling some tension, because I don't need more duties, but I feel I ought to apply for the job.*

Trent: *Why not? We'll work together and help you. I think the job will be as you want it to be.*

Jeremy: *Good. I can support you, Catherine.*

Trent: *If there's a need to write anything, we'll share the work.*

The meeting described above occurred in British Columbia in the fall of 1991. Typical or not, it exemplifies some of the concerns that surround the issue of leadership in middle school interdisciplinary

403

teams. Was the team's method of selecting a leader appropriate? Did this team and this school take team leadership seriously? Was there, in fact, any need whatsoever for a leader for this group?

These kinds of questions represent important issues for team members and schools to address as they implement or enhance teaming at the middle school level. To explore such issues, this chapter proceeds by examining the environmental conditions necessary for teams to benefit from any form of team leadership, a definition of leadership drawn from the typical duties of team leaders and a conception of effective teaming and team leadership, the various models for establishing team leaders, and recommendations to make team leadership more meaningful in middle schools. My comments arise from personal experience in teaming situations, fieldwork research with middle school teams, and research literature, particularly that from organizational theory.

Team leaders can help create a new vision of collaboration – but only as schools foster conditions that make such leadership more than tokenism.

Preconditions for team leadership: Misplaced camels?

> *What a splendid transport train they [dromedaries] would make. The aborigine would be scared to death and each warrior would feel for a hump on his back.*
> — Montana Post, June 3, 1865 (in Fowler, 1980, p. 77)

To look at much of the American West, one would think that the camel would be the perfect beast of burden, however inflated the hopes of Western settlers might have been. And, indeed, camels were introduced throughout the West, from British Columbia to Texas, from Montana to Mexico (Fowler, 1980). The use of camels, even by the military, however, never caught on: apparently the animals so frightened other beasts and people that some legislatures outlawed the presence of camels on public roads (Faulk, 1976). Moreover, the stony ground hurt the camels' feet. Camels became the stuff of legends and frightening stories.

There is a lesson for team leadership in this history: for all its perfect suitability to labor in dry places, a camel does no good if the society will not accept it. Likewise, team leaders may look perfectly suitable for middle schools, but they will be like misplaced camels if certain environmental preconditions are not met.

One key precondition for team leadership to become meaningful concerns the assumptions that constitute the social environment of schools that implement teaming. Douglas McGregor is credited with making the important distinction between *Theory X* and *Theory Y* paradigms (Fisher, 1993). A person who operates from the *Theory X* paradigm assumes that people need to be controlled and motivated because they are basically lazy, unintelligent, and not interested in doing good work. The key concept is *control*: people must be controlled, monitored, checked up on. *Theory Y* assumptions, on the other hand, credit people with being internally motivated to do good work. This perspective sees people as smart, self-controlled, and actually liking to work.

Finding a place for team leaders in a school demands the *Theory Y* paradigm. Team leaders must be the trusted co-leaders of the school, not spies or monitoring agents of the administration. To operate with a *Theory X* perspective would mean appointing watchdogs for teachers who can not be trusted. Clearly, if this is the perspective of a school system (and the principal or other school leaders), there is no need to discuss meaningful team leadership any further. At the same time, it is important to note that all the forces that might influence principals to operate from a Theory X paradigm – family patterns, employment practices, church and military experiences (Fisher, 1993) – are common to potential team leaders as well. Team leaders must reflect carefully on how they operate, the paradigm they bring to their work. As Senge (1990) points out, the mental models leaders bring to their jobs have tremendous impact on the work worlds created.

Just as important, however, is another precondition for meaningful teaming and team leadership. In the rush to "empower" teachers as site-based decision makers, we sometimes forget the double-edged nature of such "empowerment." True, to let teachers make important decisions can speak of professional trust and confidence. But as Weiss (1993) explains, there are some potential negative consequences as well: such a practice can be merely symbolic rather than actual, a way of spreading the blame for school failures, a way to bog teachers down in committees or undermine teachers' unions.

Meaningful teaming, and hence meaningful team leadership, cannot occur under such circumstances. The team cannot be a device to limit or blame teachers; it must be seen as a powerful response to the needs of our students. For meaningful team leadership to occur, the school must promote a vision of schooling which allocates authority, not blame, and opportunities, not limitations. Team leadership requires that the school's leader be willing to hand over significant authority to team leaders. Given these necessary preconditions – an environment of trust and real authority – a school is ready to foster effective team leadership.

Defining Leadership: Shaking off the Clerkship

Typical leadership responsibilities

The list of duties one typically finds for middle school team leaders consists of a fairly predictable set of activities: setting times and fixing agendas for team meetings (Porod, 1993; Whitford & Kyle, 1984), handling necessary paperwork (Merenbloom, 1991), serving as liaison with administration and other groups (Merenbloom, 1991; Porod, 1993), keeping logs and minding the calendar of events (Erb & Doda, 1989). Such "leadership" activities raise a question: does this sort of leadership represent business as usual, with minor delegation of authority, or can the activities of team leaders move our schools into a new and more collaborative paradigm?

Most of the duties listed above appear somewhat arbitrary and perhaps trivial. The suggestion implied by the team meeting described in the introduction is worth considering: is the leader nothing more than a glorified clerk, a paper-pusher fulfilling bureaucratic vagaries?

The distinction emerging here is important. The literature on teaming in the business world portrays *leadership* as a process of sparking vision and empowering team members so that a team can become effective. In contrast, middle school team leadership focuses on *duties*, carrying out someone else's priorities and interests, conducting school business, rather than building vision. The remainder of this chapter will clarify the distinction between clerking – performing necessary tasks because some one must – and leading.

Effective teaming

One possible explanation for the malaise in middle school team *leadership* lies in how teams view effective *teaming*. What constitutes a successful teaming experience? Effective team leadership demands that leaders and teams operate from a conception of effective teaming. Without this, leadership of teams consists of little more than fractured bureaucratic chores.

One lens through which we might view the potential changes brought about by teaming and what constitutes effective teaming is the business world. Businesses have been facing changes in their structures, a paradigm shift that Fisher (1993) sees not only as inevitable, but as dramatic as the industrial revolution. By some estimates, 50 percent of all employees will operate as members of teams by the year 2000 (Rayner, 1993) and productivity increases of between 30 and 50 percent in the shift to self-directed teams have been reported (Wellins, Byham, & Wilson, 1991). Indeed, the 1990s may be the "age of teaming" (Rayner, 1993).

Numerous theorists have outlined general models of what effective teaming looks like (Goodman, Ravlin, & Schminke, 1987). Hackman and Oldham (1980), for example, develop three criteria for team effectiveness: effective teams have satisfactory output (in terms of service or products), enhance the ability of team members to work together, and promote the growth and development of individuals. Katzenbach and Smith (1993) build their model of effectiveness around a carefully worded definition of a team: "A team is a small number of people with *complementary skills* who are committed to a *common purpose*, *performance goals*, and *approach* for which they hold themselves *mutually accountable*" (p. 45, emphasis added). Other theorists have taken a stages-of-development approach to understanding team effectiveness (George, 1982; Tuckman, 1965; Wellins et al., 1991; Worchel, Coutant-Sassic, & Grossman, 1992) (Figure 1).

Figure 1

Developmental Views of Effective Teaming

Tuckman (1965) stages:	Worchel et al. (1992) stages:
Forming	*Discontent*
Storming	*Precipitating event*
Norming	*Group identification*
Performing	*Group productivity*
Adjourning	*Individuation*
	Decay
Wellins et al. (1991) stages:	George* (1982) stages:
Getting started	*Organization*
Going in circles	*Community*
Getting on course	*Team teaching*
Full speed ahead	*Governmental*
	*based on middle school teams

Regardless of the approach taken, it seems to me there are a number of features that ought to be a part of each middle school team's understanding of effective teaming:

- The team identity arises from some *purpose* beyond merely being a team. Senge (1990) calls this the "purpose story." That is, there is a task or goal underlying the team's existence. Short's (1993) study of empowered middle school teams found that the interdisciplinary teams that were most successful in becoming self-managing "appeared to be the teams most able to establish clear goals and an understanding of what they were about and how to move forward" (pp. 16-17). Dyer (1995) lists clear goals and values as the number one criterion of effective teams. Harvey and Drolet (1994, p. 12) are emphatic: "Effective teams are purpose-driven. They have someplace to go and a hunger to get there." The team must keep its purpose alive through deliberate discussion of its work, and varying purposes demand the team's attention at different points in its development (Kain, 1992). *Effectiveness* is determined, in part, by the team's ability to meet its purpose and performance goals.

- The team develops productive *norms* for how it will operate. Such norms, explicit or implicit, provide direction in how decisions will be made and what behaviors are acceptable to the team. These norms influence the interpersonal relationships among team members. Effectiveness for the team, particularly in its ability to continue to work as a team, depends on establishing and adhering to these norms.

- The team will recognize or create its *boundaries* and engage in numerous *boundary-spanning activities*. Middle school teams must realize that they function in organizations comprising multiple teams and individuals (Kruse & Louis, 1995). A large portion of a team's work centers around its relating to other teams and individuals in such areas as coordinating resources and activities, developing a school culture, and representing the school to a public. Effectiveness at the team level demands a perspective that looks beyond the team level: how does this team manage and span its boundaries? (Figure 2)

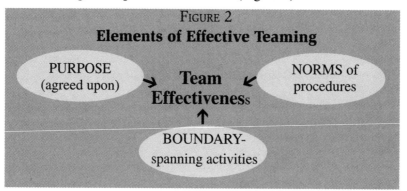

FIGURE 2
Elements of Effective Teaming

PURPOSE (agreed upon) → **Team Effectiveness** ← NORMS of procedures

↑

BOUNDARY-spanning activities

Whether a team accepts, modifies, or rejects what I have presented as the elements of effective teaming at the middle school, the important point is that *leadership* of teams cannot be effective unless there is some model or understanding of effective *teaming* that guides the leader's decisions and actions (Hackman & Walton, 1986). It is an unenviable task to lead when no one knows where you are going or why.

Leadership elements

Given a conception of effectiveness for teaming, the question of how best to lead a team to success arises. The issue of leadership has been explored thousands of times, making it the "most studied and least understood topic of any in the social sciences" (Bennis & Nanus, 1985, p. 20). I propose that for middle school teams, the most productive focus for this question is not on the psychological traits of great leaders but on the functions or process of leadership. In fact, some teams might find it more useful to conceptualize the team leader as a set of roles or a process rather than as a single person. Whether the roles are carried out by an appointed leader, an elected leader, a rotating position-holder, or the team itself (the subject of the next section), the most meaningful starting point is to explore what leadership entails in making middle school teams effective.

A useful point of comparison here is the leadership roles that have emerged in the many studies of contemporary team-based organizations. A comparison of some of these findings is presented in Table 1.

As I have indicated by my placement of the comparable qualities in rows, some parallels can be drawn among these competencies, activities, or dimensions. Some of these roles or competencies are clearly applicable to leadership of middle school teams, while others require more translation. For example, row two of Table 1, dealing with being an example, doing real work and collaborating, seems to have direct application to middle school teams. If the team leader somehow sets him- or herself apart from the team by doing less work or by operating from double standards as team leader (Messé, Kerr, & Sattler, 1992), we could expect the credibility and influence of the team leader to be diminished. Row four (dealing with business analysis), on the other hand, does not immediately seem to apply to the interdisciplinary middle school team. However, the work teachers do both with information analysis and student achievement may, on second glance, provide the basis for translation of this leadership competency.

TABLE 1

Comparison of Leadership Roles/Attributes

Seven competencies for leaders FISHER (1993) RAYNER (1993)	Six things leaders do KATZENBACH & SMITH (1993)	Eighteen leadership dimensions WELLINS ET AL. (1991)
Leader	-Keep the purpose, goals, and approach relevant and meaningful	-Ability to learn -Individual leadership -Judgment -Meeting leadership
Living Example	-Do real work	-Initiative -Collaboration
Coach	-Build commitment and confidence	-Delegation of authority -Developing organizational talent
Business Analyzer		-Analysis -Business planning -Information monitoring
Barrier Buster	-Manage relationships with outsiders, including removing obstacles	-Communication -Organizational fit
	-Strengthen the mix and level of skills	-Maximizing performance -Work standards
Facilitator	-Create opportunities for others	-Motivation to empower others -Operational planning -Rapport building
Customer Advocate		

So what can we make of this comparison to business team leadership? To start with, some caveats are in order. First, the focus of business teams is often more concrete and measurable than that of interdisciplinary teams. It is much easier to gauge success in such terms as "yielding a savings of $200,000 per year" (Wellins et al., 1991, p. 14) or "output 25 percent higher with lower costs" (Fisher, 1993, p. 24) than in the terms we use to gauge success at schools (even if we reduce success to such issues as disciplinary referrals or standardized test scores). Second, the organizational culture of most businesses is more receptive to teaming than traditional school cultures. The isolated working conditions of secondary teachers are well documented (Ashton & Webb, 1986; Goodlad, 1984; Grace, 1978; Little, 1990), and researchers frequently point out the difficulty of getting teachers to break out of isolated work patterns (Donaldson, 1993). Third, businesses are accepting of hierarchies to a greater extent than schools, where the equal status of all teachers is assumed. Thus, a team leader in a business fits into a familiar pattern of authority and behavior. Team leaders at middle schools, while not having to deal with what can be perceived in the business world as a step down the hierarchy (Fisher, 1993), may find it difficult to assert leadership due to this assumption of equality among workers (Little & Shulman, 1984; Maeroff, 1993).

Despite these differences, there are lessons for middle school team leaders in the business experience. Let me bring together the conception of effective teaming I outlined above and the elements of effective leadership as gleaned from organizational theory. A blending of these two strands is diagrammed in Figure 3.

Purpose

The central leadership roles focusing on purpose include helping the team to establish or articulate its purpose and keeping the focus of the team (in meetings and team activities) on this purpose. The various possible purposes of teaming (e.g., creating interdisciplinary experiences, improving student discipline, discussing student needs), though at times overlapping, do much to establish the direction of the team. Kain (1992) found that a team's focus on one purpose pushed other (equally valid) purposes into the background. For example, when teamed teachers worked on student discipline as their common purpose, they did not expend energy to create interdisciplinary experiences for their students. This suggests that a leader can have a dramatic influence on his or her team first by *encouraging* the team to come to an explicit agreement on its purpose and second by *reminding* and *redirecting* the group toward what it has identified as its primary purpose.

Note the striking contrast between the duties of a clerkship (bureaucratic, obligatory, "it has to be done") and the leadership associated with the team's purpose (embraced, attractive, goal-directed). Bennis and Nanus (1985) studied ninety leaders and underlined the importance of this purposing, visionary role: "Leaders acquire and wear their visions like clothes" (p. 46). A middle school team leader can help the team formulate and stick to a purpose that is worthwhile, that makes a difference in the lives of their students.

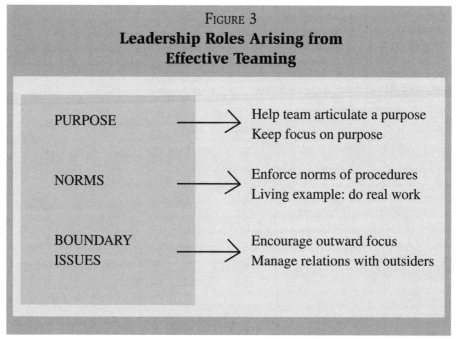

FIGURE 3
Leadership Roles Arising from Effective Teaming

PURPOSE ⟶ Help team articulate a purpose
Keep focus on purpose

NORMS ⟶ Enforce norms of procedures
Living example: do real work

BOUNDARY ISSUES ⟶ Encourage outward focus
Manage relations with outsiders

Norms

Norms are rules of behavior, explicit and implicit (Johnson & Johnson, 1994). It would, of course, not only be impossible but undesirable for the leader alone to establish the norms for how the team operates. However, the team leader can serve several important functions in relation to the norms required for effective teaming.

First, the team leader is appropriately charged with leading meetings and helping team members conform to norms. Ironically, many teams (in schools and elsewhere) simply do not discuss the norms by which they operate. Ancona (1990) reports that groups tend to norm very quickly, often in minutes. No matter how ineffective these initial norms might be, most groups do not reexamine their norms (Cummings, 1981). Pearce and Ravlin (1987) argue that groups need help in breaking a cultural norm against reconsidering their group processes. A team leader can help teams to examine norms without using intervention strategies involving outsiders (as recommended in Hackman & Morris, 1975). For example, it is not uncommon for team members to engage in other work – grading papers, writing lesson plans – during team meetings (Bell, 1990; Stein, 1978). This is a norm which, if allowed to function unexamined, can be detrimental to the team's activities. A team leader calls for discussion and reexamination of such norms in light of the team's purpose.

Second, the team leadership role in relation to norms calls on leaders to be living examples who do real work. There is evidence that merely being appointed to a leadership role is correlated with a reduction in the amount of work actually performed by the person so appointed (Messé et al., 1992), as though the title and status of leader somehow excuses one from other chores. A team leader can do much to help promote healthy norms by continuing to perform the work that contributes to the agreed-upon purpose of the group. If, for example, a team has identified creating interdisciplinary experiences as its primary purpose, the team leader should actively contribute to the creation of such experiences.

Of course, the leader needs to beware the opposite extreme: doing too much of the work. I remember once spending the Friday after Thanksgiving with two other team leaders as we put together the detailed activities for an interdisciplinary unit on Greece for some 300 seventh graders and 12 teachers. My own resentment about the amount of time this planning was taking came to a head that day, but it could have been handled better if I had acknowledged my role as a leader: to contribute real work, but not to do it all myself. It does not empower team members for leaders to do all the work.

One important part of the leader's role in being a living example is to continue to be a learner and inquirer. Senge (1990) speaks of leaders as teachers, but the key element of this is *fostering learning* for everyone. Hirschhorn (1991) sees the new role of managers as primarily being *learners* who see the effects of their actions on teams and individuals. In a school setting, particularly as we reconceptualize the middle school experience as something different from the kind of schooling we endured, it is crucial that team leaders model this ability to learn, to adapt, to adjust, to maintain an openness to the "universe of alternatives" (Sarason, 1971). Learning is the central attribute of successful organizations in an information age (Bennis &

Nanus, 1985), and leaders will be successful to the degree they encourage learning.

Consideration of the purpose and norms of the group attends to the traditional focus on task and maintenance issues in effective work groups (Hoffman, 1982). This model of group effectiveness argues that groups attend to one or the other of those dimensions. "Task" considerations focus on the purpose of the group (such as making connections for students), while "maintenance" issues focus on smooth interactions within the group. However, a third important aspect of team leadership centers around the group's boundaries.

Boundary issues

Team leaders provide the mechanism whereby teams can effectively interact with the organization as a whole. Wheatley (1992) describes the importance of a team's relating to others:

> It is well known that the era of the rugged individual has been replaced by the era of the team player. But this is only the beginning. The quantum world has demolished the concept of the unconnected individual. More and more relationships are in store for us, out there in the vast web of universal connections. (p. 38)

In her study of teams in a department of education, Ancona (1990) found that teams that isolated themselves, ostensibly to focus on team development before dealing with outsiders, had the greatest chance of failure. On the other hand, teams that initially focused on establishing and maintaining relations with other teams and individuals had the highest rates of success.

Too often, middle school teams neglect the important task of spanning boundaries. Kain (1992) describes a middle school team that became "ambassadors for teaming" at their school in order to further their own cause. Ancona and Caldwell (1988) describe a set of boundary-spanning activities that include the metaphorical roles of *scout, ambassador, sentry,* and *guard.* Such roles provide a framework for team leaders to think about in managing relations with outsiders. The nature of organizations requires that teams interact with others. The leader can build success for her or his team by attending to such things as opening lines of communication, scanning for important information for the team, and managing requests on the team's time and energy (Ancona & Caldwell, 1988) – in other words, helping to maintain an outward focus.

It is also important that teaming practices not replace individual isolation with team isolation. Mills, Powell, and Pollak (1992) report a concern that teacher teams can become isolated "islands in the stream." Kruse and Louis (1995) question whether the success of a team contributes to the whole *school's* success. They quote one middle school teacher's concern: "Years ago we had teacher isolation, and then once we reorganized, we had team isolation" (p. 4). A leader can head off such team isolation by careful attention to the team's relations to outsiders.

The decisions that generally provide the focus of middle school leadership questions – how many leaders? how should they be selected? – strike me as entirely secondary to the important base outlined above. Team leadership makes sense in a context where effective teaming governs the roles that guide a team's development. A team leader must be prepared to focus the team on its purpose, help it to develop and maintain productive norms, and deal effectively with outsiders.

Captain or Captains? How Many Leaders?

> *Our traditional views of leaders – as special people who set the directions, make the key decisions, and energize the troops – are deeply rooted in an individualistic and nonsystemic worldview. Especially in the West, leaders are heroes – great men (and occasionally women) who 'rise to the fore' in times of crises. Our prevailing leadership myths are still captured by the image of the captain of the cavalry leading the charge to rescue the settlers from the attacking Indians.* — Senge, 1990, p. 340

Conventional wisdom in the form of aphorisms argues against anything but a clear, single leader: "Too many cooks spoil the broth." "Many commanders sink the ship." "Eagles fly alone, but sheep flock together." The question for middle school teams is this: Can the functions outlined above best be performed by a single leader, or is it possible to conceive of these functions as being shared among team members? And if there is to be a single leader, how can this leader best be selected?

Before looking at some exemplars from the middle school literature, let me again turn to what organizational theorists have to say about team leadership and the question of who leads. The organizational literature reminds us that however leadership is handled within teams, this does not eliminate the need for overall leadership in the organization itself. Drawing the parallel to middle schools, whatever duties the team leader may assume, the principal still serves an important leadership function (Short, 1993). Wellins and associates (1991) argue that "shared leadership teams" is a more appropriate name than "self-directed teams" in business, since overall direction is still largely determined by leaders at a level beyond the teams of the organization.

The dominant tendency in organizational teams is for a particular person to assume the leadership responsibilities within a team. This position is often rotated among team members (Fisher, 1993; Wellins et al., 1991). For example, Fisher reports that the Boeing team designing the 777 aircraft rotated the team leadership according to the phase of the project and whose expertise was most in need at each point in the design development. While some team leaders are permanent, more than half of the 500 organizations researched by Wellins and associates (1991) used rotating team leadership. Shuster (1990), on the other hand, makes a case for avoiding any single leader: "Everyone leads in a team! Which means, of course, that no *one* leads!" (p. 25, original emphasis). Shuster argues that *leadership* must be shared, not ignored, but no one person need assume all leadership functions. Wellins, Byham, and Dixon (1994) report that shared leadership is increasingly common in team-based organizations.

The literature from middle school researchers is relatively scant on the question of a single leader versus several leaders. Lipsitz (1984), for example, articulates a traditional view of leadership, where power and vision lie in the grasp of principals as ideologues. Some researchers discuss rotating leadership among team members (Erb & Doda, 1989; Merenbloom, 1991; Parker & Lumpkins, 1987), sharing the leadership "burdens" (Merenbloom, 1991), or empowering specially trained individuals to perform the leadership tasks (Porod, 1993). We will examine these options in turn.

Rotating leadership offers a number of benefits that make it worth considering. First, it addresses the reality of the school workplace mentioned above: namely, teachers regard one another as equals, so asserting leadership is fraught with difficulties (Maeroff, 1993). By rotating leadership, there is an assumption of equality, a kind of turn-taking that effectively eliminates the hazards of status accumulation in relation to the position. Second, rotating team leadership encourages the involvement and development of each team member. The effect of taking on the leadership role can be highly motivating: people who otherwise remain detached from group work find themselves committed by virtue of owning the responsibility for the group's performance

(Johnson & Johnson, 1994).

There are, however, potential disadvantages to this approach to leadership also. For one thing, not all team members are comfortable with or willing to execute the duties of leadership. Some may not feel prepared to deal with other groups in managing boundary relations; others may not be comfortable addressing group norms. Second, to a certain extent, the use of rotating leadership – especially if the realities of team leadership are not addressed – trivializes the position. The "it's your turn now" approach to leadership reinforces the notion of leadership as performing clerical duties for the bureaucracy rather than as the meaningful route to effective teaming. A third problem with rotating leadership is that unless it is purposeful, such as having the social studies teacher lead during a social-studies centered activity, it does not take advantage of the natural strengths and interests of teachers. When team leaders can bring special talents to a phase of the team's work, their leadership gains credibility and the rotation of leaders becomes purposeful (Fisher, 1993).

Shared leadership appears to get around some of the disadvantages of rotating leaders. Clearly, by sharing leadership a team can use each member's talents and interests to the maximum extent. If, for example, the team's English teacher enjoys dealing with other teams and individuals, he might make the best boundary-spanner, and he could take on those opportunities. If the science teacher is the visionary for making interdisciplinary connections, she might assume that leadership. Thus, the leadership is purposeful rather than arbitrary.

Again, though, there are potential problems with this approach to leadership. First, unless the team has clearly articulated which leadership duties are to be addressed by which team members, it is likely that numerous important functions will be neglected. For example, in the team's initial formation, what guarantee is there that the shared leadership approach will give the attention needed to articulating the team's purpose? This crucial step gives direction to the entire team experience, and its neglect – perhaps too likely in the informal sharing of leadership – may seriously damage the team's effectiveness. Another serious disadvantage of shared leadership is the potential for unresolved conflict when too many captains are crowded together. While some teams will be able to resolve such conflict, groups too often submerge rather than deal with conflict (Senge, 1990). Shared leadership invites a team to ignore the sorts of problems and conflicts that people generally find uncomfortable to address. Yet, "One of the prime responsibilities of leadership is to induce and manage (moderate) discomfort" (Harvey & Drolet, 1994, p. 99).

This is not to say that shared leadership cannot work, especially with the assistance of the school's overall leader. Wheatley's description of a powerful team experience speaks to this: "In the interest of getting things done, our roles and tasks moved with such speed that the lines between structure and task blurred to nothing. When we speak of informal leadership, we describe a similar experience – the capacity of the organization to create the leadership that best suits its needs at the time" (p. 22). However, the disadvantages are serious enough to reconsider this option carefully. It may be that this approach to leadership requires the most input from the school's leader. When Shuster (1990) claims that sharing leadership means that "no *one* leads," he may be ignoring the possibility that *no one* leads. In the absence of a clear definition of leadership functions and assistance from the principal or some other outside leader, shared leadership is too risky for the important role teams play in middle schools, at least initially.

The final option for team leadership is that **one leader** – appointed, elected, or railroaded – assume the leadership responsibilities, ideally with extra compensation for all this involves (Porod, 1993). Such a leader is in a position, by virtue of vested authority, to establish direction for the team through a focus on the team's purpose. Furthermore, the institutional support of a formal leader (through extra pay or planning time, for example) adds credibility to the leader's position, whether that leader is working within the team (reinforcing norms) or spanning boundaries in the organization.

Two considerations deserve attention in the single-leader model. First, as noted earlier, the equal-status nature of teachers as colleagues may make it hard for teams to accept such leaders. Team members may raise legitimate questions about what sets any one member apart from others to assert such leadership. Second, in considering a new paradigm of collaboration, the use of a traditional hierarchical leader may reduce the degree of collaboration among team members. Fullan and Hargreaves (1991) call for teachers' creating together a school *vision*, like what I have argued is central to a team's success (though I used the word *purpose*). Perhaps the greatest danger of the single leader is that team members abdicate the visioning process to this leader rather than making it truly collaborative. It may be difficult for leaders and team members alike to leave behind what Belasco and Stayer (1993) call the "head buffalo" model of leadership and move to the more collaborative and empowering "lead goose" model.

Each leadership option has distinct advantages and disadvantages. The missing factor in my discussion thus far has been *context*: the social and occupational environment in which teams operate. For effective team leadership to occur, the leadership functions must be carried out in a way that harmonizes with the school and occupational culture in which the teams find themselves. For example, in a school just making the transition to teaming – where many of the variables of interdisciplinary teaming are unclear – it may be best to begin with a rotating leadership and much outside help that will be revisited when teachers and administrators can reflect on the experiences and personalities involved. It seems obvious that effective team leadership will take on different forms in different contexts. The baseline, however, is that the leadership always be directed to effective teaming.

Even the title of this section ("Captain or Captains?") demonstrates our continued reliance on traditional images of leadership. The militaristic metaphor hearkens back to Senge's (1990) comment about leading the cavalry. Instead, we might reconceptualize leadership as action arising from collaborative relations to help move a team toward its goals. Senge (1990) speaks of leadership as *designing*, *stewardship* and *teaching*; Fisher (1993) sees leadership as shepherding vs. merely herding sheep. Wellins and associates (1991) remind us of the reason for the move to teams: quality, or what the Japanese term *kaizen*, "continuous improvement." Shuster (1990) defines quality as the relentless pursuit of continuous improvement. In all these examples, leadership makes sense in the team's pursuit of a clear purpose. To focus on that purpose strikes me as the route to effective leadership.

Recommendations for team leaders – achieving greatness

> *Some are born great, some achieve greatness, and some*
> *have greatness thrust upon 'em.*
> — William Shakespeare's *Twelfth Night*
> *Historically leaders have controlled rather than organized,*
> *administered repression rather than expression, and held*
> *their followers in arrestment rather than in evolution.*
> — Bennis & Nanus, 1985, p. 16

Let me conclude with a list of recommendations for team leaders based on experiences from middle schools and elsewhere. Though such a list requires intelligent application to particular contexts, it allows me to summarize what I have been saying in a practical and brief manner.

In order to be great leaders by helping their *teams* achieve greatness, team leaders – however they got their positions – should:

1. Help the team establish and stick to a significant **purpose** – when the team moves away from this, remind team members of its importance;

2. Bring matters of **procedure** and **values** to a level of conscious deliberation in the team's operations so that everyone can live up to what the group decides is important;

3. Actively **connect** the team to other groups and individuals in the school;

4. Become a **living example** by performing the very work (but not all the work!) the team has called its goal; and

5. View leadership as **opening opportunities** and sharing power, not controlling team members. Dyer (1995) identifies the leader's central task as building the team. True leadership, he argues, resides not in a position, but in a process that can be shared with others. "Leadership is truly shared when every team member tries as much as possible to initiate an action whenever he or she sees the team struggling or getting bogged down" (p. 52).

As a caution, there are a few things a team leader should be sure **not** to do:

1. **Do not blame** team members or **excuse** shortfalls in team performance (Katzenbach & Smith, 1993).

2. **Do not submit** to the **clerk mentality** (merely keeping minutes, setting agendas, and fixing schedules) that characterizes so many teacher team leaders.

3. **Do not** fall into a **hero mentality** that sets the leader apart from the team. Messé, Kerr, and Sattler (1992) remind us how quickly the animals in Orwell's *Animal Farm* went from "all animals are created equal" to "some animals are more equal than others." The wisdom of Lao Tzu frequently finds its way into business writing on leadership: the *great* leader is the one of whom it is said, "We did it ourselves" (Bennis & Nanus, 1985; Fisher, 1993; Katzenbach & Smith, 1993; Senge, 1990).

If the prerequisite conditions for effective teaming are combined with a guiding vision of what makes for effective teaming, team leaders have the opportunity to help establish a new paradigm of teacher collaboration. The danger is that we have too long fulfilled the limited vision of clerking for others rather than building our own dreams. The challenge for team leaders is to do just that.

References

Ashton, P.T., & Webb, R.B. (1986). *Making a difference: Teachers' sense of efficacy and student achievement.* New York: Longman.

Ancona, D.G. (1990). Outward bound: Strategies for team survival in an organization. *Academy of Management Journal, 23,* 334-365.

Ancona, D.G., & Caldwell, D.F. (1988). Beyond task and maintenance: Defining external functions in groups. *Group & Organizational Studies, 13,* 468-494.

Belasco, J.A., & Stayer, R.C. (1993). *Flight of the buffalo: Soaring to excellence, learning to let employees lead.* New York: Warner Books.

Bell, N.M. (1990). *A case study of the implementation of interdisciplinary team organizations in a large school district.* Unpublished doctoral dissertation, University of Florida, Gainesville.

Bennis, W., & Nanus, B. (1985). *Leaders: The strategies for taking charge.* New York: Harper & Row.

Cummings, T.G. (1981). Designing effective work groups. In P.C. Nydstrom & W.H. Starbuck, (Eds.), *Handbook of organizational design. Volume 2: Remodeling organizations and their environments,* pp. 252-271. New York: Oxford University.

Donaldson, G.A., Jr. (1993). Working smarter together. *Educational Leadership, 51* (2), 12-16.

Dyer, W.G. (1995). *Team building: Current issues and new alternatives* (3rd ed.). Reading, MA: Addison-Wesley.

Erb, T.O., & Doda, N.M. (1989). *Team organization: Promise—practices and possibilities.* Washington, DC: National Education Association.

Faulk, O.B. (1976). *The U.S. camel corps: An army experiment.* New York: Oxford University Press.

Fisher, K. (1993). *Leading self-directed work teams: A guide to developing new team leadership skills.* New York: McGraw-Hill.

Fowler, H.D. (1980). *Three caravans to Yuma: The untold story of Bactrian camels in Western America.* Glendale, CA: Arthur H. Clark.

Fullan, M.G., & Hargreaves, A. (1991). *What's worth fighting for? Working together for your school.* Andover, MA: The Regional Laboratory for Educational Improvement of the Northeast and Islands in association with Ontario Public School Teachers' Federation.

George, P.S. (1982). Interdisciplinary team organization: Four operational phases. *Middle School Journal, 13* (3),10-13.

Goodlad, J.I. (1984). *A place called school: Prospects for the future.* New York: McGraw-Hill.

Goodman, P.S., Ravlin, E., & Schminke, M. (1987). Understanding groups in organizations. *Research in Organizational Behavior, 9,* 121-173.

Grace, G. (1978). *Teachers, ideology, and control: A study in urban education.* London: Routledge & Kegan Paul.

Hackman, J.R., & Morris, C.G. (1975). Group tasks, group interaction process, and group performance effectiveness: A review and proposed integration. In L. Berkowitz (Ed.), *Advances in Experimental Social Psychology, Vol. 8* (pp. 45-90). New York: Academic Press.

Hackman, J.R., & Oldham, G.R. (1980). *Work redesign.* Reading, MA: Addison-Wesley.

Hackman, J.R., & Walton, R.E. (1986). Leading groups in organizations. In P. S. Goodman (Ed.), *Designing effective work groups,* (pp. 72-119). San Francisco: Jossey-Bass.

Harvey, T.R., & Drolet, B. (1994). *Building teams, building people: Expanding the fifth resource.* Lancaster, PA: Technomic.

Hirschhorn, L. (1991). *Managing in the new team environment: Skills, tools, and methods.* Reading, MA: Addison-Wesley.

Hoffman, L. R. (1982). Improving the problem-solving process in managerial groups. In R. A. Guzzo (Ed.), *Improving group decision making in organizations: Approaches from theory and research* (pp. 95-126). New York: Academic Press.

Johnson, D.W., & Johnson, F.P. (1994). *Joining together: Group theory and group skills* (5th ed.). Boston: Allyn and Bacon.

Kain, D.L. (1992). *Collaborative planning of interdisciplinary experiences: A case study at the middle school level.* Unpublished doctoral dissertation, The University of British Columbia, Vancouver.

Katzenbach, J.R., & Smith, D.K. (1993). *The wisdom of teams: Creating the high-performance organization.* Boston: Harvard Business School.

Krause, S., & Louis, K.S. (1995). Teacher teaming—Opportunities and dilemmas. *Brief to principals, 11,* 1-6.

Lipsitz, J. (1984). *Successful schools for young adolescents.* New Brunswick, NJ: Transaction Books.

Little, J.W. (1990). The persistence of privacy: Autonomy and initiative in teachers' professional relations. *Teachers College Record, 91* (4), 509-536.

Little, J.W., & Shulman, J. (1984). *The instructional and professional environment of middle schools: Guidance for teacher education.* San Francisco: Far West Lab for Educational Research and Development. (ERIC Document Reproduction Service No. ED 265 119)

Maeroff, G.I. (1993). Building teams to rebuild schools. *Phi Delta Kappan, 74,* 512-519.

Merenbloom, E.Y. (1991). *The team process: A handbook for teachers* (3rd ed.). Columbus, OH: National Middle School Association.

Messé, L.A., Kerr, N.L., & Sattler, D.N. (1992). "But some animals are more equal than others": The supervisor as a privileged status in group contexts. In S. Worchel, W. Wood, & J.A. Simpson (Eds.), *Group process and productivity* (pp. 203-223). Newbury Park, CA: Sage.

Mills, R.A., Powell, R.R., & Pollak, J.P. (1992). The influence of middle level interdisciplinary teaming on teacher isolation: A case study. *Research in Middle Level Education, 15* (2), 9-25.

Parker, F.R., & Lumpkins, B. (1987). *Planning and administering a collaborative teaching program (PACT).* (ERIC Document Reproduction Service No. ED 313 333)

Pearce, J.A., & Ravlin, E.C. (1987). The design and activation of self-regulating work groups. *Human Relations, 40,* 751-782.

Porod, G.N. (1993). New roles for teachers: Instructional team leaders. *Schools in the Middle, 3* (2), 7-10.

Rayner, S.R. (1993). *Recreating the workplace: The pathway to high performance work systems.* Essex Junction, NJ: Oliver Wight.

Sarason, S.B. (1971). *The culture of school and the problem of change.* Boston: Allyn and Bacon.

Senge, P. M. (1990). *The fifth discipline: The art and practice of the learning organization.* New York: Doubleday.

Short, P.M. (1993). *School empowerment through self-managing teams: Leader behavior in developing self-managing work groups in schools.* (ERIC Document Reproduction Service No. ED 364 983)

Shuster, H.D. (1990). *Teaming for quality improvement: A process for innovation and consensus.* Englewood Cliffs, NJ: Prentice Hall.

Stein, P.J. (1978). *A participant observer study of team teacher planning behavior in a middle school study.* Unpublished doctoral dissertation, Michigan State University, East Lansing.

Tuckman, B.W. (1965). Developmental sequence in small groups. *Psychological Bulletin, 63,* 384-399.

Weiss, C.H. (1993). Shared decision making about what? A comparison of schools with and without teacher participation. *Teachers College Record, 95* (1), 69-92.

Wellins, R.S., Byham, W.C., & Dixon, G.R. (1994). *Inside teams: How 20 world-class organizations are winning through teamwork.* San Francisco: Jossey-Bass.

Wellins, R.S., Byham, W.C., & Wilson, J.M. (1991). *Empowered teams: Creating self-directed work groups that improve quality, productivity, and participation.* San Francisco: Jossey-Bass.

Wheatley, M.J. (1992). *Leadership and the new science: Learning about organization from an orderly universe.* San Francisco: Berret-Koehler.

Whitford, B.L., & Kyle, D.W. (April, 1984). *Interdisciplinary teaming: Initiating change in a middle school.* Paper presented at the annual meeting of the American Educational Research Association, New Orleans. (ERIC Document Reproduction Service No. ED 263 672)

Worchel, S., Coutant-Sassic, D., & Grossman, M. (1992). A developmental approach to group dynamics: A model and illustrative research. In S. Worchel, W. Wood, & J.A. Simpson (Eds.), *Group process and productivity* (pp. 181-202). Newbury Park, CA: Sage.

Teaming and Decision Making $\quad$ **19**

Elizabeth Pate

Teaching, in general, is a decision-making process (Borko & Niles, 1987; Clark & Peterson, 1986). Teaching on teams in middle schools is often a collaborative decision-making process. Team organization in middle schools generally involves small groups of teachers who teach a variety of subjects (e.g., language arts, mathematics, science, social studies, and humanities) for a common set of students. Collaboratively, teams of teachers share decision making regarding appropriate instruction for their students. According to Clark and Peterson (1986), on the average, "teachers make one interactive decision every two minutes" (p. 274). Interactive decision making involves teachers actively making decisions about appropriate instruction for their students.

The heart of decision making occurs during team planning and involves (a) designing the content and form of instruction, (b) helping each individual student grow not only in academic achievement but also in self-esteem, (c) promoting student behavior for a constructive learning environment, (d) communicating with parents about student progress, and (e) scheduling and grouping students (Hart, Pate, Mizelle, & Reeves, 1992). Specifically, teams of middle school teachers make important decisions regarding team organization (e.g., two-teacher, student-teacher progression), management (e.g., team rules, team consequences), curriculum (e.g., interdisciplinary, integrated), instruction (e.g., lecture, problem solving), assessment (e.g., traditional, alternative), scheduling (e.g., block, long-term) and grouping (e.g., interest, multi-age).

According to George, Stevenson, Thomason, and Beane (1992):

> *Shared decision making seems necessary for teachers to commit themselves to a total school program and mission. Social and instructional organizational schemes involve decisions that are natural priorities for teachers and best decided collaboratively. Exemplary middle schools employ collaborative decision making not only to achieve the best*

results, but to assure professionals that they are empowered
to make decisions affecting their professional work. Mean-
ingful collaborative decision making also carries into stu-
dents' school lives. Where youngsters learn to exercise au-
thority, they also learn real responsibility. Experiences that
enable all participants to resolve questions affecting their
school lives foster respect and appreciation for the values of
the democratic process. (pp. 41-42)

Teacher participation in shared decision making surfaced as a dominant theme in school reform and restructuring movements in the late 1980s when recommendations called for a more collaborative approach to decision making than in the past (Barth, 1990; Goodlad, 1984). Shulman and Carey (1984), in a theoretical perspective known as collective rationality, suggest that educational problems be addressed by groups rather than individuals. They suggest that this collaborative decision making may give groups an advantage over solitary decision making in problem solving, problem defini-tion, and work distribution. Collaborative decision making gives groups an advantage because multiple perspectives can be brought forward, a variety of ideas and solutions can be brainstormed, and participants can assume a variety of roles such as leader, documenter, or even antagonist. Many inter-disciplinary teams make decisions according to the participatory decision-making model. The participatory decision-making model (Estler, 1988) involves coming to a consensus regarding making decisions among relevant participants in order to achieve shared goals. Shared decision making and participatory decision making are largely synonymous terms referring to the practice of reaching decisions collaboratively (Dougherty, 1995).

Another prevalent theme from the school restructuring literature is the importance of the teacher's voice in the change process (e.g., Bracey, 1990; Carnegie Council on Adolescent Development, 1989; Glickman, 1991). According to Glickman (1991), the "decentralization, deregulation, site-based, empowerment movement" (p. 9) has put educators on the right track toward improving the quality of education in our country. He maintains that school improvement will not occur without the existence of schools "where the faculty wants to share in the choice and responsibilities of schoolwide decisions and where the administrators and supervisors likewise want them to share" (p. 9). The Carnegie Council on Adolescent Development (1989) concludes that in middle schools in particular:

Teachers must have greater authority to make decisions,
and responsibility for the consequences of those decisions,

regarding the day-to-day educational experiences of their students. Dramatically improved outcomes for young adolescents require individualized, responsive, and creative approaches to teaching that will occur only when teachers are able to use their intimate knowledge of students to design instructional programs. (p. 54)

This chapter presents three vignettes of teams of middle school teachers engaged in the collaborative decision-making process. Each team used collaborative decision making to design individualized, responsive, and creative instructional programs as part of middle school reform. Ferrara and Repa (1993) discovered, in their research on shared decision making, that "it is important to describe decision-making involvement in terms of both the extent of decision making and the way in which decision making is occurring" (p. 71). Therefore, for each vignette, the following is provided: the reasons for collaborative decision making, examples of the types of decisions made, how those decisions were acted upon, and what happened as a result of collaborative decision making. The chapter concludes with each teams' reflection of collaborative decision making.

Delta Project

The Delta Project involved one team of four teachers and their approximately 100 students working together throughout grades 6-8 (the 1990-91, 1991-92, and 1992-93 school years). The participants are from Elbert County Middle School, the only middle school in Elberton, Georgia.

The four teachers came together as an interdisciplinary team (language arts, mathematics, science, and social studies) at the beginning of the 1990-91 school year. Prior to this, two of the four teachers were involved in Project 2061, a large science curriculum development project funded by the American Association for the Advancement of Science and the National Science Foundation (Pate, Mizelle, Hart, Jordan, Matthews, Matthews, Scott, & Brantley, 1993).

The idea for the Delta Project evolved from the Project 2061 experiences of Sue (the science teacher) and Vicky (the social studies teacher). During a conference, Sue and Vicky learned about a restructured school in Cologne, Germany that kept students and teachers together for six years and emphasized student and teacher teamwork (Ratzki & Fisher, 1989-1990). Sue and Vicky embraced the idea of student-teacher progression. They envisioned a team of teachers working with the same group of students throughout the 6th,

7th, and 8th grades; they wanted to create a family environment with an emphasis on interdisciplinary instruction.

To help their students maintain an identity within the team, each year the Delta teachers assigned students to "base groups." Students were assigned to a group so that each group contained a heterogenous mix of students by race, gender, and achievement. Students in the same base group worked together on various projects.

The Delta teachers devised "alternative schedules" that enabled them to "team teach" large groups in extended blocks of time. Using the base groups, teachers assigned students to either Section One or Section Two. For example, one section of students might be taught science and mathematics during the morning and the other section language arts and social studies. During the afternoon time block, the two sections of students would exchange classes.

The Delta teachers made important decisions about using cooperative learning, higher order thinking and problem solving, learning strategies, and interdisciplinary units of study. They decided to involve their students in long-term projects. For example, the "Garden Unit" developed over two years. As part of the unit, six garden plots were created for the students outside their classrooms. In the sixth grade, the students were told what to plant and how to plant. In the seventh grade, each garden group designed their plot and chose vegetables and flowers they wanted to grow. The following is an excerpt from a Delta Team planning session in which decisions were made about the gardening project:

April 16, 1991

> Vicky— *The planning of the garden, ah, the planning of the ...*
>
> Sue — (in unison with Vicky) *garden, the sowing of the seeds,...*
>
> Vicky —*...we, um, set up so that in every class there are 6 groups, that's true with all of our classes, and each group had a plot, so there's six plots, but in every class, ah, someone has that same plot. So that there were six groups ...*
>
> Sue — *... shared by four classes ...*
>
> Vicky — *... shared by four classes ...six plots, so what she, what they're going to do is one day each week, each class will go out and work in the garden, and the others won't and collect data and clean up, whatever. And then on Friday, rearrange the schedule so that everybody who had one plot was together, so that they could compare and work together as sort of a ... team.*

Kim — ... *team.*

Sue — *Each one will have one piece of data from the week and they will compile it on Friday, so that they can get the big picture of the week.*

Vicky — *And we wanted to have a larger block of time, so we wanted to have two periods instead of one, so we wanted to go to another schedule.*

As you can see from this team planning session, the teachers shared thoughts and ideas, discussed details, and came to common understandings about the gardening project.

For the Delta Project, teachers made important decisions because of their commitment to meet the affective and cognitive needs of their students. During the three years, as the teachers worked with one another and with their students, some of their original decisions changed and new decisions were made (i.e., instead of having the same base groups for three years, students would be in different base groups each year). This team of teachers had a vision of what they thought middle school reform was about.

Delta team student teachers

Another decision the Delta teachers made was to supervise a team of four middle school student teachers. The following is an excerpt from one of the student teaching journals:

January 19, 1993

Tuesday

Today was planning day and we used it to the fullest extent. There were a few meetings the inservice teachers were required to attend, and we went to one of them, but the rest of the time we spent both working on our own lesson plans and on the unit. I think that we made quite a bit of progress, at least organizationally. I was surprised how long it took us to write the introduction! And we didn't even finish it after at least 2 hours! However, I think that it will be great. As we developed and solidified our ideas, we began to realize just how unique an opportunity we have here at this school. We also gained some excellent experience in planning lessons and units as a team. It's not easy at times, but at other times it's much easier. I really feel good about going into a school and implementing the middle

school concept. I think that it's needed and I know that it's
good for the students.

It was interesting to see how we all tended to get off task
at times. What was good was having another person in the
group to pull you back on task. I like this idea!

The student teachers planned as a team throughout their 10-week student
teaching experience for language arts, mathematics, science, and social
studies. During their student teaching experience, they developed an interdisciplinary unit based on Project 2061's "habits of mind" (American Association for the Advancement of Science, 1989).

Beginning teachers report that they learn about students, content, and
pedagogy from collaborative planning with a mentor teacher (Wildman,
Niles, Magliaro, & McLaughlin, 1987). All four Delta Team teachers
mentored the team of student teachers. Communication became an important
part of the student teaching experience. The student teachers learned quickly
that as a member of a team open lines of communication would have to be
established. For example, during the planning of a curriculum unit some
student teachers thought others were having planning sessions without them.
As Polly (pseudonym) stated in her student teaching journal, "Today Mary
(pseudonym) and I became frustrated with Michael (pseudonym) and Fred
(pseudonym) because we felt like they had planned a unit without us. The
teachers suggested that we should clear the air. This was a good idea because
it turned out to be a misunderstanding." Decisions about communication
were made by the student teachers to "immediately hash out problems and
clear the air," "develop a communication network with parents," and "maintain constant contact with cooperating teachers for feedback."

Decisions were also made about work assignments among the student
teachers. As they became more and more involved in planning their interdisciplinary unit, the student teachers found the need to make decisions about
who was responsible for what assignment. For example, in one audiotaped
team planning session, the conversation revolved around work assignments.
Statements were made, such as,

I volunteer to get the stamps.

I'll get the red material for the flags. Why don't you work
on the cover page?

I'll write the rationale for the unit for math.

I'll write one for social studies.

We'll write one for our subject areas.

Why don't we all look over each others to spot connec-
tions we can make in the unit?

In one team interview the student teachers discussed their decisions. Polly said, "We've decided to do a mini-unit where we use the 'habits of mind' to teach math concepts. One thing that we felt important was to find an activity that would both interest the students and be relevant. Then we tried to figure out what QCC [Quality Core Curriculum] objectives could be met within the activity. This sounds like a great way to approach this.... The topic that we chose for this unit is year-round schools." During team planning, the student teachers shared their ideas, came up with new ideas, and made decisions about curriculum and instruction.

In addition to making decisions about communication, work assignments, and curriculum and instruction, decisions were also made about the team management plan. The student teachers thought perhaps the team management plan was not as effective during the third year of student-teacher progression. As Fred stated in a team planning session, "...maybe the method is overused or maybe over the three-year period it has gotten old." The student teachers collaborated on a new team management plan they put into effect during the fourth week of student teaching. They shared management models they had seen in practice or had read about. They brainstormed ideas they would like to implement and made decisions about their revised management plan.

Because of the nature of this experience, the student teachers were making collaborative decisions about planning and implementing a variety of curriculum. They were encouraged to experiment in their instruction. Content was decided upon, deadlines were set, mini-units were developed, and appropriate evaluation was selected.

Oglethorpe County Middle School

Team decisions are also made at Oglethorpe County Middle School, another rural middle school located in Georgia. Oglethorpe County Middle School is a school where faculty want to share in the choice and responsibilities of schoolwide decisions and where the administrators likewise want them to share.

To meet this need the school adopted a shared decision making model known as the Schoolwide Instructional Team (SIT). The formation of SIT began at the start of the 1989-90 school year. This was the beginning of teachers' total involvement in substantive decision making that influenced the philosophy of the school and the curricular needs of the middle school learners. The SIT is composed of seven faculty members who are responsible for developing school philosophy, policy, and plans for continuous instructional improvement. Five of the seven members are teachers and the chairperson is always a teacher. The SIT is a decision-making body rather than a purely advisory one. The group's guidelines explicitly state that the focus is on improving instruction and student learning. As shared governance has become an essential element of the school culture, the faculty have begun participating in hiring new faculty and making budgetary and staff development decisions.

Inservice days in the spring and at the end of each school year are employed to identify areas deserving special emphasis in the following year. Goals and priorities are finalized by the SIT at its annual meeting of outgoing and incoming members held at the beginning of summer. For example, the goals for the 1993-1994 school year included:

1. Increased use of instructional technology
2. Matching instructional styles to students' learning styles more closely
3. Examination of the Georgia School of Excellence criteria.

Another layer of decision making is the "liaison group." Teachers from teams are regrouped into diverse units to meet monthly. Five SIT members divide to form the axis of each group and function as recorders. Each records the wants, needs, problems, and suggestions of the group. This information is then brought before the SIT committee at their monthly meetings and is prioritized there for attention and resolution.

Still another layer of collaborative decision making occurs at the team level. Teams of teachers first make decisions about curriculum to be presented, instructional approaches to be used, the sequencing of materials, and the selection of class textbooks and other printed or visual aid materials. The teams, during their common 120 minutes of planning time, may interview candidates for team teaching positions, develop a team discipline plan in conjunction with the school's discipline system, arrange changes in daily scheduling to accommodate team programs, establish field trip guidelines, develop schedules for the inclusion model for exceptional students, and develop team communication projects with parents.

For example, three seventh grade teachers on the Dolphin Team wrote a proposal to the principal asking for latitude regarding team formation, team responsibilities, curriculum, and instruction. The rationale for this proposal was based on information these teachers gathered regarding the middle school concept, knowledge of middle school students, and interdisciplinary instruction. The proposal requested a three-teacher team (rather than their former five-teacher team), block scheduling, and interdisciplinary unit design. The proposal was accepted, and the three teacher team was formed. One teacher taught math, science, and social studies. Another teacher taught language arts and science. The third teacher taught reading and social studies. The team used block scheduling and designed their own interdisciplinary units based on the needs of their students. This decision turned out to be such a success for the team that the next year they proposed another change. This second proposal requested the opportunity to pilot the inclusion model of instruction for students of differing abilities. Again, the team researched everything they could about inclusion. In this model, all students on the team are instructed by the three teachers and a remedial teacher. The result of the decision to participate in inclusion was that "we had a zero percent failure rate".

Teams of teachers at Oglethorpe County Middle School also decide on what additional inservice experiences they need. Recently, teachers have engaged in extended staff development on such topics as "integrating technology into curriculum and instruction," "teaching and learning strategies," "mathematics manipulatives," and "developing interdisciplinary curriculum." As a result of one of these inservice experiences, many teachers have decided to become teacher-researchers. These teachers are investigating how their students use learning strategies in their particular classes and across content and grade levels. It is interesting to note that studies have shown that involvement in research increases teachers' role in schoolwide decision making (Maeroff, 1988; Sardo-Brown, 1992).

Oglethorpe County Middle School is proud of its involvement in collaborative decision making. The teachers like participating in making schoolwide decisions and team decisions. In part, because of collaborative decision making, the school was designated as a 1994-95 Georgia School of Excellence award winner.

McHome Team

In the spring of 1992, Karen, a science teacher, and Elaine, a social studies teacher, were on a five-member eighth grade interdisciplinary team in a middle school in the suburban Atlanta area. There were 150 students on their team, class periods were 45 minutes long, schedules were inflexible, and there was hardly any connection between subject areas. Student interest was hard to get and maintain, and enthusiasm for school was low. Under these constraints Karen and Elaine felt it was impossible to think about meeting the "needs of the students."

This dissatisfaction with schooling led Karen and Elaine to make significant decisions. They began the collaborative decision-making process by seeking information about nontraditional methods of teaching and learning. They read extensively about interdisciplinary instruction, curriculum integration, alternative assessment, and innovative school programs. They discussed how they could use information gleaned from the literature to make decisions regarding schooling.

Prior to this the focus of the team had been on *what was being taught*. Content delivery was the primary consideration in every decision they had previously made to improve their teaching. Karen and Elaine consciously made the decision to focus on *what was being learned* and *by whom*. It seemed clear to them that all decisions made at the middle school level should be based not only upon the cognitive needs of middle school learners, but also upon what is known about the social needs, emotional needs, and physical needs of this age group. In other words, the whole child should be considered. Karen and Elaine wanted to make their curriculum responsive to the interests and needs of their students, as well as maintaining academically challenging standards (Pate, McGinnis, & Homestead, 1995).

After the initial decision had been made to change the curriculum to meet the needs of the student, Karen and Elaine wrote a proposal to their principal. As Elaine reflected in her journal:

> *In May, 1992, Karen and I wrote a proposal for an integrated curriculum (language arts, social studies, and science) two-member team for the school year 1992-1993 and submitted it to our principal. We asked that we be placed in classrooms with a movable curtain wall between so that we could team teach. It made so much more sense to integrate the subjects so that our students could see the connections between the subjects. Math applications were already being integrated into social studies and science regularly. Science concepts were already being talked about in social studies and social studies topics were discussed in science. So why not develop units of study that could more fully integrate these subjects in ways that made sense for our students?*
>
> *Our proposal was accepted. Both of us would teach a traditional math skills class. The rest of the academic block time, 10:05 to 2:00, was ours to develop. The only drawback*

was that our classrooms were placed across the hall from
one another so we would have to pile all 60 students into
one room to team teach.

After the proposal was accepted, Karen and Elaine decided to develop a survey for their upcoming eighth graders. The survey was designed to find out how students felt they learned best, what concerned them most at school, what they would like to learn, and what they could change about school if they could. Karen and Elaine wanted to use the student responses to help personalize learning. Students indicated they wanted "less book work," more projects, "less about what happened a long time ago," and more current issues.

As Karen and Elaine thought about integrating the curriculum, they took into account their own personal beliefs as well as educational theories about schooling. Their overarching goal for the year was to integrate the curriculum for a team of 58 eighth graders. The responses from the survey helped Karen and Elaine decide on the following long-term goals (Pate, Homestead, & McGinnis, 1997):

- *Develop a curriculum that gives students and teachers a deeper understanding of content*
- *Make connections between school and the outside world*
- *Guide students in the learning process*
- *Encourage students to accept responsibilities*
- *Help students learn to work effectively with a diversity of people*
- *Encourage students to take risks and learn from mistakes*
- *Assist students in becoming effective problem solvers*
- *Enable students to discover that learning can be fun*

Karen and Elaine then spent the summer collaborating on a framework for an integrated curriculum for the 1992-1993 school year. They consciously made the decision to develop thematic units using social studies as the organizer. The rationale for this decision was "it was easier to integrate the disciplines into social studies because it seemed to be most flexible." They developed loose frameworks for units realizing that they wanted student input in the curriculum. Each of the units began with an initial focus on the student's connection to the topic. The emphasis would then shift to a local, state, national, and world historical perspective. The units would culminate with consideration of current and future implications for all levels of society. Karen and Elaine felt this framework would address the students' desire to have "less book work," more projects, "less about what happened a long time ago," and more current issues.

Karen and Elaine made the decision to have the first unit partially designed for the students at the beginning of the school year instead of waiting for input from the students. This decision was made for several reasons: (1) they wanted to make sure they could teach content within a theme, (b) they wanted to find out if the central focus of social studies would work, (c) they wanted to model integrated curriculum for their students, and (d) they wanted to have something planned to begin the school year.

Karen and Elaine also made the decision to have a democratic classroom. A democratic classroom is one in which students and teachers collaborate. It is one in which students' voices are heard and respected. In a democratic classroom, students and teachers work together in formulating classroom management plans, setting grading policies, and developing curricula. Developing a democratic classroom on the McHome Team incorporated the teaching and modeling of these skills and concepts:

problem solving,

decision making,

listening,

respecting others,

sharing,

compromising,

discussing,

encouraging,

respectful questioning,

following directions,

explaining,

accepting others,

sensitivity to others,

taking risks, and

accepting responsibility

— Pate, Homestead, & McGinnis 1997, p. 17

Throughout the remainder of the school year Karen, Elaine, and the McHome Team students collaborated on designing integrated thematic units. The units include Human Migration, Human Interactions, Human Interactions and the Environment, Human and Civil Rights and Responsibilities, Leadership, and Communities of the Future.

The Human Migration unit enabled the students to gain a perspective of why they are where they are and to further understand the concept of diversity. The overarching questions for the unit were: "How has my world been affected by human migration?" "How are world human migration patterns correlated with the settlement and growth of our state and the United States?" and "What will be the implications of human migration on me in the future?"

During the Human Migration unit, students studied the historical reasons why their state and country were colonized and students studied how topography, climate, and natural resources influenced westward movement. Students posed questions such as, "Why are people continuing to migrate to the United States?" "Where are people migrating from?" "How will continued migration affect my employment opportunities, my standard of living, and where I might live?" and "What impact will future migration have on our environment?"

From these student-generated questions, research projects were developed. Groups of students chose migration "hot spots" around the world, studied reasons for migration to the United States and Georgia in particular, brainstormed possible implications for the future, and shared their findings with the class.

This unit helped the students discover that even though they were culturally, ethnically, and economically diverse, their families all had similar reasons for moving to the community (jobs, family ties, and the search for political and religious freedom).

The next thematic unit was Human Interactions. This unit was a study of social issues that affect students personally, as well as social issues that have affected societies in the past. Students investigated the issues of racism, abortion rights, animal testing, and world hunger. They developed questions for research, determined how they would share their information with others, kept journals, and constructed their own alternative assessments.

The McHome Team students were so interested in their study of current social issues that affected them that they wanted to continue their studies to include environmental issues of personal concern. In the Human Interactions and the Environment unit, students chose topics to learn more about. Their topics included such issues as ozone pollution, erosion due to clear cutting, acid rain, and quality of air and water.

Students shared information learned from their studies through multimedia presentations that included narrated slide presentations, student-made videos, a puppet show, photo displays (one group cataloged their efforts to mobilize their neighborhood to clean up a nearby lake), models, charts and graphs of statistical data, and student-generated computer programs detailing environmental information.

In the fourth unit, Human/Civil Rights and Responsibilities, students examined the relationships between past, present, and future human and civil rights from the 1600s to the present. These events ranged from the Salem Witch Trials to the conflict in the former country of Yugoslavia.

The fifth unit was Leadership. This unit was originally to have been an exploration of leadership qualities. However, by that time of the school year everyone was exhausted. The students asked if they could take a break and read a book for a change. The students were enthusiastic about reading the novel, *Jurassic Park*, so the team made decisions regarding how to incorporate a leadership study into a novel study.

The final unit of the year was Communities of the Future. This unit was developed because of student interest (interest in their surroundings and genuine concern for their future living conditions) and to address school-mandated curriculum requirements (governmental and economic systems and astronomy). For this unit, it was decided to focus on the following groups of skills:

1. recognize problems and opportunities; devise, implement, evaluate, and revise (if necessary) a daily plan of action
2. cooperate effectively in a group setting by generating and contributing ideas through negotiation, teamwork, and leadership
3. write to communicate personal feelings, attitudes, and ideas
4. imagine, generate, and produce new ideas, solutions, or products

During final presentations, groups of students shared details as they presented scaled drawings and 3-D models of their chosen communities of the future (e.g., where they were located, why they were located there, how they got there, their government and economic system, their constitution, details of their 3-D model).

Upon reflection on the McHome Team, Elaine said, "Most educators dabble with incorporating new ideas into their curriculum. We jumped in head first: integrating language arts, science and a newly restructured social studies curriculum; creating performance assessments, rubrics and checklists; and collaborating with students on curriculum and instruction."

The McHome Team teachers actively made decisions together in pursuit of their goal of connecting all aspects of the curriculum – the working world, subject content and skills, and social skills – for students and teachers. They decided what goals were necessary in order to guide the curriculum and shape how it is taught and learned. The team made a decision to connect the curriculum in every way it could. This meant organizing a curriculum with no artificial boundaries between content areas. It meant relating how content and skills can or will be important outside of school.

The McHome teachers also made decisions regarding when and how to use traditional and alternative assessments. They matched assessments to themes, activities, and students' needs. Through the shared decision-making process, the teachers determined appropriate pedagogy. They made a concerted effort to personalize learning. Personalizing learning included identifying learning styles, determining strengths and weaknesses in content and social skills, researching background and family information, recognizing personal interests and concerns, exploring career interests, and determining student expectations from school.

The McHome Team teachers were successful in achieving their long-term goals. Their decisions helped create a curriculum that gave students and teachers a deeper understanding of content and the connections between school and the outside world. Students were guided in the learning process and encouraged to accept responsibilities; students learned to work effectively with a diversity of people, took risks and learned from their mistakes, and became effective problem solvers.

Discussion

A common thread among these teams was collaborative decision making. The teachers on the Delta Project made important decisions about team organization (student-teacher progression), curriculum (long-term, short-term, interdisciplinary), and instruction (team teaching) *as a team*. The teachers at Oglethorpe County Middle School made important decisions about team organization (three member), curriculum (interdisciplinary), and instruction (inclusion) *as a team*. The McHome teachers made important decisions about team organization (two-member, team teaching), curriculum (integrated), and instruction (responsive) *as a team*.

When making decisions, it is important to know what you want to achieve (Conley, 1991). Teacher teams should have objectives, goals, outcomes, or a sense of vision in mind when making decisions. Each team discussed in this chapter had a shared vision and common goals to work towards. Each of the teams ultimately assumed responsibility for student learning. The McHome Team teachers, for example, had a vision of integrating the curriculum. They had eight long-term goals. Countless decisions had to be made by the McHome Team teachers in order to meet those goals.

As decision makers, teams of teachers must know what they want to do, yet be flexible enough to consider new options or directions to take. Teams must try to make the best possible decisions in a given situation at any given time. And teams should realize that every decision may not be the right one. The Delta Team, the Dolphin Team at Oglethorpe County Middle School, and the McHome Team were willing to take risks and learn from any mistakes.

The Delta Team teachers believed it was easier to make decisions as a team because

> It [collaborative decision making] moves you as a classroom teacher out of isolation. You grow professionally. You throw out an idea and it evolves into something great from input from other team members.
>
> You have more help. If you have a problem with a student, there are other teachers there to help. The team management plan is an example of how we made decisions together.
>
> In terms of effect on kids, kids benefit [from team decision making] because then you tend to do more teamwise rather than as a class. For example, the first year I was on a team we really didn't plan and work together. We weren't functioning as a team. So, during the Delta Project, we all worked together to make decisions – as a result, we were a real middle school team.
>
> The students like seeing interaction between us. I guess we are modeling collaborative decision making for them.

The Delta Team student teachers believed it was easier to make decisions as a team because they could "talk through a situation," "volunteer information that might help a situation," "disagree, agree, and compromise," "ask for examples and clarification," and "generally have other perspectives to take into consideration when making a decision."

A teacher from the Dolphin Team at Oglethorpe County Middle School believed it was easier to make decisions as a team because "You feel like you have some control over decisions. You feel ownership in what the school does."

The McHome Team teachers believed it was easier to make decisions as a team because

> It's like synergism. You know how they say that two minds are better than one? When you work together and you put

ideas together more happens than singly. Ideas spin off each other. You are more creative that way. Also, sometimes when you are making decisions – well, you know, I'm linear – this way I can see other ways of doing things.

Knowing when we are in agreement regarding philosophy, strategies, and curriculum ideas, there is more force behind the decisions. Our input regarding decisions was complimentary. Together our ideas seemed rich, full of meaning. Having a partner made risk taking seem less risky. Shared decisions made it more dynamic for the students. We played off one another. We modeled decision making for them.

Teams of teachers engaged in middle school reform take responsibility for making decisions about the use of their time, the choice of curricular materials, and the use of facilities. Teachers can and should be trusted to make decisions that are based upon the individual needs of learners in the classroom, as the nature of learning requires both flexibility and responsiveness (McDonald, 1992). The Delta Project teachers, the Delta Team student teachers, the teachers from Oglethorpe County Middle School, and the McHome Team teachers made collaborative decisions and assumed responsibility for the consequences of those decisions.

References

American Association for the Advancement of Science. (1989). *Science for all Americans: A Project 2061 report on literacy goals in science, mathematics, and technology*. Washington, DC: Author.

Barth, R.S. (1990). *Improving schools from within: Teachers, parents, and principals can make a difference*. San Francisco: Jossey-Bass Publishers.

Borko, H., & Niles, J.A. (1987). Descriptions of teacher planning: Ideas for teachers and researchers. In V. Koehler (Ed.), *Educators' handbook: Research into practice* (pp. 167-187). New York: Longman.

Bracey, G.W. (1990). Rethinking school and university roles. *Educational Leadership, 47* (8), 65-66.

Carnegie Council on Adolescent Development. (1989). *Turning points: Preparing American youth for the 21st century*. New York: Carnegie Corporation.

Clark, C.M., & Peterson, P.L. (1986). Teachers' thought processes. In M. C. Wittrock (Ed.), *Handbook of research on teaching* (3rd ed.) (pp. 255-296). New York: Macmillan.

Conley, S. C. (1991). Review of research on teacher participation in school decision making. In G. Grant (Ed.), *Review of research in education* (pp. 225-266). Washington, DC: American Educational Research Association.

Dougherty, G.W. (1995). *Principals' perspectives of shared governance.* Unpublished doctoral dissertation, The University of Georgia, Athens.

Estler, S.E. (1988). Decision making. In N. Boyan (Ed.), *Handbook of research on educational administration* (pp. 305- 319). New York: Longman.

Ferrara, D.L., & Repa, J.T. (1993). Measuring shared decision making. *Educational Leadership, 51*(2), 71-72.

George, P.S., Stevenson, C., Thomason, J., & Beane, J. (1992). *The middle school—and beyond.* Alexandria, VA: Association for Supervision and Curriculum Development.

Glickman, C. (1991). Pretending not to know what we know. *Educational Leadership, 48* (8), 4-10.

Goodlad, J.I. (1984). *A place called school: Prospects for the future.* New York: McGraw-Hill Book Company.

Hart, L.E., Pate, P.E., Mizelle, N.B., & Reeves, J.L. (1992). Interdisciplinary team development in the middle school: A study of the Delta Project. *Research in Middle Level Education, 16* (1), 79-98.

Maeroff, G. (1988). A blueprint for empowering teachers. *Phi Delta Kappan, 69,* 473-477.

McDonald, J.P. (1992). *Teaching: Making sense of an uncertain craft.* New York: Teachers College Press.

Pate, P.E., Homestead, E.R., & McGinnis, K.L. (1997). *Making integrated curriculum work: Teachers, students, and the quest for coherent curriculum.* New York: Teachers College Press.

Pate, P.E., McGinnis, K.L., & Homestead, E.R. (1995). Creating coherence through curriculum integration. In J. Beane (Ed.), *Toward a coherent curriculum: 1995 ASCD Yearbook* (pp. 62-70). Alexandria, VA: Association for Supervision and Curriculum Development.

Pate, P.E., Mizelle, N.B., Hart, L.E., Jordan, J., Matthews, R., Matthews, S., Scott, V., & Brantley, V. (1993). The Delta Project: A three-year longitudinal study of middle school change. *Middle School Journal, 25* (1), 24-27.

Ratzki, A., & Fisher, A. (1989-1990). Life in a restructured school. *Educational Leadership, 47* (4), 46-51.

Sardo-Brown, D. (1992). Elementary teachers' perceptions of action research. *The Journal of the Association of Teacher Educators, 14* (2), 55-58.

Shulman, L.S., & Carey, N.B. (1984). Psychology and the limitations of individual rationality: Implications for the study of reasoning and civility. *Review of Educational Research, 54* (4), 501-524.

Wildman, T.M., Niles, J.A., Magliaro, S., & McLaughlin, R.A. (1987). *Teachers learning from teachers: A mentor's guide.* Blacksburg: Virginia Polytechnic Institute and State University, College of Education.

Teams and Curriculum **20**

John Arnold

S urprisingly, relatively little has been written about the role that
interdisciplinary teams can play in developing and facilitating curriculum. Yet teams are the cornerstone of middle level organization
and hold enormous promise for engaging young adolescents in stimulating
and purposeful curriculum opportunities.

Though a non-teamed teacher may certainly provide meaningful curriculum, such a teacher usually affects only one period of the student's day. Even
where students have a number of good individual teachers, there frequently is
a lack of consistency and connectedness to their education. Because teams
are able to plan jointly with the totality of students' experiences in mind, they
have much greater opportunity to engage students in a rich, cohesive, and
comprehensive approach to curriculum. As compared to conventional
departmentalized arrangements, well-functioning teams enjoy the following
potential advantages relative to curriculum:

- Teams can create a more personal, positive climate where risk taking,
  initiative, and responsibility on the part of teachers and students can be
  cultivated.
- Teachers know students needs, interests, and abilities better and thus
  can tailor activities to meet individual and group concerns.
- Teachers have greater flexibility in the use of time and the grouping of
  students.
- Teachers have colleagues with whom they can develop curriculum,
  share ideas and responsibilities, learn new skills, and receive support
  from one another.
- Integrative/interdisciplinary curriculum, advisory activities, and special
  events are more easily facilitated.

Unfortunately, many teams do not take advantage of these opportunities.
While in some cases this is due to lack of resources or to teams being too
new to have developed to the stage where they could take advantage of these
opportunities, more often it is attributable to a lack of information, motiva-

tion, or effective leadership. Few current teachers or administrators attended teamed schools when they were young adolescents, nor have they had college or inservice courses which have thoroughly prepared them for teaming. Hence many schools have been thrust into teaming without adequate knowledge and support. Knowledge, understanding, and a strong desire to make teams work effectively on the part of teachers and administrators, especially the principal, are essential if team curriculum is to reach its potential.

The purpose of this chapter is to explore some of the curricular opportunities which teaming provides, focusing upon three major topics: (a) team structure and procedures which facilitate curriculum, (b) fundamental principles of developmentally responsive curriculum, and (c) appropriate teaching and learning approaches. Curriculum, a term with numerous connotations, in this context refers to the activities in which students are engaged and the methods used to engage them. Due to space limitations, issues related to articulation, assessment, and other aspects of curriculum development lie beyond the scope of this chapter.

Optimal Team Structure and Procedures

Where teams have an optimal organizational structure and well developed procedures, their curricular efforts are greatly enhanced. Where these are absent, frustration and lost opportunity are likely outcomes.

Team selection is critical to all aspects of teaming and particularly to curriculum. Keeping overall school equity in mind, teachers with reasonably compatible philosophies of education should be grouped together. Attention should also be given to seeking balance and diversity of curricular strengths and styles; including someone with art-making-building skills, for example, is a boon to any team.

Further, team size merits careful consideration. It is all too common for the typical four-teacher team to divide its time into fixed periods and isolated subjects, thus putting old wine (departmentalization) into new wineskins (team organization). In my experience, small (two- or three-teacher) teams generally engage students more meaningfully in curriculum than do larger teams. Because two-teacher teams have half as many students as do four-teacher teams, they know their students much better. In addition, it is easier for small teams to agree upon goals, to make compromises, to plan, to flex the schedule, and to facilitate integrative learning. Of course, small teacher teams are feasible only where qualified teachers who desire to work together exist. Keep in mind that team size does not have to be a constant throughout the school. Finding the best match of teachers, not uniformity, should be the goal; teachers should have considerable voice in team selection.

Students should be selected for teams on a heterogeneous basis. The evidence is quite clear that homogeneous grouping, while perhaps easier for teachers, has a devastating effect on lower level students' performance (George, 1988; Oakes, 1985). Multi-age and student-teacher progression teams, though not currently widespread, offer distinct curricular advantages over grade level teams in that they enable teachers to know students better, work with them for longer periods of time, and make various types of continuous progress curricula more feasible.

Once teams have been selected, they require sufficient *planning time, a true flexible block schedule, and well developed procedures* if they are to function optimally relative to curriculum. Ideally, teachers will have a daily team planning period in addition to their individual planning time. During team planning, an appreciable amount of time must be set aside on a weekly basis for curricular matters, including the coordination of homework and testing and the planning of advisory activities, joint projects, and special events. Planning must also be tied in with ongoing discussions of individual students' interests, strengths, weaknesses, learning styles, and overall development. Lest inordinate amounts of time be spent on the behavior problems of a few students, a good procedure is to set a limit of five minutes for discussing individuals. Those students who require more discussion or those about whom little is known are slated for advisory or parental conferences (Arnold, 1981). Where used effectively, these discussions can inform and guide curriculum planning in a powerful manner.

A block schedule which best facilitates curriculum is one where a team is assigned a heterogeneous group of students and a large block of time with the autonomy to schedule and group students as it sees fit (Figure 1).

During the block, teachers are usually responsible for four core classes, plus an additional one where all teachers simultaneously offer a reading, enrichment, remediation, or special interest course. All pullouts are ideally scheduled during this "fifth period." Note that four teachers cannot teach five sections of core subjects within a true block schedule. To do so, one elective class would have to be scheduled each period; the capacity for team teachers to alter the schedule to suit their plans would be lost. Consequently, the four teachers could schedule four sections of core curriculum activities and set aside a common period to offer the enrichment and remediation opportunities.

FIGURE 1
An Ideal Block Schedule

6th grade teams (or multi-age)	A/A (30)	Core academic subjects/lunch (280)		Exploratory courses individual & team planning (100)
7th grade teams (or multi-age)	A/A (30)	Exploratory courses; individual & team planning (100)		Core academic subjects/lunch (280)
8th grade teams (or multi-age)	A/A (30)	Core academic subjects (100)	Exploratory courses; individual & team planning (100)	Core academic subjects/lunch (180)

minutes in parentheses

The curricular advantages of such an arrangement, as opposed to the conventional "bells and cells" approach, are considerable. Teachers, not administrators, are in control of time. Teams may easily rotate the order of classes, or lengthen or shorten them according to curricular aims and student needs. To cite but three possibilities: (a) the entire block may be used for integrative curriculum or special projects; (b) a science teacher and a social studies teacher might schedule double periods for two different classes on Monday and then exchange these classes on Tuesday for double periods; or (c) team members may decide to shorten their classes to create an extra period in the block to accommodate an outside speaker, a film, or a special event. There are grouping advantages as well. Students not well adapted to a particular group could be changed easily, and special groupings can be formed for short durations for various projects, remediation and enrichment, or interest sessions (Arnold, 1991a).

A vexing problem of block scheduling is the *isolation of "exploratory teachers"* affiliated with core teams from collaborative curricular planning with them. Normally these teachers are unable to attend team meetings because they are with the students while core team teachers are planning. However, through special arrangements they can sometimes attend meetings. Also, they can communicate through circulating team minutes, share curricular goals, and schedule after school meetings (Garvin, 1989). It is highly desirable to involve exploratory teachers in core team curriculum planning, for they bring fresh perspectives, engage students in different modes of thinking, and often design hands-on activities that appeal to different learning styles.

The existence of an ideal structure and well developed policies will not automatically produce desired results. The most important ingredient of all is the *commitment* of team teachers to help young adolescents learn and grow and the willingness to devote the time and energy to make this happen.

In developing an enduring commitment, team teachers need to forge a vision of what could and should be, of what students and teachers are doing at their very best. The next step is for them to discuss frankly how much time and effort they are willing to devote to this vision (e.g. "I want us to meet daily, to discuss kids needs regularly...to really work towards integrative learning...to engage kids in independent studies..."). Finally, team members need to develop specific goals and procedures for putting their vision into action.

Fundamental Principles of Middle Level Curriculum

In developing and implementing curriculum, there are a number of basic principles which should guide practice. While these principles are not unique to teams, teams afford a greater opportunity to employ them in a comprehensive manner.

Middle level curriculum is grounded in *developmental responsiveness*, that is, the notion that curriculum must meet the developmental needs, interests, and abilities of young adolescents. However, the phrase "developmental responsiveness" has in many instances become a mindless cliche, misunderstood and used to justify vested interests or the status quo. Curriculum resulting from this latter mind set is neither developmental nor responsive. The tendency to confuse characteristics which are truly developmental in young adolescents with those that result from social forces especially plagues current curriculum efforts. Thus we see distorted beliefs about hormones and inherent storm and stress resulting in curriculum with excessive control and limited opportunities for student driven learning (Arnold, 1993), and misguided notions about adolescents' limited cognitive abilities and readiness resulting in dummied down, unchallenging curriculum (Keating, 1990).

There are two related, overarching principles that help clarify the meaning of genuinely developmentally responsive curriculum: (a) curriculum must be rich in meaning, and (b) it must relate to the individual differences among young adolescents.

Making the curriculum rich in meaning

First and foremost, middle level curriculum that is rich in meaning *helps young adolescents to make sense of themselves and the world about them* (Arnold, 1985; Beane, 1993). Relative to themselves, they want to understand their bodies, their growth, their sexuality and emotions; their peers, and how to be an individual yet part of a group without losing their souls in the process; their parents and teachers, and how to disagree with authority without breaking relationships; and their competence, and the relationship of fantasies and dreams to actions and results.

Concerning the world, young adolescents want to understand the discrepancy between what adults say and do, how to distinguish shades of grey, why there is so much injustice in the world, the relationship of competition and cooperation, what it means to be grown up, and a host of other topics. We must never submit to views which see 10 to 14 year olds as intellectually inert; they are young philosophers of a sort (Kohlberg & Gilligan, 1971) who are asking profound questions about who they are, what they can become, and what in life is worth committing themselves to.

Helping students to make sense of self and the world emphatically does not mean confining curriculum only to that which is of interest to young adolescents. As Dewey (1938) so forcefully reminds us, we have responsibilities to broaden existing concerns and to create new interests. Teaching is a matter of opening doors, of providing experiences which promote growth and development.

Curriculum that is rich in meaning thus obviously *emphasizes important issues and concepts* (Arnold, 1991b). Content does matter. Seventh graders with minimal skills have read *The Autobiography of Malcolm X* because of its compelling nature. Oakes (1985) found that providing meaningful content is one of the keys to teaching heterogeneously grouped students. Bruner (1960) admonishes us to teach the "structure of a discipline" (i.e., the way things are related, the basic principles which are involved). Teaching structure not only conveys meaning; it aids memory, the transfer of learning to other topics and intuition within and across disciplines.

Perhaps the chief reason for student boredom and disinterest in school is due the trivial nature of much curriculum. Textbooks tend to treat all material as of equal value and many teachers assume it all should be "covered." It is important to note that the official curriculum in most states is not the textbook, but is a published guide, expressed largely in terms of skills and concepts, not specific content. Hence teachers have considerably more flexibility relative to content than they may realize. The best teachers understand that texts and materials are vehicles, not ends in themselves. They select what is important from existing materials or create new ones.

James (1975) emphasized curricular focus on *knowledge, not isolated information*, pointing out that information is external to the learner while knowledge is an internal process that involves perceiving, feeling, thinking, and at times doing. Knowledge emerges from a question-and-answer procedure; content (answer) and process (question) should never be separated. Too often we disjoin content and process by giving students answers to questions they have not asked, thus giving them information, not helping them create knowledge. It is crucial that a considerable amount of curriculum enable students to explore their own questions, engaging them in "first hand knowledge" or direct experience.

None of this implies that the three R's are neglected; rather they are accentuated and made more substantive. In lieu of short reading exercises, grammar lessons, and math drills, students engaged in genuine inquiry are reading real books and articles, writing about their findings, and solving problems they have encountered.

A curriculum rich in meaning *deals effectively with values.* Values in particular are what "hook" students, for they engage students at deep levels, posing the questions, "What do *I* believe about this issue? What is right? Wrong? Why?" However, discussions must avoid the moral relativism that all ideas are of equal value, that morality is simply a matter of personal preference or cultural conditioning. In justifying a position or criticizing that of another, students and teachers must draw upon principles of justice (Kohlberg, 1975; Rawls, 1971). However, teaching students simply to reason about issues of justice is not sufficient (Lickona, 1991). Given the problems of society, it is increasingly apparent that character education – which emphasizes virtues and habits such as honesty, integrity, fairness, and compassion – is necessary if we are serious about creating good people and citizens.

Curriculum which embraces the above principles is to a considerable degree *integrative.* While it is often useful to look at reality through the specialized lenses which various disciplines provide, this fact does not imply that the best way to organize and teach the resulting knowledge to young adolescents is through separate subjects. Most often, life comes to us in terms of questions, problems, and issues. Insight frequently consists of seeing the connectedness of ideas and phenomena. Unfortunately, much that is labeled integrated or interdisciplinary in schools is an artificial pasting together of topics which have little significance for 10 to14 year olds. The key is to develop curriculum which offers the opportunity to create meaning, not simply integrate subjects.

Finally, and most importantly, curriculum rich in meaning *empowers* students by fostering their initiative, responsibility, and ownership by engaging students in curricular goal setting, planning, implementation, and assessment (Arnold (1993). Where this occurs, concerns about students' lack of motivation disappears.

Young adolescents are capable of far more than we imagine. To cite but a few examples: Seventh graders in California wrote and successfully lobbied for legislation which saves the state billions of gallons of water a year, rewrote the procedures for voting in Los Angeles county, and convinced the county to fingerprint all youth so that runaways and kidnapped children could be traced. In Indiana, seventh graders study science by managing the largest animal refuge shelter in the state from their classroom. They perform minor operations and nurse injured animals back to health. In Vermont, students plan, raise money for, conduct all correspondence for, and implement a program in which groups of seven to nine students have traveled annually an average of 40,000 miles for the past 17 years (Arnold, 1990).

Significantly, this two-teacher team from Vermont states, "We begin our teaching with the question, 'Are we doing something that students can do for themselves, and if so, why?'" The goal of adolescence is to become a grown up, and it is impossible to do this without opportunities for initiative and responsibility.

Tailoring the curriculum for individual differences

A cardinal principle of developmentally responsive curriculum is that it take into account the huge differences among young adolescents in the various domains of development. Attention to developmental differences is implied in the curricular principles discussed above; here the focus will be upon cognitive development, which strongly influences social and moral development.

The difficulty in gearing curriculum appropriately to students' *cognitive levels* stems from the fact that they vary dramatically from one another in their capacity for abstract thought. Compounding the problem is that individuals will vary considerably within themselves in this capacity, depending upon the type of knowledge investigated and the context in which it is encountered (Inhelder & Piaget, 1958).

Our inability to match curriculum to students' cognitive levels may well be the most pressing problem in middle level curriculum. There is a strong tendency to move too quickly from concrete to abstract ways of thinking. As a result students often memorize concepts, formulas, or algorithms without understanding the basic principles involved. Many textbooks, especially those in science (Spooner, 1990), are written for readers who can engage in Piaget's formal operational thought, something many middle school students are not yet capable of doing. The fact that less than one percent of all commercially designed curriculum materials have been field tested, based on research by Education Products and Information Exchange Institute (Komoski, 1971), no doubt contributes to this problem. Further, Toepfer and Marani (1978) found that about one-third of all students who had made A's and B's through elementary school made at least one grade of C or less in grade seven. This trend held for students identified as gifted and talented as well as for regular students. They attribute this phenomenon largely to our inability to "pitch it [curriculum] where the kids can hit it," that is, to make things too abstract.

The other side of this coin is failing to challenge students appropriately. Some young adolescents can handle abstract thought to a surprising degree, and many others are capable of it with good instruction. The ability of most Japanese 12 year olds to handle algebra is a case in point.

There is no one test we can administer to give us the information about students' cognitive levels which we need in order to develop curriculum. Teacher observation, reflection, and conversations with students and colleagues are the best diagnostic tools. In general terms, developmentalists agree that to promote cognitive development, four conditions need to be satisfied: (a) a manageable level of cognitive conflict, or need to know; (b) interaction with people or materials; (c) opportunities for role taking; and (d) reflection (Inhelder and Piaget, 1958). More concretely, curriculum must offer numerous options that include a range of hands-on, direct experience, demonstrative, and problem-solving activities. The cognitive level matching program, developed by Shoreham-Wading River Middle School (Fusco, 1984), presents a number of specific strategies for gearing curriculum to students' cognitive abilities.

In addition to variability due to adolescent development, there are other significant individual differences which effective curriculum planning must take into account. *Differences in learning styles* have been conceptualized in terms of student preferences about interacting with their environments along concrete/abstract and sequential/random dimensions (Gregorc, 1979), learning environment (Dunn, 1992), locus of control (Peterson, 1979), brain hemisphericity (Grady, 1990) and other factors. The "4-Mat Program" (McCarthy, 1990) is one of several curricular approaches based upon learning styles.

Gardner (1985) has demonstrated that intelligence is not a monolithic entity. Rather, at least *seven distinct intelligences* exist: logical/deductive, verbal, spatial, kinesthetic, musical, intrapersonal knowledge, and interpersonal knowledge. Our competence in and preference for these various intelligences, plus the unique way we combine them, greatly affects our learning and behavior. Gardner (1991) and others have developed curricular implications of this theory of intelligence. The Key School in Indianapolis, which pioneered Gardner's ideas in grades K-5, has just opened a middle school based upon multiple intelligence theory.

Individual differences related to *race, ethnicity, gender, and socioeconomic status* also have enormous effects on students' interests, needs, goals, and motivation. These differences interact with learning styles and types of intelligences in complex ways. Clearly curriculum that embodies the value of diversity, promotes multiple perspectives for viewing the world, and seeks to stretch students' horizons is essential in light of these differences. Such curriculum enables students to understand and respect themselves, others, and the nature of democratic society (Banks, 1994).

A final area of individual differences that affects curriculum is the enormous variability of *personal interests* among young adolescents. Stevenson (1992), in describing the four children in his family, states the case succinctly:

> While they shared a few family activities and sports interests, their primary schticks were essentially idiosyncratic, even though they were only six years apart. One of them loved mechanical things, another preferred to draw and paint....One was intrigued with mysticism and practiced meditation while another was quite literal and fundamental in terms of spiritual beliefs. One loved and read classical literature, another was immersed in medieval fantasies, another devoured war and sports stories, and one resisted reading anything at all beyond 'how to' directions....Musical tastes included hard rock, opera, reggae, disco and country and western. (p. 170)

Teaching and Learning Approaches

Given this diversity and the principles of developmentally responsive curriculum, it is obvious that business-as-usual approaches to curriculum will not engage students in the kind of learning that they need and deserve. Teachers on teams, acting collectively and individually, need to think carefully about what to teach and how to teach it, be the focus an individual student, a daily class, a particular unit, or a long term project. Such careful thinking may lead to many teachers letting go of a number of conventional assumptions: (a) all worthwhile knowledge is contained in four core subjects and a few electives; (b) teachers must always know in advance what students learn; (c) tests adequately demonstrate what students have learned; and (d) material in textbooks should be thoroughly covered (Stevenson, 1994). To be genuinely developmentally responsive, teachers approach curriculum in a variety of ways that go beyond textbooks, worksheets, and tell-drill-and-test formats.

This section will discuss a number of teaching and learning approaches appropriate for young adolescents. The word "approach" is used because some strategies imply a particular kind of content, others involve teaching methods or learning strategies, and still others are ways of organizing curriculum. In theory, all teachers, be they teamed or non-teamed, could use any of these approaches. However, the implementation of most approaches is potentially enhanced when used by teams.

Integrated studies

Integrated studies afford students the opportunity to explore topics in depth, see connections among ideas, and view learning holistically. Integrating skills and content around themes, issues, problems, and questions comprises the type of curriculum most identified with middle school teams. Because teachers represent various disciplines, have joint planning time, and can flex their block schedule, teaming provides the ideal context for this approach.

There is no correct way to develop integrated studies, nor is there a widely agreed upon terminology to distinguish the various types. Figure 2 represents Brazee and Capelluti's (1995) recent attempt to depict a continuum of strategies which range from simple, teacher-directed approaches to complex, student and teacher-directed efforts.

Figure 2
Continuum of Curricular Integration

----1-----------------------2-----------------3-----------------4------------------5------------

conventional   correlated   interdisciplinary   integrated   integrative

(adapted from Brazee & Capelluti, 1995)

1. *Conventional curriculum* involves no integration; teachers simply teach separate subjects.

2. In *correlated curriculum,* two or more teachers emphasize the same vocabulary words, skills, or concepts on a given day or week. For example, all team members might agree to stress the word "superfluous," the skill of listening, or the concept of ratio.

3. *Interdisciplinary curriculum* is planned by teachers, who teach ideas related to a central theme in their separate subjects. For example, a unit on World War II might involve reading *The Diary of Anne Frank* in language arts, following campaigns on maps in social studies, charting and graphing various statistics in math, and investigating airplanes and principles of flight in science.

4. *Integrated curriculum* is also focused on a theme chosen by teachers but activities related to it are pursued without regard to traditional subjects. For example, in a study of "Unexplained Phenomena," various interest groups might study extrasensory perception, UFO's, the Bermuda triangle, the predictions of Nostradamus, and the Loch Ness Monster. Students may be regrouped from regular classes, and the schedule may often be flexed.

5. *Integrative curriculum,* championed by Progressive Educators and recently rejuvenated by Beane's (1993) seminal work, also pursues themes without regard to subject and uses flexible scheduling and grouping. But it adds a critical element: students are involved with teachers in selecting the theme, planning activities, and in making decisions about time, materials, and assessment. Indeed, the empowering aspects of Beane's work are as important as the integrative ones, if not more so. His approach advocates the exploration of themes that are identified where students' personal concerns intersect important societal issues. For example, young adolescents' concerns about dealing with adults might intersect with the society's concerns about human rights resulting in an investigation of the theme of independence or justice. For pursuing such themes Beane proposes giving attention to personal, social, and technical skills while embracing the values of democracy, dignity, and diversity.

Quite obviously, the skill requirements for teachers escalate rapidly as they advance along the continuum presented in Figure 2. While there are no hard and fast rules, most teams, unless they are comprised of highly accomplished teachers, will find it difficult to *begin* efforts at levels four or five. More likely they will try only a short unit or two the first year, choosing topics that fit in most easily with the conventional curriculum. As they gain confidence and experience working together, effective teams will become more flexible and enlist more student initiative and responsibility. Teachers will find help for planning and implementing integrated studies in the following sources: Alexander, Carr, and McAvoy (1995); Beane (1993); Brazee and Capelluti (1995); Brodhagen, Weilbacher and Beane (1992); Springer (1994); Stevenson and Carr (1993); and Vars (1993).

Independent study

Independent study, one of the most fruitful but least used curricular approaches, allows students, either as individuals or in small groups, to pursue special interests in depth. In so doing, it can furnish enrichment opportunities for gifted students as well as a means of motivation for students who are turned off to schooling. To cite one dramatic example of the latter, I know of a sixth grade boy who received failing grades in all subjects and had been expelled from two schools. Yet he came alive when an enterprising home-bound teacher engaged him in an extensive study of falconry, his major interest, for an entire semester. Allowed to take year-end competency tests at his old school, he passed with flying colors and was promoted to grade seven.

Effective teams which discuss students regularly become well aware of individual student interests. In helping students to develop independent studies, team teachers can share in guiding them, or can enlist the help of exploratory teachers, administrators, parents, or adults in the community (perhaps tied in with an apprenticeship).

The structure for independent study will vary considerably, depending upon the student and the topic selected. In general, it is helpful for student and teacher to develop jointly a contract which specifies goals, activities to be undertaken, time frame, any final products, provisions for help, and means of assessment. Good resources for using independent study include: Kahl (1972), Renzuilli (1985), and Tomlinson (1994).

Minicourses

Minicourses offer students in a group setting opportunities to pursue interests that normally lie beyond the conventional curriculum. Folklore, small engines, tie dying, archaeology, logical puzzles, and chess are but a few of the myriad topics that can be explored.

Because students choose minicourses, motivation often runs high. Moreover, these courses afford teachers the chance to teach something of special interest to themselves beyond their specialty areas. While large teams are able to offer more choices than small teams, any team can increase its offerings by adding parents or knowledgeable people from the community as teachers. Occasionally, a student might lead a short duration minicourse such as model rocketry.

Typically, minicourses run from three to nine weeks and may be scheduled daily, on alternate days, or once a week. In a few schools, teams offer them during the "fifth period" for which team teachers may be responsible either throughout the year or for only a portion of the year. More frequently, teams operating on a block schedule will shorten existing periods, using the time gained to accommodate minicourses. The periodic creation of an extra period for these courses can be a useful strategy to help overcome the "February blahs" or other times of low energy. It is helpful for teams to make an inventory of student interests, which can be used in planning integrated studies and independent study as well as in developing minicourses. Further guidance for developing minicourses can be found in Compton and Hawn (1993), George and Alexander (1993), Stevenson (1992), and Wiles and Bondi (1986).

Teacher advisory activities

Teacher advisory activities provide opportunities for investigating young adolescent concerns and for positive group interaction in an informal setting. Teams can strengthen advisory curriculum through weekly planning sessions. Initially most teams will find that a weekly schedule that balances events that take considerable preparation with those that do not – two days of group activities, and one day each for current events, silent reading/individual conferences, and intramurals, for example – facilitates planning. Since team members can share responsibilities in preparing activities, a team can, over time, develop a repertoire of effective activities. When used judiciously, commercial materials such as Lions Club International's *Quest: Skills for Adolescence* and Alachua County, Florida's *F.A.M.E. Program* (Finding Acceptance in the Middle School Environment), or public television shows such as *DeGrassi Jr. High* and *Wonderworks* are helpful.

The best advisory curriculum, however, results from teacher advisors having meaningful talks with students or leading discussions about topics which interest or concern them. Where good rapport is established, young adolescents are often eager to talk about a school policy, a significant TV show, a disturbing community event, getting along with parents and peers, and a host of other subjects. As advisors grow with experience, they can move away from formally structured activities to more open discussions. Team meetings where colleagues share knowledge about students and advising strategies greatly aid this process as do the ideas in James (1986), and the handbook of Shoreham Wading River (1994).

Special team events

Special team events teach a variety of academic and social skills while building team morale. Team newsletters, plays, musicals, academic competitions, clubs, peer tutoring programs, assemblies, town meetings, recognition ceremonies, holiday celebrations, field days, fairs, camping trips, and career days illustrate a few of the rich possibilities available.

In conventional schools, many of these opportunities are offered as whole school, extracurricular activities that involve tryouts and hence relatively few students. But where teams offer them as special events, student participation is greatly increased (George and Stevenson, 1989; Stevenson, 1992).

Community service projects and apprenticeships

Community service projects and apprenticeships enable students to give of themselves while providing valuable assistance to agencies and individuals. This service is especially significant for young adolescents who grow up in a society where feeling needed is increasingly problematic. In addition, service projects place students in relationships with adults in the real world where they have opportunities for initiative and responsibility that are impossible to duplicate in schools. In these settings students' actions have genuine consequences. An increasing number of schools opt to have all their teams engage students in community service projects, Challenger Middle School in Colorado Springs, Colorado (Andrus & Joiner, 1989), was one of the first. Opportunities for service are virtually limitless. Students may work in nursing homes, senior citizens organizations, libraries, kindergartens and elementary schools, soup kitchens, environmental projects, and fund raisers for various causes. Apprenticeships, where students work under the mentorship of a photographer, electrician, veterinarian, and the like constitute a special type of service opportunity.

It is very worthwhile to connect service endeavors with academics thereby creating service learning opportunities (Erb, 1996; Fand, 1996; Fertman, White, & White,1996; Kurth, 1995; Obert, 1995; Sherman & Banks, 1995). For example, students serving in nursing homes might explore the process of growing and aging; those monitoring pollution in a stream might investigate chemistry and environmental law.

Because service projects are time consuming, wise teams will seek out interested parents to help arrange transportation and coordinate activities. Further, because service projects are so well received in the community, there may be opportunities for grants and donations from local businesses. Help in organizing service projects can be found in The National Center for Service Learning in Early Adolescence (1990); *Phi Delta Kappan* (June, 1991) featured section on youth service; Arnold and Beal (1995); and from Youth Service America, 1319 F Street, NW, Washington, DC 20004.

Intramurals

Intramural activities allow students, regardless of ability, to participate in numerous sports and contests. Thus they circumvent the "star system" of conventional schools, which requires tryouts and cuts those students deemed to have insufficient talent. Intramurals are usually conducted throughout a school but are best organized around teams and advisories. Team teachers serve variously as organizers, coaches, mentors, score keepers, or referees.

Intramurals may encompass traditional team and individual sports, outdoor education activities, cooperative "new" games, and in some schools academic competitions such as quiz bowl, Odyssey-of-the-Mind-type problem-solving contests, or television type game shows. The best programs I know encourage students and teachers to invent games. For example, at Cook Middle School in Winston-Salem, North Carolina (Arnold, 1990), students participate in events such as "Worms Away" where a student using only toes launches worms from a tub while a partner catches them in a bucket; "Nose Roll," where relay teams using their noses, roll a ping pong ball along a ketchup and syrup coated sheet of plastic; and "In Search of the Jello God," where relay teams enter into a wading pool whose liquid contains jello powder, spaghetti and other goodies in search of a rubber glove, bar of soap, hard boiled egg, tennis racket, and dill pickle. Resources for intramurals can be found in *Mid Sports* (newsletter), P.O. Box 207, Pittsburg, KS 66762;

NIRSA: The Journal of the National Intramural Recreational Sports Association, Oregon State University, 221 Gill Coliseum, Corvallis, Oregon, 97331.

In addition to these team-oriented teaching and learning approaches, there are other important strategies that middle level teachers in any type of organization will want to draw upon. Among these are cooperative learning, technology-based learning, simulations, self-improvement studies, book sharing groups, mastery learning, inquiries, learning centers, and field studies. The first two of these approaches deserve special attention. Cooperative learning, the best researched methodology existent, has been shown to be very effective with heterogeneous classes, improving student achievement, (especially with minorities and exceptional students), cooperation, attitude toward school and self esteem (Slavin, 1991). Its small group format, motivational capabilities, and overall effectiveness make it ideal for middle schools.

While technology-based learning has been of some help in providing self-paced, individualized approaches, its content thus far has been disappointing. Yet it has great potential. With on-line and satellite networks becoming rapidly available, students have access to a huge variety of data bases that lend themselves to substantive problem solving and firsthand learning. In addition, students are able to communicate directly with people all over the world; pen pal and mentor relationships are but two of the possibilities (see Whitaker, 1996). On the horizon lie holograms, virtual realities, and "scientific visioning" techniques which may allow students to explore highly complex concepts through visual means.

Summary and Conclusion

Because they provide a more personal, comprehensive, and flexible context, interdisciplinary teams hold enormous promise for developing curriculum that is truly responsive to the developmental needs of young adolescents. In order for this potential to be realized, teams must take the three steps described below:

First, they must work to establish and use organizational structures which facilitate good curriculum. These structures include: (a) joint planning time where student needs and interests and curricular issues are discussed on a regular basis, (b) a flexible block schedule, (c) flexible grouping of students, and (d) collaboration with exploratory teachers. Care must obviously be given to create balanced yet compatible teams. Two- or three-teacher teams seem more capable of developing innovative and challenging curriculum than do larger ones. Multi-age and student-teacher-progression teams add to this potential.

Second, teams must understand and implement the principles of developmentally responsive curriculum. Such curriculum is rich in meaning. Dealing with their questions and concerns, it helps students make sense of themselves and their world. In so doing, it emphasizes substantive issues, values, and skills. It deals with knowledge in an integrative fashion, not with isolated information or subjects. It also takes into account individual differences, including cognitive levels, learning styles, multiple intelligences, and as well as those related to gender, race, and socioeconomic status. Most significantly, it empowers young adolescents by engaging them as fully as possible in planning, implementing, and assessing their own work.

Finally, teams must use a wide variety of teaching and learning approaches in order to meet the diverse needs and interests of their students. Approaches which teams can facilitate in special ways include integrative learning, independent study, minicourses, advisory activities, special team events, service projects and apprenticeships, and intramurals.

Not all teams operate in a structure which optimally facilitates responsive curriculum development. But where educators clearly understand the advantages of such a structure, they can, through re-ordering priorities, changing hiring practices, and re-allocating resources, create it over time.

Further, no one team will be able to master all of these curricular principles and teaching and learning approaches which have been set forth. Yet over time, those who are really serious about meeting young adolescents' needs will develop a large repertoire of effective strategies. Where teachers make a commitment to use developmentally responsive curricular principles, to learn at least one new teaching methodology each year, and to examine other strategies they already know, a great deal can be accomplished.

Engaging young adolescents in stimulating curriculum that fosters knowledge of self and the world, opens new possibilities, and builds good people and a good society is our most pressing concern in middle level education. Teams must be at the forefront of this effort.

References

Alexander, W. , Carr, D., McAvoy, K. (1995). *Student-oriented curriculum: Asking the right questions.* Columbus, OH: National Middle School Association.

Andrus, E., & Joiner, D. (1989). The community needs H.U.G.G.S. too. *Middle School Journal, 20* (5), 8-11.

Arnold, J. (1981). Guidelines for discussing students in team meetings. *Journal of the North Carolina League of Middle/Jr. High Schools, 3,* 25.

Arnold, J. (1985). A responsive curriculum for emerging adolescents. *Middle School Journal, 16* (3), 14-18.

Arnold, J. (Ed.). (1990). *Visions of teaching and learning: 80 exemplary middle level projects.* Columbus, OH: National Middle School Association.

Arnold, J. (1991a). The revolution in middle school organization. *Momentum,* April, pp. 20-25.

Arnold, J. (1991b). Towards a middle level curriculum rich in meaning. *Middle School Journal, 23,* (2), 8-12.

Arnold, J. (1993). A curriculum to empower young adolescents. *Midpoints, 4,* (1).

Arnold, J., & Beal, C. (1995). *Service with a smile: Service learning projects in North Carolina middle level schools.* Raleigh, NC: North Carolina Middle School Association.

Banks, J. (1994). *An introduction to multicultural education.* Boston: Allyn and Bacon.

Beane, J. (1993). *A middle school curriculum: From rhetoric to reality* (2nd ed.). Columbus, OH: National Middle School Association.

Brazee, E., & Capelluti, J. (1995). *Dissolving boundaries: Toward an integrative curriculum* Columbus, OH: National Middle School Association.

Brodhagen, B., Weilbacher, G., & Beane, J. (1992). Living in the future: An experiment with an integrative curriculum. *Dissemination Services on the Middle Grades,* 22 (9), 1-6.

Bruner, J. (1960). *The process of education.* New York: Vintage Books.

Compton, M., & Hawn, C. (1993). *Exploration: The total curriculum.* Columbus, OH: National Middle School Association.

Dewey, J. (1938). *Education and experience.* New York: McMillan.

Dunn, R. (1992). *Teaching secondary students through their individual learning styles: A practical approach for grades 7-12.* Boston: Allyn and Bacon.

Erb, T. (Ed.). (1996). Connecting kids to communities (theme issue). *Middle School Journal, 28* (2), 3-38, 43-57.

Fand, F. (1996). Adopt-a-grandparent program teaches about life. *Middle School Journal, 27* (5), 22-28.

Fertman, C., White, G., & White, L. (1996). *Service learning in the middle school: Building a culture of service.* Columbus, OH: National Middle School Association.

Fusco, E., (Ed.). (1984). *Cognitive matched instruction.* Columbus, OH: National Middle School Association.

Garvin, J. (1989). *Merging the exploratory and the basic subjects in the middle school.* Rowley, MA: New England League of Middle Schools.

Gardner, H. (1985). *Frames of mind: The theory of multiple intelligences.* New York: Basic Books.

Gardner, H. (1991). *The unschooled mind: How children think and how schools should teach.* New York: Basic Books.

George, P. (1988). Tracking and ability grouping: Which way for the middle school? *Middle School Journal, 20* (1), 21-28.

George, P., & Alexander, W. (1993). *The Exemplary Middle School* (2nd ed.). New York: Harcourt, Brace, Jovanovich.

George, P., & Stevenson, C. (1989). The very best teams in the very best middle schools as described by middle school principals. *T.E.A.M.: The Early Adolescent Magazine, 3,* (5), 6-17.

Grady, M. (1990). *Whole brain learning.* Bloomington, IN: Phi Delta Kappa Foundation.

Gregorc, A. (1979). Learning/teaching styles. *Student learning styles: Diagnosing and prescribing programs.* Reston, VA: National Association of Secondary School Principals.

Inhelder, B., & Piaget, J. (1958). *The growth of logical thinking from childhood to adolescence.* New York: Basic Books.

James, C. (1975). *Beyond customs: An educator's journey.* New York: Agathon.

James, M. (Ed.). (1986). *Adviser/advisee programs: Why, what and how.* Columbus, OH: National Middle School Association.

Kahl, D. (1972). A fifth grade moves toward independent study. *Childhood Education, 49* (2), 80-83.

Keating, D. (1990). Adolescent thinking. In S.S. Feldman and C. L. Elliott (Eds.), *At the threshold: The developing adolescent* (pp. 54-90). Cambridge, MA: Harvard University Press.

Kohlberg, L. (1975). The cognitive developmental approach to moral education. *Phi Delta Kappan, 56* (10), 670-677.

Kohlberg, L., & Gilligan, C. (1971). The adolescent as a philosopher: the discovery of self in a post-conventional world. *Daedalus*, Fall, pp. 1051-1086.

Komoski, K. (1971). Testimony before Congressional Subcommittee on Education and Labor, May 11.

Kurth, B. (1995). Learning through giving: Using service learning as the foundation for a middle school advisory program. *Middle School Journal, 27* (1), 35-41.

Lickona, T. (1991). *Educating for character: How our schools can teach respect and responsibility.* New York: Bantam Books.

McCarthy. B. (1990). Using the 4-mat system to bring learning to schools. *Educational Leadership, 48* (2), 31-37.

Nathan, J., & Kielsmeier, J. (Eds.). (1991). Youth service (special section). *Phi Delta Kappan, 72,* 738-773.

National Center For Service Learning in Early Adolescence (1990). *Connections: Service learning in the middle grades.* New York: Author.

Oakes, J. (1985). *Keeping track: How schools structure inequality.* New Haven: Yale University Press.

Obert, D.L. (1995). "Give and you shall receive": School-based service learning. *Middle School Journal, 26* (4), 30-33.

Peterson, P. (1979). Direct instruction: Good for what and for whom? *Educational Leadership. 37* (1), 46-49.

Rawls, J. (1971). *A theory of justice.* Cambridge: Harvard University Press.

Renzuilli, J. (1985). *The schoolwide enrichment model: A comprehensive plan for educational excellence.* Mansfield Center, CT: Creative Learning Press.

Sherman, P., & Banks, D. (1995). Connecting kids to community with survey research. *Middle School Journal, 26* (4), 26-29.

Shoreham-Wading River Middle School (1994). *Advisor's Handbook.* Shoreham, NY: Author.

Slavin, R. (1991). Synthesis of research on cooperative learning. *Educational Leadership, 48* (5), 71-82.

Spooner, W. (1990). Cognitive levels and science teaching. Presentation at North Carolina State University summer curriculum institute, Raleigh, NC, June 27.

Springer, M. (1994). *Watershed: A successful voyage into integrative learning.* Columbus, OH: National Middle School Association.

Stevenson, C. (1992). *Teaching ten to fourteen year olds.* White Plains, NY: Longman.

Stevenson, C. (1994). A baker's dozen of curricular options. Presentation at North Carolina State University summer curriculum institute, Raleigh, NC, June 25.

Stevenson, C., & Carr, J. (1993). *Integrated studies in the middle grades: 'Dancing through walls.'* New York: Teachers College Press.

Toepfer, C., & Marani, J. (1978). School based research. In M. Johnson (Ed.), *Toward adolescence: The middle school years* (79th annual yearbook of the National Society for the Study of Education). Chicago: University of Chicago Press.

Tomlinson, C. (1994). Independent study: A flexible tool for encouraging academic and personal growth. *Middle School Journal, 25* (1), 55-59.

Vars, G. (1993). *Interdisciplinary teaching: Why and how?* Columbus, OH: National Middle School Association.

Wiles, J., & Bondi, J. (1986) *The essential middle school.* Columbus, OH: Merrill.

Whitaker T. (1996). Linking technology with the middle school. *Middle School Journal, 27* (4), 8-14.

Whole Language on the Team

21

Deborah Butler and Tom Liner

It's a sunny Wednesday in March. Ms. Moore's class is bright and alive. Student writing and student made books are displayed everywhere. On one wall a board covered with yellow paper announces, 'Introducing...' and it is filled with students' poems. On the other side of the room a bookcase sags under the weight of journals. Beside it another one is stuffed with paperbacks. Across one wall hangs a row of t-shirts with illustrations and slogans from the books the kids have been reading, **The Outsiders, Tex, The Mouse Rap, The Pigman's Legacy, Summer of the Swans, Hatchet.**

Virginia Monroe sticks her head in the door and looks the group over. Students are already working at the computers in the back of the room or in their journals. Melissa Moore is in one corner looking over the shoulders of a pair of girls at the computer. Virginia announces that she is sending some of her students over to work with this group editing their writings. Some have already left Melissa's room to go downstairs to the computer lab where Linda Clark will make room for them to write in her already crowded class.

Ten students or so wander in with their journals. They quickly disperse into pairs or small groups with the others in the room. There is a buzz of comfortable activity. Two girls near the door sit head to head over one girl's journal. She reads aloud, stops to make a comment or ask her partner's opinion. Then her pencil darts to the page. She reads aloud again. Something strikes them funny, and their laughter dances over our heads. They are just two kids working on their writing and enjoying each other.

A tight group of students cluster around a computer in the back of the room. A boy and a girl sit side by side look-

465

ing at 'Crunch's X-Cape' on the screen. They are editing the dialogue in the story. It's impossible to tell which one wrote the story as they talk. Three other students look over their shoulders and offer advice.

Melissa sits with two girls talking about the story one of them has just read and asked a question about. 'That might work, or you can turn it around,' she comments. Virginia is in the front of the room talking to a student about the memory piece Quanza has written about 'Auntee.' The narrative is about the death of the aunt who raised her, and it makes Virginia cry. She puts her arm around her student and praises her writing. Quanza beams.

Michael and Alfred work on their stories together in the middle of the room. Both journals are open, and they take turns reading aloud and talking about their writing. In a few minutes they go looking for a computer to type a second draft. Michael says Alfred is a 'good partner for editing.' We can't tell which boy came from the low class.

And so the work goes on in these two rooms.

Melissa Moore and Virginia Monroe teach seventh graders at Merry Acres Middle School in Albany, Georgia. They have worked across the hall from each other for several years – and in each other's rooms – with seventh grade students. Melissa teaches English and reading; Virginia teaches science and reading. They do not talk much about teaming really or educational jargon. They talk about the work they do and their kids, and it is obvious watching them that they know the benefits of the learning and growing their students do together. They do not talk much about whole language either; but what is taught in both rooms, together and apart, is always somehow connected.

And that is what is happening in this room; teaming and whole language together help the day stay flexible for the young readers and writers. Both teaming and doing whole language are a natural fit with middle schools and young adolescent learners, as Irvin (1993) has already noted in her enlightening comparison of the two movements.

These are some of the reasons why we believe this. The idea of a unique middle school curriculum is not new. Proponents for a distinct level of schooling in the middle have supported interdisciplinary instruction since the 1930s and interdisciplinary teams since the 1960s. In the 1990s George, Stevenson, Thomson, and Beane (1992) wrote *The Middle School – and Beyond* describing the new and more radical visions of middle level curriculum, ideas being described by middle level educators like Beane (1993), Stevenson (1992), Arnold (1985/1993, 1991/1993), and Capelluti and Brazee (1991/1993). These newer curricular ideas slowly finding their way into middle schools support to an even greater degree flexibility, process approaches to learning, and subject integration. The assumptions behind these curricular reforms seemed very familiar to many of us who had read the whole language literature:

> — *knowledge is constructed actively; it is not sets of isolated information bits;*
>
> — *processes are important – the process of thinking, writing, reading, and of inquiring;*
>
> — *developmental appropriateness is 'where instruction is at';*
>
> — *personal and authentic concerns of young adolescents are central to their educations. The whole of the learning act is important, that is, whole people in natural environments learning about self and others across an integrated day.*
>
> — Butler & Liner, 1995, p. 91

Likewise the whole language movement and process language arts teachers of the 1980s and 90s who base their teaching ideas on Goodman (1986), Graves (1983), Atwell (1987), and now Rief (1992), also built upon earlier ideas, specifically process writing and personal relevance and integration thrusts proposed in the 1970s in the field of English teaching (Liner, 1992). Almost in synchronization with the newer pushes in middle level curriculum, current whole language teachers argue for programs arising from kids and teachers, real books and real writing, not texts and programs. They argue, too, for developing reading and writing skills naturally as kids explore with language what means most to them. In fact, most people would agree that those tenets are the essence of whole language: to connect reading and writing, learning and thinking in all subjects. In essence, to learn naturally with language.

These newer notions of middle level integrated curricula and interdisciplinary teaming can offer structures to relate whole language approaches to everything in the curriculum. They are compatible with natural language classrooms inhabited by Melissa and Virginia and their other colleagues doing whole language with their kids in their own ways in situations you are about to see. In fact, plenty of other teams are discovering the compatibility of teaming and whole language that Melissa and Virginia experience.

Three Vignettes: More Possibilities

These are warm days in April and May when we arrive to see Jenny Froehle and Tony Smarella and their teammates at Lincoln Middle School, a 6-8 middle school in Pike Township in Indianapolis, Indiana. Both teach on seventh grade teams, teams which include core academic teachers and related arts as well as special teachers. On Jenny's team, we have a chance to talk to Suzanne Rauh, the social studies teacher, and Mary Babb, the science teacher, as well as Jenny who teachers language arts. On Tony's team, we have a chance to talk not only with Tony, who teaches science, but with Chris Wilson, and Maggie Daupert who teach social studies and language arts respectively. We had attended the Indiana Middle Level Education Association conference a month earlier and had seen Jenny and Tony in separate sessions where they talked about doing real reading and writing projects, integrated by their respective teams into their academic programs.

    Lincoln Middle School is not a new building; it is an old red brick square, three stories high with a usable basement. It has been added onto many times. Sometimes we talk in the library, sunny and with creaking floors; other times, we talk in a team room in the basement. It too is sunny, flanked by high windows on one side. Always there are kids streaming around us, busy with the day's activities.

Jenny's team: A portrait of beginning reading and writing on the team

    Jenny explains that this year (1993-94) is only the second year that Lincoln Middle School has been teaming. She is this quarter's team leader, as team chairs will rotate in the future. Her team is not only new at implementing authentic language use in the team, but new at teaming also – and perhaps not as far into interdisciplinary work and whole language as Tony's team, or as Melissa's and Virginia's, but just the same, right where they should be. Right now, every teacher on the team has an advisee group and an advisee time period; and they have begun to keep journals (ungraded, of course, but always responded to) in every advisory. Jenny says this helps everyone begin to approach student writing as readers instead of evaluators. Jenny, because she has read people like Atwell (1987) and admittedly bases a lot of her own language arts class on Atwell's ideas of reading and writing workshops, developed scoring rubrics for her classes and to share with the team. These are used by the team to insure consistency in responding to student papers.

As a team, they have begun to talk about student writing in terms of essay questions because this is a form of student writing they all assign in common. "It's a good way, because it is common ground, for all teachers to begin to talk about student writing. We've even tried to establish some common policies for prewriting in exam reviews," Jenny says. Mary shares that right now everyone is trying to encourage peer sharing and peer editing with the various projects within disciplines. Jenny has even offered to help with the evaluation of papers herself to free colleagues from the idea that they must be editors of papers. Apart from the whole team activities, Jenny and Suzanne work more often on joint projects. This year the kids prewrite their topics with Suzanne in social studies, then draft and revise with Jenny in her section. Much of the peer revision goes on during the social studies time.

Every team member focuses on reading real texts in advisory period. Kids are allowed authentic choices of reading. But beyond this, several team members are using trade books in their classes, especially Jenny who does run a reading workshop with her students, and Mary, the science teacher, who encourages students to read science fiction books as they study science with her. She offers them choices from a list and encourages independent reading alongside the subject.

It has been a real two years of learning, they all agree. The first year they spent on the students and student issues; now they are doing more with common instructional goals for whole reading and writing, inservicing and educating each other as Jenny has done this year with her encouragement of process writing and raising awareness by sharing what she does in her whole language classroom and by sharing what she reads and knows. Next year, they will do more: each team member will begin the year with reading workshop classes, and students on the team will begin to keep portfolios of their writing.

Tony's team: A second year means trying out more and trying to get it right

Tony Smarella, the seventh grade science teacher on the other team at Lincoln Middle, may not be his team's chairperson right now, but he has led the movement to team integration of whole writing and reading projects into the curricula. Unlike Jenny's team, Tony's teammates and he are known more for plunging right in and getting their hands dirty with interdisciplinary units, especially ones which involve meaningful reading and writing. In their second year too, the team has already done several interdisciplinary units. In fact, they've redone some from their first year's attempts. Tony and Chris pull down some large newsprint sheets, each having a thematic topic written in the center. Encircling it and branching off in all directions are all the team ideas for doing that integrated unit of study. For every interdisciplinary unit, they plan together this way. And some efforts to incorporate authentic reading and writing projects are shorter than the one we are about to share, like the study of the Africa and Life video, during which all the students kept personal travel journals, as if they were on the trip.

Their major team effort involving writing and reading is what Tony calls the "Interdisciplinary Magazine Project." Before teaming, Tony developed the idea and had the kids writing in his science classes. A believer in process and publication and the power of learning language and content naturally, he brought this idea to the team, shared what he did, and they have now all transformed it into something even bigger, more complex, and more like life.

The team is working on a nine week project done near the end of the year as Maggie, Tony, and Chris explain by turns. Each kid defines a topic; it can be any one of interest; it is their choice – gymnastics, cars, the environment, the Civil War – you name it. They research it, reading from real and varied sources, gleaning the best information they can. Reading the research can take several days. Generally, Tony says, two days a week in someone's class is spent on reading research, gathering data, then later drafting. Usually, this is done in his and Maggie's classes, but not always.

Once the research is done, the kids create their magazines by packaging their research in a writing format that is common to each discipline they study. They might write a short story on their subject from an English perspective or create a glossary, write a technical report from a science viewpoint, or for social studies do surveys on ethical issues using interpreted data to make their points. Mathematically, they interpret some of their research in graphs. Everyone's magazine always includes two to three visual representations as well. "Basically," says Chris, "they take what they've read and learned and shape it to all disciplines." At least one day a week is spent in a writing workshop on this project where kids are readers of their own and their peer's writing.

Tony coordinates a lot of the planning for this. He helps the team generate common guidelines for scoring/evaluating the pieces of writing. It is important that all team teachers are reading from a common vantage point because during the drafting each team member will read papers for reactions – and not always from her or his discipline. Tony will insist on process; they have already discussed the writing process long ago in team meetings. He will coach his teammates on critiquing positively as they read and circulate drafts for kids to rework and revise over the nine-week period.

Does the shared writing work for the whole team? Tony says "We've seen definite benefits. This way (with the magazine project) the whole team sees different types of writing and they get an image of the whole student."

And reading? Like Jenny's team, all of Tony's team has a reading period with the students; and, like the others, students choose their own reading and pursue their reading interests. Like Jenny's team, they are moving kids toward whole reading.

Deborah's team: The team who stays together, does more language together

Lunch for Deborah Bova's team at Creston Junior High, a 7-9 middle school in another part of Indianapolis, is at 11:30 a.m. After their usual quick lunch, by 12 noon the whole team treks up to Deborah's language arts classroom where they share their team meeting time. There are four other teachers besides Deborah on this seventh grade team: Heather Keith, who teaches science; Garmand Sowers, who teaches social studies; Mary Shelton, who teaches math; and Joan Belshwender, who teaches physical education. It is obvious from watching their brief business meeting that they have worked together for a long time, are comfortable and compatible, know each other's strengths and rely on them, work as a collaborative whole, not little parts; in other words, they are one big organism, something other than just the sum of their own selves. It is like the way Melissa and Virginia work to create that naturally interchangeable language learning flow from one class to another.

They all work and talk on two levels simultaneously. They talk about their next plans and the kids, and sometimes they break into personal conversations which weave in and out of the daily planning naturally. There is a lot of joking and teasing and hilarity. You have to be a quick listener to catch it all, this energizing and exciting banter. Today they talk about recent student reports, identifying kids who are having attendance problems. Deborah copies down the names of kids they will need to follow up on; she will take care of this. But finalizing their plans for Earth Day is their key instructional focus today. They have planned an Earth Day celebration which includes the whole team visiting the Indianapolis Zoo for a morning. The proposed activity for the return in the afternoon is primarily a writing, art, and science one. Deborah reminds everyone that the kids will have researched quotes dealing with Earth Day; they will have composed quotes in the classroom and drafted and revised them to perfection (art and writing periods will be used as labs for them to work on this). When they return from the zoo, they will take their compositions and everyone will report outside to the sidewalks where they will, before the rest of the school is dismissed to the buses, write their composed quotes, all revolving around "save the earth," on the sidewalks for everyone to read. Heather reminds everyone she has a recipe for making chalk that is environmentally safe that she got at the National Science Teacher Association convention. Deborah says they do need chalk that is environmentally safe regardless of how they get it. Mary suggests the parent chaperons from the morning be asked to stay on for the afternoon since kids will need more help of all kinds to "publish" their writing. Joan, who has been in charge of organizing permissions and other forms, passes out the parent return slips for the field trip; these forms will take care of getting chaperons as well as providing permission for the kids to leave the school.

Asking them to focus a while on what they do with reading and writing as a team is a natural question for them to answer. As a team, Joan says, they have relied on Deborah to teach them all she knows about whole language. She is their "pivotal point" for reading and writing in their teaming. They have all learned from her; they all see the benefits of doing language naturally and more often. Garmand says he does a lot more writing now that he is teamed than he ever thought about before. Apart from total team projects involving reading and writing, they all involve writing heavily in their subjects even when not doing something interdisciplinary. Mary has all the students keep math journals; this helps them communicate with her about confusions, clarity, thought processes. Joan has the students write about physical education field trips; in health, they write drug-free messages, skits, posters with slogans, or rap verses. Heather works with Deborah on helping the students learn how to write effective essays. In fact, Heather will ask students to write certain kinds of essays as she knows Deborah has worked and will work with kids on these skills. Joan does not even do her essays on sports, like the bowling field trip essays, until she knows the kids have worked with Deborah on comparisons and contrasts and flashbacks. Garmand's start of the year papers on world cultures are all coordinated with Deborah, who long ago knew the language arts workshop classes were flexible places where kids brought their work and drafted and revised and got help in peer and teacher conferences. Call it a "service area" if you like; Deborah still meets her own language arts goals, including teaching the kids how to work in reading and writing workshop, but that just helps this team facilitate integrated learning. The language arts workshop is always a place to read and write and get help on any team project.

Most of their team meetings, usually three times a week, revolve around two kinds of instructional planning. The first is a sharing of what they plan to do within their disciplines, with the others listening and often offering to rearrange their sequences to parallel the teaching of concepts and skills. As Deborah sees it, language arts is the foundation, the homebase instructionally, for all this coordination with language development. Secondly, more and more, their instructional planning has become a brainstorming session around important themes or events they can all contribute to from their curricula and their class times, so that kids study thematically across all their classes. Projects like the Earth Day are jointly planned and handled by every teacher. And there are many more.

Reflections on Teaming and Whole Language

All these four teams are at various stages in their development as teams – and in their development as whole language users within the team's instruction. And that makes a difference in what you see going on with general instruction and whole language instruction in each team. Knowing where to start with infusing whole language approaches throughout the team to some extent depends on how integrated and well-defined as a group the team already is. Nonetheless, everyone in these scenes, regardless of the stage in the teaming process, seemed to think there were some guidelines worth keeping in mind as people begin to deal with language wholly and authentically as teams.

Some guidelines: The absolute necessities

Across the board, team teachers trying to work with authentic language say these are a must:

1. Teams must not only share kids in common, but common planning time and space, too.

These are absolute essentials, the basics if you will. Melissa and Virginia remind us that teaming takes a lot of planning, especially early in the year or the term. Of course, once routines are established and comfortable, the load is lighter; but there still needs to be constant communication and troubleshooting as well as planning. Tony and his team think that planning for the magazine unit needs to be addressed when the team could talk face to face.

Issues such as how to evaluate and react to the drafts of the papers and how to grade the whole project come up in phases and in the ongoing discussion. "There are just too many questions we have for each other; we need to see each other and talk a lot."

Maybe even more important, especially for whole language infusion, is the educational function the team serves. Deborah's, Tony's, and Jenny's team all have learned from sharing with each other about what they each know about their subjects, kids, and developing lifelong skills. Having a regular space and time established somewhere helps this education get done. Thinking that a team can do this kind of intensive day-after-day work on their own time before or after school is just plain silly.

2. There need to be supportive and knowledgeable people in charge, people knowledgeable at least about middle level schooling and middle level learners, if not about whole language.

We think this comes down to the principal. Deborah says that the administration must encourage risk taking and that there needs to be support of the workshop orientation along with the realization that "grammar is no longer queen and literature does include nonfiction." Teresia Wynns, Deborah's principal, has actively supported all their community efforts and involvements for the kids. Melissa and Virginia are not only supported by their principal, but they are encouraged and applauded. Mike Manning takes an active interest in their work. He is often in their classrooms, reading with students, responding to their writings, taking part in groups. His example and enthusiasm go a long way toward making the experience a success. But there are other ways principals help. Jenny says that resources for trade books which support her reading workshop are very important in the beginning movement toward authentic language teaching. Her principal, John Maloy, has been able to provide that. All these principals support a move to a more flexible curriculum, a hallmark of middle level education, and this too is a necessary condition for teaming and whole language to flourish.

3. There needs to be "someone" who is knowledgeable about, and a believer in, whole language and who believes in its power enough to teach the team about it; someone who can begin to lead the team to transforming the curriculum by infusing it.

Joan, Deborah's teammate, was adamant about this: "You need a language arts teacher who brings these ideas to the team and gets everybody affected. That person shares those ideas – and keeps sharing and keeps us moving."

This is why Deborah believes that language arts teachers are the pivotal point of the team, the source for the growth of the most profoundly developmental skills of this age – reading and writing. Tony's team agrees; and, although Tony is a science teacher, he is well educated in language arts – from his colleague Jenny and his own outside reading, experiments in class, and values. He can play that role of pivotal point, the educator and initiator for whole language in team instruction. Virginia, a science teacher and well-grounded in Atwell and Rief, obviously agrees. Regardless of who that "someone" is, Jenny insists that "there needs to be someone very committed to the writing process and whole language approach who's willing to take the heat of the 'what about the eight parts of speech?' questions. That someone needs to be able to explain to colleagues that all of a thirteen year old's struggles to become an adept writer won't be resolved in one ten-month period of team teaching. Keeping people realistic in their expectations is an important job of that someone."

Some guidelines: Getting started

1. Go slowly! There are some prerequisite attitudes necessary for teaming and going with whole language and interdisciplinary approaches.

Even from just looking at the work of these four teams, you would have to infer that there are all kinds of levels of team experience and maturity out there. And how whole language is adopted depends on where the team is in its own development as a team. It takes time for many teams to begin to work well together. People have to come to know each other, begin to trust and respect each other as professionals, as colleagues, as human beings who are trying their best to help young adolescents learn all they can and develop all they can. We like what Jenny says about her team working together: "I would suggest beginning with raising awareness among teammates of how you conduct the writing process in your classroom. Try to speak about and share writing projects so that you show what can be done." There are other steps she suggests too: Share your writing expectations with teammates so that all of you reinforce common standards for writing, perhaps even help develop rubrics for evaluating writings of various sorts, especially since evaluation is often an area that non-language arts teammates are leery of. Essays are a good place to start since almost everyone expects this kind of writing at some point or other. Beyond that, establishing joint writing or reading projects with other teachers where part of the process is accomplished in each class can work as a kind of pilot plan that the whole team can see benefiting kids.

Jenny's teammates echo this movement. "Let it happen naturally," say both Mary and Suzanne. "It's better when it's not a forced activity, but when everyone really comes to see the value of doing reading and writing." Suzanne reflects, "We spent our first year focusing on the students and having the students in common and on getting used to each other and working as a team. We've learned to talk about what does need to happen, what doesn't happen, or what doesn't happen well. We're learning that sometimes we need to jump right in and do something unfamiliar to us, and if it bombs, we just need to try again." These are all attitudes that needed to be fostered before whole language could spread through the team. They are the kinds of attitudes that Tony's team developed early – that ability to openly communicate, that experimental edge that allows the push toward interdisciplinary work and whole language to develop. Tony's team recognizes this: "Everybody has to be sold on the idea (of doing real reading and writing and interdisciplinary projects)," says Maggie. We think they are saying ownership of whole language by the whole team, not just the language arts teacher, is necessary to become a team capable of helping kids develop their language abilities naturally and wholly.

Deborah's approach is a little different. She suggests initiating the reading and writing through a series of "brainstorm bashes." Initially the language arts teacher is on her own; and she lists and notes as many types of reading and writing experiences that she can conjure up, experiences that would occur primarily in other content classes if the teachers of those classes were teachers of language arts as well. If language arts is a workshop class where any writing and reading of the student's choice may occur, as Deborah's is, she can then assure the team members that these kinds of integrated writing and reading can be developed in her class too with her help. Using models of student writing in content areas, helping the teammates with holistic evaluation, and even generating possible rubrics for evaluating help get the reading and writing integrated into the team's curricula. While a different approach from Jenny's or Tony's team, the same underlying features are present – education, a pivotal and knowledgeable teammate who is trusted, and slow building up to success.

2. The Partner Team, a team of two friends, may be the easiest to operate when teaming and whole language are new; it may be easier for many people during the limited time of the school day.

Virginia and Melissa like each other, and they like working together. The two things are not necessarily the same. Across many teams, we see some internal pairs that just seem to naturally fall in together and do projects together. Jenny and Suzanne do this on their team, too. In fact, her advice to establish joint reading and writing projects comes from this natural move. On the other hand, Deborah's team which has worked together for quite a while, seems to move in and out of foursomes, threesomes, and duos quite easily. Sometimes, it just makes sense to pair up and do a language-based interdisciplinary unit with language arts and science, or language arts and social studies, rather than always planning a totally integrated unit. If a team is new working together or working with whole language, it is worth remembering Melissa's and Virginia's experience; when they add a third member to their planning, the planning time doubles. That is not a deterrent, just worth remembering.

3. **Think about starting with writing workshops and get the team involved before tackling reading workshop approaches as well.**

Jenny shared an insight she discovered when she began working with her teammates on reading and writing. It seemed easier to make inroads with writing. Everyone wants their students to write, and no one but the language arts teacher really has a text for language or writing that they must feel tied to using. Freed of a text, and of a pre-made written curriculum guide for writing, teams might feel freer to develop authentic approaches to writing development than reading. This is, of course, dependent on the language arts teacher's having freed herself from any imposed "part by part" writing curriculum! Jenny found that reading is harder somehow. Everyone has a state-adopted text which he feels must be used. With all that money spent on these texts and little left for trade books and other primary sources, it is just tougher for the other content people to handle the entrenchment of texts. Everyone having a session or time where reading can take place helps; it makes everyone a reading teacher. But through their own creativity and models shown by the whole language teacher, reading can become authentic and involving for kids. It just might be slower happening. Do not let it hang you up. Begin where you must.

On the other hand, as Melissa says, teaming does eventually enhance the reading workshop. Teachers share their choices of books to read, often giving a book to an interested student when they finish reading it, and frequently accepting a suggestion from the kids. With two adult book readers in their classroom, more books are shared. When other teachers in other disciplines than language arts share their reading with the group, students have an extra encouragement to read widely. It is not just something you do in reading class or language arts. It is something educated adults do. And that may be the key to the reading workshop.

Some guidelines: Sustaining the flow

1. Be consistent about encouraging the team through continued growth and movement into whole language.

We liked Jenny's thinking about beginning to use whole language in the teaming process. As the team leader for a while and as a language arts teacher all the time, she has delineated some key goals for developing whole language as part of the team's work together. But these goals cannot be achieved all at once since getting started is often slow. Instead, teams might tackle one or two important goals for them each year, slowly realizing all of them only as a more interdisciplinary approach to learning develops over time. For example, Jenny's goals last year were to share knowledge about reading and writing and to gain support from the team for her whole language approaches within the language arts classes. This year, the goals have mainly been to adopt similar approaches to writing across all disciplines, again starting with talking about how they all might help students write better essays, which includes knowing about and coming to value the writing process, and how they might evaluate consistently. Suzanne and she are, in a sense, modeling how authentic reading and writing might be shared by different disciplines on the team. Future goals include educating themselves about portfolios. Her personal goal is for her classes to function as reading-writing workshops related to the other team classes and interdisciplinary projects.

Although Jenny is the first to say that the goals she holds for whole language on the team (Figure 1) are not implemented totally, she has thought through a viable sequence of goals which a team might work toward over time. The important point here though is not only to expect that whole language will *eventually* become the primary way the kids develop their abilities, but the move toward using authentic language projects must be followed up consistently and pushed along to new heights by a persistent, patient "someone." Team teacher growth is as developmental as the young adolescents that we teach. If there was any more doubt about this, all anyone would have to do is sit in on a team like Deborah's and just watch and listen to how they plan and interact with each other. They look purposefully, consciously, for ways to do interdisciplinary instruction together. They do not want to make up unit topics, they purposefully consider themes

FIGURE 1
A Teamwide Commitment to Writing

Philosophy Statement:
Teachers on this team believe that writing is a tool for learning in all classes and that the skills involved in learning to write well are some of the most important skills we can help our students develop for future success.

Goals:
1. We will give students many opportunities for writing and will follow a process (*) model of writing.

   *In other words, no teacher will simply assign a written product, have students write it at home, collect it the next day, and mark it for errors. All teachers on team will reinforce the idea that writers must first go through some prewriting or brainstorming usually in the company of other writers to get ideas for what to write. All teachers will reinforce the idea that students should be given choices and ideas instead of ironclad assignments from teachers. Following the selection of ideas, students should draft, reread or share with others for feedback, revise, edit, and THEN produce a final draft for evaluation and for sharing or publishing. Not all writing projects will go through this process but projects which have not will not be graded as if they are perfect final drafts.

2. We will use writing to learn on a weekly basis to help students reinforce concepts and skills in class.

3. We will give students frequent opportunities for writing projects in all content areas – the message being that educated people in all disciplines need to write clearly and effectively to communicate what they know.

(Figure 1, continued)

4. We will collaborate with one another as we identify writing problems and patterns of errors in our students' written work and will help students eliminate these problems to become clearer thinkers and writers.

5. We will use team funds to publish several books of student writing each year. These will be collections of their best pieces done each quarter in all classes. Final drafts only will be included. Students will illustrate them. They will be bound with covers and placed in all classes for Silent Reading days, free time, etc. Copies will be placed on display in the office, school library, and central administration center.

6. We will develop team rubrics for scoring pieces of writing. Students may assist in developing scoring rubrics for various assignments.

7. Students will be encouraged to revise and resubmit unacceptable written work until it gains an acceptable rating. Time will be provided in language arts class each week to work on revision and editing of work for all classes. Critical analysis of student writing will take place in all classes.

8. Each student will develop, add to, and periodically reflect on a portfolio of written work. Criteria for portfolios are under development. The portfolio will go with the student at the end of the year as evidence of the thinking and learning he/she has done on our team.

based on a number of sources: a team member's curriculum in the discipline and how everyone relates to that, an event that needs highlighting, or kid's personal concerns. For the most part, the more they have looked for the interdisciplinary connections, the more the content of their teaching has become the kids themselves.

2. When the writing workshops work, encourage the reading workshops even more.

Ask that the team consider the reading they do and how they can link it to what goes on with team instruction. Already, Jenny's team uses quite a bit of self-chosen student reading and sharing of books as part of advisory period. Both she and the other language arts teacher, Maggie, use trade books heavily in their reading period. The team makes use of library days and coordinates their efforts to help kids read with that of the school media center. Tony and Chris have used their reading period similarly – to allow kids to read self-chosen books and whole pieces, none cut up and excerpted and put into a text. And Jenny, like Deborah, handles her own elective reading class as a workshop complete with self-chosen, real readings; shared responses; and short lessons when needed. Their own rooms, like Melissa's and Virginia's, are full of trade books that they make time for kids to read and enjoy as a pleasurable act as well as learning from reading and their peers as readers. They are models for future team growth and instructional sharing, models ready for the right time to begin the team dialogue about reading authentically for learning in all subjects or for all themes.

3. Realize and accept the fact that units may take longer to do now that teaming in a whole language environment exists. Not only may your old units take longer, they may actually disappear because there is no longer room or need for them in the curriculum.

This is a fundamental paradigm shift. This shift needs to occur when team members embrace teaming, interdisciplinary units, and whole language. If this happens, continued growth and movement toward whole language and interdisciplinary goals continue. Time and time again, each new team seemed to notice this. Tony's team thought this was some of the most important advice they would like to give others trying teaming and interdisciplinary teaching infused with a great deal of reading and writing. "You need to realize that you must be flexible," said Maggie. "You have to come to the point of not minding giving up some of your specialized content for the over-arching skills, really life skills, that will benefit the kids better. You need to realize that it will take you longer to do other units of your own because of the time all this takes, but the benefits are worthwhile to the kids." Jenny and her team agree totally. Jenny says, "Sometimes the team must abandon some of their favorite content in order to make authentic reading and writing activities part of their instruction. But that's all part of a natural conclusion that writing and reading are the most essential life skills kids can develop and that we can all help them develop. We are all becoming reading and writing teachers."

It takes time to grow into this identity, but teams who have been together longer, like Deborah's and Melissa and Virginia, know that assuming this identity enhances who you are as a content area teacher, not that you give up one identity as a teacher for another.

4. Continuing to educate each other is absolutely necessary!

Not only does that important "someone" introduce and share what whole language is, modeling how powerfully it works to develop middle graders' language abilities, but she keeps sharing, as do the other team members as the team continues to work together. None of us ever stops learning; we all continue our professional development. We attend professional meetings (nearby or far away, in our disciplines or in general), or we take classes, or read good things about teaching. The team cannot stop bringing up and discussing fresh ideas, fresh ways of doing things. More and more discipline areas boast sessions at national and regional and state meetings about writing and reading and their powerful relationship to each discipline. Everyone has a chance to increase the whole team's ideas – as long as the team continues to plan time to educate each other, reads and talks together, and risks and tries things. Jenny's teammates mentioned two very important corollaries to this continued education process: Suzanne said, "Anyone should expect this to be a messy process. When something fails, you need to just jump in and try it again. It isn't going to be perfect all at once." And Jenny follows, "A team needs to be willing to confess areas of individual discomfort with new procedures and to be open about this and talk it out." If, as the team continues to work together, these attitudes of openness and frankness can evolve into a positive status quo, then the team works for the benefit of teachers and kids.

A Few Cautions

It is not always easy to move toward a transformation from a teacher on a team to a teaching team and then to a whole language team. Experienced team leaders offer a few cautions along the way:

1. **Avoid coming on too strong when you begin to share ideas about whole language with the team.**

   Non-language arts colleagues are sometimes unsure of themselves as teachers of reading and writing, so collaboration on initial projects often helps teammates over their anxieties. First of all, we can all avoid making teammates feel that they have to single-handedly pull off a written project in their classes from beginning to final draft and grade it in order to encourage the writing process, or that they have to throw all texts out the window and create every bit of reading from their own pockets or the students'. Deborah thinks that team colleagues need the reassurance they will not be abandoned. Especially at first, experiences with writing and reading authentically need to be positive. You do not want colleagues feeling like whole language is a horrible thing, and that they should do text and worksheets after all!

2. **Involve your principal regularly in planning.**

   If it is at all possible, the principal should come to team meetings, especially when whole language projects are being discussed. Making sure she comes to see classes, even to work with students, is important, too. After all, the principal must be able to explain to parents why the science or math teacher assigns so much writing and why grammar texts are not coming home with their students.

3. **Communicate with parents about new teaming efforts and projects. Be especially clear with students and parents about how grades are determined**.

   Many teams already send home a team produced newsletter or heavily involve parents in projects or in field trips. Some also do a lot of detailed explaining about their teaching and team projects at open houses, or they send introductory letters home. Whole language in the team's rooms demands communication. Parents need to know what goes on in a whole language classroom; they need to see the rubrics for evaluating portfolios, for instance. Indeed, they need to read their own child's portfolio and comment and share in and promote their language growth. Melissa and Virginia at Merry Acres Middle School have parents involved in writing response groups and reading groups. Parents also help with the publishing. Do not hesitate to invite your parents into your classrooms.

Final Thoughts: In Its Broadest Sense, Teaming is Whole Language Instruction

As members of all these teams are coming to experience, language is whole in all of our learning efforts, no matter what the discipline. We do not usually read about reading (only language arts professionals or philosophers do that at all). Nor do we write ordinarily about writing, let alone language itself. We use language to learn, as well as to communicate. What is more natural than putting language together with the other subjects in the school day? While these portraits and thoughts on how to create positive alternatives may help many more teams use language more naturally, this is not our only goal. When whole language pervades the interdisciplinary team, wonderful implications for fully integrated curriculum occur. Teachers discover they have common roots, regardless of their specialist training.

But just as important, the whole language permeation in the team structurally curves back into the discipline. On Deborah's team, Heather, the science teacher, now takes time to get the kids ready to read at the early part of the year. They begin to read the text together; she teaches them the tools for reading by modeling, gradually letting them read for meaning on their own. Garmand is clear about it; he knows he now does far more writing in his classes since he has been part of a team than he ever did before.

But this kind of dual transformation of the curricula – both the interdisciplinary one and the disciplines themselves – takes a while to develop. But in the end, language and teaming working together in the middle school offers middle level students the best in literacy and thinking that we can afford them.

References

Arnold, J. (1993). A responsive curriculum for young adolescents. In T.S. Dickinson (Ed.), *Readings in middle school curriculum: A continuing conversation* (pp. 21-31). Columbus, OH: National Middle School Association. (Reprinted from Arnold, J. (1985). A responsive curriculum for early adolescents. *Middle School Journal, 16* (3), 3, 14-18)

Arnold, J. (1993). Towards a middle school curriculum rich in meaning. In T.S. Dickinson (Ed.), *Readings in middle school curriculum: A continuing conversation* (pp. 63-72). Columbus, OH: National Middle School Association. (Reprinted from Arnold, J. (1991). Towards a middle level curriculum rich in meaning. *Middle School Journal, 23* (2), 8-12)

Atwell, N. (1987). *In the middle: Writing, reading, and learning with adolescents.* Upper Montclair, NJ: Boynton/Cook.

Beane, J. (1993). *A middle school curriculum: From rhetoric to reality.* (2nd ed.). Columbus, OH: National Middle School Association.

Butler, D., & Liner, T. (1995). *Rooms to grow: Natural language arts in the middle school.* Durham, NC: Carolina Academic Press.

Capelluti, J., & Brazee, E. (1993). Middle level curriculum: Thinking sense. In T.S. Dickinson (Ed.), *Readings in middle school curriculum: A continuing conversation* (pp. 143-151). Columbus, OH: National Middle School Association. (Reprinted from Capelluti, J., & Brazee, E. (1991). Middle level curriculum: Making sense. *Middle School Journal, 23* (3), 11-15)

George, P., Stevenson, C., Thomason, J., & Beane, J. (1992). *The middle school—and beyond.* Alexandria, VA: Association for Supervision and Curriculum Development.

Goodman, K. (1986). *What's whole in whole language?* Portsmouth, NH: Heinemann.

Graves, D. (1983). *Writing: Teachers & children at work.* Exeter, NH: Heinemann.

Irvin, J. (1993). Lessons learned from the whole language movement: Parallels to curriculum reform. In T.S. Dickinson (Ed.), *Readings in middle school curriculum: A continuing conversation* (pp. 207-211). Columbus, OH: National Middle School Association.

Liner, T. (1992). Curriculum or curricula? Language arts and crafts in middle schools. *Midpoints, 3* (2), 1-12. Columbus, OH: National Middle School Association.

Rief, L. (1992). *Seeking diversity: Language arts with adolescents.* Portsmouth, NH: Heinemann.

Stevenson, C. (1992). *Teaching ten to fourteen year olds.* New York: Longman.

Inclusion and Teaming: Including All Students in the Mainstream   **22**

Chriss Walther-Thomas

Many school systems are replacing traditional special education services with more "inclusive" models of support designed to help students with disabilities to perform successfully in mainstream environments (Bauwens & Hourcade, 1995; Stainback & Stainback, 1990; Wang & Birch, 1984). Inclusive approaches provide specialized instruction and classroom support without removing students from general education classrooms (Sailor, Anderson, Halvorsen, Doering, Filler, & Goetz, 1989; Thousand, Villa, & Nevin, 1994). Inclusive models use various structures to facilitate teaming among professionals and students (e.g., peer consultation, teacher assistance teams, cooperative learning groups, buddy systems, co-teaching) (Bauwens & Hourcade, 1995; Laycock, Gable, & Korinek, 1991; Slavin, Karweit, & Madden, 1989). Effective inclusive support models are designed to provide help for all students. Consequently, these approaches provide help for many students with unmet academic or social needs; students who may be deemed "at risk" for school failure but for whom few resources exist. These are students of great concern to educators because they are the ones who frequently "slip through the cracks" without receiving any special attention or support (Giangreco, Cloninger, & Iverson, 1993; Ornstein & Levine, 1989; Slavin et al., 1989; Williams, 1992). This chapter will review factors that have led to recent changes in special education and the development of inclusive education support programs. Characteristics of inclusive schools and collaborative support structures will also be described. Finally, basic inclusive program planning considerations within schools that are already organized into interdisciplinary teams will be presented.

Middle schools are well suited for the implementation of more inclusive special education programs (Walther-Thomas, in press; Walther-Thomas & Carter, 1993). The existing organizational structure of most middle school programs facilitates professional teamwork, collaboration, and peer support (Erb & Doda, 1989; George, Stevenson, Thomason, & Beane, 1992; Lipsitz,

1984). Unique features such as interdisciplinary teams, flexible scheduling, and common planning periods provide ongoing opportunities for professionals to work together to design and deliver innovative support programs for students (Cawelti, 1988; Mac Iver, 1990). In addition, many middle school professionals share a philosophical commitment to help their students develop skills across many dimensions. This philosophy motivates teams to find effective ways to work together to meet student needs (Erb & Doda, 1989; George & Stevenson, 1989).

Special education law and the least restrictive environment

Passage of P.L. 94-142 in 1975 was a landmark in public education. This law, now known as the *Individuals with Disabilities Education Act* (IDEA), represented the culmination of many years of litigation and legislative action on behalf of students with disabilities. It guaranteed these students the right to free and appropriate public education. A key feature of this legislation was the provision for education in the "least restrictive environment" (LRE) in which students with disabilities could learn successfully (Danielson & Bellamy, 1989; Turnbull, 1993). Many advocates and educators assumed that, for most students with disabilities, the LRE would be the educational mainstream (i.e., general education classes). Success in these environments would be facilitated by the help of support specialists (e.g., special educators, reading specialists, counselors, bilingual teachers, consultants, interpreters, speech/language specialists, paraprofessionals) and the use of various classroom accommodations (e.g., taped text books, study guides, calculators, extended time for tests).

However, most states did not interpret the LRE component as a mandate for greater inclusion of students with disabilities in mainstream classrooms (Snell & Janney, 1994). More than 15 years of state and federal data have shown that most systems use many traditional "pull-out" placement options (e.g., individual therapy sessions, resource rooms, self-contained classrooms) that fit their pre-IDEA patterns of service delivery (Danielson & Bellamy, 1989; United States Department of Education (USDE), 1994). The "resource room" model has long been the most popular pull-out option (USDE, 1994). Typically, students with mild to moderate disabilities are assigned to mainstream classrooms for most of the day. During a portion of the day, however, they leave their home base classrooms and attend special resource classes designed to meet their unique learning needs.

Intervention data have shown that most resource programs have not been effective sources of support and skill remediation for students with disabilities (Bickel & Bickel, 1987; Carlberg & Kavale, 1980; Shephard & Smith, 1989; Wang & Birch, 1984; Will, 1986). These models failed to provide students with adequate help because, in part, most schools lacked the essential mechanisms that would have enabled professionals to communicate effectively with each other (Will, 1986). Few schools provided professionals with regularly scheduled time to coordinate their instructional activities and monitor student progress. Reynolds (1989) has noted that general educators and special educators rarely know what students with disabilities are learning outside their own classrooms. Minimal contact has also made it impossible for specialists to understand the daily classroom setting demands (e.g., homework requirements, weekly testing procedures, participation expectations) and provide students with adequate support and skill instruction needed to succeed in these environments (Wang & Birch, 1984).

It is not surprising to find that most students with disabilities continued to perform poorly in school after their disabilities were identified and special help was provided (USDE, 1987; Sansone & Zigmond, 1986). For example, one study of 26 large city school systems found that fewer than five percent of all identified students ever resumed full-time general education participation (USDE, 1987). Poor results from special education intervention programs have led some researchers to suggest that many students, especially those with mild disabilities, might have done as well if they had remained in their mainstream classrooms without any special assistance (Carlberg & Kavale, 1980; Lipsky & Gartner, 1989; Reschly, 1988; Reynolds, 1989; Wang & Birch, 1984).

Critics of current practices have also raised concerns about the damaging side effects created by the student "labeling" process (Coles, 1988; Gartner & Lipsky, 1987; Hagerty & Abramson, 1987; Stainback & Stainback, 1984; Will, 1986). Poor academic and social skills performance, compounded by the stigma associated with a disability label, all contribute to feelings of social isolation and inferiority that many students with disabilities experience (Coles, 1988; Lipsky & Gartner, 1989).

Pull-out models have limited opportunities many students with disabilities have had to interact with peers and develop more appropriate social skills. The movement in and out of the classroom by students involved in pull-out programs is often confusing for students themselves, their teachers and their peers. Daily disruption in the classroom routine easily interferes with identified students' participation in classroom activities and small group work. It can also contribute to misconceptions about students with disabilities and may limit their opportunities for friendship development (Stainback & Stainback, 1990).

By the time many students with disabilities reach the emotionally-charged years of middle school, participation in special education has become a source of painful embarrassment. School, at best, is often an unpleasant experience. Their confidence, motivation, and willingness to take on new challenges are all waning. Consequently, many students with disabilities, particularly those with mild disabilities, leave public schools prematurely (Edgar, 1987; USDE, 1987; Wagner & Shaver, 1989). Follow-up studies, conducted after these students leave school, have shown that many former students are ill prepared for the demands of adult life (Wagner & Shaver, 1989). Many young adults with disabilities lack critical academic, vocational, and social skills that are needed for independent adulthood (Edgar, 1987, 1988; Goodlad & Lovitt, 1993; Haring, Lovett, & Smith, 1990; Sitlington & Frank, 1990).

Prevalent special education models have fostered "two track" thinking among most public education professionals (Gartner & Lipsky, 1987; Stainback & Stainback, 1984; Will, 1986). Despite the mandate for LRE learning for students with disabilities, prevalent practices have encouraged general educators to continue focusing their teaching efforts on the skill development of typical students, while special educators have educated students with disabilities. This dual approach has perpetuated educational segregation, social stigma, and inferior learning experiences for students with disabilities (Gartner & Lipsky, 1987; Stainback & Stainback, 1984; Wang & Birch, 1984; Will, 1986).

Mounting concerns about the quality and efficacy of prevalent special education practices have led many professionals and families to conclude that there must be better ways to educate students with disabilities (Bauwens & Hourcade, 1995; Gartner & Lipsky, 1987). Since the early 1980s many school systems have initiated inclusive education programs designed to ensure that students with disabilities are *included*, not excluded, in the mainstream of public schools.

Inclusive Education Students with Disabilities

Characteristics of inclusive schools

Inclusive support services are developed and implemented by general educators and support specialists who work together to solve learning and behavior problems and implement appropriate support strategies (Bauwens & Hourcade, 1995). Inclusive support teams provide help for students with disabilities without segregating them from their peers and without calling special attention to their disabilities (Snell & Janney, 1994). These programs also provide help for other students. Consequently, these models are supported by many general educators and administrators who are frustrated by demands for greater academic excellence at a time when the number of students struggling to grasp basic concepts is growing (Bauwens & Hourcade, 1995; Carnegie Forum on Education and the Economy, 1986; Cuban, 1990; Howe, 1988; Shephard & Smith, 1989; Snell & Janney, 1994; Stainback & Stainback, 1984; Toch, 1984).

To guide the development of inclusive education programs, many state and local decision-making teams have defined "inclusive schools." Recently, the Colorado State Department of Education Special Education Service Unit (CSDESESU) developed the following definition that contains many characteristics found in other inclusive school definitions (Giangreco, Cloninger, Dennis, & Edelman, 1994; Snell & Janney, 1994; Stainback, Stainback, & Jackson, 1992; Thousand et al., 1994):

> *Inclusive school communities are those in which all students are valued members of the educational environment. All students have access to and participate in opportunities within the school and community at large, based on their needs. General and special educators within the building are prepared to teach all student members within the school community; supports and resources are available to maximize successful teaching and learning experiences. The school community is aware of and maintains responsibility for all of its student members including those who may currently be learning in settings other than the neighborhood school.* — CSDESESU, 1994, p. 1

The Colorado definition provides a useful framework for a brief examination of some characteristics commonly found in inclusive schools. As decision-making committees consider the development of more inclusive education for students with disabilities, it is important to assess local interests and determine whether or not adequate resources exist to support new program development efforts.

1. Inclusive school communities are those in which all students are valued members.

Inclusive classrooms and inclusive schools are genuinely supportive *communities*. There is a strong emphasis on the development of meaningful relationships within these settings. Learning programs are designed to create a sense of belonging for the students and adults who work in these environments (Stainback, et al., 1992). Inclusive schools are places where "...everyone belongs, is accepted, supports, and is supported by his or her peers and other members of the school" (Stainback & Stainback, 1990, p. 3).

2. All students have access to and participate in opportunities within the school and the community.

Traditional schools operate under the assumption that it is the student's responsibility to "fit" into existing academic and social structures. Inclusive schools design challenging programs to fit the unique needs of all student participants, regardless of their ability levels (Giangreco et al., 1994; Lusthaus & Forest, 1989; Putnam, 1993; Snell & Janney, 1994; Stainback, et al., 1992; Wang, 1992).

Typically, all of the students in inclusive classrooms study the same content, however, their learning goals, individual assignments, and course materials (e.g., textbooks, exams) may vary to meet individual needs. For example, Alex is a sixth-grade student with severe cerebral palsy. He has limited mobility, poor fine motor skills, and poor speech. He is also very bright, reads well, loves science, and is highly skilled with computers. When his class studied new recycling project at a nearby park Alex was a valuable member of his cooperative learning group. While he was unable to gather recycled materials in the park, he recorded data on the computer that the other members found. While he was unable to present part of his team's oral report to the class, he created a useful graphic that summarized the key points of their report on glass recycling, and wrote the introduction that another team member read orally for him. Because it takes Alex longer to write his answers than it takes many of his peers, his teachers gave him part of the final unit exam on a diskette that he completed as a take-home assignment.

3. General and special educators are prepared to teach all student members within the school community.

Staff development is a high priority in inclusive schools. Classroom teachers and support specialists may need some additional skills to team effectively with others in inclusive settings or to provide appropriate technical assistance for students.

Professionals who work well together in inclusive classrooms do not think of students in terms of "these are mine" and "those are yours;" instead, they share a commitment to provide appropriate learning experiences and support for all students (Lusthaus & Forest, 1989). Consequently, teachers share their available resources to provide students help without regard to their labels or special designations (CSDESESU, 1994; Giangreco et al., 1994; Putnam, 1993; Stainback et al., 1992). To increase their collective knowledge base, they also share their professional knowledge and expertise willingly with others. Recently, a sixth grade language arts teacher described her experiences working in an inclusive classroom with a special educator:

> During the past two years we've learned a lot from working together two periods a day. In the beginning we found that we looked at learning very differently. On one hand, I'm really good at painting an exciting 'big picture.' I can provide good content and I understand normal learning expectations. I'm also experienced at setting a reasonable pace so we can cover the required material before the end of the year. Mary Anne, on the other hand, is great at filling in the important details in my big picture. She anticipates problems and is constantly coming up with good strategies to help the kids grasp the material more quickly. Together we think we're pretty hot! We've developed a co-teaching routine that works for our students. We've told a lot of people we are **much** better teaming together than we ever were when we were teaching alone.   — Walther-Thomas, 1994

4. Supports and resources are available to maximize successful teaching and learning experiences.

Administrative leadership is an essential part of effective and lasting programs that are introduced in schools (Cook & Friend, 1994; Fullan 1991; Huberman & Miles, 1984; Snell & Janney, 1994). Ongoing division and building level administrative participation helps ensure that the professionals have the support and essential resources needed to provide appropriate support services for students (Cook & Friend, 1994).

In inclusive settings, one important administrative function is leadership in the development of classroom rosters. Special education students should be assigned general education classrooms according to the natural proportions that exist in society. Loosely translated, this means that 15 to 20% of the students (i.e., four or five students in a class of 26) may have identified mild to moderate disabilities. Because of the significant needs of students with more severe disabilities, it is generally accepted that only one of these students should be assigned to a given classroom (Giangreco, et al., 1994).

Students with disabilities, especially severe disabilities, constitute a small proportion of the general population (USDE, 1994). If students with disabilities attend their own neighborhood schools, then reasonable numbers of students with special needs can be assigned to any given school's support providers. Building level administrators can support neighborhood school attendance by welcoming students with disabilities who live within their school's boundaries and by encouraging their administrative colleagues to do the same (Snell & Janney, 1994).

Administrative involvement protects the rights of all students to appropriate education. By understanding and supporting the goals of inclusive programs, administrators can make program development a high priority in their schools rather than merely another "add on" event. Existing resources can be channeled to ensure that classroom teachers and support specialists have the tools they need (e.g., common planning time, staff development opportunities, visible administrative support, classroom aides) to create effective learning environments for heterogeneous groups of students (Snell & Janney, 1994).

Inclusive support teams that lack administrative participation often operate without critical resources. One common problem in these settings is the excessive "weighting" of classrooms where inclusive specialist support is available with students needing special assistance. Classrooms that become "too needy" undermine the professionals' work and negatively affect the learning experiences of all students (Giangreco, et al., 1994). In these settings the basic goals of inclusion are compromised and low-achieving educational ghettos are created in the process (Bauwens & Hourcade, 1995).

It is important to note that some inclusive high school classes may reflect less heterogeneity than what is possible in elementary and middle school classrooms. This is due to content offered in these courses. Based on the student's long-term goals and unique learning needs, participation in college preparation, vocational, or remedial course offerings may be appropriate. Classes aimed at low-achieving students on functional program plans (e.g., English I, consumer's math, practical writing) are likely to have more needs and will reduce additional support.

5. Inclusive school communities are aware of and maintain responsibility for all students including those who may currently be learning in settings other than their neighborhood schools.

Much like tossing a pebble in a pond and watching its impact create ripples across the surface, changing special education services in one setting is likely to create "ripples" that will extend far beyond single classrooms or individual schools. For example, if middle schools develop inclusive education opportunities for students with disabilities, how will this affect high school programs? Initially, many school divisions sponsor small pilot programs to test various inclusive support models. While small pilot projects have many merits, they also limit the number of students with disabilities who can participate. How will families, students, and professionals feel about this cautious approach? Planning teams need to anticipate possible questions and concerns professionals and families will have and develop an action plan that addresses issues and minimizes potential problems (Snell & Janney, 1994).

6. Inclusive education programs are effective learning environments.

Finally, inclusive communities are good places to learn and work. This important dimension of inclusive schools is implied but not directly addressed in Colorado's definition. Inclusive classrooms are creative and supportive learning environments where many instructional strategies and natural support structures are used to increase student confidence, motivation, and performance (Bauwens & Hourcade, 1995; Giangreco & Putnam, 1991; Putnam, 1993; Slavin et al., 1989; Stainback et al., 1992; Wang, 1992).

In a three-year study of co-teaching teams, classroom teachers and inclusive support specialists reported numerous benefits for themselves and their students as a result of participation in these inclusive settings (Walther-Thomas, in press). Teachers indicated that their participation provided them with increased professional growth, colleague support, professional camaraderie, and greater professional satisfaction as a result of increased student performance. Participants reported that their general education students benefited in the following ways: low-achieving students improved their academic performance, all students showed increased levels of awareness and acceptance of diversity, there were high levels of demonstrated support for one another, and improved social skills. These students also had positive experiences nurturing and supporting others and received more individual teacher time and attention. Students with disabilities also made improvements in self-esteem, social skills, content knowledge, and peer relationships. Teachers also reported that these students showed greater confidence in their academic abilities (Walther-Thomas, in press).

Collaboration in inclusive education programs

Schrage (1990) has described collaboration as "...the process of shared creation: two or more individuals with complementary skills interact to create a shared understanding that none had previously possessed or could have come to on their own" (p. 40).

Working together as inclusive support teams, classroom teachers and support specialists use their complementary skills and knowledge to plan, implement, and evaluate classroom support services and specialized instruction that benefits all of the students in their classrooms (Bauwens & Hourcade, 1995; Friend & Cook, 1992; Idol, 1989; Laycock et al., 1991; West & Cannon, 1988). Innovative instructional plans, practice ideas, and solutions to problems emerge from these collaborative efforts that reflect greater creativity and are more comprehensive than any one participant could have crafted on his or her own.

While general and special educators are frequently paired as primary collaborators in inclusive schools, many schools involve other members of the school community in direct and indirect classroom support activities (Bauwens & Hourcade, 1995; Sailor et al., 1989; Stainback & Stainback, 1990). Active participation by the administration, professional staff, and community (e.g., parents, retired teachers, college students) ensures greater classroom support, facilitates communication, and provides a framework for the development of a genuine learning community (Sailor et al., 1989). Broad-based support mechanisms also reduce the likelihood that too many students with learning and behavior problems will be assigned to a small number of classrooms in which special education teacher support is provided. By designating all professional staff members as potential classroom support specialists, the groundwork is laid for a strong network of collaborative relationships. Administrators facilitate the development of these relationships by providing support mechanisms and monitoring and reinforcing the teamwork that occurs.

Collaborative classroom support structures

Helping students perform well and feel good about themselves as learners are important goals in inclusive classrooms (Giangreco et al., 1994; Putnam,

1993; Stainback et al., 1992). Various accommodations and modifications, learning strategies, and collaborative learning and teaching structures are used to achieve these goals (Bauwens & Hourcade, 1995).

Many helpful modifications can be provided that require minimal teacher time and attention. Sometimes minor adjustments in classroom routines can improve both behavior and academic performance. Typical examples of low-level accommodations or modifications include preferential seating, daily homework assignments written in a box on the board, extended time on unit vocabulary tests, and the use of taped textbooks. Working together classroom teachers and support specialists can identify appropriate accommodations and modifications and supervise their implementation. Teams are encouraged to select the least intrusive accommodation that works. By doing so, greater student independence is provided and valuable teacher preparation and implementation time is preserved. When more extensive modifications are required (e.g., adapted unit study guides, behavioral contracts, daily home-school notes), the inclusive support team should divide the required preparation, implementation, and monitoring responsibilities fairly. These modifications are not just the responsibility of the classroom teacher.

Middle school students are excellent candidates for learning strategies and study skills instruction (Gaskins & Elliot, 1991; Rafoth, Leal, & DeFabo, 1993). These valuable learning tools can improve student performance during the middle school years and can prepare low-achieving students and their peers for challenging learning experiences ahead in high school and post-secondary education (Deshler & Schumaker, 1988; Rafoth et al., 1993; Thousand et al., 1994). Some of the appropriate strategies and skills students should develop during middle school include social skills, test preparation, notebook organization, reading and listening comprehension, paraphrasing, and proofreading papers (Deshler & Schumaker, 1988; Gaskins & Elliot, 1991; Rafoth et al., 1993). As classroom teachers teach new content (e.g., new science vocabulary words), support specialists can teach new strategies (e.g., mnemonics for remembering vocabulary words). Together, professional teams supervise and reinforce prompted and independent use of appropriate strategies and skills.

Many instructional procedures used in inclusive classrooms focus on collaborative work by students with each other. Use of natural support structures encourages relationship development among students and academic learning simultaneously (Giangreco et al., 1994; Stainback & Stainback, 1990). These procedures accommodate individual differences in both skill proficiency and learning abilities that are present in these classes

(Giangreco & Putnam, 1991; Harper, Maheady, & Mallette, 1994; Putnam, 1993; Schrumpf, Crawford, & Usadel, 1991). Support structures frequently used in inclusive schools include cooperative learning groups, peer buddy systems, multi-age student activities, thematic instruction, peer tutoring, and peer mediation.

Development and delivery of appropriate learning activities are the results of productive teamwork by participating professionals in inclusive settings (Morsink, Thomas, & Correa, 1994). Many teams use recognized collaborative structures to facilitate their work together (Laycock et al., 1991). These structures offer participants a wide range of possible interaction patterns. For example, many inclusive classroom teachers and specialists participate in daily co-teaching with others (Bauwens & Hourcade, 1995). Other teacher-specialist pairs engage in weekly collaborative consultation sessions in which they monitor progress, discuss student concerns, and plan appropriate interventions (Dettmer, Thurston, & Dyck, 1993; Morsink, Thomas, & Correa, 1994). Some schools also offer staff members help from designated teacher assistance teams (TAT) (Chalfant & Pysh, 1989). TAT teams are composed of master teachers who work together to provide assistance for teachers requesting help dealing with persistent learning or behavior problems.

Cooperative teaching in inclusive classrooms

A popular staff development exercise illustrates some of the fundamental problems school professionals often experience as they work together in inclusive settings. Participants are asked to select partners and then draw an imaginary line between them. Next, the session leader explains that a prize will be awarded to the first participant who can persuade his or her partner to cross the line without using any physical force. For the next minute or two, participants offer an interesting array of pleas, threats, bribes, and promises to their partners but very few move across their lines. In the discussion that follows this activity, many participants are surprised by the simple formula for success (i.e., "If you'll cross the line, so will I.").

Many of us are so accustomed to working competitively in school, jobs, sports, games, and other endeavors that professional cooperation may not be a concept we are as skilled performing as we may think we are. Initially, new inclusive support teams may find it difficult to share their classroom space, ideas, resources, and teaching "limelight" with others. It will require some initial staff development, as well as ongoing communication, practice, and feedback for collaborating teams to work together well (Bauwens & Hourcade, 1995).

Many inclusive support teams use team teaching as the basis for their work together. Bauwens and Hourcade (1995) describe this process as cooperative teaching or "co-teaching" when there is:

> ...a restructuring of teaching procedures in which two or more educators possessing distinct sets of skills work in a coactive and coordinated fashion to jointly teach academically and behaviorally heterogeneous groups of students in integrated educational settings, that is, general education classrooms. (p. 46)

Co-teaching teams work together to design and deliver classroom instruction (e.g., content, study skills, learning strategies), supervise student practice, monitor progress, and evaluate learning outcomes. Class preparation, instruction, and follow-up responsibilities are shared fairly by participants.

Effective co-teaching teams report that their roles are dynamic and flexible. While recognizing the professional expertise, experience, and preferences each co-teacher brings to these relationships, participants use these experiences to try new ideas and expand their skill repertoire (Bauwens & Hourcade, 1995). Some basic classroom roles and responsibilities shared by effective co-teaching partners are shown in Figure 1 (Korinek & Walther-Thomas, 1994).

Co-taught classrooms are active learning and working environments. Most co-teachers provide their students with a variety of direct and indirect support services. Co-teachers report that these relationships motivate them to higher levels of professional performance (Walther-Thomas, in press). For example, very few co-teachers report that they work less because there are two adults providing instruction and support in these classes; however, many indicate they are introducing new ideas and programs that they would not have undertaken on their own (Walther-Thomas, Bryant, & Land, 1995). Because of the level of activity that takes place in these settings, it is important to select competent and enthusiastic teachers who do not see co-teaching as an opportunity to spend additional time in the teachers' lounge drinking coffee and reading the morning newspaper. Typical preparation, instruction, and monitoring activities that take place simultaneously in co-taught classrooms are provided in Figure 2.

FIGURE 1
Potential Roles and Responsibilities of Co-Teachers
(Korinek & Walther-Thomas, 1994)

Some basic classroom roles and responsibilities of co-teachers are listed below. While partners need to acknowledge each other's unique skills and knowledge, effective co-teaching teams report that their roles and responsibilities are dynamic and flexible. Initially, co-teachers are likely to feel more confident performing some roles more than others but teams need to avoid getting "stuck in a rut" (i.e., Teacher A *always* introduces new concepts; Teacher B *always* corrects classroom homework). It is important to remember that co-teaching relationships are opportunities for colleagues to share expertise and develop new professional skills as they team together.

1. **Design and/or Prepare Instructional Accommodations**
   - Simplified content materials
   - Similar content with functional applications (e.g., social, vocational)
   - Graphic organizers for key concepts
   - Taped textbooks, chapters, passages
   - Supplementary handouts (e.g., chapter vocabulary lists)
   - Study guides, lecture outlines
   - Alternative curricular materials (i.e., same content but easier reading)
   - Adapted materials (e.g., size, format, devices, number of problems)
   - Models, demonstrations
   - Instructional posters or bulletin boards
   - Mnemonics
   - Learning strategies (e.g., test-taking skills, textbook comprehension)
   - Computer software
   - Behavior contracts/Management plans
   - Background information
   - Communications with parents, resource personnel, community contacts
   - Instructional resources (e.g., films, speakers, texts, field trips)
   - Paraprofessional/Volunteer preparation and supervision

2. **Develop and Deliver Co-Taught Presentations**
   Team teaching – Alternating the presenter role frequently (i.e., 5-10 minutes) both teachers teach subject content, study skills, learning strategies, and/or social skills (e.g., Teacher A presents the South's position during the Civil War while Teacher B presents the North's position).

   One teaches; One monitors – One teaches while the other monitors the class to ensure understanding, provide individual help as needed, and/or collect data on specific student behaviors.

   One teaches; One models – One teaches while the other models appropriate student behavior (e.g., Teacher A teaches a brief content lesson while Teacher B takes notes on an overhead projector using a two-column note taking method that was introduced earlier in the period).

One teaches; One clarifies – One teaches while the other asks clarifying questions or rephrases the material to increase understanding (e.g., Sensing some confusion among the students, Teacher A asks Teacher B: "Mr. Evans, do you mean you want us to discuss the diagram on page 57 with our teams?").

Role play – Teachers role play with content material (e.g., conversation between a Union soldier and a Confederate soldier) or new skills (e.g., asking for help appropriately: Teacher A plays the teacher while Teacher B plays a student needing assistance during class).

Skill demonstration – Working together teachers demonstrate the steps in completing a new task or conducting procedure (e.g., performing a lab experiment, using a new computer program).

3. **Present Content through Instruction Provided Separately**

Station teaching – Teachers present different content, skills, or practice activities at various teacher-led and independent (e.g., small group, partner, or individual) work stations. Students rotate among stations in an assigned sequence or in random order.

Parallel instruction – Teachers work with small groups on the same content to provide closer monitoring (e.g., using the telephone to make an emergency call, reviewing test taking procedures for a standardized exam).

Re-teach or enrichment instruction – Occasionally, co-teachers may need to work with small groups specifically on missed instruction or when more practice is needed on critical skills. This structure can also be used to provide extension/elaboration activities for a few students who have the content and are ready to move ahead. (NOTE: It is important that *both* teachers provide reteach and extension activities.)

4. **Design and Monitor Student Practice Activities**

Computer-assisted assignments	Partner interviewing
Cooperative learning groups	Peer practice/tutoring
Journals, diaries, book reports	Skits, models, group reports
Learning centers	Experiments
Educational games	Flash cards
Worksheets	Role plays

5. **Evaluate Student Progress**

Adapted quizzes/Tests	Individual/Group products
Homework correction	Participation grades
Classroom observations	Progress reports
Daily monitoring sheets	Report cards
Portfolios	Curriculum-based assessment

FIGURE 2

What Do Co-Teachers Do When They Work Together?

TYPICAL BEFORE CLASS ACTIVITIES:

Teacher A...	**While Teacher B...**
Checks in today's homework assignments	Greets students at the door
Writes today's warm-up and tonight's homework on the board	Sets up science activity
Calls a parent to set up a conference	Confers with a student about yesterday's lesson
Arranges desks for a small group activity	Assembles needed materials
Counts money for next week's field trip	Goes to the office to check the field trip bus schedule

DURING CLASS ACTIVITIES:

Teacher A...	**While Teacher B...**
Reviews last night's homework assignment	Discusses yesterday's lesson with three students absent yesterday
Passes back corrected papers; monitors student participation	Introduces today's lesson
Reviews note-taking strategy	Takes example notes on overhead transparency
Monitors student understanding, prompts students to ask questions, and models appropriate question-asking as needed	Leads class discussion
Role plays the part of a teacher	Role plays the part of a student asking for help
Leads a small group discussion discussion of today's reading assignment in *The Indian in the Cupboard*	Leads a small group of today's reading assignment in *The Sign of the Beaver*
Teaches a 15 minute new content lesson at Math Station A	Directs a 15 minute practice activity at Math Station B

Reviews new vocabulary words	Signs two students' daily behavior notes
Reinforces positive class behavior	Supports Teacher A's observations and points out good individual performers
Conferences with a student who had difficulty working today	Answers questions about homework assignment

AFTER CLASS:

Teacher A...	**While Teacher B...**
Grades homework on T & TH	Grades homework on M & W
Plans tomorrow's warm-up activity	Keeps track of three student behavior contracts
Calls parents if there is a problem on M & W	Calls parents if there is a a problem T & TH
Plans with teaching partner on Fridays	Plans with teaching partner on Fridays

Collaboration and classroom support at Barnhill Middle School

Barnhill Middle School is an inclusive setting that provides mainstream support for students with special needs through co-teaching, one-on-one consultation, team problem solving, and ongoing student monitoring. Barnhill has been a middle school for six years and the staff has been developing its network of inclusive support services for the past three years.

When Barnhill made its transition from a junior high school to a middle school, extensive staff development and support were provided to ensure that staff members developed essential teaming skills. Many of their positive interdisciplinary team experiences and successful student outcomes laid the groundwork for their willingness to pursue more inclusive special education and related service options. Clearly Barnhill is a positive and productive place to work and learn. Ongoing projects and activities reflect a high level of enthusiasm as well as strong commitments to collaboration and teaming by staff members, administrators, and students. Faculty turnover is minimal; most Barnhill staff members who participated in the initial middle school preparation are still on board.

Administrative support and leadership at Barnhill is strong. Administrators speak highly of the school's teachers. The principal and two assistant principals spend time working with teams and observing classrooms. Administrators speak knowledgeably about ongoing projects, individual students, team strengths, and specific areas of concern. The principal is clearly an instructional leader who is described by teachers as "dynamic," a "real go-getter," and a "visionary." She has been at Barnhill for six years. The assistant principal in charge of special education and related services has five years experience at Barnhill. He is also viewed very positively by staff members.

Four years ago Barnhill began exploring inclusive models because of encouragement from a newly appointed school superintendent. Previously he had implemented inclusive support services in another school system. He was eager to implement similar services in this system. During an early meeting with principals he asked for six volunteer schools to (a) examine inclusion models, (b) evaluate the appropriateness of inclusion in their schools, (c) develop three-year implementation plans if they determined that their schools were willing to change their current service delivery models, and (d) identify the resources they would need to make necessary changes (e.g., staff development, additional personnel, parent education). He promised to provide ongoing support for this effort.

After discussing the superintendent's proposal with her faculty, the Barnhill principal volunteered for this project. As she noted:

> Most of our faculty members read the current professional literature. They attend a lot of conferences, and they belong to professional organizations. The idea of inclusion was not totally new to many of them. I must admit some were wary – specialists as much as general educators. Most, however, were definitely interested. At Barnhill we see ourselves on the 'cutting edge' and we like that image. We work well together and most people felt like this was a logical next step for us. Fortunately, by the time the idea of inclusion was proposed, we were "over the hump" in terms of our transition from a junior high to a true middle school. We liked the changes that we had seen in the kids and in ourselves – so our school was ripe for expanding our teaming network even further.

In November the principal appointed a committee to study inclusion and make recommendations to the faculty in the spring. The all-volunteer committee consisted of one general educator and one special educator from each of the three grade levels, the assistant principal, a reading specialist, a gifted/talented teacher, and two PTA representatives. Over a four-month period the committee visited inclusive special education programs in nearby school systems. Members attended conferences on inclusion in their state. They read related professional literature and participated in several overview sessions sponsored by the superintendent.

In early April, the committee shared their findings with the faculty. Based on their study, the committee supported implementation of inclusive services for all special programs. These programs at Barnhill included special education, Chapter I reading, bilingual education, gifted/talented, speech/language, and alternative education. Working with the principal and two consultants supported by the superintendent's office, the committee and other interested faculty members designed their school's three-year implementation plan. They agreed that three years seemed like a reasonable time period for phasing in new services. As one committee member noted:

> Three years gave us time to train the staff, learn how to schedule students and teachers effectively, and pilot test our ideas. It was great to have enough time to really 'work out the bugs' of our plan. I think this approach made a big difference in how well we implemented inclusion. A slow approach helped us defuse a lot of the initial resistance that existed among some faculty members. As it turned out, most of these folks just needed time to see that it worked. Some of them were very intimidated teaching with someone else in their classrooms. When they finally realized how much help the specialists provided – and how much fun it could actually be to teach with others – their thinking changed.

The following summer the principal, assistant principal, and representatives from three grade-level teams participated in a five-day summer course on inclusive education sponsored by the superintendent's office. Teams from five additional schools also participated in this course. Each grade level team was represented by two general educators and two specialists (e.g., special educator, alternative educator, reading specialist). All participants were volunteers and they were paid for their time.

During the school district's three-year implementation period, two university consultants co-taught the annual summer courses and provided support during the school year. Support consisted of classroom observations, problem solving sessions with grade-level teams, and several advanced skill training workshops. The consultants also worked closely with a staff development specialist from the central office who was assigned to support implementation in the six schools. She met with administrators and teachers in small groups and individually throughout the year to discuss progress and concerns.

During the second year of implementation, the consultants and the staff development specialist trained additional teams from the six schools during the summer. The first-year teams attended one day of the second group's summer training course. They shared their experiences with the second-year group and made implementation plans for their second year. All teams continued to receive support from the consultants and the staff development specialist during the second year. In addition, some members of the first-year implementation teams were recruited as mentors for the second-year teams. Mentors participated in classroom observations, provided feedback, and facilitated monthly problem solving meetings for new implementers.

The same basic pattern of staff development and academic year support was also provided during the third year. The third summer training course, however, was taught primarily by members of the first- and second-year implementation teams and the staff development specialist. The consultants participated in course planning, presenter preparation, and some introductory instruction. Throughout the third year, the first- and second-year implementation teams played more active roles in providing support.

The summer course helped participants develop new skills and fine-tune their teaming and problem-solving competencies. Working with their team members they learned how to schedule students and teachers effectively to ensure that teams and individual classes were not weighted too heavily with special needs students. They learned how to evaluate available support services and develop appropriate support plans based on co-teaching and consultation. They developed fundamental co-planning and co-teaching skills and advanced problem solving strategies (e.g., negotiation, conflict resolution). Finally, participants learned new procedures for monitoring academic and social skills development.

A summary of Barnhill's 7th grade team rosters, planning times, and co-teaching schedules are shown in Figure 3. As this figure illustrates, students are divided into two heterogeneous teams at each grade level (6th-8th grades). Most of the grade-level teams consist of 110-120 students. The needs and abilities of all students are considered as team rosters are developed. Typically, students with disabilities are assigned to one team and equal numbers of students with other unique needs (e.g., low reading skills, court involvement, substance abuse, language differences, family-related issues) are assigned to the other team. All remaining students are divided equally between the two teams on the basis of their achievement (i.e., low, middle, and high achievers).

Figure 3

Student Rosters, Teachers, and Planning Time

8th Grade Comets Team
Team Students (N= 114)

7	Gifted/Talented
11	High ability
80	Average/Low average
4	Low achieving
12	Special Education (Identified students)
	8 Learning disabilities
	3 Emotional disabilities
	1 Physical disability

8th Grade Eagles Team
Team Students (N= 117)

8	Gifted/Talented
8	High ability
83	Average/Low average
4	Other low achieving
14	Alternative Education (Identified students)
	5 Court-monitored
	2 Substance abuse
	3 Foster placements
	3 Past school failure
	1 School phobic

Comets Team Teachers
Hernandez (Language Arts)
Thomas (Math)
Fisher (Science)
Burns (Social Studies)
Bryant (Special Education)

Eagles Team Teachers
Ito (Language Arts)
West (Math)
Zito (Science)
Cason (Social Studies)
Bon (Alternative Education)

Direct classroom support is also provided to both teams by a gifted/talented teacher, a Chapter I reading specialist, and two counselors. These faculty members meet regularly with each team to plan and prepare co-taught lessons and related activities.

Daily Planning Time
Individual   3rd period
Team   4th period

Daily Planning Time
Individual   5th period
Team   6th period

Weekly Co-teaching Schedule for K. Bryant, Comets Special Educator*

1st period	Hernandez/Bryant (5/25)**
2nd period	Hernandez/Bryant (5/26)
3rd period	Team Planning (M-TH)
4th Period	Individual and/or Co-planning with teaching partners
5th period	Thomas/Bryant (7/24)
6th period	Thomas/Bryant (5/26)

*   The alternative education teacher on the Eagles has a similar co-teaching schedule
**   This represents the proportion of students with disabilities in the total class enrollment.

Five or six teachers work together as a teaching team. These teachers have responsibility for math, reading, language arts, social studies, science, and inclusive support. Teams consist of four or five general educators and one or two inclusive support specialists (e.g., special educator, Chapter I reading specialist, alternative educator). Most of the specialists are assigned to their teams on a full-time basis. Some, however, may have their time divided between two teams because of limited numbers of students who qualify for their support services (e.g., bilingual, speech/language, gifted/ talented).

Administrators and teachers at each grade level work together in April to develop team rosters, co-teaching schedules, and identify co-planning periods for the following year. Active participation and early planning help minimize many potential scheduling problems. This approach also ensures that team members will have scheduled time for co-planning and consultation. Typically, designated co-teachers work together on a daily basis for one to three periods. Frequently co-teaching takes place during reading, language arts, and math classes. Most support providers co-teach with two or three colleagues. In general most co-teaching teams need an hour or more of planning time each week to ensure that they are both actively involved in planning, preparing, teaching, and monitoring student progress. In classes where students with special needs are placed but where co-teaching does not take place, it is important for general educators and specialists to schedule time to discuss student progress and address problems on an ongoing basis. Scheduled consultation helps ensure that all team teachers receive the support they need to implement inclusion effectively.

Considerations in inclusive program planning

Ensuring that new ideas become integral parts of the infrastructure of schools is a complex, slow-moving, and labor-intensive process (Fullan 1991, 1993; Hall & Hord, 1987; Huberman & Miles, 1984). As many experienced educators can attest, most new initiatives do not last in schools. Schools have tremendous difficulty embracing new ideas and changing existing patterns (Fullan, 1993). There are many reasons schools do not change easily. Some of the frequently mentioned reasons include competing priorities, lack of administrative support, poor staff development, limited implementation support, and few rewards for extra work. Because of problems associated with innovation implementation, effective program planners address fundamental aspects of program development in a systematic and sustained manner to minimize the potential roadblocks and maximize the efficacy of their efforts. The following dimensions of effective inclusive program planning will be addressed in this section: (a) integrating with existing team structures, (b) developing a collaborative base of support, (c) enlisting key administrators, (d) providing adequate preparation and implementation resources, (e) supporting small pilot projects, (f) creating realistic expectations for participants, and (g) planning and monitoring progress.

Integrating with existing team structures

Clearly middle schools are committed to many forms of collaboration and ongoing teamwork by professionals and students (Erb & Doda, 1989; George & Stevenson, 1989; George et al., 1992). Typically, new inclusive education initiatives dovetail nicely the existing organizational structure and collaborative commitment that exists in middle schools. Generally, even in schools where traditional special education services are provided, many collaborative efforts are also in place. Grade-level teaching teams often work closely with various support specialists (e.g., special educators, reading specialists, counselors) to monitor the progress of identified students and problem solve concerns that arise. To facilitate monitoring and problem solving, many schools utilize various professional support structures such as teacher assistance teams, peer coaching partnerships, and peer consultation (Laycock et al., 1991). Planning teams involved in the development of more inclusive support services should build on successful structures that are already established. Encouraging interested grade-level teams or individual teachers to volunteer for possible co-teaching assignments with specialists may identify a number of working relationships where there is a base of professional confidence, trust, and experience in place.

Developing a collaborative base of support

Participation from all significant stakeholders during the initial stages of program planning facilitates the long-term success of new initiatives (Fullan, 1993). Building or division-level committees composed of teachers, administrators, support specialists, families, and students, facilitate the development of commitment among essential stakeholder groups. These committees perform important functions in the development of new programs. First, they provide valuable leadership and help develop support networks within the school system and across the community for new initiatives (Stainback & Stainback, 1990). Second, they gather relevant information, visit model programs, review research, and present their findings to others (e.g., professionals, school board members, families, students). Third, they provide opportunities for community members to voice concerns and offer suggestions. This process ensures that potential problems are addressed proactively, contributes to greater community participation, and facilitates ownership in new initiatives. Finally, these committees synthesize the data they have gathered and develop long-range plans that represent the needs and interests of their communities (Fullan, 1993; Giangreco et al., 1993; Snell & Janney, 1994; Stainback & Stainback, 1990).

Enlisting key administrators

Administrative support is essential in the lasting success of innovations in education (Barth, 1990). Competing priorities quickly drain valuable resources (e.g., time, money, personnel) away from projects that lack solid administrative support (Cook & Friend, 1994; Fullan, 1991). New programs proposed by administrators are more likely to succeed than those initiated by teachers or families. As a result, inclusive education advocates must include administrators who have similar beliefs in the early stages of program planning (Snell & Janney, 1994).

Building administrators play important roles in facilitating the effectiveness of inclusive support programs. First, they can provide general educators and specialists with classrooms, offices, and/or work stations that are in proximity. This helps increase ongoing communication and opportunities for interaction. Second, administrators can work with their staff members to maintain team assignments. Teams need two to three years to mature as work groups. This time provides opportunities for them to fine tune their collaborative efforts and enjoy the successes from their efforts working together.

Providing adequate resources

Advanced staff development experiences can ensure that inclusive education teams have the skills, knowledge, and attitudes needed to work together (Graden & Bauer, 1992; Wang, 1992). For example, learning to resolve conflicts helps teams avoid unnecessary communication breakdowns that can limit their effectiveness. As differences (e.g., philosophy, values, education, teaching styles) emerge among team members, conflict is inevitable. Owens (1987) has noted that it is important to understand that conflict is a natural part of the team development process. Many education professionals are unfamiliar with the team development process and are likely to be unskilled in conflict resolution. Consequently, many individuals may feel discouraged and hurt when conflicts begin to emerge on their teams. They assume conflict is bad rather than viewing it as a sign of team growth. Providing all team members with basic and necessary negotiation and conflict resolution skills facilitates open and effective communication among co-teaching partners and within interdisciplinary teams. Good communication, in turn, fosters trust and enables teams to solve challenging problems more effectively (Owens, 1987).

Teams can use needs assessment tools to identify a small number of topics for in-depth staff development. This approach helps focus staff development funds on the areas of greatest need for participants. A focused approach also allows staff development specialists to continue to provide support and resources on a small range of topics following initial training sessions. Topics of interest might include collaborative problem solving, co-planning strategies, portfolio and curriculum-based assessment procedures, negotiation and conflict resolution skills, classroom accommodations, learning strategies, cooperative learning, and peer tutoring.

Professionals should be encouraged to make choices regarding their own skill development. This approach recognizes their skills, previous experiences, abilities to assess their own competence and select appropriate skill development experiences. Giving professionals choices in staff development also ensures higher levels of enthusiasm and commitment from those who do choose to participate.

Supporting well-planned pilot projects

Small and well-planned pilot programs that are carried out by willing volunteers are an effective way to implement innovations. Initial successes that teacher volunteers report to their colleagues can reduce anxiety, misconceptions, and resistance (Fullan, 1991).

Planning teams need to select the most competent and willing administrators, teachers, and support specialists for participation in initial pilot programs. The outcomes from these preliminary efforts will have long-lasting effects on future program development efforts. Sometimes division and building level administrators may recommend professionals who are not good candidates for participation in these initial projects. For example, recognized school leaders are often recommended for participation because of their skills, enthusiasm, and proven performance. Unfortunately, some of these capable teachers, specialists, and administrators may be so involved in other worthwhile projects that they may not make good choices despite the skills they possess. Sometimes well-intentioned administrators may see involvement in new projects as great opportunities to improve the skills and attitudes of weak or "burned out" professionals. Unfortunately, this improvement rarely happens and their participation negatively affects other members of the pilot program team. Effective inclusive programs are built on professional relationships that are collaborative and cooperative. Trust, respect, and confidence in each other's professional skills are essential ingredients in pilot program efforts (Cook & Friend, 1994; Friend & Cook, 1992; Fullan, 1991).

Creating realistic expectations for participants

Bauwens and Hourcade (1995) encourage schools implementing co-teaching to do so slowly to reduce potential resistance from teachers, parents, and students, gain support, and allow professionals time to develop needed new skills. The good news, as well as the bad news, is that making lasting changes in schools takes time (Hall & Hord, 1987). Fullan (1991) has suggested that successful adoption of programs may require five to ten years of hard work from division, building, and classroom supporters.

Despite the best of intentions, it is impossible for support specialists to develop productive relationships with six classroom teachers simultaneously. Realistically, inclusion support specialists need to start new services with a small number of classroom teachers. Ideally, they should begin their work with one or two volunteer teachers. More experienced inclusion specialists may find it possible to co-teach with three classroom colleagues (60-90 minutes per class per day) and consult once a week with one or two additional teachers (60-90 minutes per session).

It is important to note that some schools do not offer all of their special services for all students with disabilities within the context of mainstream classrooms. There are a number of reasons why some schools continue to provide a combination of inclusive and traditional support services. First, some students may require skill instruction and support that cannot or should not be provided in mainstream classrooms. For example, individual therapy sessions (e.g., speech, mobility, muscle continue, personal counseling) may not be appropriate in the presence of students' peers. This may be particularly true for older students who would be uncomfortable with intensive special attention within the mainstream setting. Second, a combined approach may be the best option available for some school systems involved in the development of inclusive services. A number of potential challenges must be addressed as traditional service programs change. To implement new initiatives successfully, many educators, administrators, students, and families may need new skills (e.g., communicating, problem solving, co-teaching, scheduling, organizing). Ongoing classroom support is needed during the critical early stages of implementation to ensure that appropriate scheduling, teamwork, instruction, and monitoring take place. Limited staff development and support resources may require school systems to phase in inclusive programming over a period of time.

Generally small pilot projects, as part of a larger implementation plan, provide opportunities for program planners and participants to work out many potential problems in new initiatives. Successful preliminary efforts can also help allay potential fears that some staff members and families may have about proposed changes.

Planning and monitoring progress

Teachers and support specialists need at least one hour of planning time each week to plan, monitor student progress, and evaluate their work together. These sessions ensure that teachers and support specialists agree about important classroom goals and learning objectives for their students. They also provide opportunities to discuss problems and develop appropriate intervention strategies (Bauwens & Hourcade, 1995).

Regularly scheduled planning also ensures that co-teaching roles and responsibilities are divided in a fair and equitable manner. Assigning both co-teachers responsibilities for class preparation, instruction, and monitoring also serves several important purposes. It provides opportunities for members to develop trust in each other's professional skills, demonstrates each person's commitment to the success of their collaborative work, and strengthens their working relationships (Friend & Cook, 1992).

Insufficient planning time and lack of instructional coordination can undermine inclusive support teams (Walther-Thomas et al., 1995). If planning does not occur, classroom teachers receive limited help in instructional planning and preparation for instruction. Over time classroom teachers can resent the specialist's limited participation in this effort. If planning discussions do not occur, specialists are limited in the support they can provide. In co-teaching situations if planning does not take place, co-teaching does not happen. In these cases, the general education teachers retain most of the classroom power, authority, and responsibility. Specialists work primarily as aides rather than equal partners; most feel unwelcome and quickly frustrated by these situations (Walther-Thomas et al., 1995).

In general, middle school inclusive support teams work well together because they have scheduled planning periods. Building administrators can establish common planning blocks for team members. If planning time does not exist or if additional time is needed, administrators, teachers, and members of the community need to work together to develop more time. Some creative planning time strategies that have been used by other inclusive support teams are shown in Figure 4.

FIGURE 4
Finding Planning Time for Collaborators
(Korinek & Walther-Thomas, 1994)

Ideally, schools should provide professionals with two daily planning periods: one for team planning and the other for individual planning. If planning periods are designated, one to two hours per week can be allotted for collaborative planning. If planning periods are not scheduled, school teams need to find ways to provide this valuable time for teachers and specialists to work together. Listed below are ideas generated by teams that found creative ways to provide planning time:

1. Trade time blocks with colleagues. Combine some class sessions to instruct larger-than-classroom size groups (e.g., films, speakers).
2. Recruit retired teachers. Ask volunteers to make a three hour time commitment per week for a nine week period of time. These commitments are usually renewed but short-term approach give potential volunteers, who might be hesitant to make the commitment for an entire school year, greater freedom and flexibility in planning their own schedules.
3. Provide compensation time for teachers who co-plan before or after school on their own (e.g., leave at noon on teacher work days).
4. Work with the Parent-Teacher Organization to recruit, train, and schedule family member volunteers to supervise independent work periods, use fund-raising revenues for substitutes, identify community partners who are willing to provide teachers with resources (e.g., pizza for after school planning sessions, free fast food breakfasts, sponsor substitute teacher hours). Recruit, train, and supervise high school and university student service club volunteers and future teachers.
5. Apply for division, community, state, and federal grants.
6. Plan during lunch with meal/dessert provided by the school administration.
7. Use school or PTA funds to hire a "floating" substitute.
8. Generate a monthly list of times when administrators and/or specialists will teach/supervise collaborating teachers' classes.
9. Hire only paraprofessionals with valid teaching certificates.
10. Restructure school day to create a "zero hour" planning period during the day when all teachers are required to be at school but no instruction is scheduled.
11. Reduce duty periods for teachers who are involved in co-teaching.

It has been well documented over the years that students with disabilities and many other low-achieving students are poor test-takers (Cohen & Spruill, 1990). Consequently, many successful learning experiences in mainstream classrooms may not be adequately reflected by student performance on standardized measures. To ensure team teachers, support providers, families, division evaluation specialists, and the students themselves assess how well inclusive education experiences are meeting identified academic and social learning needs, an evaluation plan should be developed. This should be a collaborative endeavor in which concerned stakeholders are involved. This plan should provide the planning team with various benchmarks of progress. Systematically, the team should collect data and discuss this information during its planning meetings. Adjustments in support can be made on the basis of the information collected.

Daily and weekly curriculum-based assessment measures (e.g., precision teaching strategies, portfolio assessment) should be used (Cohen & Spruill, 1990; Giangreco et al., 1993; Putnam, 1993) as well as some less-frequent and more standardized tools. Some typical academic measures include work samples, journal entries, test and quiz scores, book reports, and other written assignments. Individual and group work projects should be considered. Other possible "academic" measures worth considering for monitoring progress may include improved performance in student self-monitoring time on task, independent work completed, homework assignments returned, notebook organization, independent use of reading comprehension strategies, accuracy and/or speed on assignments or daily timed tests, and oral contributions during class discussions. While some of these items can be used as social measures, they form the basis for work habits and tool skills, allowing the students to ultimately perform more successfully on content materials. Some appropriate performance indicators may also be standardized achievement measures. Possible social indicators include participation in extracurricular and community activities, dressing in gym, conversations with peers, use of appropriate social skills on field trips, increased school attendance, fewer referrals to the office from gym and health teachers, fewer requests to visit the school nurse's office, and family comments.

Summary

Inclusive support programs for students with disabilities and their peers are growing in popularity in middle schools. These programs work, in large measure, because they are compatible with middle school goals, teaching philosophy, instructional grouping patterns, and are supported by the organizational structure of these settings.

In these programs, professional teams share responsibility for problem solving, intervention planning and implementation, and group recognition for successful student outcomes (Bauwens & Hourcade, 1995; Friend & Cook, 1992). Sharing these responsibilities help create a "collaborative ethic" within teams that enables members to work together effectively to meet student needs and to grow professionally (Phillips & McCullough, 1990).

These programs are designed to go beyond earlier attempts to "mainstream" or "integrate" students with disabilities primarily for the purpose of social interaction. Today, we recognize the importance of providing *all* students with challenging academic and social learning experiences and there is mounting evidence to suggest that school teams can accomplish these aims (Giangreco et al., 1993; 1994; Slavin et al., 1989; Stainback & Stainback, 1990; Wang & Birch, 1984).

Educational research has also helped us understand the importance of staff development, planning, teamwork, and administrative support in the development and delivery of appropriate learning programs (Bauwens & Hourcade, 1995; Cook & Friend, 1994; Fullan, 1993; Giangreco et al., 1994; Stainback et al., 1992). Research has shown that new initiatives have a better chance of survival if program planners (a) work with stakeholders to develop a strong base of support among key administrators and designated implementers, (b) provide adequate resources for planning and implementation, and (c) collect program evaluation data that show students perform well (Barth, 1990; Fullan, 1993; Hall & Hord, 1987; Montgomery, 1990).

Effective inclusive support programs will not mean the elimination of special education for students with disabilities. The goals of inclusion cannot be achieved by simply "dumping" students with disabilities in mainstream classrooms. What new inclusive education approaches offer, however, is the opportunity for schools to be productive and supportive learning communities that provide better academic and social-emotional learning opportunities of all students.

References

Barth, R. (1990). *Improving schools from within: Teachers, parents, and principals can make the difference*. San Francisco: Jossey-Bass.

Bauwens, J., & Hourcade, J.J. (1995). *Cooperative teaching: Rebuilding the schoolhouse for all students*. Austin, TX: PRO-ED.

Bickel, W.E., & Bickel, D.D. (1987). Effective schools, classrooms, and instruction: Implications for special education. *Exceptional Children, 52*, 489-500.

Carlberg, C., & Kavale, K. (1980). The efficacy of special versus regular class placement for exceptional children: A meta-analysis. *Journal of Special Education, 14*, 295-309.

Carnegie Forum on Education and the Economy. (1986). *A nation prepared: Teachers for the 21st century*. Hyattsville, MD: Carnegie Forum on Education and the Economy, Task Force on Teaching as a Profession.

Cawelti, G. (1988). Designing high schools for the future. *Educational Leadership, 47* (7), 30-35.

Chalfant, J.C., & Pysh, M.V.D. (1989). Teacher assistance teams: Five descriptive studies on 96 teams. *Remedial and Special Education, 10* (6), 49-58.

Cohen, L.G., & Spruill, J.A. (1990). *Practical guide to curriculum-based assessment for special educators*. Springfield, IL: Charles C. Thomas.

Coles, G. (1988). *The learning mystique*. New York: Pantheon Books.

Colorado State Department of Education Special Education Service Unit (CSDESESU). (1994). *Inclusion: A working definition*. Denver, CO: Author.

Cook, L., & Friend, M. (1994). Educational leadership for teacher collaboration. In B. S. Billingsley (Ed.), *Program leadership for serving students with disabilities* (pp. 219-262). Richmond, VA: Virginia Department of Education.

Cuban, L. (1990). Reform again, again, and again. *Educational Researcher, 19* (1), 3-13.

Danielson, L.C., & Bellamy, G.T. (1989). State variations in placement of children with handicaps in segregated environments. *Exceptional Children, 55*, 448-455.

Deshler, D.D., & Schumaker, J.B. (1988). An instructional model for teaching students how to learn. In J. Graden, J. Zins, & M. Curtis (Eds.), *Alternative educational delivery systems: Enhancing instructional options for all students* (pp. 391-411). Washington, DC: National Association for School Psychologists.

Dettmer, P., Thurston, L.P., & Dyck, N. (1993). *Consultation, collaboration, and teamwork for students with special needs*. Boston: Allyn and Bacon.

Edgar, E. (1988). Employment as an outcome for mildly handicapped students: Current status and future directions. *Focus on Exceptional Students, 21* (1), 1-8.

Edgar, E. (1987). Secondary programs in special education: Are many of them justifiable? *Exceptional Children, 53*, 555-561.

Erb, T.0., & Doda, N.M. (1989). *Team organization: Promise—practices and possibilities.* Washington, DC: National Education Association.

Friend, M., & Cook, L. (1992). *Interactions.* New York: Merrill.

Fullan, M.G. (1991). *The new meaning of educational change.* New York: Teachers College Press.

Fullan, M.G. (1993). *Change forces.* London: Falmer Press.

Gartner, A., & Lipsky, D.K. (1987). Beyond special education: Toward a quality system for all students. *Harvard Educational Review, 57,* 367-395.

Gaskins, I., & Elliot, T. (1991). *Implementing cognitive strategy training across the school: The benchmark manual for teachers.* Media, PA: Brookline Books.

George, P.S., & Stevenson, C. (1989). The 'very best teams' in the 'best schools' as described by middle school principals, *TEAM: The Early Adolescent Magazine, 3,* 6-14.

George, P.S., Stevenson, C., Thomason, J., & Beane, J. (1992). *The middle school—and beyond.* Alexandria, VA: Association for Supervision and Curriculum Development.

Giangreco, M.F., Cloninger, C.J., Dennis, R.E., & Edelman, S.W. (1994). Problem-solving methods. In J. S. Thousand, R. Villa, & A. Nevin (Eds.), *Creativity and collaborative learning: A practical guide to empowering students and teachers* (pp. 321-346). Baltimore, MD: Paul H. Brookes.

Giangreco, M.F., Cloninger, C.J., & Iverson, V.S. (1993). *Choosing options and accommodations for children: A guide to planning inclusive education.* Baltimore: Paul H. Brookes.

Giangreco, M.F., & Putnam, J.W. (1991). Supporting the education of students with severe disabilities in regular education environments. In L.H. Meyer, C.A. Peck, & L. Brown (Eds.), *Critical issues in the lives of people with severe disabilities* (pp. 245-270). Baltimore, MD: Paul H. Brookes.

Goodlad, J.L., & Lovitt, T.C. (1993). *Integrating general and special education.* New York: Merrill.

Graden, J.L., & Bauer, A.M. (1992). Using a collaborative approach to support students and teachers in inclusive classrooms. In S. Stainback & W. Stainback (Eds.), *Curriculum considerations in inclusive classrooms: Facilitating learning for all students* (pp. 85-100). Baltimore, MD: Paul H. Brookes.

Hagerty, G.J., & Abramson, M. (1987). Impediments to implementing national policy change for mildly handicapped students. *Exceptional Children, 53,* 315-323.

Hall, G.E., & Hord, S. (1987). *Change in schools: Facilitating the process.* Albany, NY: State University of New York Press.

Haring, K.A., Lovett, D.L., & Smith, D.D. (1990). A follow-up study of recent special education graduates of learning disabilities programs. *Journal of Learning Disabilities, 23* (2), 108-113.

Harper, G.F., Maheady, L., & Mallette, B. (1994). The power of peer-mediated instruction: How and why it promotes academic success for all students. In J. S. Thousand, R. Villa, & A. Nevin (Eds.), *Creativity and collaborative learning: A practical guide to empowering students and teachers* (pp. 229-242). Baltimore, MD: Paul H. Brookes.

Howe, H. (1988). *The forgotten half: Non-college youth in America*. Washington, DC: William T. Grant Foundation.

Huberman, M., & Miles, M. (1984). *Innovation close up*. New York: Plenum.

Idol, L. (l989). The resource/consulting teacher: An integrated model of service delivery. *Remedial and Special Education, 10* (6), 38-48.

Korinek, L., & Walther-Thomas, C.S. (1994). *Co-teaching: The nuts and bolts*. Unpublished training materials. Williamsburg, VA: College of William & Mary.

Laycock, V.K., Gable, R.A., & Korinek, L. (1991). Alternative structures for collaboration in the delivery of special services. *Preventing School Failure, 35*(4), 15-18.

Lipsitz, J. (1984). *Successful schools for young adolescents*. New Brunswick, NJ: Transaction.

Lipsky, D.K., & Gartner, A. (1989). The current situation. In D.K. Lipsky & A. Gartner (Eds.), *Beyond separate education: Quality education for all* (pp. 3-24). Baltimore, MD: Paul E. Brookes.

Lusthaus, E., & Forest, M. (1989). Promoting educational equality for all students. In S. Stainback, W. Stainback, & M. Forest (Eds.), *Educating all students in the mainstream of regular education* (pp. 43-57). Baltimore, MD: Paul H. Brookes.

Mac Iver, D. (1990). Meeting the needs of young adolescents: Advisory groups, interdisciplinary teaching teams, and school transition programs, *Phi Delta Kappan, 71*, 458-464.

Montgomery, J.K. (1990). Building administrative support for collaboration. In W.A. Secord (Ed.), *Best practices in school speech-language pathology* (pp. 75-79). San Antonio, TX: Psychological Corporation.

Morsink, C.V., Thomas, C.C., & Correa, V.I. (1994). *Interactive teaming: Consultation and collaboration in special programs*. New York: MacMillan.

Ornstein, A., & Levine, D. (1989). Social class, race, and school achievement: Problems and prospects. *Journal of Teacher Education, 40*(5), 17-23.

Owens, R.B. (1987). *Organizational behavior in education*, (3rd ed.). Englewood Cliffs, NJ: Prentice-Hall.

Phillips, V., & McCullough, L. (1990). Consultation-based programming: Instituting the collaborative ethic in schools. *Exceptional Children, 56*, 291-304.

Putnam, J.W. (1993). *Cooperative learning and strategies for inclusion: Celebrating diversity in the classroom*. Baltimore, MD: Paul H. Brookes.

Rafoth, M.A., Leal, L. & DeFabo, L. (1993). *Strategies for learning and remembering: Study skills across the curriculum*. Indiana, PA: National Education Association.

Reschly, 1988. Introduction. In M.C. Wang, M.C. Reynolds, & H.J. Walberg, (Eds.), *Handbook of special education: Research and practice: Vol. 2: Mildly handicapped conditions* (pp. 3-5). Oxford, England: Pergamon Press.

Reynolds, M.C. (1989). An historical perspective: The delivery of special education to mildly disabled and at-risk students. *Remedial and Special Education, 10* (6), 7-11.

Sailor, W., Anderson, J.L., Halvorsen, A.T., Doering, K., Filler, J., & Goetz, L., (1989). *The comprehensive local school.* Baltimore, MD: Paul H. Brookes.

Sansone, J., & Zigmond, N. (1986). Evaluating mainstreaming through an analysis of students' schedules. *Exceptional Children, 52*, 452-458.

Schrage, M. (1990). *Shared minds.* New York: Random House.

Schrumpf, F., Crawford, D., & Usadel, C. (1991). *Peer mediation: Conflict resolution in schools.* Champaign, IL: Research Press.

Shepard, L.A., & Smith, M.L. (1989). *Flunking grades: Research and policies on education.* Philadelphia, PA: Falmer Press.

Sitlington, P.L., & Frank, A.R. (1990). Are adolescents with learning disabilities successfully crossing the bridge into adult life? *Learning Disability Quarterly, 13*, 97-111.

Slavin, R.E., Karweit, N.L., & Madden, N.A. (1989). *Effective programs for students at risk.* Needham Heights, MA: Allyn and Bacon.

Snell, M.E., & Janney, R. (1994). Including and supporting students with disabilities within general education. In B.S. Billingsley (Ed.), *Program leadership for serving students with disabilities* (pp. 219-262). Richmond, VA: Virginia Department of Education.

Stainback, S., Stainback, W., & Jackson, H.J. (1992). Toward inclusive classrooms. In S. Stainback & W. Stainback (Eds.), *Curriculum considerations in inclusive classrooms: Facilitating learning for all students* (pp. 3-18). Baltimore, MD: Paul H. Brookes.

Stainback, W. , & Stainback, S. (1984). A rationale for the merger of special and regular education. *Exceptional Children, 51*, 102-111.

Stainback, W., & Stainback, S. (1990). *Support networks for inclusive schooling: Interdependent integrated education.* Baltimore, MD: Paul H. Brookes.

Thousand, J.S., Villa, R., & Nevin, A. (Eds.). (1994). *Creativity and collaborative learning: A practical guide to empowering students and teachers.* Baltimore, MD: Paul H. Brookes.

Toch, T. (1984). The dark side of the excellence movement. *Phi Delta Kappan, 65*, 173-176.

Turnbull, III, H.R. (1993). *Free and appropriate public education: The law and children with disabilities* (2nd ed.). Denver, CO: Love Publishing.

United States Department of Education (USDE). (1994). *Sixteenth annual report to Congress on the implementation of the Individuals with Disabilities Education Act (IDEA).* Washington, DC: U.S. Government Printing Office.

United States Department of Education (USDE). (1987). *Ninth annual report to Congress on the implementation of the Education of the Handicapped (EHA).* Washington, DC: U.S. Government Printing Office.

Wagner, M., & Shaver, D.M. (1989). *Educational programs and achievements of secondary special education students: Findings from the National Longitudinal Transition Study.* Menlo Park, CA: SRI International.

Walther-Thomas, C.S. (in press). The development of co-teaching teams: Benefits and problems teams report over time. *Journal of Learning Disabilities.*

Walther-Thomas, C.S. (1994). [Co-teaching teams: team development over time]. Unpublished raw data.

Walther-Thomas, C.S., Bryant, M., & Land, S. (1995). Planning for co-teaching: The key to successful inclusion. Manuscript submitted for publication.

Walther-Thomas, C.S., & Carter, K.L. (1993). Cooperative teaching: Helping students with disabilities succeed in mainstream classrooms. *Middle School Journal, 25* (1), 33-38.

Wang, M. C. (1992). *Adaptive education strategies: Building on diversity.* Baltimore, MD: Paul H. Brookes.

Wang, M.C., & Birch, J.W. (1984). Comparison of a full-time mainstreaming program and a resource room approach. *Exceptional Children, 51,* 33-40.

West, J.F., & Cannen, G. (1988). Essential collaboration consultation competencies for regular and special educators. *Journal of Learning Disabilities, 21,* 56-63.

Will, M.C. (1986). Educating children with learning problems: A shared responsibility. *Exceptional Children, 52,* 411-415.

Williams, B.F. (1992). Changing demographics: Challenges for educators. *Intervention in School and Clinic, 27* (3), 157-163.

Part VI

Coda

The final chapter, "The Future of Teaming," serves as a coda for the text. In it, Erb and Dickinson attempt to deal with three topics of critical importance: what we know about the status and impact of teaming, the "necessary agenda," and moving beyond interdisciplinary teaming.

Throughout this effort, the editors weave examples from previous chapters in the text with additional research and information to support their points. They close the chapter and the book with a particular view of the future:

> *The future of teaming depends on the future of schooling. The future of schooling depends on the future of education. Teaming is a means, not an end.*

The Future of Teaming   **23**

Thomas O. Erb and Thomas S. Dickinson

> *True belonging is born of relationships not only to one another but to a place of shared responsibilities and benefits. We love not so much what we have acquired as what we have made and whom we have made it with.*
>
> — Robert Finch, *The Primal Place*

Interdisciplinary teaming: Its status and impact

Interdisciplinary teaming is the hallmark of reformed middle schools. It is an organizational structure of enormous power for student learning. And should anyone question this structure that goes to the heart of middle school teaching and learning, as some are wont to do, we can demonstrate its effectiveness as well as the results of the lack of implementation of interdisciplinary teams. For interdisciplinary teams, as demonstrated throughout this text, the future is now.

Balancing planning time with teaching time

Teachers in the United States at all levels teach more hours per year and are given less planning time than teachers in any of 15 European countries. A study released by the Organization for Economic Cooperation and Development (Henry, 1995) documented that in 1992 American teachers spent an average of 1093 hours teaching at the elementary level, 1042 at the middle level, and 1019 at the secondary level. The 16-nation averages were 858 hours in elementary, 781 at the middle level, and 745 in secondary. Those critics who blame the shortcomings of American schools on lack of teaching time would do well to look at the hard facts. Teachers teach more in American schools already; what they are not given as much time to do is plan for that instruction, assess that instruction, and engage in staff development.

School board members in those nearly 50 percent of districts without middle school teaming should ponder the implications of these data. Doubling teacher planning time by adding team meeting time to individual planning time would go a long way toward addressing the problems of American middle schools.

Not yet convinced? Is doubling teacher planning time just one more way to feather the nest of members of "powerful teachers unions" as many critics of education contend? Large scale empirical studies are providing data that demonstrate that when teachers plan together and coordinate what they do with students the results are positive for student achievement.

How teams affect student performance

Though interdisciplinary teaming became part of the education landscape around thirty years ago, hard evidence that teaming makes a difference for students has been slow to emerge. As we have seen, implementing teams is subject to development through experience across time. Just putting the basics in place does not make a team. Effective teaming emerges as team members learn how to take advantage of the potential power that teaming permits.

In the 1990s we have seen a burgeoning of research on teaming. Much of it has appeared in *Research in Middle Level Education* or *Middle School Journal* and is documented in other chapters in this book. Most of the published research on teaming has focused on the processes of teaming. This follows the natural evolution of research on an educational innovation. Before researchers can assess the outcomes associated with an innovation, they have to establish the true characteristics of that innovation in practice. Before the effects of teaming can be assessed it is necessary to know, not just that the building principal claims teaming is occurring because common planning time has been provided and students are shared among several faculty, but how teaming has changed the teaching-learning process. In the 1990s we have seen documented in several studies how common planning time affects dialogue among teachers. Other studies have looked at changes in teachers as a result of teaming.

But what of the effects of teaming on the *raison d'être* of schools, student learning? Three studies over the past decade have provided empirical evidence that teaming (and the associated changes in teachers' planning, teaching, and relating to students) does have a positive effect on student performance. The first of these was published ten years ago as part of a "research on teaching monograph series" by Longman. This monograph by Ashton and

Webb (1986), entitled *Making a Difference: Teacher's Sense of Efficacy and Student Achievement*, provided indirect evidence of the impact of teaming on achievement by linking teaming to teacher efficacy which in turn was empirically linked to student achievement.

The Ashton and Webb monograph documented two separate relationships that suggested a positive link between teaming and student achievement. These researchers looked at two types of efficacy. "Teaching efficacy" is related to teachers' expectations that teaching can influence student learning. Teachers with high teaching efficacy believe that teachers can have a positive effect on student performance regardless of the students' abilities or family backgrounds. The second type of efficacy is "personal teaching efficacy" which refers to individuals' assessment of their own teaching competence. Drawing heavily on Doda's (1984) dissertation, Ashton and Webb reported that teachers on interdisciplinary teams believed that students could learn and that teachers could positively effect their students' lives. Teachers in the departmentalized situations were less confident that all students could learn or that teachers could have a lasting impact.

Later in the monograph Ashton and Webb showed how teachers' sense of efficacy influenced their teaching behavior and student achievement. In their own words: "Our findings strongly support the hypothesis that teachers' sense of efficacy is related to student achievement" (p. 138). Both language arts and math achievement were found to be related to teacher efficacy. These findings taken together suggested a link between teaming and student achievement mediated through teacher efficacy. What the Ashton and Webb study suggested, subsequent studies have empirically demonstrated.

The first real breakthrough in directly demonstrating the impact of teaming on achievement was published in *Sociology of Education* by Lee and Smith (1993). The data for the Lee and Smith study were drawn from the base year of the National Educational Longitudinal Study (NELS 88) (Ingels, Abraham, Spencer, & Frankel, 1989). The sample consisted of 8845 students attending 377 different schools representing public, Catholic, and independent schools. In schools that were less departmentalized and more teamed, students scored higher on achievement tests in math and reading. In addition, students were more engaged in learning and less bored. Finally, there was a more equitable distribution of these outcomes across social class.

To date the most massive study of the effects of middle school restructuring on student outcomes is being carried out under the direction of Robert Felner at the University of Illinois. Felner's study (the Project on High Performance Learning Communities) now involves more than 25,000 students in 52 schools ranging in size from less than 200 to about 2000. Felner (Felner, Jackson, Kasak, Mulhall, Brand, & Flowers, in press) based his definition of restructuring on the eight recommendations of *Turning Points* (Carnegie Council on Adolescent Development, 1989). Among these is the practice of interdisciplinary teaming. Felner and his associates compared three levels of implementation of the Carnegie Council recommendations: high implementation, partial implementation, and no implementation. Students in the most highly implemented settings scored higher in mathematics, language, and reading achievement than students in less implemented settings, who in turn scored higher than students in settings with no implementation of the *Turning Points* recommendations. The elements of team structure that were found to relate most highly to student outcomes were these: (a) number of common planning periods in addition to individual planning time, (b) length of common planning time, (c) teacher/student ratio and absolute number of teachers and students on teams, and (d) length of time teaming. Where teachers had more common planning time and made use of it, students not only achieved more, they showed more positive behaviors in class and reported more positive attitudes than students in less well implemented schools.

These large, well-controlled studies are providing evidence that teaming, especially when combined with other elements of restructuring, does have a positive effect on student learning. Assessment of the results of restructuring presents a major challenge. Not only is interdisciplinary teaming practiced at various levels of implementation, but other aspects of restructuring often take place simultaneously. In spite of the complexities involved, both of the major studies cited here that offer direct evidence of the impact of teaming are ongoing. Data continues to be collected for the National Education Longitudinal Study and the Project on High Performance Learning Communities. Further evidence to document the impact of teaming and other elements of restructuring on student learning will continue to emerge in the immediate future

The Necessary Agenda

There is a "necessary agenda" for middle school interdisciplinary teams. This agenda is about interdisciplinary teams moving forward in their overall development as they maximize student learning; as they contribute to building safe, secure, and effective places of learning for young adolescents; and as they shape educational life within this democracy. The necessary agenda to accomplish these goals includes:

1. Team leadership
2. Administering teams
3. Inclusion
4. Preparing teachers for teaming

Team leadership

Maximizing the effectiveness of teams is what team leadership is about. And yet, as Daniel Kain points out earlier in this volume, leadership on interdisciplinary teams has been more the mundane tasks of maintenance. And while maintenance is important, movement beyond this basic level is of primary importance. As a field we need to turn our collective attention to how to prepare and shape team leadership – both in specific individuals and in the team broadly. We need to document cases of exemplary leadership that can serve as examples for other teams. Researchers must focus on what leadership means in various contexts – two person teams, four person teams, the use of team planning time to explore curricular alternatives, how consensus is built and shared decision making, the kind that P. Elizabeth Pate writes about, is accomplished.

Vision is a wonderful possession, yet without leaders to move us toward these images and ideas of what could be, interdisciplinary teams will be mesmerized by possibilities but rooted in place. And so we need individuals with strong dispositions – bravery, courage, pluck, determination, tenacity, persistence. We need to develop, encourage, and sustain a posture of adventure – about our students and their learning, about what John Arnold calls "rich curriculum," about our peers and their own professional development.

The plan to accomplish this is at once simple and complex. In team meeting room after team meeting room, all across the country, we need individuals and groups of individuals to offer up comments like "We need to talk about where our instruction is going – not in the sense of our basic strategies – but in the underlying message that we are sending to our students." Or "I propose that we examine our curriculum in light of what students are not experiencing and for which resources exist in this building – how do we connect with our colleagues, for our student's learning." When the rush is for filling out forms, or scheduling the vast number of events that make up the life of a team, it is easy to forget questions that move us further along in our agenda to those broader and important questions of "What are we about?" and "How can we help our students learn?" But this too must become a focus, and the mechanism for achieving it will be the development of team leadership – in single individuals, in dyads and triads, in whole teams.

Administering teams

Administrators, as Mary Gallagher-Polite has informed us, have particular responsibilities in working with teams from a variety of perspectives. This will be particularly important as new educational agendas surface for middle schools and education in general – issues of performance based assessment of students, continued professional development for teachers, new technologies, and increasing issues of risk for students.

Administrators will need to create particular relationships with teams – not leave them to their own devices. While a "team" that does not meet during its designated common planning time is responsible for this egregious sin, their administrator is part of the problem as well. To move teams continually forward takes a clear agenda that is shared with the team, resources applied strategically to this agenda, and a means of assessment that holds all parties – team members and administrators – accountable. And part of this accountability must be product – we must be able to demonstrate in convincing fashion our students' learning.

As with team leadership we will need an expanded knowledge base to move us to these goals. This expanded knowledge base should include: (a) "lighthouse" case studies of exemplary practice on the part of administrators with their teams, (b) an understanding of the dynamics of an administrator's goals for a team set against the background of broader school and district goals, and (c) how administrators translate team accomplishments to various publics and various publics concerns to teams. Researchers will need to provide both qualitative and quantitative studies of administering teams with a special view to translating their findings for *both* administrators and team members. And this critical line of research should link with the previously discussed topic of team leadership.

Inclusion

In the final analysis, teams may be judged on how they handle those students most in need of help and assistance. The inclusive classroom may be the agenda for the rest of this decade and into the next; and, in our point of view, this is how it should be. Middle school educators claim that teaming offers students an opportunity to maximize their learning. Can we realistically amend this claim or qualify it with an asterisk or footnote that reads "Only certain students?"

The benefits of inclusion can be found broadly – both in the benefit that general education students derive from working with *all* their peers and in the supportive learning environment that is created in an inclusive classroom for exceptional learners. But the benefits of inclusion for teams can be found in the philosophical underpinnings of both teams and inclusive classrooms – both are democratic elements that have as their core value the dignity and worth of each individual. As a consequence, teams and inclusive classrooms are not only about "you" or "me" but are also about "we."

"We" need to attend to how we create and sustain learning environments for *all* our students as Chriss Walther-Thomas informs us. The first step may need to be how "you" and "me" feel about "we." Democratic classrooms are understood as sites of struggle, sites of growth and movement, not sites of predetermined outcomes. Therefore we need to approach inclusive classrooms with a sense of what is possible, with a strong research base, with a stance of adaptation and adjustment, and with a sense of long-term growth and development.

Preparing teachers for teaming

Middle school teachers graduating from college and university programs must bring initial skills in working as a part of an interdisciplinary team. If they do not, then the school site will be doomed to a low-level of team operation – always focusing on induction and "forming." Colleges and universities must move preservice students into middle schools where teams operate, not into departmentalized settings.

In preservice programs students should become well acquainted with the knowledge base of teaming and how this is carried forth into practice. Extensive internships, often with multiple peers on the same team, allow both the work of the middle school and the work of the teacher education program to move forward with benefits to all. Programs such as Trinity University in San Antonio, Texas (Van Zandt & Harlan, 1995), the University of North Carolina at Greensboro (Van Hoose & Strahan. 1995), and California State University San Marcos (McDaniel, Rios, & Stowell, 1995; McDaniel, Rios, Stowell, & Christopher, 1994; Stowell, McDaniel, & Rios, 1995; Stowell, McDaniel, Rios, & Kelly, 1993), are pointing the way with multiple teachers on middle school teams for extended (often an entire school year) periods of time.

Beyond the knowledge base and practice of teaming colleges and universities will need to educate their students to be "advocates of teaming." As C. Kenneth McEwin documented in his examination of teaming over the last thirty years, only about half of all middle schools use this organizational structure. Colleges and universities must help "fill the void" that currently exists by ensuring that their graduates are committed to this structure for the benefit of their students.

Getting results

> *Our concern with politics has caused us to overlook the most obvious on-the-ground concerns about our real purposes – our goals. We have launched initiatives (e.g., site-based management), provided loads of staff development in certain methods (e.g., 'Essential Elements of Instruction'), and spent untold hours drawing up visions and mission statements. All had enormous promise. But these symbolic, high-profile 'initiatives du jour' occurred in the near absence of any written or explicit intention to monitor, adjust, and thus palpably increase student learning or achievement.* **The combination of three concepts constitutes the foundation for results: meaningful teamwork; clear, measurable goals; and the regular collection and analysis of performance data.**
>
> *In this era of heightened interest in school reform, we have yet to realize that organizations typically get what they earnestly and specifically set out to get. Good-faith efforts to establish goals and then to collectively and regularly monitor and adjust actions toward them produce results.*
>
> —Schmoker, 1996, pp. 1-2 (emphasis added)

> *Two insights about teams emerged early, consistently, and very emphatically from our interviews. First, high performance teams have both a clear understanding of the goal to be achieved and a belief that the goal embodies a worthwhile or important result.*
>
> *Second, whenever an **ineffectively** functioning team was identified and described, the explanation for the team's in-*

effectiveness involved, in one sense or another, the goal.
— Larson & LaFasto, 1989, p. 27 (emphasis in original)

We Gain More Than We Give is in the final analysis dedicated to understanding the means to important ends. Teaming is not the purpose of schooling. Instead, teaming is the state-of-the art means to achieving the best results in learning for young adolescents. We must not lose sight of the fact that it is not sufficient to claim that we have a modern, up-to-date school because we are engaged in teaming. Better to be able to claim that we have students who are learning more, demonstrating pro-social behavior, and showing more positive attitudes toward themselves and others because the faculty works in teams, sets clear goals, and monitors the results of their efforts.

Successful teaming – teaching that does produce more learning for more students than conventional arrangements – is not about structures *per se*. The structural aspects – common planning time, shared students, team space, and flexible blocks – are simply bottom-line enablers that allow teams to develop to the point that they do make a difference.

To become successful, teams must be goal-directed and results-driven. While it is permissible in the early stages of team development to focus on process goals, the ultimate success of a team will be measured by how well it achieves goals directed at student outcomes. These outcomes do not need to be narrowly measured in terms of grades or standardized test scores.

> *Results should be understood as a thoroughly established, desired end-product, as evidence that something worked (or did not work). In this sense, all results – good and bad – are ultimately good, because they provide feedback that can guide us, telling us* **what to do next** *and how to do it better.*
> — Schmoker, 1996, p. 3 (emphasis in the original)

The notion that all decisions may not lead inextricably to success the first time they are tried is reinforced by Larson and LaFasto's (1989) observation that to establish trust among team members requires the norm that team members take risks and be permitted to fail.

To move beyond the rudiments of teaming in order to improve student learning, teams must set for themselves specific goals to direct their efforts. The number of goals being pursued at any given time must be limited. One worthwhile goal is often enough. More than three at a time is rarely productive because they become too fragmenting. Though long-term goals – one- or two-year goals or beyond – can be decided upon, the most useful goals will be those that guide the current semester's work. Goals should be committed to writing and be ones for which the team will hold itself accountable in the relative short run.

When written goals are ones that team members agree to accept, the team must also agree on what evidence will be necessary to assess the team's progress toward those goals. Formal tests are not always – not even often – the best source of evidence to measure the success of a goal. Appropriate evidence may consist of the following: frequency counts; records of actions taken; systematic observations of student behavior; examples of student products, especially those assessed with formal rubrics; parental feedback; data collected through action research; or notes on class discussions.

Only by collecting data related to the team's goals will the team have the information it needs to make informed decisions about student learning. Not only will the team have sufficient information to make good decisions, it will have the evidence to defend itself against those who claim that teams are an unnecessary luxury in lean fiscal times. Unless educators at all levels can show that teaming does really make a difference, it will fade away and rightly so. Just as researchers document the big picture, local teams must document their own results. Without goals and evidence to assess those goals teams cannot hope to improve student learning much less prove that improvement has occurred.

Team size and accountability

> *I thought, as we drove on east, the ice closing in more now, forcing us to run yet closer to the beach, of the geographer Carl Sauer and his concept of biologically distinct regions. The idea of bioregionalism, as it has been developed by his followers, is a political concept that would reshape human life. It would decentralize residents of an area into smaller, more self-sufficient, environmentally responsible units, occupying lands the borders of which would be identical with the borders of natural regions – watersheds, for example. I thought of Sauer because we were headed that day for a great, invisible political dividing line: 141 degrees western longitude. Like the border between Utah and Colorado, this one is arbitrary. If it were not actually marked – staked – it would not be discernible. Sauer's borders are noticeable. Even the birds find them.*
>
> — Barry Lopez, "Borders," *Crossing Open Ground*

If teams are good, are bigger teams better? Some middle school educators seem to think so. This view has teams enlarged well beyond the core team. However, how can team membership include core teachers, other staff, community workers, and parents and maintain accountability? What does such a prescription do to the organizational basis of teaming (i.e., common planning time, shared students, team space, and block schedules)? Just because a team does not contain all of the expertise it needs to function effectively, does not mean that every one that the team relates to should be a "member" of the team.

Teams should be large enough that good decision making can occur but small enough that every one knows each other and can meet on a regular basis. In practical terms this is two to six people. A permanent team can be made up only of those teachers, both subject specialists (e.g., language arts, science) and learning specialists (e.g., learning disabled, gifted), who meet regularly and are jointly *accountable* for the instruction of their shared students. From time to time the permanent team may join with others to form *ad hoc* "teams" to carry out specific tasks. A counselor may join in the discussions of a specific child's needs, a media specialist may join in the planning of an interdisciplinary unit, exploratory teachers may join in the planning of special curriculum events such as Black history month or earth day. But to consider these other people to be "members" greatly distorts the meaning of the term "interdisciplinary team." To talk of throwing in district personnel, community workers, and parents is to render the concept "interdisciplinary team" meaningless by divorcing the concept of teaming from the notion that team members are accountable for the learning that their students accomplish.

When the team does need outside expertise in order to carry out its work, it does not expand its membership, it spans its boundaries. In this regard teams function like families. Families sometimes need expertise from beyond their boundaries. Families might seek assistance from marriage counselors, physicians, pastors, and mental health professionals. These people do not become "members" of the family to offer their services. Though families may function as an *ad hoc* team with a pastor or physician to deal with a specific problem, the family remains the family. It simply goes beyond its boundaries to acquire needed services.

Teams are correctly thought of in the same way. The team is that group which meets regularly to make the joint decisions that are necessary for it to carry out the mission required by its joint accountability. All other connections are just that: connections to outside resources that the team needs to function more effectively. Consequently, counselors, media specialists, business partners, museum curators, parents, and others who work with teams from time to time are not members of the team because they are not ultimately accountable for the learning that occurs among students on the team.

Changing teaching roles

> *What natural things manifest, if observed closely enough*
> *is their nature, and their nature is to change.*
>
> — Wendell Berry, "The Long-Legged House,"
> *Recollected Essays*, 1965-1980

Acts of teaching vary from time to time and situation to situation. Socrates was a teacher. Jesus was a teacher. John T. Scopes was a teacher. Ross Burkhardt is a teacher. Each taught at different times and places and under different circumstances, yet each is recognizable as a teacher.

However, part of what Ross Burkhardt does in his work with students at Shoreham-Wading River Middle School in the 1990s is different from what John T. Scopes did as a high school teacher in the 1920s in Tennessee. The same statement would be true were Mr. Burkhardt's work to be compared to the other two teachers of centuries past. As society has changed, and education in its wake, so has the role of the "teacher."

For eons in the Western world teaching was a private enterprise, as the work of Socrates and Jesus will attest. As teaching became a vocation carried out within formal educational institutions, it has come to be characterized by such roles as these:

1. Instructing youth
2. Planning that instruction
3. Evaluating the performance of students
4. Managing student behavior
5. Carrying out communications with students' parents and guardians
6. Keeping records
7. Enforcing rules
8. Collecting fees

When teachers operate alone to educate their students within a school context, they do all of the things mentioned above. In those formerly rare instances where teachers sought to team teach, new roles were added. Teachers engaged in team teaching must do the following:

1. Planning instruction collaboratively
2. Delivering instruction jointly
3. Evaluating students interactively

What has happened to the roles associated with teaching in information age organizations such as restructured middle schools? Roles and responsibilities that have not been a part of "teaching" since the beginning of time have come to redefine what it is to be a teacher. The roles added by "team teaching" are continued while other previous roles, such as keeping records and managing behavior, have been modified to accommodate the addition of new roles:

1. Setting team goals
2. Assessing team growth
3. Planning/coordinating calendars of team events
4. Jointly managing student behavior
5. Planning and conducting joint parent conferences
6. Coordinating use of resources (e.g., team space, books, equipment)
7. Jointly diagnosing student needs
8. Carrying out coordinated responses to student needs
9. Managing one's own and the team's professional growth
10. Engaging in professional dialogue on educational issues
11. Reinforcing instruction across subjects
12. Integrating the curriculum

Though these lists are not exhaustive in defining what teaching is and has been, they do illustrate the truth that teaching as part of a middle school team is different in significant ways from teaching as a lone wolf. The work of teachers – like that of physicians, professors, publishers, and most other professionals – is currently being altered by changes in technology and organizational structure. Pining for "the good old days" may soothe the souls of those who wish for simpler times and simpler teaching roles, but it is nonadaptive behavior for these times.

Beyond Interdisciplinary Teaming

To locate ourselves, we needed to be located. If the warblers failed to arrive in May, how would we recognize our station between the continents? When we left home we could quickly join the highways and airlines of the world. They had succeeded, along with all forms of modern communication, in making a good deal of local, which is to say, connected travel unnecessary. Despite the telephone, which crossed many voids, there were areas between us and our

neighbors, near or far, which we no longer needed to ex-
plore, because they were so easily and quickly passed. This
also amounted to a loss of local hospitality, in terms of people
who could help you on your way and give your directions.

— John Hay, *The Undiscovered Country*

After 30 years of movement from cellular schools to teamed ones, where do we stand and where are we going? The answer to the first part of this question is contained in the chapters of this book. Readers should have a better idea of the state of the art in middle school organization. But what of the future? Will we see a regression to cellular school organizations? Or will we see teaming come to predominate in virtually all middle level schools in the 21st century? Or will yet new societal forces compel educators to move beyond teaming to new arrangements for delivering instruction to young adolescents?

So long as schools continue to be the main means of educating youth in the 21st century, teaming's place seems secure, particularly if information age organizations continue to revolve around teams. However, two forces may redefine education as we now practice it. The first is privatization of schooling. If voucher systems become federal and state policy, those who can afford it will send their children to private schools or engage in home school-ing. Public schools across the country may go the way of public health: a low-budget service for the poor. It takes no special insight to see this coming. For some time now in our large cities and throughout the American South there has existed a private and public split between the middle class and the poor. The notion of the common school to educate all of the children of the democracy may be on its way out. Though a public-private split would still result in the institution of schooling persisting, home schooling abetted by a second societal change might end the nation's reliance on schooling as the main means to educate youth.

This second factor to influence middle level education (as well as all of education and the workplace as well) is the rapid development of communi-cations technology. The Internet with its constantly expanding web sites, news groups, chat groups, and search engines along with instantaneous worldwide communication via e-mail may render traditional schools – "places" where students congregate to acquire information, skills, and habits of mind from university-trained subject specialists – as archaic as the tele-graph, 78 rpm records, house calls, or hitching posts. Today, using power PCs or Macs, a modem, and a cellular phone people can send e-mail from any-where in the world to anywhere in the world. Communications technology is so rapid, so flexible, and so portable that schools may have to change dramatically or disappear. The privatization issue will then take on a whole new dimension. Educators will be those who control the educational resources available on the Internet and students will be those with the means to access these resources. Some folks may be left pondering whether students should be taught by single teachers in isolated classrooms or by teams of teachers as this whole discussion becomes the twenty-first century equivalent of "how many angels can dance on the head of a pin." The future of teaming depends on the future of schooling. The future of schooling depends on the future of education. Teaming is a means, not an end.

References

Ashton, P.T., & Webb, R.B. (1986). *Making a difference: Teachers' sense of efficacy and student achievement.* New York: Longman.

Berry, W. (1981). *Recollected essays, 1965-1980.* San Francisco: North Point Press.

Carnegie Council on Adolescent Development. (1989). *Turning points: Preparing American youth for the 21st century.* New York: Carnegie Corporation.

Doda, N.M. (1984). *Teacher perspectives and practices in two organizationally different middle schools.* Unpublished doctoral dissertation, University of Florida, Gainesville.

Felner, R., Jackson, A., Kasak, D.T., Mulhall, P., Brand, S., & Flowers, N. (in press). The impact of school reform for the middle years: A longitudinal study of a network engaged in *Turning Points*-based comprehensive school transformation. In R. Takaniski & D. Hamburg (Eds.), *Preparing adolescents for the twenty-first century.* New York: Cambridge University Press.

Finch, R. (1983). *The primal place.* New York: Norton.

Hay, J. (1981). *The undiscovered country.* New York: Norton.

Henry, T. (1995, April 12). Teaching time is highest in the U.S. *USA Today*, p. 4D.

Ingles, S.J., Abraham, S.Y., Spencer, B.D., & Frankel, M.R. (1989). *National education longitudinal study of 1988. Base year: Student component data file user's manual.* Washington, DC: US Department of Education.

Larson, C.E., & LaFasto, F.M.J. (1989). *Teamwork: What must go right/what can go wrong.* Newbury Park, CA: Sage Publications.

Lee, V.E., & Smith, J.B. (1993). Effects of school restructuring on the achievement and engagement of middle-grade students. *Sociology of Education, 66,* 164-187.

Lopez, B. (1989). *Crossing open ground.* New York: Vintage Books.

McDaniel, J.E., Rios, F.A., & Stowell, L. (1995). California State University San Marcos. In C.K. McEwin & T.S. Dickinson (Eds.), *The professional preparation of middle level teachers: Profiles of successful programs* (pp. 57-63). Columbus, OH: National Middle School Association.

McDaniel, J.E., Rios, F.A., Stowell, L.P., & Christopher, P.A. (1994). Do as we do and as we say: Modeling curriculum integration in teacher education. *Middle School Journal, 26* (2), 14-20.

McEwin, C.K., & Dickinson, T.S. (Eds.).(1995). *The professional preparation of middle level teachers: Profiles of successful programs.* Columbus, OH: National Middle School Association.

Schmoker, M. (1996). *Results: The key to continuous school improvement.* Alexandria, VA: Association for Supervision and Curriculum Development.

Stowell, L.P., McDaniel, J.E., Rios, F.A. (1995). Fostering change for democratic middle schools through teacher education. *Middle School Journal, 26* (5), 3-10.

Stowell, L.P., McDaniel, J.E., Rios, F.A., & Kelly, M.G. (1993). Casting wide the net: Portfolio assessment in teacher education. *Middle School Journal, 25* (2), 61-67.

Van Hoose, J., & Strahan, D. (1995). The University of North Carolina at Greensboro. In C.K. McEwin & T.S. Dickinson (Eds.), *The professional preparation of middle level teachers: Profiles of successful programs.* Columbus, OH: National Middle School Association.

Van Zandt, L.M., & Harlan, N.K. (1995). A professional development school improves teacher preparation: Twain meets Trinity in Texas. *Middle School Journal, 26* (5), 11-16.

Author Biographies

Jacqueline Anglin is Professor of Education and Human Sciences and Director of Faculty Research and Sponsored Programs at Berry College in Rome, Georgia. A graduate of the University of Akron (B.S. and M.Ed.) and Kent State University (Ph.D.), she taught art in the Cuyahoga Falls, Ohio city schools. She has co-authored and authored several articles for *Middle School Journal* and also publishes in art education and teacher education journals. Her primary interests in middle school education include integrating the arts into the curriculum and the preparation of art teachers. She is currently working on a monograph titled *Authentic Art for Adolescents.*

John Arnold, Associate Professor and Coordinator of the Middle Grades Education Program at North Carolina State University, has had over 30 years experience as a middle level teacher, principal, professor and consultant. He has authored a number of works including *A Celebration of Teaching* (1986), *Visions of Teaching and Learning* (1990), *Best Bets* (with W. Parker, 1992), *A Curriculum For Empowering Young Adolescents* (1993), and *Service With A Smile* (with C.Beal, 1994). He is a graduate of Washington and Lee University and the University of Connecticut (B.S. and Ph.D.), and has also done graduate work in theology at Yale University Divinity School and in psychology at the University of Houston. His major professional interests focus upon innovative teaching and exemplary practice in middle level schools.

Marge Bowen holds a B.A. in Elementary Education from Mid-America Nazarene College in Olathe, Kansas. She earned her M.A.T. with emphasis in reading from Webster University. Marge was a fifth grade teacher in the Blue Valley District before coming to the middle school program as a reading and social studies instructor.

Nan B. Bowles graduated from Wake Forest University with a B.A. in English. She taught in the public schools of North Carolina as a high school English teacher, an ESL teacher, and as a middle school language arts/reading teacher. She received the M.A. degree from the University of North Carolina at Greensboro with an emphasis in middle school and literacy. She is currently employed as a lecturer at UNCG working with students in the professional development schools, and is completing work for a doctorate in education at the university. Her research interests lie in the areas of at risk middle school students, especially in the area of reading, and in the education of middle school teachers.

Ross Burkhardt graduated from Dartmouth College in 1962 and, after serving as a Peace Corps Volunteer in Tunisia (1962-64), earned his Master's degree from the University of Pennsylvania in 1966. Ross has taught eighth grade English/social studies at Shoreham-Wading River Middle School on Long Island since 1972. A founder of the New York State Middle School Association and its second President, he served as President of National Middle School Association in 1995-1996; he also is a member of the Early Adolescent/Generalist Committee for the National Board for Professional Teaching Standards. Since 1990 Ross has written a column, "musings" for *Transescence: The Journal of Emerging Adolescent Education*. He authored *The Inquiry Process* (Perfection Learning, 1993), and in 1995 he served on a committee of ten that developed NMSA's basic position paper, *This We Believe: Developmentally Responsive Middle Level Schools*.

Deborah A. Butler is Director of Teacher Education and Professor of Education at Wabash College, Crawfordsville, Indiana. A graduate of Christopher Newport College (B.A.) and the University of Virginia (M.Ed. and Ed. D.), she taught middle school students in Virginia for five years. She is the author of *American Women Writers on the Vietnam War: Unheard Voices* (1989), and co-authored *On Site: Preparing Middle Level Teachers Through Field Experiences* (Butler, Davies, & Dickinson, 1991) and *Rooms to Grow: Natural Language Arts in the Middle School* (Butler & Liner, 1995). She maintains a professional interest in middle level teacher preparation and language arts education.

Thomas S. Dickinson is Associate Professor of Education at Indiana State University in Terre Haute, Indiana. A graduate of Wake Forest University (B.A.) and the University of Virginia (M.Ed. and Ed.D.), he taught middle and secondary students in his native Virginia for eight years before moving to the college teaching ranks. He has co-authored *America's Middle Schools: Practices and Progress – A 25 Year Perspective* (McEwin, Dickinson, & Jenkins, 1996), *A Vision of Excellence: Organizing Principles for Middle Grades Teacher Preparation* (McEwin, Dickinson, Erb, & Scales, 1995), and *The Professional Preparation of Middle Level Teachers: Profiles of Successful Programs* (McEwin & Dickinson, 1995). His primary interest in middle school education is the professional preparation of middle school teachers at all levels of education.

Thomas O. Erb is Editor of *Middle School Journal* and Professor of Curriculum and Instruction at the University of Kansas, Lawrence. He holds an undergraduate degree from DePauw University (B.A.) and graduate degrees from Northwestern University (M.A.T.) and the University of Florida (Ph.D.). He began his middle school teaching career in 1967. For the past 18 years he has been engaged in middle grades teacher education. Among his most recent works are "Teamwork in Middle School Education" in *Teamwork Models and Experience in Education* (Garner, 1995), "The Middle School: Mimicking the Success Routes of the Information Age" (*Journal for the Education of the Gifted*, 1994), and "Promoting Gifted Behavior in an Untracked Middle School Setting" in *Beyond Tracking: Finding Success in Inclusive Schools* (Pool & Page, 1995). He wrote the widely-cited article "What Team Organization Can Do for Teachers" (*Middle School Journal*, 1987) and co-authored with Nancy Doda *Team Organization: Promise—Practices and Possibilities* (National Education Association, 1989).

Mary M. Gallagher-Polite is Associate Professor of Educational Administration at Southern Illinois University at Edwardsville. A graduate of Augustana College (B.A.) and Illinois State University (M.S. and Ph.D.), she has been an elementary and middle school teacher and principal before moving to the university. She is a co-author of *Turning Points in Middle Schools: Strategic Transitions for Educators* (Polite, DeToye, Fritsche, Grandone, Keefe, Kuffel, Parker-Hughey, 1996), a chapter author in *Advances in Educational Administration: Distributed Leadership: School Improvement Through Collaboration* (1995), and has written a number of articles for professional journals. She began a two-year term as President of the Association of Illinois Middle-Level Schools (AIMS) in the fall of 1996 and directs a Danforth Foundation Grant to develop an integrated teacher-administrator preparation program for the middle grades.

Judy Hainline holds a B.A. in Elementary Education from Southwestern College in Winfield, Kansas. She has a M.S. in Educational Psychology from Emporia State University and has completed Ph.D. course work in Counseling at Kansas State University. She taught at the elementary level and was a school counselor prior to joining the middle school as a sixth-grade math teacher.

Sarah Hanawald is currently a middle school technology coordinator and learning specialist at Greensboro Day School in Greensboro, North Carolina. After graduating with a degree in English literature from Duke University, she earned a Master's degree in Middle School Curriculum and Instruction from the University of North Carolina at Greensboro. As a technology coordinator, she specializes in using technology as a tool to reach all students and working with teachers in an effort to integrate technology seamlessly with existing areas of study. Within her classes, she works with a variety of students, teaching them how to understand their own learning styles and focusing on developing independent study skills.

Marla Harper, past-president of the PTA at Harmony Middle School, Blue Valley School District, Kansas, was a parent of a middle school student (now high school) when her contribution to this book was written.

Jeanneine P. Jones is Assistant Professor of Middle Grades Education at the University of North Carolina at Charlotte. Prior to graduation from the University of North Carolina at Greensboro (M.Ed. and Ed.D.), she taught for 15 years in a nationally recognized middle school. The former author of the "Teacher to Teacher" column in *Middle School Journal*, she has written several additional articles based on her experiences and research, and has shared them at numerous conferences and with more than 100 schools and districts. She is particularly interested in junior high schools that transition into middle schools, maintaining exemplary middle schools, literacy, and curriculum design.

Daniel L. Kain is Assistant Professor of Instructional Leadership at Northern Arizona University in Flagstaff, where he teaches in the Integrated Secondary Teacher Education Program (I-STEP), a program which utilizes team planning and teaching among faculty members. Prior to his university teaching, he taught mainly at the middle level in Montana. His publications on teaming have appeared in such journals as *Middle School Journal, T.E.A.M.:The Early Adolescent Magazine*, *Schools in the Middle, Research in Middle Level Education, Journal of Curriculum and Supervision*, and *Teachers College Record*. His primary research interests include teacher teaming, interdisciplinary instruction, and problem-based learning. He earned a B.A. from Montana State University, an M.A. from the University of Washington, and a Ph.D. from the University of British Columbia.

Karen King, a former elementary teacher in the Blue Valley School District, Kansas, was a parent of three middle school students (now high school) when her contribution to this book was written.

Sharon Lee is Associate Professor of Education at the University of South Dakota in Vermillion where she is currently the Director of Graduate Student Services and the Professional Development Center. Sharon received her Ph.D. in Curriculum and Instruction from Texas A & M University in 1987 after teaching middle level reading and language arts in rural schools in Texas. Her major research interests include middle level literacy, adolescent literature, rural education, and the professional development of teachers. Recent publications include "Can Educators Communicate with the Religious Right: The Nature of the Dialogue" in *The New Advocate*.

Tom Liner is Language Arts Supervisor for the Dougherty County Schools in Albany, Georgia, where he works with middle school teachers in all areas of the spoken and written arts. He has been an educator for 30 years with 18 years of classroom experience. He was educated at David Lipscomb College (B.A.), and The University of Georgia (M.A., Ed.S., and Ed.D). He has written numerous professional articles, including a series for *Middle School Journal* ("Being Among Them"), poetry, and personal essays, and is best known as the co-author with Deborah A. Butler of *Rooms to Grow: Natural Language Arts in the Middle School* (Carolina Academic Press, 1995). He also co-authored with Dan Kirby *Inside Out: Developmental Strategies for Teaching Writing* (Heinemann, 1981, 1988). Tom's professional interests always include writing and teaching writing, and he is active in the Southwest Georgia Writing Project.

Janet E. McDaniel is Associate Professor at California State University San Marcos, where she also serves as Coordinator of Middle Level Teacher Education. A graduate of Whitman College (B.A.), she taught middle school social studies for twelve years before earning her M.Ed. and Ph.D. at the University of Washington. Her research interests are middle school teaching and teacher education. With her CSUSM colleagues, she has published regularly in journals such as *Middle School Journal, Research in Middle Level Education,* and *Teacher Education Quarterly.* Her recent co-authored book is *Working with Middle School Students* (Stowell, Rios, McDaniel & Christopher, 1996).

C. Kenneth McEwin is Professor of Curriculum and Instruction at Appalachian State University, Boone, North Carolina. A graduate of East Texas State University (B.S. & M.Ed.) and North Texas State University (Ed.D.), he taught sixth grade in Paris and Arlington, Texas, and was an elementary principal in Arlington. A Past-President of the National Middle School Association (1983) and recipient of the Lounsbury Award (1989) from that association, he has co-authored *America's Middle Schools: Practices and Progress - A 25 Year Perspective* (McEwin, Dickinson, & Jenkins, 1996), *A Vision of Excellence: Organizing Principles for Middle Grades Teacher Preparation* (McEwin, Dickinson, Erb, & Scales, 1995), *The Professional Preparation of Middle Level Teachers: Profiles of Successful Programs* (McEwin & Dickinson, 1995), and *Growing Pains: The Making of America's Middle School Teachers* (Scales & McEwin, 1994). He maintains an interest in middle school teacher preparation and interscholastic sports for young adolescents.

Jane A. Page is Professor in the Department of Curriculum, Foundations, and Research at Georgia Southern University in Statesboro, Georgia, and serves as the Department Chair. A graduate of Georgia Southern (B.S.Ed., M.Ed., Ed.S.) and Mississippi State University (Ed.D.), she taught elementary grades in Bulloch County, Georgia, before joining the faculty of Georgia Southern in 1979. She has authored or co-authored numerous journal articles and book chapters and co-edited a book published by Phi Delta Kappa in 1995 entitled *Beyond Tracking: Finding Success in Inclusive Schools.*

Fred M. Page is Professor in the College of Education at Georgia Southern University in Statesboro, Georgia, and serves as Associate Dean for External Relations. A graduate of Georgia Southern (B.S.Ed., M.Ed., Ed.S.) and Mississippi State University (Ed.D.), he taught middle grades in the Marvin Pittman Laboratory School before assuming other responsibilities in the College of Education. He has co-authored a number of journal articles including publications in *Middle School Journal, Journal of Teacher Education*, and *Phi Delta Kappan.*

P. Elizabeth Pate is Associate Professor in the Department of Elementary Education at The University of Georgia. She is currently the Middle School Program Area Head. She has co-authored *Making Integrated Curriculum Work: Teachers, Students, and the Quest for Coherent Curriculum* (Pate, Homestead, & McGinnis, 1997) and chapters in the 1995 ASCD Yearbook: *Toward a Coherent Curriculum* and in *Beyond Separate Subjects*: *Integrative Learning at the Middle Level* (Siu-Runyan & Faircloth, 1995). Her primary interests in middle school education are curriculum and strategy instruction.

Richard R. Powell is Associate Professor of Curriculum and Instruction at Texas Tech University in Lubbock, Texas. A graduate of West Texas State University (B.S., M.S.) and Indiana University (Ph.D.), he taught in middle schools for three years. He has also taught high school, junior college, and university levels. Additionally, he has taught technical laboratory training in the Middle East for two years. He has co-authored several works, including *Field Experience: Strategies for Exploring Diversity in Schools* (Powell, Zehm, & Garcia) and *Classrooms Under the Influence: Addicted Families, Addicted Students* (Powell, Zehm, & Kottler). He has also co-authored a monograph published by NASSP, titled *Classrooms Under the Influence: Helping Early Adolescent Children of Alcoholics*. His research on teacher education has been published widely, including the journals *Teaching and Teacher Education, Qualitative Studies in Education, Journal of Research in Science Teaching,* and *Curriculum Inquiry.* His primary interest in middle school education is in alternative curriculum contexts and curriculum reform.

Vanessa Richardson is currently a graduate teaching assistant and Ph.D. candidate at the University of North Carolina at Greensboro majoring in Curriculum and Instruction. Her responsibilities include serving as university supervisor in the Professional Development Schools program which is a collaborative program between UNCG and the Guilford County Schools. Her special interest is in the area of middle school education, specifically programs to assist at risk students. She earned her B.S. degree from East Carolina University and two M.S. degrees from North Carolina A & T State University. She taught at North Carolina A & T State University for two years before pursuing full-time graduate study.

Stacey Burd Rogers is currently a 6-8 multiage math teacher in Scranton, Kansas. She is a graduate of Kansas State University in elementary education with an emphasis in math and science. Formerly, Stacey was a sixth grade science teacher in the Blue Valley School District, where she also taught computer classes for Blue Valley faculty members.

Stan Smith is Director of Personnel for the Olathe School District, Kansas. A former principal of Oregon Trail and Frontier Trail Junior High Schools, he was the parent of a middle school student (now high school) when his contribution to this book was written.

David Strahan has been a member of the faculty at the University of North Carolina at Greensboro since 1984. After graduating from Miami University of Ohio (B.S. and M.Ed.), he taught middle level language arts for six years and served as a reading specialist while completing his Ed.D. in Curriculum and Instruction at the University of Cincinnati. He is currently Associate Professor of Curriculum and Instruction and Coordinator of Middle Grades Education at UNCG. His areas of specialization include young adolescent development, curriculum and instruction, teacher education, and school improvement. He has written more than 60 professional articles and directed several grant projects that have explored school improvement processes. He is especially interested in improving the quality of schooling for "disconnected" students and enhancing support for their teachers.

K.O. Strohbehn, a member of the Board of Education for the Blue Valley School District, was the parent of a middle school student when her contribution to this book was written.

Deborah Thomas is Assistant Professor of Middle Grades and Secondary Education at Georgia Southern University's Graduate Center in Savannah, Georgia. She received her B.S., M.S., and Ph.D. degrees from Florida State University and is a former elementary and middle school teacher. She provides staff development and consulting services for schools on interdisciplinary teaming, advisory programs, curriculum integration, and flexible scheduling. She is currently conducting research on teacher development and curriculum reform at three high schools that are implementing interdisciplinary teaming in one or more grade levels.

Sue Carol Thompson teaches middle school curriculum and instruction and educational administration courses at the University of Missouri at Kansas City. A former Director of Middle Level Education for the Blue Valley School District in Overland Park, Kansas, she guided the district's implementation plan from junior high schools to middle schools. She has been a member of the Publications Committee for the National Middle School Association for the past six years. A former middle school teacher and principal, she has conducted numerous workshops for state and national organizations on middle school programs and practices.

Chriss Walther-Thomas is Associate Professor in the Educational Policy, Planning, and Leadership Program at the College of William & Mary in Williamsburg, Virginia. She is a graduate of programs at the University of Utah (B.A. and M.Ed.) and the University of Kansas (Ph.D.). She has taught elementary and middle school students with and without disabilities and has worked with college students with disabilities. Currently, she teaches courses related to instruction of students with disabilities and others at-risk for school failure in mainstream environments, professional teaming and collaboration, educational leadership in schools, and inclusive program development. Her research, writing, and staff development interests focus on collaboration between general and special educators, co-teaching relationships, team effectiveness, principal leadership, inclusive program development, and professional development over time. Her current research focuses on effective classroom planning to meet needs of students with disabilities and other students who do poorly in school.

George White is Associate Professor and Program Coordinator of Educational Leadership at Lehigh University in Bethlehem Pennsylvania. He is the founder and director of the Lehigh Middle Level Partnership, a consortium of over fifty middle schools and the University dedicated to creating effective learning environments for middle level students. Dr. White earned a Doctorate from Peabody College of Vanderbilt University in Educational Leadership and a Master's Degree from the

University of Northern Colorado. He has served as a middle level science teacher and team leader, an assistant principal and principal at the middle level, and an assistant superintendent. He has recently co-authored the book *Service Learning in the Middle School: Building a Culture of Service* (Fertman, White, & White, 1996) and has written numerous articles on middle level issues. His primary interest in middle level education is in the area of program design and implementation.

William G. Wraga is Assistant Professor in the Department of Educational Leadership at The University of Georgia, Athens, Georgia. He earned his A.B. at Rutgers College, M.A.T. at the University of Chicago, and Ed.D. at Rutgers University. Prior to teaching at the university he worked for over fourteen years in New Jersey schools, first as a social studies and English teacher and then as a department and, later, district supervisor. He is author of *Democracy's High School* (1994), co-editor of the *Annual Review of Research for School Leaders* (Hlebowitsh & Wraga, Eds., 1996), and a contributing author in *Readings in Middle School Curriculum: A Continuing Conversation* (Dickinson, Ed., 1993).

NATIONAL MIDDLE SCHOOL ASSOCIATION

National Middle School Association was established in 1973 to serve as a voice for professionals and others interested in the education of young adolescents. The Association has grown rapidly and now enrolls members in all fifty states, the Canadian provinces, and forty-two other nations. In addition, fifty-three state, regional, and provincial middle school associations are official affiliates of NMSA.

NMSA is the only association dedicated exclusively to the education, development, and growth of young adolescents. Membership is open to all. While middle level teachers and administrators make up the bulk of the membership, central office personnel, college and university faculty, state department officials, other professionals, parents, and lay citizens are also actively involved in supporting our single mission – improving the educational experiences of 10-15 year olds. This open and diverse membership is a particular strength of NMSA.

The Association provides a variety of services, conferences, and materials in fulfilling its mission. In addition to *Middle School Journal*, the movement's premier professional journal, the Association publishes *Research in Middle Level Education Quarterly*, a wealth of books and monographs, videos, a general newsletter, an urban education newspaper, and occasional papers. The Association's highly acclaimed annual conference, which has drawn over 10,000 registrants in recent years, is held in the fall.

For information about NMSA and its many services contact the Headquarters at 2600 Corporate Exchange Drive, Suite 370, Columbus, Ohio 43231, TELEPHONE 800-528-NMSA, FAX 614-895-4750.